Meyer Schreiber, M.S.W., is currently Associate Professor, Fordham University School of Social Service, and Chairman, Social Welfare Policy and Services Sequence. Previously he has served as Consultant on Social Services to the Mentally Retarded for the United States Children's Bureau and as Director of Group Work, Director of Training, and Director of N.I.M.H. Project with the New York City Association for the Help of Retarded Children. In 1968 he was one of six winners of the National Association for Retarded Children's Rosemary B. Dybwad International Award, under which he traveled to Uruguay to study social policy and mental retardation.

Mr. Schreiber received his B.B.A. at City College, his M.S.W. at Columbia University, School of Social Work, and has done further study at Wayne State University. He has been active in both national and local associations in his field and has served as Consultant on Child Care for the National Association for Retarded Children, Consultant on Social Work to the Maryhaven School for Exceptional Children, and Consultant on Social Work at Letchworth Village. He has written and edited numerous journal articles and conference proceedings in the field of social work and mental retardation and has conducted institutes and seminars at many universities.

Dr. Leonard W. Mayo, who has contributed a Preface to the book, is Professor of Human Development at Colby College and has served as Chairman of President Kennedy's Panel on Mental Retardation.

Social Work and Mental Retardation

EDITED BY MEYER SCHREIBER

Social Work and Mental Retardation

WITH A FOREWORD BY LEONARD W. MAYO

THE JOHN DAY COMPANY · NEW YORK

The John Day Company, 257 Park Avenue South, New York, N.Y. 10010
Distributed in elementary and high schools by
Steck-Vaughn Company, P. O. Box 2028, Austin, Texas 78767
Intext companies

Published on the same day in Canada by Longmans Canada Limited.

Library of Congress Catalogue Card Number 78-101462

Printed in the United States of America
Designed by the Etheredges

Contents

Social Work and Mental Retardation

Foreword

This volume presents a broad survey of the field of mental retardation, particularly, but not exclusively, as it relates to social work. The manner in which social work and mental retardation have gradually developed to a point approaching integration over the last few years is evident in this well-selected collection of able papers. The editor, Meyer Schreiber, has made the selection with the conviction that no other childhood disability represents such a lag between what is known and what is actually done. The papers reveal some of the progress made by social work in helping correct this lag, and appear at a critical time in the long struggle to place mental retardation in proper perspective as a major educational, social, and public health problem. Though it must be recorded that social work, as a profession, was not at first on the side of the angels in this effort, there has been substantial movement toward collaboration in the last decade by both social workers and those who labor in the vineyards of mental retardation.

This book will make a significant contribution to those whose main identification is with social work, by increasing the concern of social workers for the retarded; encouraging the development of social services for the retardate and his acceptance in all appropriate existing services; by stimulating an increasingly close relation between professional workers in social work and mental retardation; and by revealing to professional people and volunteers in mental retardation the philosophy and approach as well as the nature of social services.

Undergraduate students seeking an overview of the field will find this volume a gold mine of information on social work and mental retardation; the graduate student who desires to dig more deeply into some aspect of mental retardation will find many valuable leads here. The social work practitioner, administrator, and teacher, and those in similar positions in mental retardation cannot fail to find guidance, information, and enlightenment.

The authors of the nearly one hundred papers in this volume are among the outstanding leaders in social work and mental retardation. The editor is to be congratulated on the selection of authors, the arrangement of the material, and indeed on the entire undertaking.

LEONARD W. MAYO
Professor of Human Development,
Colby College
Chairman,
President Kennedy's Panel on Mental Retardation

Introduction

Mental retardation has had a long past, but only recently has positive and vigorous action been directed toward its amelioration, treatment, and prevention. The new interest in this complex biological, psychological, social, and legal problem is the result of several factors: the emergence of an articulate self-help parents' group, the personal interest of professionals and of prominent relatives and friends of the retarded, and political developments motivated by a general awareness of the problem.

This new interest on various levels has brought, first, new hope for the retarded. As enthusiastic workers implement new preventive measures, new ways of modifying behavior, new ways of raising levels of social functioning, hopelessness gives way to hope for all those involved. The articles in this volume reflect the enthusiasm that is changing the outlook for the mentally retarded.

Along with the new knowledge and understanding of mental retardation has come social work's realization that it has a responsibility to persons who are retarded. Beyond affirming the rights and dignity of every man, social work in the field of mental retardation affirms the human being's right to be different; it affords the same consideration of need to the socially dependent as to the socially productive; it honors the value of sustaining people even if minimal social functioning represents maximal achievement; and it accepts and promotes the belief that service must be adapted to people, not people to service.

Historically, this philosophy is related to that of the Charity Organization Societies and the settlement work of the late nineteenth and early twentieth centuries. In the 1930's, however, organized social work, under the influence of the behavioral, biological, and medical disciplines, lost interest in mental retardation. Social workers were encouraged to seek other fields of practice, and no useful guidelines were formulated for the few who did direct their energies toward mental retardation. This attitude on the part of the profession was partly an expression of the basically nonsupportive, even rejecting, attitude of society as a whole toward the retarded. Mental retardation posed problems that defied scientific understanding and therapeutic endeavors, and because so much of professional satisfaction is in seeing clients improve or get well, social workers were discouraged by so-called irreversible conditions. An overemphasis on the part of social workers on psychodynamics —for example, motivation and insight—clouded their understanding of mental retardation and limited their adaptation of social work knowledge, methods, and skills on behalf of the retardate and his family. Since social agencies and social workers were convinced that retarded individuals had little chance of improvement, mental retardation became synonymous with hopelessness.

Another factor militating against the mentally retarded was the historical precedent of separating them from others served by social welfare agencies and programs. This separation was partially the result of defining the problem as one of removal. With the exception of a few specialized agencies set up to work with the retardate and his family, social work institutions by and large bypassed such persons. Thus, the forces generated by the professional orthodoxies and by the balance of public apathy tended to restrict services to the favored few, with the mentally retarded receiving less appropriate attention and service than their representation in the community warranted, and far less than their total needs required.

During the 1960's, however, the situation changed radically. In 1962, the landmark Report of the President's Panel to Combat Mental Retardation expressed the firm—and, in a sense, revolutionary—view that mental retardation is a national problem and could in large part be prevented. The report also stated that it was necessary for government and voluntary agencies to take bold action together. Now, eight years later, social agencies and social workers are enthusiastically involved in programs that were not in existence prior to the issuance of the report. The increased activity is due, in part, to the considerable increase in federal expenditures —matched by the states and by local and voluntary agencies—on mental retardation and related problems. Advances have been made on a broad front, ranging from genetic counseling to vocational rehabilitation, and these advances give us hope that more significant gains will be made against this formidable problem in the future.

In face of the magnitude of mental retardation as a social problem and its predicted increase as the population grows, it has become increasingly necessary to define and refine the role and function of social work and to direct more of its efforts to this important sphere of human welfare. Social work, it seems to me, has recognized this challenge. That it has begun to accelerate its efforts is unquestioned. That it needs to do more is equally clear.

About This Volume

The social work student, teacher, or practitioner who wishes to review social work practice in mental retardation, or to delve into the basic concepts of social work as they relate to mental retardation, or to find clues about future directions in this field must find his way through a tangle of data contained in research reports, government documents, journals of opinion, professional journals, monographs, studies, symposia, and books of readings. Much of this data has been reported since the publication of the Report of the President's Panel. Some materials accurately reflect the current state of affairs; others are little more than self-serving statements on the part of people who are trying to camouflage meager efforts and results. The available material is more than enough—the chief problem is to understand and interpret it. There has as yet been no systematic effort to place before American social workers a carefully developed picture to indicate what has gone on in the past and what is currently reflected in social work practice with the mentally retarded and their families.

This volume, it is hoped, will be a step in that direction. It consists of articles and other materials, drawn from a variety of sources, arranged in a sequence that attempts to be relevant in terms of social work needs and interests. The selections were made with the objective of presenting meaningful background material on mental retardation from the social and behavioral sciences. Also included is material concerning the retarded individual himself and the significant individuals in his social network, as well as some basic relevant concepts from social work, some recent and current social work practices, and some of the more vital issues. These selections were made on the basis of what they add to our knowledge, understanding, and skill in social work with the retarded. They are also intended to reflect some historical development regarding social work's input during the past fifteen to twenty years. The materials are presented virtually in the form in which they originally appeared.

What is "new" about this volume and characteristic of the items selected is a sharp focus on something actually done. The contributors, many of them social workers, seek to involve us in a significant attempt as they utilize social work knowledge, methods, and skill in the process of helping retarded individuals and their families. The contributors recount real occurrences in the full richness of the actual experience. Human beings and events are dealt with here by sensitive social workers in settings of many kinds. Other contributors, including psychiatrists, sociologists, pyschologists, doctors, and a foster parent, make equally clear their unique contributions to a social problem that involves the knowledge and skills of many professionals and paraprofessionals. These contributors collectively support the observation that social work has much to contribute, that it is in the forefront of helping efforts, and that social agencies and social workers are busy grappling with both the causes and consequences of mental retardation.

I have learned much, both from my colleagues and from the other contributors as well, in the process of assembling this volume. It will have achieved its goals if the reader comes away with increased understanding, insights, and knowledge, and—above all—with a willingness to work with these vulnerable individuals.

Acknowledgments

This volume came into being through a combination of interesting and fortuitous circumstances. I was influenced by my students at the Fordham University School of Social Service, who were interested in mental retardation and found it difficult to locate social work contributions; by my colleagues in the practice settings, who were anxious to extend their horizons in the seminars that I was privileged to develop under the aegis of the Social Work Division of the American Association on Mental Deficiency; and by the interest of the publisher, The John Day Company, through its president Richard J. Walsh Jr., and his editor, Elizabeth P. Swift. All of these individuals were instrumental in the development and completion of this book.

To the authors, for their consent to republication of their materials, go my gratitude and appreciation for the cooperative way in which the products of their many hours of labor were shared with me. The periodicals in which many of these articles appeared, and the professional associations that publish these magazines, were another gratifying source of assistance.

The federal agencies, and their staffs, who made available their excellent materials merit a special note of thanks. The Children's Bureau and the Social and Rehabilitation Service of the Social and Rehabilitation Administration of the U.S. Department of Health, Education and Welfare typified and exemplified this consistently high level of cooperation.

Research in the process of assembling this volume was facilitated by the liberal assistance of Miss Corinne Freeman, Librarian, Fordham University School of Social Service; Mrs. Grace Bermingham, Librarian, Columbia University School of Social Work; and Mrs. Edith Frankel, Librarian, National Association for Retarded Children. The local libraries in Maplewood, New Jersey (my previous residence), and South Orange, New Jersey (my current residence), were extremely useful as their resources were not only readily available but of a consistently high caliber.

Finally, to the parents of the New York City Association for the Help of Retarded Children goes my deepest gratitude for the opportunity to work with them in this unique self-help group and to learn from them, in personal and human terms, what the impact of mental retardation is upon the individual, his family, and the community.

My wife, Sheila, and my daughters, Deborah and Miriam, were active collaborators in the production of this volume as they supplied the patience, enthusiasm, and support that made this activity a rewarding one.

MEYER SCHREIBER
Fordham University
School of Social Service

PART ONE

First the Person, Then the Handicap

ONE

The Handicapped Also Are People

CHARLOTTE TOWLE

All public assistance workers encounter many individuals who are chronically ill or have a physical handicap. These people present special problems, and therefore it frequently occurs that workers set them apart as persons who must be treated differently. It is important to bear in mind that, in spite of special problems which demand special services, our work with the ill and the handicapped is governed by the same basic principles as our work with any other group of individuals.

In Physical Handicaps, Timing Is a Decisive Factor

It is important, first of all, to understand the meaning of the illness or of the handicap to the individual. His life will be affected circumstantially and psychologically, in varied ways and in varying degrees. Insofar as these conditions bring change, the factors determining the nature and the degree of the individual's response are noted as age, sex, prior life experience, prior personality development, and the timing of the onset of disability in relation to other events in his life.[1] This factor of timing is sometimes decisive. For example, a man immersed in humiliation and defeat at being unemployed may sustain an injury or fall ill. At such a time the disability may be seized on and used to the utmost as a more acceptable basis for being unemployed than not being wanted in the labor market. The same mishap in time of employment might not have brought the same gratifications and therefore, not being useful, would not be clung to in the same way.

Or in old age, when the future is uncertain and life in general has become frustrating, illness or handicap may be used as a means to return to early infantile gratifications. The person may derive attention and a feeling of safety and comfort through the care which his disability conscripts. This is not necessarily the case, however, for if the person has well-entrenched patterns of self-dependence he may resist his disability or deny its existence through refusing medical care and attempting to carry on as of old. An important factor determining his choice of a solution

From Charlotte Towle, *Common Human Needs*. Federal Security Agency (Washington, U.S. Government Printing Office, 1945), pp. 72-80.

may be the response of family members to his disability. Their anxious overprotection may drive him to further lengths in denying his limitations or it may encourage regression. Their indifference and neglect may provoke regression in order to command attention or it may block him in getting help which he genuinely needs.

Likewise in adolescence when the young person has not a secure place in the adult world and when he has considerable anxiety about his status among his peers, a physical handicap or a chronic illness which limits his activity may be deeply disturbing. He may solve the problem by a regression to childhood or he too may resist the limiting reality of his handicap through overreaching himself in activity and through refusing to use measures proffered to safeguard his welfare. Again decisive factors in determining the nature of his response are his prior personality development and the response of others, notably his family and his friends, to his disability.[2] Above all, he may need help in planning realistically for the future.

Illness or Disability May Serve a Useful Purpose

If we understand the meaning of illness or of disability to the individual, we may see the purpose which it serves for him. Within the framework of his present situation and the interplay of his family relationships, we need to try to understand what *use* his disability has for him—what *unmet need* it fulfills—*now*, in his present life situation. Accordingly we ask ourselves such questions as, Why does he not want to give up his handicap? Why does he need to deny it? Is it enabling him to escape overwhelming pressures, to compensate for certain lacks, or to gain satisfaction in one way or another? We seek the answer through knowing the individual, focusing on more than his handicap; frequently we fail to understand the disabled person because we do not see beyond his disability. Perhaps our own limitations, physical or otherwise, brought us the experience of feeling different, so that as we encounter "the disabled" it may be difficult not to emphasize his difference and to stress the handicap as though it were the total person rather than merely an aspect of him, or as one problem which he presents. The worker in the case of Miss S. tended to do this.[3] You may recall that in attempting to help her see that an institution would afford her a more comfortable life, she focused on the woman's physical ineptitudes, her inability to get along, and thus, perhaps, aroused a strong defense in which Miss S. may have been driven to prove that she could and would get along on her own. Had she focused on understanding Miss S. as a person, she would have helped her express something of what her infirmity meant to her, something of the loneliness and dissatisfactions of her present life as well as her fear of institutions. Thus she might have enabled her to make this choice and thereby to realize constructively her desire to manage her own affairs. Likewise, in the D. case, the worker saw Mr. D. as a tuberculous patient rather than as a man who had been the head of his family and who still had both the inclination and the capacity for participation in the management of family affairs.

Congenital Handicaps May Shape the Personality

When physical handicap has been congenital or has had its onset in infancy or early childhood, it does not have the threat of change as when it occurs later in life. It may have been deeply influential, however, in forming the personality of the individual. The effect which it has had in these instances will depend largely on the meaning which the handicap has had for parents and other family members responsible for the care of the individual during childhood.[4] Frequently, a parent brings to the experience of having a child certain predetermined needs which may lead him to seek self-realization, or sometimes even to strive for adjustment, through the child. When the child is born handicapped or early suffers injury or chronic illness, the parent may experience great personal frustration. It may be also a threat to his pride, thus making him feel inferior. The resultant feelings of irritation, particularly if he feels at all to blame for the child's condition, may lead to feelings of rejection. This rejection may be openly expressed or, if the parent feels guilty over his hostile feelings, may be disguised through overprotective handling which eases the guilt.

If the parent has had deep feelings of inadequacy or great frustrations, he may identify himself very closely with a handicapped child, and in such an instance protective handling or unrealistic, wishful strivings may characterize his relationship with the child. In a family receiving aid to dependent children, Mr. V., unemployed because of a serious cardiac condition, had had cut short an able career in the engineering field. He responded to his son's post-infantile-paralysis handicap and mental retardation with refusal to accept a clinic's advice regarding medical care and vocational training. He needed to deny that there was anything much wrong with the boy. He blamed the school for the boy's failure and resisted placing him in a school for crippled children where it was thought that the youngster would have a better chance for some success. In aid to dependent children and other programs, as workers confer with parents on problems presented by their handicapped children, it is important that they understand what the child and his disability mean to the parent. This understanding can serve as a guide in our efforts to help parents who turn to us not only in relation to their management of children but also in such vital decisions as to whether or not they place children, allow them to have special educational opportunities, or cooperate in medical care.

When we work with the adult whose handicap has been lifelong, it may be too late to bring about basic personality change. Understanding his response may, however, enable us to be more helpful in many ways. For example, in the case of Mr. and Mrs. N., the worker encountered a young couple who were both blind. They were living in basement rooms in a dilapidated building, quarters provided by the township authorities for families receiving assistance. Mr. and Mrs. N. had met in the State institution for the blind and had been married shortly after leaving there while both were employed at broommaking in a blind and disabled-workers' shop. Mrs. N., aged 20, applied for and received aid to the blind when she became pregnant and could no longer work. Because of his age, 19 years, the husband was not eligible for aid to the blind. When she was unable to accompany him back and forth from the shop and in their rounds in broom selling, he gave up his work, maintaining that he could not get along without her. During the subsequent months he became increasingly dependent on her. He became increasingly irritable and difficult after the birth of a child with normal sight, since the mother became quite absorbed in this fulfillment of her fondest hopes.

Parental Responses to Children's Handicaps Are Decisive Determinants in Personality Development

It was at this point that Mrs. N. unburdened to the worker her great discouragement over Mr. N.'s inability to assume the responsibilities of a husband and father. She described him as always having been childish, which she attributed to the fact that he lost his parents during infancy and was left to the care of a grandmother who gave him excessive care because of his disability. Upon marriage he immediately looked to her to plan for both of them. She contrasted her own situation with his in that she had come from a family in which there was hereditary blindness, five of eight members having been sightless or having had markedly impaired vision. She said that her disability had been taken for granted. Her family was sociable and of great solidarity. The children took responsibility and participated almost normally in the life of the community. Mrs. N. impressed the worker as being an outgoing sociable woman with unusual self-dependence in managing her affairs and in caring for her child.

As Mrs. N. talked of her concern over her husband the worker directed her to consider what the child meant to him, and she was able to identify his difficulty as one of rivalry, though at the time this did not help her to feel any more tolerant of his limitations. The worker's suggestion that she put more responsibility on him did not bring results. Later the worker tried to get acquainted with Mr. N., who had until this time remained almost unknown because all financial planning had been done with Mrs. N. She found him very unhappy because he was not working and earning, and also because his wife had money and he did not. He disliked broommaking. He claimed to be mechanically inclined and said that he enjoyed working on old radios. He recalled his life in the institution with some pleasure, particularly as he talked of having studied the violin, of having played in the orchestra, and of having participated in musical activities at the church. In this community he had missed his religious and musical activities and had wanted work of a different sort but had felt that he would not be considered for anything. He was discouraged and depressed about their physical surroundings, and the worker got the impression that their living arrangements had operated against community contacts. The worker agreed that there might be difficulty in getting a job but, in view of the labor shortage and the fact that some industries were now employing blind workers, held out hope that he might get work. She made suggestions as to where he might apply. She showed interest in his musical ability also, and interest in the possibility that they might find community activities and church connections similar to those which they had enjoyed in the past. Later Mr. N. obtained work, and shortly thereafter the worker helped him apply for residence in a housing project.

Some months later the worker learned from Mrs. N. that he had continued to be fairly regularly employed; that they were planning to have the child admitted to a nursery-school group; that Mr. and Mrs. N. had become affiliated with a group of young married couples who lived in the housing project and gave parties. Both Mr. and Mrs. N. were playing in the orchestra for their dances. In their last conversation Mrs. N. stated that her husband had become tolerant of the baby; that he had bought him an electric train for Christmas and, since the baby was too young to enjoy this toy, Mr. N. was playing with it a great deal. She complained that he had spent a considerable sum of money on a watch, which was foolish in that he could not use it. The worker directed her to consider the importance of this possession to him in terms of "being like other men." Mrs. N. reported general improvement in their relationship, their only present difficulty being over the spending of money. She recounted that their worst quarrel had occurred over some curtains—Mrs. N. wanted pink ones, while Mr. N. wanted blue!

The Meaning of the Handicap Will Influence the Individual's Uuse of Public Assistance.

This case affords discussion of a number of important points in our work with the handicapped.

1.   Basic personality differences in Mr. and Mrs. N. result in part from their differing life experience with the same handicap. It is clear that each brings different needs to adulthood. There can be no great change in the personality of Mr. N., but, insofar as his needs are met, he functions more adequately within the limits of his personality.

2.   Because Mr. N. was not the recipient of aid, he apparently was ignored. That aid had meaning for him, however, in that it became a disturbing factor in his relationship with his wife. The worker's eventual recognition of him as a person, important in the family scheme, apparently brought a ready response. Perhaps because of his handicap and also because of his dependency, he needed this recognition all the more.

3.   We note also that marked change had come into the lives of Mr. and Mrs. N. through transferring from the protected regime of an institution, where they lived among the handicapped, to a competitive community in which they must find their place among those who are not handicapped. This adjustment was probably more difficult for Mr. N. because he was basically a more dependent person than his wife. He had clung to her to support him within the community, so that when she was withdrawn from work he had to accompany her. He needed encouragement and supportive help from someone who represented the community. One might expect that in our work with blind individuals who have lived in an institution there frequently might be a need for help in using community resources and in

finding some of the interests of their past life in the strange situation. In this connection the difficult problem introduced by living in wretched housing, stigmatized as township property for the use of the indigent, deserves our careful consideration. The value for these people of the community life which obtains in many housing projects is worth noting.

4. This case also emphasizes the deeply significant fact that "the blind" are not necessarily helpless, and that in spite of, or perhaps all the more because of, their difference from others, they long for identification and association with those who have normal vision. They try to see the world through our eyes, to a greater extent perhaps than we try to see it through theirs. Watches and colors and respectable surroundings still matter. All Mr. N.'s needs were needs frequently encountered in our work with sighted fathers and husbands. The blind individual is a *person* who happens to be blind. We need to know the person in order to help with the problem of blindness.[5] This same principle would apply with handicaps other than blindness.

5. This case presented the need for more adequate rehabilitation measures in State schools and for use of State rehabilitation resources. Correspondence with the State school in the case of Mr. N. revealed that there had been no attempt to determine his intellectual capacity, his vocational aptitudes, or to learn his aspirations and interests. It is obvious that persons with a major handicap need special help and special opportunities which may enable them to overcome their limitations insofar as possible. Dependence, actual and psychological, is an inevitable result of a lack of preparation for the life of the community. When the person's prior life experience has been such as to induce dependency, he may have all the more need for this help.[6] We note the importance also of using all available community resources both for preventive and remedial care.

It Is Important How the Worker Feels About Handicaps

In our work with disabled people, traditional attitudes, certain time-honored emphases, frequently obstruct us, perhaps because we feel deeply about them. We encounter our own mixed feelings about persons who are different. In many of us there probably are vestiges of our early childhood anxiety about difference. In any group of children we can note anxiety about the child who is a stranger until they have felt him out and been assured of his likeness to them. We have all observed their reactions to the child who is marked different, in dress, in ways, or in language. A disabled child frequently becomes the target of much hostility. They cannot permit themselves to identify themselves with him. Perhaps this is because of an unconscious fear that whatever happened to him might happen to them. Therefore, they taboo him in one way or another as a protection against entering into a relationship which is somehow threatening. As they grow older parental disapproval checks their savagery. Also, as they mature they become more socialized, and guilt over past feelings toward or treatment of those who are less fortunate may bring a reversal of attitudes and behavior. They may become as overprotective of the handicapped person as they were rejecting of him in earlier years.

Adult attitudes toward disabled persons are characterized by an inability to take handicaps for granted, by overprotective tendencies, and by a degree and kind of emotional involvement which tends to set the disabled person apart. These feelings are reflected in disability-conscious efforts to help them. Perhaps these feelings explain our studied attitudes, our concentration on *just how* to treat the handicapped as though they were a species. Perhaps they determine our tendency to view these individuals in terms of their disabilities and to plan for them primarily with reference to their difference, thereby frequently enhancing their discomfort and feelings of isolation.

Much work with the handicapped has been done with the self-conscious conviction that certain attitudes should be maintained by individuals who work with them. Long have we been aware that some handicapped persons have tended to become dependent. The prominence of regressive impulses in response to the obstacles or the change incurred in the individual's life led to a creed against infantilizing the disabled. Workers have been cautioned to avoid sympathizing with them and to encourage a certain bravado through reassuring them and "bucking" them up. In accordance with this, some workers have avoided discussing the handicap lest the individual become too centered in his disability. One could cite a number of such attitudes which bespeak our studied efforts to help those who *we feel* are different. Our helping efforts have swung from the extreme of coddling and sympathy which weaken to the discipline and denial which also may not strengthen. The decisive point is that these stock attitudes are not valid for general use. They meet the needs of some individuals but to the same degree frustrate others. We will help the handicapped individual only as we understand his *needs as a person*, not only the needs created by his handicap but also those which he has in common with other human beings. This focus implies readiness to acknowledge his difficulties, readiness to help him express his feelings about them, readiness to offer protective measures and supportive help in accordance with his need, and readiness to let him use his strengths and his resourcefulness in managing his own affairs. The same principles which we use in helping people with other problems are appropriate in work with those who are chronically ill or physically handicapped.

References

[1] For further discussion of the social and emotional problems of the physically handicapped, see Fitzsimmons, Margaret, "Treatment of Problems of Dependency Related to Permanent Physical Handicap," *The Family*, Vol. 23, No. 9 (January 1943), pp. 329-336; Ohmann, O. A., "The Psychology of the Handicapped," *The Crippled Child*, Vol. 18, No. 1 (June 1940), pp. 3-4 f.; and Reznikoff, Leon, M.D., "Emotional Factors in the Rehabilitation of the Physically Disabled," *American Journal of Psychiatry*, Vol. 94, No. 4 (January 1938), pp. 819-824.

[2] Richardson, Henry B., M.D., *Patients Have Families,* New York, Commonwealth Fund, 1945.

[3] See Chapter 4, pp. 69-70, *Common Human Needs* by Charlotte Towle.

[4] For a picture of how family reactions determine in considerable measure the child's response to physical disability, see *The Little Locksmith,* by Katherine Butler Hathaway, Toronto, Longmans, Green & Co., 1943; and *Of Human Bondage,* by Somerset Maugham, New York, Doubleday, Doran & Co., 1936.

[5] See Emerson, Ruth, "In the Interest of Preventing Blindness: Psychological Attitudes of the Visually Handicapped Toward Treatment," *Social Service Review*, Vol. 16, No. 3 (September 1942), pp. 477-496.

[6]For further consideration of vocational guidance, see Davis, J.E., *Principles and Practice of Rehabilitation*, New York, A. S. Barnes & Co., 1943; Hoppock, Robert, "Vocational Guidance," *Social Work Year Book, 1941*, pp. 581-584, New York, Russell Sage Foundation, 1941; Horton Evelyn, "Preparing for the Job; How the Medical Social Worker Aids in a Vocational Guidance Program," *The Crippled Child*, Vol. 19, No. 6 (April 1942), pp. 151-152 f.; Martens, Elise H., "Guidance for Physically Handicapped Pupils," *Outlook for the Blind*, Vol. 33, No. 2 (April 1939), pp. 40-45; Pintner, Rudolf, Eisenson, Jon, and Stanton, Mildred, *The Psychology of the Physically Handicapped*, New York, F. S. Crofts & Co., 1941; Super, Donald E., *The Dynamics of Vocational Adjustment,* New York, Harper & Brothers, 1941.

TWO

The Meaning of Handicap

ASSOCIATION FOR THE AID OF CRIPPLED CHILDREN,
NEW YORK

Perhaps the term "handicap" can usefully be defined as *an undesirable deviation from normality*—a deviation in function, in behavior, or in appearance, or any combination of these, that makes it difficult for the individual to lead (or be allowed to lead) a normally satisfying and productive life. Such a definition is not a new one . . . but it has come, in recent years, to cover a much broader range of disabilities and disorders than the visible orthopedic defect.

One reason why the visibly handicapped—the deformed, the lame, the blind—received early attention was that they could be readily identified and that some sort of service for them—medical treatment, orthopedic devices, education—was available. Moreover, in terms of our definition of handicap, the "cripple" represented a strongly undesirable deviation in a society which was not highly mechanized and which, therefore, placed a premium on motor skills and physical strength. The non-visibly handicapped, by contrast—the retarded, the emotionally disturbed, the individual with a circulatory or metabolic disorder—remained untreated because his defect could not be diagnosed or because he could not be helped.

The growth of medical knowledge, changes in social attitudes and the increasing complexity and mechanization of society in the twentieth century, however, brought about considerable change in the nature and significance of "handicap." The "cripple" provided with a prosthetic device and living in a society in which machine power had largely replaced human physical effort, found himself slightly less disadvantaged. And society's experience with two world wars led to somewhat greater acceptance of the individual with an obvious physical defect. The non-visibly handicapped, on the other hand, came to public attention in greater numbers as scientific knowledge and diagnostic acumen increased. And, because of the greater complexity and mechanization of society and hence the greater need for skilled labor, the mildly retarded or the slight behavioral problem fitted less easily into the educational, economic and social structure. In terms of the definition of handicap,

Reprinted from "Annual Report, 1960-1961, Association for the Aid of Crippled Children, New York," pp. 3-9. By permission of the Association.

such deviations became more apparent, more undesirable and of greater concern to society as a whole.

Biological and Social Factors

Even the schematized account given above indicates the inextricable relationship between biological and social factors in defining handicap and determining its degree. This relationship becomes clearer when one examines it in detail.

Virtually all handicapping conditions are determined by a combination of biological and social components. The degree of handicap of the individual who is completely incompetent mentally or physically will, of course, be little influenced by the social environment, but in most cases, even those involving severe physical defect, the degree of handicap is strongly influenced by social as well as biological factors. The child born without a leg, for example, will be handicapped to a degree determined in large part by social, cultural and psychological factors. How will his parents respond to his malformation, and how will their response affect his rearing? Will society regard him as a legless child or, let us say, as a child with considerable intelligence and a pleasant personality who lacks a leg? Will he be offered an opportunity for employment and social acceptance? And how will he respond to society's treatment of him? To what extent does his view of himself correspond with society's view of him? Will he withdraw from proffered acceptance or will he overcome rejection? If he is provided with a prosthetic device that permits him to function well and conceals his defect from outward view, will he still regard himself as handicapped? And how will others respond to his view of himself?

In the case of a non-visible and subtler defect, the role of society in determining handicap is even clearer. The child with a moderate degree of retardation, for example, could probably function quite adquately in a non-mechanized agricultural society in which the major requirements are the basic physical skills in food-gathering and shelter-building. But in a modern society, which places a higher value on intellectual skills than on physical strength and which requires even the least skilled laborer to sign a payroll and file an income-tax return and "get along well" with his foreman, he will be handicapped to a considerable degree. An ironic footnote to this situation is the fact that modern society seems to be increasing the numbers of such children: improvements in obstetrics, the widespread use of antibiotics, and the wider availability of good medical care save the lives of many children stricken with diseases which used to be fatal, but a considerable proportion of these survive with irreversible damage to the nervous and other body systems. Such children are handicapped because they cannot cope with the multiplicity of tasks that make up the normal day in modern society.

Both the child without the leg and the child with the intellectual handicap are, of course, quite measurably handicapped with respect to certain tasks or activities. The one is unlikely to become a track star, the other unlikely to become a philosopher. But what of the biological defect—a severe facial disfigurement, for example —which involves no loss of function? Such a person is likely to be discriminated against in situations in which his physical appearance is irrelevant. And, if the individual begins to reject himself as others reject him, he is likely to become even further handicapped.

Even the individual who begins life biologically intact can be physically damaged—and thus handicapped—by society. Perhaps the most dramatic organic damage produced by society is caused by war or by accidents, both leading causes of childhood handicapping. The child who becomes paraplegic as a result of military bombing or an automobile accident, the child who may become diseased from exposure to uncontrolled radiation or to toxic substances that he ingests, the child who is permanently disfigured by an oil-heater explosion—all these have been injured by a society that operates automobiles, owns firearms, manufactures inherently unsafe mechanical products, tests nuclear devices, and remains either unaware or indifferent to the toll being extracted.

Another source of physical damage wrought by society stems from simple neglect or from failure to use existing knowledge, techniques and facilities for either treatment or prevention. Such neglect or disregard can cause or aggravate or fail to correct a biological condition that may become a handicap. The unwed mother who is forced by society to conceal her condition or the migrant mother who cannot get adequate prenatal care is likely to suffer pregnancy complications that are in large part preventable but that, unprevented, can handicap her child from birth. It is easy, of course, to blame society as a whole for such a situation and to hope for a Utopia in which the best medical care will be available to all. But this view overlooks the fact that many preventive and therapeutic techniques and services—Salk vaccine, seat belts, well-baby clinics—are being disregarded by many individuals. The problem of medical neglect will not be solved then, until more is known about individual attitudes toward the utilization of available resources.

Thus far we have oversimplified the interaction between biological and social factors by describing them unilaterally—as though one influenced the other relatively simply. In reality, however, these factors sometimes interact with one another in a viciously cyclical fashion. The child who has dysfunction of the central nervous system may have difficulty in learning to read, even though he appears "intelligent" in other aspects of his behavior. His own sense of failure at this socially crucial task, coupled with the effects of his parents' and teachers' reactions, may then produce emotional problems which are not only intrinsically handicapping but which can aggravate the original reading difficulty. In similar fashion, a mother of low socio-economic status is more likely, for a variety of social and biological reasons, to produce a biologically defective child and then, again because of her status and the attitudes that accompany it, be reluctant or unable to use facilities which might correct the defect or maximize the child's physical and social functioning and abilities.

Thus far, although we have recognized the influence of social factors in determining the degree of handicap, we have nevertheless viewed handicap as involving at least to some extent an organic defect. But organic defect is not an essential component, for social factors alone can produce severe handicap even in the individual who is physically intact. There is evidence to suggest, for example, that healthy children reared in orphanages where they received the best of diets and medical care but less personal attention and social stimulation than in a normal family environment show a measurable degree of social and intellectual retardation. The deleterious effects of environmental deprivation are evident also in refugee, migrant and slum children, whose environment is impoverished in terms of the quality of their family life, their living conditions and their schooling. Less apparent, but well worth investigation, is the effect of the lack of social stimulation on children who are not "deprived" in the usual sense but who are isolated from a rich and intimate relationship with the social environment by their geographic location, parental idiosyncracy, social ostracism—or even extreme wealth.

The phrases "broken homes" and "slum neighborhoods" have become cliches used in glib explanations of juvenile delinquency, emotional disturbance and other pathologies. Nevertheless, it seems clear that certain kinds of family and community dysfunction can produce or aggravate undesirable deviation. James B. Conant, in *Slums and Suburbs*, makes clear the almost insuperable educational and vocational handicaps produced in children by the inadequacies of their schools and their neighborhoods. And it seems highly probable that the emotional climate in certain homes—whether broken or intact—can handicap the children both immediately and in terms of their own future parenthood.

Good physical health—or, at least, the absence of physical defect—is more or less definable. Freedom from social or emotional handicap, on the other hand, is difficult to define or measure, and the etiology of such handicap now lies largely in the realm of speculation. These facts alone would justify an acceleration of research. But two further points reinforce them: first, if medical progress continues at its present pace, there will undoubtedly be further decreases in the incidents of physical impairment, and, as a result, social and behavioral factors will loom even larger as features of handicap than they do today; secondly, with the continuing urbanization and mechanization of the entire world, such deviations are likely to become even more severe handicaps than they are now.

PART TWO

Mentally Retarded Persons and Their Families: A Social Welfare Concern

Portrait of Median City

THE WELFARE ADMINISTRATION

Social welfare is commonly thought of as those organized activities and direct services to individuals, groups and communities which help, in the words of a United Nations definition, "towards a mutual adjustment of individuals and their social environment."

In a broader sense, however, social welfare may be regarded as encompassing the total spectrum of society's efforts to improve, enhance and protect the well-being of its individual members and their interrelationships. In such a context, social welfare includes also social insurance, education, medical care, public health services, housing, and related functions.

Viewed within this larger context U.S. expenditures under public programs came to more than $66.5 billion in 1963, nearly 12 percent of that year's gross national product. Of this sum, $8.4 billion fell within the categories usually thought of as social welfare. The antipoverty program, which did not get under way until 1964, currently adds another $1.5 billion to this figure. To this sum of approximately $10 billion in public expenditures for direct welfare services must also be added some $1.6 billion in private philanthropic contributions by individuals, foundations, and business corporations.

It seems reasonable to ask why, in a nation which has attained the highest living standards the world has ever known, such staggering outlays should be needed for welfare programs. The explanation lies in the fact that the role of social welfare in all nations is conditioned not only by measurable political, economic, and demographic characteristics, but also by those intangible factors which reflect the mood, tempo, aspirations and expectations of the nation's people.

The viewpoint expressed in the phrase "the American way of life" stems both from a democratic system of government based on constitutional guarantees of each man's right to equal freedom and opportunity, and from a national history that has produced a fluid, steadily upward-striving society. The free exercise of individual initiative conquered an empty continent, explored and developed its rich natural

From *Portrait of Median City*. The Welfare Administration, U.S. Department of Health, Education and Welfare (Washington, U.S. Government Printing Office, 1966), pp. 2-8, 33-37.

resources into a productive, highly industrialized society. Social and physical mobility were both essential to the development of the United States, and both continue to characterize the American ethic. Tradition is cherished less than progress; unlike older, more deeply rooted societies where generation after generation cultivates the same plot of land or engages in the same occupation, Americans are constantly changing their place of residence and their means of livelihood in quest of greater economic opportunity, better living conditions, brighter prospects for their children.

This kind of free and mobile economy, which is neither centrally planned nor centrally controlled, does not grow at a measured pace, nor are its benefits evenly distributed. Spurts of expansion and change exact a price in the form of social stresses and imbalances. Those unable to keep pace with the majority experience not only deprivation but discouragement and discontent. Vital social and economic values are threatened by this kind of imbalance. To ignore or tolerate apathy, loss of motivation or restless ferment in any significant segment of the population is to endanger the entire structure of society.

Social welfare services in the United States, therefore, are designed to aid both those weakened by the common misfortunes of mankind: the very old, the helpless young, the sick and infirm, the physically or mentally handicapped—and those whose difficulties stem from economic and social factors: the undereducated, the economically displaced and technologically unskilled, the racial minorities struggling to overcome a heritage of discrimination and exploitation, the individuals and families thrown off balance by the stresses of urban living, the culturally backward, the socially rebellious.

To understand how these services operate one must keep constantly in mind the nature of the United States political structure.

The 50 States which form the American Republic retain wide domestic powers, among which is control of the tax-supported welfare programs operating within their borders. For geographic, political, and social reasons, the States do not share equally in the Nation's wealth, nor do they have a common outlook or follow common practices with respect to public welfare services.

There is, consequently, no uniform social welfare pattern in the United States, no single city or State which can be said to characterize the rest of the country. However, an arbitrary device may serve the purpose—a device developed along the following lines.

With more than 70 percent of Americans already living in urban areas and the percentage steadily on the rise, urbanization is the dominant feature of present-day life in the United States. The essential nature of social welfare services can therefore be seen in action through construction of an imaginary city to serve as a microcosm of the Nation as a whole.

The characteristics of this imaginary city are determined by locating the median in a list of the 130 American cities which have populations in excess of 100,000. The midpoint in this list turns out to be about 200,000. Our imaginary microcosm, which we will name Median City, is thus assumed to have a population of 200,-

000. As it happens, this is a convenient figure for use because it is one one-thousandth (0.0001) of the U.S. population, currently approaching 200 million. National figures are thus easily projected onto a local scale, and vice versa. Reading the figures ascribed to Median City in the chapters which follow, one need merely add 000 to see the national picture.

Profile of Median City

SOME SOCIAL CHARACTERISTICS

A look at some of the basic social characteristics of Median City will show the following:

Among its 200,000 people there are 70,000 under the age of 18 and 18,000 over the age of 65. The population of working age numbers 112,000.

All but about 18,000 of Median City's people are members of its 47,000 family units. Families start young: two out of three women, and one out of three men, marry before the age of 21.

About 8,500 of these 47,000 family households are manless. The family heads are childless single women, widows, divorced, deserted or separated wives, or mothers of out-of-wedlock children.

Racially, 89 percent of 178,000 of Median City's people are white. Of the 22,-000 nonwhites, 20,000 are Negro and the remainder of Oriental, American Indian, or mixed ancestry.

In terms of religion, the large majority of Median City's people were born into a Protestant denomination. Only about 60 percent of the population have current active church affiliations: 67,000 Protestants, 45,000 Roman Catholics, 5,500 Jews. Less than 2 percent belong to other religions.

The population of Median City is growing at the rate of 3,000 persons a year; for every 10 deaths, there are 20 births. Children born today can expect to live until 70 if male, 73 if female. Of the 4,000 children born each year, nearly 250 are born out of wedlock.

Many of the city's residents were born elsewhere. If Median City reflects the national average, 26.4 percent of its people were born in a different State or country. Depending on its geographic location in the United States, however, this figure may be much lower or much higher. If Median City is situated in a southern State like Alabama or Kentucky, or in the northeastern State of Maine, its percentage of non-native residents is only about half the national average. If, on the other hand, it is situated in a fast-growing western State, such as California, Nevada or Arizona, its percentage of non-natives may be as high as 50-70 percent.

About 10,000 Median City people were born outside the United States; 24,000 others are members of families in which one or both parents are of foreign birth.

How much education have Median City people had? Applying the national yardstick for urban areas, whites have had 11 years of schooling, nonwhites just over 8 years. Median City's children, however, are getting more schooling than their parents. Of every 10 students who start high school, 7 graduate (i.e., have 12 years of education) and 3 of these 7 go on to college. Nevertheless, 1,000 Median City youngsters leave school every year, 300 of them before they have even completed the 8 years of grade school.

Some 11,500 Median City residents suffer from mental illness at some time in their lives; 300 or more enter a mental hospital each year. There are, in addition, close to 6,000 mentally retarded children and adults.

Nearly 900 children between the ages of 10 and 17 are brought into Median City's juvenile courts each year because of acts of delinquency. Also brought under the court's jurisdiction each year are some 300 children who are adjudged dependent because they lack parents or their parents cannot provide a home for them, or who are adjudged neglected because of parental incapacity or abuse.

SOME ECONOMIC CHARACTERISTICS

What are some of the economic facts of life in Median City?

Applying the 0.001 formula to the gross national product, we find that in 1966 the value of all the goods and services produced in Median City, plus its share of Federal production, was at the rate of more than $700 million a year.

About 71,000 of Median City's 112,000 adults are in the labor force, 22,000 of them women. Three out of five of these employed women are married and living with their husbands.

Employment is high. Less than 4 percent of the employables are without a job at any given time, although the unemployment rate is twice as high among Negroes as it is among whites. About 3,700 Median City workers hold more than one job; this double employment, known as "moonlighting," is particularly prevalent among civil servants, especially teachers.

Despite high employment, more than 30,000 of Median City's 200,000 people are deemed to live in poverty.

Poverty is, of course, a relative term. An income classified as at the poverty level in the United States may easily be considered near-affluence in another part of the world where living standards, living costs and, even more important, popular expectations are at a lower level. Nevertheless, in every nation those people are poor who do not share in the average proportion of the nation's bounty. In the United States the poor are those who, for whatever reason, lack sufficient resources to keep themselves and their dependents decently nourished, housed, clothed, protected against health hazards, educated for effective participation in the Nation's economy.

By this yardstick, the "poverty line" in the United States has been drawn at an annual income of just over $3,000 for a family of four, although obviously a higher figure would pertain to larger families. Median City has 7,500 family units whose incomes are under $3,000; of these, more than 1,000 contain five or more children.

In 1964, the median income of a nonfarm American family was $6,832 if the family was white and $4,467 if nonwhite. Although nonwhites are only 11 percent of the Median City population, their percentage of the city's poor is very much higher.

In a simpler age, in a simpler society, perhaps all that would be needed to minister to the many social ills of Median City would be a sufficient distribution of money. The complex forces at work in a modern industrialized urban society, however, make alleviation of financial need only a first step. Experience has shown that unless basic causes are attacked, unless proliferating side effects are curbed, the pattern of social dependency is passed on from generation to generation, with each succeeding cycle more difficult to dislodge.

Social welfare services in the United States consequently have a three-fold aim: (1) amelioration of urgent temporary or permanent subsistence needs, (2) social rehabilitation of those who have failed in, or have never even attempted, the struggle to help themselves; (3) prevention of future social dysfunction through detection and removal of causes.

In the American microcosm which we have named Median City, we will find these three aims pursued by a complex network of public and voluntary agencies and services.

Services for the Handicapped

In no area of social need is there a greater multiplicity of services than in the field of help for the physically or mentally impaired.

Medical, paramedical, hospital, vocational, social welfare and mental health services are all brought to bear on behalf of the more than 9 percent of the Nation's population suffering from long-term chronic illness or impairment which renders them partially or totally unable to work, keep house or go to school. For Median City, this means 19,000 incapacitated men, women and children.

The efforts to meet the needs of the orthopedically handicapped, the blind, the deaf, the sufferers from chronic cardiac or rheumatic or arthritic disease, the mentally ill and the mentally retarded involves an extremely wide range of welfare and health services: Federal, State and local public agencies of various kinds plus national, regional, State and local voluntary organizations.

FINANCIAL NEEDS

Help with the financial and medical costs of disablement comes from a number of sources.

As previously noted, aid to both the blind and the permanently disabled are specific categories of public assistance. In Median City, 100 "legally blind" persons and 500 permanently disabled persons are sufficiently needy to be eligible for these two categories.

About 400 disabled children receive medical treatment and nursing services under the federally aided crippled children's programs. These programs, which operate in all States, aid youngsters with orthopedic handicaps, neurological and muscular impairments, cerebral palsy, rheumatic fever, epilepsy, hearing loss, congenital heart conditions, and other crippling conditions.

Many of the chronically ill are also aged. In Median City in 1964, medical and nursing home care for persons receiving old age assistance involved an expenditure of about $450,000 plus an approximately equal sum for medically indigent aged persons served by the medical assistance to the aged program. The advent of Medicare and the extension of medical assistance to children and others in low income groups will mean substantially increased sums in years to come.

Under the social security provisions for disabled workers, about 700 such persons in Median City receive monthly benefits, with additional benefits paid to their spouses and children. Disabled veterans are treated free of charge in Veterans Administration hospitals and institutions. For 500 Median City people temporarily or permanently disabled by industrial accidents, medical treatment or equivalent payments are provided under workmen's compensation insurance.

SERVICE PROGRAMS

Medical and financial needs are only part of the story, however. A large number of public and voluntary agencies are engaged in meeting the social, psychological and vocational requirements of the handicapped; in conducting programs of research, prevention and public education to reduce the incidence and impact of disabling conditions; in recruiting and training professional and other personnel to staff the rehabilitation services and in coordinating the multiple services entailed in rehabilitation of the handicapped.

In an urban center like Median City such activities involve—in addition to the tax-supported hospitals, health services, welfare and vocational rehabilitation agencies—independent local organizations or local chapters of national agencies concerned with specific disabilities and diseases: blindness, deafness, orthopedic conditions, cancer, heart disease, tuberculosis, cerebral palsy, multiple sclerosis, kidney disease, birth defects, mental illness, mental retardation and others. Patient care and services may or may not be included in the programs of these agencies, but all are active in casefinding and in efforts to insure that adequate community provisions exist for medical and social treatment of the conditions they specialize in.

Voluntary family and children's agencies, the school system, community planning bodies and civic groups are also active sources of referral and after-care services for the handicapped. There are civic and business groups, not usually thought of as social welfare bodies, that have taken certain types of disability "under their wing," so to speak, supplying funds and, in some instances, services on behalf of victims of the particular disability. Such groups range from businessmen's associations like Rotary, Kiwanis and Lions, to fraternal organizations like the Masons, Elks and Moose, to membership groups as diverse as the American Legion and the Junior League.

REHABILITATION SERVICES

Due largely to the special-interest agencies and groups, many specialized rehabilitation services have been developed to assist persons suffering from particular handicaps in adjustment and reorganization of their lives. Median City has, for example, one or more agencies for service to the blind, offering some or all of the following services: casework and psychiatric counseling, education for blind children and youth, teaching of communications methods and mobility skills, psychological testing, vocational guidance and training, sheltered employment, braille transcription, reading services and a host of others. Comparable separate facilities may exist for the crippled, for persons which chronic cardiac impairment, for mentally retarded children or adults or for other handicapped groups.

With the recognition that better and more efficient results can be attained through centralization and coordination, there have been developed in recent years more than 100 comprehensive rehabilitation centers, usually attached to a medical school-teaching hospital complex. If Median City is one of the cities which has such a comprehensive rehabilitation center, resident patients and out-patients are served through:

Medical, surgical and restorative treatment, including nursing care; physical, occupational, recreational and speech therapy; prosthetic services; instruction and training to achieve maximum independence in self-care and activities of daily living.

Social casework and group work to assess and ameliorate the social effects of the disability on the patient, his family and their interrelationships.

Psychological and psychiatric services to evaluate the factors which condition the disabled individual's rehabilitation potential and to counsel the patient on problems of personal, family and community adjustment.

Vocational services to evaluate, establish goals for, and provide training or retraining in the vocational field suited to the disabled person's interests and capacities.

The modern trend is to place increasing emphasis on extension of these services beyond the walls of the rehabilitation institution into the patient's home. Home care programs involve visiting teams of specialists—doctors, nurses, therapists of various kinds, social workers—to bring the necessary treatment services to the patient and to teach him and his family the techniques of basic care. Such home care programs have the dual effect of expediting the handicapped person's reintegration into normal living while simultaneously freeing hospital and institutional beds for treatment of emergency and short-term illness.

VOCATIONAL REHABILITATION SERVICES

For psychological, social and economic reasons, vocational rehabilitation services are basic to all programs for the handicapped. Through the Federal-State rehabilitation system, which restores employment people with mental or physical disabilities, Median City spent $375,000 to help these handicapped people in 1965, with the Federal Government paying $300,000 of this amount.

In addition, one or more voluntary agencies helped the handicapped. Through the public and voluntary programs about 135 handicapped persons in Median City were rehabilitated in 1965. Over the years ahead, because they can now work, they will pay taxes of $5 for every $1 invested in their rehabilitation, thus, repaying, many times over, the aid they received.

Median City has one or more of the Nation's 900 sheltered workshops which provide training and employment to handicapped persons not yet able to hold jobs in open employment. Its handicapped citizens also can use one of the Nation's 500 rehabilitation centers. Some of the centers are comprehensive. Others are units in mental hospitals, and some specialize in such disabilities as speech and hearing impairments.

Vocational rehabilitation goes beyond the maintenance of physical facilities and primarily is concerned with providing services. These include evaluation, counseling, physical restoration, training or retraining in specific job skills, development of work tolerance, job placement, and follow-up service.

MENTAL ILLNESS AND RETARDATION

A major emphasis in rehabilitation is the reintegration into normal community life of persons formerly isolated. This is of particular significance to the recovered mental patient, for whom special facilities to promote resocialization include day hospitals, night hospitals, halfway houses, foster care arrangements and various therapeutic group services conducted in the community. Similar integrative efforts are increasingly being made on behalf of the mentally retarded, many of whom can be satisfactorily assimilated into community life if given assistance, guidance and training at an early stage.

Median City, as has been noted, has close to 6000 mentally retarded men, women and children. By far the largest number, more than 5,000, fall into the mildly retarded (IQ 50-70) classification. Of the others, about half are confined to public and voluntary residential institutions or in mental hospitals, and the remaining half are in family care, some of them on a waiting list for institutional admission.

Much research effort is currently being invested in finding ways to prevent the spread of mental retardation as well as methods of effective treatment. It has been found that there is a causal relationship between prenatal care and retardation. Impoverished mothers who receive little or no prenatal care are three times as apt to have premature babies as those given proper care; small premature infants are 10 times more likely to be mentally retarded than full-term infants of normal weight.

Poverty is not only a contributory cause of retardation but tends to accentuate and prolong the condition. In deprived families, children with mental deficiencies are less apt to be identified at an early age, and thus less apt to receive the stimulation, guidance and remedial education services that can help them make the most of their limited abilities.

In Median City we may expect to find one or more clinics for diagnosis and treatment of retarded children. The city may also have a special nursery program for preschool retardates, although there are only a limited number of such facilities in existence thus far. Some, but not all, of Median City's retarded school-age children are taught in special educational programs under the school system; however, a nationwide shortage of teachers trained in the special techniques of working with the retarded makes it probable that other mentally deficient children in Median

City attend regular school classes in which their learning opportunities and achievements are necessarily limited.

Some of Median City's retarded young adults are in vocational training programs, but here, too, there is a shortage of facilities and not all can be served who need to be.

In all it may be said that, compared with the facilities available to the physically handicapped, the mentally handicapped need many more social welfare services than are presently available in Median City or elsewhere.

As a result of recent legislation, increased Federal aid is now available for a broad range of programs to prevent mental retardation and to serve the mentally retarded.

FOUR

Hypothetical Community

OFFICE OF THE SPECIAL ASSISTANT ON MENTAL RETARDATION, THE WHITE HOUSE

In the *average*American community of 100,000, not less than 3,000 mentally retarded persons of all ages and all degrees of retardation would be found. The services needed by these persons are many and vary greatly depending upon age and the severity of retardation. This hypothetical community would be confronted with large numbers of retarded pre-schoolers, retarded of school-age, and young adult and adult retarded.

	PRE-SCHOOL under age 6	SCHOOL AGE age 6-19	YOUNG ADULTS age 20-24	ADULTS age 26 & over	TOTAL all ages
Mildly	341	596	150	1,416	2,503
Moderate	54	95	24	226	399
Severe	13	23	6	56	98

Just a few of the major services this community must have if it is to combat the problem of mental retardation are:

Diagnostic and counseling services for all retarded and their families.

Welfare, social and educational services to enrich the learning opportunities of the 341 mildly retarded pre-school children, many of whom live in slums or in otherwise depressed circumstances.

Public health nursing and homemaker services to assist in caring for the 54 moderately and 13 severely retarded infants and young children.

Forty special education classes for the 596 mildly retarded pupils who with specialized training will become self-sufficient adult citizens.

Twelve special educational calsses for the 95 moderate or trainable retarded who with appropriate training will also become productive workers in protective, supervised settings.

Reprinted from "Hypothetical Community." Office of the Special Assistant on Mental Retardation, The White House (Washington, 1962).

A day-care, recreation center for the 23 severely retarded children of school-age who are unable to profit from formal schooling.

Vocational counseling, job training and placement services for the 150 mildly retarded young adults who can become self-sufficient, independent, working members of the community.

Sheltered workshops for the 250 moderately retarded adults of all ages who can contribute to their own and the community's welfare if given an opportunity to work in a protected environment.

Activity centers for the 56 adult severely retarded who may never take their place as workers in the community, but who are not less important from the humanitarian and social viewpoint.

Residential centers to meet the needs of those of the retarded with problems of care and training so complex as to require 24 hour effort.

FIVE

The Concept of Mental Retardation

VOCATIONAL REHABILITATION ADMINISTRATION

The person attempting to acquire a knowledge of the field of mental retardation can scarcely avoid becoming confused by the bewildering variety of terms, definitions, and estimates of prevalence. He will encounter such terms as feeble mindedness, moronity, mental deficiency, imbecility, idiocy, amentia, etc. All of these terms have been popular at one time or another and have been advocated by various experts in the field. Shifts in popularity from one term to another have come about because of the stigma which has invariably become attached to a particular term after a period of use. The advocacy of any new "name" is a misdirected effort because no term can, for long, escape the stigma which comes to be attached to a label as a result of misunderstanding of the essential nature of that which is being described. The current most widely used term is "mental retardation." It is suggested that this term be used by the counselor to refer to the broad group under consideration.

Mental retardation can be described simply as *an inadequacy of general intellectual functioning which has existed from birth or childhood.* The *principal tool* for establishing the presence of mental retardation is the tests which have been constructed to measure intellectual functioning. However, it has been found that the level of a person's adaptive behavior (how well the individual solves problems in his environment, and how well he adapts to the behavioral expectation and standards of society) can be predicted with only *moderate* efficiency from knowing his measured intelligence (test score). In other words, our current tests of general intelligence are not a foolproof measure of adaptive behavior. And, it is the deficiency in adaptive behavior, not a subaverage test score, which draws society's attention to an individual and creates a need for social or legal action on his behalf. Consequently, the official definition of the American Association on Mental Deficiency requires that a suspicion of mental retardation established on the basis of measured intelligence be confirmed by a clinical judgment as to the individual's actual adaptive behavior.

From *Special Problems in Vocational Rehabilitation of the Mentally Retarded.* Vocational Rehabilitation Administration, U.S. Department of Health, Education and Welfare (Washington, U.S. Government Printing Office, 1964), pp. 11-18.

Measured intelligence greater than one standard deviation below the mean (a statistical term which expresses the dispersion of scores in the standardization sample) is arbitrarily set as the cutoff point for *consideration* of possible retardation. This cutoff point is equivalent to a test score of about IQ 84 on the most commonly used individual tests of general intelligence. It is important for the counselor to bear in mind, however, that this figure will vary from one test to another depending upon the standardization characteristics of the particular instrument.

In addition to subaverage measured intelligence, a diagnosis of mental retardation requires that there be a significant impairment in adaptive behavior. What constitutes a meaningful impairment in adaptive behavior varies as a function of the age of the individual. In identifying mentally retarded children below school age, maturation is of prime importance. At this age level, significant lags in the maturation of the self-help skills of infancy and early childhood (development of locomotion, eating, dressing and communications skills) are the principal bases upon which a judgment of impaired adaptive behavior is made. At the school age level, disability in rate of learning of academic skills constitutes the major basis upon which a judgment of retardation is made. At the adult level, adaptive behavior is considered to be inadequate if the individual is unable to maintain himself independently in the community or meet basic performance standards in employment when presented with an opportunity to do so. In practice, few persons *near* the cutoff point in measured intelligence (that is minus one standard deviation below the mean of IQ about 85) are diagnosed as mentally retarded in as much as their adaptive behavior is not called into question. As measured intelligence becomes lower, increasing percentages of persons are identified as mentally retarded. This relationship between measured intelligence and impaired adaptive behavior is illustrated below.

In actual practice, then, the counselor will be able to regard most persons with IQ's below or near minus two standard deviations (about IQ 70 for the most com-

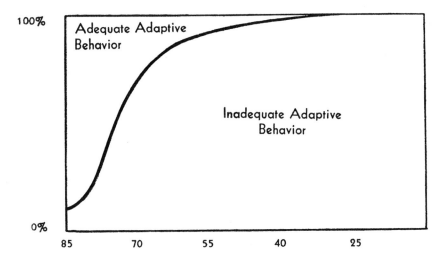

mon tests) as mentally retarded. Persons whose measured intelligence is between minus two and minus one standard deviation (about IQ 70-85) may be considered retarded if their adaptive behavior so indicates.

Mental retardation, as with other disabilities, varies in degree of severity. The prognosis and rehabilitation objectives are, of course, in part determined by the degree of mental retardation. Current official usage arbitrarily classifies measured intelligence in terms of five levels which extend from the cutoff point (minus one standard deviation or IQ 85) to the zero point on the test. More useful from the point of view of rehabilitation and management is the degree of impairment in the adaptive behavior of the individual.

Current usage favors a classification in terms of four levels of impairment in adaptive behavior; mild, moderate, severe, and profound. The mildly impaired group is comprised of those who, with proper preparation, can be fully capable of independent living in the community and gainful competitive employment. They require supervision and guidance only under conditions of unusual social or economic stress. The moderately impaired are those retarded adults capable of maintaining themselves in the community and performing adequately in unskilled work but who need some continuing supervision and assistance in adjusting to even the mild social and economic stresses in their lives. The severely impaired are considered capable of productive work activity but only under sheltered noncompetitive conditions in a protected environment. The profoundly impaired group is comprised of those persons who are incapable of any significant productive work activity and who require complete care and living supervision.

These gross groupings of impairment in adaptive behavior of the mental retardate are useful with respect to program planning; a broad classification, of course, cannot reflect the variations in the individual's skill among different categories of behavior. It is these variations which are taken into account by the counselor in setting objectives and planning rehabilitation programs for individual clients. The schools, being concerned principally with academic skill learning, have found it more useful to classify mentally retarded pupils in terms of the programs which have been devised for their special education; educable, trainable, and nontrainable. Pupils who are labeled as educable will often fall into the mild or moderate categories of adaptive behavior in adult life while children labeled as trainable during the school years will often demonstrate a severe adaptive impairment as adults. Persons regarded as nontrainable during the school age period almost always present a profound impairment in adaptation as adults. However, this correspondence between school classification and adult vocational classification is not invariable and should never be assumed in individual cases.

Prevalence

No comprehensive survey of the number of mentally retarded in a community has ever been undertaken using satisfactory techniques for identification. The most common figure cited, one based on expert opinion, is 3 percent of the total population. In actual practice, that figure has never been reached for an unselected segment of the population in any study where rigorous criteria of mental retardation were employed. Two other factors must be borne in mind in considering prevalence: (1) the percentages of *identified* mental retardates vary dramatically as a function of age, and (2) prevalence figures vary markedly as a function of the socioeconomic level of a community or neighborhood. The percentage of identified mental retardates increases gradually from birth to age 6, jumps significantly at the age of school entry and continues to rise reaching a peak in the 14-16 year age period. The prevalence then drops rather dramatically from age 16 on. The high prevalence of identified retardation among school age persons is probably a function of the facts that: (1) schools are the only community agency which has access to, and the means to assess, all persons in the population belonging to a particular age group; and (2) schools, in their academic expectations, apply a more rigorous standard of adaptive behavior than is demanded either of the preschool or adult age groups. The prevalence of mental retardation will be found to be considerably greater than 3 percent among the lowest socioeconomic levels (for example, census tract areas with median education levels of 8 years in school or less and median family income levels of $3,000 per annun or less) while neighborhoods or communities characterized by high incomes and education levels will often have prevalences of less than 1 percent. Consequently, an estimation of the total prevalence of mental retardation in a given community must involve consideration of factors such as the socioeconomic and age distributions.

Statistical compilation of all of the mental retardates now known to every private and public agency (schools, institutions, vocational rehabilitation, welfare, etc.) would doubtless not yield a total greater than 1 percent of the general population of the United States. School systems considered to be providing the most adequate specialized educational services for retarded children serve no more than about 2 percent of the total school population. At the same time, it is generally acknowledged that all services for the mentally retarded fall far short of demand. No service for the mentally retarded has yet been inaugurated in any community and found itself with a shortage of clients once the availability of the program was known. In the absence of definitive surveys, perhaps the best statement regarding prevalence that can be made at this time is that: *it is sufficiently greater than the approximate one percent now known to all agencies to suggest that the continued demand and need for service will exceed the availability of such services for many years to come.*

One further factor is of interest with respect to prevalence. That is, the proportions of the total population of mentally retarded persons falling into each of the four levels of adaptive behavior vary radically different. This is illustrated in the figure below. The figure is intended to be illustrative rather than suggestive of precise figures. However, it does point out the need for considering program planning, not in relation to some overall prevalence figure such as 3 percent but, in relation to prevalences of the various levels and subcategories of the mentally retarded.

Level of Adaptive Behavior Impairment		Percent of Total Population of Mental Retardates

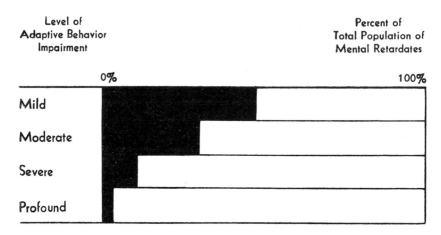

The Cause of Mental Retardation

From 10 to 20 percent of the total group of mentally retarded are known to have some demonstrable pathology in the structure or function of the central nervous system. This pathology is presumed to be directly responsible for producing the mental retardation. There are literally scores of specific diseases and conditions which have been known to produce damage to the brain and eventuate in retardation. All of these, however, can be grouped in the following categories:

> infections which involve the central nervous system of the infant or young child;
> physical injuries to the brain before, during or after birth;
> an array of disorders of metabolism, some of which are genetically determined, which damage the nervous system;
> conditions of genetic or unknown cause which involve abnormal growths within the brain;
> diseases of genetic or unknown origin which result in a progressive degeneration of the nervous system; and
> an array of prenatally determined conditions which involve physical defects of the brain or skull or which present distinctive physical characteristics which have their origin from before the time of birth.

The presence of this type of retardation, in which pathology of central nervous system is a presenting feature, is fairly evenly distributed throughout all socioeconomic, ethnic, and racial groups. Further, it is generally although not always associated with measured intelligence below IQ scores of about 55 (greater than three standard deviations below the mean). Affected persons tend to function as trainable or nontrainable pupils in school, and as profoundly or severely impaired in adaptive behavior in adult life. They are also likely to have associated secondary physical disabilities which complicate their rehabilitation problems.

By contrast with the group above, about 80 to 90 percent of all mental retardates *do not* present *obvious gross* pathology of the central nervous system. A small number from among this group appear retarded because of long-standing emotional or psychotic disorders of childhood which have interfered with learning. A few are retarded because of a secondary disability such as impaired vision or hearing or cerebral palsy which has resulted in a restriction of learning opportunities essential to normal intellectual development. The *great proportion* of this group, however, are persons who appear quite normal in the physical sense but who function as mentally retarded. These persons invariably derive from and have been reared in socially and economically disadvantaged environments. They are heavily represented in the slums of the metropolitan centers of the country and in depressed rural areas. Their greatest concentration is among minority groups residing in city slums.

The basic cause of this type of retardation is unknown except for the fact that its roots are to be found among the concomitants of deprived social and economic circumstances. Factors of inheritance of intelligence are undoubtedly significant. Poor, or nonexistent prenatal care among low socioeconomic group mothers, high rates of prematurity, inadequate infant health supervision, etc., may be factors related to producing mild central nervous system insults which are simply not demonstrable by present methods of examination. There is evidence to suggest that failure to acquire a motivational structure and a value system consistent with intellectual development and achievement, along with restrictions in learning opportunities, are also contributing etiological factors in this group.

These persons will most often have mild degrees of impairment in measured intelligence, that is between IQ about 50 or 55 and the upper limit, IQ 84. They usually are considered as educable children in school and generally will fall into the mild and moderate degrees of impairment in adaptive behavior in adult life. The major factor complicating the rehabilitation of this group is to be found in their low socioeconomic group membership. The self-defeating values and motivations characteristic of socially and economically deprived cultures are frequently superimposed on the basic intellectual disability.

Related Disabilities

Mental retardation is frequently encountered in combination with secondary physical or *behavioral disabilities*. These *secondary disabilities* are no less important for consideration in rehabilitation than are the *fundamental characteristics* of mental retardation. The most frequent supplementary physical impairments to be taken into consideration are:

   I. cranial anomalies—defects of the skull such as hydrocephalus, microcephaly, etc.,
  II. impairments of special senses—vision or hearing, losses,
 III. convulsive disorders,
 IV. motor dysfunctions—such as cerebral palsy.

These secondary physical disabilities are most common among those retarded with demonstrable central nervous system pathology who also tend to be more severely retarded.

Secondary behavioral disabilities are a major factor among all categories of mental retardation. They are particularly important with respect to those retarded who demonstrate mild or moderate impairments in adaptive behavior and who generally come from adverse environments in which they have learned to be defeated, unmotivated, and hostile. The retardate with mild degrees of retardation in measured intelligence will often be brought to the attention of the rehabilitation counselor not because of the intellectual defect *per se* but, rather, because of concomitant behavioral disabilities. Every retarded client should be evaluated with respect to the following supplementary behavioral impairments:

I. *Personal-social factors*
   a. Impairment in cultural conformity—refers to behavior which does not conform to social mores, standards of dependability, reliability, or trustworthiness; or to behavior which is persistently asocial, antisocial, or excessively hostile.
   b. Impairment in interpersonal relations—inadequacy in the way in which the individual relates to peers and/or authority figures; or to an inability to recognize the needs of other persons in interpersonal interactions.
   c. Impairment in responsiveness (motivation)—an inability to delay gratification of needs or a lack of long range goal striving or persistence with response only to immediate or short term goals.

II. *Sensory-motor skill impairments.*
   a. Motor skills—disability in gross or fine motor movement.
   b. Speech skills—defects in vocalization such as a lisp. stuttering, stammering, etc.
   c. Auditory skills—a disability in understanding and responding to speech (over and above the performance level expected on the basis of measured intelligence).
   d. Visual skills—a disability in responding meaningfully to visual stimulation (over and above the performance level expected on the basis of measured intelligence).

SIX

Significance of the Problem

REPORT OF THE PRESIDENT'S PANEL TO COMBAT MENTAL RETARDATION

Mental retardation ranks as a major national health, social, and economic problem:

It afflicts twice as many individuals as blindness, polio, cerebral palsy, and rheumatic heart disease, combined. Only 4 significant disabling conditions—mental illness, cardiac disease, arthritis, and cancer—have a higher prevalence, but they tend to come late in life while mental retardation comes early.

About 400,000 of the persons affected are so retarded that they require constant care or supervision, or are severely limited in their ability to care for themselves and to engage in productive work; the remaining 5 million are individuals with mild disabilities.

Over 200,000 adults and children, largely from the severe and profound mentally retarded group, are cared for in residential institutions, mostly at public expense. States and localities spend $300 million a year in capital and operating expenses for their care. In addition, they spend perhaps $250 million for special education, welfare, rehabilitation, and other benefits and services for retarded individuals outside of public institutions. In the current fiscal year, the Federal Government will obligate an estimated $164 million for the mentally retarded, about three-fourths for income maintenance payments and the rest for research, training, and special services. Federal funds for this group have nearly doubled in 5 years.

The Nation is denied several billion dollars of economic output because of the underachievement, underproduction, and/or the complete incapability of the mentally retarded.

The untold human anguish and loss of happiness and well-being which result from mental retardation blight the future of millions of families in the United States. An estimated 15 to 20 million people live in families in which there is a mentally retarded individual. Economic costs cannot compare with the misery

Reprinted from *A Proposed Program for National Action to Combat Mental Retardation.* The President's Panel on Mental Retardation (Washington, U.S. Government Printing office, 1962), pp.1-2.

and frustration and realization that one's child will be incapable of living a normal life or fully contributing to the well-being of himself and to society in later life.

SEVEN

The Distinction Between Mental Retardation and Mental Illness

THE SECRETARY'S COMMITTEE ON MENTAL RETARDATION, U.S. DEPARTMENT OF HEALTH, EDUCATION AND WELFARE

It should be emphasized that mental retardation and mental illness are in most instances separate problems. There has been much misunderstanding on this point among the general public. Mental retardation is usually a condition resulting from developmental abnormalities that start prenatally and manifest themselves during the newborn or early childhood period. Mental illness, on the other hand, includes problems of personality and behavior disorders especially involving the emotions; it usually manifests itself in young and older adults after a period of relatively normal development.

There is always a deficit in intellectual function in mental retardation; mental illness may or may not involve such a defect. If there is an involvement of intellectual function, it is usually not of the nature and degree found in mental retardation.

The two problems are related in that they may occur in the same individual and frequently involve some of the same kinds of professional skills to diagnose or assist the person. On the other hand, each problem does occur independently of the other and adequate professional skill to deal with one problem does not assure competency to deal with the other. The ability to distinguish clearly between these problems in a given person and to deal with each appropriately is often the crux of good care.

From "New Approaches to Mental Illness and Mental Retardation." The Secretary's Committee on Mental Retardation, U.S. Department of Health, Education and Welfare (Washington, 1963), p. xvii.

EIGHT

Ann Landers Column

PUBLISHERS-HALL SYNDICATE

A Cruel Reaction

Dear Ann Landers:

Our sixth child was born six weeks ago—a Mongoloid. We are doing our best to adjust to a heartbreaking situation.

Not one member of my husband's family sent a note expressing consolation or sympathy. Not one of them picked up the phone to comfort us.

Yesterday my husband received a letter from his mother. She wrote: "Clara is too old to be having babies. She should have stopped with the last one. Five children are enough for people in your financial bracket. When I told your sister Barbara about the Mongoloid she said she had just read that older women run the risk of having abnormal children."

My husband is furious. I am sick of the whole bunch. When an abnormal child is born, what should friends and relatives say and do?

—GA.

Dear Ga.:

When an abnormal child is born, friends and relatives should send a gift as they would for a normal child. Letters of condolence or sympathy are not in order at such a time. . . .

Retarded Brother

Dear Ann Landers:

Some friends of ours have a retarded son. The boy is ten years old, but his mentality is at the four-or-five-year-old level. He is usually pleasant and well behaved; but it is apparent that the child is mentally deficient.

The problem is the boy's 16-year-old sister. She is ashamed of her brother and fearful that if her friends see him it will hurt her socially. She insists that the boy be in his room when she comes home from school—in case she brings a friend. When she has a date the retarded child must be kept out of sight.

[1]Reprinted by permission of the author and Publishers-Hall Syndicate.

The parents want to be fair to the girl, but they want to be fair to the boy, too. They don't know what to do. Can you help?

—NEWARK

Dear Newark:

The attitude of the 16-year-old girl is a sorry reflection of ignorant parents. The daughter should have been taught years ago that her brother needs love and kindness. To treat the little fellow as something to be hidden is shameful.

Write for literature to the National Association for Retarded Children. . . . The parents, as well as the daughter, need educating.

Needs Supervision

Dear Ann Landers:

A lovely family moved next door to us last March. Their youngest is a girl whom I will call Jody. She is 12 years old, but has the mentality of a five-year-old.

Our eight-year-old daughter (I will call her Margaret) gets along fairly well with Jody. She understands that her friend is mentally retarded and makes allowances for her. Yesterday Margaret came home in tears. Jody got mad because she couldn't get her doll's clothes on right. She tore the doll apart and bit Margaret on the arm. The skin was not broken but the teeth marks were there.

Jody has had temper tantrums before but she has never actually hurt our daughter. My husband is very upset. Jody's mother is sick at heart over it. She says it is important that Jody play with normal children and she has begged us not to keep our child away. Will you please give us some advice? We cannot be objective.

—PERPLEXED

Dear Perplexed:

Retarded children present a heartbreaking problem to parents. Those who have normal children should try to understand and help as best they can.

Tell Jody's mother you will cooperate if she does her part. This means that she must promise to supervise the two little girls every moment they are together and separate them at the first sign of trouble.

Ignorant Relatives

Dear Ann Landers:

My wife and I have been married 13 years. Our 11-year-old daughter is retarded. We have a fine 7-year-old son who understands his sister's problem and treats her beautifully.

The doctors have told us that our daughter is teachable and have urged us to put her in an institution where she will be among children on her own mental level and can be trained to do many things for herself. We could visit her at any time we choose and talk to her on the telephone.

It's heartbreaking to give up this dependent child but we know we must do it now while she is young enough to be taught.

The problem is our relatives. They say we are heartless and selfish—that we are getting rid of the girl because she is a burden. We feel this is the best for the girl but it is going to cost us the love and respect of several members of the family.

Will you say something in your column to let people know how difficult it is to give up a retarded child and that we need understanding and moral support at such a time—not criticism and hurtful remarks.

—BRENDA'S FATHER

Dear Father:

. . . Don't waste time or energy attempting to justify your actions. Your decision is the wise one, based on the recommendation of your physician. Parents must always act in the best interests of their children. And this is precisely what you are doing.

Doctor Should Decide

Dear Ann Landers:

The letter from Brenda's father hit close to home. He was distressed because the doctors advised him and his wife to put their retarded child in an institution. Their relatives were violently opposed. Perhaps we can help Brenda's father because we had a comparable experience.

Our doctor advised us to put our retarded son in an institution but we disregarded his suggestion for years because our relatives thought it would disgrace the family name. When we finally decided to take the doctor's advice we realized how foolish we had been.

Jimmy now has his own friends 24 hours a day. He also has around-the-clock care and love. And his progress has been remarkable.

My husband and I have peace of mind. We know if anything should happen to us Jimmy will be in the hands of loving friends and competent people.

Which one of those relatives offered to take the child if anything happened to the parents? None, I'll bet.

—JIMMY'S MOTHER

Dear Mother:

Some retarded children do well at home—depending on the level of retardation, the temperament and disposition of the parents and the parents' capacity to work effectively with the child.

Every retarded child should be checked out by a physician. He is the best qualified to decide if the child should remain at home or be institutionalized because the doctor's decision will be objective, untouched by emotion.

Care for Retarded

Dear Ann Landers:

I am a 16-year-old girl with a mentally retarded brother. He is seven years older than I. Lately I've been wondering what will become of him when Mom and Dad pass on.

In addition to being retarded, my brother has a spinal problem and is completely helpless. He needs to be bathed, fed and dressed like an infant. I'm beginning to wonder if the responsibility will fall on me. Please don't think I am selfish or cruel, but I don't want the burden of my handicapped brother. It could spoil my chances for marriage.

I never heard of a place that cares for people who are both retarded and crippled. Have you? I wouldn't dare discuss this with my parents. Please help me.

—CLOUDY FUTURE

Dear Cloudy:

You must discuss this with your parents. It is their responsibility to see that your brother is provided for after they are gone. An insurance policy purchased early would guarantee good care in a private institution. It would also give your parents peace of mind. I hope they have such a policy.

If there are no funds for private care, and no willing relatives, the patient becomes a ward of the state and is sent to a state institution.

NINE

Who Will Tie My Shoe?

TRAINING CENTER AND WORKSHOP OF THE NEW YORK CITY ASSOCIATION FOR THE HELP OF RETARDED CHILDREN

Sometime in November 1965, six retarded young people and a social worker got together in a television studio of station WABC in New York City and held a two hour discussion. This is an abridged script of that discussion.

The discussion was conducted in the form of a panel rather than a counseling session. The group leader was much more directive than she would have been in a counseling session, actively canvassed the group for opinions and attitudes and refrained from actively encouraging the members to explore significant thought and feeling in depth.

About twenty minutes of this discussion were telecast the following month as part of an hour long program on mental retardation which a year later won an Emmy Award of the New York City Chapter of the National Academy of Television Arts and Sciences. The program, which was largely concerned with the projects of the New York City Association for the Help of Retarded Children, was called "Who Will Tie My Shoe?" The title originated in a line spoken by one of the discussants.

The program dealt mainly with the Shop* and with the habilitation program of Dr. Jack Gootzeit. The Shop was primarily represented by this panel discussion. The discussants—all young adults—were either trainees at the Shop at the time or had once been trainees and were still very much involved with it as members of the Alumni Club which is operated by the Shop Friday evenings. The leader of the discussion, Mrs. Gerda Corvin, the chief of social service at the Shop, had been the social worker for four of the discussants and knew the other two very well through Alumni Club contacts. We are giving the six discussants pseudonyms in this paper and they will be known as Beth, George, Jack, Jim, Joan and Rose.

From "Who Will Tie My Shoe?" Training Center and Workshop, New York City Association for the Help of Retarded Children (New York, 1967), pp. 1-10. By permission of the Association.

*The Shop is what we call the Training Center and Workshop of the New York City Association for the Help of Retarded Children. This is an agency which provides remunerative work as the core of a training and treatment program for some 250 mentally retarded young adults who are helped to achieve outside employment or adapt to sheltered employment, and in any case, who are helped to improve their social competence and emotional stability. The Shop has three centers, two smaller ones in Brooklyn and Queens, and the central setting—which has between 160 and 200 trainees—in Manhattan.

Perhaps the main point of the entire discussion is that many mentally retarded people, with prolonged periods of intensive help and encouragement and opportunity, can come to express important thoughts and feelings about themselves and the world around them. This expression is part of a process which enables them to modify their behavior and attitudes so that they can become more mature and socially competent and happier people. I doubt that these six persons are particularly atypical. They all show strong signs of organicity, have IQs in the sixties, and had failed to make vocational, educational and other social adjustments before coming to the Shop. These are not "pseudoretarded" people.

Of the six, four are single. Two, the only Negroes in the group, were already married when the discussion took place but have no children. All come from working class families with low to low middle incomes and one comes from a family receiving public assistance.

The discussion was spontaneous although the group had met together one afternoon a few days earlier to consider the issues they would explore. Actually much of the material in the televised discussion had not been anticipated. Of course all of the discussants had had intensive individual and group counseling so that it was not new for them to talk about significant experiences, thoughts and feelings. Had it been their first exposure to such a discussion—particularly for television—they probably would have frozen.

The Shop brought to bear upon them a certain climate and a constellation of programs and services. All of the trainees had intensive individual and group counseling, as did some of their parents. The trainees were exposed to treatment-oriented individualized relationships with their nonprofessional work supervisors. They participated in a number of group activity programs. Work assignments were often made for psychological rather than directly vocational reasons, especially in the early phase of their training. They experienced a range of monetary, status and recognition rewards on the one hand and another range of deprivations, limitations and restrictions on the other. Some were examined by our neuropsychiatrist and given medication. All were tested by our psychologist. Some received instruction in traveling in the streets and subways and some were tutored in work-related reading, writing and arithmetic. They attended job orientation classes and went through a bimonthly treatment-oriented evaluation process. When designated employable, they received selective placement services which included in some cases intervention with the employer to salvage jobs which seemed headed for disaster.

All were actively encouraged to understand themselves and express themselves and to be creative in ways useful to themselves as persons and to the Shop. They were all paid. They were given opportunities for leadership and helping roles. While encouraged to verbalize problems, they were also expected to participate in their solution. And of course staff tried to relate to them with real patience, a genuine acceptance of their retardation and their trying personalities, a sensitive recognition of their worthwhileness simply by virtue of their being people, and with a warmth and humor which hopefully imparted to their whole experience in the Shop a pervasive quality of humaneness and optimism.

Almost all of these young people in varying degrees came to the Shop immature, tight, angry, suspicious and pessimistic. Judging from the outcomes and from the discussion which follows, something worthwhile did happen inside of them. What happened to them is happening to other retarded persons receiving similar treatment and training, and would happen to many more if they could be provided with adequate resources for similar habilitation processes.

Jerome Nitzberg, MSW
Assistant Director

January 27, 1967

CORVIN	Well, look, if you remember, when we talked last time on Tuesday, we discussed the question, "Suppose you had to have a handicap, which handicap would you pick?" Would you want to be retarded rather than anything else?
JOAN	Of course. I can use my hands and I can see and I can do plenty of things, help around the house, and you know, when I'm married, to help out. I can do more things. That's why I'd pick retarded.
CORVIN	How about George?
GEORGE	You can use your hands. You can work. That's about it. About everything else that you would do.
CORVIN	You think that retarded people can work and use their hands and do many things which other people mightn't be able to do—other handicapped people mightn't be able to do?
GEORGE	Yes.
CORVIN	How about you, Jim?
JIM	I agree with George. I think it's the same thing. Because when you're crippled in a wheelchair, you can't walk. At least I'm retarded. I can walk and move my hands and work with my hands.
CORVIN	How about Beth?
BETH	I agree with all of them. Retarded, I can do a lot of things—hold a job, do all different kinds of work, take care of housework, shop, and do everything.
CORVIN	Make a budget. (Laughter)
JACK	I feel the same way as everybody else. Because you can use your hands. You can move around and do a lot of things. Where, if you were the other way you wouldn't be able to do it.
CORVIN	And Rose?

ROSE	I agree with all of them because people that are in wheelchairs and some of them can't see, they can't do nothing for themselves. They need somebody to work for them. And us, we could work for ourselves. We can help around the house with the cooking and cleaning, and go to the store sometimes, and sometimes go out with friends. Like them that can't see and can't walk, they can't go out by themselves.
CORVIN	You think they need someone to take care of them all the time?
ROSE	Yes, yes.
CORVIN	Now all of you have been saying that retarded people can work, they can use their hands, they can do many kinds of different things. In what way would you say then are retarded people different from normal people?
ROSE	Well, some retarded people like myself are slow in work. Some—I can't say which ones—but I know myself, like when I went to school, I was slow, so they put me in a special class.
CORVIN	Uh-huh. How did you feel about being put in a special class?
ROSE	Oh, I didn't feel so bad because there was others like myself in the class. And I didn't feel so bad. But when the kids in the street used to tease me I felt real bad, and sometimes started to cry.
CORVIN	Beth is nodding her head and George is nodding. Did you have a similar experience?
BETH	Yes.
CORVIN	You mean the kids teased you?
BETH	Yes.
CORVIN	And what else happened?
BETH	Well, I—when I went to school my high school years, the teacher always told me not to feel sorry for myself, to go out and try, because you can do if you want to.
CORVIN	Well, how would you say, Beth—in what way would you say a retarded person is different from a normal person?
BETH	Well, some retarded people—they can use their hands and walk around but they can't concentrate. A lot of them have slow concentration.
CORVIN	Why do you think they have this slow concentration?
BETH	Well, some of them feel sorry for themselves and that makes a conflict on them, makes them feel that they can't do, but they can.

CORVIN	Jim, you're nodding as if you agreed.
JIM	I do.
CORVIN	That's unusual for Jim to agree with us.
JIM	Especially with women.
CORVIN	Especially with women.
JIM	I used to feel sorry for myself all the time. It's no good.
CORVIN	Well, do you remember when you stopped feeling sorry for yourself?
JIM	I guess when I came to the Shop and started learning things that I didn't know before, got away from the house. When you're sitting around the house watching television and don't know what to do with yourself, you start feeling sorry you got nothing else to do.
CORVIN	Before you came to this Shop, you were just sitting around, doing nothing, watching TV? I hope it was Channel 7. (Laughter)
	What about you, Joan? In what way would you say retarded people are different from normal people?
JOAN	Well, they're slow with their hands.
CORVIN	Well, think of the people in the Shop or of yourself, for that matter. In what way would you say that you are different from a normal person?
JOAN	I'm slow.
CORVIN	What are you slow in?
JOAN	Slow in my work, using my hands.
CORVIN	You're pretty fast in many ways, aren't you?
JOAN	Yes, in clerical work.
CORVIN	How about Jack? In what way do you think retarded people are different from normals?
JACK	Just that they're slow, I think.
CORVIN	When you say they're slow, really what do you mean?
JACK	Like they're not as fast as other people. Like if you put a not retarded person next to a retarded person and you gave them some-

thing to write or something they feel, probably they could do it faster than the other one, the other person.

CORVIN   You mean the normal person could write it down faster?

JACK   Yes, yes, that's right.

CORVIN   And suppose the retarded person were given enough time? Do you think he might be able to write things down or read things just as fast as everybody else?

ROSE   Yes.

CORVIN   You think—

JACK   Learning is actually what it means. I mean slow in learning things.

CORVIN   Rose, I think you wanted to say something.

ROSE   I found out when I went out to make an application one time that some bright people can't write, neither, because one man came over to the man at the desk and said, "Would you make this out for me?" He said, "Can't you try and write your name?" He says, "I don't know how." And I said to myself there, "I try." I make out the form. If I don't know, I just leave it and they help you.

CORVIN   Who helps you?

ROSE   The person that interviews you. I had it already.

CORVIN   So you had a very nice interviewer and he helped you fill out the application?

ROSE   Yes.

CORVIN   I think some of you have had different experiences when you were asked to fill out forms. Jim?

JIM   I was looking for a job and I tried and filled out a form and I said I couldn't fill it out because I couldn't read, so they said they couldn't use me, and that was that.

CORVIN   Did anybody try to help you fill out the form?

JIM   No.

CORVIN   They just said nothing doing.

JIM   "If you can't read, we can't use you. Tell him we can't use him," the boss said to his secretary.

CORVIN	Were you angry at them?
JIM	Well, if they can't use me, they can't use me, that's all. What can I do about it?
CORVIN	How about Jack there? Were you ever asked to fill out anything that you couldn't fill out or you didn't know how to read—didn't understand the paper?
JACK	A couple of times. But they helped me.
CORVIN	Did you feel badly about having to ask them to help you fill out the forms? Yes, Rose?
ROSE	Well, I didn't because I know I told them I couldn't understand, and some words I couldn't read. Like my birthday I put down, and the year I was born, and my social security number. And he said if I had a phone. I couldn't read that because I didn't understand that. So he helped me.
CORVIN	You mean it's a long word—telephone number?
ROSE	Yes. So I said—I went over to him. He gave me a number and he said as soon as he called me he'll help me make it out. He said do I feel bad about asking somebody this? I said, "Well, they always tell us if we need help we should always come and ask somebody."
CORVIN	Who tells you this?
ROSE	This is what we were taught in the orientation group in the Shop. If we need to go to somebody, they help us with a form. And I learned it.
CORVIN	Well, what about this—you know, having trouble reading things and understanding things? Do you feel that this is something that makes retarded people different from normals?
JIM	Yes, very much. Most normal people know how to read and write, I think.
CORVIN	Well, how do you feel about not being able to read so well, Jim?
JIM	Lousy, miserable.
CORVIN	Miserable?
JIM	Like a stupid little kid.
CORVIN	Have you been able to learn anything in class at the Shop within the last year or so?

JIM	Learned a little bit of reading and how to write my name. The Shop aide taught me.
CORVIN	Do you think she helped you feel any better about reading than you felt before, or do you still feel so miserable?
JIM	Well, I feel a little bit better because I know how to read a little bit but not enough, as much as I should or want to know.
CORVIN	Do you feel that not being able to read might make it difficult for you to find a job?
JIM	Yes.
CORVIN	Have you ever looked for work?
JIM	Especially in the thing I've been trained for—as a messenger. It's very hard. I found that out for myself. It's very hard to get a job as a messenger on the outside if you can't read because most messenger jobs call for reading.
CORVIN	Are you actually saying that it's not a good idea to train you as a messenger because you can't read?
JIM	Well, yes, in a way, because when I first came to the Shop I didn't think I could do it because I couldn't read. But the supervisor said I could. There were other boys there that could, but it's a little hard. It's much better if you know how to read better. It might be much easier to be a messenger.
CORVIN	But we also know that some of our very best messengers are people unable to read and somehow they get around.
JIM	Yes.
CORVIN	And you get around beautifully.
JIM	Yes, because they tell me how to travel.
CORVIN	How can you travel if you don't know how to read?
JIM	You travel—know how to take the trains to different places.
CORVIN	How do you know where to get off?
JIM	Well, if somebody prints the name of the station, prints it the way it is on the sign, I can read it, but if they write it in regular writing, I can't make head or tail out of it. But if they print it, I can find it.
CORVIN	Tell me, when did you first find out—any of you—first find out that you were retarded? In school?

JOAN	In school.
CORVIN	Do you remember how old you were?
JOAN	I was around ten years old. And I was up—I was in a regular class in the fifth grade and then I couldn't catch up with the other class. I was slow. The teacher told me that I had to go down to a special class. And the following month I was in a special class ever since.
CORVIN	But you didn't like it?
JOAN	I didn't like it.
CORVIN	Did you like it in the regular classes and not being able to keep up with them?
JOAN	Yes, because I wanted to catch up with them, but I couldn't. I was too slow.
CORVIN	Well, you couldn't keep up with the other kids in the regular classes?
JOAN	In the reading and arithmetic.
CORVIN	What about the special classes? Were you able to do as well as the others there?
JOAN	In the special classes?
CORVIN	Yes.
JOAN	I did very good in the special classes. It was easy work but I didn't like the idea of being sent to one, because I felt I could do the work. But I was there in special classes ever since.
CORVIN	You stayed in special classes until you left school?
JOAN	Until I left high school.
CORVIN	How about you, Rose? When did you first find out?
ROSE	When I was nine, when I was nine years old. My mother—no, my father—took me to a doctor to see why I used to cry. Every time I come from school I always complained that one of the little boys or girls used to hit me in school. And I would never want to hit them back. I was one of those that never wanted to defend themselves. So my father one day kept me from school and took me to the doctor and the doctor took all sorts of tests. He even took a how-do-you-call-it?
CORVIN	Electroencephalogram?

ROSE	No, brain wave. And he then told my father that I had some kind of a seizure and they told my mother. My father had to bring my mother and they told my father and mother that you should be put in some institution until I grow out of it. But I was away from nine, from nine and a half until about seventeen.
CORVIN	That's when you were sent to Willowbrook?
ROSE	Yes. I was there for six years straight. I didn't learn no reading, no writing, but I learned how to sew and cook and how to keep a house.
CORVIN	So you think that in a way maybe it was good that they sent you away?
ROSE	No, no.
CORVIN	No?
ROSE	It was a waste of time.
CORVIN	You think it was?
ROSE	I feel that it was just a waste of time and waste of money.
CORVIN	Did you get along with the kids in Willowbrook?
ROSE	I never got into trouble. I got along with everybody. I still have friends that write to me from the school.
CORVIN	They're still there?
ROSE	Yes. That they don't have nobody—no parents, no brothers, no sisters. They're all by themselves. They work. I feel that people like us should be proud of ourselves what we can do for ourselves, and what the state or what anybody can do, the social workers and everybody.
CORVIN	You're really saying you're sorry for the people who still are at Willowbrook?
ROSE	Yes.
CORVIN	And who have no families to go back to?
ROSE	That's right.
CORVIN	We'll get back to this a little bit later. But let's get to Jack. When did you first find out about being retarded?
JACK	When I was in grammar school. See, I stayed in the same class and the kids were, you know, they were going ahead of me and I couldn't like understand it. And my mother told me and she took

me to doctors and they said that I was, but it wasn't, you know, a real bad case. But I was. And then that's when I was in about the fourth grade, not even that.

CORVIN   Do you remember how you felt when—

JACK   Well, I felt a little bad because the other kids were going to other grades and I was just sitting there, and at the beginning I didn't, you know, care. But then later on as the time went by I felt down, you know. Like they were better than me. And why was this happening? And I never used to want to go to school.

CORVIN   You know, this must be a question I think all of you must ask yourselves again and again—why is this happening? Why did it have to happen to me of all people? Yes, Rose?

ROSE   You know, a lot of my friends—they're braver than me and they say to me that I don't act like I'm retarded because I have a mind, that I talk to people clear as day, they tell me. Like my friend yesterday, I told her I was going on a show. I told her I don't know when they were going to show it on television. She said to me I don't act like I was retarded or anything, because I talk like a normal person should, like a normal adult should.

CORVIN   Wait again. We'll come back to this, Rose, O.K.? But let's get to George. When did you first find out about being retarded?

GEORGE   Well, I think when I was about nine.

CORVIN   Also in public school?

GEORGE   In public school, yes.

CORVIN   Well, how did you find out about it?

GEORGE   Well, when I went to this special class there, and all the other kids were there. I felt pretty bad then.

CORVIN   Did they tell you why they were sending you to special classes?

GEORGE   No, they didn't tell me that. I was sent there. I knew why, though.

CORVIN   You knew why, but you didn't ask them? You didn't want to be told?

GEORGE   No.

CORVIN   How about you, Beth?

BETH   Well, I came all the way through elementary, all the way through high school, and I graduated. But I was a little slow. But all the tests that the doctors had given me say that I am mostly handicapped more than retarded.

CORVIN   You mean with your arm?

BETH   Yes, because they say you are very, very, you're slow, but you're very, very smart in some ways.

CORVIN   I think this is true of everybody here. How about Jim? When did you first find out about being retarded?

JIM   I think I found out when I was about fifteen.

CORVIN   Fifteen?

JIM   Although I was going to grammar school and I kept getting left back in classes, but I didn't know why. Nobody ever told me. They just thought I was playing stupid, that's all.

CORVIN   They thought that you were playing stupid?

JIM   That's what the kids used to call me, too. I just thought they were right. But I went into a special school for one hour a week when I was fifteen. That's how I found out I had to go to special school to learn how to read, but it didn't do too good.

CORVIN   Well, did you go to any doctor or psychologist?

JIM   There was one in the special school. He told my mother, and I was standing there, he told my mother that I would never work in the school. Like a psychologist I think he was.

CORVIN   He told your mother in your presence that you would never be able to work?

JIM   Yes.

CORVIN   Well, you fooled him, didn't you?

JIM   (Depressed) I fooled him. I'm working in the Shop, though. I had one or two jobs on the outside but never really kept them.

CORVIN   You don't feel that the psychologist was wrong?

JIM   Well, I do in a way. I proved that I can work but so far I haven't been able to keep a job yet.

CORVIN   What happened when you were in school, Jim? Or any of you, when you were in school as long as you were in regular classes, and all of you were in regular classes to begin with at least.

ROSE   For two weeks.

CORVIN   For two weeks?

ROSE	I went from the sixth to the fifth.
CORVIN	Well, you said something before, Rose, that the kids would tease you.
ROSE	Uh-huh.
CORVIN	What did they say? Just what did they do to you?
ROSE	"You're stupid. You can't read and can't write, ha-ha." So I used to say, "If I can't read . . ."
CORVIN	Sounds familiar.
ROSE	I used to say to them like this—tears used to come out. I used to say, "If I can't read, do you think you could do better?" Then they used to gang up on me and then I'd run home. Of course, I don't like to fight with nobody. Now I go to school now, night classes, three nights a week, and well, my mother said I am improving in my reading and writing now.
CORVIN	Do you feel that you are improving?
ROSE	Yes. Now this year I am in a class that I am going to graduate and I am proud of myself. I've been going for three years. Like this year to study. But after I make . . .
CORVIN	That's a big project.
ROSE	If I pass the test this year, I go into Junior High School in nights.
CORVIN	Uh-huh.
ROSE	So I said to my mother, "If I pass, it will be a miracle."
CORVIN	You don't think you'll be able to pass?
ROSE	Well, last year I passed all the tests that he gave me—the teacher —except one, except one.
CORVIN	Which one was that?
ROSE	Spelling.
CORVIN	Spelling?
ROSE	Four, four. I passed my arithmetic, my reading and my social studies, but my spelling was poor. He said I got a 53.
CORVIN	Oh.
ROSE	But I didn't feel so bad. I didn't feel so bad as long as I knew I passed my writing.

CORVIN	I think George is sympathetic. How's your spelling? I really don't know. No good?
GEORGE	No good.
CORVIN	Is it keeping you from working now? When you were in school, George, do you remember when you were in regular classes the first two or three years? Did the kids tease you? Did they get after you?
GEORGE	No, they didn't bother me.
CORVIN	They didn't bother you. How about later on? Were you ever teased by anybody?
GEORGE	No.
CORVIN	He was lucky, huh? How about Beth? Did you ever get teased by people?
BETH	No. I wasn't because I always felt to myself that if I can learn how to be faster and do things then I wouldn't be teased. But the teachers always said, "No matter what anyone says, you are just as good as anyone else is, and you can learn to do and you can take care of your own self. Don't never let no one tell you that you can't, because you can."
CORVIN	And you believed them?
BETH	Yes.
CORVIN	And you proved that you can.
BETH	That's right.
CORVIN	How about Jim? You had a rough time?
JIM	Yes, a very rough time.
CORVIN	Well, do you want to talk about it a little bit?
JIM	Well, they used to always tease me, call me stupid, can't read and all that stuff. Big guys used to beat me up and all because I couldn't fight too good either. They never wanted to let me play ball. They said, "You can't catch. You can't play. I went through a lot of stuff when I was a kid.
CORVIN	Did they tease you any other way at all?
JIM	What do you mean? What other way?
CORVIN	I don't know. I can think of many other ways in which people can tease others.

JIM	I don't know.
CORVIN	Did they make fun of the way you talk?
JIM	Sometimes. Some say I got buck teeth and everything else.
CORVIN	Buck teeth?
ROSE	I don't think that was nice. Not nice at all.
CORVIN	Well, what did you do?
ROSE	Ignore them.
CORVIN	You can ignore them?
JIM	I wasn't much for ignoring. I had a bad temper when I was a kid. I used to throw things at them.
CORVIN	You threw things at them?
JIM	I once threw a lunch chair at one guy once. Missed him.
CORVIN	Did you ever hurt anybody?
JIM	Sometimes. Not real bad, but I hurt them. I think I got beat up more times than I fought back. I used to be—I'd more or less run away. I was a coward, as the saying goes.
CORVIN	What about you, Jack, when you got teased, or did you get teased at all?
JACK	Oh, I didn't get teased. Not much. Once in a while the kids in the neighborhood, like if they were running for something, like, you know, running around and I couldn't go so fast, they'd say, "What's the matter?" And I'd say, "Well, I can't help it. What do you want me to do?" Then they won't say nothing to you. Like I more or less ignored them, you know, and they'd say, they ask me something to which I had no answer. And they'd say, "Well, how come?" Well, I could try the best I can, that's all I used to say to them. But I didn't get teased.
CORVIN	Do you feel, any of you, later on, after you left school and you went to special classes and then later on when you came to the Shop, that people made fun of you? Yes, Jack?
JACK	Well, if they made fun of you at the Shop, they were talking about themselves, too, because if they did that they were there for the same reason we were, or some other reason. Because everybody that comes here has a reason, that's true.
CORVIN	What kind of reason?

JACK	Maybe they're a little slow, maybe, you know. It's all different cases, I guess.
CORVIN	You don't agree, Jim?
JIM	I agree some of them are different. They say you're stupid or something. You say, "Well, what are *you* doing here? You must be the same thing." And they shut up.
CORVIN	Three hands at the same time. All right, Joan.
JOAN	That's why we're all at the Shop, because we're all slow—no one special. So if they make fun of us, they're only talking about themselves, like Jack said. They call us retarded. They're retarded, themselves.
CORVIN	Do people use the word "retarded"—do you think—as a kind of cuss word?
JOAN	When they get mad—as an expression. But they only talk about themselves when they call other people that.
CORVIN	How about Rose?
ROSE	This is one of the things you was talking about when I came for my interview. You said if somebody would ever call you names, they'd be calling themselves names because, like yesterday, a boy was calling another boy stupid. And I interrupted. I says, "That's not right. If he's stupid, so are you stupid." I said, "Because if you call another person stupid, you're calling it to yourself," I said. So the boss told us that if you call another person stupid, that's not nice anyway. You're making fun of another person. They act like children there.
CORVIN	Who acts like children?
ROSE	A lot of them.
CORVIN	Anybody at the Shop acts like children?
SEVERAL	Yes.
CORVIN	When they tease you, they're like children?
JIM	They're just acting like children, growing up.
JOAN	They like to make others get mad. They tease. Others can't take it and some can take it. And they tease you.
CORVIN	Do you think they like to see people get mad?

JIM	Sort of.
JOAN	Sort of, yes. (Laughter.)
CORVIN	What's so funny?
JIM	Temperamental.
CORVIN	Temperamental, huh. That rings a bell.
JOAN	Of course, it makes you feel very bad about being in the Shop.
CORVIN	Jack?
JACK	I think the reason why they say that is because they're not thinking and they're not realizing—well, they're calling it to somebody else, but if they stop to think, it's themselves, too. I mean the ones that are saying it to you at the Shop, it's themselves, too, and they're not thinking about themselves being that way and they wouldn't want no one else to say it to them.
CORVIN	Well, Beth, you have your hand up.
BETH	Well, I feel this way. If you hear them say that in order to avoid a fight or argument, walk away. Because it's better to walk away than to fight. Because you have always told us in the Shop if we feel that it's going to be an argument or they something against us, our social workers are there, and that's what they're there for, to get us both together and discuss our problems and to see what it's all about. Because if you get mad at each other and fight all the time, then you'll never be able to be friends. You'll always constantly remember that some fight every time you get together.
CORVIN	So you are really saying they ought to have it out with the social worker?
BETH	Yes.
CORVIN	You did?
BETH	Isn't this the truth, Mrs. Corvin, that that's what the social workers are there for, to help the trainees with problems like this here? And that's what the supervisors are around for, to watch your work, what you do, and to prevent fights? Whoever gets into a fight, you're supposed to stop it and bring them to their social worker.
CORVIN	That's right. And then what does the social worker do?
BETH	Well, the social worker talks to you, and if she can't talk to you, they suspend you. That's what I guess. I don't know. I was never suspended.

CORVIN   I think Joan disagrees.

JOAN   The social workers don't suspend you. The social workers will talk to you, you know, and try to help you see what's wrong. But if it continues, if they keep getting into the same fight and you have to keep talking to them and it doesn't do any good, then it's either to the director of the Shop to suspend the trainee if he should continue fighting. You know, like I say, he gets into a fight every day and loses his temper, or there's something wrong.

CORVIN   Would you say that retarded people have more fights or get into hot water more easily than other people?

JOAN   No. Other people—normal people—get into just as many fights as we do. Millions fight all over the city.

JIM   Even social workers.

CORVIN   Even social workers.

JIM   Guys who want to work, fight. Who's going to talk to social workers when they fight?

CORVIN   That's a good question, Jim. The social workers' social worker?

ROSE   This isn't true. I've seen a picture one time on TV. I don't remember, I remember it was about a social worker. He went to a psychiatrist and the psychiatrist told him that he was going to have a breakdown. I don't want to say anything else, no more.

CORVIN   So what you are saying is that social workers have problems just like trainees or other people.

ROSE   There's another thing. That normal people I've read in the papers, that people that are, you know, okay and all of that stuff—normal—they rob things, they take dope, they take, I don't know, all sorts of things. They get in trouble with the law and all that.

CORVIN   You think retarded people get into this kind of trouble, too? It could happen.

JIM   I never said it. I never seen anybody or heard anybody, but it could happen.

ROSE   At least we have a Shop to come to.

TEN

It's Tough . . . To Live with Your Retarded Brother or Sister

BROTHER AND SISTER GROUP, ASSOCIATION FOR THE HELP OF RETARDED CHILDREN, NEW YORK CITY CHAPTER

1. How do you tell your friends about your brother or sister? This is how we do it.

We tell the truth about this mental handicap which can happen to any family and we are selective in the friends with whom we share these facts. . . . We say:

Our brother or sister does not learn as much or as quickly as we do; they require more time and patience from their loved ones. Formal schooling may start later. Reading and writing skills, if achieved, are accomplished laboriously and speech is often impaired. . . .

Our brothers' and sisters' interests are limited and very often they are hyperactive.

We don't drag the subject in from left field. . . .

2. How do you accept the situation? This is how we accepted it.

We accepted our parents' explanation. Although at first it was a shock we tried to learn more about retardation. We tried to understand that "the world had not suddenly come to an end," and that we would try hard to help our parents as well as our brother or sister live with this situation. If the brother or sister is younger you move into the role of directing and helping more naturally and make every effort to afford him or her every protection. You must learn to set limits on your own and his activity so that he will not become "spoiled" and will learn acceptable social behavior. . . .

If he or she is older, the helping role does not come as easily since he or she might resent constant advice from a younger brother or sister.

Both older and younger brothers and sisters need to feel wanted and should be encouraged to participate in family activities in a helping way. Although they should be helped to perform up to their maximum capacity you should not take advantage of them. Their learning capacity may be limited but their feelings are not and can be easily hurt.

Reprinted by permission of the New York Association for the Help of Retarded Children (New York, 1963).

GUIDING THEM: We teach our brother or sister by good example in words and actions. We help them to read, write, and to speak more clearly. We show them how to take care of their personal needs. We take pride in having them look attractive at all times. We carry their pictures with us to show to friends. When we bring our friends home, we introduce them. . . .

3. How do you help your family cope with the demands of the situation? This is how we do it.

We try to understand how they feel about circumstances of having a child who learns slowly. We know they are probably sensitive about this and may feel guilty about the condition of our brother or sister. We share the care of our brother or sister with our parents. When the situation arises we try to offer comfort by talking to them. This helps relieve some of the anxiety and tension that is often present when the care and attention required by our brothers and sisters at times becomes too overwhelming. . . .

4. What do you and your brother or sister do together? This is what we do.

We have fun together as a family group and as individuals. Our retarded brother or sister is included in all family activities. . . .

OUTSIDE THE HOME: We go on walks with our retarded brother and sister; go to the park for games; windowshop; have fun in the snow; eat pizza in restaurants; attend a movie or bowl. As a family we go to the beach to swim, to the country for picnics, to church or synagogue to worship. . . .

AT HOME: We listen to music and records. We have our disagreements over TV programs and other things about which all families may differ from time to time. We play family games, enjoy visits with friends and relatives and participate in the ceremonies of religious holidays. . . .

How do You Think Your Brother or Sister Feels About You?

We think our brother and sister have the same kind of feelings about us that older brothers and sisters usually have toward each other. . . .

One of the most important things is that we know they love us as much as we love them. . . .

Sometimes they may have a feeling of *inferiority*, especially when they are unable to do the same things that we are able to do such as:

To learn sports as quickly,

To have "dates,"

To be creative,

To do things on their own. . . .

Sometimes they feel *equal* to us especially in situations when they are able to do such things as

    chores around the house
    participate in family fun
    run errands
    answer the phone

Sometimes they even feel better than us—especially when they can work and hold down a job; and do things well.

We hope other brothers and sisters will have an opportunity to meet in a group as we have done for the past several months.

We have made new friends. We met and talked to other brothers and sisters who had the same problem.

We learned how other retarded brothers and sisters behaved in the family group.

We helped each other.

We learned how to "talk" about retardation and felt free to discuss our problems.

We helped each other to become better prepared for any unexpected behavior of our brothers and sisters.

We knew that we were not alone.

ELEVEN

Five Days As a Retarded Laundry Worker

BERNARD POSNER

I apologize to the C----- Industrial Laundry, in a dreary old section of the city surrounded by gray rowhouses, a grocery store featuring chicken backs at 19 cents a pound, and a grease-spattered gas station.

And I apologize to Rebecca with the motherly eyes, who carried her red wallet in a paper bag so it wouldn't wear out. And to George who hummed rock-and-roll music in a high falsetto while he worked. And to Mr. Howard, a supervisor who couldn't bring himself to meet my glance. And to Sid and Larry, owners of the laundry, the only ones to know the truth. And to all the hundred-or-so men and women in the laundry who became used to seeing me wander through the plant.

I defrauded them all. I worked in the laundry for a week as a retarded person. They all accepted me as retarded, each in his or her own way: with sympathy and scorn, patience and impatience, studied attention and studied neglect. I apologize for their misplaced reactions.

I masqueraded as retarded for good reasons. My assignment on the President's Committee on Employment of the Handicapped is to promote jobs for the mentally retarded and mentally restored. Recently, acting as a bureaucratic matchmaker, the Committee arranged for a meeting of the Institute of Industrial Launderers, the Bureau of Apprenticeship and Training of the U.S. Department of Labor, and the Vocational Rehabilitation Administration. It was love at first glance. Together, they developed a $344,000 project of training and hiring 1,000 retardates in industrial laundries over the next 18 months.

A great breakthrough; the first national trade association ever to take such action. But how would it be for a retarded person to work in a laundry? How were working conditions? How would he be treated by his bosses? By his fellow workers? I wanted to see from the inside what problems a retarded worker might face in an industrial laundry. So I pretended to be one.

How can a clumsy, pink-cheeked public relations type who can't even play charades at a party pass himself off as mentally retarded? It was easier than I thought.

From *Rehabilitation Record,* Vol. 7, No. 3 (May-June, 1966), pp. 1-5. By permission of the author and the Vocational Rehabilitation Administration.

In your eyes, who am I? You've heard that I write publicity for a living so you've already half-formed a mental image of me. When you do meet me, a computer in your mind rings up those facts about me that reinforce your image: horn-rimmed glasses, button-down shirt, loud neckties. Bzzz bzzz bzzz, out comes a computer-sketched portrait of me; not the real me, but a stereotype that you've decided ought to be me—Posner, public relations type.

What we do, psychologists tell us, is perceive people not as they really are but as we think they should be. We select a prefabricated mental image and we search for a few facts to strengthen it.

That's what happened in the laundry. The day before I reported for work, Sid and Larry, the owners, spread word that a retardate was going on the payroll for a week's trial, so please be kind to him. Bzzz bzzz bzzz went a hundred built-in mental computers and the next day, when I showed up, I already had been tagged as mentally retarded—and the tag would stick almost no matter what I said or did.

To reinforce the stereotype, however, I wore a red knit stocking cap and I spoke but little. I chewed gum; it calmed my anxiety. I acted normally; I didn't know how to act any other way. I did indulge in the pleasant luxury of not comprehending too fast, of asking that things be explained over and over again until I was sure I had grasped them.

The first morning, I parked several blocks away (the story was that someone brought me and picked me up each day). I trudged slowly past the rowhouses. What if I couldn't take a week's physical labor, me, pushing fifty? Then there was the laundry, the door, I was inside.

A man was loading laundered blue workshirts onto a dolly. I handed him a slip of paper with Sid's name. I didn't trust myself to speak. He looked me over from head to foot and said: "first door on your right."

There was Sid, without an eyeblink of friendship. He spoke loudly to me, or rather *at* me, as though the louder the talk the clearer the comprehension. "Oh, you're the new man from the sheltered workshop," his voice blasted. "We're glad you're here. Tomorrow you come a little earlier. We start at 8 o'clock. It's 7 after 8, now. Tomorrow, 8 o'clock." I nodded.

Sid escorted me to the folding and packaging department to meet Mr. Howard, the supervisor. Mr. Howard spoke with feigned heartiness, also many decibels louder than normal. He wouldn't look in my eyes. "Here, I'll hang up your jacket, Bernie," he shouted. "Oh, you're wearing a short-sleeved shirt. You'll be cold."

"Not cold," I said. They were my first words, flat and hollow.

"Meet George. He'll tell you what to do. If you have any question, you come see me." With that, Mr. Howard disappeared. He seemed glad to escape.

George was even quieter than I. A Negro in his late teens he didn't quite know how to react to a white man in his late forties. The first time he called me "sir," but he knew this wasn't right. I was retarded, wasn't I? After that, he didn't call me anything; but every time he told me what to do, I could sense him swallowing the "sir."

Here was a table heaped high with four sizes of laundered wiping rags, used in factories, gas stations, and wherever else dirt and grease accumulate. They had to be folded, inserted in a machine which encased them in plastic, and stacked on shelves. Three women worked in the room along with George. They paused to glance at me with open curiosity, then went back to work. There was much to be done.

"Fold the big cloths this way, then this way, then this way," said George. My fingers fumbled. Four or five times he explained without a trace of impatience, as though slow comprehension was not unusual. Finally I caught on. "Fold only the big ones," he said. "Chuck the others in here." He pointed to a bin.

He folded, softly crooning rock and roll in a high falsetto; the girls folded; I folded. The girls bantered among themselves, teasing George occasionally. Lehola, across the table, watched me curiously. Later in the morning, George showed me how to stack packaged cloths on the shelves.

A buzzer; lunchtime. I went on working, waiting for someone to tell me it was time to eat; nobody did. I folded one more cloth, gave it a resounding pat, found my lunch bag and sat in a corner. Would the rest ask me to join them? No. I ate alone.

After lunch, I learned to fold a second-size cloth. The third and fourth sizes, however, were too much for me. Fold, fold, fold. Fold, fold, fold. As soon as the table was clear, along would come another load, and another. The minutes trudged by, second by reluctant second. "Does time pass slow?" I asked Lehola. "Some days it does, some days it doesn't," she said. Bit by bit, the girls drew me into their conversations; even taciturn George spoke to me. From time to time, Mr. Howard, the supervisor, would come into the room. I tried to catch his eye and smile, but he carefully avoided my glances. How strange: the workers weren't unsettled by my presence; the supervisor was.

The minutes crept on, and so ended the first day.

The second day I forgot my lunch. I was in such a hurry to arrive on time that I left it home. Rebecca was at work in the folding department that day; Rebecca in her late fifties, with kind, warm eyes and a strong chiseled face. She sat with Lehola across the table from me and whenever she thought I wasn't watching she looked at me with such compassion that I yearned to explain "Rebecca, Rebecca, I am not retarded." All over again, she explained the folding procedures to me, for I told her I had forgotten overnight. "You'll catch on, Bernie," she reassured me, "It took me a long time too." Whenever she asked me to stack the shelves, to wheel in a load of freshly laundered cloths, to do anything, she pointed to the exact place I was to go and smiled "thank you" when I finished—a born lady.

Lunchtime was different today. "Won't you share my fried chicken?" asked Rebecca. "And take a piece of my sandwich," offered Lehola. We perched on a worktable, eating together. "Were you tired when you got home last night?" they asked. "Yes, ma'am." "Where, your legs?" "All of me." There was warm laughter.

After lunch, Rebecca said: "Bernie, you've been folding two kinds of cloths. I'm going to show you how to fold the other two kinds. Now watch me." She folded. "You do it." I tried and fumbled. "Again." Again I fumbled. "Again," she persisted, while my fingers clumsily gripped the wrong corners. At last I mastered them. "Now try them yourself." I did. "Again." I did.

With that, she cried out to the entire room: "Bernie got it! Bernie got it!" The girls came over to see and to shake my hand. Even George permitted himself a little smile. This was a day to remember—for Rebecca, for the girls, and for me.

Before going home that day, Rebecca called me over. She whispered: "You learned a new thing today. Aren't you proud of yourself? You can learn many new things. Only you have to believe in yourself." Pride and hope were in her words.

The third day. Today I had a new job, in the washer-extractor-dryer room. Four mammoth washing machines stood on one side, their gaping mouths capable of gorging a thousand pounds each. Lined up on the other side were four giant extractors and four dryers, taller than I, fed by a vicious gas flame. Four men handled the equipment.

Sid introduced me to my new boss, Mr. Ross, slightly built, harried, always on the run. "Keep an eye on him," said Sid, and I could feel Mr. Ross wince. At one end of the room dirty work clothes, cloths, rags, and mops poured in. After passing through the washers, extractors, and dryers, they poured out again to other parts of the laundry—pressers, folders, packagers. Income and outgo had to balance. If the washing machines slowed down, traffic jams would occur. Dirty clothes would pile ceiling high; pressers and folders would be idle. The boss would bluster out of his office to find out what went wrong. With one dryer on the verge of giving up, the last thing Mr. Ross needed that morning was me—a green hand, nonproductive. "Keep an eye on him, Joe."

The work was easy and he explained it clearly. "Take these wiping cloths and put them in these two dryers. Fill the dryers only up to here." He pointed to the level. Off he shot, to handle a crisis in some other part of the department. But he came back frequently to watch me. I had overloaded both dryers. "If you put too much in, the dryers won't dry," he explained, removing the excess. "Fill 'em only up to here." His instructions were clear enough for any retardate to understand. But why did he, too, have to speak in a voice louder than natural?

The first morning I was slow and clumsy. But I was willing. The work came in spurts and, between spurts, I asked for more. I'm not ambitious, just compulsive. I can't bear to stand about idly. My willingness pleased Mr. Ross. Overlooking my clumsiness, he volunteered, "You're doing fine."

Later I was loading mop rags into the dryers, absorbed in my task, when I felt eyes focused on me. I looked up. The supervisor of the pressing department, cross the aisle, had come over to watch me work. Unblinking, puffing a cigar, he eyed me the way he might have eyed a new piece of machinery. He said not a word. I looked at him as if to say, "Well?" He shrugged and sauntered off, embarrassed. He hadn't expected a retardate to behave like a human.

That afternoon, Mr. Ross beckoned to me. "Bernie, help Slim, here, load the washing machine." Nineteen or so, Slim had the beginnings of a fresh goatee under his chin. Once in a while he would walk over to a mirror to comb it. Together, Slim and I wrestled greasy coveralls into the machine, untangling recalcitrant arms and legs, shoving, pushing.

Slim spoke. "Say, are you—uh—mentally handicapped?" "Yes." "How long you been mentally handicapped?" "Long as I can remember." Silence. Then Slim said: "Me, I took an exam for a job in the Post Office. A supervisory job. I got a high mark in the mental test. A *very* high mark."

I knew what Slim was doing. Here he was, working shoulder to shoulder with a retardate. To soothe his ego, he was "unidentifying" himself from me. He was convincing not me, but himself, that although we were doing the same work, we were not in the same mental bracket. He was placing himself notches above me.

After that, we got along fine. Secure in the knowledge of his superiority, he could talk to me, work with me, he could tell me the story of his life.

Fourth day. I walked in at 8 and the laundry was beginning to feel comfortably familiar. The man loading workshirts by the front door said, "Hi, Bernie." There were the offices, a bustle of white-collar activity behind closed doors. Behind the offices, on the right, were the long rows of steam pressers, a symphony of high-pitched hisses; the feminine side; women working with deft fingers, draping shirts onto forms for automatic pressing, arranging trousers in pants pressers; their magpie chatter-chatter adding brightness to the cavernous plant tinged with dust and lint and grease. And on the left, across the aisle from the pressing department, was the folding and packaging room. I walked through on my way to the washers and dryers.

Rebecca looked up. "Here's Bernie! How you doin', Bernie?" "Okay." "Like your new job?" "I guess." "We wish you were back, Bernie, don't we, Lehola?" "We sure do!"

Talk about acceptance of the retarded!

I was unloading wet work pants from the washing machines. A good-humored, stocky man passed by. I had noticed him the past few days—a happy word for everyone. But when he approached me, he wiped off his smile as though with an eraser, replacing it with an expression of mournful pity—a perfunctory gesture, the way you automatically tip your hat in the presence of a lady. "Be serious when you pass handicapped," his code of behavior told him. And he was true to his code.

All the machines in the room were busy. Nothing to do but wait for them to finish their cycles. I was sitting on an empty crate. Mr. Ross approached. "Nice winter we've having." "Yes, sir." "No snow." "No." "Don't want snow either, do you?" "No, sir." We both were uncomfortable at his attempt at small talk. He was trying to bridge the chasm and probe this creature with the willing spirit and the backward mind. I was trying to play my role safely and prevent the give-and-take of conversation. I was relieved, and I know he was, too, when one of the washers stopped and I put on my rubber apron to unload it.

The fifth and last day. By this time almost everyone in the plant had formulated his own personal set of attitudes toward me, the mentally retarded newcomer.

Some would self-consciously turn their heads when I passed by; others just as self-consciously would greet me with a forced cheerful "hello." The stocky man with the ready smile would dial M for Mournful when he passed me. Mr. Howard, my first supervisor, would avoid my eye; but he no longer felt embarrassed about it. Mr. Ross would hail my willingness and almost overlook my ineptness, because he needed willing men. Rebecca would consider me as a human person and not as a stereotype marked "retarded." Most of them didn't go out of their way to be kind; nor did they go out of their way to be unkind. I was just one more worker—a bit "different," to be sure—in the stream that flowed in at 8 every morning and out at 4 every afternoon.

I liked this kind of acceptance—not the heart-on-your-sleeve variety, but the more genuine matter-of-fact sort.

What more could I learn at the laundry? One more day or one more week wouldn't make much difference; attitudes already were pretty much crystallized. And I had proved many points to myself about acceptance and rejection of human beings.

Four o'clock came. Goodby, Rebecca and Lehola. Goodby, George. Goodby, Mr. Howard and Mr. Ross. Goodby Slim. And goodby, Bernie, the willing retardate who didn't catch on fast but who certainly tried hard.

Folding thousands of wiping cloths, loading and unloading tons of work clothes, I had plenty of hours to think:

1. *What's in a name?* Plenty. At the plant, I constantly told people: "I don't learn so good." "I don't catch on very fast." "I'm pretty slow." These descriptive phrases everybody understood and most could accept. I'm not sure as many would have accepted the cold, barren abstraction of the phrase "mentally retarded."

2. *Acceptance, bottom to top.* I was accepted more quickly at the bottom than at the top. Those who worked with me—the semiskilled and low-skilled—more readily opened their hearts than did my bosses. Perhaps lower skilled people, often living on the wrong side of the tracks, see so much culturally caused retardation all around them that slow learners like myself are not strange to them.

3. *Dreariness of repetition.* Lehola, on the job 8 months, had the longest seniority in the folding department. And no wonder; repetitive work is monotonous and unchallenging. And it's endless.

The mentally retarded, properly trained, have a high tolerance for this kind of work. They're likely to stay, not quit. They can be an answer to the boss' prayer.

4. *The willing worker.* Willingness, I found, ranked high with the bosses. You can train the willing, even though retarded; you cannot train the foot-draggers.

The retarded can offer the asset of willingness.

5. *The pressures of bossism.* Pity the poor line supervisor; he's the one under constant pressure. He's the one who has to meet production schedules, whose greatest fear is falling behind. He's the one the front office points to should anything go wrong.

If he is to accept the retarded, he has to be assured that the retarded are willing, that they can work, that they are not going to slow his operations.

So ended my topsy-turvy week, a week that put me at the absolute bottom of a "pecking order." Every creature on earth has the need to look down upon somebody: the chickens in the barnyard, the monkeys in the zoo, man in his society. In the laundry, everyone had the opportunity to look down upon me: the school drop-outs, the semiliterates, the alcoholics drying out for a couple of weeks.

I was stripped naked of all the trappings and symbols by which so many of us measure our neighbors. I was myself.

It was a humbling experience. It was refreshing to my spirit. I shall cherish its memories all my days.

TWELVE

The Parents of Retarded Children Speak for Themselves

CHARLOTTE H. WASKOWITZ

Within the last decade there has been vast development and rapid progress in the total area of mental retardation—more and better resources; specialized clinical and counseling services; training, educational, and recreational facilities; medical research; and financial aid. Concomitantly, there has been widespread interest in professional circles as well as in the community, increased understanding, acceptance, and tolerance of the mentally retarded child and his family. Much of the credit for the impetus to this important movement belongs to the parents of retarded children who, because of their persistence, perserverance, and courage, have shown the way. It is the parents themselves who have given us clues about their own capacity and strength to find the solutions and resolutions to their problems.

Although much has been accomplished, one area that is a constant source of difficulty is that of communication between parents and professional personnel. Frequently the parents of a retarded child go away from a contact with a physician, psychologist, or social worker with a good deal of justifiable dissatisfaction. This is not an isolated occurrence but tends to be rather widespread and, as professional persons, we must assume the responsibility and blame for these difficulties. The services that are offered can and should be improved. As a means of improving these services, the author enlisted the participation of the Maryland Society for Mentally Retarded Children and interviewed the parents in the following exploratory study.

With the approval of the officers and members of the Society, a letter was sent to every fourth member stating the purpose of the study. A questionnaire was developed as a general guide, with the full knowledge that this study would produce qualitative material of importance although not statistically impressive. In general, the guide fell into the following categories: (1) identifying data, (2) when retardation was first suspected by parents, (3) consultations by specialists, (4) counseling by professional persons and parents' reactions to counseling, and (5) value of group organization to the parents. Interviews were held by the author in the Harriet Lane

Psychiatric Clinic; the average length of interview time was approximately 1 hour and, with few exceptions, it was the mother who came for the interview. Of a group of 50 to whom letters were sent and follow-up contacts made, 40 were seen; of the 10 remaining, the majority could not be reached and only 3 refused to participate. It should be noted that the group was a highly selected one, and the material is based on recall; therefore, the study does not lend itself to usual statistical methods.

In general, the parents can be described as an intelligent group of young and middle-aged people, with small families of 2 and 3 children, of the white race, and the middle socioeconomic class. Diagnostically, the children could be placed into the following categories; 19 mongoloid, 15 brain damaged, 1 epileptic, 1 seriously emotionally disturbed, and 4 of unexplained etiology. There was 1 instance of a family with two retarded children.

Answers to the factual questions of "When did you first suspect something was wrong?" "Was someone professionally consulted at that time?" and "Who really told you your child was retarded?" produced difficulty in pinpointing answers. One explanation is the time lapse and the problem of recall, since this material was gathered from several months to many years after the patient was diagnosed as retarded. However, other factors that bear consideration are (1) problems in diagnosing, and (2) the parents' reactions to the seriousness of the problem of retardation, to their feeling of difference from other parents, and the resultant feelings of fear and anxiety.

Often there is much uncertainty around diagnosis because many different factors must be weighed and evaluated such as (1) physical, (2) emotional, and (3) limitations in the tests themselves and the difficulties surrounding the testing, particularly of young children. The process of considering physical factors that complicate accurate evaluation frequently involves referral to many different specialists with their variety of opinions and, certainly, their uniquely different ways of handling the parents. It was not unusual to hear such expressions as: "My doctor did not know whether his slowness was due to his mental condition or to his physical sickness." "The doctor was confused as to whether the child could hear." "The doctor's first impression was muscular dystrophy and then in another examination he thought he was just retarded." Occasionally the influence of emotional factors must be considered, which necessitates intensive involvement of the parents in recapitulation of bitter life experiences. The limitations of the tests themselves, just in terms of evaluating intelligence, lend another element of doubt. Certainly the innumerable difficulties in having the child perform at his best and obtaining as much as possible from him create questions and doubts. In other words, are the test results representative of the child's intelligence? And, lastly, the adequacy and skill of the tester add another problem to the welter of confusion.

Mention of retardation creates a serious impact on parents, which is understandable in view of the attitude of society and the problems of the intellectually limited child achieving a safe, secure place in our culture. The very practical aspects of everyday living, training, schooling, recreation and, lastly, occupation and self-support have been almost insurmountable. It is no wonder then that usual responses were: "It's like someone came to you and told you your child was dead." "When we were told, it was a terrible shock—you stop living." "I was on the verge of a nervous breakdown." It was not surprising, therefore, that these reactions were followed by acute feelings of "aloneness," "difference," being set apart from the rest of the world, rejection, and lack of interest in the children and their problems. This is vividly illustrated by such comments as: "None of the doctors said anything to me; I couldn't even get any schooling for him." "We got so nervous—everywhere we went nobody would help us." "We then thought it was God's will and we did not go anywhere." "I feel the doctors brushed me off." "I feel that the medical profession did not want to be bothered, were impatient and annoyed." "We did not find anyone who sat down and told us what the problem was." "They just push you from one person to another." Is it any wonder then that there were expressions of anxiety, embarrassment, and guilt? As one parent said, "The doctor did not want to be bothered. I was embarrassed to go to his office. I had to sit with other people's children. I was always treated with the attitude: 'Here comes this woman with this child.' The doctor did not like him and did not mince any words about it." Another said, "The majority of professional people we dealt with left us with the feeling that if you had a child who wasn't normal, you should be ashamed of it."

Of the total group of 40, in 30 of the cases studied the parents suspected or were aware of retardation in the first year of life. Of the mongoloid group of 19, in 13 instances the parents were aware of and/or were told of the serious deficiency within the first month. The brain damaged and the etiologically unspecified cases of mental retardation took longer to diagnose. In the brain-damaged group, 12 were suspected of retardation under 1 year of age (3 of whom were known under the age of 1 month) and the remaining 3 took up to 3 years to diagnose. In the cases where no specific cause of retardation was known, 1 was diagnosed at age 20 days, 1 at 8 months, 1 at 1 year, and 1 at 18 months. In the two remaining cases, the epileptic was diagnosed at 10 months and the other was diagnosed as questionable retardation due to emotional factors. Therefore, we must conclude that mental retardation was serious enough to be detected reasonably early in this age group of children.

As one would expect, it was the pediatrician who was most frequently consulted first (in 25 instances). This was followed, in order of frequency, by the family doctor in 7 instances, the obstetrician in 3, the neurologist in 1, and the child guidance clinic in 1. In 3 instances the parents "just knew" and did not consult anyone at the time. "Were others consulted and at what ages?" prompted a succession of medical specialists too numerous to record. Illustrative is one parent's comment, "I must have had Billy to over 100 different doctors." Another replied, "I must have spent over $8,000.00 for various consultations to no avail." Unfortunately, parents did not seem to obtain the help they needed early enough to prevent the trauma of endless pursuit of answers to their problems. Perhaps significant is the fact that the "end of the road" seems to be the child guidance clinic, psychologist, or psychiatrist, whom the parents finally seek in desperation, usually after the child is 2 years of age. Also significant is the fact that one-half of these patients finally reached these specialists.

"Who really told you?" produced only one significant point, namely, many parents "just knew" or suspected serious pathology long before affirmation by specialists. The author has found that it is not an unusual occurrence in clinical work for a parent to be able to state fairly accurately the intellectual level at which his child is functioning at the time he is seen. What the parents are really asking for is not just a diagnosis, but total handling of the problem.

The question "How were you told your child was retarded?" evoked the most intense responses indicative of the traumatic experiences suffered by so many of these parents. The striking thing that permeated this section was that the different reactions to what parents considered good and poor handling varied according to their own individual needs, so that one is forced to conclude that the most important consideration is the ability of the counselor to individualize, to be sensitive to where the parents are emotionally at a particular time, in other words, to empathize with the parents. Some parents wanted to be told directly as soon as retardation was suspected. A typical comment was, "The doctor was very frank about it. It was very positive and in no way abrupt. We were aware of what the situation was, and we appreciated knowing this." Another commented, "I was told right at the beginning. We were always thankful to the doctor who did tell us." On the other hand, many parents indicated their wish to be prepared gradually, as follows: "The doctor was very tactful. He implied things right along. At first he said she was not holding her head up, not sitting up, etc. Not until two or three years later did he really tell me the child was seriously defective and had to be in an institution. He prepared me well." Another parent reported, "A pediatrician told us the child was retarded. He told us in the nicest way it could be explained. He told us it was far too early to say how much he would progress. We returned for visits frequently. As the child grew older, we were told what the future held." Apropos of this discussion, it should be pointed out that frequently parents inadvertently mentioned the names of the doctors they had consulted (in spite of the request that no names be mentioned). It is of interest to note that a parent would condemn a doctor while another would highly praise the same doctor. This obviously casts no reflection on the doctor but emphasizes the need to individualize each situation. Another observation is that in almost every record there is an admixture of good as well as poor handling, which again emphasizes the premise that each situation should be handled individually.

Important to note is that, when questioned specifically, only 25 per cent of the parents indicated that their contact with professional people was satisfactory. The most important factor in this regard was that these parents were counseled not only sensitively and directly, but also their questions were answered, particularly those relating to implications for the future. A typical expression was, "Our family doctor was wonderful. He talked to us for about an hour. He said our child was a dull boy and to give him regular care, but to give him a little bit of extra love. He answered all my questions and told me just what to do. He prepared me well for the future." Another stated, "A psychiatrist told me for the first time my child was retarded. It was a shock, a bitter disappointment, but it was accepted. He told us what to expect and gave us wonderful advice." Another 8 also indicated they were told directly, frankly, tactfully, sensitively, or slowly, but in most instances, questions pertaining to implications for the future were not answered. In 3 cases parents were not informed by anyone, "they just knew."

In 16 instances parents clearly described how poorly they were told with such adjectives as cruel, abrupt, confused, blunt, upsetting, contradictory. The adjectives the parents used are graphically illustrative of descriptions of their experiences, and they reacted to them with such comments as: "They tell you your child is an idiot and everything else. There should be a nice way to tell parents. When they told us roughly, we stopped going." "The doctor said he will never be any good to you or to himself. I told him I was raised with the feeling where there's life, there's hope." "I was told my child was mongoloid without any preparation for it. I thought he was perfectly normal, and it came as a complete surprise. We had just stopped in for a checkup. The doctor said I should have him in an institution because it would be better for the child and everybody else. All I wanted was to get out, I was stunned. My husband was overseas at the time, which certainly did not help. When you think back, you can't believe anyone could be so blunt." Two parents commented that they were told over the telephone: "My husband was told over the telephone that the child was a mongoloid when the child was 4 days of age." "The doctor said our child was a mongolian idiot over the telephone. He acted as though it was your problem, buddy."

Numerous references were made to examinations which were considered too hasty and careless: "It was an assembly line fashion." "The interview was not at all satisfactory. He saw us very quickly and did not even give us the results of the electroencephalogram. He sent us a note and suggested we buy a book he wrote. Good God, we still don't know whether he is epileptic or not." "I didn't have the feeling wherever we took her that they thoroughly examined the child." "The doctor gave her a 3-minute examination and said she was brain injured and threw her out." "The mother knows first of all what the child is. She's around the child all the time. She knows him thoroughly. How can a doctor, who sees a child for one-half an hour, know about the child?"

One other complaint, that was outstanding in the study, was a tendency on the part of professional persons to evade the issue. As one parent said, "The doctors gave me no clue that anything was amiss. In fact, they assured me everything was going to be all right."

Other complaints pertained to complicated medical terminology.

As indicated in the preceding section, there are certain generalities that can be made, namely, that parents would want to be handled gently and warmly at all times, in language that they can understand, without evasiveness, after thorough examination and, with enough time to digest the significance of such important material. This was reinforced by the parents in response to the question: "What type of service would you advise for people who are faced with this problem and are just beginning?" The material indicates that they need gentler, more sensitive handling than the usual patient. This is supported quite vividly, as they expressed intense feelings and reactions. Particularly they stressed that their "children be treated as individuals" and that the counselor be interested in their problems. What they seemed to be expressing is the need for more responsible, integrated services in this field. Professional people are becoming aware of this, as special diagnostic centers are developing in various parts of the country. Parents are able and willing to accept the uncertainty involved in diagnosis in an area which is not clear-cut if they could depend on a centralized resource rather than to be left to shift for themselves in an endless search for answers which are not possible.

In the instances where parents indicated the wish for frank, direct diagnosis as early as possible, they felt they could accept the worst if the counselor was compassionate and respected them as parents with strength and dignity. They needed time to take in the extent of their problem, and they needed to work out solutions step by step. Questions did not arise in an organized, crystallized fashion, but gradually as the child grew. As one parent put it, "This is a lifetime thing."

Some of the comments of the parents are indicative of their keen feelings of anxiety and guilt, and it is important to emphasize that this is not resolved simply by articulating it for the parent. One parent said, "I got angry at people who told me not to feel guilty. It only made me feel guiltier." There seems little question that, for many parents, the highest degree of specialized skill is indicated in the area of counseling. If we, as professional persons, really listen to what parents of mentally retarded children say, we can take our clues from them. It was not unusual to find parents express relief as they learned their children could at least be toilet trained and could express such simple needs as to ask for water, etc. As one parent said, "I used to lie awake and pray that my child could say a little word like 'water' because I was so afraid he would be thirsty and could not help himself." It is interesting to note that two parents spontaneously commented that they were relieved in "spilling over to me," although they had innumerable, previous opportunities to talk about their problem.

Two observations worthy of mention were related to terminology. One is that parents showed severe reaction to such terms as idiot, imbecile, and moron, and hoped for terminology that would avoid such negative connotation. Another is their request for simpler explanations in terms they could understand, particularly, practical, tangible suggestions relative to everyday living. Perhaps we need a greater appreciation of the little achievements of the retarded child and its meaning to their parents. Still another request was for clearer explanations, the full meaning of which they could take in. Parents often interpret such terms as "the child is slow" to mean that the child "will catch up in due time." In my clinical experience I have found that a better way of helping parents to understand what is really meant is to use the word "behind," connoting that the child will not catch up.

A discussion of the material would be incomplete without giving some illustrations of the continuous history of the parents' search for help. Comments taken out of context and categorized cannot possibly present the full meaning of the total impact of accumulated frustrations on the parents on the one hand, and their strength and capacity to handle their problems on the other. Only as we can appreciate and accept this can we be fully helpful in developing adequate services. Two records have been selected to illustrate this: the first one concerns a child diagnosed as mongoloid and the second one a child diagnosed as brain damaged.

Mrs. Martin, the mother of five children, is a warm, motherly person, of limited educational background but, nevertheless, of good intelligence. She is a thoughtful, sincere individual.

She begins as follows: "I knew Johnny was a slow child, but I thought he was a sick child. During infancy he slept for the most part and we couldn't awaken him." Early he was taken to the clinic; however, no mention was made of retardation. "They said he was just sick. He was not a well baby, but would probably pick up, but they never gave me a reason." However, an attendant kept repeating, "If only I had your faith." Apparently this comment seemed so inappropriate at the time that it made an impression on the mother.

When Johnny was about 2 years of age, a doctor was called about another sibling and casually commented that Johnny was mentally retarded. The doctor referred him to the hospital where the opinion was that the child was a mongoloid, very retarded, and that the best thing for us to do was to put him in an institution because he would forget us very quickly and if we had other children, it would have an effect on the whole family, particularly that our children would be embarrassed because of Johnny. On this statement, Mrs. Martin comments, "I thought that was abrupt and cruel."

Mrs. Martin continued, indicating her upsetness over this experience. She said, "After I got home, I wanted to know how retarded he was because I was too upset to ask any questions while I was at the hospital." She returned to her pediatrician because apparently she had a warm relationship with him. He disagreed with the opinion of institutionalization, suggesting that it was the parents' prerogative to decide such a drastic move. His opinion was that the child needed the love which could not be received in an institution. He explained Johnny's mentality, cautioning her not to spend any money on Johnny, but to center her financial resources on the other children. The doctor's most meaningful comment, and Mrs. Martin says this with much warm feeling, was, "Remember, when your other children have left, you will always have Johnny." (In response to the question, "Who gave you the most help?" Mrs. Martin unequivocally said it was this pediatrician.)

The parents explored every school possibility without any success until he was 10 years of age when he was accepted in a special class in the public school. He stayed there four years and was withdrawn when the center closed, and was then placed in another school. According to the mother, considering his limitations, he has made a good adjustment at school. He mixes well with the other children who have encouraged him in this respect. He even writes, spells, and does a little arithmetic. Mrs. Martin feels that the school has been instrumental in giving Johnny confidence, and enabling him to do some of the things normal children are doing. She glowingly describes her relationship with the teacher as "wonderful," particularly the help to the parents in allowing them to sit in class, observe, and learn.

In response to the question "Do you feel that your contact with professional people had been satisfactory?" Mrs. Martin's first point was, "Parents need all the kindness you can give them."

She also felt that parents should know exactly what is wrong as early as possible. If known at birth, it should be told at that time because one can be more helpful to the child.

She regretted the information being withheld from her. She described it as "not fair." "It's yours, your baby, you want to know right at the beginning." Mrs. Martin had the feeling that everyone knew that her child was mongoloid except herself. It bears emphasis that she was not informed that the child was a mongol until he was 2 years of age.

She further emphasized that "if there is a ray of light, it should be told." When the pediatrician told her Johnny could reach the mental age of 8, it was helpful to her. "Every word we took hold of."

Still another area of importance is to handle questions pertaining to heredity. The Martins were very much concerned whether to have additional children, and it was with great relief that after repeated contacts with professional people, she finally got her questions answered.

"What type of service would you advise for people who are faced with this problem and are just beginning?" brought forth the seriously traumatic experience of first being told bluntly and insensitively. "I felt it could have been handled a little more kindly. If you can speak to anyone in the medical profession for a while, it's wonderful. If they can't help the child, maybe they can help the parent."

About institutionalization, she commented, "I think too many children like this are put in institutions. It frightens the parents to think of institutions. I don't think an institution should be mentioned at first. Couldn't it wait to see how a child progresses before it is mentioned? I am truly as proud of Johnny as I am of my boy who graduated from college."

The second record is as follows:

This is one of the few situations in which both parents participated in the interview. The Allans are intelligent, fairly young people, in their middle thirties, and have a family of three children. In spite of all of their struggles, their charm and zest for living comes through.

Bobby was about 7 months of age when they had some vague suspicion that all did not seem quite right. They consulted their pediatrician who said that he was a little slow—not responding, not sitting up. "But the pediatrician said nothing to allay my fears, he said Bobby would be all right." Then, with much feeling, Mrs. Allan adds, "He didn't say this because he didn't know—he did know."

After much "badgering," on the mother's part, and insistence that there must be something wrong, they were referred to a neurologist. Bobby was about 1 year of age by this time. The examination showed that he was nearsighted.

Further consultation with two doctors indicated that there was nothing wrong. Mrs. Allan said, "I thought I would work harder and teach him more. Then began the most frustrating period of my life. Trying to teach a child when it was not possible to teach him was like knocking my head against a stone wall. My heart just aches when I think what we have been through. I pushed him. I spent a lot of time with him. I would try to feed and toilet train him and we got just no place."

The Allans returned to the pediatrician, whereupon they were referred to an orthopedic man. At that time, Bobby was about 1 ½ years old, and Mrs. Allan estimates his intelligence at about 1 year. The orthopedic man found his feet were quite flat and suggested corrective shoes. He also offered the following advice, "He will catch up, he will be all right." Mrs. Allan, however, felt all was not so rosy because she mentions that at 19 months he was beginning to walk but "still there was not a flicker any place else."

When Bobby was 2 years of age, the family was referred to a psychiatric clinic. Here she describes her experience as "wonderful." The doctor spoke to her at some length and "it was almost a relief for me to hear it. At least I knew where I stood." By this, Mrs. Allan means she had her suspicions confirmed, namely, that Bobby was retarded. However, he was described as being only mildly retarded, with a good prognosis, but the years have proved otherwise. At least she knew she didn't have a normal child.

Mrs. Allan described meeting her pediatrician on the street and berated him for not telling her the truth. His comment was, "You couldn't have done anything about it anyway. I knew that you would find out soon enough." Mrs. Allan emphasized how deeply disturbed she was during that time.

Although Mrs. Allan felt she was reasonably well handled by the psychiatrist, her questions were not answered. When questions arose regarding other children, Mrs. Allan consulted her pediatrician and he advised her against having another child. Their obstetrician, however, encouraged her to have another one. She subsequently became pregnant, and describes this period as one of great fear of having another retarded child. In the sixth month of pregnancy she contracted mumps, and "nearly went crazy." "The baby was wonderful. Anyway it had a happy ending."

At about 3½ years of age, Bobby had his first convulsion, his condition was followed at the seizure clinic, where he was put on medicine for convulsions. The parents were told nothing about his condition, and were critical of the fact that he did not have a complete work-up. They ". . . were not even told what the EEG showed."

There was further pursuit of medical exploration until finally they consulted a psychiatrist. The psychiatric consultation was described as being reasonably satisfactory, although the psychiatrist was "cold, he told us the brutal facts. At least I could start living after that rather than just hoping. Even so, he was optimistic." He recommended institutionalization, but the parents indicate their disapproval of this with much vehemence. The psychiatrist also pointed out that they were concentrating too much on the retarded child to the exclusion of the normal sibling. The indications are that they could accept this.

In answer to the question, "Was your contact with professional persons satisfactory?" the response was "absolutely not." Then they added, "In fact, we have lost a great deal of respect for the medical profession; we have had nothing but frustration every place we have turned."

"What type of services would you advise for people who are faced with this problem and are just beginning?" brought the immediate response, "Gently, but the truth." Mr. Allan felt that the counselor should evaluate the type of parent and the intellectual capacity of the parent, have a few visits with them if necessary, and handle them accordingly. They both agreed that the parents should be informed just as soon as the doctor knows. He said, "The attitude is of paramount importance. If the parents sense sympathy in the professional person and willingness to understand, this has a great deal of meaning. After all, most parents want to respect their doctor."

One further comment revealed the magnitude of the burden for parents when Mr. Allan said, "After all, you have a whole lifetime to worry about this, and you can only take it by degrees."

The discussion of the questions of institutionalization produced much negative response on the part of the parents, especially when the counselor had no direct knowledge of the resources but, even more important, little understanding of the family and discriminately advised it as a solution. Illustrative are such comments as: "They all spoke of institutional care as though that was the only thing we could do. They acted as though we had no choice." "If the child can be cared for at home and is not a burden on other members of the family, then they should keep him. I look at the happiness Billy has given us—he is so sweet and kind. The other children in the family adore him." "I honestly think that Tommy would not have gotten anywhere in an institution. There is no difficulty in having him at home." Without exception these parents wanted what was best for their children. They wanted to know whether the resources would help their children to achieve their capacities, however meager, and help them grow up as well as possible considering their handicaps. When necessary, they can come to terms with institutional care if that is the soundest way of helping their children. They asked whether their children need more than their share to enable them to assimilate whatever training and education are available. Also, they are able to provide the tender, loving care to make this possible. So many parents cannot be interviewed without the interviewer being greatly impressed with their love for their retarded children, and their ability to accept and handle frustration. It is important to note that in 21 of the cases institutional care was recommended early, but in only one was it followed through. The obvious conclusion is that they were not ready or interested in this solution to their problem.

It is significant to note that there is important research going on in the field on the families who can best use institutional care for their retarded children. One study, still in progress, considers the effects of a severely retarded child on family integration, the results of which can be of help to counselors in evaluating the kind of family who can keep their child with them and those who might best be directed toward institutionalization.

Apparently there has been more change in the attitudes of society toward retarded persons than we realize. The prevalent assumption has been that families cannot accept too much difference and that the higher the cultural and intellectual achievement, the less possibility there is for the retarded child to be cared for at home. This is not supported by this study. On the contrary, a place has been found for these children in their families, neighborhoods, and schools. I do not believe that it is being too omniscient to say that many of these children have gotten as good a start in life as is possible under the circumstances. I should doubt that any one would challenge the fact that the institutionalized child does not have his emotional needs met.

Needless to say, parents spoke glowingly of the local state Society for Retarded Children. They have found a way to share their experiences, to be supportive to each other, to resolve their feelings of difference, and, most important, to speak for retarded children and crusade in their interest. This has been an invaluable group therapeutic experience for many parents, an important factor in enabling families to live more comfortably with these children and to be helpful to them. They have proved parents need to be no longer isolated as individuals and families, with the serious emotional problems which set them apart from the rest of the world. These parents have paved the way for community understanding and acceptance of the problem, and have achieved an important role in community welfare by spearheading the need for specialized services in education, recreation, parent education facilities, and in programs of financial aid. They have discovered so much for themselves that they want to share their experiences and to be helpful to others.

THIRTEEN

Emotional Reactions of Handicapped Children

ROGER D. FREEMAN

Introduction

It is now well recognized that a child's emotional development, behavior, and reaction to his handicap may be more significant in determining· whether he may be able to remain in the community and achieve a degree of independent functioning than the extent of the physical handicap itself. Rehabilitative procedures often require the child to subject himself to months, or even years, of unpleasant or painful experiences without the assistance of motivation and understanding as may reasonably be expected of the adult patient. Parents are becoming increasingly aware of the possible consequences of early "traumatic" experiences and ask penetrating questions of the professional worker. New technics in the modification of behavior and controversies over treatment methods and their efficacy baffle and frustrate parent and professional alike.

The present report is an attempt to communicate some general principles that may be helpful to those working with handicapped children. While much is yet unknown and it is rightly considered hazardous to fit a person into the Procrustean bed of a generalization, it is also true that much that has been established has never been put into practice.

There is an enormous literature on personality studies, normal and abnormal child development, intelligence, counseling, psychotherapy, behavior therapy, and preparation of the child for hospitalization. A review of this material is obviously beyond the scope of this discussion and will be presented elsewhere.

We shall assume that early experiences in life may have profound effects upon later functioning, that development may be affected by the attitudes of parents and society, that a person's thoughts and feelings about himself and his body are significant and merit consideration, and that the professional worker's understanding, or lack of it, may be an important variable in the outcome of the rehabilitative process.

From *Rehabilitation Literature*, Vol. 28, No. 9 (September, 1967), pp. 274-282, with permission of the author and the National Easter Seal Society for Crippled Children and Adults.

Diagnosis

In recent years emphasis has been increasing on "early diagnosis." Unfortunately, this can be a mixed blessing or an actual disservice. Unless it results in some meaningful program, it may have only academic interest and result in potentially harmful distortions in parental attitudes, expectations, and child-rearing practices. This is particularly true of a wrong diagnosis; in some instances the child's needs would be better served by providing ongoing diagnosis and parental support without firm prognostication.

In the event no diagnostic label is applied, a major task involves clarifying for the parents the reasons for uncertainty and an explanation of the process by which the diagnosis will be arrived at. Reassurance that lack of a "label" will not mean lack of a program of management is a basic requirement. Explanations may also be necessary when diagnostic terms (sometimes deliberately incorrect) must be used for administrative purposes (*e.g.,* when a "brain-damaged" child is reported as having "cerebral palsy" for purposes of state aid).

The most tragic cases of misdiagnosis are those in which the parents have been told the child has a progressive disease that will result in death. Most parents go through a gradual emotional detachment from the child, a kind of "mourning in advance," only to discover that the child does not die but may continue at an even more handicapped level for an indefinite period of time. In such a situation the parent may never be able to achieve the previous level of emotional investment, and considerable bitterness may ensue.

We have found that the vagueness of the term *emotional problem* is itself an issue that must be dealt with. Many parents misunderstand the meaning, assuming that it signifies a "mental block," unhappiness, insanity, or a neurotic type of "mental conflict," as seen in adults. In many instances the professional person uses the phrase *emotional problem* to mean a developmental deviation, which may or may not have an important environmental or "psychogenic" component in its etiology. Unless this is fully discussed, the parent may assume that he or she has been an inadequate or unworthy parent and has thereby produced the deviation in some way.

Problems in differential diagnosis are often quite complex in young handicapped children. There is little agreement as to criteria for establishing many diagnostic categories. In fact, there is dispute over whether some categories exist (as in aphasia of developmental type, minimal brain dysfunction, and developmental lags in speech). Where the developmental process is still so unpredictable, diagnostic certainty may indicate the professional's own insecurity rather than acumen.

Since many of these youngsters are nonverbal, highly dependent, immature, and anxious, hospital or office visits may be of very limited value, particularly where evaluation of behavior is indicated. Unless an older child is highly verbal, we have found it much more helpful to evaluate the child in his natural home setting, in school, or both. We have been interested in comparing impressions gained from office visits with those from the home. The differences in some cases are striking;

more important, the recommendations emerging from the evaluation may be quite surprising after the home visit. Pessimistic prognoses may be altered in a positive direction as hitherto unsuspected assets are discovered. Interpretation to the family of the diagnostic impressions and recommendations is also facilitated when they feel evaluation has been performed in a situation in which the child feels most secure. In the past three years this type of home evaluation has been routine for preschool age children requiring psychiatric evaluation, where practical from the standpoint of distance.[4] Other professional workers have also used these methods (social workers, speech therapists, nurses, pediatricians, nutritionists).

Areas of Vulnerability in the Development of the Handicapped Child

Even before the child's birth, many parents have a desire for a specific set of characteristics and sex for the child, and they may go through a more or less complicated process of choosing a name. If the child is conceived out of wedlock or at a time of marital crisis, or for any other reason is unwanted, these feelings may be complicated and exaggerated by the birth of a defective child. In particular, attempts by the mother, or sometimes even the wish, to obtain or perform an abortion may be linked up with subsequent guilt feelings surrounding the handicap.

From the time of birth the mother normally develops a sense of pride in her child, fostered by intimate contact and the attitudes of those around her, which convey the feeling that she has produced something special and worthwhile. The infant becomes a psychological extension of the parent. Prematurity may make this process much more difficult. If the handicap is obvious at birth, maternal depression and working-through of grief over the loss of the anticipated normal child make appropriate stimulation by the mother less likely. Wounded pride, feelings of guilt, and even revulsion may predominate. Anything the parents are told at this time may be crucial because of heightened vulnerability.

In the first few months, when innate reaction patterns are primary, the handicapped child may show alterations that are puzzling and even frightening to the parents. The mother's efforts to respond to the baby's cues may be partially or almost totally unsuccessful. The physician in charge of the case may not yet be able to explain this or may attribute it to a "nervous mother." Some mothers are bothered more by excessive passivity or placidity; others by restlessness and demanding behavior. Rhythmicity of certain functions may not be so readily established in the handicapped child and may further interfere with smooth mother-child interaction. Hospitalizations, illnesses, and differing professional opinions may further jeopardize an already precarious situation. While the normal child is presumably developing a sense of "basic trust" that his needs will be met, the child with developmental deviations may sense the world as chaotic, painful, unsatisfying, or capricious. It may be that this contributes to later efforts at stabilization that may be looked upon as maladaptive: withdrawal, stereotypy, ritualistic behavior, perseveration, and other forms of rigid control.

Late in the first year of life the normal mother begins to frustrate the normal child in a progressive fashion, in keeping with the increase in predictability and ability to delay gratification that the child shows. The depressed or anxious mother may not do this, or may overdo it, failing to provide the developing personality with a basic resource for coping with future tensions and developmental crises. The need for optimal frustration is no less for the handicapped than for the normal child.

Separation problems often develop at the end of the first year. The average parent deals with this by leaving the child at times, but in a way that does not produce excessive anxiety that cannot be mastered. Fear of strangers is considered normal while the infant is developing his first sense of separateness from mother. Associated medical problems of the handicapped child (*e.g.*, seizures) may prevent such separations from being undertaken by the parents, or they may feel an excessive need to avoid anything upsetting to the child. When this occurs, the child rapidly learns how to control the parents and a vicious circle is begun that leads to annoyance on the part of the parents and to ever-increasing insecurity for the child, leading to increased efforts at control of the situation and so on.

The "milestones" of motor development may be skewed in the handicapped child, producing parental concern and sometimes resulting in inappropriate "pushing" before the child is maturationally ready (as in early speech development or walking). Cues from the child that he is ready to attempt a new developmental step may be missed by the parents because of depression, overindulgence, fear of hurting the child, or a variety of other reasons. Yet these early motor activities are basic to exploration, curiosity, learning to play, and stimulation for cognitive development and for self-initiated separations from the mother. The handicap or procedures involved in the child's management may also lead to limitations of exploration and motoric expression of aggression (*e.g.*, bracing, casting). Infantile frustration and satisfaction patterns may persist beyond the usual time (such as rocking, mouthing, smelling, temper tantrums, and breath holding). The normal two-year-old is developing speech rapidly, which assists in gaining more control over impulses and actions. Where speech is delayed, problems in impulse expression frequently occur. Early moves toward independence may be inhibited by some of the foregoing factors but also if the parents fear the child will hurt himself or die (*e.g.*, parents who fear death from a seizure and sleep with the child). Usually the parental anxieties are mixtures of realistic concern and their own distorted, confused concepts.

In the early preschool years the average child shows many signs of pride in his body functions and this provides an impetus or reward for practice and new successes. The handicapped child may not be so fortunate: neither he nor his parents may feel a sense of pleasure and pride. The impetus for trying new activities may be greatly reduced. "He just won't try anything and gives up so easily" is a common parental complaint. Often it is easier for child and parents to let the adult do it, rather than watch the child go through repeated and often unsuccessful attempts at mastery.

Early socialization with peers and play become increasingly important in the preschool years, but this may be a very restricted area for the handicapped child.

Isolation, social anxiety, and failure to make an adequate identification as a worthwhile human being of a particular sex may ensue. Negative attitudes of parents or others may be adopted and internalized. Outbursts of poorly controlled aggression are not uncommon, especially since the child may not be presented with the consequences of his actions. Sibling rivalry problems may be difficult to deal with, since the parents often find it difficult to apply the same standards to their normal as to their handicapped children. Whereas play activities normally assist the child to master anxiety, fears, and passivity (as in receiving injections and operations) and to learn imitative patterns, much of this may be denied the handicapped. Better methods of compensating for some of these limitations need to be studied and made available to those who counsel parents.

Between the ages of three and six years, transient fears ("phobias") are quite common but usually of no pathological significance in the average child. Some handicapped children develop multiple or persistent fears. The "normal negativism" of this age may also be distorted, in the direction of either excessive compliance and passivity or truly extreme resistance in which any submission or agreement seems to be akin to unconditional surrender.

Many handicapped children of this age have marked reactions to being surpassed by their normal younger siblings. This seems to be concurrent with the dawning realization of their being different from others. When this occurs parents ask many difficult questions about how to cope with the needs of their normal children for praise without increasing feelings of inadequacy on the part of the handicapped child. The answers are rarely simple and often require an understanding of the particular family structure, feelings, and attitudes.

By the time the child reaches elementary school, less allowance is being made for the individual; he must learn to fit into situations he would rather avoid, learn and abide by group rules, and become aware of, and respect, the needs and wishes of others. Appropriate outlets for his impulses must be found and a well-established conscience should guide much of the child's behavior. This presupposes experiences with peers in which he has learned the consequences of his actions and the development of some sense of self-esteem.

Dependency, passivity, and persisting immature patterns may make socialization and peer-group acceptance of the handicapped child much more difficult, apart from the "visibility" of the handicap itself. Special educational settings may not provide the child with the social skills to deal with nonhandicapped children. Parental anxiety over school and social performance may increase the child's worries. Social anxiety, compensatory fantasies, daydreaming, "acting-out," and impulsivity may all reduce the child's ability to concentrate on learning. Problems with abstract thinking, when they occur, often become evident in the third or fourth grades and may lead to considerations of tutoring, summer school, repeating a grade, or changing schools, all of which contribute their share to social difficulties.

There should be little need here to point out that adolescence is usually a time of crisis, turmoil, rebellion, and change, as the struggle to establish a separate identity and true independence progresses. Peer-group acceptance is a necessary transition and many conflicts over social and sexual problems arise. Love objects outside the family must be found and marked changes in the body image integrated. The handicapped person, during this period, may show a greater awareness of his handicap, associated with a feeling of lack of attractiveness or physical strength, or both. Earlier, the child may have had the fantasy and wish that when grown up he would somehow become completely normal. Now, his sense of time has changed and he must adopt more realistic ideas as to his future. The adolescent who *in fact* is more dependent upon his family has a much more difficult task in becoming independent and may have more conflict over desires to remain a child and avoid the unknown terrors of maturity and responsibility. Denial of mild handicaps with compensatory acting-out, even in antisocial directions, may be seen. Refusal of habilitative measures that increase his feelings of being different may become a point over which struggles with parents and professionals occur. Parents become increasingly (and often realistically) anxious over sexual expression, marriage possibilities, and what degree of independence will be achieved.

The normal child and adolescent has probably toyed with many vocational possibilities in fantasy, at play, in part-time jobs, in school experiences, in conversations, in camp, and in other ways. Usually this leads to some choice that is in keeping with reality. The handicapped youngster may have lacked both these experiences and appropriate parental attitudes. He may have unrealistic fantasies or limited reality-testing ability, make outright denial of limitations, or he may, on the other hand, assess his limitations too pessimistically. Obviously, more needs to be considered than merely IQ.

The preceding general description has a discouraging tone. But it should not be assumed that most of these vicissitudes of normal development are inevitable for the handicapped. There is a need for much more research into the antecedents and consequences of deviant development. If one keeps in mind that the maturational forces themselves may tend to overcome developmental obstacles, a more balanced view is possible.

Some Differences Between the Thinking of Children and Adults

Some understanding of how children's thinking differs from that of adults is basic to any work with handicapped children. Inability of an adult to comprehend how he used to think and feel as a child is normal and probably adaptive. It is even a problem where fewer years intervene: How many adults can sympathize with the feelings and behavior of the adolescent? Thus, some study of what might be obvious is necessary. Treating children as though they think the way we do is common and potentially harmful, since it may lead to mistrust if not outright hostility.

In the following discussion it must be remembered that *relative* differences are being pointed out; some adult thinking still carries the childish stamp.

The young child operates largely on the basis of immediate pleasure or pain. He finds it difficult, if not impossible, to plan ahead or *choose present discomfort for a promised future relief.* He cannot easily distinguish between the pain or discomfort caused by an illness or handicap and that caused by treatment or therapy aimed at improving the problem.

Egocentrism is prominent and obvious: The world seems to revolve around him and his family. (He may state that the sun or moon follows him, because it is present both before and after a change in his location.) It takes several years before he can appreciate another's point of view, understand his effect upon another, and learn to tolerate the limitations and foibles of his parents.

Wishes, fantasies, and thoughts are really confused with reality and actions. Things happen to us *for a reason.* The concept of a chance, fortuitous occurrence that cannot be blamed upon someone is usually not developed in the young child. Primitive morality is based upon experiences with reward and punishment, good and bad. The unpleasant consequences of a handicapping condition may, therefore, be viewed by the child as a punishment.

Children may fear the intensity of their own wishes, especially if they are socially unacceptable and directed toward the parents upon whom they must depend.

Because of dependency, limited knowledge and experience, poorly established inner controls, and a rather restricted repertoire of coping mechanisms, *regression* to previous patterns occurs much more easily than in the adult. "Trauma" (experiencing his inability to master successfully an anxiety-provoking situation) is also more common.

Sense of past and future time is not well established. Psychologically, there appears to the child to be a real possibility of being changed into someone else, "outgrowing" a handicap at maturity, "catching" a handicap, or being influenced or changed (physically or mentally) by someone else. Explanations given to the child are likely to be drawn into his current fantasies and distorted. Some repetition, at appropriate intervals, as well as inquiring as to what the child understands from the explanation, may be helpful.

More mature thought processes gradually evolve, but, in the areas of greatest emotional import, more primitive thinking tends to persist, even into adult life (as in sex, birth, and death). A child who is sophisticated in some areas of relatively conflict-free thinking may concurrently and surprisingly demonstrate less mature or even bizarre ideas in more emotionally "loaded" areas. Causal thinking matures rapidly and at ages 7 to 9 years approaches adult concepts (at least in conflict-free areas).

There is still too little appreciation of the extent and depth of a child's distorted fears and the threat he may perceive due to his small size, enforced passivity, limited experience, and poorer reality-testing. Adults often assume that a child cannot be adversely affected by medical procedures or discussions in his presence. This sometimes leads to almost unbelievable situations. Adults can sue, and often collect from, a doctor who does not inform them of the nature of the procedure to be done and its risks. Not respecting the child's needs in this regard may not be legally actionable but constitutes an "assault" in every sense of the word.

Role of Play

We frequently lose sight of the crucial role of play in child development. Sometimes it is regarded as a regrettable waste of time or is replaced by more "constructive" activities supervised by adults. Pearson[5] has clearly outlined the need for play and warns of the increasing trend away from unsupervised play during the elementary school years. Harlow's research on primate development seems to confirm the importance or peer interactions and is reviewed by Pearson. Failure to play may contribute to continuing dependency, failure of individuation and redirecting of fantasies, excessive daydreaming, and inability to form strong emotional ties to others. This would seem to be a particular hazard for physically handicapped children. In working with parents, ways should be found to provide for play experiences, even for the severely restricted child.

Aspects of the Handicap

There are certain aspects of the handicapping condition itself that may be relevant to the development of emotional disturbances in the child or parent. These are outlined in *Table 1.* Apart from these, the child's original endowment, areas of uninvolved functioning, position in the family, family stability, and nature of previous professional contacts may all play a part.

In general, factors leading to intellectual, social, and physical restrictions and limitations (whether due to the nature of the handicap, its management, or parental attitudes) tend to result in what is loosely called "emotional immaturity," passivity, dependency, poor reality-testing, poor impulse control, and, frequently, stereotyped activities such as autoerotic patterns, mannerisms, tics, and head-banging. Because the handicapped and restricted child may show these features (which seem to be more common with multiple handicaps), he is quite likely to resemble the psychotic child, who also has areas of massive immaturity, primitive fixations, and mannerisms. The differential diagnosis is often difficult. There is still controversy as to whether the psychoses associated with handicapping conditions are the "same" as childhood schizophrenia.[1] The most dramatic work on this area has been reported by Elonen and others,[2,3] who worked with the deviant blind child. They found that the *majority* of such children given a diagnosis of ineducable and requiring institutional care could be sufficiently changed with intensive work to attend special or regular day schools.

Incidence and Nature of Emotional Problems

There is no general agreement regarding the incidence of emotional disturbance with each type of handicap. Where figures are available, they usually indicate an increased risk, at least for handicaps with early onset. Research studies are extremely difficult to perform, however. There is at present no reason to believe that a specific personality type or reaction pattern is inevitable for a child with a particular handicap. Multiple factors are undoubtedly operative. The most meaningful

TABLE 1.—ASPECTS OF THE HANDICAP RELEVANT TO EMOTIONAL REACTIONS

Aspect	*Consequence or Example*
1 Severity of physical limitation	May reduce contact with environment and adversely affect cognitive development
2 Age at onset	Congenital defects are more likely to produce diffuse personality alterations, acquired handicaps, and "acute" disturbances
3 Duration	May affect degree of personality change or distortion
4 Course	
a Stationary	Blindness; deafness. May be easier to cope with than when future is unknown
b Progressive	Muscular dystrophy, degenerative diseases of many kinds. Reaction may depend upon central nervous system involvement or sparing
c Improving	Benign hypotonia, some cases of mild brain damage and cerebral palsy
d Episodic with periods of normality	Seizures, diabetic reactions. May be especially distressing because of extreme fluctuations
5 Appearance or "visibility"	Important in child's self-regard, social functioning, parental adaptation
6 Involvement of central nervous system	May directly impair coping mechanisms, integration, thinking, emotional control
7 Special features	
a Weakness	Tendency towards passivity and isolation may be obstacle in development
b Involuntary movements	Athetoid cerebral palsy, dystonia. Impairs sense of body mastery and control
c Predictability	Seizures. Lack of predictability may lead to protective efforts that hamper development
d How affected by stress	Many neurological, dermatologic, gastrointestinal, and allergic-respiratory conditions are exacerbated by stress; optimal frustration may not be imposed because of parental fear of worsening condition
e Threat to life	Seizures, asthma, heart disease. Excessive degree of protection is common
f Incontinence	Alert children may be very upset by inability to control processes of elimination
8 Therapeutic measures used	Need for rest, drugs, separations from family and friends, operations, and painful procedures all may impose their own obstacles to normal development

work, from the emotional standpoint, has been done in blindness, mental retardation, muscular dystrophy, convulsive disorders, "minimal cerebral dysfunction," cleft palate, bronchial asthma, and cystic fibrosis. There is relatively little that is helpful concerning cerebral palsy, and there are no adequate studies, in depth, on the deaf child. Many of the contributions were of a multidisciplinary nature and by no means solely to the credit of psychiatry.

General Principles of Management

This section outlines some suggestions that might be useful in the management of the handicapped child. They will not be found helpful or sufficient in every case, since there can be no substitute for adequate investigation, in depth, of an individual and his family. While it is hoped that these will be of assistance, they are not intended to replace professional consultation in the area of mental health. Some criteria for referral to a psychiatrist will be listed later.

A study of great potential significance was described by Shere and Kastenbaum.[6] They investigated mother-child interaction in a group of severely involved, nonambulatory, nonverbal cerebral palsied children. They found that the mothers, often without realizing it, fostered passivity in their children. They did not automatically know how to stimulate their children so as to provide maximum experience for cognitive development. These children lived in an environment in which they had much too little contact with objects. Physicians and others had tended to focus exclusively on physical or speech progress, so that the mothers were unaware to what extent their children depended totally upon them for object contact. It was felt that special procedures needed to be employed for the development of insight in these parents. The implications of this pilot study regarding other and less severe handicaps should be further investigated. It is probable that we often fail to provide early and meaningful direction to parents regarding stimulation, exploration, play, and appropriate play materials.

We need to understand the "working-through" process in children and parents. This applies to diagnosis and treatment. Short cuts and "one-shot" evaluations leave much to be desired because of neglect of this basic principle. Unfortunately, shortage of personnel and time are realistic factors that often prevent ideal care.

The professional worker should learn to recognize his own needs and feelings in work with a handicapped child. "Rescue fantasies" may easily develop, with the need to prove one's superiority to the parent. (It's easy when you don't have to live with the problem!) Negative feelings of anger and disgust may become a problem for both parent and worker as the child grows older. What was formerly "cute" may not evoke the same response later.

Since both child and parents have angry, frustrated feelings that they may transfer to a particular worker or institution, understanding and refraining from retaliation may be most helpful. Remember that, while parental love for their child is natural, feelings of a negative sort because of the abnormality are also natural, though unacceptable in our culture. The child's parents' defenses against anxiety or depression need to be respected, not battered down, unless and until there is something better to offer.

Where possible, substitute outlets for a child's motoric and fantasied aggression, competitive impulses, and needs for success should be provided. Boredom, sensory and social isolation, and apathy are to be avoided, as are shame and humiliation as disciplinary or motivational technics.

While understanding ease of regression, we should do everything possible to avoid practices and procedures that are unnecessary but may force the child into a regressed position (*e.g.*, wheelchairs, bedpans, day-time use of pajamas, and unnecessary bed rest in hospitalized children).

Cooperation and compliance may be very convenient but at times may be expressive and pathological. A child who protests vehemently against a painful procedure that he does not understand is not necessarily "disturbed"; in fact he may be healthier than the "perfect patient."

Parents need to be told about the results of routine procedures that we take for granted. It is rare for a routine skull film to turn up unexpected pathology but parents and child may believe that it can determine whether something is "wrong with his brain."

Serious problems should be referred early. (*See Table 2.*)

Preparation for Surgery or Other Procedures

Elective procedures should be deferred until the child and family are ready; inquiry should be made as to the stability of the home situation and other current problems. Most authorities agree that surgery is least traumatic before the age of one year and after the age of five or six. Adequate preparation involves corrections of distortions, wherever possible, as to what to expect before, during, and after the procedure and should not precede the procedure by more than a few days in most instances (for the child). Of course, the child may know that an operation is contemplated, but the *detailed* preparation should adhere to the previous stipulation. The parents need more time than this. They should have one person they can contact, rather than a "team." Mounting anxiety before a procedure, despite preparation, is often encountered and not necessarily a problem. Lying to the child should be avoided. The parents should also be prepared for the possibility of emotional reactions of a transient nature after surgery (*e.g.*, hostility to the parents, or clinging, demanding behavior, sleep difficulties, and other regressive patterns). Parent-child contact should be fostered by permitting rooming-in with the very young child or frequent visiting with the older child. A familiar object (doll or toy) from the home environment may help.

Preparation need not be done by the psychiatrist, psychologist, or social worker, except in special circumstances. A sensitive pediatrician, general practitioner, orthopedist (or other surgical specialist), or even a nonmedical person or parent may do the job successfully, provided the information is available to them.

Psychiatric Referral

When general principles of good management fail to prevent or modify a pathological emotional reaction, referral or consultation may be in order. Depending upon the availability of a child psychiatrist with experience in this area, consultation with a knowledgeable general psychiatrist, pediatrician, or psychologist might precede this step. Consultation prior to referral has certain advantages, perhaps the most significant being the avoidance of stirring false hopes or fears in the child and family. (Many parents see a psychiatric referral as indication that a new "cure" is possible, or, alternatively, that a new and crushing burden has been added to the existing handicap.) Treatment of the persistent and severe problem is in the province of the mental health professional and will not be discussed here.

The same principles applying to any referral are pertinent: Some specialists are competent and helpful, others are not. Unfortunately, most psychiatrists have not had adequate training in working with the handicapped child until relatively recently. Some criteria for referral are listed in *Table 2*.

TABLE 2.—SOME CRITERIA FOR REFERRAL TO A PSYCHIATRIST

1 Suicidal threats, preoccupations, or attempts.

2 Severe and persistent depression or withdrawal, out of proportion to any known precipitating factors

3 Self-punitive behavior, pleasure in painful experiences, "accident proneness"

4 Severe and persistent behavioral regression without known physical cause

5 Marked resistance to habilitative measures, which cannot be modified by a flexible therapist; evidence that "psychological gain" from the handicap is producing, or adding to, such resistance

6 Severe and repeated acting-out or delinquent behavior

7 Severe separation anxiety in the school-age child; "school phobia"

8 Evidence of possible incipient psychosis: bizarre behavior, withdrawal to extreme degree, delusional or paranoid thinking, habit deterioration

9 Differential diagnostic problems. A few are:
   a Psychosis with (or versus) mental retardation;
   b "Bizarre behavior" in children with sensory handicaps;
   c Deafness versus psychosis or "elective mutism;"
   d Convulsive disorder versus "conversion reaction" or "hysteria."

Factors in Good Adjustment

After so much emphasis upon problem behavior, it is appropriate to consider some factors that seem to be conducive to successful adjustment. These are listed in *Table 3*. It is true, though not always well understood, that the most competent team of professionals may be unduly pessimistic about a child's development and potential. There is, as yet, no way to predict consistently eventual "good" or "bad" adjustment. Until this goal is achieved, it is best to give every child and family a reasonable chance to maximize all areas of functioning. The factors listed, it should be stated, rarely all occur together, and successful adjustment may take place without all of them.

Conclusions

It is probable that the handicapped child, by reason of his difficult developmental process, is more vulnerable to emotional disturbances (of either developmental or acute types) than the nonhandicapped. Reliable statistics are not available, however, and it has not been possible to demonstrate a clear relationship between a particular handicap and a specific personality pattern or developmental deviation.

The amenability of emotionally disturbed handicapped children to various forms of intervention has never been adequately established. It is probably better than many have thought. Too many clinics and mental health workers have assumed a pessimistic outlook or excluded such children from services they needed. Environmental factors can be assumed to be of at least as much importance in the genesis of emotional disturbances of the handicapped as that of the nonhandicapped.

It is hoped that the recently increased interest in the handicapped child by psychiatrists and in emotional development by nonpsychiatric professionals working with such children will result in better communication and will eventually benefit children and their families.

TABLE 3—FACTORS CONDUCIVE TO GOOD ADJUSTMENT

---

1 Favorable endowment and "temperament" (hard to define or determine)

2 Stable family situation

3 Parent-child relationship predominantly positive; sense of "basic trust" established in child; parents who are sensitive but not overly intellectualizing

4 Parents and professionals working cooperatively, rather than at cross-purposes

5 Realistic information about the handicap available to child and family

6 Adequate preparation of child and parents for hospitalization and painful or complicated procedures

7 Adequate opportunities for exploration, peer contact, and play

8 Development of effective coping mechanisms to deal with anxiety

9 Minimal (but sufficient) number of professional evaluations and absence of marked differences of opinion among those who have seen the child

10 Realistic acceptance by the therapist of his own role, expectations, and needs in working with the child

---

References

1. EATON, LOUISE, and MENOLASCINO, FRANK J. Psychotic Reactions of Childhood: A Follow-Up Study. *Am. J. Orthopsychiat.* Apr., 1967. 37:3:521-529.

2. ELONEN, ANNA S., and CAIN, ALBERT C. Diagnostic Evaluation and Treatment of Deviant Blind Children. *Am. J. Orthopsychiat.* July, 1964. 34:4:625-633.

3. ELONEN, ANNA S., and POLZIEN, MARGARET. Experimental Program for Deviant Blind Children. *New Outlook for the Blind.* Apr., 1965. 59:4:122-126.

4. FREEMAN, ROGER D. The Home Visit in Child Psychiatry: Its Usefulness in Diagnosis and Training. *J. Am. Acad. Child Psychiat.* Apr., 1967. 6:2:276-294.

5. PEARSON, GERALD H. J. The Importance of Peer Relationship in the Latency Period. *Bul.*, Philadelphia Assn. for Psychoanalysis. 16:3:109-121.

6. SHERE, EUGENIA and KASTENBAUM, ROBERT. Mother-Child Interaction in Cerebral Palsy: Environmental and Psychosocial Obstacles to Congnitive Development. *Genet. Psychol. Monogr.* May, 1966. 73:2:255-335.

Suggested Reading

BAER, PAUL E. Problems in the Differential Diagnosis of Brain Damage and Childhood Schizophrenia. *Am. J. Orthopsychiat.* Oct., 1961. 31:4:728-737.

BLUMBERG, MARVIN L. Emotional and Personality Development in Neuromuscular Disorders. *A.M.A. J. Diseases of Children.* Sept., 1959. 98:3:303-310.

CAPLAN, HYMAN. The Role of Deviant Maturation in the Pathogenesis of Anxiety. *Am. J. Orthopsychiat.* Jan., 1956. 26:1:94-107.

CAPLAN, HYMAN. Some Considerations of the Body Image Concept in Child Development. *Quart. J. Child Behavior.* Oct., 1952. 4:4:382-388.

CROTHERS, BRONSON, and PAINE, RICHMOND S. *The Natural History of Cerebral Palsy.* Cambridge, Mass.: Harvard Univ. Pr., 1959.

CRUICKSHANK, WILLIAM M., ed. *Psychology of Exceptional Children and Youth. (ed. 2)* Englewood Cliffs, N.J.: Prentice-Hall, 1963.

DENHOFF, ERIC. Emotional and Psychological Background of the Neurologically Handicapped Child. *Exceptional Children.* Mar., 1961. 27:7:347-349.

FLAVELL, JOHN H. *The Developmental Psychology of Jean Piaget.* Princeton, N. J.: Van Nostrand, 1963.

FREUD, ANNA. The Role of Bodily Illness in the Mental Life of Children. *Psychoanalytic Study of the Child* (New York: Internatl. Universities Pr., 1952), 7:69-81.

GREEN, MORRIS. Care of the Child with a Long-Term, Life-Threatening Illness: Some Principles of Management. *Pediatrics.* Mar., 1967. 39:3:441-445.

MORROW, ROBERT S., and COHEN, JACOB. The Psycho-Social Factors in Muscular Dystrophy. *J. Child Psychial.* Apr., 1954. 3:1:70-80.

PHILIPS, IRVING. Psychopathology and Mental Retardation. *Am. J. Psychiat.* July, 1967. 124:1:29-35.

PINCUS, J. H., and GLASER, G. H. The Syndrome of "Minimal Brain Damage" in Childhood. *New Eng. J. Med.* July 7, 1966. 275:1:27-35.

ROSS, ALAN O. *The Exceptional Child in the Family—Helping Parents of Exceptional Children.* New York: Grune & Stratton, 1964

SCHECTER, MARSHALL D. The Orthopedically Handicapped Child: Emotional Reactions. *Arch. Gen. Psychiat.* Mar., 1961. 4:2:247-253.

SHAW, CHARLES R. *The Psychiatric Disorders of Childhood.* New York: Appelton-Century-Crofts, 1966.

TISZA, VERONICA B., Selverstone, Betty, Rosenblum, Gershen, and Hanlon, Nancy. Psychiatric Observations of Children with Cleft Palate. *Am. J. Orthopsychiat.* Apr., 1958. 28:416-423.

TUREEN, LOUIS L., and WOOLSEY, ROBERT M. Some Psychiatric Aspects of Convulsive Disorders. *Missouri Med.* Feb., 1964. 61:2:91-98.

WATSON, E. JANE, and JOHNSON, ADELAIDE M. The Emotional Significance of Acquired Physical Disfigurement in Children. *Am. J. Orthopsychiat.* Jan., 1958. 28:1:85-97.

WERRY, J. S. Studies on the Hyperactive Child. IV. An Empirical Analysis of the Minimal Brain Dysfunction Syndrome. Read before the American Psychiatric Association, Detroit, May, 1967. To be published.

FOURTEEN

The Meaning of a Retarded Child for His Parents: A Focus for Counselors

DAVID B. RYCKMAN AND ROBERT A. HENDERSON

Within the professions concerned with the problems of the mentally retarded, there has been an awakening of concern for the problems of the parents of retarded children. The last 20 years have produced a relatively large body of literature on these problems. Much of this literature has been comprised of professionals' opinions based on their experience with parents of retarded children. With the exception of the Farber studies (Farber, 1959; Farber, 1960; Farber, Jeene, and Toigo, 1960), few attempts have been made to conduct research experiments or to develop theoretical conceptualizations about these problems.

Most writers in this area have pointed out a relatively standard group of reactions of parents when they learn their child is retarded. There is general agreement in the literature that the fact of having a retarded child places considerable strain on the psychological adaptive mechanisms of the parent. Most of the literature describes the various parental reactions in terms of psychopathology. Parental reactions which deviate from some "idealized normal" response of parents to a "normal" child are viewed as basically pathological.

The purpose of this paper is to analyze the ideas expressed in the literature concerning the meaning of retarded children to parents and to suggest several factors which may effect the degree of parental reaction.

Recognition of the primary contribution of the parent to the development of the child has stimulated most writers to concentrate their efforts on the effect of the parents on the child. Information on the parental influence has formed the basis for working with parents toward developing healthy child-rearing practices. However, some understanding of the reciprocal influence, i.e., the influence and meaning of the child to the parent, is needed if professional workers are to make the most effective use of parent contacts. This paper will approach parent-child relationships from the meaning and influence of the child on the parent.

1. *The parent views the child as a physical and psychological extension of himself.* This is either stated or implied in much of the literature. Kozier (1957, p. 184)

---

[1]Reprinted by permission from *Mental Retardation*, Vol. 3, No. 4 (August, 1965), pp. 4-7, a Publication of the American Association on Mental Deficiency.

stated, "In our culture, a parent makes a great emotional and material investment in the preparation for the birth of a baby. In many ways, a child represents to the parent an extension of his own self." This concept has many ramifications to the parent, especially when the child is defective (Cummings & Stock, 1962; Rheingold, 1945; Solnit & Stark, 1961).

The child is a physical production of the parents. He is a product of the combined characteristics inherited from the parents. Assuming for the moment that there are no environmental factors operating, the child is a combination of the positive and negative characteristics of the parents. If something is "good" about the child, it is a reflection of the "good" in one or both parents. Conversely, if something is "bad" or "wrong" with the child, it is a reflection of the same trait, overt or covert, in one or both of the parents.

Many of the authors in this area point out the almost universal feeling of inadequacy of parents when they learn that their child is retarded, i.e., that something is wrong with the child (Goodman & Rothman, 1961). Hersh, 1961; Kelman, 1953; Mayer, 1956; Stone, 1948; Willie, 1961). Dalton and Epstein, (1963) specifically discuss this reaction as "well-nigh universal" among parents of retardates. If this feeling is so universal among these parents, one might speculate that this identification with the child as an extension of self may be a normal reaction of parents. Hence, this may be one relatively universal meaning of children to parents in our culture.

2. *The child is a means of vicarious satisfaction to the parents.* The parents may experience or expect to experience satisfaction of their wishes and desires through the life experiences of their children. Cummings and Stock (1962) listed some core problems of parents of retarded children which include specific mention of the disappointment, loss, and sense of bereavement associated with having a child which cannot fulfill the parents' wishes and desires. Rose (1958) discusses the deviations between the "expected" child and the "real" child and the problems inherent in separating the two.

Blodgett and Warfield (1959) refer to the "rewards" which children may offer parents as they watch their children and relive their childhood. Various authors have noted the loss which parents feel when they realize that their child cannot fulfill their hopes and desires (Begab, 1956; Michaels & Schueman, 1962; Olshansky, 1962). Auerback (1961) makes reference to the almost universal expectation among parents that their children can fulfill these hopes and dreams. The parents of the retarded child are denied these rewards. If these expectations and desires are relatively universal within our culture and parents expect satisfaction and reward from their children, this would indicate that vicarious rewards are a second area of meaning to parents.

3. *The parents can "transcend" death through their child, i.e., derive some measure of immortality.* This area of meaning of children is not widely discussed in the literature directly but it is implied in relation to the two concepts described above. Blodgett and Warfield (1959, p. 42) state that children are highly valued in our culture, not only because of the ego-extension and vicarious satisfactions for

the parents but because "They also project themselves, through their children, into a future they will not live to see."

Roos (1963) suggests the importance of this aspect in his comments on the significance of the existential conflicts of parents of retarded children, especially when they become aware of the diagnosis. He also points out that although this concept is not as readily observable in the reactions of parents a diagnosis of retardation, it seems to have significant implications in terms of how the parents can be expected to react. Some indications that this may be relatively universal in our culture are the expressed concern that children have a better "chance" than the parents, and the hoped-for climb in status which many parents have for their children. Such things as concern for family names and traditions are also indications. All of these aspects may imply some concern of parents for achieving immortality through their children.

4. *A fourth area of meaning of children for parents is the concept of a personalized love object.* Although not directly stated in the literature, this area of meaning is implied in the widespread discussion of guilt. Dalton and Epstein (1963) describe guilt feelings of parents in terms of their inability to love the defective child wholeheartedly. Because the parent cannot do this, as he believes he should, he feels guilty. The problem of guilt becomes heightened if the parents consider institutionalization (Schipper, 1959).

Inherent in this guilt is the element of rejection, i.e., failure to love the child, accompanied by anger and frustration. There is general agreement in the literature' that parents feel guilty, at least in part, because they do not love their defective child as they believe they should (Grebler, 1952; Hastings, 1948; Hersh, 1961; Zwerling, 1954). The guilt reflects their feelings that the child should be a personalized love object. The widespread reports on paternal guilt in the literature suggests that it is relatively universal in our culture that a parent views his child as a personalized love object.

5. *A fifth meaning of children is the parental feeling of worth in meeting the dependency needs of the child.* Although Stone (1948) refers to this directly, it is most often expressed in terms of the overprotectiveness observed in many parents of retardates (Cummings & Stock, 1962; Grebler, 1952; Mahoney, 1958; Willie, 1961) Overprotectiveness is a means of compensating for the child's handicap, i.e., a means of achieving some satisfactions from the child. Waterman (1948) describes the "chosen people" or "martyr syndrome" in which the parents maintain some feeling of self-worth through extreme devotion to the needs of the retarded child. It is hypothesized that most parents derive some sense of worth through meeting the needs of a dependent child. This may be another relatively universal meaning of children in our culture.

6. *Negative feelings about the limitations and demands of child rearing are a sixth area of meaning of children.* Retarded children are an added burden to parents. The demands and limitations on the parents are realistically increased when rearing a retarded child (Coleman, 1953; Murray, 1959; Sheimo, 1951). When one considers the needs of a retarded child, especially a trainable or custodial child,

it is not surprising that the added problems warrant attention in the literature. However, child rearing places demands and limitations on almost all parents. Thus, one might consider the negative factors of child rearing as being a relatively universal meaning of children to parents within our culture.

These six areas of meaning were extracted in reviewing the literature on the reaction of parents to their retarded children. Some of these areas were directly stated in the literature and others were felt to be implied. However, if these six areas are relatively universal, and it is hypothesized that they are, then these would have important implications in the evaluation and expectation of the parents of a retarded child.

Effect of the Birth of a Retarded Child

Self-Concept. All of the areas of meaning described above, with the exception of the negative concept of the limitations and demands of child rearing, are very closely connected with the self-concept of the parent. The parent is more or less exposed to himself through the child, especially in the role concept of a parent. It should be noted that the parent also performs in other roles which may not necessarily give the parent the same exposure of himself. However, since there is usually some overlap in an individual's various roles, one might expect some overlap in reactions if one role is severely threatened.

When the parent becomes aware that his child is retarded, a number of rewards which the child may bring to the parent are denied and his self-concept may be severely shaken. The parent can be expected to react to these threats and loss of rewards. Only a very unusual individual would fail to react to this kind of trauma or threat (Cohen, 1962). To continue to react in the usual or culturally expected patterns would be somewhat abnormal for the parents of a retarded children, especially during the initial recognition stages (Olshansky, 1962).

Because of the lack of sound scientific knowledge about some causes of mental retardation, many parents cannot absolve themselves of the possibility that they have contributed to the retardation through hereditary transmission or improper conduct of some sort during pregnancy or infancy.

Since there are no cures available for mental retardation, the problems will of necessity be of a long-term nature. The parent is left with the prospect that the child will never perform to parental hopes and expectations. Thus, he is also denied the prospect of immortality in an adequate form. He is placed in a position of being expected to love a child which is unacceptable to him.

Alternatives. The parent of a retarded child has two general courses of action as alternatives; he must either change his method of viewing the child, and/or develop ego defense mechanisms to insulate himself against the threats of a defective child. Initially one would expect the parent to develop some strong defense mechanisms—such as denial, rationalization, or repression—to the traumatic situation of a diagnosis of mental retardation. At best, one could anticipate the need for considerable time before the parent's view of the child was changed appreciably.

To expect the parent to alter his ideas immediately is unrealistic in view of the meanings which the child has for the parent. It appears that the term "acceptance" is used very loosely in the literature. The professional worker needs to define this concept as he works with parents if realistic goals and expectations are to be developed.

It would be unrealistic to expect that parents should be happy about having a retarded child. The retarded child cannot offer the parents the same rewards and satisfactions that a normal or gifted child can offer. It would appear reasonable to assume that there are limits to the extent to which a parent can emotionally respond to the retarded child in the same manner as he would to a normal offspring.

Factors that Effect the Emotional Involvement of Parents

It is hypothesized that there is a point beyond which the parent cannot healthfully involve himself emotionally with a retarded child. There is a limit to the stress that an individual can handle, and once past that point the individual will develop defense patterns which allow him to cope with the situation. No single factor will determine this point and it will vary from parent to parent. Several factors will combine to determine the amount of stress which a parent can handle before regressive defenses become necessary.

Parental Variables. Kanner's description of parental reactions to a diagnosis of retardation indicates one important variable, the emotional adjustment of the parent. Referring to parents of retarded children, he states, "Their own life experiences, which have helped to shape their personalities, have contributed to the manner in which they adjust to the pleasant and unpleasant realities in general, and to the presence of a handicapped child in particular (Kanner, 1953, p. 382)." Nitzberg (1958) similarly indicated that personal adjustment of the parents would be a factor in determining toleration limits. However, general life experiences of the individual, will also help determine the relative order and intensity of the six areas of meaning of children to parents.

The Retarded Child Variables. Another factor which may affect the involvement or toleration capacity of the parent is the deviation in intelligence of the child from the parent. Michaels and Schueman (1962) report that it is their impression that the lower intelligence groups are apparently better able to accept the fact of retardation than the more intelligent parents. As the deviation in intelligence becomes greater between the parent and child, the probability that the children meet the expectations and standards of the parent becomes less.

The social class of the family may affect the relative importance of intelligence as a criteria of parental expectation. Parents of upper-grade mentally retarded children may display considerable confusion in attitudes because the deviations and differences are not as clear-cut as with the more severely mentally retarded children. The lack of a clear-cut distinction probably emphasizes the parent's ambivalence toward the child and postpones the necessity of adjusting to the retarded child.

The social adjustment of the child may effect the reaction of the parents. If the child's social behavior is such that it calls attention to the deviance of the child, the parent is forced into acknowledgment of the difficulty either through his own perception or the reactions of other people. Consequently, certain of the areas of meaning listed above such as the "extension of self" or the "means of vicarious satisfaction" may be altered for the parent.

The sex of the retarded child would probably be another factor which would influence the amount of stress and tolerance level of the parent. Boys have been found to be a more negative influence on marital integration than girls (Farber, 1959; Farber, 1960). Parents may expect more of the boy in terms of carrying on family tradition and "getting ahead." Consequently, areas of meaning such as the physical and psychological extension of self, means of vicarious satisfaction, and means of transcending death may be more seriously affected when the retarded child is a boy.

Another factor which would probably influence the meaning of the child on the parents is the age of the retarded child. Age of the retarded child has been negatively correlated with marital integration (Farber, 1959; Farber, 1960; Farber et al., 1960). The older severely retarded children increase the child-rearing problems for the parents.

Sibling Variables. The number and order of siblings may be a significant factor in the parental reaction to a retarded child. Research has indicated that there is a linear relationship among higher socio-economic families between the number of siblings and willingness to institutionalize a severely retarded child (Farber et al., 1960). Parents may be able to come to grips with problems if there are normal children who can meet the parents' expectations.

Community Variables. Community pressures can be determinates of the relative importance of any of the areas of meaning of children discussed above. Research has indicated that community pressures can be either supportive or non-supportive (Farber, 1959; Farber, 1960). Various authors have expressed the idea that community pressures can influence the direction and degree of parental reaction to a retarded child (Begab, 1956; Hutt & Gibby, 1958; Kelman, 1953; Sheimo, 1951; Stone, 1948; Waterman, 1948; Weingold & Hormuth, 1953; Zuk, 1959). Professional workers need to be aware of the general community attitudes toward retarded children as well as the pressures of the "specific" community of the parents when evaluating the problems involved in this area.

Summary

The many articles on the problems of parents of retarded children indicate the awakened concern of professional workers in dealing with these problems. This paper has analyzed ideas expressed in the literature concerning the meaning of children to parents.

Six areas of meaning have been described which may help to organize an approach to these problems from an understanding of the effects of the child on the parents. A number of factors have been suggested which may help to estimate the degree of the effect of these six areas on the parents and their capacity to adapt to the existence of a retarded child.

With an appreciation and understanding of the problems of the parents, the professional worker may be able to plan more realistic goals for the parents and thus make more effective use of professional contacts.

References

AUERBACK, A. B. Group Education for Parents of the Handicapped. *Children,* 1961, *8*, 135-140.

BEGAB, M. J. Factors in Counseling Parents of Retarded Children. *American Journal of Mental Deficiency,* 1956, *60*, 515-524.

BLODGETT, H. E., & WARFIELD, G. J. *Understanding Mentally Retarded Children.* New York: Appleton-Century-Corfts, 1959.

COHEN, P. C. The Impact of the Handicapped Child on the Family. *Social Casework,* 1962, *43*, 137-142.

COLEMAN, J. C. Group Therapy with Parents of Mentally Deficient Children. *American Journal of Mental Deficiency,* 1953, *57*, 700-704.

CUMMINGS, S. T. & STOCK, D. Brief Group Therapy of Mothers of Retarded Children Outside of the Specialty Clinic Setting. *American Journal of Mental Deficiency,* 1962, *66*, 739-748.

DALTON, J. & EPSTEIN, H. Counseling Parents of Mildly Retarded Children. *Social Casework,* 1963, *44*, 523-530.

FARBER, B. Effects of a Severely Mentally Retarded Child on Family Integration. *Monographs of the Society for Research in Child Development,* 1959, *24*, No. 2.

FARBER, B. Family Organization and Crisis: Maintenance of Integration in Families with a Severely Mentally Retarded Child. *Monographs of the Society for Research in Child Development,* 1960, *25,* No. 1.

FARBER, B., JENNE, W. C. & TOIGO, R. Family Crisis and the Decision to Institutionalize the Retarded Child. *CEC Research Monograph,* Series A, No. 1. Washington, D.C.: Council for Exceptional Children, 1960.

GOODMAN, L. & ROTHMAN, R. The Development of a Group Counseling Program in a Clinic for Retarded Children. *American Journal of Mental Deficiency,* 1961, *65*, 789-795.

GREBLER, A. M. Parental Attitudes Toward Mentally Retarded Children. *American Journal of Mental Deficiency,* 1952, *56*, 475-483.

HASTINGS, D. Some Psychiatric Problems of Mental Deficiency. *American Journal of Mental Deficiency,* 1948, *52*, 260-262.

HERSH, A. Casework with Parents of Retarded Children. *Social Work,* 1961, *6*, 61-66.

HUTT, M. L. & GIBBY, R. G. *The Mentally Retarded Child: Development, Education, and Guidance,* Boston: Allyn and Bacon, Inc., 1958.

KANNER, L. Parents' Feelings about Retarded Children. *American Journal of Mental Deficiency,* 1953, *57*, 375-383.

KELMAN, H. Parent Guidance in a Clinic for Mentally Retarded Children. *Social Casework,* 1953, *34,* 441-447.

KOZIER, A. Casework with Parents of Children Born with Severe Brain Defects. *Social Casework*, 157, *38*, 183-189.

MAHONEY, S. C. Observations Concerning Counseling with Parents of Mentally Retarded Children. *American Journal of Mental Deficiency*, 1958, *63*, 81-86.

MAYER, E. Some Aspects of Casework Help to Young Retarded Adults and Their Families. *Journal of Social Work Process*, 1956, *7*, 29-49.

MICHAELS, J. & SCHUEMAN, H. Observations on the Psychodynamics of Parents of Retarded Children. *American Journal of Mental Deficiency*, 1962, *66*, 568-573.

MURRAY, MRS. MAX. Needs of Parents of Mentally Retarded Children. *American Journal of Mental Deficiency*, 1959, *63*, 1078-1088.

NITZBERG, J. Some Different Emphases in the Role of the Social Worker in a Workshop for Mentally Retarded Adolescents and Young Adults. *American Journal of Mental Deficiency*, 1958, *63*, 87-95.

OLSHANSKY, S. Chronic Sorrow: A Response to Having a Mentally Defective Child. *Social Casework*, 1962, *43*, 190-193.

RHEINGOLD, H. L. Interpreting Mental Retardation to Parents. *Journal of Consultant Psychology*, 1945, *9*, 142-148.

ROOS, P. Psychological Counseling with Parents of Retarded Children. *Mental Retardation*, 1963, *1*, 345-350.

ROSE, J. A. Factors in the Development of Mentally Handicapped Children, Counseling Parents of Children with Mental Handicaps. Proceedings of the 1958 Woods School Conference, May 2-3, 1958.

SCHIPPER, M. T. The Child with Mongolism in the Home. *Pediatrics*, 1959, *24*, July, 132-144.

SHEIMO, S. L. Problems in Helping Parents of Mentally Deficient and Handicapped Children. *American Journal of Mental Deficiency*, 1951, *56*, 42-47.

SOLNIT, A. J. & STARK, M. H. Meaning and the Birth of a Defective Child. *The Psychoanalytic Study of the Child*, Vol. XVI. New York: International Universities Press, 1961.

STONE, M. M. Parental Attitudes to Retardation. *American Journal of Mental Deficiency*, 1948, *53*, 363-372.

WATERMAN, J. H. Psychogenic Factors in Paternal Acceptance of Feebleminded Children. *Diseases of the Nervous System*, 1948, *9*, 184-187.

WEINGOLD, J. T. & HORMUTH, R. P. Group Guidance of Parents of Mentally Retarded Children. *Journal of Clinical Psychology*, 1953, *9*, 118-124.

WILLIE, B. M. The Role of the Social Worker. *American Journal of Mental Deficiency*, 1961, *66*, 464-471.

ZUK, G. H. Religious Factor and Role of Guilt in Parental Acceptance of the Retarded Child. *American Journal of Mental Deficiency*, 1959, *64*, 139-147.

ZWERLING, I. The Initial Counseling of Parents with Mentally Retarded Children. *The Journal of Pediatrics*, 1954, *44*, April, 469-479.

FIFTEEN

Profile of Failure

MAX DUBROW, JEROME NITZBERG, AND JACK TOBIAS

The central fact of life of the person coming to us is his history of failure. He is likely to have failed his parents by having been a late walker and a late talker, and by having soiled himself much longer than did the neighbor's children. He is likely to suffer from physical handicaps. He fell behind in school. The chances are that he began in regular classes but was transferred to special classes, which, while they protected him from hopeless academic competition, probably accentuated for him and his family his difference from other children, and his membership in a blemished part of the population.

As he grew older, he lost the few friends he may have had, for his friends absorbed and acted out the cultural values emphasizing the differences between them. As his normal playmates ventured away from the home block, he probably remained behind, restrained by his parents, and by his own fears and deficiencies. School chums went on to higher grades while he stayed still and at 17 or before, he left school altogether. As others paired off into heterosexual couples and groups, he was likely to stand out in his loneliness even more obviously. And when others went off to work, he stayed at home. He made few if any efforts to find work, and if he did get a job, he did not hold it for long. He quit or was fired, probably the latter, and felt it was hopeless to try. In all likelihood, his parents felt the same way.

Thus, when he comes to us, our client is apt to be friendless and jobless, suffering from various physical handicaps, bored with life at home, unhappy with his parents and they with him, and unhappy with himself. He is "slow" and often looks it. However, he is likely to know that he is a failure and wherein lies his failure, and in this knowledge lie both his pain and his hope.

Fifty-seven percent of the clients in this group reported in intake that they had no friends at all (38 of the 67 for whom we had such information). Thirty-one percent claimed several friends and the remaining 12 percent claimed one friend. A closer look at the friends revealed that many of them were much younger, a few much old-

From Max Dubrow, Jerome Nitzberg, and Jack Tobias, "Working for Maturity" (New York, New York City Association for the Help of Retarded Children, 1962) pp. 25-31. By permission of the authors and the Association.

er, many only casual acquaintances, and some merely tolerated the retardate as a lovable, pitiful mascot.

Sixty-seven percent of the group, or 57, shared among them 81 physical problems, of which 17 were speech problems, 11 visual deficiencies, 11 epilepsy, nine thyroid deficiencies, seven motor coordination difficulties, five noticeable physical deformities and five obesity. Less frequent were asthma, hearing deficiencies, cardiac ailments. The physical handicaps do double damage: they interfere with physical functioning and they contribute to emotional problem. Those with speech and hearing deficiencies suffer still another kind of damage for they are deprived of the optimal use of a principal habilitation tool—client-worker communication. Of 66 trainees who started with us, seven suffered from speech problems of sufficient severity to obstruct communication seriously.

In a city like ours, the ability to travel alone by bus and subway is important. It is vital for working, for acquiring goods and services, for utilizing opportunities for recreation and socialization. It is one of the criteria of adult functioning and its absence is not only a deprivation but a blow to one's self-esteem. Forty percent of this group (30 of 76 for whom we have such data) did not travel anywhere alone by bus or subway. It was apparent that at least 21 of these persons were very anxious about traveling alone.

One aspect of this anxiety stems from the fear of exposing one's ignorance and inviting humiliation. One trainee explained what he expected from a stranger to whom he might appeal for directions:

> "What's the matter, boy? Can't you read the signs? So I blush and feel bad. Getting lost is wanting to cry like a kid." (Age 28 IQ 50)

It is sometimes said that retardates do not know that they are different and intellectually handicapped. This is not true of our population. Of 74 persons whose intake responses are recorded, 46 or 62 percent acknowledged their awareness that they were different in an undesirable way, and that this difference lay in their slowness to learn. Nine others denied their handicap but so equivocally or inconsistently as to suggest at least a sporadic awareness too painful to verbalize. Only 19 or 26 percent denied their handicap unequivocally and consistently. Of these 19, 12 were considered psychotic and employed denial extensively as a defense mechanism.

Those who admitted the handicap did so with distress. The following are typical definitions of mental retardation offered in intake interviews:

> "They can't help each other. They can't do things in school. They need help like they can't write and do things." (Age 19 IQ 64)

> "Needs help with everything." (Age 18 IQ 64)

> "It means difficulty in walking, in working with the hands. It means some can't think so good. You're slow in getting things out and thinking." (Age 21 IQ 68)

> "That's me! Something in my head makes it hard for me to learn, like a 12-year old kid." (Age 18 IQ 48)

"You're back in everything, in work. Sometimes I feel, sometimes I feel I'm not." (Age 19 IQ 48)

"Yeah, it means a little slow in thinking, reading, a little slow. The mind don't function so good. You can't have friends like everybody else." (Age 19 IQ 48)

Often trainees prefer to consider themselves "slow" rather than "retarded," reserving the latter term for the more severely retarded or for the severely disturbed. From time to time, trainees propose at shop meetings that the name of the Project be altered to omit the word "retarded." Many invent places of work and schooling in order to conceal from friends and neighbors their attendance at the Shop. A trainee explained that he had knocked down a sign bearing the name of the Project because it revealed to visitors that this was a place for retarded persons. When certificates of achievement were introduced—which some of the clients at once dubbed "diplomas"—several were happy that no reference to retardation had been made. They could hang it on their wall or show it to their friends without embarrassment.

Occasionally "retarded" is used to describe the physically handicapped. Said one person, "A retarded is like you don't know how to use your hand or have difficulty with your legs or need help. I'm not retarded. I'm a slow learner." (Age 20 IQ 61)

Often the trainee admitting retardation takes some comfort in partializing the handicap, in seeing others as worse off than he, and in claiming some superior abilities.

"Like my mother says, we should thank God we are not the worst. I feel sorry for them." (Age 18 IQ 64)

". . . but I can read real good." (Age 18 IQ 70 Reading Grade 4.2)

Some admit only to a temporary deficiency caused by poor habits or bad luck.

"I could be smart. Maybe go to college. I didn't study or do homework like other kids. I don't pick up so good but I shoulda studied. If I studied, I coulda been a cop or a detective or an engineer or a drummer." (Age 18 IQ 68)

"Boy! You have to have luck in this world. They didn't work and got through (school) and I worked and didn't. (Age 20 IQ 61)

Many trainees are aware that more social stigma is attached to mental retardation than to physical handicaps or even serious emotional disturbance. In one instance, epilepsy is the preferred problem. In another it is "clumsy hands." One mentally ill retardate whose stay with us was an interlude between mental hospitals, held forth lucidly in group meetings that he was not mentally retarded but mentally ill. Sometimes the parents of severely disturbed retardates prefer to see their children as ill rather than retarded.

Our trainees come to us with the knowledge that society expects them to have a job although they themselves are not likely to have accepted this proposition with as much conviction as their intellectually normal peers. They usually have a fairly accurate idea of how many days they may expect to work, how many hours and what their beginning pay is likely to be. In the main they express an interest in jobs which are realistic for retarded persons although a large minority is somewhat unrealistic and a small number, grandiose.

Eighty-one percent (50 of 62) expected to work five days a week, eight hours a day. Fifty-two percent (32 of 61) entertained realistic vocational objectives such as packer, stock clerk, messenger, simple factory work, porter, domestic, unskilled hospital helper, laborer, car washer, general helper in a factory. Thirty-nine percent entertained somewhat unrealistic job objectives such as nurse's aide, office clerk, auto-mechanic, counterman, store clerk. The grandiose choices included secretary, veterinarian, chemist, actor, candy store proprietor. A few talked vaguely about wanting to work with their hands, using tools, working with copper and wood, caring for children. One young man would settle for nothing except a job at an airport but ultimately accepted something less romantic—delivering stationery supplies in midtown Manhattan.

While most persons asserted an interest in regular employment, the intake worker judged that just under half asserted such an interest with language and affect suggesting conviction. Forty-nine percent of the persons interviewed for whom such data was recorded (36 of 73) seemed strongly desirous of regular employment. Twenty-six percent seemed equivocal and twenty-five percent admitted their disinterest or were obviously disinterested despite some token claim to the contrary.

It is significant that virtually no one in this group expressed surprise that he should be asked why he wanted a job. The principal reasons given for wanting work were: occupying one's time, making money and preparing to support oneself in the future. The trainees had difficulty in explaining how they would spend their money. Most mentioned buying clothing. Few mentioned contributing money to the home. Rarely was a hobby mentioned or spending money on a date. A few envisaged trips to distant places, buying cars, houses and businesses. Some might buy more ice cream sodas or comic books or go to the movies more often.

One trainee said:

"What do I need money for? I got nothing to spend it on. No girl, no car, no place to go. Nothing." (Age 20 IQ 80)

The quest for social experience in employment was expressed by one young woman as follows when she explained why she wanted factory work:

"Because that's where boys and girls are and it's fun and you work with your hands." (Age 19 IQ 59)

A specific material objective with psychological meaning to the trainee:

"I want to buy cuff links so I can look like a salesman. You know—well groomed." (Age 19 IQ 58)

Themes of seeking work to keep busy, to feel self-esteem and to achieve normalcy occur in the following responses:

"I tried sitting at home and don't like it. I want to earn for myself and not have to ask my mother for everything." (Age 18 IQ 65)

"I want to show I can do something." (Age 28 IQ 64)

"I want to be like other people. I want to marry, have kids, have money. . . . I don't want to sit home and just sleep and eat and walk. . . . If you don't get money, you're a nobody. I can't go out with friends without money. I like nice clothes. I want to be like other people." (Age 18 IQ 48)

There is a striking difference between stated interest in employment and actual experience in having sought and sustained it.

Thirty-eight percent of this group (23 out of 60) had never sought work before coming to us. Thirteen of these people had been out of school for less than one year before coming to us and one could assume that they had been awaiting the outcome of their application to DVR. Ten others, however, had been out of school for periods ranging from one to 11 years before coming to us in intake. Even allowing a year for the application process and for normal post-school idleness, their average period of "staying at home with nothing to do"—without employment—was 4 ½ years.

We have no reliable information about the number of times the 37 others, who had looked for work, had actually applied for jobs. Our impression is that most of them attempted one or two interviews, had been easily discouraged and in any case had acted upon the parents' initiative.

Of the 37 who had sought work, 31 had found it. They represent half of the persons for whom we have reliable information concerning work history. These 31 persons had done some kind of paid work: full time, part time, sporadic neighborhood chores, jobs with relatives, regular jobs.

The most meaningful job would be the regular full time job with an employer who is not a relative or particular friend. Only 19 persons held such jobs. In the main they had been messengers and unskilled general helpers in a variety of settings. One had been a chicken killer and another a store guard.

What had been the experience of these 19 full timers? A dismal one marked by failure. They had held 36 jobs among them. Eliminating two atypical persons who had held jobs for six months and two atypical persons who had held jobs for just one day, the remaining 15 had held jobs for an average of just over four weeks per job per person.

Fifteen of the 19 full timers had experienced 20 dismissals among them for unsatisfactory work and 11 of them had experienced quitting 16 jobs among them. Generally, their quitting was a symptom of low tolerance for psychological or physical distress. They would not remain long enough to determine whether the distress could be reduced, tolerated or outweighed by compensations. In popular shop parlance, they had failed to "stick it out."

How slight the experience of even the full timers is becomes apparent when one compares how much time they had spent in working with how much time they had spent in idleness before coming to us. Six persons may be excluded on the ground that the time elapsed between school and Shop, after deducting working time, was less than a year—again allowing for post-school idleness and the application process.

For the 13 others, after allowing the year of grace, the problem is apparent. They averaged three years of idleness for ten months of employment.

Thus, half of our trainees came to us with no regular, competitive employment which was full time. The half who had such work experience, had precious little. A large minority had never sought work and the majority who had, had done so sporadically and half-heartedly.

PART THREE

Perspectives on Our Current State of Knowledge About Mental Retardation

SIXTEEN

Twofold Nature of the Problem of the Handicapped

JESSIE BERNARD

Income Maintenance

The problem which arises in connection with the handicapped is twofold in nature. One aspect has to do with providing income for those who cannot work; the other has to do with re-establishing role relationships, or rehabilitation. Of these, the first is by far the simpler to deal with. Indeed, as the following summary indicates, the problem of providing income may be on the way to solution.

Public provisions to offset the actual or potential wage loss among these millions of persons and their dependents have been extended somewhat in the past two decades. In 1935, protection through public programs was confined to work-connected disabilities under State and Federal workmen's compensation laws, to service-connected and non-service-connected disabilities under the veterans' and Armed Forces programs, to sickness and disability under programs for employees of Federal, State, and local governments, and to special programs for the blind in about half the States.

Since that time, both permanent and temporary disability benefits have been provided under the railroad retirement system, and temporary disability insurance programs for industrial and commercial workers have been adopted in four States. Federal grants for aid to the blind were provided under the original Social Security Act and in 1950 for a new assistance program of aid to the permanently and totally disabled. . . .

The number of persons in the age group 14-64 with long-term total disabilities who are receiving some support from public programs designed to maintain income in case of disability has increased, it is estimated, from something less than 200,000 in 1934 to about a million in 1954, or from about 1 in 10 in 1934 to about 1 in 3 such persons in 1954.

Insurance benefits for extended disability were paid in December 1954 to about 266,000 persons (some of whom were aged 65 or over) under the railroad retirement and public employee retirement systems. There were 224,000 persons receiving assistance under the program of aid to the permanently and totally disabled and 102,000 receiving aid to the blind. These figures contrast with the 33,000 receiving aid to the blind in December

From *Social Problems at Midcentury* by Jessie Bernard. Copyright 1957 by Holt, Rinehart & Winston. Reprinted by permission of Holt, Rinehart & Winston, Inc. I p. 203-205, 230-233.

1934. Additional disabled persons and their dependents receive payments under the aid to dependent children and general assistance programs. There has also been a large increase in the number of persons receiving veterans' compensation. About 470,000 totally disabled veterans under age 65 are now receiving veterans' benefits, compared with 100,000 in 1934. (The large number of veterans receiving benefits for partial disabilities is not included in these figures.) With the aging of the veteran population of World War I, the growth in the number of recipients of non-service-connected disability pensions has been particularly striking. The veterans' and public assistance programs are bearing the brunt of the public burden of income maintenance for the long-term totally disabled.[1]

In 1956 the Social Security Act was amended so that a person who becomes disabled at, let us say, age fifty, no longer has to wait until he is sixty-five before he is eligible to draw retirement benefits.

In evaluating income maintenance we must not forget the effect of rising standards. We once thought it satisfactory for handicapped persons to make their way by begging or by selling pencils or by other means we now consider degrading. No matter how many benefits the physically handicapped receive, so long as these benefits are less than the amount of income the unhandicapped receive, we shall probably consider the disabled a problem.

Re-establishing Role Relationships

But to maintain income is easier than to create or re-establish satisfying role relationships. For most handicapped persons it is not enough simply to be kept alive, even on a generous level. They want to perform dignified roles; they want to maintain as nearly normal relationships as possible. And those who have worked with handicapped persons have noted that morale—to be referred to below—is by far the most important factor in rehabilitation. The government can, and does, offer rehabilitation opportunities;[2] but it cannot force people to take advantage of them nor can it restore role relationships.

Two kinds of role trauma are especially serious in the case of handicapped or disabled persons, namely those associated with the role of the worker and those associated with family roles. . .

Reasons for the Difference in Role Performance

How can we explain the differences in the two sets of data? Why was the role performance so poor in one set and relatively good in the other? The conclusion seems to be warranted that the differences shown between the mentally deficient who succeed in life and those who do not cannot be explained in terms of their mental handicap alone. It is suggested here that two explanations must be used, one referring to other than mental pathologies in those who perform their roles poorly and one referring to the supporting role network of those who perform their roles well.

The Personality of the Mentally Deficient

We are likely to be so impressed by mental deficiency that we tend to forget that these human beings have personalities also, that they have hopes and fears, frustrations and anxieties. Indeed, it is likely that because their frustrations are more frequent than are those of people with more ability to cope with problems, much of their handicap is emotional rather than intellectual. Anyone who has ever visited an institution for the feebleminded must have been impressed by the tremendous affection the inmates show. They cling to a visitor who shows a sympathetic manner. Their capacity for affection, at least on this surface level, seems inordinate. With such need for affection we can well imagine how devastating their experiences must be to them, rejected as they are likely to be.

Even a cursory reading of the first set of cases presented above suggests that these people were suffering from far more than mental deficiency alone. Symptoms of psychopathic personality, that is, inability to feel anxiety, seem prevalent also, as well as other disorders. In brief, the poor role performance of these cases seems to be associated far more with other pathologies than with mental deficiency alone.

It has been usual among clinicians to consign mentally deficient cases to institutions, on the theory that they were not good prospects for therapy. But one of the interesting results of recent research is that many of these patients are amenable to therapy. It has been found to be remarkably effective in some cases, even in those that were institutionalized. Some cases originally diagnosed as mentally deficient, in fact, prove themselves to be normal; and some which exhibited seriously delinquent, or at least antisocial, symptoms became more nearly normal in their behavior or role performance, even if they are not normal in intelligence as measured on tests.

How many and what etiological types of an institutional population are amenable to and can benefit from psychotherapy cannot be answered at this time because of the absence of the necessary research. What evidence is available suggests that a fair number of cases diagnosed as mentally defective are in need of and respond favorably to psychotherapeutic procedures.[3]

Not mental deficiency in and of itself, then, but mental deficiency associated with pathologies may explain the poor role performance of many individuals.

Supporting Role Network

Because of their handicap, many mentally deficient persons never get experience in proper role performance. But when sympathetic and supporting roles are supplied to them, they can and do learn complementary role behavior. In the training of the men in the Army's Special Service Units, to be discussed below, advantage was taken of group roles and group support. At first the men with low IQ were very shy, since they had never associated closely with other men. But "gradually the spirit of teamwork and cooperation . . . developed and within a few days the men . . . made an adjustment sufficient to enhance learning."[4] Their instructor remained with them twenty-four hours a day; he wrote letters for them; he gave them advice on their personal problems. He had a special role: he was their kind father. It paid off in their improvement.

Of two people with equal handicap, one succeeds, the other does not. We suggest that something in the role network in which they find themselves must explain the difference. Some light on this problem is cast by a study of young parolees from an institution for feebleminded women in Pennsylvania, which found that success or failure on first parole seemed to be determined on a chance basis. That is, with respect to all the variables studied—IQ, family background, medical record—there was no difference between those who succeeded and those who failed. The conclusion was drawn that these young women were at the mercy of their environments; they themselves contributed little to the success or failure of their lives. They responded to the stimuli that presented themselves almost indiscriminately.[5] With respect to a policy for dealing with the mentally deficient child, the implication is that the very things which make it difficult for him to learn in the first place also make it difficult for him to change. Thus, if he is not properly role-trained in early life it will be hard to effect a change in him in later life.[6]

Because of the differences in family background reported in the experimental and control groups in the Connecticut study referred to above, one critic of the study feels that the project is really a study of differences between morons coming from unfavorable backgrounds and non-morons coming from less unfavorable ones. Moreover, he considers that since unfavorable background influences intellectual efficiency and social adjustment, the differences reported cannot be considered the result of differences in intelligence alone.[7]

In any event, the contrast in life patterns shown by the two sets of data reported above demonstrate that mental deficiency in and of itself cannot be taken as proof of social or role inadequacy. The crucial problem appears to be one of finding roles in which those who are mentally deficient can perform satisfactorily. . . .

References

[1]Lenore Epstein, Dorothy McCamman, and Alfred M. Skolnik, "Social Security Protection, 1935-1955," *Social Security Bulletin*, 18 (Aug. 1955), p. 11.

[2]Workmen's compensation laws gave some relief to disabled workers, but did not provide for rehabilitation. In 1918 the federal government passed a law which provided for vocational rehabilitation of wounded servicemen under the direction of the Veteran's Bureau; it aimed to see that men were trained for productive work. Between 1918 and 1920, twelve states also passed rehabilitation laws; in 1920 a federal law was passed establishing an agency under the Federal Board for Vocational Education to promote rehabilitation of civilians also. Federal funds were made available to states that had rehabilitation programs which met certain standards. In 1943 this law was amended to provide more generously for civilian programs. All veterans come under the jurisdiction of the Veterans' Administration program; but civilians come under the jurisdiction of the several states. "The central idea of the laws for both veterans and civilians is: A vocationally handicapped person should be made able to go into productive work unhandicapped by his present injury or illness as far as his economic future is concerned—if that is possible. All necessary steps toward (1) vocational counsel in the choice of work at which a man may be under no economic handicap, or under the least possible handicap (2) education, training, or retraining, as the case may be, for the work he is to perform, and (3) help in finding and getting himself

placed in a suitable job when he is ready for it." (Edna Yost and Lillian M. Gilbreth, *Normal Lives for the Disabled* [Macmillan, 1944], pp. 79-80.) In addition to these federal and state laws, three laws were enacted by the 83rd Congress to assist those with long-time disabling injuries. One expanded the federal-state program; one provided for more hospitals and facilities for rehabilitation; and the third, one of income security rather than rehabilitation primarily, safe-guarded old-age survivors insurance status of individuals with long-time disabilities. The American Medical Association opposes federal programs of this type. A bill which was passed by the House in the summer of 1955, for example, was branded as part of "piecemeal approach to socialization of medicine" by the *Journal of the American Medical Association,* July 1955.

[3] Seymour B. Sarason, *Psychological Problems in Mental Deficiency* (New York, Harper, 1949), p. 310.

[4] Eli Ginzberg and Douglas W. Bray, *The Uneducated* (New York, Columbia University Press, 1953), p. 72.

[5] Unpublished study by Robert Clark and Jessie Bernard.

[6] Sarason, *op. cit.*, pp. 310-311.

[7] *Ibid.*, p. 112.

SEVENTEEN

Notes on Sociological Knowledge About Families with Mentally Retarded Children

BERNARD FARBER

Few sociologists have shown an interest in mental retardation. Yet, many phenomena connected with retardation can be of legitimate concern to them. This paper will discuss two potential sociological concerns. These are (a) the effect of the presence of a retarded child on patterns of social mobility of other family members and (b) consequences of labeling a child as severely mentally retarded.

Social Mobility of Parents and Siblings

Most studies on the effects of a severely mentally retarded child on family relationships have focused upon the emotional problems and personal difficulties generated by the child. Another perspective that can be applied pertains to the place of the retarded child's family in the social structure. From this viewpoint, research is framed in terms of the question: How does the presence of a severely mentally retarded child in the family affect the social destinies of the other family members? An effort can then be made to determine the conditions under which various consequences occur.

Social destinies have been described in sociological literature in terms of the concept of life chances.[1] Ordinarily, life chances means the probability of an individual to attain a successful social and economic position in the society. The meaning of "a successful position" is vague and varies with the particular social structure. In a society which honors its wealthy individuals, life chances would refer to the likelihood of attaining much wealth; in a society which glorifies political power, success is measured in terms of a position held determining the major decisions of the society. Additionally, the concept of life chances implies the probability of reaching a particular position in society through achievement rather than through ascription. By definition, an individual cannot change a status which has been ascribed to him through birth or marriage. In a society based on caste or closed social classes the life chances of an individual are not problematic—everyone knows what his life

Presented at the Annual Meeting of the American Association on Mental Deficiency, 1967. Reprinted by permission of the author.

chances are. However, in a society which is organized to facilitate upward social mobility, life chances are no longer fixed. Yet, since an individual's life chances are determined in large measure by the socioeconomic position of his parents and the place of his family in society, there is much variation in life chances for the different segments of society.

A student—Max Culver—is completing a Ph.D. dissertation on social mobility patterns of parents with severely mentally retarded children.[2] He has compared the occupations of fathers of retarded children with those of the grandparents. This study utilized the data collected on approximately 400 families with severely mentally retarded children living either at home or in an institution. The data were gathered in the Chicago metropolitan area in 1957-1958. This investigation showed that the timing of the birth of the mentally retarded child was related to the upward or downward social mobility of the parents. The earlier in the marriage that the child was born the greater were the chances of him having a depressing effect on social mobility. Thus when a couple had a retarded child early in their marriage the husband's chances of getting ahead occupationally were impeded. If his father was in a blue-collar occupation, his chances of remaining in a blue-collar job were greater than those of a father whose retarded child was born later in the marriage.

This study on social mobility utilized very gross categories and presented little analysis of the occupational history of the retarded child's parents. Insight into the impact of the retarded child on the destinies of his parents and siblings would be enhanced by a study of the occupational and educational histories and aspirations of fathers and mothers, brothers and sisters, and grandparents.

The concept of life chances is also relevant for the study of institutionalization. The findings indicated that among families in which the grandfathers of the retarded child have had a white-collar occupation, those parents who keep their severely retarded child at home are more often downwardly socially mobile (as indicated by the husband's occupation) than are those parents who institutionalize their retarded child. Moreover, the investigation by Culver found a greater tendency for parents who have attended college to place their retarded child in an institution than for parents with a high school education or less. These findings suggest that when the probability of upward social mobility is high, families tend to rid themselves of impediments to occupational and social success and, accordingly, institutionalize their severely mentally retarded children. Lower class parents of retardates are less motivated toward effective outward social mobility and therefore do not regard their retarded child as an impediment to their socioeconomic aspirations.

Accordingly, consistent with this speculation, in his study of reactions to institutionalization, Downey found that when middle class parents institutionalize their severely retarded children, they tend to ignore them and in many cases regard them as "deceased."[3] On the other hand, lower class parents of retardates tend to maintain contact with their children and, as Mercer reported, they try to reintegrate the retardate into family life after release.[4]

The concept of life chances can also be applied to the effect of the retarded child on his siblings' lives. Downey reported that many parents institutionalize their retarded child because of its possible harmful effect on the siblings.[5] The parents may believe that they cannot devote sufficient attention and care to the retarded child's siblings. Hence, there is a convergence of findings to the effect that families with retarded children tend to restrict the number of additional births,[6] and siblings about the same age as the retarded child appear to be more profoundly affected than are older brothers and sisters.[7] The implications of this set of findings have not been specifically investigated. Presumably, the older siblings would have higher rates of upward social mobility than would the younger siblings.

The concept of life chances can be applied in still another way in regard to siblings of the retarded child. Children who interact constantly with their retarded siblings seem to have a more serious outlook on life than do other children. A study by Farber and Jenne showed that both boys and girls who interact daily with their retarded siblings emphasized as life goals "devotion to a worthwhile cause" or "making a contribution to mankind," while those who do not interact so frequently with their retarded siblings are more oriented to success in personal relations.[8] In the performance of their duties as parent-surrogates, the normal siblings apparently internalize welfare norms and turn their life careers toward the improvement of mankind or at least toward the achievement toward goals which will enhance social welfare. It might be valuable to determine the extent to which siblings of retarded siblings differ in their occupational and leisure time patterns from others. Such a study might reveal how such factors as relative age, frequency of interaction and sex of the child affect the life changes of the retarded child's siblings. In some social circumstances, parents may be more tolerant of deviance of normal children and their lack of achievement and in other instances the parents may apply great pressure toward achievement.

The effect of the retarded child on the life chances of his siblings extends not only to occupation but also to marriage. Especially where the siblings of a retarded child have a close relationship with him, the presence of the retarded member may influence the choice of marriage partner. Presumably, the sibling would not marry an individual who could not tolerate their retarded sibling. Yet, the extent to which the presence of a mentally retarded child influences mate selection has not been investigated. If the presence of a retarded child is more disturbing to an upwardly mobile individual than to someone whose ultimate socioeconomic status has generally been attained, the retarded child's sisters may pass up marriages which would enhance their life chances.

Knowledge about life chances of families in which a retarded child is present is necessary in order to assess the long run effect of a retarded child on his parents and siblings. An earlier study described three types of family organization developed by parents to cope with the presence of a retarded child. These types were parent-oriented, child-oriented, and home-oriented.[9] The parent-oriented families focused upon the father's and mother's occupational and social careers and gave to the retarded child a secondary position in determining life chances of family members. In the parent-oriented family, the husband and wife acted as colleagues in the family enterprise. A second group of families was classified as child-oriented. These families subordinated the activities of the parents to the maximization of the life chances of children. This subordination often meant a complete devotion by the husband to his job. The division of labor in these families was most often that the husband would specialize in work activities while the wife cared for the home and family. Here again, great expenditure of time and effort compensated for the depressing effect of the retarded child on upward social mobility. The third kind of family organization, the home-oriented family, sacrificed the parental life chances for those of the children. In home-oriented families the husband sacrificed his own personal career in order to maintain family unity. In these families, the life chances of all the members might be markedly affected. However, there was a larger proportion of families in the investigation which did not present a clear-cut type of orientation. The families in the fourth or residual category were not consistently parent-oriented, child-oriented, or home-oriented. There was considerable disagreement between the parents with regard to orientation, and in many instances the orientation itself was not crystallized. The families in the residual category were probably the most affected in their life chances. Perhaps, the numerous problems which beset these families interfered with any concerted effort to promote upward social mobility. The long-run consequences of the type of family organization on the life chances of family members should provide important knowledge about families with retarded children.

In summary, the concept of life chances would facilitate the study of the long-run effects of a retarded child on his family. Research on health problems suggest a relationship between poor health and downward social mobility. However, little is known about the circumstances under which chronic illness or severe disability of a child interferes with social mobility of the family. Institutionalization, birth order, family organization, and parents' position in the social structure represent only a few of the factors that could be studied. Investigation of families with severely retarded children would produce the knowledge necessary for an adequate understanding of the relationship between a child's disability and his family's life chances.

Effects of Labeling a Child as Mentally Retarded

Another topic about which there is a dearth of knowledge is the effect of labeling a child as mentally retarded. Some sociologists, such as Lewis Dexter, consider labeling a self-fulfilling prophecy.[10] By labeling an individual, the authorities define for that individual a particular life career and they thereby determine his life chances. If they had not labeled him, possibly his life would not have been perceptably affected by his deviant behavior. Accordingly to Dexter, just as people discriminate against dope addicts, alcoholics, the mentally ill, or ex-convicts as outsiders so do they discriminate against the mentally retarded because of their label. He suggests that "there is also the experience which may be observed over and over again of the denial of employment, of legal rights, of a fair hearing, of an opportunity, to the stupid because they are stupid (e.g., have a low IQ or show poor academic performance), *and not because the stupidity is relevant to the task, or claim, or situation.*"[11]

The topic of labeling raises several questions about the relative importance of the label as compared with incompetence in affecting the life chances of a mentally retarded person and his family. Deviant individuals can be regarded as motivated to act contrary to the cultural norms. On the other hand, incompetent individuals are seen as trying to conform to the accepted standards of conduct, but because of some impediment, they cannot do so.

The act of labeling implies a value judgment about the persons whose behavior is regarded as deviant.[12] This label imposes a stigma upon the individual which marks him for special kinds of interaction and tends to segregate him from individuals without this stigma.[13] There is little question that the active labeling an individual as severely mentally retarded by a physician or psychologist generally produces much emotional turmoil in the parents. The area about which there is little knowledge, however, concerns the long-term effects of labeling.

In modern society the life chances of individuals depend on many labels such as race, religion, occupation, age and sex attributes, as well as personal attributes. Different groups within the society differ with respect to the importance attached to these labels. Among some groups the label of mental retardation may assume a greater importance in determining participation than in other groups. Probably, in modern society the combinations and permutations of socioeconomic and other social class labels are probably more significant in determining life chances for the mentally retarded than the label of mental retardation itself. Viewing the label of mental retardation as one in a series suggests that this label will have different consequences for family relationships to the extent that it represents a contrast to other labels. These remarks suggest the following hypotheses:

The first hypothesis is: The higher the socioeconomic status of the family the greater will be the impact on family relationships of labeling the child as mentally retarded. This effect emerges through the discrepancy between the mental retardation label and the other labels ascribed to family members. In low socioeconomic status families, the label of mental retardation is not greatly divergent from the other labels associated with low status. Therefore, the label of mental retardation will have less impact on family relationships in low socioeconomic status families. This hypothesis is consistent with an earlier finding that there tended to be a greater initial emotional reaction of the parents of high socioeconomic levels to the diagnosis of retardation, whereas low socioeconomic level mothers were often not as severely shaken by the diagnosis.[14]

The second hypothesis is: The potency of child care problems associated with mental retardation in affecting family relationships is associated with socioeconomic status. For high socioeconomic status families, as long as parents are uncertain about the potential intellectual development of the retarded child, they will not be profoundly affected in their family relationships. However, as soon as the child is diagnosed as severely retarded, the discrepancy between his other familial, social, and economic labels as contrasted with his intellectual label is so great as to produce great emotional impact. On the other hand, if the child is considered as an educable retarded individual, the discrepancy is not so severe and family relationships may be not as profoundly affected. For low socioeconomic level families, however, since the label itself is presumably not the primary crisis-evoking factor, care problems themselves would provide the basis for family tension. Regardless of the degree of retardation, if the physical disabilities of the child do not require a great deal of effort and attention, the consequences for family relationships would not be severe.

This hypothesis is consistent with an interpretation of data in an earlier study that the kinds of crisis which mothers face varies with socioeconomic level.[15] For middle class mothers, the major problems concerned the frustration of aims and aspirations for themselves and their families. They see the retarded child as interfering with the accomplishment of the ends in family life. They regard the situation as tragic. In contrast to the tragic crisis faced by many middle class mothers, low socioeconomic status mothers are confronted with a different kind of problem. They are concerned with their inability to organize their domestic roles in ways which would permit them to have an acceptable family life. As the mother is drawn into caring for the retarded child, she becomes more alienated from other family members. The lower class mother is often faced with a role organization crisis. The differentiation between the tragic crisis and role organization crisis thus seems to hinge upon the part played by the label of mental retardation in influencing family relationships.

To summarize, the relative impact of the child's intellectual incompetence versus the label of mental retardation on family relationships has received comparatively little attention in research. The hypotheses suggested in this paper refer to differential impact of incompetence and labeling by socioeconomic class. Other factors which might influence the consequences of labeling include religion, ethnic background, number of children in the family, sex of the child, urban or rural residence, family organization, and relationship to kith and kin.

Conclusion

Research on the relative effects of severe incompetence and labeling on family relationships and on life chances of parents and siblings of retarded children may be helpful to professionals dealing with the mentally retarded. Physicians and psychologists who must communicate diagnoses should have insight into consequences of their labeling the child. School administrators and teachers should also be aware of the effects of their decisions on the families of the severely retarded. Social workers and rehabilitation workers must also be sensitive to the implications of their work for the retardate's family.

References

[1] H. H. Gerth and C. Wright Mills, *From Max Weber: Essays in Sociology,* New York: Oxford University Press, 1946, pp. 181-183.

[2]Max Culver, "Integenerational Social Mobility among Families with a Severely Mentally Retarded Child," Unpublished Ph.D. dissertation, University of Illinois, 1967.

[3]Kenneth J. Downey, "Parental Interest in the Institutionalized Severely Mentally Retarded Child," *Social Problems*, 11 (1963), pp. 186-193.

[4]Jane R. Mercer, "Social System Perspective and Clinical Perspective: Frames of Reference for Understanding Career Patterns of Persons Labelled as Mentally Retarded," *Social Problems*, 13 (1965), pp. 18-34.

[5]Kenneth J. Downey, "Parents' Reasons for Institutionalizing Severely Mentally Retarded Children," *Journal of Health and Human Behavior*, 6 (Fall, 1965).

[6]K. S. Holt, "The Influence of a Retarded Child on Family Limitation," *Journal of Mental Deficiency*, 2 (1958), pp. 28-36; J. Tizard and Jacqueline Grad, *The Mentally Handicapped and their Families*, New York: Oxford University Press, 1961.

[7]Bernard Farber, "Family Organization and Crisis: Maintenance of Integration in Families with a Severely Mentally Retarded Child," *Monographs of the Society for Research in Child Development*, 1960, 75.

[8]Bernard Farber and William C. Jenne, "Interaction with Retarded Siblings and Life Goals of Children," *Marriage and Family Living*, 25 (1963), pp. 96-98.

[9]Farber, "Family Organization and Crisis," *op. cit.*

[10]Lewis A. Dexter, "The Sociology of the Exceptional Person," *Indian Journal of Social Research*, 4 (January, 1963), pp. 31-36.

[11]Lewis A. Dexter, "On the Politics and Sociology of Stupidity in our Society," *Social Research*, 9 (Winter, 1962), p. 224.

[12]Howard S. Becker, ed., *Outsiders*, New York: Free Press, 1963.

[13]Erving Goffman, *Stigma: Notes on the Management of Spoiled Identity*, Englewood Cliffs, N.J. Prentice-Hall, 1963.

[14]Bernard Farber, "Perceptions of Crisis and Related Variables in the Impact of a Retarded Child on the Mother." Journal of Health and Human Behavior, 1 (1960), pp. 108-118. Reprinted in Marvin Sussman, ed., *Sourcebook in Marriage and the Family*, Boston: Houghton Mifflin, 1963.

[15]*Ibid.*

The Attitude of the Retarded Person Towards Himself

HENRY V. COBB

When we consider the stresses on family life caused by retardation in one of its members, we are likely to think only of the feelings and attitudes of the parents and siblings and the effects on family structure as a whole. We may overlook the stress experienced by the retarded member himself. To *be* a mentally retarded person in a family of normals obviously has its difficulties, not least of which is the limited ability of the retarded to understand precisely how and why he is different.

There has been very little research on the attitudes of the retarded toward himself, although the "self-concept" has been a popular subject in the psychiatric literature. Perhaps this neglect stems from the assumption that the retarded are incapable of any significant awareness of themselves. Consider, however, such incidents as these, which are commonplace in their behavior.

A group of retarded children excitedly look at photographs of themselves, pointing out and identifying their own faces and those of their friends to one another.

Mary asks plaintively, on her way to the special school, "when will I not be retarded any more so I can go to school with the other children?"

John, a twenty-year-old employee in a sheltered workshop, says with pride, "I know I'm not very good at some things, but I can sure do *this* job all right!"

Five-year-old David, leaving his own home for a residential school, commented sadly, "Throw away old broken David; get a new one now, I guess."

Nanette, in an experiment, when asked to choose one of three mirrored faces as her own, persistently and definitely rejected her own image.

Danny, ten years old, a severely retarded mongoloid boy, hides with shame, his left hand with clubbed, syndactylic fingers.

Rosa, a mongoloid girl of thirty, remarked after returning from the cinema, "I liked the nurse; she helped the people; I know how nice that is for someone who needs help."

Reprinted from "Stress on Families of the Mentally Handicapped." *Proceedings of the Third International Congress, International League of Societies for the Mentally Handicapped* (Paris, 1966), pp. 62-74. By permission of the author and the League.

> A group of workshop trainees commented on a television show depicting mental retardation. Beth said, "It was an interesting show until the parents talked and said that deep in their minds they didn't want their retarded children. A sister of a retarded boy said that she regrets having a retarded brother. The doctor didn't defend the retarded children when the parents and sister said those things . . . I think the show should be on again, but without the parents. I resented what they said."

Hundreds of other examples could be given. They represent degrees and kinds of awareness which the retarded have of themselves. Although the ability to conceptualize the self in abstract terms may indeed be limited in a degree corresponding to the extent of intellectual impairment, nevertheless the retarded person does develop a complex set of self-referent perceptions, attitudes and behaviors which permeate and profoundly influence his relationships with the world around him.

As with those of normal intelligence, the self-attitudes of the retarded are the product of learning which occurs in the developmental years. The normal child discovers himself as a consequence of his striving to cope with a world which at once satisfies and thwarts his needs; a world which nurtures and comforts him, but at the same time imposes expectations and punishes failure. In the case of the retarded child, the process is essentially similar but many of the components are modified: the developmental stages of maturation tend to be delayed but not uniformly for all functions; the efforts to cope with the environment are limited by intellectual and often by motoric disabilities; the expectations and demands of others reflect the ways in which they perceive—or fail to perceive—the child's disabilities. Excessive nurturance, excessive demand or excessive neglect may impede and distort the normal processes of self-discovery and self-evaluation.

The image of self is not something over which the person, especially the retarded person, has voluntary control. Rather, it becomes itself a controlling factor in the personal history of the individual. It becomes deeply rooted as the core of personal existence, permeating all other attitudes, judgments, and decisions, the choice of goals, the strength of effort, the selection of associates. It is formed normally through two major stages of development: the foundations and main outlines are established in early childhood around the core of personal identity; then the image thus formed is later revised in adolescence, sometimes with a good deal of stress, as the role of dependent childhood is repudiated and the role of independent adulthood is assumed. The elements of this image are derived from all levels of experience, from the most primitive of interactions between person and environment, to the most abstract conceptualizations of self and world. Hence, mental retardation does not eliminate the formation of self-image, but only modifies it, limiting it to whatever level of functioning the person is capable of. The established institutions of family and community life are geared to normal developmental rates and the adaptations made to the needs of the retarded never quite eliminate the discrepancy between normal expectancy and the actual performance. This further complicates self-discovery. In order to develop some guidelines which may assist in fostering the most desirable self-attitudes in the retarded, we shall consider briefly six aspects of development in the child's psychological world and see how these are modified in the experience of the retarded.

1. *Primitive Differentiation.* The elemental separation of self from not-self occurs as a baby learns to cope with a world that is necessary to satisfaction of his needs. It is probable that this differentiation would not occur without some experience of thwarting and the differential reinforcement of effort—yet if frustration is too great, the infant is helpless to attain gratification and the coping self cannot emerge. It is here that nurturant care, especially by the mother, mediates between the infant's needs and the thwarting or satisfaction which the world provides. Thus the mother assists in the infant's organization of his world by keeping his ability to cope with it within manageable limits. How rapidly this organization takes place and the form which it takes depend on a number of elements vital to our understanding of the retarded: (a) the vital energy (drive strength) of the infant; (b) the flow of stimulation from all sources through all the sensory modalities; (c) the infant's maturation rate, especially of the central nervous system, which makes possible the differentiation and integration of behavior; (d) the pattern of thwarting and attainment, especially as this is mediated and regulated by the nurturant mother.

In the retarded we can expect both delay and impairment in coping behavior and hence in the differentiation of self and not-self. This will, of course, depend on the degree of retardation and its specific characteristics. In the great majority of instances, especially in the mildly retarded, impairment at this stage will be minimal and usually not obvious. In the profoundly retarded, at the other extreme, environmental adaptation may be insufficient to sustain life at all without total nurturance. Where vital energies are low or physical disabilities seriously reduce motoric output, the infant may have little opportunity to experience himself as active agent in attaining gratification. Even though integrative functions may be impaired the flow of sensory stimulation in the retarded can be essentially normal except where there is specific sensory disability, or where the child is socially deprived of normal experience. Sensory deprivation from either organic or social sources, can result in the secondary retardation of mental functions and may well affect the primitive differentiation of self and not-self.

It is in the maturation of the central nervous system, however, that the retarded differ most from normal children. This is, of course, one of the primary criteria for the diagnosis of mental retardation. Consequently, we find not only that it takes the retarded child longer to differentiate himself from the world around him, but that he will have greater difficulty in establishing stable differences, his pictures of both self and world will be more limited in scope and clarity and will be subject to various distortions depending on the precise nature and extent of intellectual impairment. Moreover, the retarded child is likely to experience an unusual thwarting of his needs and drives; hence he is more extensively dependent on nurturant care for the satisfaction of his needs over a much greater length of time. The lag in development of self-resources, coupled with prolongation of infantile care impedes the formation of the self-image. This is further complicated by the extent to which the mother perceives or fails to perceive the child as defective. She may, depending on both her perception of defect and her feelings about it, subject the child to unusual experiences of neglect or of excessive nurturance or to confusing alternations of the two, thereby adding to the child's helplessness in learning to cope with the world around him.

What then can be done by the family to promote the best possible development of the personality of the retarded child at this early stage? Unquestionably of first importance is a realistic attitude towards the child's disabilities, neither exaggerating nor minimizing their importance. The existence of defect should be allowed to interfere as little as possible with the normal flow of stimulation. Responses of the child himself which lead to the satisfaction of his needs should be encouraged and reinforced as consistently as possible. The nurturing role of the mother and of others in the family should be limited to supports which supplement but do not displace the developing abilities of the child to cope with his own world. Within the encircling arms of a warm, welcoming and comforting world, the retarded child needs to experience his own developing powers, however limited they may be.

2. *Identity.* As the normal child develops, language emerges and naming becomes possible. The clusters of experience which constitute familiar objects and surroundings now, in being named, acquire identity and a degree of permanence. Similarly, the child's own name, at first only a signal which induces attention, now becomes a symbol which identifies the permanence and ubiquity of himself. "Danny—that's ME!" Thenceforward, the child's name serves as a powerful integrator of his self-structure.

For the retarded child, too, this takes place. He is given a name, but the length of time in which he responds to this only as a signal may be greatly prolonged. Only as he comes to the point of internalizing his name into the self-core, does it take on the quality of personal identity. Every means by which this can be hastened or encouraged should be sought, in view of the powerfully integrating effect which it has on the organization of a child's life. Any form of management of the retarded which contributes to anonymity or to confusion of name acts as a strong deterrent to the formation of the sense of personal identity and of all that derives from it.

Closely associated with a child's name in establishing personal identity is the recognition of his own body, with its palpable existence, its sensitivity and its characteristic appearance. A child typically identifies self with body, and the emergence of self-awareness is enhanced by recognition of bodily appearance. Normally, a child is able to recognize his own image in a mirror or photograph at about the age of three years. In a recent experiment by this author, it was found that retarded children tend to recognize their own image at a *mental age* of approximately three years. But it was also found that this was hastened or further retarded by the presence or absence of mirrors in the environment, by the amount of emphasis placed upon neatly groomed appearance, and by the experience of being photographed and seeing their own pictures and those of others.

In this same experiment, it was also found that a significant number of retarded children in a residential institution explicitly and definitely rejected their own mirror image, selecting the image of another person in preference to their own. The retarded are not insensitive to the way in which others have regarded them!

There can be little doubt, then, that retarded children need an environment which identifies them by name and by appearance, and which fosters in them a positive recognition and acceptance of their own identity. To live in large numbers in regimented, impersonal routines, in mirrorless surroundings; or shut away in lonely isolation, regarded as repugnant by those who care for them and by others who might see them—how can these things fail to do violence to the struggling human spirit?

3. *The Self-Portrait.* Around the core of self-identity, the normal child builds an elaborate self-portrait. This is made up of all that the child perceives as belonging to himself: his body and its various differentiated parts, aptitudes and experiences (the body image); his describable attributes of all sorts, seen and unseen; his abilities and limitations; his clothes and his possessions, even his surroundings and the objects and persons in them in so far as he identifies them with himself. The boundaries of the self-structure are usually difficult to determine precisely because, as they are perceived at increasing psychological "distance" from the self-core, they become ambiguously self and not-self.

Much of what goes into this developing self-structure is assimilated from the environment by the process of identification. These identifications serve in the satisfaction of emerging needs in the developing personal-social life of the child. Among the most important identifications is that of the sex role in which the child sees himself.

Knowledge of this phase in the development of the self-structure of the retarded is very limited. For the most part it is derived from clinic files rather than from controlled research. Existing techniques for the assessment of personality variables are of diminishing value with increasing severity of retardation, since they rely heavily on the uses of language and on conceptualizations of experience. For this reason also, psychiatrists and psychologists have tended to find the retarded uninteresting subjects for the assessment of personality, an unfortunate bias which robs the retarded of needed understanding and deprives the investigator himself of richly rewarding experiences.

As we might expect, the self-structure of the retarded tends to develop more slowly and to remain both less highly differentiated and less closely integrated than the normal. Because of a reduced ability to make perceptual and especially conceptual discriminations, the retarded often tolerate ambiguities and inconsistencies in the self-image which would be rejected or a source of anxiety to a person of more nearly normal mentality. Robert, for example, consistently and eagerly responds to any request for volunteers to do a task, but just as consistently blunders and fails in the execution—with no apparent evidence of confusion or discouragement. This appears to be a prolongation of egocentricity which Piaget defined as a cognitive state in which the subject sees the world (and himself) from a single point of view—his own—without awareness that any other point of view is possible. Without the corrective of objectivity, the self-percept can happily entertain contradictory elements. But a child normally passes through various stages of cognitive development, from the more concrete to the more abstract, and hence may be objective on one level but remain egocentric with regard to more abstract concepts. The retarded child tends to remain egocentric at each developmental stage over far longer periods of time than the normal child, and may remain so in important aspects at full maturity. This is a major source of the apparent ineptitude and "stupidity" of the retarded: when he attempts to operate in contexts requiring conceptual objectivity, his persistent egocentricity interferes with adequate adaptation.

As a consequence, the self-structure of the retarded child tends to be more stable and consistent in relation to more immediate and concrete elements of experience. A typical mongoloid child for example, seems to live rather exclusively in the immediate present, responding happily to praise and despondently to blame, but not looking very much to past or future. Similarly the mimicry and play-acting of the mongoloid is an expression of the immediacy of the present moment, an ability to assume a role in concrete behavior which does not conflict with an idealized self-image.

Yet the retarded child does experience stress, confusion, and unhappiness in his self-portrait. He lives in a world that is often thwarting and frequently baffling in his relationships with other persons. In most of the world's cultures, mental retardation is negatively valued, sometimes mildly, sometimes in the extreme. In the United States, for example, there is a widely held stereotype of the mentally deficient for which the community has a very low tolerance. The retarded person is perceived by many people as having a variety of undesirable, even threatening, characteristics. Few of these traits can be perceived directly; they are imputed to the person because they are contained in the stereotyped image. "All retarded people," so an extreme form of this attitude goes, "are not only stupid and incompetent, they are degenerate, prone to delinquent and criminal behavior, lacking in any moral sense, with sex drives both unlimited and uninhibited." Even in milder form, the prevailing view of the retarded person endows him with negatively valued characteristics. This places the retarded person in a peculiar position. He finds himself an object of negative or ambivalent evaluation in terms which he has no way of assimilating into his self-portrait. He experiences the attitudes of others in episodes of exclusion, rejection or even attack, but there is nothing concrete to which he can attribute these events; he can only take them at face value as a rejection of himself. If adjustment to a disability requires that it be integrated into the self-image in such a way as to leave the essential self-structure intact, where the disability is invisible and intangible and pervasive of the person, how is this to be done? The retarded person, is further limited in the very trait which would enable him to conceptualize the nature of his disability and thus view it realistically. What generally happens is that the negative attitudes of others become associated with his failures in accomplishment, so that his self-image is likely to be dominated by a generalized sense of inability to compete.

How can this be avoided? It would seem that mental disability can be assimilated into the self-structure, not directly as might be the case with an amputation or a facial disfigurement, but indirectly through the incorporation of positively valued traits. Characteristics which can be viewed as assets rather than liabilities, which bring success rather than failure, social and self esteem rather than disparagement, can be brought into the foreground. Negatively valued traits and incapacities can then become background facts with the status of limiting conditions of attainment, at a distance from the self-core. In order to have not only a positive but a *realistic* effect on self-structure, such traits must be experienced in fairly concrete terms and involve positive reinforcement; otherwise, the child viewing experience egocentrically is at the mercy of factors beyond his comprehension, and success with its consequent esteem can quickly turn to failure.

4. *Level of Aspiration.* As the self-structure is formed in normal personality development, accumulating experience furnishes a guide to what one may expect of oneself in the way of accomplishments. This estimate, or level of aspiration, is incorporated into the self-structure. It reflects the need to achieve success and to avoid failure, and is determined by a great many variables, including cumulative experiences of success and failure, the nature and strength of socially induced standards, the status-value of various goals and of the traits required to attain them. These variables determine the stability and realism of levels of aspiration, both specific and general; the strength of motivation and inhibition, the extent to which success or failure is attributed to oneself or to external agencies; and the way in which specific estimates of capability are generalized into an overall self-image of success or failure. "Self-concept" in the literature of personality usually refers to this inclusive estimate of personal worth.

In so far as the retarded child is exposed to the usual standards of expected achievement, he is subject to chronic failure. When his disabilities are recognized, however, he may be reared in a controlled environment which, in supplying his needs, protects him from the experience of failure. Both excessive exposure to failure and excessive protection from it result in unrealistic self-estimates, a tendency to under-perform and a self-image in which success or failure—and consequently one's status—are independent of one's own efforts. Thus, to fail again and again leads to the expectation of failure and a feeling "No matter how hard I try, I cannot succeed. Why, then, make an effort?" Overprotection from failure has much the same result. Success, guaranteed by a manipulated environment yields a generalized expectancy of success, independent of effort. "No matter what I do, I'll not fail. Why, then, make any effort beyond demanding that the world continue its benevolent support?" There seems, indeed, more danger in this latter case than in the former. The overprotected child who has never experienced and therefore never expects failure is extraordinarily vulnerable if the sheltering arms are removed. Forced to rely on his own resources, he is helpless, his world dissolves, his personality tends to shatter and disintegrate. The chronic failure, may on the other hand, when success occurs, discover the fruitfulness of his own efforts and make a partial recovery. Nevertheless, it is the child trained in situations where his own efforts have always made the difference between success and failure who shows the greatest stability and makes the most progress. Having discovered that in most situations success is available but failure is possible *depending on his own efforts*, he has learned to attribute the outcome to himself rather than to external agencies. He develops a more realistic self-estimate, shows a higher level of effort and efficiency and has a greater tolerance to failure when it occurs. Family life which accepts the retarded child as a responsible member, expecting from him what he *can do with effort*, allowing him to experience failure but keeping success within reach; rewarding his accomplishments with praise and joy, but letting his shortcomings and errors stand in an equally clear light—all this creates in the child a satisfaction in self-reliance but also a feeling of security and well-being.

5. *Systems of Control and Defense.* In normal development, the self-structure reaches a fairly stable fruition in childhood. The self-core has been firmly established around a central sense of personal identity for which the childhood name is the symbol. Around this has evolved an elaborate structure of attributes toward which the child has developed attitudes, estimates of effectiveness and judgments of worth. He views himself altogether with a generalized self-regard which is usually positive in esteem. In some instances, typical of the "emotionally disturbed" child, the self-image may be negatively valued and unstable, reflecting unresolved stresses of childhood. In most cases, however, the self-system tends towards equilibrium which is fairly stable, but which is still in varying degrees vulnerable to external pressures or internal conflict. Preservation of self and control of self emerge as twin motives dominating self-referent behavior in the older child. On the other hand, the child needs to defend himself against hurt, to preserve the integrity and esteem of the self from external threat and internal disruption, and to this end he will develop and utilize systems of defense. On the other hand, he feels a strong need to be in command of his resources in coping with the situations with which he is confronted and in pursuing the objects of his desire; and to this end he will devise systems of control. The need for defense and the need for control tend to be inversely related to each other. The more successful the child becomes in controlling and utilizing his resources in coping behavior, the less vulnerable he feels to hurt and disruption. On the other hand, the more he protects himself from stress and external attack, the more "encapsulated" the self is likely to become, with a consequent reduction in effective operational controls. When neither defensive nor controlling systems are effective in meeting the contingencies of life, severe personality disturbance, panic and disintegration of the self may ensue.

What of the retarded child? Does he follow these same patterns of self-development? Is he capable of self-defense and self-control? Or does retardation render the child too dull to feel the threat of psychic hurt, or to imagine the fruits of controlled attainment? All too frequently we deny to retarded children the possibility of feeling as other children do in the face of threats to self-esteem. All too often, the emotional disturbances seen in the retarded is attributed solely to their inherent "nature" or to the organic lesions responsible for their mental defects, rather than to the products of experience, to thwarting, loss of esteem and an overwhelming feeling of inadequacy. It is true that organic defect may make for increased impulsivity, reduced behavioral controls, hyperemotionality. It is true also that retardation reduces the ability to imagine threats and to foresee the results of effort. It is true also that the retarded child is less adept at devising defensive systems, just as he is less adroit at coping with problems in general. The retarded child, just as the normal child, attempts to defend himself against hurt, but the things that threaten him are more direct and concrete and he is more vulnerable to them. The retarded child, just as the child of greater endowment, attempts to cope with whatever confronts him, but he cannot see as far, understand as clearly or manage as effectively. It is precisely because his defensive systems are weak and crude that they are easily penetrated and he suffers hurt; it is precisely because his attempts to cope are more inept and illogical that they are easily thwarted and he suffers defeat and humiliation. For these reasons, the retarded frequently find themselves defenseless in a world with which they cannot cope: small wonder then that we so often see in them severe personality disturbance, drastically irreal adaptive behavior, disintegrated personality and tragic unhappiness.

When we compare the defenses of the retarded with those of normal and bright children, we find them usually much simpler, more direct, less subtle and devious. Where the normal learns to rationalize, the retarded is more likely to deny or to lie. Where the normal tends to justify or excuse, the retarded is likely to remain silent. Where the normal projects his hostility into others or expresses it in displaced aggressions, the retarded is more likely to attack the source of frustration directly or beat a hasty retreat. The retarded is more likely to seek escape in direct physical flight or in obdurate silence, while the normal seeks escape through subtler and more subjective routes. As a consequence the defenses of the retarded are more easily seen through and outwitted by those in authority over him, who may through punishment or other means reduce him to docility or to the silence which is his last refuge. It is, however, for the same reasons much easier to understand the defenses of the retarded, to see what it is that threatens him, to assist in the development of his ability to cope and to generate means of defense which are appropriate and adequate to his needs. For there is much in the world that the retarded person cannot cope with, for which his resources will always be too meager. Hence he must have defenses if he is to survive as a human person.

Similarly, the controls of the retarded will tend to be simpler, more direct and concrete than those of the normal child. For example, a normal child may develop a "social intelligence" which enables him to adapt to a new situation by applying selectively a wealth of previous social experiences, and through observing the effects of his actions gradually work out an adequate solution. The retarded child, on the other hand, is likely to seize upon some particular behavioral model, which he then employs uncritically as a means of control. Only when it obviously fails will he beat a defensive retreat or try a new model. An example of this is seen in the case of Bart, a fourteen-year-old mongoloid boy, on admission to a new school. Bart had been very rigorously trained by his mother in a simple clear-cut delineation of "goodness" and "badness"; those acts (and persons) which Mother approves and permits are Good, those of which she disapproves and does not permit are Bad.

On the first day away from home, Bart showed a disturbed, restless, rather harshly aggressive behavior, quite different from anything we had observed when the mother was present. Halfway through the day, Bart changed his identity to that of "Frank Dubek," who turned out to be a thoroughly bad character from one of the more gruesome television programs. Bart took the name of this villainous character and, over a period of some days, adopted him as a model, proceeding to act out the kind of behavior he had witnessed on the screen. This developed as a channel for Bart's aggressive feelings as well as his means of attempting to control his environment. It became alarming when the script called for a really violent attack, and intervention was obviously necessary. An attempt was then made to modify Bart's behavior. It turned out to be rather surprisingly easy in view of the intensity of his dramatic identification with Frank. Bart was allowed to verbalize the entire story of which he had a remarkably vivid and detailed memory. Throughout, the counselor continually distinguished between Frank Dubek as a "bad" man, and Bart himself as a "good" man. To this Bart readily assented: "My mother does not like Frank Dubek; he is a bad man; Jesus does not like Frank Dubek." From that time on Bart completely repudiated the character and would not allow anyone to call him by that name; he adopted a quite different model for his social conduct which became very friendly and effective.

In both roles, it should be noted, Bart was behaving as a responsible agent responding to a need to be in command of his resources in coping with a new situation. In the one case his model was socially unacceptable, in the other it was appropriate: in either case it reflected a view of himself. Coping behavior, and the systems of control which make it possible, requires anchorage in self-concepts which provide a sense of identity and of worth, and the means of selecting operational techniques which are appropriate to objective realities.

In the management of the mentally retarded, the central aim should be towards the development of adequate and appropriate systems of control, because these are in the last analysis the best defense against a wounded ego. But where control is insufficiently advanced to give him strength and confidence, and where his resources leave him vulnerable to external pressures and internal stress, extreme care must be taken not to rob him of his defenses. On the contrary, every effort should be made to assist him in acquiring means of defense which are effective and socially acceptable, which supplement his controls rather than substituting for them. Perhaps most important of all is to enable him to feel that his weaknesses are understood while his strengths are recognized and admired. The most devastating thing of all is to feel that his weaknesses are condemned and the limitation of his abilities a cause for shame.

6. *The Adolescent Transition.* One final aspect of self-development must be noted. The child does not remain a child but becomes an adult, and this is true of the retarded as of other children. For the retarded, however, there are some important differences of which we must take careful note.

During the later years of childhood, with the self-concept pretty well established, the child is a familiar person to himself. He is accustomed to his appearance, his name, his attributes and possessions. Depending on the quality of his personal development, he has familiar feelings of comfort and unease, of self-approval and shame, of competency and esteem or of ineptitude and inferiority; and he has at hand his well-established methods of coping and defending. But all of this is cast in the *image of childhood,* with its correlatives of inferiority in stature, strength and authority in relation to the adult world around him.

There comes a time in early adolescence, however, when this child-image dissolves. The passage to adulthood means not only radical adjustments to changing body-image, but a repudiation of the dependency roles of childhood and the acquisition of the mature roles of adult status. The adolescent characteristically goes through a period in which his status is ambiguous, in which he is neither child nor adult, but something of both. In the words of Matthew Arnold, he is "suspended between two worlds, one dead, the other powerless to be born." The passage of adolescence and the turbulence of its course varies widely with cultures and with the personalities of those who go through it; but the net result is a final reintegration of the self-image on a higher level of maturity. The adult image reinstates the essential structures formed in childhood but with revised estimates of attributes, capabilities and status. To be seen by the world and to see oneself as a man or woman, no longer as a child, is the foundation of adult responsibility.

There are, of course, those who, for a variety of reasons, fail in this transition; whose personalities remain immature, or who break down under the stress of adult responsibility. There are those also who, despite their growth to maturity have difficulty in attaining to recognized status as adults and are forever regarded as children. This is unfortunately still the lot of many who are mentally retarded. The combined effects of limited intellectual capability, subnormal social adaptation and perpetuation of dependency, creates a social bias which makes the transition to adult status for the retarded extremely difficult. Because the retarded person on reaching maturity remains child*like* in some of his attributes, there is a mistaken tendency to regard him as a child in all respects except for physical size and physiological functions.

The period of adolescence is indeed apt to be a difficult one for the retarded boy or girl. Because the whole process of self-formation is likely to have been slowed down through the years of childhood, the child-image may not have been fully formed before physical maturity, with its changes in stature and sexuality, occurs. This confuses the image before it has had time to stabilize. In addition, the extent of his disabilities results in a corresponding or even exaggerated dependency. If, on top of this, the social environment views his sexual maturation with alarm while in other respects fails to acknowledge his growing up, it is not surprising that his self-image becomes highly confused.

Most of the research on the self-concept of the retarded has been concerned with the self-appraisal of mildly retarded adolescents and young adults. It has shown a general tendency toward confusion and lack of realism, but has failed to trace this to its roots, citing only the difference between retarded and normal subjects. In the absence of more precise knowledge, we can at least surmise that the view a retarded person has of himself will reflect the view taken of him by others. If he is viewed as an overgrown child in a world of adults, he will act like one; if he is viewed as a man or woman with assets as well as liabilities, he will see himself as less dependent on others and more capable of self-direction. If he is viewed with respect for his positive qualities, rather than with pity for his negative ones, he will respond with social pride and respect for himself. If his limitations are not hidden from him but viewed in the perspective of his assets, he is likely to be more realistic in his own self-estimates. These are hypotheses for the researchers to verify.

When we ask, then, what should a family do to improve the experience of *being* a retarded member of the family, perhaps these things suggest themselves:

To provide an infancy rich in experience, flowing in through all the senses, and flowing out in effort, assisted and encouraged by a wise nurturance which sees the child as more important than the defect.

To foster the sense of identity, by giving the child a name which he can internalize as a symbol of himself, and by encouraging familiarity and pride in his own appearance.

To help the child build a self-portrait in which assets override limitations in importance, and self-esteem grows through confidence in the acceptability of accomplishment.

To manage the child's experience in such a way that success or failure depends upon his own efforts, and aspiration grows realistically with goals that are attainable with effort.

To encourage the developing child in the growth of self controls through confidence in the use of his resources for coping with life, and to allow him to learn those defenses which will reduce his vulnerability to hurt in a world that is often less than sympathetic.

To recognize his growth to manhood or womanhood, assisting in those transitions from dependency to independency which are possible, and never allowing the limitations of intellect to detract from his place of dignity in the family of mankind.

NINETEEN

The Demonstration and Measurement of Adaptive Behavior

H. LELAND, K. NIHIRA, R. FOSTER AND M. SHELLHAAS

In 1961, the American Association on Mental Deficiency incorporated the concept of Adaptive Behavior into the definition of mental retardation, as follows: "Mental retardation refers to subaverage general intellectual functioning which originates during the the developmental period and is *associated with impairment in adaptive behavior*" (our emphasis) (Heber, 1961).

Adaptive Behavior was defined as the "effectiveness with which the individual copes with the natural and social demands of his environment . . . [and includes] 1, the degree to which the individual is able to function and maintain himself independently, and 2, the degree to which he meets satisfactorily the culturally imposed demands of personal and social responsibility" (Heber, 1961).

However, there were no adequate measures of adaptive behavior available and no precise criteria of impairment (Leland, 1964b). It became apparent that this notion of Adaptive Behavior had to be developed by a special program of research. The purpose of this presentation is to discuss the progress of this research, to provide historical antecedents of the concept, to discuss the critical sociocultural elements which bear upon the concept, and finally, to bring these considerations together for the development of a measurement scale. Further, we will present general suggestions for the application and use of the concept of Adaptive Behavior in planning rehabilitation for the mentally retarded.

A special five-year project was developed at Parsons State Hospital and Training Center, Kansas, under the combined auspices of the American Association on Mental Deficiency, the National Institute of Mental Health, and the Kansas Division of Institutional Management through its participation at Parsons. The purpose of this special project is to demonstrate new information on the use and function of Adaptive Behavior. This project is now in its third year. We are using this opportunity to expose to you the present state of our thinking and the progress we have made toward achieving the long-range goals of the project. These goals are to establish the concept of Adaptive Behavior as a major dimension in the measurement and classification of mentally retarded, socially incompetent individuals.

From *Proceedings, First Congress, International Association for the Scientific Study of Mental Deficiency* (Montpelier, 1967), pp. 74-80. By permission of the authors and the International Association.

The complete overview of the historical antecedents of the concept of Adaptive Behavior cannot be presented in the amount of time available today. The realm of adaptation and behavior in relationship to the mentally retarded has emerged as a major point of interest in some periods and declined to almost no interest in others. One of the earliest attempts to measure that which today we might call "Adaptive Behavior" is found in the work of Felix Voisin (1843) who developed a rating scale in this general area. From the early part of the nineteenth century to the present, many writers have dealt with the question of social incompetence and the relationship of maladaptive behavior to the acceptance and understanding of the retarded individual and his total relationship within his community. These contributions have kept the topic alive, but there has not been a systematic attempt to utilize the information available either from the psychology of measurement or from the area of child development to bring a rigorous measuring process to bear on the question of Adaptive Behavior.

The work in the area of social maturity by Edgar Doll (1953) and that of others in related fields has demonstrated that the manner in which the individual copes with his problems is a much more effective way of defining mental retardation than the limited measurements represented by the I.Q. Yet there has been a continued reliance on the I.Q. Although there have been excellent discussions about why the I.Q. is not effective, no one has come forth with an appropriate substitute to provide a more humane indication of the retarded individual's needs in relationship to society than the shelving kind of classification represented by the I.Q. We are not thinking of a dimension to be added to the present dimension of Measured Intelligence, but of a new dimension which eventually might replace the present ways of looking at the mentally retarded individual. Thus, there is a need to be able to say of a retarded individual that he fits a particular pattern or that his behaviors are developing in a particular way. This new dimension should help in deciding whether he is to remain in the community or is to be institutionalized. It should help in deciding where in the community he might remain; what kinds of special programs, sheltered workshops, or other services he might need. If he must be institutionalized, it should help decide for how long and what processes will be required during the institutionalization. We recognize that, at least in the United States, most of the individuals admitted to institutions for the mentally retarded are there because of maladaptive behavior, and we presume that this is true in other countries who followed similar practices. Historically, the individual institutionalized for maladaptive behavior nonetheless was expected to spend most of his life in the institution. The concept of dealing with his problem and sending him back to the community has only recently been accepted. Vast numbers of able individuals have been deprived of their right to be contributing members of society merely because an I.Q. number said that they are retarded. Their adaptive behavior directed·the community to put them into a special kind of institution. This same maladaptive behavior without that I.Q. number might have placed them in another service.

This aspect of Adaptive Behavior becomes particularly apparent if we look at the extensive prevalence count done in Onondaga County, New York (1955). There, it was found that there was a low percentage of mentally retarded individuals below the school-starting age, that there was a gross increase of individuals—approaching 10 % during the compulsory school ages, and that this figure dropped to around three % after school age. Obviously, these youngsters did not become mentally retarded by being sent to school and they certainly were not cured of retardation by being released from school. Rather, a child was considered retarded at the preschool level only if he had obvious disabilities. If he looked normal, developed ambulation, etc., he was not identified as retarded. When he came to school and flunked sandpile, he began to be recognized *as scholastically retarded* and later, through his inclusion, following I.Q. testing, in a special education program, *as mentally retarded.* He carried this label throughout his school history, but on leaving school, people no longer asked him to read and write or to pass scholastic achievement tests and he was absorbed into the community and no longer labeled mentally retarded. What is apparent from this discussion is that we are dealing with the same individual throughout and the question is not whether he was *really* mentally retarded but whether there was beside the subaverage intellectual functioning also an impairment in adaptive behavior. When this impairment in adaptive behavior was not present the individual did not need to be identified as mentally retarded; he did not need to carry the stigma.

In order to understand what types of adaptation are required, we must look at the sociocultural elements within our society which establish for us the label of mental retardation. It can be accepted by most that mental retardation is not an absolute, but is, rather, a social concept derived from the critical demands and specific needs of communities, which sort out individuals who interfere with the maintenance of those communities. A rural, underdeveloped community has different kinds of critical demands, different kinds of needs than a sophisticated, industrialized urban community. Take, for example, crossing the street. There are areas in Southern France where a retarded child can wander into the road without the least worry about a truck or automobile striking him. Were he to do this in Paris, there is a high probability that he would be struck.

There is another type of critical demand which might be said to be based on the survival of the community itself; certain types of social behaviors, certain types of moral behaviors, certain types of functional activities have to be carried on if the community itself is going to survive. An individual who seems incapable of these behaviors is thought to endanger the existence of the community and historically it was felt that he must be separated from it. Today we know that his presence is not an ongoing danger to the survival of the community. Mental retardation does not rub off as though it were poison ivy. If the most critical demands—those specific demands on which the community places the greatest importance—can be defined, it is possible to help the individual meet these demands. For example, if certain areas are not to be trespassed upon, windows are not to be broken, objects that are placed out for public use are not to be carried off, then following these rules is necessary for the social survival of the individual in the community. The rock-throwing, stealing, trespassing individual can be helped through specific kinds of training and treatment without being separated from society. These behaviors can be modified regardless of etiology, and the retarded person can be considered acceptable. There is no question here of I.Q. All of you know children with an I.Q. of 50 who are polite, do not throw rocks, do not kick dogs, keep their zippers closed on their trousers, and in general, present themselves in an acceptable manner, and you know individuals with I.Qs. of 50 who do exactly the opposite and who cause a great deal of grief and make you feel that you want to run when you see them coming. Which of these two youngsters would be institutionalized? Obviously, it is not the I.Q. that is bringing about these phenomena. It is the rock-throwing, the inappropriate maintenance of clothing, the inappropriate language, the general filth of the individual that causes the disturbance. These can be changed; they are the reversible aspects of mental retardation and it becomes our responsibility to try to bring about this reversal.

In addition, there are age critical demands for special kinds of coping strategies. Thus, you would not be particularly worried—back to the child crossing the street —if the behavior referred to a three or four-year-old. One expects a young child to be conducted across the street. He is not expected to handle stoplights, etc. It becomes more disturbing when it is a seven- or eight-year-old, and if it is a 12- or 15-year-old we have a serious problem. It is not a matter of mental age in the old sense; it is a question of the critical demands that society places within age ranges. Or, in another example, it is not sufficient to say that certain types of dress must be maintained. Rather, it is necessary that certain types of dress be maintained by certain groups of certain ages in certain places.

Here, we need to recognize that there are currently available a number of measurement devices which do some of the work which we have outlined. Those which come closest to meeting the needs include the Vineland Social Maturity Scale (Doll, 1964), the Progress Assessment Chart (Gunzburg, 1965), the Cain-Levine Social Competency Scale (1963). These and others have been listed and discussed in another paper (Leland, Shellhaas, Nihira, and Foster, 1967).

The difficulty is not so much the lack of efficiency of these other devices, but rather, that to be able to include "impairment in adaptive behavior" in the definition of mental retardation, it is necessary that the full concept of Adaptive Behavior be subject to measurement. We recognize the enormity of this task, but accepting the principle that all observable behavior can be measured, we are sure it is a task which can be completed. Such a measurement instrument must be based upon a clear conceptualization of the critical demands of the environment and the results must be interpreted in the light of the age critical behaviors required of the individual to survive in a variety of environments.

Such a scale must include the major aspects of independent functioning. Does the child walk, dress himself, feed himself? Can he care for himself alone? Does the adolescent function independently, taking care of most of his general needs and all of his personal needs? Does the adult function in a wage-earning, socially contributing manner? Does he have sufficient self-concept to perform in a variety of independent functioning activities so that he does not have to be a burden on someone else for his personal, social and psychological survival? These questions have to be built into a scale.

Beyond that, presuming the individual knows how to do these things, that his level of independent functioning has been established, we also need to know whether he will do them. We need questions which test the motivation of the individual. How much personal responsibility for his own well-being and for his own behavior is the individual willing to accept? If the child knows how to dress himself, will he dress himself? If the adolescent knows how to cook a meal, will he cook it? If the adult knows how to work at an occupation, will he do so? How much personal responsibility will any of these individuals assume in terms of their relationship to other individuals?

Also, an adequate scale must measure the social responsibility of the individual. How much responsibility does the individual demonstrate toward the community as a whole, as separate from specific relationships to individuals therein? This category involves the ability of the individual to carry out behaviors because they are supposed to be done. This is a measure of social conformity to the accepted mores of the community. A socially responsible person has learned that this is what is expected and he has also learned if he does what is expected his chance of survival is greater. Social responsibility has three categories: 1, social adjustment, 2, civic responsibility, 3, economic responsibility. A scale has to tap all of these to determine whether the individual of sub-average intellectual functioning is also sufficiently impaired in his adaptability to be labeled mentally retarded and thus be in need of public services.

It is not possible to eliminate the bookkeeping aspects of classification. It is necessary to know how many of a certain etiology one has in a particular setting. Research has to be conducted and individuals have to be matched according to certain kinds of functional abilities, etc. Appropriations have to be created by governmental bodies and the needs of one type of retarded individual are different than those of another, and if these appropriations are to evolve sensibly these numbers have to be known. Therefore, one of the gains that must come from an Adaptive Behavior measurement scale is a bookkeeping system. The system which the AAMD suggested was a system of levels whereby individuals with the least impairment in adaptive behavior would be considered to be functioning at Level 1 and individuals with the most impairment would be considered to be functioning at a lower level, which in terms of our present research is Level V (Leland, 1965). It may be that this is a magic number of levels depending on how the research progresses, but the level system does give an opportunity for the bookkeeping procedures to be maintained without utilizing these labels as shelving categories as the I.Q. was used (Leland, 1964b, and Leland, Nihira, Foster, Shellhaas, and Kagin, 1966). Of greater importance is the development of an appropriate mode of diagnosis to indicate where an individual should be placed for treatment or training. The I.Q. has never served this function. The ideal type of diagnostic grouping would group individuals who are similar in certain aspects of adaptive behavior which are amenable to modification by a given treatment program. Two individuals who are classified under the same diagnostic grouping might be expected to function in a similar area of social competence, demonstrating similar types of personal and social responsibility, and to have approximately the same types of abilities leading to similar levels of independent functioning. It would be possible to evolve effective rehabilitation planning around these individuals. In an institution it would be possible to group individuals together into living units so that programs can be developed on a group basis and thus help deal with the severe manpower shortage and still serve the individual needs of each patient. In a community center or comprehensive clinic it would be possible to provide treatment-oriented programs concerning specific kinds of needs so that the individual can receive help for the behaviors for which he was referred to the center. Or, in a local setting, we may have only one professional who, in the typical sparsely populated area, is not expert in mental retardation. If the child could be assigned a certain level, the local professional, regardless of his discipline, would have some idea of the kind of treatment or training program needed and might be able to apply certain aspects of it himself.

Thus, we have *first* the measure of those behaviors within the retarded individual's personality which are *reversible. Second,* we have the basis for curriculum development throughout the special education, special training, special treatment realm. Since we are not concerned with teachability so much as with the individual meeting the critical demands of his community, then different kinds of curricula must be evolved (Edmonson, Leland, deJung, and Leach, 1967). This training leads to the major and *third* aspect of this question—the achievement, for the mentally retarded, of social invisibility. The individual who is not known as mentally retarded because he has achieved a sufficiently high level of adaptive behavior is, in effect, socially invisible. This means that he has learned enough about the use of verbal cues and strategies that he is not immediately identifiable in his milieu. It means also that he has learned appropriate coping strategies so that he appears to be functioning in the same manner as other people around him even though his intelligence may not permit him to fully function in that way. The ability to deal with verbal cues and strategies and the possession of appropriate coping strategies becomes the main rehabilitation goal of a program based on the modification of adaptive behavior.

The measurement device which we have described will diagnose the adaptive level of the individual so that people in helping professions can set up training and treatment programs to modify the reported behaviors.

References

CAIN, L. F. LEVINE, S., and ELZEY, F. F. (1963) *Cain-Levine Social Competency Scale.* Palo Alto, California: Consulting Psychological Press.

DOLL, E. A. (1953 *The Measurement of Social Competence: A Manual for the Vineland Social Maturity Scale.* Minneapolis: Educational Test Bureau, Educational Publishers.

DOLL, E. A. (1964) *Vineland Scale of Social Maturity.* Minneapolis: American Guidance Service.

EDMONSON, BARBARA, LELAND, H., DEJUNG, J. E. and LEACH, ETHEL M. (1967) Increasing social cue interpretations (visual decoding) by retarded adolescents through training. *Amer. F. Ment. Defic.*, 71: 1017.

GUNZBURG, H. C. (1965) *Progress Assessment Chart for Children Unsuitable for Education at School.* London: National Association for Mental Health.

HEBER, R. (Ed.) (1961) A Manual on Terminology and Classification in Mental Retardation. Monograph Supplement, *Amer. F. ment. Defic.*, Second Edition.

LELAND, H. (Ed.) (1964a) *Conference on Measurement of Adaptive Behavior.* Parsons, Kansas: Parsons State Hospital and Training Center.

LELAND, H. (1964b) Some thoughts on the current status of adaptive behavior. *Mental Retardation*, 2: 171.

LELAND, H. (1965) Some modifications in the us of adaptive behavior definitions. *Project News,* Parsons State Hospital and Training Center, Parsons, Kansas, 1: 1.

LELAND, H., NIHIRA, K., FOSTER, R., SHELLHAAS, M., and KAGIN, E. (1966) *Conference on Measurement of Adaptive Behavior:* 11. Parsons, Kansas: Parsons State Hospital and Training Center.

LELAND, H., SHELLHAAS, M., NIHIRA, K. and FOSTER, R. (1967) Adaptive Behavior: A new dimension in the classification of the mentally retarded. *Mental Retardation Abstracts*, 4: 359.

NEW YORK STATE DEPARTMENT OF MENTAL HYGIENE. (1955) A special censure of suspected referred mental retardation, Onondaga County, New York. *Technical Report of the Mental Health Research Unit.* Syracuse, New York: Syracuse University Press, 84.

VOISIN, F. (1843) *Del'idiotie chez les enfants.* Paris: J. B. Baillière.

Basic Problems and Issues in the Differential Diagnosis of the Mentally Ill-Mentally Retarded Child

STELLA CHESS

The upsurge of interest in mental retardation during the past decade has swept away many outworn dogmas in various disciplines concerned with the problem. Some healthy soul-searching has also been going on among child psychiatrists. Many of them have begun to re-examine their role in the diagnosis and rehabilitation of retarded youngsters.

Until recently most child psychiatrists had a very limited conception of this role. They tended to believe that their main responsibility was to differentiate between so-called "pseudo retardation" and "true retardation." The label "pseudo retardation" was rather indiscriminately slapped on children whose intellectual deficiency was presumed to be secondary to one or another emotional disorder. Once this judgment was made, the psychiatrist proceeded to diagnose and treat the emotional disturbance, all too often without reference to the cognitive issue. On the other hand, if the child was found to have a structural incapacity for age-appropriate intellectual functioning the psychiatrist's involvement was minimal. He considered his responsibility fulfilled when he recommended that the child be placed in a special school or institution.

This narrow approach reflected the faulty view of mental retardation as a diagnostic entity. The term is still widely used as if it referred to a unitary condition existing in a homogeneous group of persons. We certainly know better. The more we learn about the anatomy and biochemistry of the brain, the metabolic processes of the body as a whole, and the mechanisms of genetics, the more clearly do we recognize that mental retardation is not a disease entity but an outstanding symptom of syndromes that may stem from a diversity of causes.

Similarly, we have become increasingly aware that it is essential to take into account individual differences in the temperament and behavioral style of retarded children as of all other youngsters. Closer study has exposed such global myths as

Reprinted from "Basic Problems and Issues in Differential Diagnosis of the Mentally Ill-Mentally Retarded Child" (East Orange, N.J., Essex County Unit, New Jersey Association for Retarded Children, 1968), pp. 1-12. By permission of the author and the Unit. This work was conducted under N.I.M.H. Research Grant MH 12711-02.

that of the "quiet and contented Mongoloid." No longer is it considered sufficient to say, "He is slow intellectually; this explains his behavioral difficulties."

And I like to think that we have all become more wary of such grab-bag diagnoses as "emotional block." As Leo Kanner once noted, "somewhere along the line, the term 'emotional block' was coined to indicate the masking of innate intellectual assets by psychotic or near-psychotic disturbances." Perhaps the term had some pertinence in calling attention to the fact that low IQ scores could be based on emotional factors such as anxious perfectionism or preoccupation, just as the test results could be affected by visual, auditory, and neuro-orthopedic handicaps. But some professional persons, Kanner adds, have gone to the extreme of "ascribing primary emotional etiology to children who, by all standards, were, are, and will remain defective in the sense of an inherent minus." And naturally the mother was blamed for causing the block—another illustration of what I like to call "mal de mere." A large body of research in the past few years has reinforced our clinical awareness that the coexistence of mental subnormality and behavioral abnormality does not necessarily imply primary emotional disorder and secondary reversible retardation.

The diagnosis of retardation is based essentially on the history, clinical observation, and psychological test data.

The history may reveal that the child's development was slow from birth onward. The mothers of many children in this category have histories of difficult pregnancies or deliveries. There may be mention of neonatal stress. In many cases, however, the history may be one of normal pregnancy, delivery, and neonatal period. Yet one finds that all these children have been delayed in their developmental phases, that speech in particular is slow, and that their behavior in learning situations has always been appropriate to a younger age. Physically, these children may appear normal and show no neurological evidence of cerebral dysfunction. The vast majority of mentally retarded children fit into this category of undifferentiated or familial retardation.

A second group comprises retarded children who show neurological signs of brain damage. This may be of a specific nature, with a special area of dysfunction, which may be neuromuscular or may involve a particular sense organ. In other cases, the symptoms may be generalized and indicate diffuse damage, with resultant disorganization of functioning that may take various forms: heightening of irritability, or decrease in capacity to respond to stimuli, lessening of impulse control or decline in spontaneity.

A third category comprises children with signs of hormonal imbalance. The defect in cognition is one symptom of an endocrine malfunction that modifies the brain chemistry and physiology. Psychological tests of intelligence identify their impaired functioning.

Another group includes children who begin life normally but show a slowing up, cessation, or regression in mental development following some traumatic event, such as infection, inflammation, injury, neoplasm, or degenerative neurologic disease affecting the brain. In such cases, there is a history of normal development in all areas up to the time of the brain insult. Thereafter there is a change in the tempo of development and, eventually, a discernible pattern of retarded intellectual functioning. Clinical observation shows the child as behaving in an immature manner, and the psychological tests confirm this finding.

These categories are useful insofar as they distinguish the kinds of problems that will confront the children as well as their parents. A child who has always been slower than average will not face the same demands as the one who has functioned normally for a number of years and only then begins to display a lag. Similarly, a child who looks normal will not necessarily have the same social difficulties as one who is palsied or has some other physical stigmata.

In making a differential diagnosis of retardation, one must be alert to certain pitfalls. A closer examination of the history may reveal that the apparently backward child is one who has always been slow to warm up to new situations. Such a child could give the impression of being retarded when he is shifted from one learning situation to another. Or a child may have a reactive behavior disorder involving his school work. He may be frightened by the newness of a classroom situation or a bad approach by the teacher. It is possible that he has been over-pressured at home or been overpowered by a superior sib. A full history and clinical observation may reveal adequate cognitive ability in other social situations.

The diagnosis of mental retardation must also take into account the specific nature of the child's developmental lag. For example, if he has a language lag, is this part of a general pattern of retardation or does the child handle other situations well? The diagnostician must also make sure that a child who appears retarded has intact vision and hearing. A child who is disorganized in his thinking processes is not necessarily retarded and may respond to a therapeutic program.

Children with cerebral damage may have normal IQ scores and yet be unable to handle material appropriate to their age group. They may be highly distractible and may have memory deficits or difficulty in shifting their mental set. The psychiatrist must define the handicap by estimating which learning capacities are damaged and which are intact.

For this purpose, psychological testing is important, so long as its results are not overrated. As we all realize today, IQ test scores must be appraised with care. The tests were designed to measure a child's ability to learn in school, and there are many possible reasons why a youngster may attain a low score. I have already referred to the fact that low scores may reflect physical handicaps, specific learning disabilities, and emotional factors. In addition, cultural and social biases in the tests may limit their application.

And, as Sarason has pointed out, IQ scores "do not enable one to state in what ways a particular individual is different from others with an identical score, what his differential reactions are to a variety of situations, his attitudes toward himself and others." The crucial role of the psychiatrist in assessing test scores is to ask why this particular child and not others with identical IQ's behaves the way he does, and why certain situations rather than others elicit his backward response.

Nevertheless, such psychometric testing can be of great clinical value. In some cases the test results suggest a diagnosis markedly different from what is suggested by other information available to the clinician. The person who appears dull and "looks defective" but is of average or superior IQ, the child who seems bright and glib but who fails at school and whose test results indicate that he is really a dullard despite his ready tongue; or the child who does not speak very much but whose test scores give otherwise unsuspected glimpses of latent mental capacities—these are the cases in which mental testing opens up avenues for further investigation and for remedial treatment.

The diagnosis of retardation is only the beginning of psychiatric exploration, not the end. Once he has identified the deficiency the psychiatrist's major responsibility still remains. This is to make a behavioral assessment of the youngster. Here his task is to determine how the fact of retardation relates to the child's over-all adaptation and development.

In considering the special problems of retarded children, I have found the following psychiatric classification useful:

1. Mental retardation with no behavior disorder.

2. Mental retardation with behavior symptoms that are a direct expression of organic brain damage.

3. Mental retardation with reactive behavior disorder.

4. Mental retardation with nuerotic behavior disorder.

5. Mental retardation with psychosis.

While such a classification is necessarily oversimplified, it is convenient for our present purpose. I shall comment on each of these five categories.

1. Mental retardation with no behavior disorder.

Some investigators would deny that there is such a category. They assert that all retardates suffer from some specifiable psychiatric defect. For example, Thomas Webster, in a study of 159 retarded children from three to six years of age, suggests that there is a primary psychopathology of mental retardation. Not one of the children, he found, was "simply retarded." Webster concludes: "The slow and incomplete unfolding of the personality is associated with partial fixations which result in an infantile or immature character structure. This particular style of ego development is accompanied by special descriptive features: a nonpsychotic autism, repetitiousness, inflexibility, passivity and simplicity in emotional life."

In my own clinical and research experience, I have been unable to identify any emotional or behavioral characteristics that are specifically and necessarily associated with retarded children. Moreover, not all retarded children who do have behavioral disturbances show the same symptoms. Most other workers in this field have reported varying percentages of behavior disorder among retardates, though all indicate a higher prevalence than in the general population.

What is true, of course, is that one must take into account the stresses from an environment organized primarily for the non-deviant youngster. Before his defective development has been accurately identified, the retarded child experiences a host of inappropriate demands for higher levels of performance, judgment, and impulse control that lie within his capacity. Even after retardation has been established, such youngsters continue to face situations in which their inability to function in accord with age expectancy is met by displeasure and statements of disapproval. As a result of such stresses, the retarded child can be considered at risk for the development of behavioral disorders. It is the child who develops disorders that is likely to come to psychiatric attention.

Of crucial importance is the fact that behavior which is abnormal in terms of a child's chronological age may be appropriate to his mental age. In that case, the behavioral deviance can be understood primarily in terms of the slowness in cognition. Parents are often confused about this. They may be aware that their 12-year-old son is intellectually unable to assimilate formal learning, and yet may complain that he needs excessive help in dressing, whines if he is denied what he wishes, and prefers playing with the 5-year-old children in the sandbox. This youngster is at an integrated 5-year-old level both cognitively and behaviorally. To reduce the risk that this child will develop a secondary behavior disorder, it is necessary to revise the inappropriate expectations and demands. In this respect, the technique of parent guidance is to be classified as preventive psychiatric treatment. (I shall say more about this later.)

2. Mental retardation with behavior disorder due to brain damage.

The presence of brain damage does not in itself necessarily mean that there will be disordered behavior. Some youngsters with clinically demonstrable brain damage, as evidenced by the various types of congenital cerebral palsy, may be behaviorally well adjusted. Others may show a wide range of behaviors that are direct symptoms of faulty cerebral functioning. Similarly, retarded children with brain damage may exhibit such diverse symptoms of organic dysfunction as hyper- or hypo-motility, brevity or excessive length of attention span, high distractibility or imperviousness to environmental stimuli, hyperirritability or hypoirritability, lability of mood or monotonous sameness, excessive dependence on people or inappropriate independence. Obsessive thoughts and compulsive behaviors are also to be seen in such children, as manifested in repetitive questions, stereotyped gestures, or mechanically rhythmic body movements.

Some of these symptoms can be modified by psychopharmacologic agents. It may be possible, for example, to decrease activity, increase attention span, lessen emotional lability, and ameliorate depression through a drug regimen. In large part, however, the treatment of organically determined symptoms involves milieu therapy; that is, organizing a way of life with appropriately modified expectations that take into account the child's vulnerabilities as well as his abilities. Thus, the child with short attention span should be presented with new demands only in brief teaching episodes; the hyperirritable child must be shielded from intense scolding; the hypoactive child be given intense stimulation.

3. Mental retardation with reactive disorder.

When the retarded child enters the world of his peers, the social meaning of his slowness begins to take form. Even if he escapes being made fun of in his preschool years, his inability to keep up in the area of formal learning will make him a target for jeers in the classroom. The child's parents, reluctant to accept his handicap, may handle him inappropriately. Misunderstanding his capacity, embarrassed about community reaction, they may keep the child from joining groups made up of his intellectual peers.

It is not surprising that intellectually handicapped children tend to build up a host of defensive behavior patterns. Retarded children, like the rest of us, may be happy or sad, aggressive or docile, adventurous or timid. But an unhealthy interaction between child and environment can distort feelings, turning happiness into clowning, sadness into depression. Either docility or aggression may become a way of life, and timidity may be converted to fear and anxiety.

Unfortunately, we do not have nearly enough systematic information on the factors responsible for the development of behavioral disturbances in mentally retarded children. A great deal has been written on the influence of emotional factors on intellectual functioning, but very little on the effect that mental retardation may have upon psychological functioning and personality development. The influence of parents on the retarded child's emotional life has been extensively described, but one-sidedly in terms of acceptance versus rejection of the child and the effect of guilt and anxiety feelings.

That parental love and acceptance are essential for the healthy psychological development of any child is well established. But it is a dangerous simplification to jump to the conclusion that parental love can always overcome the stressful effects of all difficulties confronting the child. Parents of retarded children must cope with special demands of time, energy, emotional giving, ingenuity in planning, and money. To offer parents the illusory hope that these stresses will disappear with love and acceptance can lead only to cruel disappointment, confusion, and self-blame.

In planning a therapeutic program for retarded children with reactive behavior disorders, one must identify the specific functioning of the child that has led to and exacerbated the negative interaction of child and environment. One must define the aspects of behavioral organization that bear on the child's capacity to respond to environmental demands.

Few attempts have been made to do this in a systematic way. One such attempt is a research project that I have directed for the past five years under a grant from the National Institute of Mental Health. We have been studying a sample of 52 retarded children living at home with their middle-class intact families. The chronological ages of the children range from 5 ½ to 11 ½ years; their IQ scores from 50 to 75; and their mental ages from 4 to 6 years. All the children attend special classes in public and private schools. The nature of the sample has been advantageous for the purpose of identifying features of behavioral organization that bear a relationship to mental abnormality as such. It has been possible to exclude a number of variables that could contaminate the behavioral findings. Such possible contaminating variables include: a) environmental stress produced by marginal economic status or family disorganization; b) past failure to diagnose the existence of retardation, resulting in a history of unrealistic demands and expectations; c) institutionalization, which may in itself affect behavioral development; and d) the existence of significant degrees of motor handicap or physical stigmata, which may create special stresses in attempts at environmental mastery and social functioning.

Thirty-one children were diagnosed as having a behavior problem. Of these, nine had behavior problems that were direct symptoms of cerebral dysfunction, 19 had reactive behavior disorders, two had neurotic behavior disorders, and one was psychotic.

One striking finding has been the frequency with which professional workers consulted by the family had avoided the diagnosis of mental retardation. This phenomenon became evident as we established contact with special schools, recreational facilities, and organizations for mentally retarded children, and as we received reports from psychiatrists, psychologists, social workers, and educators. Parents had often been told that the child's basic problem was one of emotional disturbance and that the mental retardation was a secondary phenomenon; i.e., our old friend "pseudo retardation." In general, the professional literature deals with the problem of parents who refuse to accept the diagnosis of retardation in their child. Very little attention, however, is given to the problem of professional workers who show this bias in favor of a diagnosis of emotional disturbance.

We also found to our surprise that there is a widespread lack of understanding that the *degree* of intellectual retardation is a significant factor in determining the child's adaptive capacities and potential for coping with the demands of his environment. This would appear to be self-evident, but we have noted many instances in which psychiatrists and social workers gave guidance and treatment without obtaining a reliable psychometric evaluation.

To determine the children's levels of functioning in self-care, socialization, play, etc., we found it necessary to distinguish between the level of habitual functioning and the child's actual capacity. This differentiation is not made in the performance scales currently in use, such as the Vineland Maturity Scale. Our data indicate that this distinction is an important one. For example, a child was reported by the parent to be able to dress himself completely. However, this was not a routine accomplishment but possible only under optimum conditions at home. At school, faced with many distractions and noise, the child required help. Overestimation of a youngster's abilities, by confusing his highest level of functioning with his routine level, may lead to excessive expectations and demands. On the other hand, exclusive consideration of the child's routine abilities may lead to an underestimation of his capacities and the setting of inadequate goals.

Among the significant factors entering into any child-environment interactional process is the attribute of temperament. This term refers to a child's characteristic style of reaction to varied situations of day-to-day living. That children differ in their characteristic reactions, even in the newborn state, has been generally recognized. However, little systematic study has been devoted to the delineation of these typical reaction patterns and the elucidation of their significance for psychological development.

Together with my colleagues Dr. Alexander Thomas and Dr. Herbert Birch, I have been concerned for a number of years with a longitudinal study of 136 children, the results of which have just been published in a book, *Temperament and Behavior Disorders in Children.* We have been able to define individuality in temperament from 2 months of age onward in terms of 9 characteristics: rhythmicity or regularity of biological functions, activity level, initial reaction to a new stimulus (approach-withdrawal) adaptability, intensity of reaction, threshold of responsiveness, quality of mood, distractibility, attention span and persistence. These temperamental qualities have been found to enter significantly into determining the normal child's responses to child-care practices and to intra- and extra-familial environmental demands.

The behavioral records in the study of 52 retarded children has shown that these youngsters, too, can be characterized in terms of the 9 categories. Qualitative analysis of the data in the children with behavioral disturbances indicates quite clearly that temperamental factors play a significant role in the development of such disturbances, in interaction with environmental stresses and, in some cases, the special behavioral consequences of brain damage.

To illustrate, one child had frequent tantrums which expressed a characteristically negative response to the new and unfamiliar. The parents dealt with this problem by shielding her from new experiences. She had few tantrums, but the lack of new stimuli and learning experiences resulted in a level of functioning below her potential capacity. The parents were advised to expose her to selectively graded new situations by stages and gently, and to expect tantrums the first few times. With this appropriate management, the child was given the optimally structured learning atmosphere for her temperament and intellectual level.

Another child, on the other hand, adapted quickly to new situations and functioned easily with simple routine tasks. He was also an extremely persistent child, and this, in combination with his retarded level of learning, resulted in his sticking to a difficult task in a perseverative, repetitive fashion without mastery. As a consequence, his IQ level gradually decreased from a score of 75 at 6 years to one of 57 at age 9 years, 6 months, and he also developed a number of perseverative behavior patterns. Treatment involved guiding his parents and teachers to divide every new task into small sequential segments, each of which he could master in turn and then pass on to the next segment.

It should be noted that in some cases diminished intellectual function may be a consequence of a reactive behavior disorder. For example, a child may react directly to an abrupt shift in environmental circumstances by developing a defensive maneuver of intellectual immobility. Thus one Negro child from the South having his first classroom contact with a white teacher in the North was frightened into temporary paralysis of his learning ability. Another youngster, who was very shy, was shocked into protective immobility by a shouting teacher, only to return to good functioning with a soft-spoken teacher.

4. Mental retardation with neurotic behavior disorder.

While the reactive behavior disorders can be modified by altering the environmental organization, neurotic behavior disorders show more firmly fixed patterns and may not be so amenable to change. Neurotic manifestations may reflect anxieties or defenses against anxiety. The child may be fearful in all new situations or in specific types of situations. He may have phobic reactions or rigid attitudes inappropriate to the intentions or actions of those around him.

In all cases, however, one must guard against misinterpreting acts that are appropriate to a given mental age as neurotic behavior in a retarded child. These acts may appear to reflect neurotic attitudes only because they are incongruous with a youngster's actual age and physical appearance.

For the mentally retarded child who is indeed neurotic, direct psychotherapy may be advisable. Although psychotherapy is not commonly recommended for mentally retarded children, I can report a measure of success with this approach. To be sure, the techniques of psychotherapy with normal children require modifications for effective application to retarded youngsters. The goals of such treatment must be individualized, with full recognition that the child will continue to function on a retarded level. It is important that we do not give false hopes to the parents, who are sufficiently traumatized and bewildered by their problems without these being added to iatrogenically.

However, in many cases the anxiety and fears of retarded children can be alleviated, no matter how limited the child's intelligence, so that he can be included in some facsimile of normal family life. In general, the child's intellectual level will determine whether it is possible to reach him in conceptual terms, or whether relationship therapy or some form of conditioning will be more effective.

Strong, deep-set neurotic defenses may cause poor use of a child's intellectual capacity. If this is severely inhibited, the functioning level of the child may be that of mental retardation. The average child is keenly interested in the world around him and has spent his preschool life in very active learning experiences. But if his experience in the course of eager exploration has created the concept that the world is a dangerous place, he may feel that safety lies in sticking to the tried and proved, an attitude that interferes with the acquisition of knowledge and gives the impression of incapacity to learn. Similarly, a child who has found that mistakes are not to be tolerated may be so afraid to hazard a guess that he will not reach out for new experiences. An extreme degree of competitiveness or fear of authority figures may interfere with the learning process. A sense of inferiority engendered by rivalry with a sibling who is alert and obviously smart may cause a youngster to take for himself the role of the stupid one. These and a host of other neurotic mechanisms may be the cause of retarded function in a child of normal or better than normal capacity. In such cases, adequate treatment of the neurotic difficulty may result in more successful use of the intellectual potential. By the same token, a retarded child may be functioning below his capacity as a result of neurotic defenses, and successful treatment would enable him to function at a higher retarded level.

5. *Mental retardation with psychosis.*

With the coexistence of subnormal intellectual functioning and childhood psychosis, the decision as to which is to be considered primary and which secondary is often purely semantic and non-determinative of treatment plans or goals. For the youngster with an effective disorder of the autistic type, one may postulate that the achievement of increased awareness of the people and activities around him would result in better cognitive functioning. Planned stimuli in this direction would indeed be appropriate treatment. This can be attempted through enrollment of the child in a recreation group, specified parental interaction, speech, music, or dance therapy, or direct psychotherapy. How much any of these programs will accomplish, however, may depend on the severity and irreversibility of the syndrome, factors about which our knowledge is still limited. Other children with both psychosis and subnormal cognitive functioning may require treatment designed to give them maximum superimposition of structure with a view to limiting their freely wandering flights of thought and activity.

In recent years, much attention has been focused on childhood schizophrenia as a cause of retardation. We have long lists of youngsters whose condition is diagnosed as "childhood schizophrenia." The belief that schizophrenia is relatively treatable is so firmly held by parents, as well as some professional groups, that the psychiatrist is often pressured into replacing a diagnosis of mental retardation by one of childhood schizophrenia. Inattention and unresponsiveness to the environment is called "autism," peculiarities of speech and motility are dubbed "bizarre," an occasional response of obvious relevance and logic is seen as a "flash of normal intelligence," and a diagnosis is born which is invoked almost as a magic talisman to ward off the evil of permanent disability.

It is certainly true that a portion of the population in institutions for the mentally retarded are basically schizophrenic and functional retardates. Since learning requires communication of knowledge from one person to another, a severe interference with interpersonal communication will decrease one's ability to learn. The highest degree of this difficulty is found in autistic youngsters.

But it is sometimes difficult to make a differential diagnosis. A retarded child may have a vacant look in his eyes that may make him appear to be autistic. But his failure to respond does not necessarily mean autistic in the sense that he is self-preoccupied. It may merely mean that his degree of retardation is such that he does not have the capacity to react to certain external stimuli. Such terms as autism, echolalia, and echopraxia have become so firmly associated with childhood schizophrenia that they impede careful thinking. Once a child has been described as exhibiting echolalia, the diagnosis of schizophrenia has to all intents and purposes been made. The fact that echolalia is a normal way of learning speech and that it is therefore not unexpected in a retardate who is mastering speech may easily be forgotten in the reliance on the presumed pathognomonic symptom.

In our study of 52 retarded children we observed that their language functioning was more retarded than their non-verbal behavior. Also notable in our sample was the degree to which speech was repetitive, perseverative, and stereotyped, even though other aspects of their behavior were organized and affectively responsive. Since there is a penchant for using such verbal indices to diagnose emotional disturbance and autism, it is important to note their presence in psychiatrically normal but mentally retarded children. If these speech characteristics are automatically assumed to be signs of emotional disorder or disorganization of thought process, there is a great danger that psychiatric treatment will be arranged for a child who really needs an effective educational and management program.

While much perseverative verbal behavior is to be found in both retarded and autistic children, there are essential differences in the kind of repetition as well as in the behavioral context. Autistic repetition appears to have no aim beyond the activity itself and resembles the pre-intentional behavior patterns which occur in early infancy of normal children, whereas the delayed echolalia of retarded children does have some relevance and is less purely a matter of lifting phrases out of context and repeating them. Schizophrenic children show affective withdrawal and deficient socialization, but the retarded children in our study tried to convey ideas, had competence in the tasks of daily living, and displayed appropriate affectivity.

A grossly retarded child may appear bizarre. The incongruity between physical appearance and aimless running about or repetitive actions can be very striking. But if the observed behavior of a retarded child would seem appropriate in a child of a younger chronological age, then it cannot accurately be called bizarre.

Nor does the existence of single repetitive pattern mean that the child is autistic. The same child may be observed helping his mother put the groceries away and participate in all sorts of sensitive social acts. This is not a schizophrenic child, but a retarded youngster with peculiar habit patterns.

It must also be remembered that childhood schizophrenia is itself not a single disease, and its treatability varies. Even if a child is correctly transferred from the retardate to the schizophrenic group, the prognosis may not be altered. In any case, the issue is not whether the diagnosis makes the prognosis more hopeful, but whether the diagnosis is correct. If a retarded child is treated for schizophrenia, appropriate plans for management and vocational guidance may be unnecessarily postponed.

In conclusion, I would like to emphasize that the diagnosis of retardation and the degree of severity should be conveyed to parents without camouflage. The prevention and treatment of emotional problems of the retarded child requires an orientation toward using the parent as a colleague. The important therapeutic procedure that has crystallized out of our studies consists of a new approach to parent guidance. While an extensive literature does exist on the counseling of parents of retarded children, it concentrates, as I have indicated, on helping parents accept their retarded child and on parental anxiety and guilt.

Our approach to parent guidance has been quite different. To begin with, we make a detailed inventory of the data available for each child including 1) IQ level and any special characteristics of perceptual and cognitive functioning revealed by the psychometric testing; 2) the level of functioning in various activities of daily living—both the maximum and the habitual level; 3) temperamental characteristics; 4) learning pattern, including the manner in which the child himself identified errors and sought to correct them, as well as his response to correction by others; 5) patterns of parental practices and techniques of dealing with the child's problems; 6) special intra- or extra- familial environmental stresses; and 7) pertinent features of medical, neurological, and psychiatric examinations.

We evaluate the child's problems in terms of the interrelationship and interactions of these factors. On the basis of this analysis, the discussion with the parents focuses on making them aware of the demands and expectations that are easy, difficult, or impossible for the child to master. A program of activity is then laid out with the goal of increasing the child's ability to master difficult demands and to cope with stress through an alteration in parental functioning. The extent of this program is of course contingent on an estimate of the parents' capacities to follow concrete directions for change in their handling and on their ability to maintain a new approach consistently.

With only a few exceptions, the parents have responded favorably to this program. While generalizations regarding acceptance of the retarded child may be useful, they are of limited value. I believe that a program of altered parental function, spelled out concretely and based on an analysis of the individual child-environment interaction, offers useful possibilities for helping the retarded child cope most constructively with the special stresses and demands in his life.

TWENTY-ONE

Family Processes in Mental Retardation

D. RUSSELL DAVIS

Lecturing 101 years after his birth, I belong to a generation to whom Adolf Meyer was a grandfather. Many of our teachers had been taught by Adolf Meyer. *Henderson* and *Gillespie* and *Muncie* were our textbooks. Psychopathology became my special interest through the influence of John Thompson MacCurdy, for nine years (1913-1922) an assistant to August Hoch at Ward's Island and then Lecturer in Psychopathology at the University of Cambridge.

We were fortunate in that for our teachers, discussion of psychopathology was not just an academic exercise, but the means by which therapy might be made more effective. The questions "Why has this patient become ill?" and "Why at this time?" led on to the questions "What can be done for him?" and "What could have been done to prevent his illness?"

We were taught in the tradition of psychobiology to look for answers in the history, not so much in what the patient is by reason of his genetical constitution but in what have been his circumstances. What has happened to him? What have been the crucial experiences? Especially, what attachments has he made? What has happened to these attachments? The findings are summarized in the style of Adolf Meyer in a life chart, which shows at a glance when there were crises in the family.

Social Policy and Theory

First observations, then conclusions, Adolf Meyer used to insist. But before the facts comes the theory, which decides what observations we make, what facts we seek to establish. Our choice of theory, whatever we may like to think, is liable to depend not on the sober evaluation of the experimental evidence but on attitudes which are essentially political. The theory is thus a set of assumptions, justified by their relevance and usefulness in rationalizing and making more efficient social movements to reform.

The theory dominating research throughout the last quarter of the last and the first quarter of this century attributed mental retardation to the inheritance of an

From *American Journal of Psychiatry*, Vol. 124, No. 3 (September, 1967), pp. 340-350. By permission of the author and the *Journal*. Copyright 1967, the American Psychiatric Association.

inferior constitution. The mentally handicapped were regarded as being of inferior stock and owing their survival to a civilization which prevented the struggle for existence and natural selection from following their normal course. The evidence brought forward to justify the theory, notably by Galton in England and Goddard in America, is now seen to be equivocal and inconclusive. Much of it was assembled after the influence of the theory had begun to decline. Yet the theory explained and supported the social policies which led to the establishment before the First World War of the special hospitals where the mentally handicapped could be cared for over long periods.

The inheritance theory gave meaning to such terms as mental defect, oligophrenia, and subnormality, put the emphasis on the familial occurrence of cases and the constancy of the I.Q., and supposed that inferiority is congenital and lifelong. Adolf Meyer seems to have accepted the theory without serious questioning, although he did issue the warning: "Mental abnormalities are frequently, too frequently perhaps, attributed to heredity" (8, p. 325). He had little to say about the "oligergasias," which he concluded were "implastic and nonmodifiable" (9, p. 124). Psychobiology has contributed little to the study of mental defect, as Sir Aubrey Lewis (5) pointed out in the Adolf Meyer Lecture of 1960. The more positive attitudes towards treatment it encouraged in other branches of psychiatry were not extended to cases of mental retardation.

The time is ripe for a reappraisal. The political climate has been changing rapidly during the last two decades. In the U.K., less advanced economically and industrially, the inheritance theory has been held to more strongly than in America and has retained its predominance longer. One turning point came in 1941 with Gregg's demonstration of the association of rubella in the first trimester with mental defect. This served as a sharp reminder that mental defect could be the result not of an inferior constitution but of what had happened to the child. It reawakened interest in the causes of damage within the uterus, at or near birth, or in the first year or two of life. Infection, trauma, or error of metabolism have been identified as causes in a substantial minority of cases, but for the majority, the undifferentiated, without detectable organic defect or metabolic error, resort is still made to the inheritance theory, sometimes for lack of any better alternative.

There are alternative theories. Maudsley (7, pp. 341-342) indicated one in a famous passage about those causes of "non-congenital idiocy without physical defects" which he supposed lie in epileptic convulsions, syphilis, febrile diseases, bad food and starvation, toxic effects of soothing narcotic syrups, and interestingly, "the shock of fright and the violent emotion." He went on:

> There is no remedy notwithstanding that its victims may be bright-looking, well-shapen in body and features, without deformity of any sort, for the injury done to the very fine tissues of the brain and their occult molecular processes, although impenetrable by our most subtle means of research, is still so serious as to be irreparable.

Brain mythology? Or promising line for biochemical research? There is another theory more appropriate to the setting in which contemporary psychiatrists work.

This setting is very different from what it was. Perhaps the greatest achievement of the 1950s—one that would have pleased Adolf Meyer—lay in the incorporation of psychiatric hospitals of all kinds into mental health services which have made care in the community their main concern. The problems immediately in front of us in the U.K., and likely to preoccupy us during the next decade and longer, lie in the transformation of a variety of more or less independent, but overlapping services for individuals, whether children, adults, or elderly—patients, offenders, or indigent—into an integrated service which provides for families as units and which strengthens the capacity of families to retain within themselves their disabled members.

Family Processes

For the support and instruction of this policy, we need to work out with some urgency a new psychopathology which gives due weight to the part played in causing and perpetuating disabilities by psychosocial processes in the family and which indicates how these processes may be modified by treatment.

Of course, psychosocial processes in the family are not the only causes of mental retardation. Every modern theory accepts that causes are diverse. Causes of several kinds may cooperate to produce retardation. Psychosocial causes are likely to be of the greatest importance in "undifferentiated" cases in which evidence of organic and metabolic abnormality and sensory defect is lacking.

They should not be assumed to be of little importance when there is unmistakable evidence of other causes. They may play a part in these cases too, for often the degree of retardation is out of proportion to the organic defect. However, an exclusive concern with psychosocial processes is permissible in this lecture. It is convenient, although not strictly necessary, to restrict consideration to undifferentiated cases. What we learn from these cases may be applied in other cases.

There are two types of theory which explain how psychosocial processes may affect the rate and pattern of mental development. One is the *stimulation* theory, the other, the *disorder* theory.

The stimulation theory—the characteristic theory of North America in the mid-20th century—supposes that the rate and pattern of mental retardation may result from lack of stimulation, lack of opportunities, or deprivation. This theory tends to be associated with political attitudes that the community should do more to create stimulating conditions for its young children and to provide for the deprived. It has much to offer towards the explanation of intellectual and educational retardation of lesser degree.

The Disorder Theory

The disorder theory(4), which governs this account, reflects the political attitudes that have led to the social welfare movement in the U.K. during the last two decades. It regards mental retardation as the result of disorder in mental processes, this disorder being the result of the failure of the family to give sufficient protection from stress (i.e., overstimulation)·during the critical periods of learning in early childhood.

Protection of the young child from stress depends upon the *security system,* of which the mother is usually the key member, and to which contributions are made by the father and others, perhaps grandparents, especially the mother's mother, aunts, older sibs, neighbors, and family friends. If the security system is weak or disorganized, the young child is subjected to stresses, to which he reacts in various ways in attempts to adapt.

Some of the facts are explained by all three theories. A disproportionate number of cases of undifferentiated mental retardation come from families of low social status or of abnormal composition or that function badly in other respects. The inheritance theory explains this fact by supposing that the parents, themselves poorly endowed genetically, transmit unfavorable combinations of genes to their children. The stimulation theory supposes that such families provide poor conditions for learning, a poor discipline for their young children. The disorder theory supposes that they give inadequate protection to their young children, who tend to suffer also from bronchitis, pneumonia, and infective diarrhea and to sustain accidents with undue frequency. Moreover, they tend to be alienated and socially isolated, and hence to be denied the support of neighbors and friends.

The theories are not in conflict. To choose one is not to deny the validity of the others. But the choice does decide to what aspects of cases attention is directed. The disorder theory refers to processes rather than states, and processes in families as well as in individuals. It does not prescribe the age at which the disorder arises, or whether the onset is acute or insidious. It allows that the onset may be after birth. It explains why there is variety in the patterns of disorder and relates the pattern to the age and the character of the stresses.

It supposes that the processes may be modified by circumstances or through treatment. It turns attention to the experiences associated with slowing of development and to the factors which tend to weaken the security system or make the child vulnerable in other ways. It explains also why cases of severe retardation of undifferentiated type occur in families of good status which provide adequate stimulation and educational opportunities and why one child in a family may be affected, and others escape.

Sensitive Learning Periods

Theories attributing retardation to unfavorable circumstances are not new. A theory like this guided Itard who, in the political climate of France after the revolution at the end of the 18th century, undertook the training of Victor, the wild boy from the woods of Aveyron. The argument against these theories is still that used by the more conservative Pinel, that the improvement made when the child is removed into more favorable circumstances tends to be small. Victor's behavior did improve in many respects, but he did not learn to use language except for a few words.

Yet to expect improvement is to take too simple a view towards learning in early childhood and to neglect important characteristics of it. It is not necessary to assume, as Pinel did, that those who can learn do so whatever the circumstances and that those who have not learned have been unlucky, not in their circumstances, but in their endowment or in being handicapped by brain disease. On the contrary, the conditions in which learning takes place in early childhood are probably much more specific than has been supposed.

To describe the limitation of learning in time, Tinbergen, Lorenz, and others have introduced the concept of sensitive (or critical) periods. Thus for some habits there appear to be optimal periods during which learning proceeds rapidly, although at other times the habits are learned only slowly or not at all. Once the optimal period has passed, the capacity to acquire the habit wanes. There are authenticated examples from animal studies. As they become sexually mature, dogs, for instance, learn territory habits rapidly. The first copulation, the first defense of territory, and the first avoidance of strange territory may all occur within a week(14).

If there are sensitive learning periods in man, as there appear to be, then a child may fail to learn when removed into favorable circumstances because the sensitive period had passed, just as, to takeThorpe's (13) example, chaffinches prove incapable of learning songs if they are kept in isolation until after they are 13 months old. Too late is no better than no opportunity at all.

Normally the young child attaches himself to his mother during a sensitive period beginning in the third quarter of the first year(12). If he fails to do so then, for one reason or another, his capacity to form attachments appears to decline. Normally he learns to listen and to discriminate speech sounds towards the end of the first year; this sensitive period probably does not extend much beyond the end of the second year.

Learning proceeds rapidly at certain times, probably because of special conditions which do not recur. A child learns to speak in his second year, perhaps because the need to do so arises when his growing powers of locomotion take him away from his mother, with whom he then has to communicate across space, and bring him into contact with strangers. If he fails to learn to speak at this time, he may learn other ways of dealing with the anxieties these experiences arouse. He may then turn away from social contacts.

Why the capacity to learn declines becomes a crucial question but one that may prove difficult to answer immediately. The first task is perhaps to define more precisely the conditions in which learning can take place. If this can be achieved, it may be possible to go on to discover how to recreate the conditions for those who have not learned.

Learning proceeds rapidly when a habit first appears. If it is arrested because circumstances are unfavorable, it tends not to be resumed after the optimal period has passed, even when circumstances have returned to normal. Habits are thus vulnerable while they are being acquired and before they become established.

Adverse circumstances may lead not only to failure to acquire the habit but also to its regression if it has recently been acquired. Skills disintegrate. A child who has been speaking becomes mute. One who has gained control over urination starts to wet again. A two-year-old child may stop talking, begin again to wet his bed, and cling again to his mother after a stay in the hospital, or a family move, the birth of a sib, or other disturbance in the family.

The pattern of the disorder of development depends upon the stage reached when adverse circumstances make their impact. Knowing which functions are preserved and which affected, the clinical investigator may arrive at a hypothesis stating the age at which development became disordered. Hypotheses so arrived at tend to be confirmed by the histories given by the parents.

A Series of 50 Cases

In order to illustrate this lecture, I have taken a series of 50 cases. Every child has been examined by me at the Bristol Royal Hospital for Sick Children before he or she had reached the seventh birthday. The intelligence quotient of each child was less than 75. Cases were excluded in which there was unequivocal evidence of organic defect or metabolic abnormality, of birth weight less than 2.5 kg., or complications of delivery or postnatal signs.

The series is thus one of cases of undifferentiated mental retardation. A diagnosis of psychosis or autism might have been made in some cases. Incidentally, the disorder theory resolves the problem of the relationship of psychosis to mental defect by supposing that psychotic processes may play a part in any case of retardation. Sticking to the broad term disorder, we can avoid using the terms psychosis and autism.

There were 36 boys and 14 girls. The median age at referral was 49 months, the median I.Q. about 55. There was a significantly greater proportion of firstborn than in the general population in England and Wales. The mean maternal age at birth (25.1 years) was close to the mean in the general population.

AGE AT ONSET

Of the 50 children, 22 had been sitting without support at seven months, and of these, 18 had been walking without help at 15 months. Nine had also established full control over urination by day before their second birthday. Judging by the ages at which these milestones were passed, slowing up or arrest in development had occurred in 28 cases before the age of seven months, in another four cases before the age of 15 months, and in another nine before the age of 24 months. The onset in the remaining nine was after the second birthday.

As Table 1 shows, the timing of the onset in this way agrees well with the timing based on the answers given by the mothers to the question "At what age do you think his development began to fall behind?" The series thus contained a number of cases in which there was evidence of normal progress up to a certain age; this could be specified more or less precisely.

Full records are available of the examination of Lucy, for instance, when a few days after her first birthday she was removed to a foster home because her mother had to be admitted to a hospital for what was probably a depressive illness. Lucy was found to be a normal child; she was walking and speaking, with a vocabulary of a few words. Her development ceased, and there may have been some regression. She was reunited with her mother after about three months, and progress was resumed after a while. Her I.Q. at about five years of age was 65.

TABLE 1 AGE OF CHILD AT ONSET OF RETARDATION

In Mother's Opinion	*As Judged by the Passing of Milestones*				
	Before 7 Months	*7-15 Months*	*16-24 Months*	*After 24 Months*	*Total*
Before 7 months	25		1		26
7-15 months	1	3	1		5
16-24		1	5		6
25-36 months	2		2	6	10
After 36 months				3	3
Total	28	4	9	9	50

When James was 22 months old, his brother died after an illness of about six weeks, during which James was largely neglected. He had hitherto been regarded as a lively boy whose development was well up to his age. He became mute and did not speak again until immediately after the first consultation at 49 months of age. At five years, his I.Q. was about 60.

Arrests occurring after seven months of age are more easily dated precisely than those occurring earlier. The evidence tends to be clearest when the arrest is relatively late, but there is one case in the series of arrest at 14 weeks old, when the infant developed what was thought to be an allergy to cow's milk and was admitted to the hospital.

Arrests in the first year affected sitting up and walking. About half the children did not walk until after 18 months; one-fifth, not until after 24 months. Yet once the children started walking, they made rapid progress and became normally agile so far as could be assessed by the methods available. Other psychomotor functions showed a similar tendency to improve rapidly. In more than half the cases the establishment of handedness was delayed until the age of four or five years, and as is usual, a disproportionate number, about a fifth, were then either ambidextrous or left-handed.

Arrests after the first birthday affected language, social behavior, and control of urination especially. Failure to comprehend speech appears to be associated with arrest in the first year and did not seem to improve. These children did not listen and were largely or wholly inattentive to speech. Those who had acquired habits of listening might stop talking, as did Lucy and James, but begin again after a while. Disorganization of speech without muteness appears to be associated with arrests in the third and fourth year. The establishment of habits of control over urination was delayed in nearly all the cases, except in those in which the arrest had not taken place until after the second birthday.

EVENTS ASSOCIATED WITH ARRESTS

There were 22 cases in which the parents mentioned one or more events as having been associated with arrest, slowing up, or distortion in development.

Illness was mentioned in nine cases (in five of which the child was admitted to a hospital). Convulsions occurred in three cases.

The birth of a sib was cited in eight cases. In six of these cases the patient was the first child and the sib the second.

Separation from the mother occurred in five cases, in every one because of her admission to a hospital.

Loss of other significant person was cited in five cases (death of or removal from maternal grandmother—three; death of sib—one; death of playmate—one).

Other crises in the family were mentioned in five cases.

No such events were mentioned in the majority of cases. The events mentioned by the minority were mundane and within the experience of many normal children. Two out of three firstborn children have the experience of the birth of a second child into the family. Admission to hospital has been the experience of one in five children of five years of age in the U.K. It is not unusual for a young family to remove from a grandmother's home. It would hardly be reasonable, therefore, to argue that the events associated with arrests constituted stress of unusual severity, even if the arrests had been associated with a combination of events. Some authorities reject the idea that events like those mentioned are causal in any way and regard them as coincidental.

Yet such experiences as separation from mother, move to another home, admission to the hospital, or the birth of a sib do appear to have significant, even if ordinarily short-lived, effects on the behavior of some children. Development is generally resumed within a few days, but the effects may be more persistent.

Events like those mentioned cannot be dismissed as coincidental only and may be held to be causal of arrest, delay, or distortion in development. But if this view is to be sustained, it has also to be supposed that the children affected are especially vulnerable by reason of their genetic constitution, their previous experience, or the way in which their reactions to the events are managed. The events hold perhaps some interest as indicating the nature of the child's vulnerability.

THE FAMILIES

In nearly every case the mother was depressed at the time of the first consultation and gave a history which suggested that she had been more or less depressed for the greater part of the child's life. An immediate benefit of the consultation was often the restoration in some degree of the mother's morale and optimism. It is hardly surprising that depression was the general rule, since persistent failure of a child to thrive imposes serious stress on the parents.

Few would doubt the generality of the finding of depression, but some would argue that the main significance of the depression is as a reaction to the realization of the child's abnormality. Yet depression cannot be so readily dismissed as an effect of the retardation. It is surely reasonable to suppose also that it reduces the capacity of the parents to provide favorable conditions for the child to learn. Moreover, it is likely to weaken the security system. There is a vicious circle, the retardation of the child adding to the depression of the parents and thus producing conditions in which the retardation becomes worse.

The important question is: are there causes for the parent's depression preceding or lying outside the child's retardation? To pose the problem differently, Bowlby (2), among others, has argued persuasively that the essential condition for the mental health and development of the child is "a warm, intimate and continuous relationship with his mother in which both find satisfaction and enjoyment." Are there factors which reduce the capacity of the mothers of retarded children to form such a relationship?

In order to find answers to this question, we depend on the histories the mothers give of themselves, supplemented by the histories the fathers and other informants give. Did the mother resolve the conflicts with her parents during adolescence in such a degree and in such a way that she became free to transfer her affections from her father to her husband? Did she become reconciled with her parents so that she has been able to receive and accept the help and support of her kin in caring for the child? Has she had the support of her husband? Is it a good marriage? Did the revival of conflicts prevent her from forming a good relationship with the child during the critical period of the puerperium?

The histories tend to show that there have been conflictful attitudes towards marriage, childbearing, and care of the child before the child was recognized as being retarded. One or both parents may have grown up in disturbed circumstances. Adolescence may have been stormy, or unresolved conflicts may have existed in relationships with their parents.

The marriage may have been contracted for unsatisfactory reasons, to get away from an unhappy home, for instance, or on the rebound, because of a pregnancy, or as an attempt to solve other problems. A parent may have suffered from a psychiatric illness. The marriage may have been in difficulties; separation may have been considered. The pregnancy may have been unwelcome. An attempt may have been made to bring it to an end, illegally or by seeking a therapeutic termination. A parent may have become depressed during the puerperium. Mother and child may have been separated at this time.

Do the parents of retarded children differ from the general run of parents in these respects? A confident answer cannot be given for several reasons. Comparable information is not easily obtained from normal parents. Suitable control groups are not easily assembled for this and other reasons. Some of the factors to which significance is attached cannot be defined precisely enough to make comparisons possible. Certainly more studies are required before conclusions are reached. However, a few findings can be brought forward in support of the hypothesis that the families of retarded children do differ from those of normal children in respects relevant to the disorder theory.

I shall not try to review here a diffuse field (but see 3), and shall do no more than to report a few findings as illustrations of the kind of evidence that might be brought forward.

Mismatching. It is well known that husbands and wives tend to be similar to one another in respect to age, country of origin, religion, social class, education, and intelligence, i.e., to show homogamy. In nine of the 50 cases in the series, husband and wife had grown up in different countries (e.g., England and Germany, England and Italy, Lebanon and England). This is found in less than five percent of other cases attending the clinic, and the association of retardation and mismatching in this respect is a significant one statistically.

There is also an excess of cases in which there was mismatching in other repects, such as age, although this association was not significant. The reasons for going far afield in choosing a spouse are likely to be complex, and any interpretation of the finding is speculative.

Relationship between mother and maternal grandfather. Over and over again in the clinical investigation of these cases, the mothers told of serious difficulties in the marriage before as well as after the birth of the patient. One way of seeking to understand why a woman has met difficulties in her marriage is to ask her about her relationship with her father during her adolescence. In a high proportion of the cases her relationship had been terminated by his death or departure, i.e., desertion, separation, or divorce.

Table 2 presents the findings in a systematic form. It will be seen that in more than one-third the relationship had been terminated before her 16th birthday. This proportion may be regarded as unduly high and as corroborating the clinical impressions. Conclusions from data of this kind are of course notoriously uncertain because of the unreliability of the proportions found in control samples.

TABLE 2   RELATIONSHIP OF MOTHER AND HER NATURAL FATHER

Status of Relationship		*Number of cases*
Terminated before age of 11		11
Death	2	
Departure	9	
Terminated during period 11-15		
years of age		6
Death	3	
Departure	3	
		—
		17 (34 percent)
Continued after 16th birthday		30
No information		3
Total		50

Support from maternal grandmother. The maternal grandmother usually plays an important part in the life of a new family and makes a special contribution to the security system of the young children. The new family tends to live near the wife's relatives and to visit her relatives more often than her husband's (e.g., 15). The wife's attachment to her mother tends to be preserved more strongly than any of the other attachments to parents.

Clinical impressions suggest that the mothers of retarded children have had little support from their mothers and other relatives, from whom they have been alienated. Systematic ratings of the support given by the maternal grandmothers have been made on a scheme modified from that used by Elizabeth Bott(1) in her studies on *Family and Social Network*. Support is described as intimate when the maternal grandmother lives nearby and visits frequently, as effective when she is available on call, as ineffective when there is little or no contact, and as unfamiliar when she is not available at all.

Table 3 shows the distribution of ratings in the series of retarded children and, for purposes of comparison, the distribution in a series of children studied under similar conditions who presented with a simple delay in the development of speech without intellectual retardation. Fewer of the families of the retarded, less than one-half, have had effective support from the maternal grandmother. The proportion in the general population is probably about three-quarters.

TABLE 3   SUPPORT TO FAMILY FROM MATERNAL GRANDMOTHER DURING
CHILD'S LIFE FROM BIRTH TO THREE YEARS

Degree of Support	Retarded Children	Simple Delay Control Group
Intimate	3	6
Effective	15	16
Ineffective	17	5
Unfamiliar	7	2
Maternal grandmother dead	3	1
Removed from maternal grandmother during period	2	0
No information	3	0
Total	50	30

$$x^2 = 8.77, p < .01$$

This finding accords with the hypothesis that the security system provided for the retarded children has been inadequate. The clinical evidence suggests that the reasons lie in the relationships within the families, which tend to be strained, rather than in geographical factors.

Prevention

The disorder theory shifts the emphasis from the intellectual defects of retarded children to the disorders they show in social behavior. It is surprising how much emphasis traditional theories have put upon the intellectual defects and how little upon the disorders of social behavior. Many retarded children show a marked detachment, much of their behavior in a social setting being autonomous. They are largely unaffected by the signs of pleasure and displeasure which ordinarily serve as rewards and punishments and thus bring about learning.

Others display a high level of anxiety in all social contacts, and others cling to their mothers and are difficult to separate from them. These and other tendencies make it difficult to establish with a retarded child a relationship that makes cooperative and educative play possible, and serious limitations are placed upon learning.

Not only do retarded children appear to be detached from their mothers, but also the mothers tend to be detached from their children. Sometimes the father or a grandmother or older sister has taken over the mother's usual role in tending the child, more often not.

Are we right when we suppose that the essential failure in mental retardation lies in disorder in social behavior? A substantial amount of experimental and clinical research in man and other mammals over the last two decades has shown that experiences disturbing the normal formation of attachments to mothers or others, or of mothers to the newborn, may have profound effects upon all aspects of development of behavior. These effects may resemble closely those seen in retarded children (6,11).

Bowlby's monograph *Maternal Care and Mental Health,* first published in 1951, gave impetus to this new way of looking at the problem of mental retardation and has had considerable influence. Many of the researches on social behavior in mammals have been widely publicized. Nevertheless, cases in which development is delayed or distorted are still not being referred for investigation of the social processes until very late. In my own series the median age of referral was 49 months.

The reasons for late referral are several. In many cases, general medical practitioners reassure the parents that all will be well. Optimistic opinions appear to be the rule. It still seems to be accepted generally that expert investigation of delay in the development of speech can be postponed until after the third birthday.

In some cases, there is a fatalistic acceptance that the child is mentally defective and that there is nothing to be done. In the U.K. cases tend to be referred first to pediatricians who embark on intensive investigations in a search for rare metabolic abnormalities. In order to facilitate these investigations children, who may be highly vulnerable, are sometimes admitted to a hospital. By the time the disorder in social behavior is recognized as serious, the critical periods in the first and second year have passed.

Risk registers. Inclusion in risk registers—intended to bring about the early detection and diagnosis of disease or defect, if possible before symptoms are noticed by parents—tends to be decided by criteria which are almost exclusively physical (10). Mention is occasionally made of problem families as candidates for inclusion, but little is yet being done to identify the families in which the mother is handicapped by her attitudes or the difficulties in her marriage or by lack of support from kin. Even serious depression of the mother is not always seen as a warning that a young child is at risk.

We need to know much more about the family processes which, when they go wrong, result in retardation. More immediately, we need to spread widely the knowledge we have so that all the nurses, midwives, doctors, health visitors, and others who work with young mothers and infants understand the importance of the mother's attachment to the child and the child's attachment to the mother in promoting the healthy mental development of the infant. We need to direct attention to the organization of the family so that those cases in which the security system is weak are identified early and included in risk registers.

The number of physically stunted children had declined steeply during the last two or three decades. The pale, thin, small child, with discharging ears and adenoidal facies has become exceptional as a result of measures of many kinds: better nutrition, better housing, and better care in many respects.

There are still far too many children who are mentally stunted because of the circumstances in which they are brought up. In the forefront of the tasks of the improved family service lies the support, help, and encouragement of those mothers and fathers who are handicapped in carrying out their functions of protecting their young children during the vulnerable stages of mental development. To treat early is sometimes to prevent mental retardation.

Treatment

In the circumstances in which we work, it is unlikely that we shall ever have sufficient trained staff to provide intensive treatment for the individual children. This is one of the reasons for turning much of the treatment over to the families and especially to the mothers. One task for the expert is then to help the families to help the children. They have more and better opportunities to do so at home than can ever be arranged in the clinic.

The parents of a retarded child are nearly always seriously depressed and discouraged. They tend to feel that the child's retardation detracts from them and to be keenly aware of the possible faults in the care they have given the child. Notwithstanding their sensitiveness, inquiries into the family's history have to be made, and the interactions of the parents with each other and with the child explored and discussed.

A few sessions with the parents, usually separately but occasionally together, may be sufficient in some cases to bring about major changes in the pattern of interactions in the family. Sometimes it does no more than reveal the severity and extent of the disturbances. There may then be a gradual shift in attitudes. Sometimes no progress can be made at all. Improvement in the way in which the family functions may give a better chance to the younger children to develop normally, even if it is too late to do much for the already retarded child.

The objectives of the direct treatment of the parents may be limited. One may try to do more than open up discussion of the problems the child's retardation raises. This may help the mother and father to talk to each other about them and encourage them to give each other greater support in the care of the child. To break down the barriers of reticence and shame may make it possible for them to accept more help from neighbors and friends and thus to broaden the child's security system.

Given encouragement, the parents may renew efforts to get the child to walk or to establish toilet habits. A degree of success may do much to build up their morale. It is usually helpful to explain to them that the disorder in social behavior is the means the child uses to protect himself from what to him is a perplexing and perhaps frightening world. Usually they accept readily that to create or restore his confidence in social relationships is the essence of the job they have to do.

Another lesson for the parents to learn is to refrain from trying to control the child's activity too directly. They have to learn to be patient and passive and to await initiatives and approaches by the child. All too often they make great efforts to teach him to count or to recite nursery rhymes, even though what little he learns is meaningless and useless to him. It is hardly surprising that, in their efforts to help their child, parents are guided by caricatures of old-fashioned theories and the hangovers of traditional beliefs.

They have also much to learn in the clinic about how to play with the child, how to communicate with him, and how to encourage him to communicate with them. They can learn through participation in play sessions, during which the therapist can show them by example how to behave towards the child, how to make use of cuddling and physical contact, how to combine communication through speech with that through touch and vision, and so on.

Through simple, ordinary measures like these, we can do something towards creating the conditions in which learning can take place. The child's behavior may show marked changes towards normality in many respects. Yet in the acquisition of language functions progress tends to be slow. Itard did as well with Victor as we are likely to do now.

The opening during the last decade of training centers, which handicapped children may begin to attend daily at the age of three years or younger, gives us great opportunities to improve our methods of special education, which are still crude. The staff of these centers is growing in skill and understanding, and efforts are of course being made to elaborate methods in practical everyday ways.

But we cannot expect to do much better until we know more about the reasons for the decline in ability to learn after the critical period has passed. Does the decline occur, as I have suggested, because the child has acquired other, less favorable habits of reaction to people? How can these habits be corrected? Physicians and educators must cooperate in seeking answers to these questions.

Conclusion

Adolf Meyer (9, p. 12) wrote:

> The physician is seriously and practically involved in the hangovers of traditions and the tragedies of their failures, and it is easy to see why he must revalue the traditional facts, concepts and methods for practical medical purposes.

My hope is that this lecture contributes towards the revaluing of the part played by family processes in causing and perpetuating mental retardation in early childhood.

References

1. BOTT, E.: Family and Social Network. London: Tavistock Publications, 1957.

2. BOWLBY, J.: Maternal Care and Mental Health, WHO Monogr. Ser. 2:1-179, 1951.

3. CLARKE, C. M., and DAVIS, D. R.: The Families of Mentally Retarded Children, Develop. Med. Child Neurol. 5:279-286, 1963.

4. DAVIS, D. R.: An Introduction to Psychopathology, 2nd ed. London: Oxford University Press, 1966.

5. LEWIS, A.: The Study of Defect, Amer. J. Psychiat. 117:289-305, 1960.

6. LIDDELL, H. S.: "Experimental Neurosis in Animals," in Tanner, J. M., ed.: Stress and Psychiatric Disorder. Oxford: Blackwell, 1960.

7. MAUDSLEY, H.: The Pathology of Mind. London: Cassell, 1895.

8. MEYER, A.: Collected Papers, vol. 4. Baltimore: Johns Hopkins Press, 1952.

9. MEYER, A.: Psychobiology. Springfield, Ill.: Charles C. Thomas, 1957.

10. OPPE, T. E.: Risk Registers for Babies, Develop. Med. Child Neurol. 9:13-21, 1967.

11. PFAFFENBERGER, C. J., and SCOTT, J. P.: The Relationship Between Delayed Socialization and Trainability in Guide Dogs, J. Genet. Psychol. 95:145-155, 1959.

12. SCHAFFER, H. R., and EMERSON, P. E.: The Development of Social Attachments in Infancy, Monogr. Soc. Res. Child Develop. 29:1-77, 1964.

13. THORPE, W. H.: "Sensitive Periods in the Learning of Animals and Men," in Thorpe, W.H., and Zangwill, O.L., eds.: Current Problems in Animal Behavior. London: Cambridge University Press, 1961.

14. TINBERGEN, N.: The Study of Instinct. London: Oxford University Press, 1951.

15. YOUNG, M., and WILLMOTT, P.: Family and Kinship in East London. London: Tavistock Publications, 1966.

Poverty and Mental Retardation: A Causal Relationship

RODGER L. HURLEY

Welfare: The Cycle of Dependency

Any attempt to understand the conditions which can impede the mental development of the poor must consider one of the most pervasive and destructive elements in their lives—that which they call "the welfare." In New Jersey, where more than 187,000 persons receive some form of public aid and where welfare rolls continue to rise, the problem is particularly acute. For beyond the view that the State has been able to give financial assistance to a large number of people in need lies a growing recognition that what the State does not give and the way it uses what it does give are of great significance in making the lives of the poor intolerable.

The general failings of public assistance are too familiar to require extensive discussion. Senator Robert F. Kennedy, for example, struck a responsive chord in an audience when he described the situation this way: "We have created a welfare system which aids only a fourth of those who are poor, which forces men to leave their families so that public assistance can be obtained, which has created a dependence on their fellow citizens that is degrading and distasteful to giver and receiver alike." [1]

The degree to which this dependence is distasteful to the receiver has been well illustrated by recent demonstrations on the part of the welfare recipients in our nation's cities, Newark and Paterson among them. The demands of these groups have been many; they have called for higher grant levels based on a national minimum standard, for the participation of recipients on local welfare boards, for improvements in food-distribution programs, for an end to "spying" by social workers, and for the establishment of procedures that would eliminate arbitrary, almost whimsical, treatment of applications by welfare departments. But the essence of their feelings was captured in a sign carried by a New York marcher: "We Want to Be Treated Like Human Beings."

Reprinted from Rodger L. Hurley, *Poverty and Mental Retardation: A Causal Relationship* (Trenton, N.J., New Jersey Department of Institutions and Agencies, 1968), pp. 124-134. By permission of the Division of Mental Retardation. This publication was produced under a grant from the Social Rehabilitation Services, U.S. Department of Health, Education and Welfare.

The distaste for the present welfare system on the part of the giver, outside as well as inside the government, is also apparent. The attitude of many intellectuals is typified by that of Charles E. Silberman, who has indicated a welfare state which gives its greatest benefits to groups other than the poor. For Silberman, the three primary aspects of welfarism in this country are its middle-class bias, its inability to present the poor with a coherent program of funds and services, and its refusal to allow the poor to assume a meaningful role in the operation of the system.[2]

These criticisms have not been lost on the government itself, at least on the higher levels. The New Jersey Division of Public Welfare, in a 1966 Statement of Objectives, called for "a more integrated, more comprehensive more simplified, more constructive, and more acceptable structure of public social services for New Jersey citizens."[3] The Federal government has gone deeper; the Advisory Council on Public Welfare—reporting to the Secretary of Health, Education, and Welfare in 1966—advocated a system of public assistance given according to a nationwide standard—as a matter of their right—to individuals whose eligibility is determined solely on the basis of need.[4]

Unfortunately, many on the giving end of the welfare process, particularly on the local level, are less willing to recognize its degrading aspects. For these people, the most vital reforms are those which will assure that there is no cheating on the system. The well-publicized attempt to weed out potential cheaters in Newburgh (N. Y.) has had brutal sequels in Mississippi—where the traditional niggardliness of welfare administrators and other public officials has led to conditions of outright starvation—[5] and in Baltimore, where a number of welfare recipients, often illiterate and ill-informed, have been fined and given jail terms because of alleged frauds. In New Jersey, a Monmouth County Freeholder demanded that welfare records be used to prosecute the fathers of illegitimate children, and the Burlington County Welfare Board voted to cut off Aid to Dependent Children if it could be shown that there was a "man-in-the-house."

These instances of "welfare backlash" reflect a large segment of public opinion; they illustrate precisely why the dependency involved in welfare is so destructive of human dignity. American attitudes on the subject of welfare are, in a word, ambiguous: "While admitting that Society is, in some sense, 'responsible' for the culture of poverty so that social aid is necessary and proper, most Americans vaguely suspect that poverty could be relieved if the poor only tried to do something about it."[6] In view of the spirit in which aid is given, it is not difficult to understand the pain with which it is received.

Perhaps the most important relationship between welfare and mental retardation is the similarity in the popular approach to both problems. There is a tendency to keep the poor shut away in ghettos, just as the retarded are often shut away in institutions; to absolve society of guilt by blaming poverty on laziness, just as retardation is blamed on heredity; and to avoid, in both areas, the steps which would lead to prevention and rehabilitation.

If the subject of retardation can be discussed largely in terms of rigid institutions, the same is even more true of welfare. The public assistance system in the United

States can best be described in terms of two self-perpetuating structures. First, there is the social service bureaucracy, preoccupied with its own procedures, concerned with its own survival, and operating with machinery that it designed to move slowly, if at all.[7] Second, there exists the subculture of poverty, increasingly dependent on welfare and forced, by necessity, to adapt its style of life to the demands of the welfare system. Completely beyond the specifically harmful aspects of welfare, therefore, is its greatest single failing: it helps to produce an unhealthy overall environment for poor people.

The way in which welfare contributes to the ability of the poverty subculture to breed mental retardation is most clearly described in practical terms—that is, dollars and cents. The financial assistance provided by welfare is so inadequate that while it may succeed in sustaining life, it achieves almost nothing in the way of ameliorating the hardships of poverty. As the Advisory Council succinctly stated, "Public assistance payments are so low and so uneven that the Government is, by its own standards and definitions, a major source of the poverty on which it has declared unconditional war."[8] The implication of this statement is that the whole range of factors which characterize poverty and which may lead to retardation—factors such as inadequate nutrition, poor prenatal care, psychological and cultural deprivation, and unsanitary living conditions—are left intact by our public-assistance program. Small wonder that in Newark's welfare case-load, which consists largely of people in the second, third, or fourth generation of those on relief, three out of ten are suffering from serious congenital defects.[9] The same situation was revealed in a California study: "A senate committee in 1961 disclosed an alarmingly high incidence of physical and social pathology in families receiving Aid to Needy Children funds. Among ANC families in a study in Santa Clara County, it was reported, 13 percent had problems of mental deficiency, as compared with the estimated average of 3 percent for the general population."[10] Beneath such statistics lie deplorable instances of human misery, as is shown in this Monmouth County case study: "Mrs. S., mother of five children was deserted by her husband after his final unemployment insurance check had been spent. For seven weeks Mrs. S. and the five children lived on a $30 a week food order from the municipal welfare officer. This occurred during the winter while three of the children had infectious hepatitis."[11] The obvious difficulty of welfare recipients may, with considerable delay and inconvenience, acquire help for specific diseases, mental retardation is not itself regarded as a disease. The health and nutritional causes are allowed to persist, due to the lack of appreciation of their long-range effect on human development.

The failure of welfare to deal with these long-range problems is best illustrated by reference to the financial situation of the people on relief. A family of nine in New Jersey, consisting of a mother and eight children ages 13, 11, 9, 7, 5, 3, 2, and 6 months—a not uncommon welfare family—received the rather meager monthly allotment of $359.60, according to State guidelines.[12] This figure does not include a number of special allowances which may be granted to the family under certain circumstances, but those may act to the detriment of the family. For rather than being able to live with the assurance that all the difficulties normal to any large family can be comfortably met, the welfare mother must rely on the dubious generosity of the welfare board in order to deal with each additional circumstance.

The basic monthly allotment is also exclusive of rent; the position of welfare boards is that they set no rigid guidelines on the monthly cost of rent. The practical effect of this position, however, is that the welfare board makes no effort to see that the recipient is provided with anything better than sub-standard housing. Indeed, the board may require that a welfare family move to "comparable housing" in which the rent is lower. The agony of dislocation seems to have less importance than the expenditure of fewer dollars.

One need not rely on cases as drastic as that of the Monmouth County mother, therefore, in order to demonstrate the inability of welfare to allow recipients to lead normal lives. Even under the best of circumstances, welfare provides only the barest minimum in the areas of food, clothing, shelter, and other necessities. A handbook prepared by the New Jersey Community Action Training Institute tells recipients that their food allowance is based on a very low-cost diet plan, and it warns them, as it must, that "buying a birthday cake may mean [that a woman on relief] has to do without something she really needs."[13] Certainly the inability of a welfare child to eat birthday cake with the happy abandon of a middle-class child bears no direct relationship to mental retardation. But it would be as absurd today to claim that the poor may enjoy the style of life led by the middle class as it once was to respond to the needs of the poor by crying "let them eat cake."

The disadvantages of life on welfare, whether concerning hepatitis or the absence of birthday cakes, have the most severe psychological effects on the children of the poor. The inability of public assistance to combat the physical and psychological deprivation associated with poverty, along with welfare's disruptive effect on family life, serve as a guarantee that the formative years of the poor child will not be suitable for normal development. The cycle of poverty—and retardation—starts with the child, and the influence of welfare on the child is such that it helps to perpetuate and intensify this cycle rather than to terminate it.

An improvement in the financial assistance provided by welfare—as one means of combating the poverty cycle—is not beyond the means of society. It was estimated in 1962 that the cost of raising every individual in the nation above the subsistence level would be about ten billion dollars a year—one fifth of the cost of national defense.[14] Although public assistance expenditures in the nation have been rising, the proportion of personal income spent on public assistance declined from one percent to 0.7 percent from 1950 to 1965. New Jersey itself has no greater claim to excessive generosity: though eighth among the states in 1964 in average per capita income, it ranked 34th in per capita expenditure on public assistance. This placed the state well below Mississippi, which was last in per capita income.[15] Once again, the characteristic public approach to welfare—the refusal to place a high priority on the needs of the poor—lies at the heart of the welfare problem.

The public approach is based on the myth that the largest numbers of those on relief are the shiftless and the lazy, a myth which was rudely shaken by a recent Federal study which showed that less than one percent of recipients are capable of being employed.[16] The same point had been made earlier in New Jersey in response to public dismay about increases in welfare costs despite the expenditure of seventy-seven million dollars in the State in anti-poverty programs. The New Jersey Office of Economic Opportunity, in addition to noting that few on the relief rolls are employable, correctly argued that relatively small amounts of anti-poverty funds were aimed directly at manpower training rather than longer-range programs and that, in fact, the *rate* of increase in welfare costs had slowed since the beginning of the War on Poverty.[17] The view that public assistance in New Jersey is wasteful and unnecessary is also belied by the Division of Public Welfare, which reported that in fiscal year 1965, its "program operations continued to be crisis-orientated."[18]

In addition, if there is some lack of motivation on the part of recipients a large part of the blame belongs to the welfare program itself. The long pattern of dependency, in combination with the unavailability of steady employment, is not likely to spur incentive or any other ingredient of success in middle-class society. One New Jersey analysis demonstrated that motivation to work, as one would expect, is partly a function of expectancy to work.[19] For many on relief, unskilled and broken by dependency, that expectancy has been entirely lacking for years. At the same time, reports the Newark study, "the popular feeling is that the individual on relief should gratefully accept any job."[20]

While the public continues to express its indignation over the expense of welfare, a disturbing truth is that relatively few of the nation's poor are being assisted at all. Senator Kennedy's estimate seems conservative; it is more likely that only a fifth of the poor are actually receiving help.[21] If this smaller group suffers from the popular misconception that all of its needs are being handled, so, too, the remaining four fifths suffer from the unchecked fury of all the disadvantages of life in poverty.

What groups comprise this four fifths? Many are simply individuals whose incomes exceed a state's eligibility standard but which fall below the Federal poverty level—another indication of the need for a national standard. But many others fall victim to the stringent residency requirements of the states. Despite the increasingly mobile nature of American society, despite the fact that the poor are often forced constantly to move in search of work, and despite their frequent forced relocation, many fail to qualify for assistance merely because they do not meet the residency requirements of a particular state or area. A strange paradox is that such requirements may stand in the way of eligibility when the lack of American citizenship generally does not.

This problem is especially troublesome in New Jersey, where twenty thousand of the most needy persons—the migrant workers—cannot possibly meet the one-year-residency requirements for most assistance. Recognition of this may be the first step (though there are many others) in understanding the staggering degree of apparent "retardation" among this group. Residency regulations also present difficulties for people newly arrived in urban areas and even for people who change their residence within the state.

The problem lies deeper than that, however; many persons who do not qualify for Categorical Assistance—Assistance for the Blind, Disability Assistance, Assistance for Dependent Children, Old Age Assistance and Medical Assistance for the Aged—are eligible for General Assistance. But this program, though intended to meet emergency needs and to fill in gaps left in the Categorical Assistance program, is administered by municipal welfare boards which are usually even less eager to help the poor than are those on the county level. Moreover, of 567 municipalities in New Jersey, only 386 accept State funds and are required to report their programs to the State. In the rest, General Assistance, especially for transients, is often minimal or nonexistent.

Even more significant than residency requirements and the local autonomy of General Assistance is the division of the bulk of public assistance into rigid categories. Because of this division, welfare fails to reach most needy unemployed adults under sixty-five and most incapacitated adults who are not considered permanently and totally disabled. An additional effect of the rigidity of categories leads to absurdities. In Newark: "When individuals are rejected by the county as candidates for Disability Assistance, Aid to the Blind, etc., the city has no recourse but to classify them as 'suited for light employment.' Alcoholics, extremely obese persons, retarded people, and, occasionally, narcotics addicts are also classified, by default, as employable."[22]

The categorical approach, along with the system of matching Federal and State funds, also means that "welfare programs are defined and developed to fit the available funds rather than the need for assistance or measures adequate to meet the need."[23] This means that states are more reluctant to participate in Aid to Dependent Children programs than in programs for the aged, blind, and disabled, for which the Federal Government provides a greater proportion of the cost. The use of matching formulas also presents difficulties in non-Federally-funded welfare, in which the cost is shared by State and local governments. Accordingly, the New Jersey Division of Public Welfare has emphasized the need for (1) "a single formula of State-County sharing of the costs of all categorical assistance," and (2) a greater assumption of welfare costs by the State, in order to relieve the disproportionate burden on local governments. Additionally, in order to avoid the long waiting period for Categorical Assistance—a period during which other help is often difficult to obtain—the Division urges that payments begin immediately on the basis of the principle of "presumptive eligibility."[24]

In New Jersey and in thirty-two other welfare jurisdictions, an even more serious problem remains that most severely affects children. For these areas have refused to take part in the program of Aid to Dependent Children with Unemployed Parents, a program intended to allow unemployed fathers to remain with their families without risking loss of welfare. The effect of this refusal has been disastrous for the poor family, and the policy has been decried by the New Jersey Welfare Committee in these terms: "Our public welfare program in New Jersey today operates in such a way as to perpetuate the matriarchal structure of the Negro family which existed throughout the period of slavery in America. It is structured so that the thousands of children growing in A.D.C. families are damaged by the absence of their fathers from the home, and by the knowledge that this absence is the basic premise of their eligibility for a minimum amount of economic security."[25]

This absent-father element of welfare in New Jersey lies at the heart of the link between welfare and retardation, and it merits further consideration. Daniel P. Moynihan stated the problem this way: "In essence, the Negro community has been forced into a matriarchal structure which, because it is so out of line with the rest of American society, seriously retards the progress of the group as a whole."[26]

Moynihan's use of the word "retards" is significant; he goes further, describing the situation as a "tangle of pathology" which ensnares the Negro youth and which is due primarily to the weakness of the Negro family.[27] This pathology often takes the form of an apparent mental dullness, evidenced by the consistently poor performance of disadvantaged Negro youth on IQ tests. But Moynihan goes on to cite the work of Martin Deutsch and Bert Brown which shows that "the IQ's of children with fathers in the home are always higher than those who have no father in the home."[28]

The validity of IQ tests is, of course, debatable, and the Deutsch-Brown study illustrates perfectly their uselessness as an indicator of a fixed intellectual capacity. But noting that the tests demonstrate the difficulty of a child from a broken home in performing according to middle-class standards, the results are significant. The denial of ADC-UP funds to New Jersey's children does more than deprive them of an opportunity to escape the physical hardships of poverty; in a real sense it seriously jeopardizes their chance to develop normally.

The financial inadequacy of welfare, however, is only a part of its detrimental effect. Equally important are the circumstances under which it is dispensed. The welfare recipient, it must be understood, lives an extremely insecure existence. In the light of potential disintegration of family life as discussed by Moynihan, it would be a mistake to minimize the fact that recipients are entirely at the mercy of welfare boards. Living on the whims of a group of individuals who often are not committed to the idea of welfare itself—and who must justify their decision-making by thinking up reasons *not* to grant assistance—is not likely to help to stabilize the lives of the poor. The welfare mother who is able to obtain employment and to arrange for some sort of day-care for her children does so at the risk of losing her welfare grant and even of being accused of fraud. The fact that she is often driven by necessity to augment her slim dole in this way has little effect in softening a welfare view which is geared to saying "No."

Moreover, the recipients' primary contact with the system is through the visitations of caseworkers whose function is often more investigative than sympathetic, and who are often poorly trained for their positions.[29] Welfare agencies make almost no effort to discover additional needy members of the community; they are quite active in declaring ineligible, however, those who believe themselves to be in need. A Monmouth County survey reported that only 9.5 percent of the recipients felt that caseworkers did anything more than determine eligibility.[30]

The Monmouth study also emphasized an equally important failure of the welfare program. "There is little or no attempt," it revealed, "to ascertain the causes of dependency, to ascertain the strengths of the recipients which could be built upon and bring about personal or economic independence, or to help the recipient plan toward a better way of life."[31] The fact is that welfare has a record of general failure in breaking the cycle of dependency because it concerns itself with peripheral services and not with the concept of rehabilitation and prevention.

The implications of this failure to mental retardation are vast. On the national level, the Advisory Council on Public Welfare has noted that "the lack of adequate social services for families, children, young people and individuals isolated by age or disability is itself a major factor in the perpetuation of . . . the widely deplored climate of unrest, alienation, and discouragement among many groups in the nation."[32]

This viewpoint was echoed more specifically in Monmouth County, where the study revealed an extensive need for services to dependent children and their families. Four crucial services mentioned were prenatal, confinement, and post-natal medical care for mother and child; guidance and counseling for dependent children; improvement of home conditions; and, significantly, special programs for "individual children damaged by neglect or rejection."[33] That these services have been lacking in the past goes far to explain the perpetuation of the poverty-welfare-retardation cycle.

It is not surprising then that in Neward, where this cycle has been so persistent, "the City DPW (Department of Public Welfare) has been unable to provide its clients with the type of intensive long-range rehabilitative services that are prerequisite to achieving a goal of independent community living."[34] The anti-poverty program and related programs have made a start in the direction of providing needed services and opportunities, in areas ranging from day-care to manpower training. But essentially the problem is related to a popular attitude which places a low priority on eliminating degradation and dependency in the welfare system. Until society is able to disabuse itself of the myths of welfare—as well as those of poverty and retardation—the old cycle is likely to continue.

The destructive results of the attitude of society has no better illustration than in the area of child and youth welfare services. New York City authorities learned that the children who need help the most—"the losers"—are the ones most rejected by the city's agencies. These are children who wind up at the Children's Center, a badly equipped, greatly overcrowded building where many youngsters remain indefinitely. It is not surprising that "their sense of rejection is overwhelming."[35] Nor would it be surprising if the great majority of these children are characterized, now and later, as mentally retarded.

The situation in New Jersey is scarcely better. The Passaic County Children Shelter in Wayne Township is a clean, modern building with pleasant surroundings. It would seem, at least superficially, to be a showpiece of enlightened treatment of deprived children. But it is severely overcrowded; it houses children ranging from murderers to those who are the victims of badly broken homes. All who can fit live in tiny cells; the others live together on temporary cots in a large room.

No education is provided for the children; the only recreation area is a patch of blacktop completely enclosed by screening. No child is allowed out of doors. Those in charge seem more concerned about a single child escaping from the Shelter than about the probability that not a single child will escape from the maze of his own fears and frustrations. One child leaving the Shelter with his parents, was told that if he were sent back he would never be allowed to leave again, "no matter how much you cry and scream." Another, requesting permission to read during a period set aside for resting, was thrown into his cell, the heavy door slammed behind him.[36]

"Social welfare," wrote a historian of the subject, "is special services supplied and material assistance given by all or part of society to a human being thought to be in need."[37] The ideal is a simple, yet noble one; but somewhere along the way it has soured. The helping hand characteristic of an earlier day has, for too many in society, become the slammed door. The effects of this kind of treatment on the human mind as well as on the human spirit have only recently begun to be realized.

References

[1]SENATOR ROBERT F. KENNEDY, Address to the Day Care Council of New York (May 8, 1967), p. 3.

[2]CHARLES E. SILBERMAN, *The Myths of Automation* (New York, 1966), pp. 83-84.

[3]*Statement of Objectives* (New Jersey Division of Public Welfare, 1966), p. 1.

[4]*Summary of Recommendations to the Secretary of Health, Education and Welfare,* The Advisory Council on Public Welfare (June 29, 1966), pp. 6-7. Hereafter referred to as *Summary of Recommendations.*

[5]RICHARD A. CLOWARD and FRANCES FOX PIVEN, "Starving by the Rule Book," *The Nation,* CCIV (April 3, 1967), 429-431.

[6]ISADORE SILVER, "Poverty As A Crime," *Commonwealth,* LXXXV (October 21, 1966), 74.

[7]MARTIN REIN, "Social Science and the Elimination of Poverty," *Journal of the American Institute of Planners,* XXXIII (May, 1967), 160.

[8]*Summary of Recommendations,* p. 6.

[9]GEORGINA M. SMITH, *On The Welfare* (New Brunswick, N. J., 1967), p. 3.

[10]*Report of the Senate Fact Finding Committee on Labor and Welfare: Aid to Needy Children Program,* 1961, p. 48.

[11]*Report of the Findings and Recommendations Related to the Public Assistance Program of the Monmouth County Welfare Board,* conducted by Greenleigh Associates, Inc. (New York, 1963), p. 18. Hereafter referred to as *Report of the Findings.*

[12]Personal Communication, Mr. Gerald Malanga, Public Welfare Consultant, New Jersey Division of Public Welfare, July 11, 1967.

[13]*Public Assistance; Rights and Responsibilities,* prepared by the New Jersey Community Action Training Institute (February, 1967), p. 12.

[14]JAMES N. MORGAN, MARTIN H. DAVID, WILBUR J. COHEN, HARRY E. BRAZER, *Income and Welfare in the United States* (New York, 1962), pp. 3-4.

[15]HELEN E. MARTIN, "National Blueprint for Public Welfare," *Department of Health, Education, and Welfare Indicators* (Washington: U. S. Government Printing Office, 1966), pp. 6 and 10.

[16]JOSEPH A. CALIFANO, Address to the Washington Chapter of Sigma Delta Chi, April 19, 1967.

[17]"The Relation of New Jersey's War on Poverty to Rising Costs and Caseloads," New Jersey Office of Economic Opportunity Background Memorandum, (February 24, 1967), pp. 1, 2 and 5.

[18]1965 Annual Report, New Jersey Department of Institutions and Agencies, in *The Welfare Reporter*, XVII, No. 3 (July, 1966), 30.

[19]BERNARD P. INDIK, *The Motivation to Work*. (New Brunswick, N. J., N. D.), p. 4.

[20]SMITH, p. 5.

[21]MARTIN, p. 5.

[22]SMITH, p. 39.

[23]MARTIN, p. 9.

[24]*Statement of Objectives*, pp. 2-4.

[25]BERT HUNTER, "The Case for the Aid to Dependent Children Program," *New Jersey Welfare Council Bulletin*, XXXVI (December, 1966), 2.

[26]DANIEL P. MOYNIHAN, *The Negro Family; The Case for National Action* (Washington: U. S. Government Printing Office, 1965), p. 29.

[27]MOYNIHAN, p. 30.

[28]MARTIN DEUTSCH and BERT BROWN, "Social Influences in Negro-White Intelligence Difference," *Social Issues* (April, 1964), p. 27, quoted by Moynihan, p. 37.

[29]*Report of the Findings*, p. 31.

[30]*Report of the Findings*, p. 27.

[31]*Report of the Findings*, p. 4.

[32]*Summary of Recommendations*, p. 5.

[33]*Report of the Findings*, pp. 46-48.

[34]ANNETTE O'FLAHERTY, in Smith, p. 65.

[35]KATHLEEN TELTSCH, "Welfare Services for Problem Children Under Study," *The New York Times* (June 29, 1967), pp. 45, 48.

[36]Personal visit by author.

[37]VAUGHN DAVIS BORNET, *Welfare in America* (Norman, Oklahoma, 1960), p. 30.

TWENTY-THREE

The Doubly Disadvantaged: A Study of Socio-Cultural Determinants in Mental Retardation

CHARLES MEISGEIER

In the previous chapter, several statistical differences among the three major ethnic groups of Texas were pointed out. It can be safely assumed that these differences have a bearing on the problem of mental retardation and the way in which this problem is perceived and handled by persons of the different ethnic groups.

It is possible, however, that an even greater influence on perceptions and attitudes about the problem of mental retardation is exerted by factors of culture and tradition which may vary from one ethnic group to the next. It would appear to be necessary to study the cultural beliefs and practices of the Negro and Latin-American groups in Texas in order to determine the nature and degree of any divergence of their beliefs and practices from those of the Anglo group. From such a study it might be possible to infer the effect which any existent cultural differences might have on the incidence, perception, and reaction to the problem of mental retardation.

It was felt that two approaches would be needed to accomplish such a study. First, a review of the literature on the subject of cultural practices would be helpful as a base from which appropriate inferences could be made. Second, it was felt that the experience and knowledge of welfare and service agency personnel who serve primarily Negro and Latin-American persons would be of value in testing those inferences made from the review of the literature. This chapter, then, is arranged in three sections: the first two summarize a review of the literature on the Latin-American and Negro cultures respectively; the last section summarizes the ideas of a three-group discussion of this subject.

Factors of Latin-American Culture Affecting Mental Retardation

SOURCES OF INFORMATION

In attempting to study the affective relationship between the Latin-American culture of South Texas and the problem of mental retardation, one is immediately

From Charles Meisgeier, *The Doubly Disadvantaged: A Study of Socio-Cultural Determinants in Mental Retardation* (Austin, University of Texas, 1966), pp. 115-127. By permission of the author.

struck by the almost complete lack of information in the literature about this specific affective relationship. A report of the President's Panel on Mental Retardation, the *Bibliography of World Literature on Mental Retardation*, contains over 16,000 references, none of which pertains to this subject in the strictest sense, and only a handful of which were relevant in an even broader sense. Likewise, a bibliography of materials relating to the education of Spanish-speaking children compiled by Professor George I. Sanchez listed no appropriate references to this topic among its 882 annotated entries. A few sources do exist in the area of culturally oriented health practices, but several of these are repetitive and overlapping since they draw their material from the same source. The Hidalgo Project, an anthropological study of the health beliefs and practices of the Latin Americans of Hidalgo County, Texas, furnished the source for the reports of Albino Fantini (1962), William Madsen (1964), and Arthur Rubel (1966).

Exploration of the literature on such varied other subjects as medical care for, and education, cultural practices, cultural deprivation, and mental retardation of Latin Americans produced only a very few general references dealing with this subject area. The literature, then, is helpful in studying this subject only to the extent that it enables one to make inferences about this specific area from the general discussions of some of the above named topics. For example, there is a great deal of literature on the effects of cultural deprivation and the remediation of these effects by special education techniques; obviously, it can be inferred that much of this information about culturally deprived children in general will also hold true in the specific case of the Latin-American child of South Texas. One must, however, avoid the pitfall of overinference and concomitant overgeneralization about this unique cultural group.

Complicating the problem even more is the lack of homogeneity among the Latin Americans of South Texas, precluding any generalized statements about what "they" believe or practice. People of Latin-American descent obviously exist along the entire spectrum of education, socioeconomic status, and acculturation to the Anglo middle-class standard of values. Gonzales, Ratliff, and others have shown a rather high correlation between advanced education and middle and above socioeconomic status with Anglicization; conversely, low education and low socioeconomic status are generally associated with more traditional Mexican folk beliefs and practices (Gonzales, 1932; Ratliff, 1960). But these correlations are only generalized trends and should not be allowed to obscure the complexity of interrelationships which obviously must be determined for each and every individual who is affected to any extent by his antecedent culture. It should be kept in mind, then, that many of the cultural beliefs and practices which will be discussed below may be held by only some of the people of this culture and may be held by them with varying degrees of intensity and modification at different times in their lives.

DISEASE THEORY AND HEALTH PRACTICES

With these limitations, Fantini describes the disease theory and practice which is generally associated with the Latin-American culture of South Texas and which has many implications for the diagnosis, care, and treatment of mentally retarded persons. Oversimplifying, diseases are seen as of being of two general types: natural and unnatural (*mal puestos*). Among the former are those infirmities which can be judged to be natural occurrences and, therefore, amenable to the routine cures of home remedy or Anglo physician. The latter group, *mal puesto*, includes the unnatural diseases which result primarily from problems of social interaction. These are, for example, *mal de ojo*, which may be caused by a covetous glance from friend or foe; *susto* or *espanto*, which are the "fright" diseases; and there are many others. This latter group can sometimes fall into the category of "witchcraft" in that they can either be caused accidentally or be the evil design of some angry or jealous rival. These diseases are seen by the *Mexicanos* as being unique to their culture; since the Anglo physician does not have understanding of these diseases, he is very rarely consulted for their remediation (Fantini, 1962).

It is possible that until recently mental retardation may not have existed as a specific medical entity in the traditional folk medicine of the *Mexicano* culture. Various conditions which could be technically diagnosed as mental retardation may be considered by the *Mexicano* to fall into several different groups of infirmities in his framework of disease theory. Thus retardation could be thought of as having variable etiology in folk culture, including being "natural" infirmities or disabilities, being the result of a divine punishment for some transgression, or being the end result of a curse or bewitchment made manifest in a *mal puesto*. Fantini noted that the *males puestos* most often were manifested "as a neural injury or psychic ill such as epilepsy, nervousness, paralysis, dementia, and feeble mindedness. Congenital deformities . . . may also be attributed to witchcraft." He further noted that "Defects of many kinds and even mental retardation may often be regarded the same as any other innate physical characteristic. The mentally retarded child may be described as *flojo* (lazy) or *distraido* (inattentive, absent minded)." (Fantini, 1962)

Obviously, this variability of etiology has considerable implication for treatment. Rubel noted that the *Mexicano* looks upon disease and illness in pragmatic terms. That is, he does not consider himself to be ill unless he feels significant pain or discomfort. His goal then becomes the removal of this pain or discomfort, and whatever means serves to accomplish that end is viewed as efficacious medical treatment. The sufferer may explore many different resources for alleviation of his illness; and being treated by an Anglo physician and a *curandero*, or folk healer, simultaneously is not at all uncommon. It is also quite common for the *Mexicano* to experiment with all different kinds of patent medicines, herbs, teas, and other folk medicine preparations while simultaneously taking medicine recommended by a physician. This eclectic approach to medical treatment is mentioned by Madsen and Rubel as being one of the paramount characteristics of this cultural group (Madsen, 1964; Rubel, 1966).

Another major characteristic is the idea of the inevitability of disease. Again quoting from Fantini, "Fatalism pervades the life of the Latin-American population . . . in cases of illness where a cure seems hopeless, the problem may even be ignored by the Mexican." The implication for the mentally retarded child is obvious as he further states that "Seldom does one consider that the (mentally retarded child) might be helped. Seldom is therapy or rehabilitation considered. The afflicted must learn to fare as best he can with the endowments he possesses." Fatalism also has implications for the whole area of preventive medicine. In a culture which holds to the belief that disease is an inevitable part of a life which at best is often miserable, the whole concept of taking preventive action to forestall illness is largely absent. As stated above, medicine of all kinds, folk and technical, is relied upon only for the alleviation of existing pain or discomfort, and the possibility of preventing the illness in the first place is apparently not generally accepted in the *Mexicano* culture. (Fantini, 1962)

Thus it can be seen that the whole concept of disease theory which exists among the Latin Americans in South Texas has many negative implications for effective prevention and treatment of mental retardation. There are many other practices and aspects of this culture which impinge upon different areas of retardation, affecting its incidence and treatment. Primary among these is the whole area of prenatal care and birth process. Since pregnancy is not regarded as a disease, the necessity for medical care is not recognized among most of the women of this culture. There are many folk beliefs concerning pregnancy, ranging from the rather bizarre belief that the moon consumes portions of the unborn fetus and causes deformities on birth (Fantini, 1962) to the idea that mothers should avoid eating certain foods during pregnancy for fear of creating a permanent digestive problem for their future child (Kelly, 1965). To protect her child the mother may wear a string around her waist, holding a piece of metal over her abdomen. The fact, then, that physical ailments and most forms of mental illness and abnormal behavior of any kind are attributed to supernatural causes that require special kinds of folk medicine has obvious important implications for the diagnosis and treatment of mental retardation.

THE ROLE OF THE MIDWIFE

The actual birth of the child is traditionally assisted by a midwife in the mother's home rather than in a hospital. There seem to be several reasons for this. One is that childbirth is considered a rather normal process; and many mothers, particularly those who have already had several children, simply appear not to see the need for any special provisions. Also, the atmosphere of the maternity ward of hospitals is so alien and different to many of these women that the fear of this strange world may outweigh any fear of problems they may have during the birth process. There exist throughout the Latin-American community older women, *parteras,* who are widely known for their experience in midwifery. They usually charge very nominal fees and give much service additional to that which the mother could expect from an Anglo doctor and hospital, including staying with the mother for a week or two after the delivery of the child. This preference for delivery by midwife seems to be dying out, however, and more young Latin-American mothers are starting to go to the hospital to have their babies. The art of midwifery is apparently somewhat on the decline, since in one study of a small community there was much concern about the fact that all of the local *parteras* were above 50 years of age, and no young women were going into the "profession" (Saunders, 1954).

Midwife and home deliveries for the Spanish-surname population declined dramatically over the years 1948-1965. In 1948 approximately 1/3 of all Spanish-surname births were midwife deliveries, whereas in 1965 this figure had dropped to about 1/10 of all births. There was a corresponding decline in home deliveries over the same period from 61.7% to 11.2%.

NUTRITION, ETHNICITY, AND MENTAL RETARDATION

Another whole area, influenced by culture and affecting mental retardation, is that of diet. The President's Panel on Mental Retardation has called attention to the relationship between poor maternal and infant nutrition and mental and physical disability and retardation. Blazek studied the food habits and living conditions of Latin-American families of different income levels. The diets were found to be extremely poor, even at the higher income levels; there was a significant absence at the low income levels of all vegetables, fruits, milk, and other protein and vitamin substances (Blazek, 1938). Although this detailed study of diet and nutrition is now somewhat out-of-date, there is more recent, albeit less thorough, data indicating that dietary deficiencies are still very common among the lowest socioeconomic group of the Latin-American population. One can infer the relationship between the diet of an expectant mother and the health of her baby; there is also the problem of inadequate diet for children after birth which would be related to certain types of mental retardation. Indeed, Pasamanick questioned all the studies comparing *Mexicano* and Anglo children because such factors as significantly poorer diet, lower birth weight, and inherently inferior socioeconomic status were uncontrolled variables in these studies which, in his opinion, undoubtedly worked against the Latin-American groups (Pasamanick, 1951).

SOCIAL VIEW OF ILLNESS

A corollary area to medical beliefs and practices is the social context in which illness and treatment in the Latin-American culture takes place. Several authors (Clark, 1959; Fantini, 1962; Rubel, 1966; Spielberg, 1959) place great emphasis on the fact that all illness in the traditional *Mexicano* culture is a matter of social concern, especially to the immediate family of the ill person. For instance, when a child becomes ill, the first resource is the mother who has been trained from her own girlhood to provide simple home remedies and care to her family. If the child does not respond fairly soon to this home treatment, however, his illness becomes a matter for concern of the whole family. In particular, the older female members of the extended family, such as grandmothers, aunts, godmothers, etc., will all be brought in for consultation as to what should be done next in the treatment of the illness. In most families, the patriarchal system is still sufficiently present so that the father is most likely to have final say in the course of treatment. The important factor, however, is that the illness of one member of the family is seen as a problem for the entire family, and the family's resources may be mobilized to seek whatever treatment is decided as necessary, whether it be the services of a *yerbero* (herbalist), a *curandero*, or an Anglo physician. Thus the family is seen as the primary treatment agent of an ill person, even though they may solicit advice and services from persons outside.

Such traditions have definite implications for medical care necessitating hospitalization and probably are directly related to institutionalization of mentally retarded persons by the Mexicano people. Spielberg noted that hospitals are fairly universally regarded among the Latin Americans as places where one goes to die; and, indeed, many Latin Americans do not resort to hospitalization until their illness may be in terminal stages. As described above in connection with pregnancy, the hospital is seen as a very alien environment with strange rules and practices which the *Mexicano* may not understand (Spielberg, 1959). When this is complicated by the fact that many hospitals in South Texas view their mission as converting *Mexicanos* to modern Anglo medicine by exhortation and ridicule (Fantini, 1962), it is not difficult to understand why the services of the hospital are not more frequently sought by the Latin Americans.

There is some evidence that this fear of hospitalization and what might be conjectured to be a concomitant reluctance to utilize institutionalization for mentally retarded persons exists throughout the *Mexicano* culture. Spielberg studied responses to proposed hospitalization for the treatment of tuberculosis among the Latin Americans, defining as an "approrpiate response" their voluntary submission to hospitalization. He found that "appropriateness of response" was not directly correlated with the degree of acceptance of folk medical culture but was highly inversely correlated to the degree to which the patient was integrated into the nuclear family. Thus in closely knit and well-integrated families, cultural proscription would seem to preclude hospitalization and institutionalization of ill or handicapped members of the family (Spieldberg, 1959). If true, this would present interesting consequences for any studies of Latin Americans in institutions, since this would presumably be a sample biased by a preponderance of subjects from disorganized, disrupted families. Any measure of social deprivation of such children would then be questionable in its representativeness.

Another interesting reaction to the problem of mental retardation is the sort of ambivalence alluded to above which the *Mexicano* might have in attempting to remedy the problem. The consensus of the numerous studies of health practices (Clark, 1959; Fantini, 1962; Madsen, 1964; Rubel, 1966) seems to indicate that while the *Mexicano* may be fatalistic and at times accept the condition as inevitable and irreversible, he may at the same time, without any inconsistency in his mind, proceed from a doctor to a *curandero*, utilizing a wide variety of remedies. Fantini felt that in cases where a cure appeared to be hopeless, "the 'Mexican' is more prone to make a vow to the Almightly rather than to continue in his own attempt to cure" (Fantini, 1962). Langerhans studied special education in Mexico and found that, in general, the attitude of parents and society toward mentally retarded children was one of pitiful charity, with no concept of training to become useful members of society (Langerhans, 1959). This, when considered with the family context in which the illness is viewed as described above, lends even more support to the conjecture that well-integrated Mexicano families would be reluctant to institutionalize their mentally retarded children. In their frame of reference, if nothing can be done, the institution would be seen solely as providing custodial care for an apparently unwanted child. They would tend not to view institutionalization as a resource for training and improvement.

SUMMARY

In summary, one can infer that there is relationship between some of the aspects of Latin-American culture as it exists in South Texas and the incidence, treatment, and acceptance of the condition we call mental retardation. Certainly the consequences of the many cultural beliefs and attitudes regarding medical care, especially for expectant mothers and during the delivery of infants, are apparent. Treatment of childhood diseases which may develop complications related to mental retardation is also influenced by cultural beliefs and practices, including theories of the cause of disease and utilization of *curanderos* as healers. The strong family cohesion which exists in the majority of *Mexicano* families has many implications for hospitalization of expectant mothers, ill children, and institutionalization of mentally retarded children. The fact that these practices are seen as alien and probably gratuitous helps to explain the fact that proportionately fewer Latin-American children are hospitalized and institutionalized.

Factors of Negro Culture Affecting Mental Retardation

The consensus of most of the literature describing the Negro culture in America is that this culture is basically American and has little other frame of reference. In his major study of the American race problem, Myrdal concluded that, ". . . in his cultural traits, the Negro is akin to other Americans" (Myrdal, 1944, p. 928). Allen has reported that "The Negro group in America has no distinctive and no peculiar social institutions. It knows only the culture of America, and the points at which its behavior differs can be attributed to external influences such as the social and economic limitations which have been imposed upon it and the resultant inevitable psychological effects of such limitations" (Allen, 1957). This identification with American culture is not accidental but appears to be the universal motivation of most members of the Negro group. According to Manning, the Negro wants to belong; and his institutional and cultural traits are similar to the corresponding group in the Anglo society. He wants to adopt and has adopted the way of life of the Anglo group as he perceives it and to the extent that he is allowed to do so (Manning, 1960).

Despite this basic identification with American culture, there are many significant ways in which Negro practices and cultural patterns are different from the larger Anglo society. Chief among these is the widespread instability of many Negro families. Reports from public welfare agencies show that public assistance under the A. F. D. C. program has an overly large proportion of Negro recipients. It is also known that almost a fourth of Negro families are headed by a woman, and nearly one-quarter of all Negro births in the nation are now illegitimate. About one-third of all Negro children live in broken homes. These and many other facts emphasize the problem that contrary to the stability achieved by most Anglo families in America, Negro family structure appears to be highly unstable in too many instances; and in a large number of cases, the family structure has broken down.

Frazier has traced the cultural heritage of Negroes and has indicated that the process of destruction of the African family system began in Africa. The relocation of Negroes on relatively small plantations and farms provided them with little opportunity to continue their ancestral culture. Marriages and mating became subject to control of white masters, so that the resulting family system was dependent upon the requirements of a slave system. Frazier points out that in many instances the slave family acquired considerable stability, with the process of assimilation beginning with household servants and gradually working its way to the others. The Civil War and Reconstruction disrupted this established system, and only a few families had the stability to continue as such.

Frazier continues by pointing out that the Negro then began to develop a rural folk family life; and he suggests that among the lower class, which today comprises between 60 and 70 percent of the Negro population, family relations still reflect the influence of these rural folk traditions. But many Negroes were beginning to move to large communities, so that by the time of the beginning of World War II nearly half the Negro population of the United States was located in large metropolitan areas. It has been difficult, if not impossible, for most Negroes to transplant their rural folk family life background into their new city environment (Frazier, 1948).

It would seem safe to conclude that much of the problem of family breakdown described above has as its cause the difficulties encountered by Negroes from a rural environment in striving to adapt themselves to urban living.

One interesting point made by some writers is that even though some Negroes have successfully adapted and do identify with middle-class values, they are constantly affected by the problem of continued association with other Negroes who have not been so successful in their adaptation. Frazier indicates that approximately 25 to 30 percent of the Negro population can now be classified as middle class, and he points out that it is this middle-class Negro group which has stabilized and adapted to conditions of city life and which has identified most closely with Anglo middle-class values (Frazier, 1948). Because of factors such as housing segregation, however, it is very difficult for this stable group to escape from the cultural influences of the less stable majority. Middle-class Negro children are constantly being exposed to the pathology that is so widespread in Negro communities and are in danger of being drawn into it.

There are many implications of this discussion for social agencies, including those dealing with the problem of mental retardation. Manning has indicated that the middle- and upper-class Negroes closely identify with the values of the Anglo middle and upper classes and, therefore, present no unique problems to social agencies. He points out that they, as the Anglos, view organized charity in the worst sense of the word. Manning further points out that there are many psychological and cultural resistances in obtaining services traditionally viewed by the public as being for the "down-and-out." More important, however, Manning continues that regardless of the socioeconomic level, Negroes tend to bring their suspicions to social agencies, which they may view as an instrument of white domination. Often there is a problem of communication between agencies and Negro clients, particularly those coming from lower-class backgrounds. The clients may be unaccustomed to a middle-class vocabulary and may lack understanding of the expectations of the professional staff, which may create a passively expressed hostility. Manning feels that Negroes' failure to use agency services, in addition to the reasons indicated above, is many times due to ignorance of the services that are available. Complicating this problem is the fact that many Negroes feel considerable resignation toward problems that they have, and most agencies are not sufficiently aggressive to help them overcome these feelings (Manning, 1960).

Suchman made the same points in his study on medical deprivation. His study indicated that cultural values were found to affect both the perception and interpretation of symptoms and the seeking of medical treatment. He further stated that among the low-level socioeconomic group, medical deprivation is characterized by narrow health horizons, a low level of aspiration concerning preventive care, and a low level of expectation of avoiding disease (Suchman, 1965).

SUMMARY

The Negro culture can perhaps be described as one which is undergoing much change. As Negroes move from a rural setting to an urban environment their cultural patterns and traditions may no longer be appropriate, and the difficult development of new cultural patterns has often been accompanied by the breakdown of family structure and many other social problems. Some Negroes have achieved stability and, in the process, appear to have identified rather closely with the predominantly Anglo middle-class system of values and attitudes. For those who have not, social agencies must recognize the often confusing complex of cultural influences and strive to combat the feeling of hopelessness which so often characterizes the lower-class Negro.

Report of Group Meetings Concerning Cultural Differences of Negro and Latin-American Groups of Texas

To help identify attitudes, reactions, and perceptions of the problem of mental retardation in Texas' minority ethnic groups, three meetings were held with specialists from community welfare and service agencies; many of the group members were themselves leaders of the ethnic groups being discussed. The meetings were very loosely structured; a few questions had been prepared in advance, but the discussion was generally freewheeling. One meeting to discuss the Negro ethnic group was held in Austin; two meetings were held to discuss the Latin-American group, one in Corpus Christi and the other in San Benito. A third field trip was made to several West Texas cities to determine whether or not major regional differences existed.

REPORT OF THE LATIN-AMERICAN GROUP

The two meetings of welfare and service agency personnel concerned with the problems of the Latin-American group are summarized together in the following paragraphs. Although both groups were generally in agreement, the group in San Benito, which is in the Rio Grande Valley, tended more to feel that there were some differences in the way Latin Americans reacted to the problem of mental retardation than did the group in Corpus Christi. This difference may be coincidental, or it may possibly indicate that within one ethnic group there may be regional variations in cultural patterns. The Rio Grande Valley is immediately adjacent to Mexico, and there is much communication and constant movement of people from both countries back and forth across the border. It is possible then that there is a more distinct cultural atmosphere among the Latin Americans here than in Corpus Christi, 150 miles removed from the border, where the group felt that cultural differences were less significant.

Many different areas of concern were represented at the meetings. As an example, the meeting in Corpus Christi was attended by 13 persons: five welfare workers, two ministers, two vocational rehabilitation counselors and the director of Goodwill Industries, one public health nurse, and two physicians—one the director of county public health services, the other a psychiatrist responsible for the mental health division of the City-County Health Department. Of the 13, seven were themselves Latin American, six were Anglo.

This group seemed to be of the opinion that there were no real differences that would distinguish the Latin-American ethnic group from any other in regard to perception and feeling about the problem of mental retardation. A few tentative, subtle differences were advanced, but these were advanced hesitantly and were generally challenged by some of the other members of the group. For example, it was conjectured by one or two of the members that the similarity of response of persons of this group to that of the Anglo group was dependent upon the degree of Anglicization of the Latin Americans; thus those most unacculturated to the Anglo system of values would be less likely to, for example, institutionalize a retarded child. This thesis was fairly generally accepted, but the premise that it was uniquely Latin American was challenged, with the point being made that various subgroups of the Anglo ethnic group and the Negro ethnic group might also be called "unacculturated," and that they would also likely respond in this same manner.

Another tentative thesis advanced was that there might be some difference in response according to age; it was felt that acculturation to Anglo standards was generally closely correlated with economic levels among younger persons, but that some older persons tended to cling to "the old ways" regardless of their income level.

This idea was corroborated by an example given by a Latin-American professional person in one of the groups, who admitted that her daughter had been treated by medical specialists for epilepsy. The girl's grandparents, who were well-educated, respected, upper middle-class members of the community expressed doubt at the medical treatment and treated the child by having her jump three times over a broom handle and a candle placed together on the floor.

This example could tend to confirm the belief that older persons might respond differently to the problem than younger, more acculturated persons. This idea was rather insecurely accepted by the group, but was attacked on the premise that the social mores and values with which this was being contrasted were of the predominantly younger Anglo society, and that older persons of any ethnic group might tend to hold to old ways of looking at problems and dealing with them.

One group indicated that the low socioeconomic group is more apt to relate illnesses of all kinds to folk beliefs. One member related that recently a friend had not gone to a funeral because his fingers were cut and bandaged, and he feared that the fumes of the corpse would enter the cuts, and he would die of the same cancer that had caused the friend's death.

Concerning the acceptance of the mentally retarded child in the community, the group pointed out that the term "mental retardation" was relatively new to their language and understanding. They indicated that the mentally retarded child, called *tonto* (stupid), is generally sympathetically accepted, but the mentally disturbed child, *loco* (crazy), was not so readily accepted. Some stigma is attached to *locos,* and the group indicated the need for an educational campaign to explain the difference between the two problems. They pointed out that the trainable mentally retarded child is very often mistakenly categorized as *loco.*

A possible difference most securely advanced, but by no means accepted unanimously, was the idea that regardless of acculturation, economic level, educational level, or any other factor, there was a slightly higher degree of family cohesiveness among Latin Americans in general which would tend to exert a little more pressure on families with retarded children to keep them at home. While this idea was generally accepted, it was stressed by several of the members that this should not be overly exaggerated, that family disorganization was common, particularly at the very low income level, in the Latin-American group just as it was in other groups. They felt it would be more appropriate to think of this difference more in terms of degree rather than substantive differentiation of this ethnic group.

Conversely, many different opinions were advanced to the effect that there were no differences in how the problem of mental retardation was perceived by the Latin-American ethnic group or in their attitudes toward it. It was, of course, recognized that these feelings and attitudes are very strongly affected by educational and economic level, but many of the persons in the group felt that there were no *cultural* differences in feeling or attitude about the problem.

The most important point to emerge from the meetings, however, was the very strong feeling of the groups that there were many differences in services provided to the Latin-American group and in their utilization of these services. Specifically, it was felt that many agencies serving the retarded were not adequately prepared to meet the needs of the Latin-American ethnic group because they were not able to adequately communicate with them. One idea stressed over and over again by the group was that social agencies had to have more staff persons who were themselves Latin American and therefore able to communicate. The question was asked whether the staff members would have to be Latin American or only able to communicate with Latin Americans; the answer was generally unanimous that anyone who could communicate, be he Latin, Anglo, Negro, or whatever, could do the job, although it might take him somewhat longer to communicate his sincere interest and concern in the Latin-American family with the problem. It was felt that the most important thing, however, was his desire to help and his ability to communicate, and that these were sufficient regardless of his ethnic background.

SUMMARY

In summary, it was the feeling of these two groups that the Latin-American person would have the same feelings and attitudes toward his having a mentally retarded child that any other person of any other ethnic group would have. It was recognized that his feelings and attitudes, and even more his responses to the problem, would be affected by his understanding of the problem, which in turn would probably be dependent upon his educational level and highly correlated with his economic level. It was stressed rather strongly at the Corpus Christi meeting, however, that there were no major differences in the feelings or attitudes of people of any ethnic group, and that in this regard the Latin American would be no different from any other person.

As mentioned above, it was felt conversely that there were many differences in the services offered to this ethnic group and in their utilization of these services, with the general trend being toward much poorer service for the Latin American than for some others.

REPORT OF THE NEGRO GROUP

The third meeting, concerned with the Negro ethnic group, was held in Austin and was attended by 11 persons, all of them Negro. Of these 11, two were welfare workers; one a vocational rehabilitation counselor; five from education, including two special education persons, one regular teacher, and two school principals; one minister; one physician in public health; and one representative from the state Office of Economic Opportunity. In this meeting, the discussion was likewise very freewheeling and only very loosely structured by the questionnaire.

In the Negro group, too, the idea seemed to be prevalent that there are no differences in the feeling or attitudes of persons toward a mentally retarded child in their family. Here again, there was the strong idea advanced that the attitudes of people were significantly affected by their understanding of the problem, which in turn depended on their education and was correlated with their economic condition. But it was felt that this was not a basic difference and that the total range of responses would exist within any ethnic group.

The idea was tentatively advanced that there might be some tendency toward keeping the child at home, with a "this is my burden to bear" attitude on the part of the family. This idea was not generally accepted as a very fundamental and basic difference existing in this ethnic group, although several persons did tend to feel that there might be a somewhat stronger feeling of this kind in the lowest socioeconomic group of Negroes than in other ethnic groups. This idea was challenged, however, by the idea that the most severely disadvantaged persons simply lack motivation to do anything about their problem; that is, their compounded frustration causes them to be somewhat more resigned to this and other problems and therefore less prone to do something about them, a characteristic which would not be unique to this or any other cultural or ethnic group.

The entire discussion seemed to echo that of the Latin-American group that, basically there are no major differences in personal feelings or attitudes about the problem of a mentally retarded child among persons of different ethnic groups. However, as in the Latin-American group, it was felt by the Negro group members that there was considerable differences in services provided to Negroes and their utilization of these services.

The group felt that the lingering effects of segregation, and the holdover effects of previous segregation accounted for some of this difference. It was pointed out that the state institutions for the mentally retarded were formerly very strictly segregated, with all Negroes living in segregated units. Although this has not been the case for several years, it was surprising to learn that some professional personnel in this group were not completely aware of the extent to which integration had been accomplished, and they used this to very graphically illustrate the fact that members of the lay Negro community would be even less aware of the fact that this change had taken place. Likewise in other areas of service, it was noted that feelings engendered among Negroes as a result of past practices of segregation were still significant in affecting their attitudes toward services. The ramifications of segregation seemed to be the most significant aspect of the discussion of the Negro group. They indicated that services for the retarded and the Negroes' utilization of these services were affected by ingrained feelings toward past injustices.

One of the recommendations of the Negro group was the need for much more public education about the problem of mental retardation and the resources which exist for it. They expressed the need for more Negro staff persons in social agencies to aid in communicating to Negro families the availability for resources for help with this problem. Other suggestions, such as transportation to special education classes, transportation of rehabilitation clients to their jobs, and other general recommendations, seemed to be not significantly different from those made by many groups in the Texas Mental Retardation Planning Study and appeared to be not especially related to the Negro ethnic group as opposed to any other.

In summary, the same attitude seemed to prevail among the Negro group as among the Latin-American groups—that human feelings and attitudes of any parent toward a handicapped child transcend ethnic group lines, but that provision of services by society and utilization of services is very obviously different among the different ethnic group populations.

It would, of course, be a mistake to assume that this is a definitive and unassailable answer to the question of the existence of differences in attitudes, feelings, and reactions of different ethnic groups to the problem of mental retardation. The true picture may yet remain to be discovered.

PART FOUR

Philosophy and Values Regarding Mentally Retarded Persons

TWENTY-FOUR

Individual Rights

INTERNATIONAL LEAGUE OF SOCIETIES FOR THE MENTALLY HANDICAPPED

STOCKHOLM SYMPOSIUM

Individual Rights

The Symposium considered that no examination of the legislative aspects of the problem of mental retardation would be complete without general consideration being given to the basic rights of the mentally retarded, not only from the standpoint of their collective rights and those of their families, but also from that of the individual rights of the retarded person as a human being. The Symposium affirmed the following:

1 GENERAL PRINCIPLES

a. The mentally retarded person has the same rights as other citizens of the same country, same age, family status, working status, etc., unless a specific individual determination has been made, by appropriate procedures, that his exercise of some or all of such rights will place his own interests or those of others in undue jeopardy. Among the rights to which this general principle may apply are: the right to choose a place to live, to engage in leisure time activities, to dispose of property, to preserve the physical and psychological integrity of his person, to vote, to marry, to have children, and to be given a fair trial for any alleged offence.

b. The retarded person has, furthermore, a right to receive such special training, rehabilitation, guidance and counselling as may strengthen his ability to exercise these rights with the minimum of abridgement.

c. Some persons may be able to exercise all these rights, in due course, even though they are, or may have been, at one time or another, identified as mentally retarded. Others may, as a result of a serious degree of mental retardation, be unable to exercise any of these rights in a meaningful way. There remains a number of retarded persons for whom modification of some or all of these rights may be appropriate.

Reprinted from "Legislative Aspects of Mental Retardation, Conclusions." Stockholm Symposium, International League of Societies for the Mentally Handicapped (Brussels, 1967), pp. 15-18. By permission of the League.

d. When modification or denial of rights is necessary, certain compensating special or alternative rights should be acquired. In cases where a number of fundamental rights are to be abridged, the special rights include the right to have a guardian appointed, who will have the legal and moral obligation to make necessary decisions on behalf of the retarded person who cannot act for himself.

e. In respect to any right which it is proposed to deny or modify, the retarded person is entitled to the benefit of special procedures, in accordance with the general legal code of his country, which will ensure that:

1. an evaluation of his social capabilities to exercise the rights in question has been made by persons professionally qualified to do so;
2. both he and members of his family or other interested persons are advised in advance of the process;
3. rights of appeal to higher authorities, and especially the courts, are kept open;
4. the benefits of these and related legal provisions are not limited by the economic status of the retarded person;
5. the possibility remains of restoring at a later date any right which is denied, should the circumstances later justify restoration;
6. there is provision for periodic review of the necessity to restrict rights;
7. the physical and psychological integrity of his person is preserved.

2   GUARDIANSHIP

A retarded person, whether he is an adult or a child who is an orphan or abandoned, and who has a general inability to manage his life has a right to have a guardian who is legally and actually qualified to protect his interests and promote his personal welfare. The following points should be included in developing a system of guardianship for the mentally retarded:

a. In the case of an adult there should be provision for having him declared a legal minor.
b. The procedure should be as simple as is consistent with the proper weighing of the information concerning the actual and prospective intellectual and social competence of the retarded person and the qualifications of the prospective guardian.
c. The procedure should be without cost to the retarded person or to his family.
d. The guardian appointed should be one who will render conscientious service to the ward in the light of modern understanding of the nature of his condition; no person should be appointed who is responsible for rendering a direct service to the retarded person.
e. There should be provision for continuity of the guardianship and in particular for the appointment of suitable successor guardians when no member of the family remains available. A representative or member of a parents' organisation or a parent may prove suitable.
f. Guardians other than parents should be compensated for expenses incurred. In

addition, they should receive fees for their services to the person. These should be in accordance with the actual duties performed, rather than based only on the income of the retarded person. Basic costs should be paid from public funds.

g. Guardians should consider the wishes of their wards to the extent that these may be reasonable, having in mind the concept of an "extended minority".

h. A guardian should, in general, be empowered to use his discretion on behalf of his ward to initiate and consent to any action which a competent adult might undertake for himself.

3 CUSTODY

a. A parent of a person under 21 years of age or a guardian of a retarded person may arrange for his admission to a suitable facility for his care, training or treatment, in which case the institutional authorities may exercise immediate custody and control over him during his attendance.

b. However, without prejudice to a child's normal educational rights, no retarded person should be legally committed to any institution without his consent or that of his parent or guardian, unless it has been demonstrated that his behaviour constitutes a danger to himself or others or that he is in need of special education and that such restriction of his activity is required in his own or in the public interest.

c. In such a case he should be committed only to such a facility (whether it be an educational, psychiatric, penal or other rehabilitation institution) as has a programme adopted to his training and treatment needs.

d. Indefinite commitments without provision for periodic review or renewal should not be permitted.

e. Contacts between the mentally retarded and their parents and guardians should not be unduly restricted. On the contrary, they should be encouraged in order to preserve the ties which are so essential to the well-being of the retarded person and his family. Visiting rights of parents and guardians of mentally retarded persons living in residential institutions should be as liberal as possible. When there is no particular medical or other reason to the contrary, a resident in an institution should be allowed to visit his parents or guardian or to leave the institution temporarily for other suitable recreational purposes.

4 RESEARCH

a. Mentally retarded persons, as well as normal or volunteer patients are first of all human beings and medical or psychological sciences should be deeply protective of human dignity, human integrity and human life.

Accordingly, the Symposium recommends that the Declaration of Helsinki (1964), Code drawn by the World Medical Association should be observed as follows:

"In the field of clinical research a fundamental distinction must be recognized between clinical research in which the aim is essentially therapeutic for a patient, and clinical research the essential object of which is purely scientific and without therapeutic value to the person subjected to the research.

The subject of clinical research should be in such a mental, physical and legal state as to be able to exercise fully his power of choice."

b. The Symposium draws attention to and recommends the adoption of the English law, in which parents or guardians have no right of giving consent to treatment if the procedure is not for the child's direct benefit.

TWENTY-FIVE

The Law and the Retarded

REPORT OF THE TASK FORCE ON LAW

The Social Context

Growing understanding of a broad disability such as retardation usually sets off three altogether different processes, each of which affects the others, and has a bearing on practical decisions.

First, general understandings, the presumptions on which people operate every day, are altered so that human behavior comes to be seen in a substantially different light. This has occurred in relation to what we have learned both about mental disease and mental retardation. Second, important institutions such as school, church and home alter their views, doctrines and practices in the light of new knowledge. Lastly, new, specialized social institutions and services designed to deal with the problem are brought into being.

Ours is a society in flux. It accommodates the mentally retarded in changing ways, both in its ordinary social institutions and by special provisions for the retarded. These provisions and accommodations—present and projected—are the subject of much of the full Report of the President's Panel, to which this Task Force study is an adjunct. The law must consider not only new knowledge concerning the retarded but also the new contexts in which such knowledge is found.

What especially needs discussion is the bearing of our problem of changes in our ordinary social institutions. These institutions are of two kinds: those addressed to other social problems such as delinquency, dependency, chronic disability, etc., and those not concerned with "problems" as such, but with wider aspects of living, such as the church, the school and the law generally.

Thus, what the public school system does, or leaves undone, influences what it means to be or to have a mentally retarded child. It also affects the burden laid on more specialized institutions.

A major principle of the American school system is free education for *all* children. Many state constitutions guarantee each child the right to basic educational oppor-

From *Report of the Task Force on Law, The President's Panel on Mental Retardation* (Washington, U.S. Government Printing Office, 1964), pp. 10-28.

tunities at public expense. These mandates do not specifically exclude children because of physical or mental handicapping conditions. Obviously, retarded children require special educational services and programs if they are to receive opportunities equal in value, if not in kind, to those received by normal children. The responsibility for applying this principle has been placed upon the local school systems with stimulation and support being provided from the state and federal governments.

In varying degrees, and with more or less success, local school boards have tackled the problem of providing services for educable, mildly retarded children. But on the whole, they have fallen short of what we conceive to be their obligation to moderately and severely retarded children. To the extent that the moderately retarded can learn academic skills, they may be provided for. But they, and the severely retarded, can profit by *training* both in personal habits and in simple unskilled occupations. The moderately retarded, for instance, may sometimes be trained to undertake semi-skilled work. It is in providing for these trainable retarded children that our public school systems have generally failed.

The emergence of governmental and non-governmental service programs, not specifically addressed to retardation, profoundly affects the context of the retardation problem. The various social security and disability insurance programs have already had a notable effect. Even things as seemingly remote as the formation or extension of a Boy Scout troop, a family service association, a factory inspections service, or a state program to provide visual aids in schools, are all relevant.

The richer these general services, and the more easily available they are, the less the need for special services for the retarded. (It should be noted, however, that even where general services exist, they may in practice be "unavailable" to the lower classes simply because their procedures are not adapted to lower-class life, and their vocabulary and way of looking at things may be incomprehensible to lower-class people.) The general services remove from the special services for the retarded only that part of their burden which the special services were not organized to bear, but are required to bear if others will not. The optimum condition obtains only when each fulfills its proper function, e.g., when mental hospitals have to accept non-psychotic retarded persons because waiting lists are too long at residential care facilities, both the mentally ill and the retarded are hurt, and the hospital is crippled because it is trying to perform a function for which it was not intended.

What is true for general services and institutions is also true for general law. For instance, to the extent that the law protecting minors generally is adequate, the burden of providing special legislation for the retarded minor is reduced. Such general protective legislation is from "strangers" towards "kin," from the specialist towards the non-specialist—in general, as far as possible towards the resources of the person himself, his family, friends, neighbors, etc., strengthened and buttressed, as need be, by more formalized resources.

Laws and their administration influence the extent to which the mentally retarded are permitted to benefit from these trends and advances.

Justice for the Retarded

We are a nation pledged to "liberty and justice for all." But we do not conceive "liberty" as license; unlimited liberties for all are untenable in theory and in practice. Justice is concerned, in part, with achieving maximum liberties, within the limitations of physical and biological circumstances and the needs of an orderly society. We regard the law as an instrument of justice reflecting, although imperfectly, the principles of fair play acceptable to most members of society. Yet laws differ among the fifty states. These differences sometimes reflect inadequacies in formulation, or delay in reformulation of laws to express current understanding and mores. They also reflect differences in social and political values.

It is deceptively easy to measure liberty by the relative lack of physical confinement. This is but one, and not always the most important, aspect of liberty. More fundamentally, liberty is freedom of choice within the general system of laws and social values. The individual's liberty is impaired when he is not permitted the same range of choices as his peers. Many people in our society, the retarded included, suffer from unauthorized or unsanctioned curtailment of their liberties. It must be our constant concern to correct and offset these, especially since the people directly concerned are often unable to struggle effectively on their own behalf.

In a system which values order and consistency, the interests of individuals are intertwined, and all of us are threatened when the rights of any of us are abridged. To the extent that the citizen sees himself or his child or his friend potentially in a similar situation, to that extent is his interest in justice intensified. Conversely the citizen is least likely to protect the rights of another with whom he has trouble identifying. Therein lies some hazard to the retarded.

To say that the interests of different individuals and the assurance of their respective liberties are intertwined is not to deny that they may sometimes be competitive and even antithetical, at least in the short run. When the disparate needs of the retarded and normal child compete, the way of justice may be very difficult indeed.

If there were no antithesis of interests among the members of society, there would be little need for laws, and less for lawyers. The antithesis between individual and individual is usually the focus of the civil law and the antithesis between the individual and society is usually the focus of the criminal law. Both must be explored. The resolution of inequities between persons is likely to revolve around damages and restitution; the resolution of conflict between the individual and society involves the ambiguous concepts of "guilt" and "punishment," which have altered meaning for some of the retarded.

"Equality before the law" is predicated on the assumption that everyone has roughly comparable capacities to invoke its protections and to abide by its proscriptions. The minimum set of personal characteristics, which the law ordinarily takes for granted, may not be totally present in the mentally retarded person, but neither will it be totally absent. He will have, in some measure, "subaverage general intellectual functioning" and "impairment in adaptive behavior."

From "impairment in adaptive behavior" we must infer some inability to handle one's affairs with ordinary prudence and foresight. Bertrand Russell has noted that, "Forethought, which involves doing unpleasant things now for the sake of pleasant things in the future, is the most essential mark of mental development." In those with limited mental development, forethought is erratic. In the majority of the mentally retarded, foresight, and the ability to act upon it, is partial and distorted. Many are influenced by immediate prospects and ignore the distant consequences.

The results of the disability are not necessarily predictable, and are of varying significance in different situations. Some mentally retarded adults can handle money, but show no judgment in the selection of companions and models for their own behavior, while in others the situation may be exactly reversed. Some of the mentally retarded can, through ordinary forms of discipline, learn to modify their behavior; others do not distinguish punishment from accidental misfortune. One may report truth, another fantasy; one may be capable of recollecting a temporal but not a logical sequence of events, another neither. One may be capable of forming intent to harm; another neither intends nor foresees the consequences of his act.

This variability has long been understood by those who work with the mentally retarded, and has been the subject of much specific investigation in the last half century. While legislators, lawyers and judges have not been ignorant of this developing knowledge, the law itself has tended to deal in absolutes. Before it, the retardate is either incompetent or competent, committed or free. The defendant is either responsible or not responsible, triable or not triable, punishable by ordinary standards or not at all.

With the development of new alternatives in treatment, our community and residential institutions are in a better position to overcome the rigidities of the law in the interest of giving the retarded individual the benefit of modern knowledge concerning his growth, development and ability to learn, and to modify his behavior in response to various social stresses and situations.

We recognize that, for practical purposes, provision must be made for forms of mental retardation so severe as to cause complete lack of responsibility for criminal acts, general incompetence, total inability to participate in a trial, and so on. But these are extremes. The law must take more explicit account of less severe cases, which are, after all, the majority.

It has been said that the constitutional mandate of equal protection under the law requires that "all persons . . . shall be treated alike, under like circumstances and conditions, both in the privileges conferred and in the liabilities imposed."[1] Sometimes it is apparent that some specific factor is needed to provide equal treatment for the unequally endowed. If a stenographic record of trial proceedings is necessary for an adequate appeal, the defendant who cannot afford one is entitled to receive a free copy in order that he may appeal on an equal basis with others. If height is an advantage, the short man may at least be given a box to stand on. But bolder and more far reaching supplements may be needed where intellectual stature or social adaptability lies far beneath customary standards.

To give a person liberty to choose between alternatives of which he can have no appreciation is to defeat and mock the concept of liberty. It goes without saying that restitution of a missing capacity in the person himself, through every available form of treatment, should be the primary objective. But for those among the mentally retarded for whom restitution of the capacity to use liberty is not now and not foreseeably possible justice requires an effort at substitution. Just as a paralyzed limb may be amputated and a prosthetic device which functions with comparable effectiveness substituted, so occasions arise when a vitiated legal right must be excised and some substitution made. Protective intervention may be the device which maximizes liberty in such a case. But as the surgeon conserves all usable tissue, and removes only that which interferes with the patient's human function, so the court must adjust its determinations and dispositions.

The possibility of doing justice, and thus fulfilling the function of the law, turns upon at least two conditions: correct appreciation of the relevant circumstances, and a suitable range of possible dispositions. Failing the first, justice is truly blind; failing the second, it is impotent. Justice is blind if it does not inquire into the significance of mental retardation as a relevant circumstance, and impotent if it has no dispositional variants suited to the conditions it finds.

For convenience, we can say that justice, like all public policy, must deal with immediate problems, with short-run problems, and with long-run problems. The immediate problem is the disposition of the specific case which has brought the retarded individual into court, taking into account both what has brought him there and the services available to rehabilitate him. This is a matter, so to speak, of minimum injustice under immediate unalterable conditions. Short-run concerns would include for example, improvements in the special education system for the retarded and provision of recreation or counseling services to prevent the accentuation of retardation. Such action partially offsets prior injustice by providing improved solutions.

The long-run problem for justice in regard to retardation is to ensure that every American child has the opportunity to be "created equal"—in the sense that he be neither born so badly that his equality is destroyed before he comes into it, nor born into such circumstances that the promise of his equal birth is broken before his life is fairly begun. The state cannot assure a child a good set of genes; nor can it assure every child that he is born, wanted, to loving parents, who have the means both material and spiritual for his succor. But it does not lie beyond the reach of justice to insist that no child be negligently born (without elementary pre- and post-natal care) or negligently exposed after birth to surroundings, physical or social, that alter his chances for a rewarding maturity.

To fail to supply, as quickly as possible, as specifically as possible and as efficiently as possible any reasonable medical, social or legal remedy for retardation is to impose upon a child the greatest injustice of all.

Mental Retardation and Civil Law

Before discussing specifics we shall briefly mention some general principles which we think should control the application of civil law to the mentally retarded.

We would minimize intervention by the law insofar as possible. The courts should be regarded as a residual resource, if not a last recourse. Clearly, the intervention of public authorities is not required where social or personal interests can be served by other means.

Legislation to protect all the disabled under one rule or provision is, where practicable, clearly preferable to legislation for special classes of the disabled. Where, for instance, identical legislation would equally serve the needs of all "exceptional" children, this should be preferred to ad hoc legislation on behalf of each of the subgroups of this class.

There will nevertheless remain a need for some legislation dealing with specific disablements. This legislation should be such that nothing is done for the retarded person, his family, kin, guardian or community organization that they can do for themselves. On the other hand if we are thus to devolve responsibility, we must insure that they have means at hand to perform their tasks.

We would minimize mandatory requirements wherever voluntary compliance can be obtained. As we have said, the richer and better the services available to the retarded, the less need there is of coercive intervention to provide care. It is rare nowadays that the law has to be invoked to force a necessary operation or blood transfusion on an objecting person. Unfortunately, it is not rare for the law to be brought into play to secure needed action where mental disorder is concerned. This is partly because some of the people affected are in no position to make judgments about what is best for them, partly because there are real doubts in the public's mind about the value of admitting the disordered individual to a mental hospital. But, as the mental hospital improves, and as people are made aware of its improvement, it can be predicted that the necessity for involuntary commitments will lessen. Indeed, this has already begun to happen. A similar trend should be fostered with respect to the retarded. The need for coercion thus stands in inverse proportion to the value of the services offered and the current public knowledge about them. While one branch of law provides for, and to some extent insures the improvement of services, another branch of law benefits by a reduction in the unpleasant duty of forcing decisions that should be voluntary.

Assuming the necessity of special law directed toward the mentally retarded, some additional principles must be observed if that legislation is to be efficient and effective.

First, there must be a precise identification of the group to whom the special laws will apply. This identification, and any sub-classifications, must reflect the purpose and function of the law, not merely some abstract definition of mental retardation. For example, if the law is designed to make available special education services, the definitions should reflect the educational objectives, recognizing that these objectives are to be accomplished differently with children of different intellectual capacities or patterns. If the purpose of the law is to protect society from behavior of a socially unacceptable variety, then the law should define those retarded persons who present this threat and specify the procedures by which they will be identified.

If the purpose of the law is to compel the use by a retarded adult, not otherwise incompetent, of a therapeutic or educational program, the law should describe in functional terms the characteristics of those who may be the subject of this compulsion. If the law is to define long-term protective supervision, then eligibility and sub-classification should be clear. Such classifications will lean heavily on our knowledge of impaired adaptive behavior.

Experience has shown that when several handicapping conditions coexist, law and administrative practice may, by classification, create a no-man's land. An example is the blind mentally retarded child who receives service neither from the agency for the blind nor from the agency for the mentally retarded. Hence, two qualifications add up to a disqualification. These oversights and injustices are best met by legislative and administrative attention to defining the functions of agencies so that every person having a right to service on any count will receive it from some source.

Even when the gross category to which a person belongs has been established, there still remain substantial differences among individual needs. Legislation should not only allow for but direct attention to such personal differences, and to the ways in which they change with time.

The law must also face the difficult task of encouraging flexibility of operation in all institutions and services for the retarded without abandoning its beneficent protection of their rights. The way of appeal to it is never to be foreclosed, and the law must always be able to command information essential for the defense of the defenseless. Judicial intervention should be reserved for significant and critical occasions when instrumentalities "down the line" have failed, however. Justice will be better served when those instrumentalities are bolstered within a network of authorized checks and balances. We shall propose later some specific ways in which this network may be strengthened.

The critical issue between the law and the caretaking professions is the question of authority to impose "superior" judgment on an unwilling, unconscious, unprotected or uninformed subject. Society has worked out some general rules which cover most of these situations: the willingness of the parent is substituted for that of his minor child, the consent of next of kin suffices for the unconscious adult, and so on. Concurrence of a professional and a partisan of the patient protects all of them. But mental disability in the adult lends itself to no such relatively easy solutions. The advances of science have complicated rather than simplified the debate between the law and the caretaking professions—medicine, social work, administration and the rest. This is not to be deplored, so long as the patient's benefit remains the goal of each.

Constant communication between the law and the other professions is essential for proper accommodation of their competing concerns. Law and medicine are among the most valuable disciplines on which the retarded have a claim. Their capacity to do good is great but by no means boundless. It can be dissipated in a system which demands needless formalities and which, through the abrasion of routine, dulls the professional acumen which should be the retardate's greatest defense.

A just society will allocate to the cause of the retarded a fair share of the time and attention of its precious corps of talents in science and social management. But a system which requires like rules to be applied to grossly unlike situations wastes time and talent and destroys liberty. The processes of commitment to mental institutions in many states are inadequate and wasteful. They actually impede justice.

Because of the nature of retardation and because of the many advances in dealing with it, it is essential that the whole body of relevant law be reviewed from time to time in each jurisdiction. Indeed, it would be wise to provide machinery for more and more frequent review.

It is a basic democratic principle that no diminution of human rights and human dignity can be countenanced by the law for any person—let alone any class of persons—except for good reason, following due process, and then to the minimum degree necessary and for the shortest period possible. A correlative principle is that, where human rights have lapsed from disuse, the law should revitalize them and provide alternatives for those that cannot be exercised as the law originally intended. The primary justification for limitation of the retardate's rights must be that he lacks minimum capacity to assess and act upon his own self interest and to assert his own human and legal rights upon which the law otherwise applicable to him is predicated. A second justification lies in the jeopardy in which his incapacity may place the rights of others. The retardate needs protectors who place his interests first and look to his rights above others, but the law must serve the interests of all impartially.

Protection of these rights cannot, in our opinion, be completely delegated by the courts to non-judicial personnel. Where there is a partial delegation, as when a retardate is placed in the custody of the superintendent of a residential center or under the care of a guardian, an appeal by or on behalf of the retardate must always be available from their decisions.

Those charged with the care and custody of the mentally retarded will naturally urge that the patient be left to their ministrations. They will argue sincerely—especially the competent and devoted workers among them—that the patient will receive maximum benefit when the experts are allowed to exercise full discretion without interference from outside agencies and without the necessity of cumbersome formalities. Cumbersome formalities—especially where they are unnecessary—we would all be willing to dispense with. Regrettably the law cannot deal in good intentions. The law is always the ultimate recourse where rights are in any way suspended.

Our basic position is that all rights normally held by anyone are also held by the retarded. We turn now to a specific discussion of the nature of limits that must be placed upon the retarded in some circumstances and to the problem of protecting their rights in those circumstances.

1. ACTIVITIES

The retardate must have unhampered access to all lawful activities, except those for which he is disqualified by lawful restrictions.

Such restrictions may be of several kinds. The first includes activities for which some general "capacity," "competency," "soundness of mind," or similar standard is the legal touchstone, such as the right to enter into enforceable contracts or to make a valid will. A second category relates to special restrictions which have no direct reference to "general competence" and which most adults, but only some who are retarded, can satisfy. Some retarded people can drive a car safely, for example, others of equal "general competence" cannot. A third category concerns activities for which the law requires a named competence beyond the customary knowledge and achievements of the general population, e.g., licensing requirements for a wide variety of businesses and professions, particularly where the licensing requires formal examination, or the demonstration of special experience or skill.

The retardate may thus be excluded from a number of activities, or precluded from the exercise of what would be his rights if he were not retarded. This can happen without any formal challenge, or identification of retardation. But it does not render the procedure contrary to his interest, or to the public interest, provided the statutory or administrative requirements are reasonably related to the performance of the regulated activity. It is, however, important to avoid indiscriminate disqualification from a particular activity because of a finding of "incompetence" under a statute regulating other activities of a different type.

2. SOCIAL RELATIONS

a. *Marriage:* Mental retardation in and of itself should not be a legal disqualification for marriage. A study carried out in one state on persons identified in school as retarded showed a normal proportion successfully married. State laws qualifying the right of the retarded to marry vary considerably, only eight being entirely silent on the subject. Statutes prohibiting the marriage of "idiots and imbeciles" are common. A few states disqualify the "feeble-minded," although it is not always clear how they are supposed to be identified. Other states disqualify persons who have been confined in an institution because of "feeble-mindedness."[2] The statutory exceptions to the prohibitions are sometimes impossible to fulfill. For instance, a "feeble-minded" person would ordinarily be unable to show that he had been "cured," as one statute requires. But the principle objection to this type of legislation is that disqualification in one sphere can be translated into disqualification in another without further review.

Here again justice must weigh the rights of the retarded and the rights of others. There are three questions to be answered. Can the retarded prospective spouse assume the responsibilities of marriage? Will the minimum expectations for care and nurture of any children be realized? Will the genetic risks be so small that society can permit them to be taken? There are no general answers to these questions, for the answers do not necessarily depend on the degree of retardation. We merely point out that the rights and dignity of the retarded, their access to permissible activities, and to the comforts, companionship and protection of marriage, must be considered. Generally speaking, we suggest that marriage by a retarded person who is under guardianship should be permitted only with the consent of the court, acting with the advice of the guardian. Certainly it should not be categorically denied to all retarded persons.

b. *Sterilization:* Sterilization is a surgical procedure, otherwise harmless, which physically prevents conception. There are operations applicable to men and to women. Even with the intervention of additional surgery, the operations are very rarely, if ever, reversible in women; and reversible in men only in a very small percentage of cases.

Distinction must be made between voluntary and involuntary sterilization. To the extent that voluntary sterilization may be considered a right, as it is by some people, it is one to which the mentally retarded person should have access if he is capable of voluntary action.

The arguments put forward in favor of sterilization of some mentally retarded persons are usually either social or eugenic. The social argument addresses itself to the right of every child to be born to parents who can give him at least minimum opportunities, and conversely to the right of a mentally retarded adult not to be deprived of marriage when the complications of child rearing would tip the balance against him in a marginal case. A limited number of voluntary sterilization operations have been performed on such grounds in recent years.

Laws authorizing involuntary sterilization of some retardates are in effect in more than half the states today. These laws were passed early in this century and their purpose was primarily eugenic—to prevent the retarded from reproducing other retarded persons in or out of wedlock. There are serious questions about both the validity of the scientific assumptions on which these laws were based and the way in which it is decided who should be sterilized.

Only a small percentage of retarded children inherit their condition from retarded parents. Thus even if sterilization of the retarded were total, the incidence of mental retardation would drop only slightly. Types of retardation vary, and their heredity characteristics, if any, vary as well.

Most of the statutes which authorize involuntary sterilization apply only to persons who are at the same time confined in institutions. The procedures by which selection for sterilization is made vary widely. In practice, great discretion is placed in the superintendent of the institution. Legal protections for patients range from the slightest to a very careful system of judicial review. In view of the general irreversibility of sterilization, no laxity in protecting the retarded can be allowed.

Although the basis of laws providing for involuntary sterilization is usually claimed to be eugenic, and as such should apply equally to men and women, they are in practice applied more frequently to women. It is clear that in cases where the retarded woman is able to be maintained or to maintain herself economically in the open community, the real issue being decided is whether procreation is to be prevented by segregating her in a controlled environment instead of by surgical means.

We do not take a position on whether sterilization can ever be ethically justified. Our recommendations are limited to urging that the operation not be allowed to result from misjudgment as to its scientific need or from inadequate opportunity for administrative and judicial review.

c. *Adoption:* Some laws operate to the detriment of retarded children by making overly difficult their adoption by informed and willing prospective parents. On the other hand, parents who unwittingly adopt a retarded child may, under some laws, seek annulment of the adoption at any time within five years. We doubt that the rights of the child are adequately protected by such laws. It would be more equitable to hold that from adoption forward the risks which adoptive and natural parents are expected to sustain should be the same.

3. PRIVACY AND DIGNITY

In the case of many of the disabled, the retarded among them, rights to privacy and dignity are peculiarly difficult to preserve. The term "retarded" is frequently stigmatic in the minds of the ill-informed. The establishment of a differential legal status, even if necessary for beneficial purposes, frequently entails the attachment of a damaging label. We therefore recommend that judicial and administrative procedures be adapted to provide as much privacy as possible for the retardate and his family.

4. SERVICES

The retardate must have unhampered access to programs and services appropriate to his particular needs. Unhampered access is not to be construed to mean forced use.

5. LIBERTY

The transcendent question of liberty must not be obscured by the development of social services and programs of care which now grade into one another, with varied degrees of restrictions in each. Nor may liberty be truncated on the ground that a hearing whose results could deprive the retardate of liberty may be harmful or even traumatic; nor on the ground that he failed to object to a decision affecting him. This last should be avoided with particular care since retardation too often implies an incapacity to make a proper objection.

References

[1]*Hayes v. Missouri*, 120 U.S. 68, 71-72 (1887).
[2]See Lindman and McIntyre, *The Mentally Disabled and the Law*, Table VII-A, p. 207 (1961).

TWENTY-SIX

The Law of the Retardate and the Retardation of the Law

JOHN R. SEELEY

We expect the law now to lead (as in the desegregation decision), now to lag (as in the case of capital punishment). Perhaps, in general, we must expect it to be more laggard than not. But we hardly expect the law's delays to extend so far as to confront the facts of this century with presuppositions of the middle ages. Much law is retarded, but little is so absolutely retarded as the law regarding the relatively retarded themselves.

I hope it does not sound callous to say that, from the viewpoint of law reform and the consequent improvement of human life, the retarded seem as if sent by God. For, as the retardate confronts the law, he poses—unless Justice gives a strange new meaning to her blindfold—the problems of all mankind, in a form only more highly visible and only more purely pathetic. To deal with him seriously, we may have to reconstitute society. If so, he may well be a hero of history, just as the little chimney-boys, the little mine and factory slaves of England were the heroic figures who broke the iron logic of the "Economics" that would shortly have made of all men everywhere mere commodities if it had been permitted to endure. There is a straight line from the law's taking count of the factory-children's moans to the vast network of protective and social services of today. There may be a similar straight line from the present plight of the retardate, once legally taken count of, to a more generous, reasonable and noble society altogether.

For the retardate, as he faces the law, raises clearly (bless him!) a number of vital issues which all men raise indeed but none so clearly and unambiguously. And the clarity of the retardate's case makes more difficult the evasion of the law-man's duty.

The retardate poses the first issue by what he is. A retardate is merely (a) a person classified as belonging to that X% of the population who (b) *do certain defined things* worst, because (c) they *cannot* do them any better. I put the matter so because I want it to be clear (a) that it is a social classification we are dealing with, and not a "natural fact" like, say, the taste of salt; (b) that the X% is or can be 1%, 2%, 5% or 25% . . . according to social convenience; (c) that the social test depends

Reprinted from *Mental Retardation,* Vol. 14, No. 2 (June, 1964), pp. 6-9. By permission of the author and the Canadian Association for Retarded Children. Copyright John R. Seeley.

on what things are socially defined (like schoolwork, say) to be peculiarly impor- ↓
tant; and (d) that the test that distinguishes those who *can not* from those who *will
not* is itself a very subtle social test. I want to be clear on these points because they
are important to seeing clearly what is at stake. The whole question of who is or is
not "retarded" depends on social desire (or "need") to classify in this way at all; it
depends on the percentage arbitrarily chosen; on the tasks held to be sufficiently
vital to justify the discrimination; and on the techniques accredited for distinguishing between "won'ts" and "can'ts."

These points may seem primarily "philosophical" but, as with all well-taken
points, they are pre-eminently practical. For "retardation" cannot be "wiped out,"
because it is defined in relative terms. If all those presently defined as retarded were
whisked out of sight tomorrow, then society would simply turn its attention to a
new group to whom it would give the same label, the same worry, the same treatment—or neglect.

We must recognize the damage that is done by the defining process itself, in ↓
which a human being becomes very largely what he is said to be as a consequence of
what is said about him. And we must also recognize that, as society becomes more
complex, the tasks which it uses for the retarded-unretarded test become ever more
complex, abstract and difficult, so that the proportion of the "effectively retarded"
becomes continuously greater. And as affluence rises, permitting us to be more
"merciful" to more people, and as automation increases, making more and more
people productively irrelevant, the class of the "functionally retarded" that comes
into sight is some very sizeable fraction of the population. The retardate functions
thus, at least, as a forecast case for us all; all of us in most respects, and most of us
in all respects, are going to be confronted with problems identical with or nearly
analogical to his. So whatever we do or fail to do for the retardate now will speak
one way or the other for the greater part of the population soon.

But indeed we need not wait so long. For the retardate raises in his proper person—without any futher social changes—questions that are proximate and pressing for every person even now.

If the retardate raises, as he must in his confrontation with the law, questions
about even justice in relation to uneven capacity, he raises the question for all of us.
Whether the issue is to "know right from wrong," to foresee the remoter consequences of present acts, to understand the law's own complexities, to read and
write "adequately," to dress or express ourselves appropriately, either with social
competence or to meet the law's demands, we all of us fall on a continuum which
can only by a strained and useless legal fiction, be separated into discontinuous
classes: "retardate" and "non-retardate." Just as the U.S. Supreme Court doctrine
that State Courts *must* provide counsel in felony cases only under "special circumstances" had to be stretched and stretched (illiteracy, to mental defect, to complexity of the case, to virtually anything), so the meaning of "retardation" will have to
be stretched and stretched as the obvious and intractable facts require. Just as this
doctrine had recently to be reversed (in the Gideon case), so that all defendants
under felony charges must have counsel (i.e., all circumstances are special), so will

the law finally have to concede *for all,* what is so obviously true for the retarded—that capacities affect cases. When that day comes, the retarded will have led us into a new and humane law, as children are said to lead us into the Kingdom of Heaven.

But as in criminal cases, so in civil.

The same logic will similarly force us to revise our doctrines of "fair trade," taking advantage, false representation, fraudulence and fraud. If we raise a question of capacity to make a contract for *some,* said to be of lesser capacity to understand the tricks of trade and the force of technical language, we are only a step away from raising the relevant question for *all,* depending on the relation of their defensive capacity to the trickiness and complexity of the contract or contractor. The gross principle is admitted that contracts are void that rest upon gross inequality in the contracting capacities of the parties. The fine principle cannot be far off that "fair" (and enforceable) is defined by a similar decency. (Actually the Gideon case goes in that direction; no layman, necessarily legally incompetent, may any longer be pitted against a trained public prosecutor.) When that day comes, the retarded will have led us openly and on principle into a state of law and human relations that we had been approaching piecemeal and pusilanimously anyway via pure food laws, security exchange regulations and other disability-equalizing measures in unconnected matters and bits and pieces.

But even as with the central principles of civil and criminal law, so with such "special law" as appears to be written for the peculiar protection of the retarded; from the laws of guardianship, to proper hearings in the assessment of "competence" (particular or general), to the particular provisions it is appropriate for the general educational system to make for those who do not so readily fit is over-procrustean bed. Every one of these questions is only in the crudest first instance a question for a special class of people; it is almost instantly a question for all. It concerns the proper care of children or those anyhow handicapped ("all sorts and conditions of men," but especially "all those in any ways afflicted or distressed," as the Prayer Book rightly has it); it concerns the adjustment generally of social resources to *all* differences, whether of "capacity" or desire. So may the retarded lead us into that "to everyone according to his need" which must precede the hoped for "from everyone according to his capacity."

Lastly, the retarded pose for us generally another problem. So vast a proportion of them are (in an opinion which I share) wholly and solely the product of cultural (and emotional) deprivation that they cry aloud to Heaven in their needless misery that such systematic blighting cease. But the deprivation is itself the fruit of concentrated poverty, based on unpardonable neglect. The relief of retardation thus calls, at least in an era of affluence, for the wiping out of every such pocket of poverty, every such focus of social infection of childhood, everywhere in the world, now and for ever. That, too, is a task for the law. So perhaps may the retarded lead us from a shameful night of otherhood into a prologue at least of a dawn of brotherhood.

And who will do these things? Perhaps the parents of the retarded who have done so much, together with those professionals who realize what they are about. Not for nothing, do I believe, are these children given into their care; at least, not for nothing if they care enough!

PART FIVE

Social Welfare Policy Dealing with Retarded Persons

Message from the President of the United States Relative to Mental Illness and Mental Retardation

JOHN F. KENNEDY

FEBRUARY 5, 1963.—REFERRED TO THE COMMITTEE ON INTERSTATE AND FOREIGN
COMMERCE AND ORDERED TO BE PRINTED

To the Congress of the United States:

It is my intention to send shortly to the Congress a message pertaining to this Nation's most urgent needs in the area of health improvement. But two health problems—because they are of such critical size and tragic impact, and because their susceptibility to public action is so much greater than the attention they have received—are deserving of a wholly new national approach and a separate message to the Congress. These twin problems are mental illness and mental retardation.

From the earliest days of the Public Health Service to the latest research of the National Institutes of Health, the Federal Government has recognized its responsibilities to assist, stimulate, and channel public energies in attacking health problems. Infectious epidemics are now largely under control. Most of the major diseases of the body are beginning to give ground in man's increasing struggle to find their cause and cure. But the public understanding, treatment, and prevention of mental disabilities have not made comparable progress since the earliest days of modern history.

Yet mental illness and mental retardation are among our most critical health problems. They occur more frequently, affect more people, require more prolonged treatment, cause more suffering by the families of the afflicted, waste more of our human resources, and constitute more financial drain upon both the Public Treasury and the personal finances of the individual families than any other single condition.

There are now about 800,000 such patients in this Nation's institutions—600,000 for mental illness and over 200,000 for mental retardation. Every year nearly 1,500,000 people receive treatment in institutions for the mentally ill and mentally retarded. Most of them are confined and compressed within an antiquated, vastly overcrowded, chain of custodial State institutions. The average amount expended

From Document No. 58, 86th Congress, First Session, House of Representatives, 1963.

on their care is only $4 a day—too little to do much good for the individual, but too much if measured in terms of efficient use of our mental health dollars. In some States the average is less than $2 a day.

The total cost to the taxpayers is over $2.4 billion a year in direct public outlays for services—about $1.8 billion for mental illness and $600 million for mental retardation. Indirect public outlays, in welfare costs and in the waste of human resources, are even higher. But the anguish suffered both by those afflicted and by their families transcends financial statistics—particularly in view of the fact that both mental illness and mental retardation strike so often in childhood, leading in most cases to a lifetime of disablement for the patient and a lifetime of hardship for his family.

This situation has been tolerated far too long. It has troubled our national conscience—but only as a problem unpleasant to mention, easy to postpone, and despairing of solution. The Federal Government, despite the nationwide impact of the problem, has largely left the solutions up to the States. The States have depended on custodial hospitals and homes. Many such hospitals and homes have been shamefully understaffed, overcrowded, unpleasant institutions for which death too often provided the only firm hope of release.

The time has come for a bold new approach. New medical, scientific, and social tools and insights are now available. A series of comprehensive studies initiated by the Congress, the executive branch, and interested private groups have been completed and all point in the same direction.

Governments at every level—Federal, State, and local—private foundations and individual citizens must all face up to their responsibilities in this area. Our attack must be focused on three major objectives:

First, we must seek out the causes of mental illness and of mental retardation and eradicate them. Here, more than in any other area, "an ounce of prevention is worth more than a pound of cure." For prevention is far more desirable for all concerned. It is far more economical and it is far more likely to be successful. Prevention will require both selected specific programs directed especially at known causes, and the general strengthening of our fundamental community, social welfare, and educational programs which can do much to eliminate or correct the harsh environmental conditions which often are associated with mental retardation and mental illness. The proposals contained in my earlier message to the Congress on education and those which will be contained in a later message I will send on the Nation's health will also help achieve this objective.

Second, we must strengthen the underlying resources of knowledge and, above all, of skilled manpower which are necessary to mount and sustain our attack on mental disability for many years to come. Personnel from many of the same professions serve both the mentally ill and the mentally retarded. We must increase our existing training programs and launch new ones, for our efforts cannot succeed unless we increase by severalfold in the next decade the number of professional and subprofessional personnel who work in these fields. My proposals on the health professions and aid for higher education are essential to this goal, and both the proposed youth employment program and a national service corps can be of immense help. We must also expand our research efforts if we are to learn more about how to prevent and treat the crippling or malfunction of the mind.

Third, we must strengthen and improve the programs and facilities serving the mentally ill and the mentally retarded. The emphasis should be upon timely and intensive diagnosis, treatment, training, and rehabilitation so that the mentally afflicted can be cured or their functions restored to the extent possible. Services to both the mentally ill and to the mentally retarded must be community based and provide a range of services to meet community needs.

It is with these objectives in mind that I am proposing a new approach to mental illness and to mental retardation. This approach is designed, in large measure, to use Federal resources to stimulate State, local, and private action. When carried out, reliance on the cold mercy of custodial isolation will be supplanted by the open warmth of community concern and capability. Emphasis on prevention, treatment, and rehabilitation will be substituted for a desultory interest in confining patients in an institution to wither away.

In an effort to hold domestic expenditures down in a period of tax reduction, I have postponed new programs and reduced added expenditures in all areas when that could be done. But we cannot afford to postpone any longer a reversal in our approach to mental affliction. For too long the shabby treatment of the many millions of the mentally disabled in custodial institutions and many millions more now in communities needing help has been justified on grounds of inadequate funds, further studies, and future promises. We can procrastinate no more. The national mental health program and the national program to combat mental retardation herein proposed warrant prompt congressional attention.

A National Program To Combat Mental Retardation

Mental retardation stems from many causes. It can result from mongolism, birth injury or infection, or any of a host of conditions that cause a faulty or arrested development of intelligence to such an extent that the individual's ability to learn and to adapt to the demands of society is impaired. Once the damage is done, lifetime incapacity is likely. With early detection, suitable care and training, however, a significant improvement in social ability and in personal adjustment and achievement can be achieved.

The care and treatment of mental retardation, and research into its causes and cure, have—as in the case of mental illness—been too long neglected. Mental retardation ranks as a major national health, social and economic problem. It strikes our most precious asset—our children. It disables 10 times as many people as diabetes, 20 times as many as tuberculosis, 25 times as many as muscular dystrophy, and 600 times as many as infantile paralysis. About 400,000 children are so retarded they require constant care or supervision; more than 200,000 of these are in residential institutions. There are between 5 and 6 million mentally retarded children and adults—an estimated 3 percent of the population. Yet, despite these grim statistics, and despite an admirable effort by private voluntary associations, until a decade ago not a single State health department offered any special community services for the mentally retarded or their families.

States and local communities spend $300 million a year for residential treatment of the mentally retarded, and another $250 million for special education, welfare, rehabilitation, and other benefits and services. The Federal Government will this year obligate $37 million for research, training and special services for the retarded and about three times as much for their income maintenance. But these efforts are fragmented and inadequate.

Mental retardation strikes children without regard for class, creed, or economic level. Each year sees an estimated 126,000 new cases. But it hits more often—and harder—at the underprivileged and the poor; and most often of all—and most severely—in city tenements and rural slums where there are heavy concentrations of families with poor education and low income.

There are very significant variations in the impact of the incidence of mental retardation. Draft rejections for mental deficiency during World War II were 1-4 times as heavy in States with low incomes as in others. In some slum areas 10 to 30 percent of the school-age children are mentally retarded, while in the very same cities more prosperous neighborhoods have only 1 or 2 percent retarded.

There is every reason to believe that we stand on the threshold of major advances in this field. Medical knowledge can now identify precise causes of retardation in 15 to 25 percent of the cases. This itself is a major advance. Those identified are usually cases in which there are severe organic injuries or gross brain damage from disease. Severe cases of mental retardation of this type are naturally more evenly spread throughout the population than mild retardation; but even here poor families suffer disproportionately. In most of the mild cases, although specific physical and neurological defects are usually not diagnosable with present biomedical techniques, research is rapidly adding to our knowledge of specific causes: German measles during the first 3 months of pregnancy, Rh blood factor incompatibility in newborn infants, lead poisoning of infants, faulty body chemistry in such diseases as phenylketonuria and galactosemia, and many others.

Many of the specific causes of mental retardation are still obscure. Socioeconomic and medical evidence gathered by a panel which I appointed in 1961, however, shows a major causative role for adverse social, economic, and cultural factors. Families who are deprived of the basic necessities of life, opportunity, and motivation have a high proportion of the Nation's retarded children. Unfavorable health factors clearly play a major role. Lack of prenatal and postnatal health care, in particular, leads to the birth of brain-damaged children or to an inadequate physical and neurological development. Areas of high infant mortality are often the same areas with a high incidence of mental retardation. Studies have shown that women lacking prenatal care have a much higher likelihood of having mentally retarded children. Deprivation of a child's opportunities for learning slows development in slum and distressed areas. Genetic, hereditary, and other biomedical factors also play a major part in the causes of mental retardation.

The American people, acting through their Government where necessary, have an obligation to prevent mental retardation, whenever possible, and to ameliorate it when it is present. I am, therefore, recommending action on a comprehensive program to attack this affliction. The only feasible program with a hope for success must not only aim at the specific causes and the control of mental retardation but seek solutions to the broader problems of our society with which mental retardation is so intimately related.

The panel which I appointed reported that, with present knowledge, at least half and hopefully more than half, of all mental retardation cases can be prevented through this kind of "broad spectrum" attack—aimed at both the specific causes which medical science has identified, and at the broader adverse social, economic, and cultural conditions with which incidence of mental retardation is so heavily correlated. At the same time research must go ahead in all these categories, calling upon the best efforts of many types of scientists, from the geneticist to the sociologist.

The fact that mental retardation ordinarily exists from birth or early childhood, the highly specialized medical, psychological, and educational evaluations which are required, and the complex and unique social, educational, and vocational lifetime needs of the retarded individual, all require that there be developed a comprehensive approach to this specific problem.

1. PREVENTION

Prevention should be given the highest priority in this effort. Our general health, education, welfare, and urban renewal programs will make a major contribution in overcoming adverse social and economic conditions. More adequate medical care, nutrition, housing, and educational opportunities can reduce mental retardation to the low incidence which has been achieved in some other nations. The recommendations for strengthening American education which I have made to the Congress in my message on education will contribute toward this objective as will the proposals contained in my forthcoming health message.

New programs for comprehensive maternity and infant care and for the improvement of our educational services are also needed. Particular attention should be directed toward the development of such services for slum and distressed areas. Among expectant mothers who do not receive prenatal care, more than 20 percent of all births are premature—two or three times the rate of prematurity among those who do receive adequate care. Premature infants have two or three times as many physical defects and 50 percent more illnesses than full-term infants. The smallest premature babies are 10 times more likely to be mentally retarded.

All of these statistics point to the direct relationship between lack of prenatal care and mental retardation. Poverty and medical indigency are at the root of most of this problem. An estimated 35 percent of the mothers in cities over 100,000 population are medically indigent. In 138 large cities of the country an estimated 455,000 women each year lack resources to pay for adequate health care during pregnancy and following birth. Between 20 and 60 percent of the mothers receiving care in public hospitals in some large cities receive inadequate or no prenatal care—and mental retardation is more prevalent in these areas.

Our existing State and Federal child health programs, though playing a useful and necessary role, do not provide the needed comprehensive care for this high-risk group. To enable the States and localities to move ahead more rapidly in combating mental retardation and other childhood disabilities through the new therapeutic measures being developed by medical science, I am recommending:

a. A new 5-year program of project grants to stimulate State and local health departments to plan, initiate, and develop comprehensive maternity and child health care service programs, helping primarily families in this high-risk group who are otherwise unable to pay for needed medical care. These grants would be used to provide medical care, hospital care, and additional nursing services, and to expand the number of prenatal clinics. Prenatal and post partum care would be more accessible to mothers. I recommend that the initial appropriation for this purpose be $5 million, allocated on a project basis, rising to an annual appropriation of $30 million by the third year.

b. Doubling the existing $25 million annual authorization for Federal grants for maternal and child health, a significant portion of which will be used for the mentally retarded.

c. Doubling over a period of 7 years the present $25 million annual authorization for Federal grants for crippled children's services.

Cultural and educational deprivation resulting in mental retardation can also be prevented. Studies have demonstrated that large numbers of children in urban and rural slums, including preschool children, lack the stimulus necessary for proper development in their intelligence. Even when there is no organic impairment, prolonged neglect and a lack of stimulus and opportunity for learning can result in the failure of young minds to develop. Other studies have shown that, if proper opportunities for learning are provided early enough, many of these deprived children can and will learn and achieve as much as children from more favored neighborhoods. This self-perpetuating intellectual blight should not be allowed to continue.

In my recent message on education, I recommended that at least 10 percent of the proposed aid for elementary and secondary education be committed by the States to special project grants designed to stimulate and make possible the improvement of educational opportunities particularly in slum and distressed areas, both urban and rural. I again urge special consideration by the Congress for this proposal. It will not only help improve educational quality and provide equal opportunity in areas which need assistance; it will also serve humanity by helping prevent mental retardation among the children in such culturally deprived areas.

2. COMMUNITY SERVICES

As in the case of mental illnesses, there is also a desperate need for community facilities and services for the mentally retarded. We must move from the outmoded use of distant custodial institutions to the concept of community-centered agencies that will provide a coordinated range of timely diagnostic, health, educational, training, rehabilitation, employment, welfare, and legal protection services. For those retarded children or adults who cannot be maintained at home by their own families, a new pattern of institutional services is needed.

The key to the development of this comprehensive new approach toward services for the mentally retarded is twofold. First, there must be public understanding and community planning to meet all problems. Second, there must be made available a continuum of services covering the entire range of needs. States and communities need to appraise their needs and resources, review current programs, and undertake preliminary actions leading to comprehensive State and community approaches to these objectives. To stimulate public awareness and the development of comprehensive plans, I recommend legislation to establish a program of special project grants to the States for financing State reviews of needs and programs in the field of mental retardation.

A total of $2 million is recommended for this purpose. Grants will be awarded on a selective basis to State agencies presenting acceptable proposals for this broad interdisciplinary planning activity. The purpose of these grants is to provide for every State an opportunity to begin to develop a comprehensive, integrated program to meet all the needs of the retarded. Additional support for planning health-related facilities and services will be available from the expanding planning grant program for the Public Health Service which I will recommend in my forthcoming message on health.

To assist the States and local communities to construct the facilities which these surveys justify and plan, I recommend that the Congress authorize matching grants for the construction of public and other nonprofit facilities, including centers for the comprehensive treatment, training, and care of the mentally retarded. Every community should be encouraged to include provision for meeting the health requirements of retarded individuals in planning its broader health services and facilities.

Because care of the mentally retarded has traditionally been isolated from centers of medical and nursing education, it is particularly important to develop facilities which will increase the role of highly qualified universities in the improvement and provision of services and the training of specialized personnel. Among the various types of facilities for which grants would be authorized, the legislation I am proposing will permit grants of Federal funds for the construction of facilities for (1) inpatient clinical units as an integral part of university-associated hospitals in which specialists on mental retardation would serve; (2) outpatient diagnostic, evaluation, and treatment clinics associated with such hospitals, including facilities for special training; and (3) satellite clinics in outlying cities and counties for provision of services to the retarded through existing State and local community programs, including those financed by the Children's Bureau, in which universities will participate. Grants of $5 million a year will be provided for these purposes within the total authorizations for facilities in 1965 and this will be increased to $10 million in subsequent years.

Such clinical and teaching facilities will provide superior care for the retarded and will also augment teaching and training facilities for specialists in mental retardation, including physicians, nurses, psychologists, social workers, and speech and other therapists. Funds for operation of such facilities would come from State, local and private sources. Other existing or proposed programs of the Children's Bureau, of the Public Health Service, of the Office of Education, and of the Department of Labor can provide additional resources for demonstration purposes and for training personnel.

A full-scale attack on mental retardation also requires an expansion of special education, training, and rehabilitation services. Largely due to the lack of qualified teachers, college instructors, directors, and supervisors, only about one-fourth of the 1,250,000 retarded children of school age now have access to special education. During the past 4 years, with Federal support, there has been some improvement in the training of leadership personnel. However, teachers of handicapped children, including the mentally retarded, are still woefully insufficient in number and training. As I pointed out in the message on education, legislation is needed to increase the output of college instructors and classroom teachers for handicapped children.

I am asking the Office of Education to place a new emphasis on research in the learning process, expedite the application of research findings to teaching methods for the mentally retarded, support studies on improvement of curriculums, develop teaching aids, and stimulate the training of special teachers.

Vocational training, youth employment, and vocational rehabilitation programs can all help release the untapped potentialities of mentally retarded individuals. This requires expansion and improvement of our vocational education programs, as already recommended; and, in a subsequent message, I will present proposals for needed youth employment programs.

Currently rehabilitation services can only be provided to disabled individuals for whom, at the outset, a vocational potential can be definitely established. This requirement frequently excludes the mentally retarded from the vocational rehabilitation program. I recommend legislation to permit rehabilitation services to be provided to a mentally retarded person for up to 18 months, to determine whether he has sufficient potential to be rehabilitated vocationally. I also recommend legislation establishing a new program to help public and private nonprofit organizations to construct, equip, and staff rehabilitation facilities and workshops, making particular provision for the mentally retarded.

State institutions for the mentally retarded are badly underfinanced, understaffed, and overcrowded. The standard of care is in most instances so grossly deficient as to shock the conscience of all who see them.

I recommend the appropriation under existing law of project grants to State institutions for the mentally retarded, with an initial appropriation of $5 million to be increased in subsequent years to a level of at least $10 million. Such grants would be awarded, upon presentation of a plan meeting criteria established by the Secretary of Health, Education, and Welfare, to State institutions undertaking to upgrade the quality of residential services through demonstration, research, and pilot projects designed to improve the quality of care in such institutions and to provide impetus to inservice training and the education of professional personnel.

3. RESEARCH

Our single greatest challenge in this area is still the discovery of the causes and treatment of mental retardation. To do this we must expand our resources for the pursuit and application of scientific knowledge related to this problem. This will require the training of medical, behavioral, and other professional specialists to staff a growing effort. The new National Institute of Child Health and Human Development which was authorized by the 87th Congress is already embarked on this task.

To provide an additional focus for research into the complex mysteries of mental retardation, I recommend legislation to authorize the establishment of centers for research in human development, including the training of scientific personnel. Funds for 3 such centers are included in the 1964 budget; ultimately 10 centers for clinical, laboratory, behavioral, and social science research should be established. The importance of these problems justifies the talents of our best minds. No single discipline or science holds the answer. These centers must, therefore, be established on an interdisciplinary basis.

Similarly, in order to foster the further development of new techniques for the improvement of child health, I am also recommending new research authority to the Children's Bureau for research in maternal and child health and crippled children's services.

But, once again, the shortage of professional manpower seriously compromises both research and service efforts. The insufficient numbers of medical and nursing training centers now available too often lack a clinical focus on the problems of mental retardation comparable to the psychiatric teaching services relating to care of the mentally ill.

We as a Nation have long neglected the mentally ill and the mentally retarded. This neglect must end, if our Nation is to live up to its own standards of compassion and dignity and achieve the maximum use of its manpower.

This tradition of neglect must be replaced by forceful and far-reaching programs carried out at all levels of government, by private individuals and by State and local agencies in every part of the Union.

We must act—
to bestow the full benefits of our society on those who suffer from mental disabilities;
to prevent the occurrence of mental illness and mental retardation wherever and whenever possible;
to provide for early diagnosis and continuous and comprehensive care, in the community, of those suffering from these disorders;
to stimulate improvements in the level of care given the mentally disabled in our State and private institutions, and to reorient those programs to a community-centered approach;

to reduce, over a number of years, and by hundreds of thousands, the persons confined to these institutions;

to retain in and return to the community the mentally ill and mentally retarded, and there to restore and revitalize their lives through better health programs and strengthened educational and rehabilitation services; and

to reinforce the will and capacity of our communities to meet these problems, in order that the communities, in turn, can reinforce the will and capacity of individuals and individual families.

We must promote—to the best of our ability and by all possible and appropriate means—the mental and physical health of all our citizens.

To achieve these important ends, I urge that the Congress favorably act upon the foregoing recommendations.

JOHN F. KENNEDY.

The White House, February 5, 1963.

TWENTY-EIGHT

Mothers-at-Risk—Social Policy and Provision: Issues and Opportunities

VERA SHLAKMAN

During the past few years, under pressures from some very stubborn problems, we have seen developing a grand inquiry into the effectiveness of our health and welfare policies and institutions. Hardly a field of activity has been left untouched by discussion, reappraisal, or action, whether it involves new kinds of social agencies, new uses for non-professional personnel, new model social workers, new methods of reaching out to connect people with services, new ways or organizing communities, new attempts to put knowledge to work. Our present concern here with the state of maternal and child health is one example of the ferment. In this context, developing opportunities to improve the quality of health and welfare services for preventing casualties of reproduction can be grasped.

My charge is to suggest a frame of reference for discussion of the planning task, to which, like the rest of you, I will bring my own biases and preferences. I do not suggest that what I offer is either the correct or best way of getting at our problem, but it is one way of starting to think about it.

We do not now have a good, comprehensive maternal and child health policy implemented by an effective network of health and social services. What are the prospects of starting one? Can we make better use of what we have now? To answer these questions, it is helpful to start from an assessment of how we see the problem, and of the larger social conditions that shelter and nourish it.

Our central concern can be recapitulated quickly: Too many women are not receiving adequate medical care, especially, but not only, during pregnancy. Too many women, reared in poverty and deprivation, have poor nutritional histories, and many of them are marrying and having children too young, or not marrying and having children. Too many children are being born premature. The causative factors associated with reproductive casualties, extending from fetal death to a wide range of handicapping conditions, are interrelated, and the problem is widely recognized as social rather than medical in nature.[1] For when we reverse the telescope to look at the mothers who are *not* at risk, we find, to quote from the Expert Committee on Maternal and Child Health of the World Health Organization, that

Reprinted from *Mothers-at-Risk* (Garden City, N.Y., Adelphi University School of Social Work, 1966), pp. 60-80, with permission of the author and the School.

"what is very striking . . . is the high degree of reproductive efficiency shown by women born, reared and reproducing in a good environment."[2]

Social problem analysis does not always offer such apparently neatly defined targets for prevention as does the mother-at-risk. But the specificity of the target groups should not divert us from what is common to most of their situations. For practical planning and operating purposes, this specificity is an advantage, so long as the larger population of which these targets are a part is also kept in focus.

Our findings on the distribution of reproductive casualties in the population are often drawn from comparisons based on ethnicity or marital status, which reflect socio-economic status. In the absence of satisfactory data arranged according to socio-economic status, this is a useful procedure. But interpretation of the findings, influenced as it may be by prejudicial values of the community, can serve to obscure the larger target of low-income women, of which the identified subgroup of mothers-at-risk is a part. For example, Bernstein and Sauber estimated that in 1959 in New York City some 38 per cent of women pregnant out-of-wedlock had prenatal care late or not at all, compared with only 17.4 per cent of the married women who were similarly deprived.[3] The contrast is striking, but the fact is that two targets were identified, not one. Because, while some 5,000 babies were born out-of-wedlock to women without benefit of proper medical care, about 27,000 were born to married women who also did not have adequate care. In addition, teen-age girls who become mothers out-of-wedlock present a special problem of their own. Still, we should note that if young mothers are at risk, many more of them are married than unmarried. In other words, if we fix attention too closely on special groups, we will be in danger of losing larger targets.

It might be useful to ask at this point, if our approach to the problem of adequate provision and use of maternal and child services has not been moved off center by the magnetic attraction of illegitimacy. A helpful corrective is to develop the habit of thinking first of *low-income women*, regardless of marital status, who do not receive adequate health supervision during their pregnancies, many of whom have never received enough preventive or curative medical care, and many of whose health and nutritional status has been impaired by poverty. It is, therefore, within the context of this common experience that we should examine the ways in which prenatal and maternity services are used, and in which social and medical services are constructed, to find the directions that social policy must take.

When we look into the reports on how medical and related social services, including those for maternal and child health, are provided and used, we find that the literature is replete with accounts of dysfunction of long standing. A central task of social planning is to remove obstacles to use of service and to keep it functional. This requires, in the first instance, the support of a coherent and beneficent social policy. This is prerequisite to the incorporation of new knowledge into practice and to experimentation with new social inventions. Of equal importance may be the adoption of new or different perspectives. I would like to approach the problem by way of analysis and review of five sets of factors or conditions that we have to work with: (1) factors associated with the organization of medical services; (2) factors associated with the organization and provision of social welfare services; (3) factors associated with the attitudes and motivation of consumers of services; (4) factors associated with the preconceptions of suppliers of services; and (5) factors associated with the social and economic situation. All of these are, of course, interrelated.

1. *Factors Associated with the Organization of Medical Services*

It is easier to catalog the entrenched and deterrent policies of many prenatal and maternity clinics than to explain their persistence. They have been documented with dreary repetition—restrictive policies; interminable waiting; inaccessibility; refusal to accept applications after the second trimester of pregnancy, and refusal to accept applications prior to the twentieth week of pregnancy; impersonality and failure to explain procedures; failure to use an appointment system; lack of adequate physical facilities such as chairs, toilets, food service; too short contacts with doctors; unavailability of the mother's record at delivery, even in cases where she attended the prenatal clinic in the same hospital.[4] This not only tells the story of the kind of maternity care available to mothers-at-risk, but describes as well the kind of medical care that low-income people experience throughout their lives. And it is poor-law medicine.

The emergency room of municipal hospitals has become the family doctor for increasing numbers of low-income families. Clinics are disease-oriented, rather than person- or family-focused. Medical care sought on an emergency basis is episodic and discontinuous. Only a minority of hospitals has social service departments. Medical services are delivered by a bewildering variety of agencies and institutions to a degree that Dr. Leona Baumgartner characterized as "medical and social anarchy and chaos":

> Preventive care is obtained from one source, therapeutic care from another; "well babies" are served in one place, sick youngsters in any one of several other agencies or institutions. For one of his ailments a handicapped child goes here, for another, there, while for some conditions there may not be any place from which to obtain what is needed for a particular child. This applies not only to tax-supported, but also to privately-supported agencies, to children in families receiving public assistance as well as to children in self-supporting families.

> Part of this complex lack of organization, this "jungle," arises from the way in which funds are provided. Both service and administrative costs are repeatedly duplicated. For example, federal funds for health services to children in New York trickle through the State Departments of Health, Mental Health, Education and Welfare, and in the city itself are distributed by the Department of Health, the Department of Hospitals, the Department of Welfare, the Comptroller's Office, the Mental Health Board, and a Vocational Rehabilitation service of the state educational authority; and this takes no account of funds coming via the armed forces, the Veterans Administration or other special agencies.[5]

Medical services provided in the way that Dr. Baumgartner describes cannot meet the standards for maternal care prescribed by the Expert Committee of the World Health Organization:

> The object of maternity care is to ensure that every expectant and nursing mother maintains good health, learns the art of child care, has a normal delivery, and bears healthy children. Maternity care in the narrower sense consists in the care of the pregnant woman, her safe delivery, her postnatal examination, the care of her newly born infant, and the maintenance of lactation. In the wider sense, it begins much earlier in measures aimed to promote the health and well-being of the young people who are potential parents, and to help them to develop the right approach to family life and to the place of the family in the community. It should also include guidance in parent-craft and in problems associated with infertility and family planning.[6]

The medical component of care of this kind, in a form that is both acceptable and accessible to consumers, cannot be provided outside a framework of comprehensive, high quality practice. Whether we can attain it short of a national health service designed to bring both preventive and curative medical care to all who need it, without inquiry into other than medical need, will be determined by what happens with the new programs we are starting to institute. But the past history of two-track ("separate but equal") medical care systems, one for the indigent and one for the rest of us, does not augur well. In the meantime, we will have to make optimal use of what we have and what we can develop and improve in the short run. But if we take too narrow a view of what constitutes maternal and child health, or of prenatal care, we shall lose the battle. As a matter of expediency and immediate necessity, we can concentrate on improving the present "system" of maternal and child health service, the basic component in producing healthy babies and keeping them healthy. But we will have to come to terms with the fact that maternal and child health cannot be kept separate from, and superior to, the mainstream of medical services, public and private.

2. Factors Associated with the Organization of Social Welfare Services

The most important single social agency in contact with tens of thousands of mothers-at-risk and their children is the department of public welfare. In April, 1965, about 3,375,000 children and more than a million adults were supported by the AFDC (Aid to Families with Dependent Children) program. AFDC cash payments ranged from $9.31 per recipient per month in Mississippi to $47.14 in New Jersey, with a national average of $31.02. In some states, low needs standards are further reduced by imposing dollar limits on total family allowances, thereby placing larger families at still greater risk with regard to nutrition. Medical needs are met at comparable levels, with monthly vendor payments averaging $3.32 per recipient.[7] Income levels for millions of families with children, on and off the welfare rolls, are such as to impose a choice between food and another necessity. Large families are exposed to greater risk of protein deficiency.[8]

As for medical care, a 1961 survey concluded that "far too many states provide little or none of the essential health services required by all children, let alone those who have been deprived or who currently live on minimum or substandard incomes."[9] Effective use of such medical resources as are available depends on alert, informed, and willing caseworkers. That public welfare workers often provide good health information, but that such information is not necessarily followed by use of service, was suggested by a report from Syracuse. Here it was found that AFDC families, as compared with industrial middle-income families, "had considerably more knowledge of immunization, maternity, chest, well-baby, dental and psychiatric clinics . . . but that *receipt* (my emphasis) of child health supervision was lower in the ADC families."[10] Health facts learned are not necessarily the facts acted on. Sometimes lack of money is the impediment; sometimes other inescapable and immediate problems override. In health, as in other behavior, doing is a powerful way of learning—to experience medical care is to learn to use it.

Even if we assume that caseworkers in the big public agencies have the time, knowledge, and attitudes that might alert them to when and where to refer women and young girls for medical care, there are other inhibiting constrictions of social policy. Unmarried women are reportedly reluctant to report pregnancy and accept referral for health service lest this be interpreted as violating suitable home regulations, a device that has been used skillfully and extensively to keep needy women and children off the rolls. Nor do we know how many vulnerable women who are not on the rolls because of fear of agency policy, are thereby excluded from medical information and care.[11] Many states still place a premium on family breakup by excluding unemployed fathers from programs. And public welfare departments are only now beginning to refer for family planning services.

It is important to understand that this public agency, charged with the care of so many children, has from its inception operated under a policy that discriminates against children. When the Social Security Act was passed, the intention, presumably, was to maintain the home. This objective was compromised, however, by the original failure to provide a maintenance allowance for the mother of the child. This policy was corrected in 1950, but the Federal contribution to the states for children continued to be disproportionately smaller than for adults in other programs, and has remained so to this day. This is reflected in the national average money payment of $62.32 to an aged recipient as against the $31.02 paid to the AFDC recipient. Similarly, while grants for other categories, including MAA (Medical Assistance for the Aged) have been open-ended, money limits were placed on the Federal contributions for crippled children's services, maternal and child health, and child welfare.

Departments of welfare operate under restrictive and often contradictory mandates. Though they must provide much of the case-finding, health education, nutrition counseling, and referrals for medical services that are needed for realization of maternal and child health programming, the fact is that welfare departments are punitive and deterrent in philosophy and practice. Indeed, this is one of the contradictions that undercuts the 1962 amendments, that to many seemed to offer so much promise. These are not reaching-out agencies. In New York City (and, I suppose, throughout the country), advertising posters in subways and elsewhere solicit my health insurance business and advise me to my rights to hospital care; they have been placed there by the Social Security Administration. Annually, the Internal Revenue Service in the same way offers to help me with my tax returns. Occasionally, I have been invited by voluntary family service agencies to bring them my problems. But I have yet to be asked by a department of welfare if it can do anything for me.

Large numbers of women who should be reached for preventive services are not in touch with departments of welfare because they fail to qualify, or they don't know they're eligible, or for some other reason. More vulnerable women are off the rolls than on, but they are not in regular contact with social agencies. Other agencies do offer specialized services, including shelter care and adoption service, to women pregnant out-of-wedlock; but their facilities are limited, and they serve only a small minority of the women who need help, for their services are not available to the great mass of low-income women.

Thus social welfare services have either been tangential to the population-at-risk, or deterrent in philosophy and practice.

3. Factors Associated with the Attitudes of Consumers of Service

It is a fact that significant numbers of the women who constitute the population-at-risk do not attend prenatal clinics early enough in their pregnancies, or at all. They may not be seen prior to labor, or may not present themselves for postpartum care. Some have become discouraged by the fees and the administrative practices and policies of clinics and social welfare agencies, to which reference has already been made.

It is undoubtedly true that improvement of clinic practice would not of itself remove all of the obstacles to use, even if supported by the enabling services of other agencies, through provision for carfare or transportation to those who live at a distance or who are on subsistence budgets, or through caring for children while the mother attends clinic. There are those who have been through it all before, and, as veterans, do not see the need for themselves. There are others who are ignorant of the importance of medical supervision to themselves and to the child. Others are fearful of the examination. In the case of some women pregnant out-of-wedlock, delays may be caused by shame, or the desire or need for concealment (as in the case of working women). Delays may also be caused by pending attempts to induce abortion, reluctance to receive confirmation of pregnancy, fear of telling parents, fear of being expelled from school, fear of reporting to caseworkers of public agencies, lest welfare assistance be jeopardized.[12] But important to recognize is the fact that the various attitudes that affect the use of prenatal services early or regularly, do not operate independently of the terms, including the financial cost, on which the service is offered.

We should be cautious about making easy or quick generalizations about lack of motivation, though this is a factor, among low-income women. If the child is not wanted, we cannot assume that a successful outcome of the pregnancy is desired; indeed, the contrary may be the case. On the other hand, one study has shown that when the child was wanted, even dysfunctional clinic procedures were less deterrent than when it was not wanted.[13]

One piece of motivation may relate to ignorance and apathy. Another is hardly separable from the discouraging procedures of public clinics; another relates to the punitive and moralistic response that illicit pregnancy evokes. But we should also consider that women who have been brought up in poverty, or who have known deprivation and medical indigence all their lives, simply have never become habituated to the use of medical care except in emergencies, and they are not necessarily going to start when they become pregnant. This is why it is so important that we see prenatal and pre-conceptional care as extending back to birth and childhood, through adolescence and adulthood. This is why the issue basically resolves itself into the question of the general health status, preventive use of medical care, and the larger question of the organization, delivery, and utilization of *all* medical services as a normal component of family functioning.

This is not to argue the need to overcome as many as possible of the obstacles to utilization of medical care. In some cases it will require modification of clinic policy and methods of delivering service. In other cases it will require modification of the attitudes of those whom we want to use the service. Both approaches are necessary.

The strategy for effecting change will depend on many interrelated factors. The public health emphasis on the value of good health has traditional sanction. How effective it is, under different circumstances, is apparently a rather complex question, as numerous studies have suggested.[14] There may be ways of spurring motivation other than by appeal to the value of good health. One example, perhaps, is the appearance in an official organ of the Black Muslim movement[15] of a recent Public Health Service release on Negro-white differentials in low birth weight, and the consequences. It suggests that perception of the problem here was as much affected by political and social sensitivities as by health values per se. The implications may be worth study, in the light of the need for new planning approaches.

Attitudes are not easy to change, but the task might be facilitated if the women could see some quick concrete benefits that accrue to them from attendance at maternity clinics. The chief of the Children's Bureau reported recently that there are "hopeful indications that the institution of family planning services more than doubles attendance at postpartum clinics and, in some programs at least, seems to have a favorable influence in attracting women to prenatal clinics early, as word gets around that the services are available."[16] Other incentives might be explored. Would it be absurd to reduce clinic and delivery charges for early and regular attendance? Or give a bonus, such as equipment for the child, on meeting of basic attendance standards, antenatal and postpartum? Or provide a cash maternity grant that would permit mothers to buy their care privately? In France, maternity benefits are made conditional on attendance at prenatal clinics. The United States is almost the only country in the world that does not have an institutionalized maternity benefit plan.

4. *Factors Associated with the Attitudes of Suppliers of Service*

It takes skill and objectivity of a high order to stand back and look at the social policies, programs, and agencies that we have brought into being. More difficult, as we turn to planning for improvement, is the task of examining the preconceptions that we carry around. Social planning must be based, of course, on understanding the problem, but that, in turn, depends on our perception of it and of the people who are to be served. We have access to hard information, but we also use a lot of soft data, and how we interpret the information, and what conclusions we draw, are affected by the preconceptions that bind us.

The importance of really knowing what we think we know can hardly be overstated. Profile construction is a hazardous activity, opening the door to stereotyping. We come up with the dangerous article "the"—"the" out-of-wedlock mother, "the" multi-problem family, "the" hard-to-reach, "the" poor, "the" Negro family.[17]

Helping professions that do a lot of individualizing and pride themselves on their capacity to individualize, can sometimes settle for free-swinging generalizations. Sometimes, for purposes of comparison, we group individuals by reference to certain social characteristics that they share, such as income, education, marital status, or race. Similar characteristics are also found among other groups. We then look for significant variations in the frequency of the findings in both groups. This is a useful procedure for identifying deviance for planning purposes, so long as we remember that the characteristic in question overlaps both groups. If we are not careful, we run the risk of drawing imperfect or wrong conclusions from the data. But the danger of drawing wrong conclusions is compounded if we approach the data with a built-in bias. Because then we run the risk of asking the wrong questions or stopping too soon in our questioning, or failing to understand some of the answers that we get. A classic example is the construct of "the" out-of-wedlock mother as someone who is giving vent to acting-out disturbed mother-daughter relations, a model growing out of experience with a particular social group known to particular agencies with particular clienteles. As a universal, this construct has been laid to rest, I think; but it served, in its time, to facilitate talk about a rather unrepresentative out-of-wedlock mother, and to distort development of services. I wonder if this could have happened if the professions serving this particular group had not been sensitized by preconceptions, shaped by partial experiences and by commitment to a particular view of psychodynamics, to accept it with less scrutiny than might have been the case in the absence of such preconceptions.

Similarly, in our concern with under-utilization of prenatal services by low-income women, if our perceptions are filtered through a lens of alleged differences in culture and value systems, we may come to a conclusion that projects the task of increasing use of service in terms of "culture change," a solution that may not be sufficiently relevant to the reality. To repeat a point made earlier, if we were to correlate use of prenatal services by low-income women with use of other medical services throughout the life cycle, instead of correlating it with marital status, we might see the problem of prevention and treatment somewhat differently.

In a recent study of obstacles to the introduction of family planning services in developing areas, Stycos[18] gave high place to the distorted perceptions of lower-class behavior that prevail in upper-class circles. Hill and Jaffe,[19] starting from this observation, have provided a graphic description of the operation of this bias in an area of relevance to our problem:

> Perhaps nothing better illustrates elitist and class-biased attitudes, such as Stycos found in the developing countries, than our society's differential treatment of the issues of sexual morality and illegitimacy. Almost without exception and whatever the author's point of view, books, magazine and newspaper articles, and TV shows about sexual morality and/or immorality are concerned with what are regarded as lowered sexual standards in a middle- or upper-class setting (*Sex on Campus, Sex in Suburbia, Sex and the Single Girl, Sex in the Office,* etc.). It is the *changed nature* of the sexual activity itself which is criticized, approved or explained, and the psychodynamic impact of this change on "relationships" of boy to girl, man to woman, husband to wife. It is striking that the question of illegitimacy is almost never raised in this setting since it is presumed (sometimes wrongly) that middle-class couples have access to effective contraception, and if they slip, to competent abortion. . . .
>
> In the context of lower-class (and usually nonwhite) behavior, on the other hand, illegitimacy is *always* discussed; it is *never* seen as a different adjustment to the same sexual revolution which has changed the attitudes and practices of all Americans in the last 40 years, but rather is presumed to be the outcome of a historic, unchanged, and unchanging lower-class promiscuity that can only be dealt with moralistically and punitively. Deluged by this veritable flood of double-standard literature (Freud and interpersonal relationships for the upper class, Calvin and judgmentalism for the lower), James Baldwin has been led to comment: "White people seem to ask us, if they ask us anything. 'Come into my nightmare with me; be like me; have abortions instead of illegitimate children.' " To our knowledge, no one has yet responded to the policy implications of his observation.

It is in the nature of things for upper classes to hold lower classes in contempt and disesteem. It can hardly be otherwise. And it is a crucial factor, because it affects the provision of service, an upper-class enterprise. The kinds of programs we plan will be based on our perceptions of the problem and of the people we serve. Many of those served are poor, or working class, or Negro, and middle-class people like us are often unable to see them and their problems as clearly as we should. But we can grant this without resorting to exaggerated notions of cultural exceptionalism. Our awareness of the problem may lead us to overcompensate, one example of which is the currently popular use and misuse of Oscar Lewis's concept of the "culture of poverty." Protection against overcompensation lies in recognition of the "material determinants" of behavior that may be "a realistic response to the *facts* of poverty,"[20] and in recognition of a shared human condition and of living in the same society. The social equivalent of self-awareness is a *sine qua non* for planning services for people who may be alienated, but are not alien; who may have values of their own, but not to the exclusion of those that they share with us. Their life situation, of course, is different.

5. *Factors Associated with Socio-Economic Conditions*

It is this difference in life situation that brings me to the all-encompassing conditions surrounding the mothers-at-risk—poverty and deprivation. Here are generated the conditions that rule the vulnerables, determine their physique and health status, govern their life cycle, frustrate their aspirations, and shape their perceptions of the larger society and its institutions.

Certain aspects of the problems of various poor families merit comment for reasons peculiar to our central problem. I have already suggested that targets for special preventive action should be selected in awareness of the situation of many low-income working class women. It has passed out of fashion to discuss the problems of working class women, so perhaps a reminder is in order. If they have young children and do not work, the family is penalized by having only one breadwinner; in actuality, however, and to an increasing extent, higher standards of family living are supported by two wage-earners. When these women enter the labor market, they are at a competitive disadvantage; they do not have access to homemaker service in crises; and they do not have the use of adequate child-caring facilities. They may, therefore, work too hard and too long during pregnancy, both on the job and in the home. They cannot afford to buy private medical care and are often repelled by public clinics. When they are themselves heads-of-households, they tend to have more children than when the husband is in the home. [21]

The Negro woman carries a multiple burden: she is disadvantaged as a Negro, as a woman with a low command price over her labor power in the marketplace, and also as head of a single wage-earner family when such is her situation. And she has been exposed to a greater and increasing risk of family disruption (the rate of which for nonwhites increased from 15 to 21 per cent between 1940 and 1964, while the rate for whites remained stable at 5 per cent). [22] In this connection, it should be noted that, following improvement during the war years, there has been a deterioration in the relative economic position of the Negro male in all parts of the country. [23]

The prevalence of poverty and deprivation has been recorded by various measures of the distribution of income. The families of the vulnerable number nearly 5,000,000 with about 15,000,000 children. Most of the children are born in wedlock; most of the families are intact; most of them are headed by fathers. Of those headed by fathers, almost all have year-around, full-time employment. Most of the families are not known to social agencies and struggle to avoid contact with them.

Social indicators record the condition of poverty by whatever test is used—shorter life span, more chronic illness, higher rates of handicapping conditions of children, higher mortality rates at all age levels. Under pressure of industrialization and the urban condition, all families need the support of a broad range of institutionalized social services (social utilities, to use Alfred J. Kahn's phrase) to prevent pathology and enhance functioning. But poor families have available to them only second-class hospitals and medical care, second-class schools, second-class garbage collection, second-class social welfare services, and second-class dollars. [24] Hence they are denied equal access to decent housing, jobs, family planning services (including abortion), other social services—and life.

The historic reductions of maternal and infant mortality and the conquest of epidemic disease were brought about not primarily by the advance of medical science, but by rising standards of living and improvements in sanitation, housing, and nutrition. The prime movers in fostering change were the nineteenth-century sanitarians and social reformers.[25] If comparable ameliorative forces are to operate now, then top priority for prevention of reproductive casualties is to move the mothers-at-risk into higher income categories. There they will behave like the women who have the means to provide themselves with contraceptives and other advantages. They will space their babies better, turn sometimes to abortion, use medical care preventively, eat better, have access to a family doctor, have a better health and nutritional history, have fewer complications of pregnancy, and what they have will be treated. They will produce fewer children of low birth weight. And, if they reach the right income level, they will give their children a head start by placing them in nursery schools!

Those who now carry primary responsibility for maternal and child health cannot also be expected to reform medical and social services, reduce poverty, and abolish ghettoes. But they can be charged with the obligation to act on the facts and to see the problem in its whole social context. Nor do I suggest that we neglect short-run possibilities and objectives. But if the big targets are kept in sight while we turn to the immediate possibilities, and there are a good many, we will know that we are only taking first steps—but we will know where we are going.

I have argued that the social policies and provision to support maternal and child health are inseparable from the broad range of medical, educational, and welfare institutions and services that all families need for healthy functioning. Even coordinated medical and related social services cannot compensate for the permanent depression of the poor; while individual poor people may be worked with, poverty as a condition must be reduced. Primary responsibility for policy improvement belongs, of course, to the national government. Whether the task is done well, whether problems are anticipated on the basis of social trend projections, whether priorities are selected in accordance with the criteria that we would advance, will depend on how alertly and effectively the informed professional and lay communities do their jobs.

At the national level, we need to work for the shaping of a coherent policy for families and children. Practically speaking, this means modification of existing policies that discriminate against children. It means moving toward a national health service instead of providing care on the basis of medical indigence, with separate arrangements for those who buy their care in the marketplace. New mechanisms will have to be explored, such as the institutionalized provision of maternity grants and some form of children's allowances that we can disengage from present disabling practices. For instance, we might want to examine the creative suggestion made by Alvin L. Schorr to institute some kind of social insurance against the risk of family breakdown, so as to provide income to those he called the "socially orphaned," as we now do under OASDI (Old Age and Survivors' Disability Insurance) for the actually orphaned.[26] And also at the national level, we will want to consider the relative costs of the welfare benefits that are available to the poor in comparison with the "fiscal welfare" benefits and family supports that go to higher income people through the various exemptions and deductions allowed in the personal income tax. These amount to billions of dollars in tax subsidies.

At state and local levels, we move closer to actual provision of services and the planning role will be somewhat different. Implementation of national policy in critical areas depends on state sanction and one of the planning tasks is to ensure state participation. Where state legislation has been the source of punitive and deterrent policies, plans should include the mounting of a drive to seek their abolition or modification. If we have to live with public assistance for some time yet, it is most important to find ways to change the spirit and tone through different methods of determining eligibility and budgeting.

The first step is to plan at state-local levels for creative use of the new opportunities for expanded medical services and for connecting people and services more efficiently. While we may criticize the principle of a two-track medical system, we still have to make optimal use of it.

One can understand the excitement and gratification of the Children's Bureau and the whole Welfare Administration at the new opportunities for expanded and improved services that have opened with the passage of the Social Security Act Amendments of 1965—the provision for increased authorizations in the established children's programs, the special projects grants for comprehensive treatment of children in low-income areas, as well as the basic Title XIX provision for medically-indigent children. Together with the special provisions for the maternity and infant care projects enacted in 1963, the specially-focused programs can exert leverage on the wider field of practice and influence standards of practice favorably. But we should keep in mind that the health needs of the mass of low-income people are still to be served outside the medical market economy, through departments of welfare which many people distrust, and which many low-income people who are not money recipients may be reluctant to use. However, a climate favorable to shaping enabling rather than punitive and deterring policies seems to be in the air, and certainly it is one that professional administrators in these departments are trying to foster under adverse circumstances. Despite its promise to meet medical needs, it will be quite some time before Title XIX offers other than fragmented care. Indeed, its successful administration is going to be something of a challenge to the ingenuity and coordinating talents of medical care administrators.

Within this framework of new opportunity, the planning tasks at the operational level have to be directed toward the improvement and extension of services, and the education of the suppliers as well as of the consumers of service. The particular mechanisms will vary from community to community, and will be appropriate to their levels of operation. The central core of the planning bodies will clearly be drawn from health facilities, social agencies, and schools. While professionals will have to make the decisions that demand professional expertise, those for whom the services are to be provided will have to find the decisions acceptable and comfortable to use. Therefore, consumer representation is necessary and can be sought through several avenues.

While we know the target populations for whom we plan, we should not beam delivery of service to them exclusively, or too narrowly. We should not plan on the assumption that there is a sharp dividing line between married and unmarried mothers, between the poorest and the less poor, between the deprived and many of the modestly comfortable. Within and across these groups, individuals know and are in touch with each other, they advise each other, they refer each other to better clinics and services. A broad spectrum approach can therefore have a multiplier effect. Hence consumer representation in planning might draw on existing organizations which in different ways, and at different points, have their contacts with the vulnerables—church groups in low-income areas, minority groups, youth groups, fraternal orders, trade unions that have particularly large memberships or contact with women in low-income occupations, community action groups organized by the Office of Economic Opportunity, and so forth.

Reference has been made several times to the terms on which help is made available, and this a question for consideration at all planning levels. One of the traditional ways has been to transform gratuities into rights through the mechanism of social insurance, as in the case of the aged, and through social utilities, as in the case of education, environmental health, and school health. Enlarging the right of access to service through citizenship entitlement is important. When services are used by everyone, their tone changes and they are likely to be of higher quality than when they are reserved for the indigent—and good quality encourages use.

Assuming appropriate organization of planning mechanisms with such subgroups as are needed, exploration can be undertaken to identify what first steps and what next steps can be taken to effect change in policy, agency structure, attitudes, and motivations. All planning bodies will naturally concern themselves with short-, middle-, and long-range objectives. Guideposts will be suggested by assessments of community resources and identification of strengths and weaknesses. For purposes of discussion, the following areas are suggested as meriting exploration for quick action:

1. What steps can be taken with regard to medical practica, registration policy, and physical facilities to remove the dysfunctional quality of maternity clinics? What concrete incentives to early and regular attendance could be offered?

2. How can we proceed to institutionalize the provision of family planning services as a normal component of family medical care?

3. How can the scope of family life education be broadened from middle-class groups to others, and how should it be linked to improve school programs for health and family education?

4. What practical steps will be necessary in welfare departments to make medical care easy of access for preventive and curative care, and not something to be used on an emergency basis? Could medical care start at intake instead of waiting for illness?

5. Is there room for strengthening social services at well-baby clinics, and is this a strategic location for family planning services as well as in postpartum clinics?

6. Since the vulnerability of young girls to the hazards of pregnancy has been established, the post-war increase in frequency of teen-age marriages is of some concern. Such marriages, many of them forced, produce more children more closely spaced than other marriages, and through pressure of early responsibility, family size, inadequate education of the young parents for work, life and child-rearing, they are at high risk of dissolution and poverty.[27] In the circumstances, a special approach to preventive work with adolescents is a high priority.[28]

7. Despite prior comments, out-of-wedlock births are a continuing problem. School policies with respect to girls who may become pregnant, and provision for continuing education, will have to be examined. It is also possible that there is a need for a new type of publicly-supported maternity shelter, not for concealment or necessarily to facilitate placement of the child, but for better provision of medical care, physical protection, rest, nutrition and child-rearing education, transition to employment, and the like.

8. How can we more effectively reach the women at risk, wherever and whoever they are, to develop awareness of the importance of medical care? The message, of course, will have to take into account that some are not motivated through reluctance to accept what they regard as "charity," and some because they do not want the child.

9. Some thought must be given to ways of reaching men, for they are not disinterested in the size of their families or in the health of their wives and children. They should be included in informational drives. If women are reached in beauty shops and supermarkets, men can be reached in bars, barber shops, bowling alleys, trade union halls, and factories.

It remains to make some observations about the tasks of social workers in the planning enterprise and to emphasize their special contributions to the provision of a range of community services.

The social action base of the profession of social work has been said to lie in the power of knowledge. As an organized profession it can advise, speak, protest, reject, criticize, inform. It can address these actions to Washington, the state capital, city hall, and to social agencies, public and voluntary. There is nothing new about this except, possibly, the suggestion, diffidently offered, that vigorous social action may need to be better informed about the range of program effort, about the problems of the populations served, and about alternative approaches to organizing services, than has sometimes been the case.

New opportunities are opening for modifying or changing the disabling philosophy of some social agencies, and for challenging the relevance of policies and welfare structure to social problems and to the needs of clients. Part of the planning task must, therefore, include an approach to the organization of special efforts to maximize the social work contribution. Attention might therefore be directed to some areas in which social work might make its influence felt more decisively.

While it is not the business of social work to reform the organization and quality of medical services, social agencies, as purchasers of medical service, can insist on getting their money's worth.

For a long time, our public welfare agencies have faced formidable tasks. In the next few years, they will be involved in phasing in massive new medical care programs that will make great demands on the coordinating skills of the staffs. Someone will have to come to grips with the question of how to make maximal use of the professional and of the social work technician.

One need not be unsympathetic to the burdens carried by workers in the public agencies to insist on the need for testing the availability and accessibility of services, the extent to which maternal and child health is fostered, the adequacy of budgets from the nutritional viewpoint.

In the voluntary field, social work will have to stimulate examination of policies as they relate to the various facets of maternal and child health programming, perhaps beginning with a look at family life education, perhaps looking at the relations that might fruitfully be developed with schools in services to adolescents.[29] And, in this connection, school social work may require some re-evaluation to see if its present stance is the best possible one.

Social work education will certainly be alert to incorporating into its curricula knowledge content from the fields of maternal and child health and mental retardation. Perhaps room could be found for some study of demography. More problematic is the suggested need for a second (or different) kind of medical social worker who is involved in medical care administration, coordination of services, and cooperative relations with many different kinds of community agencies which have a concern with health. The new health programs will have to lean heavily on coordinated use of existing facilities.

Perhaps social work, with its past experience in operation and use of a central index, may have something to contribute in developing community medical inventories of mothers- and children-at-risk.

A final *caveat* is in order against falling into the trap of looking at our problem as though it is exclusively an out-of-wedlock problem or a Negro family problem. It is a problem of low-income families. It is not just a problem of prenatal care but of the health, ill-health, and poverty of the total community. It is not just a question of dietary supplements during pregnancy, but of life nutrition. It is not just a problem of the organization of maternal and child health services, but of the organization of family health services. It is not, therefore, a question of a quick, or even a considered, referral to a prenatal clinic, but of the way in which social agencies concern themselves with all issues of health, and whether they encourage use of medical services preventively and curatively. And it is not exclusively, or even primarily, a question of the lack of motivation of the consumers of service, but of the often distorted perceptions and attitudes of the suppliers of service. And while we have several times referred to the right of low-income women to contraceptive information as part of normal medical service, we should not clutch at this as a magical substitute for other basic policies.

There are many more ways of detailing areas for discussion, and I hope that, as they are suggested, they will be discussed and analyzed always in the context of the social situation.

Can we expect to single out one episode in the life history of poverty and seek to neutralize its debilitating effects for the period of pregnancy, while leaving the larger condition unchanged? And, if we could, what happens at the end of the episode? Can we develop a special attitude toward the use of medical care during this one brief period in life, one which is different from that held at other times?

Can we really expect to provide excellence of medical care under maternal and child health auspices without establishing it in other areas of medical practice? Can we rely on poor-law medicine to provide high quality, continuing, comprehensive care?

Can we narrowly define prenatal care as what happens between conception and delivery without concern for the health and nutritional status of the mother prior to conception?

Can we expect social agencies to develop an exceptional attitude toward clients for the period of pregnancy which it does not apply in relation to other needs and problems? And to which of the postures will the client be expected to respond?

Can we expect to have a viable social policy for women during pregnancy apart from social policy toward women and their special problems as wage-earners, disadvantaged mothers, homemakers, mothers?

Can we change the life chances of a Negro child without changing the life conditions of the Negro people?

Can we tolerate the waste of such gains as are made through improved medical care? Will we reduce fetal death, complications of pregnancy, birth anomalies, and mental retardation, only to dissipate these gains by the subsequent neglect of the saved children?

References

[1]Benjamin Pasamanick, "Epidemiologic Investigations of Some Prenatal Factors in the Production of Neuropsychiatric Disorders," in *Health and the Community*, eds. Alfred H. Katz and Jean Spencer Felton (New York: The Free Press, 1965), pp. 199-211; also *Proceedings*, University of California, School of Public Health, Bi-Regional Institute on Maternity Care—Primary Prevention, Berkeley, California, June 21-25, 1964.

[2]*Public Health Aspects of Low Birth Weight*, World Health Organization Technical Report Series, No. 217 (Geneva, 1961), p. 4.

[3]Blanch Bernstein and Mignon Sauber, *Deterrents to Early Prenatal Care and Social Services Among Women Pregnant Out-of-Wedlock*, New York State Department of Social Welfare (Albany, N.Y., 1960), p. 44.

[4]*Report of Conference on Prenatal Clinic Care in New York City, May 9, 1963*, Maternity Center Association (New York, 1963).

[5]Leona Baumgartner, "Medical Care of Children in Public Programs," *Medical Care in Transition*, Vol. II, U.S. Department of Health, Education and Welfare, Public Health Service (Washington, D.C., 1964), pp. 311-319. *See also* Alonzo S. Yerby, "The Disadvantaged and Health Care," address delivered at White House Conference on Health, November 3, 1965, Washington, D.C.

[6]*Social Aspects in the Teaching of Obstetrics and Gynecology*, World Health Organization, Technical Series, No. 266 (Geneva, 1963), p. 4.

[7]Table 13 in *Welfare in Review*, July, 1965.

[8]Mollie Orshansky, "Counting the Poor: Another Look at the Poverty Profile," *Social Security Bulletin*, January, 1965, pp. 4, 8.

[9]Pearl Bierman, "Child Health Services in Public Welfare Programs," in *Medical Care in Transition, op. cit.*, pp. 4, 8.

[10]*Ibid.*

[11]Winifred Bell, *Aid to Dependent Children* (New York; Columbia University Press, 1965), pp. 179-181.

[12]Elizabeth Herzog and Rose Bernstein, *Health Service for Unmarried Parents*, Children's Bureau Pub. No. 425, U.S. Department of Health, Education and Welfare (Washington, D.C., 1964), pp. 11-33.

[13]Andie L. Knutson, *The Individual, Society and Health Behavior* (New York: Russell Sage Foundation, 1965), pp. 185, 186.

[14]*Ibid.*, pp. 380ff.

[15]*Muhammad Speaks*, February 11, 1965.

[16]Katherine B. Oettinger, "This Most Profound Challenge," address, New York City, September 9, 1965.

[17]See discussion on Negro family in Elizabeth Herzog, "Is There a Breakdown of the Negro Family?" *Social Work*, January 1966, pp. 3-10.

[18]J. Mayone Stycos, "Obstacles to Programs of Population Control—Facts and Fancies," *Marriage and Family Living*, February 1963, pp. 5-13.

[19]Adelaide Cromwell Hill and Frederick S. Jaffe, "Negro Fertility and Family Size Preferences: Implications for Programming of Health and Social Services," mimeographed (publication pending in *The Negro American*, eds. Kenneth Clark and Talcott Parsons, Houghton Mifflin).

[20]Alvin L. Schorr, "The Nonculture of Poverty," *American Journal of Orthopsychiatry*, October 1964, p. 907.

[21]Orshansky, *op. cit.*, p. 16.

[22]James D. Cowhig, "Marital Instability Among Women in the United States," *Welfare in Review*, July, 1965, pp. 12-14.

[23]Alan B. Batchelder, "Decline in the Relative Income of Negro Men," *Quarterly Journal of Economics*, November 1964, pp. 525-548.

[24]"Poverty: The Special Case of the Negro," *American Economic Review*, Papers and Proceedings, May 1965, pp. 530-539.

[25]Rene Dubos, *Mirage of Health* (Garden City, N.Y., 1959), pp. 31, 139, 140.

[26]Alvin L. Schorr, "ADC—What Direction?" *Child Welfare*, February 1962, pp. 72-78.

[27]Alvin L. Schorr, "The Family Cycle and Income Development," *Social Security Bulletin*, February 1966, pp. 14-25.

[28]See Dale C. Garell, "Adolescence as an Opportunity for Primary Prevention," in University of California Institute on Maternity Care, *op. cit.*, pp. 132-137.

[29]Frances Mauney, Mary Ella Fox, and Mary Ann Vines, "Tenth-Grade Girls and Early Marriage: A School-Agency Project," *Social Casework*, February 1966, pp. 98-103.

TWENTY-NINE

Some Issues Related to Long-Term Disability: A Position Paper

ELIZABETH M. BOGGS

Introduction

The National Association for Retarded Children is concerned with the problem—mental retardation—which is the major cause of long term disability originating in childhood. For the individuals involved and for their families, the dependency arising from this kind of disability is particularly onerous. It is our thesis that a rational approach to the problems engendered by long term disability must be incorporated in the changing principles and practices in the public welfare field in this country.

Precisely because its interests do extend importantly into all the major fields of health, education and welfare, NARC is particularly sensitive to the need for a certain degree of consistency in the basic principles underlying the relationship between government and the individual citizen, between federal, state, county and local governments, between different agencies within the same level of government, and between public and voluntary or non-profit service agencies. We recognize that during a period of social change, and certainly the second half of the twentieth century is proving to be such a period, experimentation in one area will run ahead of that in another and that accentuation in one facet of service is nearly always accompanied by some dislocation in another. All of us are concerned to maximize both equity and efficiency in the process of change.

Mental Retardation as a Factor in Marginal Employment and Poverty

It is roughly estimated that about three percent of the population, or nearly six million people in the United States, should be or should have been identified as mentally retarded before they are fifteen years old. This figure does not include the borderline or dull-normal groups in our population who account for another fifteen to twenty percent of the total. Even among the three percent the majority are capa-

Adapted from a 1965 Statement to the Advisory Council on Public Welfare of the U.S. Department of Health, Education and Welfare. Reprinted by permission of the author and the National Association for Retarded Children.

ble of social and economic independence, assuming there is a reasonable market for their simpler skills. Their problems are in many ways similiar to those of other marginally employable people, whose jobs are characterized either by instability or by earnings which, even at a full level, are scarcely adequate to sustain a reasonable standard of living. Our Association has recognized that many of the mildly retarded are to be found in the target populations of the Economic Opportunity Act, in the programs on behalf of selective service rejectees and other programs designed for marginally inadequate adults. We, also, recognize the potential for the prevention of a significant proportion of mild retardation through improvement in child health and child welfare services to low income families.

Without minimizing the importance of all the foregoing programs, it is necessary also to focus attention on the less prevalent but more severe and unresponsive forms of disability and associated dependency found among the minority of the retarded. There are approximately 120,000 adult retardates between 18 and 65 who are receiving Social Security benefits because of total disability, and about 80,000 receiving Aid to the Permanently and Totally Disabled (APTD). These figures do not measure the numbers of those adults who are equally disabled, but who are supported by a working parent. About two-thirds of all adult childhood disability beneficiaries under the Social Security Program have mental retardation as a primary or major component of their disability. Of all adults under thirty-five years of age receiving permanent and total disability assistance, the majority are mentally retarded. These two facts accentuate the role of mental retardation as a cause of lifetime disability.

The adult with this type of disability differs from the person suffering from one of the chronic disorders characteristic of advancing age in that he or she never enjoys a period of substantial earnings, out of which savings can be accrued or an insured employment status developed. Such people are ineligible for family or other group health insurance coverage in most cases. Moreover, since they infrequently marry, they seldom have spouses or children who can contribute to their support. The burden of their support, therefore, falls almost exclusively on their parents, except to the extent that this burden may be mitigated by social insurance or public health and welfare programs. Thus the period of dependency on parents, which ordinarily runs for the eighteen or twenty years of minority, may, and frequently does, run for fifty years or more in these instances. This dependency places on the family a burden which often goes far beyond board, lodging, and routine medical care, since in many cases a degree of personal care or supervision is required which seriously limits the mobility of other members of the family.

Until recently it has usually been presumed that most adolescents and adults in these severely handicapped categories were being given care in public institutions which substantially relieved the burden on the families, both for direct care and for maintenance. We now recognize, however, that this is a false assumption, for more than two-thirds of those who are receiving social security benefits as adult disabled children of insured workers who have died or retired are *not* in institutions. The APTD recipients constitute an almost completely non-institutionalized population. The records of admissions to institutions for the mentally retarded show that, while the majority of residents are admitted prior to age eighteen, many continue to be admitted thereafter even to late middle-age. Moreover, as will be demonstrated later, admission to a public institution by no means necessarily relieves the family of a significant financial burden.

Insurance Coverage for the Risk of Lifetime Disability

The 1957 Amendments to the Social Security Act have made an important contribution to the well being of the retarded through the disabled adult child survivors provisions. These provisions are important not only for the financial benefits they accord to certain retardates, but also because they established a beach-head in the domain of providing by social insurance for a risk not otherwise coverable by private insurance. They seem, however, to be predicated on the assumption that the retarded person should be regarded as an eternal child who is somehow arrested at the stage of entitlement to parental support and protection which he enjoys up to age eighteen. There has been considerable progress in social thinking in the past eight years, and we would submit that the economic model, in the case of the totally disabled adult retardate, should rather be that of a person who moves instantly from childhood to old age—from age twenty-one to age sixty-five—without benefit of an intermission of economic independence. We believe that consideration should be given to the rationale of affording the adult who is disabled from childhood and his relatives some of the benefits now being accorded to aging members of our population and *their* relatives. After all, his inability to participate in the fruits of his own remunerative employment arises through no fault of his own, but rather through the fault of society which was not able to protect him from severe disability.

The permanently and totally disabled person has literally or figuratively been forced to retire early. The Advisory Council on Social Security, in its 1965 report, made one recommendation which reflected this assimilation. It proposed that persons eligible for social security benefits because of disability should have the same hospital coverage as the aged. Unfortunately this recommendation was not incorporated into the 1965 "Medicare" legislation, (P.L. 89-97).

Although Social Security benefit payments averaging $46 a month are now being made to adult children disabled by mental retardation who survive their parents (assuming the parent had been insured under social security), there is no way in which the parent can protect himself and his family from the financial impact of the disability of his child during that major portion of his child's life which extends from the child's twenty-first birthday to the moment of death or retirement of the parent himself. To most persons of modest income the major risks to family fiscal stability are insurable, but not this one. The normally functioning adult who suffers a disability in the course of his employment is significantly compensated. An employed adult disabled otherwise than at work becomes eligible within a few months for benefits in his own right under Social Security. To the child (and his family) who suffers permanent disability associated with damage to the brain or nervous system resulting from provable negligence of another, the courts not infrequently allow damages in the hundreds of thousands of dollars. These payments are also usually covered by insurance. But the risk of long term dependency originating in childhood from natural or unknown causes is not insurable.

As a result of the expenditures of millions of dollars in tax and contributed funds, thousands of families in the years immediately to come will be spared the burden of permanent disability due to infantile paralysis, yet those families in which there is a member whose disability society is not yet able or alert to prevent are asked to bear its continuing financial as well as emotional burden. This burden goes far beyond the limits covered even by the much touted "major medical" coverage which has been gaining favor in recent years. While there are a few "major medical" policies which can be applied against the costs of care in a medically oriented residential facility for the retarded, their time and dollar value limits fall far short of the risks. Paradoxically we are told that the risk is too great to be incorporated in existing coverages without incurring an intolerable increase in rates; therefore it is held that those who actually experience this catastrophe should bear its full effects, unless, of course, it places the parents as well as the disabled child in the "medically needy" category.

It is our observation that catastrophes of proportions which exceed the capacity of private insurance systems are usually covered out of public funds. For example, substantial federal aid will be made available to the victims of the recent natural disaster in the mid-west. We doubt whether the middle aged owner who lost his small store valued at $25,000 will be asked about the capabilities of his parents to make good his loss. Yet when the uninsurable catastrophe of lifetime disability strikes, rendering its victim unemployable and without any resources of his own, this predicament in itself is not enough to justify help from society under our system. His parents' resources must be substantially committed for the remainder of their lives before society begins to share the financial risks.

Entitlement of the Individual vs. Liability of Relatives

Concepts of the proper legal liability of relatives for other adults who are dependent are undergoing marked change. As Elizabeth Wickenden has pointed out, this is a consequence of the maturation (rather than the decadence) of our social system. Here analysis covers the issue of social advantage as well as that of individual equity:

> Almost universally the growing reliance on cash income directly related to production puts the nonproducers at a heavy disadvantage. Even though the wage-earning members of a family may continue to contribute to the support of their aged, disabled, widowed, orphaned or unemployed relatives, the nature of the relationship has created a new kind of dependency which is satisfactory to neither the giver nor the receiver . . .
> Those whose contribution to the new society as active producers is badly needed may be

inhibited by the heavy family responsibilities and tensions involved in the change. Family solidarity itself is often weakened or broken with tragic impact on those outside the source of income.

The gradual transfer of certain social costs from the individual or family to social programs serves to relieve these tensions between family members. Non-producers are given the dignity of a social entitlement not dependent on the good will or generosity of their relatives. Income-earning heads of families are freed from the burden of responsibility for a wide circle of relatives; this becomes increasingly important as the requirements and expectations of a modern society impose a heavier and more prolonged burden of expenditures in the rearing of their own children. But even more important than these factors of personal relationship is the democratizing impact of social expenditure. Without some equitable social sharing in the cost of assuring income to persons unable to support themselves at work, the cost of assuring such support falls most heavily upon the lowest income group thus aggravating its disadvantaged situation. This can only serve as a drag on the developmental process, the success of which depends upon a widening participation in its benefits. It is for these reasons that social programs for assuring income to those outside the wage and market economy are an essential part of the developmental process. The same logic applies to those social expenditures which supplement income through direct benefits considered essential to the social good.

The complexity, specialization, and interdependence of the modern economy inevitably involve a higher degree of vulnerability for individuals which can only be offset by social measures. The most obvious risk in a wage-earning economy is inability to work either because of personal incapacity or because jobs are unavailable. Social insurance is a social measure directly geared to protection against this risk and under a contributory system makes the cost of this protection a direct charge on production itself.

(Social Welfare in a Changing World: WICKENDEN, ELIZABETH, United States Department of Health, Education and Welfare, Washington, 1965, pp. 42-43)

The Accentuation of Discrimination in the 1965 Social Security Amendments

The legal changes now taking place at the federal level in response to this philosophy nevertheless appear to be accentuating discrimination against those with lifetime disabilities and against their families. For example, under the new Title XIX of the Social Security Act, providing to the states the option of a combined medical assistance program, it is expressly provided that a state may hold responsible the parents of an adult blind or disabled person even though parental responsibility toward other applicants or recipients is limited to their children under age twenty-one, and responsibility of children for parents is set aside unconditionally. Thus, under P. L. 89-97, the parents of a twenty-five year old woman who has a dependent child are not to be held liable for her support or that of her child. On the other hand the parents of a permanently and totally disabled mentally retarded woman of the same age (twenty-five) are to be held liable for her support indefinitely. There appears to be something illogical about this distinction and we would raise the question as to whether this is not the denial of equal protection of the laws.

The 1965 Amendments to the Social Security Act also continue the discrimination against those with lifetime disabilities resulting from mental retardation who require institutional care. The new Act (P. L. 89-97) continues the provision of present law under which, for example, a needy cerebral palsied mentally retarded person, under age 65, who is cared for in a facility for the chronically ill, is officially eligible for federally aided maintenance and medical care, whereas a similar person cared for in a facility designated for the mentally retarded is considered beyond the pale of such aid. Heretofore needy persons being cared for in mental institutions, public or private, have been ineligible for federally aided assistance programs. P.L. 89-97 for the first time makes eligible persons in mental institutions who are over 65. This will permit public assistance payments to or on behalf of about 30% of the mental hospital population, most of whom become thus disabled relatively late in life, but this relaxation will be applicable to less than 5 percent of the institutionalized mentally retarded. There are more than 150,000 people over 65 in our mental hospitals, and it is estimated that the states will be able to use $75 million annually of the resulting federal aid for the needy among them to improve hospital and other forms of care. The extension of the principle to those adults with permanent disability arising prior to age 18 would be a next logical step, and one whose lesser cost could be as readily estimated. There are about 90,000 persons between 21 and 65 who are so disabled and are in mental institutions. Almost all of them are mentally retarded. If something of the order of $40 million from federal sources were to be made available to qualifying states, it would for the first time give the federal government a stake, albeit a relatively small one, in an area of service whose costs have heretofore been borne exclusively by states (and counties) and a few exceptionally unfortunate families.

Under P.L.89-97, states taking advantage of the new federal assistance to aged mental patients already under public care, must show improvements in their mental health services both in and out of hospital and must provide for periodic review of the status and needs of the patients whose public assistance payments are to be used to pay for their care in public mental hospitals. These conditions will provide a desirable incentive to improvements that are certainly needed. The fact that few of the mentally retarded are eligible not only denies them the thrust of this incentive but continues a negative pressure which has already been demonstrating its ill effects. We refer to the indiscriminate push to discharge and "put on welfare" (federally aided) hundreds of residents of institutions for the retarded without proper selection or safeguards.

Title XIV and Title XVI of Social Security Act continue to exclude from APTD any person who is a patient in an institution for mental diseases, (Section 1405 and Section 1605), but permit such payments to flow when a disabled person is placed in a boarding home, family care, or private nursing home. The law encourages this exodus, but without due regard for the hazards. The mentally retarded are particularly vulnerable because by the nature of their disability they are unable to protest exploitation or abuse or neglect. The cloak of "return to the community" is a mockery when applied to those for whom residential care was originally sought as a means of assuring long term protective supervision. The use of smaller "community" facilities can only be justified when there has been individual case work to determine both the initial suitability of the placement, and follow-up to assure that the well-being of the retardate is at least as well served in the new setting as in the old. Such protective services have been conspicuously lacking in some states. In one state it was, in fact, proposed that eligibility for a mass placement would hinge on eligibility for federally-aided public assistance; since a component of this eligibility was financial need, and since this automatically selected those either without families, or whose families were themselves without resources which facilitate visiting, it will readily be seen that these placements would, in practice, have resulted in even greater risks of alienation and obliteration from the public conscience and view than has resulted in the past in public mental institutions. There is frequently cause for difference of opinion as to what is indeed in the best interest of a disabled person, but there should be no incentive, even incidental or accidental, for placements which do not have that interest as their first justification. If federal aid is to encourage sound trends, it is urgent that it be made available in the near future on behalf of those disabled persons who are properly placed in mental institutions as well as those who are placed elsewhere, and that it be conditional on well developed protective services for the mentally incompetent.

Protective Services for the Mentally Disabled Adult

The President's Panel on Mental Retardation recommended that:

Each State should establish a protective service for the Retarded in an appropriate state agency.

The term "protective service" has in the past had a rather narrow connotation focused on authoritative intervention. A more general view is developing around the problems actually encountered, in practice, with some older people, as outlined, for example, in the federal publication "Protective Service for Older Persons." Many of these needs are found among the adult retarded under 65.

One important component of protective service is continuity. The aged person may have such a need for a period of a few years—perhaps as many as twenty. But there are half a million to a million retarded adults who need protective supervision, in or out of institutions, for periods up to 50 or 60 years. More responsibility must be assumed for these services by the states. Federal participation in APTD and related programs should foster developments in that direction. There is little time to lose, for the post-war cohorts with their larger component of lifetime disability are beginning to reach adulthood now.

It is important that those institutionalized, those cared for in nursing homes and in the community, and those cared for in their own homes should have the benefit of services designed to reduce their need for personal care and attendance. Here we find another bias against the adult with a lifetime disability. The distinction between education and medical treatment is clear in principle but not always in practice. Speech correction may be effected by "therapy" or by "instruction." This would not be of more than semantic interest were it not that social philosophy concerning responsibility for costs makes significant distinction. This is illustrated in Section 1901 of the Social Security Act which states that it is the purpose of the new Title XIX to enable each state "as far as practicable under the conditions in such state, to furnish . . . rehabilitation and other services to help such . . . (totally disabled) individuals obtain or retain capability for independence or self-care." So far as the mentally retarded are concerned, reduction of personal dependence is largely a matter of training, even in the severely disabled. The implications are, however, that such "rehabilitation and other services" are part of "medical aid" and this will be available only to those adults whose parents (or spouses) are found unable to pay for them. This constitutes a discrimination against the severely disabled as compared with those whose lesser disability makes them eligible for training and vocational rehabilitation under the Vocational Rehabilitation Act. Under the Vocational Rehabilitation program, training services which improve the individual's skills and independence are not subject to a means test imposed on the rehabilitant's family. In the jurisdictional tug of war between Welfare and Vocational Rehabilitation over the concept of "independent living" services, Welfare won, but the clients apparently lost. The gap will be further widened by the Vocational Rehabilitation Amendments of 1965 which eliminate the distinction between "training" and other rehabilitation services.

Inconsistency of State Practice on Charges for State Residential Care of the Retarded

The patterns established by the federal government in these matters are of tremendous importance not only for themselves but for the precedents they set for action by the states. Certain provisions of P.L. 89-97 are clearly designed to offer inducement to the states to bring order and consistency into categorical and other public assistance. The states are being invited to make uniform their criteria for eligibility and standards for medical assistance under those categories. The system by which the states collect from parents for the cost of long term care of the adult retardate in state operated institutions for the mentally retarded should be reviewed in the light of these objectives. For example, the limitation on liens on property specified in Section 1902 (a) (18) is violated in a number of states with respect not only to the institutionalized mentally retarded but with respect to their relatives as well.

Except for recent entitlements under Social Security, the person disabled by mental retardation very rarely has resources of his own. Therefore, the reimbursement system is, in fact, aimed at the parents and grandparents. The generally chaotic state of the system of recovery from parents of the mentally retarded in state institutions is documented in an NARC study issued in 1963 on *Charges for Residential Care of the Mentally Retarded*. A number of states have applied the principle of social responsibility for major catastrophes to the point of eliminating charges to parents for the cost of care for the mentally retarded (minors or adults) in state residential facilities; some have established a statutory maximum charge; others continue to escalate the maximum charge to cover rising costs. Those costs include education, rehabilitation, and research, along with board, lodging, and medical care. The study also showed that whereas some states have placed some time or age limit on the liability of families, others hold a family liable for full costs for the entire life span of the disabled institutionalized individual. Moreover, in some states there is no statute of limitations applying to this liability and the possibility of retroactive recovery of the cumulative difference between what was actually paid and the maximum possible payment is upheld by law without limit.

When a charge less than "maximum" is assessed against the parent of a retarded person in state residential care, the official basis is "ability to pay." However, the criteria show no consistency and the procedures frequently fall short of acceptable social welfare practice, inviting abuse and political intervention. To bring some objectivity and dignity into this "system," two states (Connecticut and Michigan) in 1965 passed laws which establish a table of rates based on net taxable income as reported on the federal return. In both cases the liability of parents ceases when the retardate reaches age 21.

Following the study mentioned above, and after lively debate, the NARC Delegate Assembly in 1962 adopted a policy which calls either for the elimination of all charges or for limitation to minor children and to an approximation of the costs of caring for such a child at home. The full text is appended to this statement.

The recent decision of the California Supreme Court in the Kirchner case[1] is relevant. The court held unconstitutional the California laws making relatives liable for the cost of care in state mental institutions, holding that the application of these laws constituted denial of equal protection of the law. In its decision, the Court said:

> Lastly, in resolving the issue now before us, we need not blind ourselves to the social evolution which has been developing during the past half century; it has brought expanded recognition of the parens patriae principle . . . and other social responsibilities, including the California Rehabilitation Center Act . . . and divers other public welfare programs to which all citizens are contributing through presumptively duly apportioned taxes. From all of this it appears that former concepts which have been suggested to uphold the imposition of support liability upon a person selected by an administrative agent from classes of relatives designated by the Legislature may well be re-examined. . . A statute obviously violates the equal protection clause if it selects one particular class of persons for a species of taxation and no rational basis supports such classification. . . . Such a concept for the state's taking of a free man's property manifestly denies him equal protection of the law.

Consistency suggests that the same principles apply to retardates cared for "in the community." We are far from any consistent approaches at the present time, however.

Needed Amendments to the Social Security Act

Although the final responsibility for policy and administration of public welfare programs rests with the states, who are free to accept or reject federal participation on the terms specified in federal statutes, the conditions set by federal law and regulations have important influence not only on those states which conform and qualify for federal aid, but on all states by virtue of the expression of a social consensus on a nation-wide level. It is therefore important, both for practical reasons and for reasons of social philosophy and justice, that the inequitable treatment of disabled adults under age 65 under various titles of the Social Security Act be remediated. Specifically, the following amendments should be made in Titles XIV, XVI, and XIX at the earliest opportunity:

a. delete "tb and mental insitution" and "public institution" exclusion with respect to permanently and totally disabled clients who were disabled prior to age 18.
b. require that state plans for APTD *disregard resources of relatives* (other than spouse) in determining eligibility.
c. give permanently and totally disabled adults the *same hospital and health coverages* as the aged. (Title XVIII)
d. make above changes *applicable within state only if state maintains at least prior level* of program support for residential care.

Summation

Mental retardation is the most important single cause of permanent and total disability originating in childhood, and is a significant component in marginal disability and poverty. Present law and custom places a lifelong liability on the parents of persons so disabled, a liability and risk which may be measured in the hundreds of thousands of dollars, but which is essentially uncoverable by any social or private insurance now in effect. Movement in the direction of social responsibility for those who are involuntarily non-productive is irregular and at the present time appears to be overlooking or discriminating against those who are most seriously and catastrophically affected, i.e. those whose disability originated early in life. It overlooks and discriminates against their families as well, for example:

1. The 1965 amendments to the Social Security Act specifically maintain the liability of parents of the adult disabled, while relaxing both filial responsibilities and parental responsibilities toward other eligible persons over age 21.
2. The same amendments continue to exclude from the federally assisted APTD programs all of that significant portion of adults under age 65 with lifetime disabilities who receive care in public institutions for the mentally retarded.
3. As a result of this exclusion, members of this group will continue to be subject

to pressures for inappropriate placements without proper safeguards in care facilitites which are not especially designed for the care of the mentally retarded.

4. The inclusion of services designed to develop personal self care and independence under the heading of medical assistance within the welfare program makes these services, which for the retarded are most likely to take the form of training, subject to the means test rather than an entitlement of the handicapped, such as the person with lesser disability may receive under the State-Federal vocational rehabilitation programs.

5. The practices of the states in establishing family responsibility for the cost of continued care of the adult retarded in institutions are inconsistent with one another and with emerging social philosophies.

The disabled are a relatively small category under Public Assistance and Social Security. Those with long term disabilities are a still smaller group. Their individual tribulations are, however, the most serious. For the most part they are unable to bespeak their own needs and their own humiliation. It is therefore all the more important that a searching study, such as the Advisory Council on Public Welfare is now undertaking, should reach the issues—social, ethical, legal and fiscal—which are peculiar to this group.

References

[1]California v. Kirchner: 36 Calif. Repts. 488, 388 pp. 2d 720 (1964).

Mental Retardation and the Family Service Agency

THE FAMILY SERVICE ASSOCIATION OF AMERICA

A national plan to combat and prevent mental retardation was set in motion by the recommendations of The President's Panel on Mental Retardation in 1962. Since then, a total program, including a wide range of activities designed to attack mental retardation simultaneously from many vantage points has developed through Federal legislation and funding for the Federal, state and local public and private agencies in health and welfare fields that can bring the best professional and technical knowledge and administrative experience to this new undertaking.

There are two million mentally retarded children in America; the number of adults is more difficult to ascertain but it can be safely said that the presence in the general population of such individuals is at least 3%.

In the light of the incidence of mental retardation and its impact upon the life of the individual, his family and community, family service agencies generally view services to such people as coming within their agency's scope and function. As the individuals affected by retardation (retardates, their families and their associates) are of all of ages and present a wide variety of psycho-social problems, the services needed span the entire spectrum of social services, especially family counseling and homemaker service. Among the major contributions of the family agency is its emphases on a family-centered and community-oriented approach, in addition to the individualized approach to the person and his problems.

In 1963 a one-time appropriation of 2.2 million dollars was made for State comprehensive mental retardation planning. Fifty-one States and Territories were awarded initial grants for this planning by the Mental Retardation Branch, U. S. Public Health Service. Federal legislation made available additional funds to state planning groups for implementation of these plans. In some states, planning for comprehensive mental health services included mental retardation; in others, there have been two distinct and separate groups. At this time, the states are involved in implementing their plans, with funding from the Federal Government.

Family Service agencies have generally not been included in such planning. Involvement in this long range blueprinting of services and a voice in the way in

Reprinted by permission of The Family Service Association of America.

which the plans will be put into effect locally are of vital concern for family agencies. They can contribute considerably from their accumulated wisdom and from experience gained in family service programs. The family agency can make a significant contribution to the prevention, diagnosis and treatment of mental retardation, particularly in its social consequences. Moreover, the agency has an opportunity and responsibility for stimulating staff and board to perceive the challenge of serving such individuals and families, and for exercising leadership in advancing service to this group.

Staff should be helped in their understanding of mental retardation, through an emphasis that basic social work concepts apply to mentally retarded individuals, as well as to others. These basic concepts include: the inter-relatedness of the bio-psycho-social factors which produce mental retardation—especially economic and social deprivation, the dynamic nature of retardation and its consequent responsiveness to social intervention; the growth potential and the ability to change in the retarded person and the existence of individual differences among the retarded.

Consultation Available: In a number of Federal departments there are specialists on retardation available for consultation regarding family service programs as they relate to mentally retarded children and their families, and for help to parent groups and social planning bodies and schools of social work.

Most states also have a consultant on mental retardation attached to their Departments of Mental Health or Welfare and, in addition, many states have planning personnel for mental retardation responsible for assisting in the planning process for comprehensive services for mental retardates and their families.

The National Association for Retarded Children, 420 Lexington Avenue, New York, is a national agency attempting to professionalize and establish, extend and improve services for the mentally retarded child and his family. There are 1100 local units and 50 state units interested in closer and cooperative relations with family service agencies and may be a source of assistance in starting needed programs. Many members of the staffs and boards of family service agencies are already closely identified with their local unit of ARC.

THIRTY-ONE

Child Welfare Services for Mentally Retarded Children

THE CHILD WELFARE LEAGUE OF AMERICA

Many children and their families who are affected by mental retardation need child welfare services. Since we consider involvement in long range planning and implementation of services for them to be a vital area of concern to the child welfare field, we are sending this memorandum to call the following information to your attention.

National planning to combat and prevent mental retardation, set in motion in 1962 by the recommendations of the President's Panel on Mental Retardation, has made notable progress. Since 1962, a total program of activities designed to attack this social disability simultaneously from many vantage points has been evolving through federal and state legislation and the funding for public and private health, education and welfare agencies at federal, state and local levels. Together these activities hold potential for bringing the best professional and technical knowledge and administrative experience to the new undertaking.

Child welfare agencies generally have not played major roles in developing their states' comprehensive mental retardation planning that was initiated in 1963 by grants from the Mental Retardation Branch of the U.S. Public Health Service.

Nearly all states provide some child welfare services for mentally retarded children. Children's Bureau statistics of 1965 indicate that 43,000 children recognized as mentally retarded were being served by public and voluntary child welfare agencies. In addition, it is considered likely that a number of mentally retarded children are being given some services by agencies without their handicap having been diagnosed. In either event, the sum total of those served falls far short of the estimated 2,180,000 retarded children in the United States today.

Of special significance to those involved in child welfare is evidence that the incidence of mental retardation in low income families is as high as 10%, more than three times the national average, and that as many as three out of four of the students in classes for the educable mentally retarded come from low income families.

In spite of the fact that the number of retarded children who are receiving child welfare services represents only a small proportion of those who need them, the

Reprinted by special permission of The Child Welfare League of America.

services that have been provided have demonstrated a valuable impact. Of additional significance are reports that experiences of agencies involved with the retarded indicate that only slight adaptation of basic child welfare principles, knowledge and methods has been required in their work with retardates and their families.

As many member agencies already know, the Research Center of the CWLA is currently engaged in a national study of foster care within which children with various mental handicaps, inclusive of retardation, are being studied with reference to the nature and extent of services received from public and voluntary child welfare agencies. When completed, this study should contribute much to an increased recognition of existing needs and means by which they can be met.

The CWLA views the development, extension, and improvement of child welfare services for the mentally retarded child and his family as being an appropriate and timely area of concern for League affiliates. The League thinks it is important for the child welfare field, with its concern for the problems of all children, to be able to contribute its accumulated wisdom and experience to concerted planning efforts with other professional groups involved in this social problem.

THIRTY-TWO

Concerning Misplacement of Children in Classes for the Mentally Retarded

A STATEMENT OF THE SOUTHERN ARIZONA CHAPTER OF THE NATIONAL ASSOCIATION OF SOCIAL WORKERS

Throughout the southwest, in particular, parents are expressing resentment concerning the placement of their children in classes for the mentally retarded. This is especially true of those whose native language is other than English or whose background is different from the middle class Anglo-American. Social workers, teachers, psychologists, staff of Neighborhood Centers and others in close contact with the less privileged have had reason to agree. Articles in the Los Angeles *Times*[1] and *Atlantic Monthly*[2] and studies on local district levels have likewise pointed up the same problem.

Psychological tests, designed for majority children, have been routinely applied. Students from Spanish-speaking homes frequently score average on the performance part of a test and far below in the verbal. Disregarding the language factor, and averaging the scores serves to define the child as a mental retardate. Misplacement of a normal or bright youngster in a retarded class can handicap his self-image for life. So long as the best professional judgment favors small, special classes for those defined as mentally retarded, we can applaud additional state reimbursement to make possible such facilities; but never if it serves as an incentive for schools also to include children of average potential.

Because of the harmful effect of improper placement on children and the corrosive result in inter-group relationships, *the Southern Arizona Chapter of the National Association of Social Workers* would go on record, drawing this matter to the attention of the National Association of Social Workers and offering for consideration the following suggestions:

1. that legislators on National and state levels give serious consideration to a bilingual program where there are heavy concentrations of children speaking Spanish or Indian languages.
2. that the Department of Health, Education and Welfare, together with appropriate state departments having responsibilities of the same general nature,

Reprinted, with permission, from Statement of Southern Arizona Chapter, National Association of Social Workers, 1968.

seriously re-examine definitions of Mental Retardation and curricula designed for "educable" and "trainable" retarded.

3. that a particular responsibility rests upon state departments of education to furnish meaningful supervision to insure that school districts function within present regulations and to recommend legislative changes when indicated. It would behove a state department of education to be especially watchful when audits reveal highly disproportionate numbers from minority groups identified as "mentally retarded"; to be certain that re-testing is done as prescribed; that reimbursement be conditioned on such careful safeguards rather than by simply honoring local claims.

4. that local school districts consider recommendations already noted and, in addition, be quick to question the appropriateness of routine psychometrics[3] when applied to children from a non-English speaking or culturally different background. It is on the local school level that psychological assessments are made which may place children of good intellectual potential in classes for the mentally retarded.

Adopted April 1968

References

[1]"False 'Retardation' Label on Latins Charged"—Los Angeles *Times*, page 1—12/15/67.
[2]"A Minority Nobody Knows," Helen Rowan, *Atlantic Monthly*, June 1967, pp. 47-52.
[3]"Who Are the Mentally Retarded?" Gunnar Dybwad. *Children*, March-April 1968, pp. 43-48.

PART SIX

Models of Service Delivery Directed to Retarded Persons

Special Community Programs for the Mildly Retarded: Acceptance or Rejection?

STANLEY C. MAHONEY

The long-range, fundamental goals in our work with all the retarded should be maximizing capacities and minimizing the effects of impairment. A dilemma confronting attempts to provide special help for the retarded is that of how to give special service without increasing the social and psychological distance between the retarded and their more normal peers. This is especially relevant for the mildly retarded where the goal is to help them to become productive members of their communities functioning in a nearly independent manner.

When children are separated from their peers on the basis of their exceptionality, there is always the danger that we are accentuating their perception of their difference and others' perception of their difference far beyond the areas where it has some objective basis.

In establishing separate programs to provide special services, careful evaluation of the need for the separate program is of the utmost importance. It is not enough to be able to say that the separate and special program will be helpful; we should also be able to state that it was not possible to achieve the same objectives without separation and that the deterimental effects of separation do not outweigh the positive effects. For educational purposes some separateness is probably warranted so that instruction can be provided at the pace and level that would be most beneficial. However, even here there is conflicting evidence as to the long-range impact and effectiveness of such special programs. Whether the special class is perceived as parasitic, endophytic, or symbiotic in relation to the school, to use the terminology of Goldberg and Blackman (1965), will be an important factor in determining its overall effect.

When attention is directed to areas other than education—to recreational and social activities—the trend toward an increase in providing special help through special and separate programs is noted as well as an absence of studies evaluating the effectiveness and impact of such programs. More often than not a child is admitted to the special program on the basis that he was in a special program for the

Reprinted by permission of the author from *Mental Retardation,* Vol. 5, No. 3 (October, 1965), pp. 30-31, a publication of the American Association on Mental Deficiency.

retarded in the public school system. There is an uncritical generalization that if he needed special and separate help in the school, then he needs special and separate programs elsewhere.

What is overlooked is that while the child usually received examinations and evaluations to determine whether he needed special education in a separate classroom in the school system, such evaluations were not directed toward determining his need for special and separate programs in other areas. Diagnosed and labeled in the school system for the purpose of opening a special door for his greater welfare, the child and his family may find this open door becomes a one-way turnstile that leads to a labyrinth of one-way turnstiles in many situations far beyond the school system.

At the risk of seeming cynical, it must be noted that special service on a separate basis can sometimes indicate rejection more than acceptance.

The situation is not unlike that which is sometimes found with respect to referral practices. Referring a client to a specialist can be an ethical, reasonable act based on consideration of the client's best welfare, or it can be a rejecting act reflecting the referring person's desire to be rid of a troublesome client. An analogous pattern is also seen in some families wherein the children are given all the material advantages but little or none of the parents' time, attention and love.

Rejection wears many masks, not the least among which is an overproviding for at the expense of doing with. Special and separate can mean "we do care," but it can also mean "we don't care—we're all for you just so long as you stay out of our way and don't bother us."

It is worth remembering that the Joint Commission on Mental Illness and Health (1961) emphasized in its final report that attitudes of rejection toward behaviorally deviant members of our society by both citizens and professionals alike has been a major problem that has permeated the best-intentioned efforts. It is often easier to have a special troop, or dance, or Sunday School class, or tour for the retarded than to make a place for them in regular peer-group activities. It is often easier to have a special party or gifts for retarded children than to invite them to participate in celebrations shared by other children.

It becomes all too easy in an affluent society to isolate deviants and to ease them into compartmentalized activities in the name of providing special programs to meet their needs. Because it is easier, however, because it is more comfortable, because it is more administratively efficient, does not mean that it is better—either for the mildly retarded child or for the rest of society.

Unless we are very careful in our programming, we are in danger of perpetuating the long theme of "casting out" that has characterized society's attitude toward the behaviorally deviant since recorded history. In an affluent, sophisticated society "casting out" is accomplished not so much by crude physical expulsion nor by geographical isolation to distant institutions as by organizational and administrative exile via special and separate programs.

The most common reason given for providing separate recreational and social programs is that normal children tend to isolate and reject the retarded when the two are placed together. Since this occurs, the argument runs, it is more beneficial to the retarded to provide them with separate and special programs where they can obtain a sense of personal worth and "belongingness." The issue is seldom faced that in accepting this reasoning we are also accepting the premise that the retarded will be rejected by their more normal peers. Such a premise, it must be noted, runs counter to the verbalized purposes and values of many churches and groups as well as, ironically, our own public education efforts. While acceptance and understanding is preached, rejection and isolation via special and separate programs is practiced.

It is submitted that our ideals are not as unattainable as we sometimes think, and that we have confused what is with what must be. We must be careful not to give the empirical finding that many normal children today do isolate and reject retarded children in play and social activities the status of an eternal truth. To do so may be to participate in the perpetuation of a myth, just as we would have perpetuated a myth if we had accepted as ultimate truths the empirical findings of 50 years ago that children do not like school and children find learning painful.

The sensitivity of children to adult values and expectations cannot be underestimated; our children today still live in a society that expects them to reject retarded children and acts accordingly by removing the retarded children via separate programs.

The basic issue at point is the extent to which we may be fostering alienation, increasing differences, and contributing to rejecting attitudes by developing a myriad of special and separate programs for the retarded. Special programs that are highly visible, that can be pointed to as tangible indications that we do care, are tempting. And some are necessary. But in and of themselves they are not enough. They are a step forward from punitive rejection to toleration, but they are not acceptance.

If, with an increase in special and separate programs, the mildly retarded find themselves more and more excluded from activities available to their more normal peers, their plight will not have been lessened. On the contrary, their differences will have been accentuated and institutionalized at a community level and they will remain strangers in their own land.

References

GOLDBERG, I. I., and BLACKMAN, L. S., The Special Class—Parasitic, Endophytic, or Symbiotic Cell in the Body Pedagogic. *Mental Retardation*, 1965, 3, April, 30-31.

Joint Commission on Mental Illness and Health, *Action for Mental Health*, New York; Science Editions Inc., 1961.

THIRTY-FOUR

Safeguarding the Retarded from Isolating Effects of Special Programs

STANLEY C. MAHONEY

The needs of the retarded require that some use be made of special and separate programs wherein the retarded are provided appropriate help that could not be provided equally well in groups with their more normal peers. It must be recognized, however, that undesirable side-effects of increased isolation and alienation from more normal peers are potential dangers wherever special and separate programs are found. These dangers have been discussed by the author in earlier papers (1965, 1965).

The concept of isolation always implies a separateness or apartness from something or someone. Isolation is seldom an all-or-none affair, but usually occurs to varying degrees along several dimensions. The simplest dimension is probably that of geographical distance. A more important dimension of isolation is the psycho-social distance between an individual, or a program, and the mainstream of socio-cultural activities in a given community. Both the community and the individual are strengthened and enhanced to the degree that the individual is an involved participant in the on-going, primary activities of the community, such as school, church, recreational, and vocational programs. To the degree that the individual is not accepted in these regular, on-going programs and activities, or is unable to participate in them, he becomes alienated and isolated from his community and his more normal peers, with consequent loss to both the individual and the community.

Geographical proximity can be expected to decrease psycho-social isolation, and geographical distance can be expected to increase psycho-social isolation, other things being equal. But other things are never equal, and specific instances can be found where retardates in a special program in a populous community are more isolated from regular, on-going events participated in by their more normal peers than are some retardates in institutions relatively remote from populous centers. Organizational barriers can be as real, and even more painful, than geographical barriers. Physical closeness accompanied by psycho-social distance because of organizational barriers can result in feelings of non-belongingness, alienation, difference, and rejection far greater than is engendered by physical distance alone.

[1]Reprinted by permission of the author from a paper presented at the 1966 Annual Meeting of the American Association on Mental Deficiency.

Geographical distance makes it more difficult for the retardate to participate appropriately in the mainstream of community life with his more normal peers, but it is not the crucial factor. The size of an institution or program, also, is not the crucial factor although there is probably some tendency for larger institutions and programs to become more isolated because of greater internal resources. Relatively small programs and institutions geographically located in or near centers of population make it easier for psycho-social isolation to be minimized, and for this reason are more desirable than large institutions geographically remote, but they do not guarantee in themselves that debilitating isolation will not occur.

The crucial factor in minimizing isolating effects of special programs on the retarded is the awareness of all concerned—governing boards, staff, and parents—that such psycho-social isolation can and does take place if specific steps are not taken to prevent it. The degree to which special programs become isolating and alienating will reflect, to a large degree, the extent to which governing boards, staff, and parents allow them to become so. Planned action based on the will and desire to prevent needless alienation and isolation is necessary. Where there is an obliviousness or indifference to the possibility of isolating effects occurring, they can be expected to occur with inevitable regularity.

The following seven guidelines are presented for preventing and combating the isolating effects of special programs on the mentally retarded.

1. *Placement evaluation.* A comprehensive placement evaluation should be conducted when a retardate first applies for admission to a special program or facility. This evaluation would include three essential aspects and would be broader in scope than the usual admission evaluation. First, a clinical assessment of the retardate's condition by qualified persons in the various relevant professions. Second, an evaluation of resources in the area that offers services relevant to the retardate's needs. Third, an evaluation of the specific program and services of the facility to which the retardate is applying for admission. Such a three-pronged evaluation should be conducted or reviewed by an interdisciplinary group with representatives from both the facility to which application is being made and outside agencies and interests. Attention would be given not only to what the special program could do for the retardate, but also to what disadvantages might be involved (as, for instance, increased isolation from more normal peers). The question would not be the more narrow one of whether the special program could help the retardate, but the broader one of whether placement in the special program would be the best choice available at the time with potentiality for greater help and less harm than any other placement.

The principle that the retardate should receive needed services with the least possible disruption to normal life patterns should guide the decisions made about appropriate placement. Where possible, placement should be made in programs that are integrated parts of regular, on-going programs for more normal peers. For example, placement in a special education class in a school also serving more normal children would be preferable to placement in a special education class in a facility serving only retarded children.

2. *Periodic Re-Evaluation.* At the time the retardate is admitted to a special and separate program serving only the retarded an estimate should be made as to the length of time he will need the special placement and a definite plan for periodic re-evaluations should be made. Periodic re-evaluations, at time intervals considered reasonable in view of the retardate's needs and potentials and in view of changing resources and programs, would include clinical evaluation of the retardate's progress in the special program, appraisal of changing patterns of resources in the community, and appraisal of changes with the special program. An appropriate placement for a retardate at one time may no longer be the best possible placement a year or two later if more appropriate resources have been developed in the community.

3. *Planned Counteraction for Undesirable Side-effects.* Programs and facilities, like people, are not perfect. It should be assumed that every program and facility has weaknesses as well as strengths. Program weaknesses are usually dangerous to the extent that they are not recognized and corrected or compensated for. One weakness of any special and separate facility or program is its tendency to further isolate retardates served from their more normal peers. This tendency can be expected to increase the more the facility approaches the concept of a total institution, i.e., one where the individual sleeps, works, and plays on a 24-hour a day basis.

Placement evaluations and periodic re-evaluations should contain precise statements as to what undersirable side-effects might be involved if the individual were admitted to the program. Definite plans and commitments should be made by all concerned for counteracting these side-effects at the time of placement. For example, a severly retarded child might need institutional care for a period of several years. One undesirable side-effect might be separation from parents and family. Definite plans should be made for counteracting this undesirable side-effect at the time of placement, perhaps through systematic visitation by the parents and/or regular home visits by the child.

Just as there are iatrogenic illnesses, there are also what might be called organizationogenic disturbances wherein secondary deviation and impairment occurs as a consequence of the nature of the organizational structure which is brought to bear on the primary problem. Definite ways and means of evaluating how well counteraction plans are succeeding should be made at time of placement. Too often the pressure of day-to-day activities leads to such plans not being implemented unless they are systematically reviewed.

4. *Staff Responsibility for Opening Doors Elsewhere.* Professional staff members in a separate and special program have a responsibility beyond that of providing high-quality service to the retarded in the program. They have a responsibility, or should have, to devote some time and energy to opening doors for the retardates in regular, ongoing programs and groups in the community where this is appropriate. Staff should be concerned and work actively to see that retardates are admitted and accepted in ongoing, regular community groups while they are participating in the special program to counteract isolating effects and to pave the way for later integration in the community if this is feasible. Such activities on the part of staff

should receive reward and recognition from governing boards and other groups. Only as such efforts are expected, and openly recognized, by governing boards will they be undertaken to an effective degree by administrative and professional staff. For example, teachers of educable children should be concerned, and take active steps to see that the children participate in other classes, extracurricular activities, clubs, sports, and so on wherever appropriate. In particular, the special program staff member should not perpetuate the self-defeating philosophy that the retardate will not be accepted elsewhere.

5. *Appropriate Agency Sponsorship of Special Program.* Governing boards, community planning councils, and others must give consideration as to whether the appropriate agency is sponsoring and/or providing the special program. In general, it is probably better that special and separate programs be provided by agencies that also serve the general community rather than by specialized agencies. For example, special camping programs for the retarded should be sponsored by camps that also serve more normal children rather than by a camp that serves just retarded children. Special education classes should be embedded in a school program serving all children, not in a facility serving just retarded children. A social group might better be conducted for the adult retarded by a civic or church group than by a specialized mental retardation association. Isolation from more normal peers can generally be expected to be greater when special services for the retarded are provided by agencies serving only the retarded than when provided by agencies also serving others.

6. *Comprehensive Statistical Reports and Informational Brochures.* Statistical reports and information brochures about special programs should go beyond information pertaining to quantity and quality of services rendered to individuals in the program. Information should be presented to show what is being done to counteract isolation while individuals are in the program and to provide for continuity and follow-up services after the individual leaves the program. For example, special education classes should report on the number and kinds of experiences children in the program have in integrated sessions outside the special program. Data should also be presented regarding the experiences of graduates after they leave the special program. For retardates in institutions, data should be presented regarding number and kind of integrated experiences with groups from nearby communities, as well as information about what happens to individuals after they are discharged. Such information should be meaningful to governing boards as well as staff in evaluating and planning programs. The systematic presentation of such information tends to heighten awareness as to the need for concern beyond the immediate special program and tends to focus all concerned on the total needs of the retarded rather than on just the specifics of the special program.

7. *Support of Staff Activities Outside Special Program.* The isolating effects of special programs are due to a multiplicity of factors, many of which tend to reinforce each other. Overidentification of staff with their particular program to the extent that they become relatively isolated from their colleagues in related areas can be a contributing factor to the isolating effect of a program, but not overidenti-

fied to the extent that they lost perspective on the role of their program in the greater community. Staff in highly specialized programs, such as teachers of special education classes or clinicians serving the retarded in a residential center, need involvement in at least some outside professional and community activities. Interdisciplinary planning groups, study groups, conferences, and workshops help meet some of this need. Active support and encouragement of such activity should be reflected in board and administrative policies and practices regarding time for travel, reimbursement of expenses, and so on. This is especially important when the special program is a facility approaching a total institution relatively isolated geographically.

References

MAHONEY, S. C., *Special community programs for the mildly mentally retarded: open doors or one-way turnstiles?*, paper presentation, Amer. Assn. on Mental Deficiency, Miami Beach, Florida, June 1965.

MAHONEY, S. C., *Special community programs for the mildly retarded: acceptance or rejection?*, "Issue at Point" section, *Mental Retardation,* No. 5, Vol. 3, October 1965, pp. 30-31.

THIRTY-FIVE

Children, Mental Retardation and Planning

IRVING PHILIPS

About a century ago there was great enthusiasm in the field of mental retardation. Interested citizens formed many groups to develop better care for the handicapped child. This was perhaps best expressed by Dr. S. G. Howe in 1848 in a report to the governor of the Commonwealth of Massachusetts:

> . . . no idiot need be confined or restrained by a force; that the young can be trained to industry, order and self respect; that they can be redeemed from odious and filthy habits, and that there is not one of any age, who may not be made more a man and less of a brute by patience and kindness directed by energy and skill. . . [1]

This enthusiasm continued for at least two decades, only to be followed by a period of marked apathy that continued almost until the present time. Mental retardation, an area of great public health concern, was neglected by all professional groups: medical, psychological, educational, social welfare, public welfare and governmental institutions. The retarded were considered different, in need solely of institutional care, and generally were isolated from their peers and family. The retarded became segregated citizens lacking services, generally isolated in their communities, or institutionalized far away from their home. Little was expected of them by society and consequently they accomplished little. This philosophy was exemplified by the situation in World War II, in which the retarded were hardly used in this country either in the Armed Forces or in a much needed civilian war effort. In contrast, in Great Britain pioneer battalions manned by retarded people were formed to perform vital functions, e.g., fire fighters, dairy and farm workers cleanup crews, etc., in both urban and rural centers.

After World War II, the citizenry of this country was aroused by the general neglect and poor care of both the mentally ill and the mentally retarded. Periodic hospital scandals resulted in the awakening of a lethargic public. In our more affluent society there was now time to be attentive to the needs of the handicapped. Righteous indignation was expressed with increasing recognition that the popula-

From the *American Journal of Orthopsychiatry,* Vol. 35, No. 5 (October, 1965), pp. 899-902. Copyright, the American Orthopsychiatry Association, Inc. Reproduced by permission.

tion who supported these institutions supported them poorly and with minimal budgets. There was little recognition that the hard working civil servants who were employed at these institutions were giving their patients the best care possible with the limited funds available. Minimal standards of care scarcely could be met in most hospital settings.

The organization of parent groups gained great impetus, and these exerted pressure for change. Redress was sought for the many grievances that were apparent in all states. The pendulum, too long stationary, was beginning to move. This movement was climaxed by the interest of the late President John F. Kennedy, who called for the passage of legislation to develop better care and facilities for the retarded population. This public health concern, once an area of neglect, now was publicized as an area requiring close scrutiny. Attention was being paid to the development of better and coordinated services to help the retarded lead more successful and productive lives when possible in their community. National panels and statewide study groups were organized to develop better and more fruitful programs. For instance, the Governor of the State of California appointed a study commission to formulate long-range plans for the retarded. This commission recommended a program board of lay and professional persons, subsidized by a two-million-dollar expenditure, to recommend and coordinate programs for the retarded. It also recommended appropriate statewide diagnostic and counseling centers for the retarded. The departments of health, education and welfare of many states examined their own participation in the field of mental retardation in an effort to develop better programs. Federal legislation has furnished funds to implement programs for the retarded. Professionals who neglected this area for many years now began to vie for control of funds and the development of programs for the retarded population. The retarded are thus becoming a "popular" area of professional concern!

There is a paradox in this concern. Needless to say, the historical neglect of the retarded demands correction. It is necessary to educate society, to reduce prejudice and misinformation concerning retarded people. The retarded population must be brought into the mainstream of the community. However, the efforts of many state commissions and departments, although laudable in their intent, tend to move the retarded into still greater isolation by recommending and developing many programs specifically related only to the retarded population. This serves to emphasize the differences between the retarded and their more favored peers thereby enhancing still further isolation. This not only maintains but exaggerates the fiction that few if any similarities exist between the child with intellectual defect and the child with normal intelligence. Esquirol in the early nineteenth century remarked that "mental retardation is a condition not a disease." Retardation is a condition which is primarily first noted in childhood and only one of many belonging to childhood. But the great clamor is for help for the retarded as a preferential group.

As programs develop, there will be many services for people who are retarded but little provision for the many other needed services for children. For example, in California there are plans for the development of a Bureau of Mental Retardation in the Department of Mental Hygiene. Services for children other than the retarded will be relegated to the bureau of that department which deals with clinical services for all age groups. Federal legislation has provided for the separate development of both mental retardation and mental health centers. In some cities, counties and states these facilities will exist as separate entities. Duplication of personnel, facilities, programs, funds, training and research will thereby needlessly develop in an area in which funds and skilled manpower are in short supply. The best service would be secured not by such competition but by integrated, coordinated planning to meet the broad medical and paramedical needs of all of our citizens.

With the development of separate programs for special groups the specific condition of a child will determine what sort of services he will get. For example, if he "passes" the implicit means test of intellectual deficiency, a wide gamut of services will be available to him. If his intelligence quotient is normal, however, his opportunities for help will be more limited and he will have to compete for the few available services and probably will be placed on one of the long waiting lists to secure vital health needs. What a child is labeled will determine what he gets.

If we instead develop programs providing for all the particular services children need, in the long run we will develop the best services for all children, including the retarded. The retarded are most in need of services that all children need with the addition of some specialized services. Programs should provide for all areas of concern, without isolation of particular diagnostic groups. Better and more comprehensive programs for our total child population, regardless of their condition or severity of their disorder, should be the aim of any program. Plans should be discussed to meet the needs of children which would include, for example, such facilities as children's hospitals, children's centers, school programs and recreational and rehabilitation facilities. This would be consistent with sound medical care and would stimulate programs to benefit all children. The needs of the child and his family and his neighborhood must be considered if we are best to provide and secure the benefits of good health to all children so that they may develop their fullest capability within their innate potential.

In planning programs another consideration deserves attention. The retarded form a diverse group. Eighty-five per cent of them are only mildly retarded; most of them come from urban and rural pockets of poverty and economic deprivation. Unfortunately, the programs already developed and those being designed will reach primarily that 15 per cent of the retarded who are moderately and severely retarded. The great pressure for care has been traditionally directed towards the severely retarded who need primarily medical and rehabilitative care throughout their lives. This group poses major problems to their families. Medical research may result in the prevention of many conditions which comprise this group. The 85 per cent group, the mildly retarded, are often neglected. There is too little if any voice to speak for their needs. This group is often doubly segregated both because of their sociocultural situation as well as their intellectual condition. Few programs are developed for this large fraction of the retarded. Acctive organizations of parents most frequently represent the 15 per cent group. As a result of justified requests and publications they demand and tend to obtain services for this segment of the population with resultant neglect of the mildly retarded. No child should be without adequate care but we must consider all groups and not overlook major areas of concern. The 85 per cent group present a serious problem to society and may comprise a significant number of school dropouts, chronic unemployables, recidivists and social outcasts. Early and intensive efforts may bring great rewards to this group and society.

The pendulum is swinging too far to one side and in two dimensions, the separation of the retarded from the mainstream of community care as a preferential group and the neglect of the vast majority of the mentally retarded in planning programs. We should not and must not develop programs that will further isolate already isolated groups. Comprehensive planning must include all children who need care regardless of their condition. Facilities must be developed and supported at levels consistent with good medical practice. We must not short-change our deprived and handicapped citizens, especially during their developmental years when they most need the best programs we can offer and our imagination can develop. These programs will cost money, but we must not compromise the concept of adequate care. We must consider all of our population in need of treatment and not preferential groups. We must consider the totality of childhood and not particular conditions that occur in children. We must look at the child in this society and help him reach the fullest development of his potentiality.

Reference

[1]R. H. HASKELL, "Mental Deficiency Over a Hundred Years," *J. Amer. Psychiatric Association*, 100: 107-118.

Basic Principles for Planning and Programing

U. S. PUBLIC HEALTH SERVICE

Planning of services and facilities is a process through which all factors relating to the needs of the mentally retarded can be identified and considered as an integrated whole. In this process, adherence to basic principles is a fundamental requirement. These principles must be realistic, timely, and most important, productive of tangible results. The process necessitates definition of the nature and scope of the problem as manifested locally. It calls for awareness of the resources available to deal with the problem and identification of those aspects of the problem that remain to be solved. The process also enlists services and skills of professional and community leaders, including those with particular interest in the mentally retarded.

Planning affords opportunities for developing greater awareness of the needs of the retarded and for stimulating the action necessary to achieve a comprehensive pattern of services for them. Effective planning cannot be done in isolation. Plans for the development and coordination of appropriate resources must relate to other planning efforts and to other health, education, and welfare activities in the planning area. These efforts and activities have an important bearing on the need for services and facilities for the mentally retarded.

Principles sufficiently broad to encompass the needs of the mentally retarded, yet consonant with the cultural and economic patterns of the areas to be served, should be formulated. Factors to be considered include the types of services and facilities best suited to meet the particular needs of the retarded within these areas, based upon the best knowledge available, the feasibility of providing these services and facilities within the limitations of existing and anticipated community resources, and the degree to which acceptance and support can be expected.

Planning must address itself to the balancing of conflicting objectives. For example, the objective of making maximum use of scarce professional talent may be in apparent conflict with the objective of bringing services close to the homes of retard-

Reprinted from "Planning of Facilities for the Mentally Retarded." Public Health Service, U.S. Department of Health, Education and Welfare (Washington, U.S. Government Printing Office, 1964), pp. 11-14.

ed individuals. The process of planning should be organized to identify explicitly and weigh the relative importance of such factors in a particular situation.

Once these basic determinations have been made, the development of the definitive plan to achieve specified objectives should take into account the following principles:

1. Planning of services and facilities for the mentally retarded should involve full participation of any governmental, voluntary, or other agency having a major responsibility to the mentally retarded, to the end that effective coordination be achieved. Any agency or group which is considered to have a significant potential for contributing some element to the overall program for the retarded should also be encouraged to participate in the planning process.

Only through coordinated effort can adequate programs providing the widest possible services be developed. In addition, effective use of available funds to support construction and operation of needed facilities and services can be fostered through cooperation and participation of all interested agencies and organizations in planning to meet the needs of the retarded. The extent of involvement will necessarily reflect the degree of responsibility and commitment of the particular agency toward the retarded.

2. General community services and facilities should be available to the mentally retarded to the fullest extent possible.

Many of the medical, health, educational, and social service needs of the mentally retarded are similar to those of the general population, and maximum use should be made of general services which meet such needs. In many cases, the usefulness of these services can be extended and enhanced with the advice of a person having special knowledge of the character and needs of the retarded, or through some minor modification of procedure. To the extent that general services and facilities are thus made more widely useful and adapted to the special needs of the retarded, it will be possible to avoid capital outlays and operational costs for separate services and facilities. Moreover, available professional staff, in many areas a scarce commodity, is utilized more fully.

Such provisions, however, do not obviate the need for certain specialized services and facilities. Even when maximum adaptation of general services has been achieved, there will remain in any community or area certain needs which can and should be met by services especially designed for the mentally retarded, either in association with other services or "freestanding."

3. Existing services suitable for the retarded (whether general or specialized) should be identified and considered in relation to one another; priority should be established for the organization of new services to complete the array necessary for a comprehensive program.

Since the needs of the retarded vary widely, planning agencies should recognize that a wide range of services will be required.

4. Planning of services and facilities for the retarded should be related to other forms of community planning and to social and economic trends.

The development and utilization of services and facilities for the retarded will be affected by many aspects of community life, such as trends in population growth, shifts in age composition, and changes in land utilization and patterns of commercial and industrial growth. The demand for services and facilities for the retarded may also be influenced by any shift in the content of programs of other health, education, and welfare agencies. Practical and realistic planning calls for an understanding of all potentially influencing factors.

5. Planning agencies and organizations should stimulate the development of programs for the prevention of mental retardation concurrently with programs providing facilities and services for the retarded.

The extent and impact of mental retardation can be minimized through preventive measures. Such programs as those providing maternal and child care, particularly in "high risk" areas, and programs for early diagnosis, evaluation, and case finding can do much to lessen the incidence of retardation. Through preventive programs, even today, individuals can be spared much mental and, frequently, physical damage, and their families will be spared great emotional stress. The cost of preventive programs will be far less than the total cost of providing the spectrum of facilities and services needed for those who might otherwise be retarded.

6. Adequate data should be developed to provide a base for projecting the extent, character, and location of services and facilities which will be needed.

The soundness of quantitative decisions and the effectiveness of evaluative interpretations in planning services and facilities for the mentally retarded are contingent upon the adequacy of available data. The development of long-range goals depends on knowledge of the broad needs. To proceed toward these long-range goals, the planning body needs to project in detail the immediate steps to be taken. This requires data about needs, such as general information regarding number and distribution of retarded children under school age whose families could and would avail themselves of a nursery school situation, or the number of adult retardates who could be maintained in the community with minimal social supervision, for the lack of which they would be admitted to 24-hour residential care. The capacity of each existing service should be compared to the extent of need for that type of service.

Need should be distinguished from demand, however. Demand should be assessed with special reference to the way in which the existing service is perceived by those whose needs it is intended to meet. It is well-known that a good service tends to call forth the expression of need through demand for the service, whereas a poor service suppresses demand even where need exists.

In addition, the data should (1) provide criteria for interpreting potentials for expansion and upgrading of existing facilities and services, and (2) permit determination of resources available within the area to maintain quality programs at efficient levels.

7. Planning should be based on the total and complete needs of the mentally retarded for services and facilities rather than on the availability of financial support.

The primary objective in planning services and facilities should be consideration of the total and complete needs of the mentally retarded. The recognition of these needs should not be limited by existing policies of governmental or sponsoring agencies or the funds available. Priorities for meeting these needs must be established, and this involves the development of both long-range and short-range goals.

8. Short-range planning involves the selection of the higher priorities in the long-range plan.

Factors influencing the selection of high priority activities for inclusion in the short-range plans include urgency of needs and feasibility of meeting these needs quickly. Feasibility, in turn, is influenced by available resources of facilities, funds, personnel, leadership, and public acceptance. Attention should be given to cultivation of community resources through continuing involvement of community leaders and groups in the planning process. Short-range steps should not be taken which tend to defeat long-range goals.

9. Where feasible and appropriate, existing facilities should be improved.

A detailed evaluation of the effectiveness and efficiency of existing services and facilities should be an integral part of all planning activity. This evaluation should cover effectiveness of program, adequacy of staff, relation of size to objectives, suitability of structure and location, and potential for improvement or adapatation. New services may often be added to existing facilities rather than being established independently. Oversized institutions may often advantageously be reduced in capacity or made more versatile in their services. All such possibilities should be carefully weighed during the planning process.

10. Facilities and services for the mentally retarded should be planned to meet or exceed existing standards.

Facilities should be planned to meet or exceed any generally accepted minimal requirements which may already exist for accreditation, eligibility for licensure, or grants-in-aid or loan programs. If the accreditation or licensure standards are lacking or inadequate, the support for their development should be stimulated.

11. As far as practicable, facilities for the mentally retarded should be located so as to be readily accessible.

To the extent appropriate and feasible, services and facilities for the mentally retarded should be planned so as to be accessible to the population to be served and to professional staff. Travel time and expense for the retarded should be minimized, especially where daily travel is involved. Residential facilities should be located where families may visit easily. Careful consideration should also be given to the distribution pattern of needed professional personnel and the factors which attract and hold staff.

The location of facilities should be planned to permit effective coordination and interrelationships with other related health, education, and welfare services. Decisions on the location of facilities should be based not only on the present distribution of population but also on a consideration of population trends and growth and projected development of transportation systems.

To provide opportunities for research and training of personnel, the potential for productive interaction between facilities for the retarded and the higher education system should be cultivated. Accessibility of such resources will contribute notably toward the primary purpose of bringing the best possible service to all the retarded in the State in a community setting.

12. Projected needs for continuing inservice training of personnel should be explicitly considered as part of State and community planning for the retarded.

Some centralization of such training may be advantageous. Proximity to existing schools, colleges, and universities is a relevant factor. In any case, the possible need for suitable space for training activities in appropriate facilities should be considered.

13. Planning groups should develop procedures to evaluate their activities on a continuing basis.

By the process of continual evaluation, overall needs will be kept in constant focus and changes can be made whenever justified. This will also contribute to new and more effective means of meeting needs, particularly as consideration is given to new knowledge. Planning bodies should be alert to the significance of lessons to be learned from experience in other communities and in other areas of the country, as well as from their own activities. Full use should be made of resources which may be mobilized from beyond the area directly under study.

The development of such procedures to evaluate their own activities will assist planning groups in withstanding undue influence by special interests, whether they are professional, religious, civic, or proprietary. It will also help restrain any tendencies toward rigidity on the part of planning personnel, especially in dealing with long-range plans. The planning process should be responsive to changing conditions.

THIRTY-SEVEN

Community Planning

MICHAEL J. BEGAB

The development of a community plan to combat the problem of mental retardation must, if it is to achieve long range goals, make effective provision for *prevention* through community services. This is not a responsibility social agencies can carry alone. Nevertheless, the high vulnerability of social agency clientele to the forces which cause or contribute to mental retardation and the overwhelming prevalence of this condition in low income groups, imposes a responsibility which cannot be overlooked. To fulfill this responsibility, the social worker in conjunction with other disciplines and research personnel, must systematically identify and substantiate the family and environmental conditions inimical to child development. Needs must be more effectively interpreted and citizen and legislative support more skillfully sought.

A promising area for prevention lies in the strengthening of basic maternal and child health services. The relationship of low income to dietary deficiencies, prematurity, complications of pregnancy, infectious diseases and mental retardation is firmly established. To avoid as far as possible these potential stresses to maternal health and child growth, the community must see to it that resources for adequate medical care are available. And the social worker must help the parents understand the importance of prenatal care for the mother and pediatric attention for the child and insure that these resources are used. Close cooperation between the social worker and public health nurse can achieve these objectives in individual cases. Cooperation between health and welfare agencies on local and State levels in promoting public and professional education, disease control and expanded resources, can achieve the same results for the total community.

The prospects for preventing non-organic retardation are also promising. Many of the environmental and psychological variables involved can be controlled, or at least minimized in their effect. Here too, the social worker can apply his skill in strengthening family life, improving child-rearing practices and in providing stimu-

From Michael J. Begab, *The Mentally Retarded Child: A Guide to Services of Social Agencies*. Children's Bureau, U. S. Department of Health, Education and Welfare (Washington, U.S. Government Printing Office, 1963), pp. 125-130. By permission of the author and the Children's Bureau.

lating opportunities for child growth. But higher level policies of social agencies affecting the welfare of their clients must also be reexamined. Are welfare grants adequate to support basic nutrition and health needs? Do clients know of existing resources and are they located where they are reasonably accessible? Do the laws properly safeguard children from emotional and moral neglect? As solutions to these and other questions are found and social conditions are upgraded, fewer cases of retardation are likely to occur.

The prevention of primary retardation through community services or through research, is but one phase of a preventive program. Where the child is already retarded and his basic condition is irreversible, his overall level of functioning may still be markedly influenced by secondary handicaps of an emotional nature. These are sometimes equally disabling in their impact, but they can be prevented by the skillful application of the various social services already described. To do so with any measure of success however, these individuals must be reached as early in life as possible, before behavior patterns become too well crystallized. This calls for *early identification* and skilled case-finding techniques.

Many sources for early case finding exist—private physicians, well-baby clinics, public health nurses, child welfare workers, schools. The problem in many communities is that these sources are not always aware of the potential development of secondary disabilities and fail to invoke the necessary preventive services. Sometimes they have little appreciation of what is needed or where to find it.

To overcome this defect in community planning, organized systems of referral need to be developed. Many possibilities exist, depending on the structure of services in the given community. Information centers are one useful technique—an office identified by parents and professionals alike, as a place to get information on available resources, for help in referral, for literature on the subject, and so on. Social workers have extensive experience in the area of referral and should play a leadership role in this aspect of community planning, thus enabling retarded children and their families to get to the right agency at the right time.

Systems of referral are effective only as there are resources to refer to and resources that are properly coordinated. In many communities retarded children are compelled to accept second and third choice treatment plans because the first cannot be carried out. One child stays at home because the school has no special classes; another spends years in an institution because foster family care resources have not been developed; a third idles away his time in useless pursuits because he does not meet the qualifications of the agency for training. Sometimes resources are in short supply for all children. More frequently perhaps, restrictive intake policies limit the extension of these services to the retarded.

The dearth of services is not a phenomenon that is unique to the retarded. Other handicapped children are faced with shortages too, and in some communities the normal child fares no better. For all of these children, the community needs to *consciously* plan a network of services and facilities to prevent pathology and to promote the highest level of social usefulness and self-fulfillment in them and their families. To the extent that such planning is comprehensive and embraces the total spectrum of problem situations and the entire range of health, education and social welfare programs, many of the basic needs of the retarded will be met.

This global approach, however, tends to obscure children with special needs. When program limitations are compounded by acute shortages of professional personnel and inadequate financing, agencies tend to set priorities regarding the categories of children to be served. In this process, the retarded child rates low and his parents too, are often denied help. Basic services, ostensibly developed for all children, find limited application, *yet the extension of basic services is the most effective way for meeting the needs of the retarded.*

Focus on community planning for the retarded can help overcome these discriminatory practices—a need widely recognized in the establishment of special legislative committees, community surveys, and subcommittees of local planning bodies. Concentrated attention to this problem area can stimulate agencies to a reexamination of their policies, identify unused but potential resources, and help set forth those services needed for which no regular provision is made. At the same time, this specialized approach runs the risk of "vertical" planning for different categories of children, duplication of services and uneconomical use of scarce professional staff. These effects can be avoided by centering planning responsibility in local health and welfare councils who are concerned with overall community needs. Viewed as an integral part of the total State and local program for all citizens, the development of programs for the retarded are more likely to gain public support and acceptance.

It is a truism that no single agency or discipline can meet the complex needs of the retarded and that community planning must therefore be a shared responsibility. This highlights the importance of communication between professions and coordination between agencies, factors which rely ultimately on mutual respect, understanding of each others' area of competence and commitment to a common cause.

While no discipline has a "corner" on coordinating techniques, the social worker frequently carries this role. Indeed, social work, which is one of the very few professions that receives special training in this area, seeks to perform an integrating function for which no other provision is made in contemporary society, by enlisting the cooperation of all existing social institutions, facilities and services on behalf of those who need help. This responsibility is carried out through referral procedures, case conferences, community planning and social action and by identifying specific social ills and the need for appropriate remedial and preventive services.

Effective integration of services rests ultimately on the success of community planning efforts, for one can coordinate only what exists. In mental retardation, programs have too frequently been characterized by sporadic and uneven development without full awareness of the relatedness of a given program to total needs. These differences result from the lack of a blueprint for a comprehensive program. Individual children not only are deprived of essential services, but a distinct possibility exists that the benefits of available programs may be minimized.

Before blueprints can be developed—whether for a small rural community or a large industrial State—the diversity of needs must be identified and interpreted. The community must not only know how many retarded persons they have, but must know their outstanding characteristics, the proportion that need service and what kind, and the resources that can be brought to bear on the problem.

The community planning process is an excellent, and indispensable, device for bringing together the agencies, individual workers and lay citizens who represent the essential interrelated parts and interests underlying a comprehensive program. Of the lay representatives, the delegate from the local or State parent group is often the most important. These groups are in the vanguard of public education programs and are a potent force in stimulating legislative action, supporting research, and sponsoring pilot demonstration projects. Their specialized character and intense motivations—properly harnessed—can be a spur to progress. Through dynamic interaction with the professional community in the planning process, better understanding of one another may be achieved. In this way, the total community is able to move toward commonly defined goals. Agencies are able to reflect on what they are doing or can do with additional staff and budget, and priorities for action can be formulated. When, however, parents and professionals do not communicate and negotiate where necessary, resistances often arise that hinder effective planning or the implementation of a specific program.

Each community has a unique personality as reflected in its overall organization of programs, prevailing social philosophy, size of population, economic and cultural condition, and attitudes toward the retarded. For this reason, each may face somewhat different problems, though many similarities undoubtedly exist. For example, the number of severely handicapped children in a relatively small town may be too small to warrant setting up a day care center. Or a sheltered workshop may not be feasible in a small community or one lacking industrial resources. In both of these instances, some other type of program may be necessary. The important consideration is not to overlook the needs of these groups and to experiment with new ways of meeting them.

Each community too, while its long range goals may be similar, may set different priorities for immediate fulfillment. Various factors are involved such as community readiness to accept and support a new program, availability of staff, and financial aspects. How many persons need the service is less important than how many would actually use it were it available. Parent interest and attitudes, or practical obstacles in using the service, need to be assessed in the planning stages. Here too, the social worker has much to contribute.

One of the major factors to be considered by community planners is cooperation and coordination between local and State services. Many local communities lack the fiscal capacity to support certain programs which may be more costly for retarded than for non-retarded children. Special education is a good example, but many other illustrations are possible, such as day care, diagnostic services, sheltered workshops. Some services can be provided on a regional basis, involving the cooperation or joint sponsorship of several communities, but others must be provided where the individual lives and may call for partial State subsidy. No set pattern would apply to every State or community, but local planners should be familiar with State resources in order to make maximum use of them.

Another consideration in planning relates to research, and the evaluation of existing services. Not every community can undertake basic research, but all should recognize the importance of testing the efficiency of programs, experimenting with new techniques and discarding programs that achieve no useful purpose. Finally, the success of any community program rests ultimately on the knowledge, skill and understanding of those responsible for the provision and administration of services. If the retarded are to be integrated to the highest degree possible in existing programs, then the professional staff involved must be trained accordingly. In-service training and educational opportunities in institutions of higher learning must therefore be an integral part of the community plan.

The task confronting many States and communities in providing for the retarded child and his family the services needed, is great. But the task is not impossible, and significant progress is being made. In time, we may realize the goals expressed by the World Health Organization:

> Every child has the right to expect the greatest possible protection against the occurrence of preventable physical handicap before, during, and after his birth.

> Every child also, regardless of the nature of his physical handicap, has the right to develop to the maximum of his abilities, in spite of his disablement. This implies that the child with a physical handicap should have ready access to the best medical diagnosis and treatment, allied preparation, and employment. In this way he should be able to satisfy the needs of his own personality to the maximum, and become as far as possible a useful and independent member of the community.

THIRTY-EIGHT

Recommendations of the Conference on Mental Retardation

THE COUNCIL OF STATE GOVERNMENTS

State Administrative Organization

The problems of the mentally retarded are not and cannot be the sole responsibility of any one department of state government. They are important concerns of several departments and require a multiple, but coordinated attack.

1. *The conference, therefore, recommended that each state establish an interdepartmental agency, such as an interdepartmental committee, council or board for the joint planning and coordination of state services for the mentally retarded. This interdepartmental agency may be established by the Governor or the legislature, depending upon conditions prevailing in the state.*

2. Such departments as education, mental health, health, welfare, labor, corrections, and institutions of higher education offer programs and services for the mentally retarded. Within a given state there may be other departments concerned with the mentally retarded. *Within each of these departments there should be a division or bureau for services to the mentally retarded or a special consultant with specific responsibility for the development and administration of these services.*

3. In order to implement these recommendations, the conference recommended that

a. Each department head or his deputy should report to the interdepartmental agency on the responsibility of his department for services to the mentally retarded and on the extent to which these services are provided.

b. The interdepartmental agency should submit reports periodically, with recommendations for legislative and administrative action, to improve services for the mentally retarded.

4. A comprehensive program for the mentally retarded should include intensive efforts to prevent mental retardation in the first place. This means: services to prevent birth defects; prenatal care; pediatric care; child health supervision and safety provisions. The state program also should include diagnostic services for develop-

Reprinted from "Report and Recommendations of the Conference on Mental Retardation." Interstate Clearing House on Mental Health (Chicago, The Council of State Governments, 1958), pp. 2-4. By permission of The Council.

ment evaluation, an extensive research effort, provisions for the training of professional personnel, and intensive programs for the care, training and welfare of the mentally retarded.

5. To increase the efficient use of personnel and facilities in research, training and treatment, the states should explore the potential of pooling resources within regions for cooperative, interstate efforts.

6. Wherever possible, services for the mentally retarded should be provided at the community level, with state assistance where needed. State provision should complement services provided at the community level.

7. Any program providing a comprehensive approach to the problems of the mentally retarded must include provision for joint planning between state agencies and local government agencies.

8. Particular attention should be given to the problem of providing appropriate services to the mentally retarded in the rural areas of the states.

9. An effective program for the mentally retarded will give emphasis to services for very young children.

10. Lay groups concerned with the problems of mental retardation should participate in an advisory capacity to those agencies established by the state to deal with the problem.

PART SEVEN

The Parent Self-Help Group: A New Social Organization of Relevance to Social Work

THIRTY-NINE

The Role of Parent Groups in Services to Mentally Retarded

ALFRED H. KATZ

The emergence and rapid growth of "self-organized" groups of parents and relatives of the physically and mentally handicapped has been one of the most striking phenomena of the United States social scene since the end of World War II. Similar groups have also appeared in many other countries with such differing cultures as England and Turkey, Indonesia and Uruguay, New Zealand and Norway. It is apparent that in spite of national differences, these groups have arisen in response to some urgent problems experienced by parents in many diverse social settings, and that it is important for professional workers in the health and welfare fields to understand their dynamics of origin and growth so that mutually beneficial relationships can be established.

In the brief time availabe to me, I propose to discuss four aspects of the groups in the U.S.:

    A.   Their sociological significance as a form of self-help;

    B.   The psychological effects of participation for parents;

    C.   Principles of professional-volunteer collaboration in service to the patients served by the groups; and

    D.   The need for cross-cultural studies of the groups.

The data on which my remarks are based are set forth in much greater detail in my recently-published book, "Parents of the Handicapped," available in the U.S. from C.C. Thomas Publishers, Springfield, Illinois, and in England from Blackwell Publishers, Oxford.

A. Significance of the Groups

In the U.S. the parent groups arose first in the field of mental retardation and then have spread to many other handicapping conditions, such as cerebral palsy, childhood schizophrenia, the muscular dystrophies, hemophilia, cystic fibrosis and many others. Now such groups are being organized, almost every time a new clinical entity of a chronic or congenital character is differentially diagnosed.

From *Proceedings, Second International Congress on Mental Retardation, Part II* (Vienna, S. Karger, 1963), pp. 208-211. By permission of the author.

Why do such groups come into being? The data of my study show that their origins "lie in the needs felt by parents of children with a similar handicap to receive greater assistance in the diagnosis, treatment and care of their children than had hitherto been available from professional and community sources. In banding together for action on their problems, these parents achieve a sense of shared purpose (1)."

Thus, the groups originate for mutual aid—they achieve results no individual parent could accomplish alone. Some of these accomplishments are in the area of the initiation of services—clinics, special education, various para-medical therapies, social programs; others, in the area of influencing the Government to provide these things; still others, in professional and public education around the needs of and desirable services for patients; and still others in the raising of funds for demonstration and both basic and clinical research.

In the United States, in contrast to many European countries, there have not been many examples of social welfare programs on the mutual aid or self-help pattern that these groups exemplify. Instead of a vertical pattern of someone—a private philanthropist or Government agency doing something for those in need of help—the self-help pattern is a horizontal one in which the recipients of help are on the same level as those who provide the help. This is of great sociological and psychological significance, for it means that the "consumers" of service have something to say about what they receive, and it is easier for the recipients to accept and utilize the help given.

B.   Effects of Participation for Parents

The psychological effect on parents of participation in the groups has been found by myself and other investigators to be a profound one. In the first place, feelings of having been singled out by providence or fate for a special lifelong burden, feelings of isolation and consequent helplessness are overcome. Secondly, even in the absence of professional counselling or guidance, parents get much help from other parents—whom they can readily trust. They receive help with practical problems of information, methods of bringing up their children, rates of growth, expectations and problems to be anticipated at different ages; and also in the area of emotion and feelings about themselves and their child. Many of the meetings of the groups have a character similar to that of more formal group counselling and group therapy, with their attendant therapeutic benefits. Finally, for parents, the groups represent an opportunity for constructive social action—which has been demonstrated to be one of the most important ways of overcoming feelings of guilt, anxiety, helplessness and defeat.

Thus, in summary on this point, for individual parents, the groups become an extension of the nuclear family—a "quasi-family", in Cottrell and Foote's term (2)—which simultaneously enables the harried parents to discuss their problems, receive advice and emotional support, engage in constructive actions and help bring about some remedial and beneficial arrangements for their own and other children.

C. Professional-Volunteer Collaboration in the Groups

Despite these and other positive aspects, the self-organized groups are viewed by many professional workers in my country—as I found out in the course of interviews for my study—with considerable suspicion, hostility and distrust. To some, the emotional drives of the parents mean that they cannot achieve objectivity regarding their children, and accept a prognosis and appropriate therapeutic programs for them. To others, the groups seem to be undisciplined competitors with the leadership of professionals. To still others, they are only "pressure groups" unable to accept any limitation of realistic planning.

While there is some basis for all these attitudes, I would urge my professional colleagues to remember that the parents would not have created these groups if the needs of the patients were being adequately met. These parents have suffered a great deal; they have not always had a sympathetic response from professional workers; they often face burdens of lifelong care, which means they are constrained to an abnormal kind of parenthood. Under these circumstances, emotionalism is understandable and to be expected.

What my study has shown, however, is that when there is professional guidance that understands what these parents have endured, and also appreciates what can be learned about the children and their potential from those who know them best, the parents—then, a fruitful collaboration is possible between professional workers and parent-volunteers. We have in the United States a number of impressive examples of such collaboration in the fields of mental retardation, cerebral palsy and others.

In these cases, parents retain a strong role as volunteers and in the management of the organization they have created; they offer many suggestions around the programs to be offered, but the ultimate decisions concerning technical aspects of program planning and the operation of services are left in the hands of professional personnel or consultants. What is true is that open-minded professionals realize they can learn from the daily experience of the parents with their children.

D. Need for Further Research on Parent Groups

I conclude with a plea for cross-cultural and further national studies of parent groups in mental retardation and the other fields of handicap.

My study showed that in the United States these groups arose at least partly in response to a vacuum in public provision of necessary therapeutic and educational services. Yet in many countries of Europe where there are strong Governmental programs of this kind, the parent groups have also come into being. Why should this be so, and what role do the parent groups play under such circumstances?

Can it be that there is an underlying need for democratic participation in small group life, no matter what the national culture or social system, and that these groups of parents of the handicapped serve such a need? The groups have significant meaning for those who participate in them and also are an excellent source of data and information regarding the participants and their problems. As such they merit serious interest and further study by social scientists.

Another question: can the groups be brought together instead of remaining separate disability-centered as at present? If so, how—by what instrumentality? Can professional workers play a role in this?

These and many other questions seem to me of great sociological significance, as well as of great significance for policy and planning, and I hope in future to be able to devote some study to them in European countries.

References

1. KATZ, A. H.: Parents of the handicapped, p. 123 (Ch. C. Thomas, Springfield, Ill. 1961).
2. COTTRELL, L. and FOOTE, N. N.: Identity and personal competence, p. 85 (University of Chicago Press, Chicago 1955).

FORTY

Organizational Dynamics

BERNARD FARBER

The developments in the past two decades in the areas of institutions and mental retardation may be best understood by observing change from the perspective of a social movement. This movement can be seen in a large sense as a national phenomenon involving the National Association for Retarded Children and in a more restricted sense as social events pertaining to individual parents associations.

The National Unit

The emergence and change in the National Association for Retarded Children can be studied in terms of its implications for understanding the organizational aspects of social movements. The inclusion of the word *children* itself suggests the limitations of the functions and goals of NARC. The growth of NARC can be examined against the background of such investigations as the Sills study of the National Association for Infantile Paralysis. Specifically, systematic study should be made of this growth. The following statement presents some hunches about NARC.

After the Second World War, the focus of efforts in dealing with mental retardation shifted from the mildly retarded to the severely mentally retarded and from problems of deviant behavior (such as delinquency) to medical problems. Henceforth, the mental retardation movement became identified with agencies and personnel dealing with health problems and only secondarily with delinquent and criminal behavior, family instability, and poverty. The movement became dominated by the middle class parents deeply involved in providing schools and services for their severely retarded children. With this domination by parents, it seems inevitable that NARC would have a federated structure rather than a unified corporate structure. The federation gives considerable power to the member groups and emphasizes the diversity of needs of the retarded. This diversity requires an everexpanding liaison with other agencies in the community and a constant pressure upon government. The effectiveness of NARC in government was enhanced considerably

Reprinted from H. J. Prehm, L. A. Hamerlynck, and J. E. Crosson, eds., *Behavorial Research in Mental Retardation* (Eugene, University of Oregon, 1968), pp. 103-107. By permission of the author and the University of Oregon.

by the election of President John F. Kennedy, who facilitated the association's striving for prestige as a health agency and the redefining of mental retardation as a health problem.

In forming close alliance with health agencies, philanthropic foundations, and governmental bodies, the national unit (NARC) has been able to reduce its dependence upon state and local associations for funds and stability. In this way, the national unit tends to avoid the constraints placed upon it by the federated type of organization. However, the demands of the health agencies, foundations, and government units with which the NARC staff does its business offset to some extent the gain in autonomy. These national alliances create pressures upon NARC to develop programs different from those of the local associations. Whereas the local associations are interested in schools and diagnostic clinics, the national association tends to focus its energy on research support and cooperative programs with other agencies. These programs enhance NARC's reputation and position among health agencies. The tendency toward autonomy of the national unit creates a tension between it and the member association over the allocation of staff and financial resources.[1] Consequences of this tension for the program of the movement should be investigated.

Local Parents Associations

The mental retardation movement can also be investigated by giving attention to the development of local parents associations. For example, Alfred Katz (1961) reported on a study of four parents associations dealing with different kinds of handicaps. The description by Katz is consistent with the view generally attributed to Max Weber and Roberto Michels regarding the development of organizations.[2]

Briefly, as presented by Zald and Ash (1966), the Weber-Michels position applied to organizations associated with social movements is this:

> As an MO (movement organization) attains an economic and social base in the society, as the original charismatic leadership is replaced, a bureaucratic structure emerges and a general accommodation to the society occurs. The participants in this structure have a stake in preserving the organization, regardless of its ability to attain goals. Analytically there are three types of change involved in this process; empirically they are often fused. The three types of change are goal transformation, a shift to organizational maintenance, and oligarchization.

The transformation of goals refers to the accommodation of the goals of the organization to those considered "practical" in the society. The shift to organizational maintenance means an increasing emphasis on the requirements for sustaining the organization—funds, keeping members, bureaucratization of activities. Oligarchization is the concentration of power in a minority of the organization's members (Zald and Ash, 1966, pp. 327-328). Zald and Ash suggest that "pragmatic leadership replaces unattainable goals with diffuse goals so that the organization can pursue a broader range of targets."

Centralization of control in local organizations seems to be related to leadership patterns in the division of labor which develops in parent groups.[3] Two types of leadership will be discussed here. Some of the participants show greater interest in problems related to ends or programs or purposes whereas others become more involved in the means of organization, that is, ways of making the institution "work." Those participants involved in ends devote a considerable amount of time and energy in promoting new programs, in proselytizing others, and, in short, in making "the cause" a primary occupation in their lives. The organizing leaders both mobilize the potential membership and try to convince other agencies and the larger community of the legitimacy of their cause. They may become known as Mr. Mental Retardation or Mr. Cerebral Palsy to outsiders and either as charismatic leaders or "fanatics" to others within the movement. In contrast to the "fanatics" are the business-like leaders who are more concerned with sustaining the organization than in defining its purposes. The business-like leaders are interested in developing a corporate structure for the local organization, whereas the fanatics or organizing leaders are more interested in proliferation and improvement of treatment or educational programs. The business-like leaders are more involved in providing a stable financial base and physical plant for maintaining a staff of workers to carry out existing programs of the agencies. In most organizations, it is relatively easy to distinguish the organizing leaders from the business-like leaders.

In the classical descriptions of the routinization of charisma, the charismatic leader maintains control until his death or retirement from the organization (Zald and Ash, 1966). The extent to which routinization of charisma has been successful is indicated by the smoothness with which the succession of leadership occurs. However, my observations of the organizing leaders of parents associations suggest a different sequence of events. Perhaps even at the beginning of the association there are dissident members who remain in the organization for instrumental reasons but who dislike some personal attributes or plans of the organizing leader. The total involvement of the organizing leader prevents any attempt to displace him. Almost immediately some of the dissidents begin to undermine his influence. In the groups I observed, this undermining generally included a transformation of goals to those which were considered practical, a pressure toward bureaucratization and routinization, and a movement to make the organizing leader a figurehead.

In the course of those efforts, members of the organization took sides for or against the organizing leaders, and factions developed. The groups seemed to split into factions focusing on the handling of the business of the organization and those interested in mobilizing the membership to expand the functions of the organization. These observations suggest the hypothesis that, in spite of pressures toward oligarchy and bureaucratization, the organization of parents associations is generally characterized by an ongoing struggle between the organizing-mobilizing factions and bureaucratizing-routinizing factions.

This hypothesis is presented as an alternative to one formulated by Zald and Ash (1966), namely, "Routinization of charisma is likely to conservatize the dominant core of the movement organization while simultaneously producing increasingly radical splinter groups." (Zald and Ash, 1966, p. 388). Zald and Ash (1966), following the Weber-Michels theory, regard routinization as a way of maintaining the program of the charismatic leader; the splinter groups emerge over disagreements in program. My observations, however, suggest that the movement toward routinization in the parents associations is created in *response* to the emphasis upon expansion of functions and mobilization of personnel by the organizing leaders. If routinization represents a movement to counteract the power of the organizing leaders, these leaders themselves may personify major dissident factions in the association.

Perhaps the difference between the Weber-Michels (1946, 1949) statement of leadership and organization and the one presented here stems from the kinds of problems which necessitated the organization. The classical statement is based on political social movements, in which there can be as many organizations as there are solutions to political problems. The associations for the mentally retarded emerge mainly to promote a single solution—to develop school, welfare, and health services for the severely retarded. Hence, developing competing organizations would be unfeasible, and parents must join the existing movement to accomplish their ends. Almost immediately, such a situation will force persons who do not regard the organizing leader as charismatic to join his movement and possibly to create an opposing faction. The focusing of organization on specific problems and generally accepted treatments may differentiate health-social movements from political movements in terms of patterns of leadership and organizational dynamics. This possible difference should be investigated.

The factions created by rallying around the organizing and business-like leaders suggest the existence of a mutual contempt and suspicion within the subgroups of an organization. Research could be undertaken to indicate the consequences of this split for the power structure of the organization. Since the organizing-leader faction finds its legitimacy in the recruitment and stirring up of members, this faction would tend to favor democratization of power. The business-like faction, on the other hand, operates most efficiently as an oligarchy; it would rely more upon committee structure and the appropriation of offices for its maintenance. The accrual of specialized knowledge, the appropriation of resources, and skill in the management of others seem to favor the faction supporting business-like leaders (Michels, 1949, p. 16). The tendencies of oligarchization and bureaucratization would not eliminate the organizing leaders' factions from the association, but would stabilize the factional aspects of the organization unless splinter associations are formed.

The various descriptions of types of leadership suggest that the organizing and business-like leaders differ in personal style and in social and personal characteristics. Inasmuch as the organizing leader must stir up interest in the "cause" both within and outside the interest group, he probably resorts to expressive and dramatic language and activities. His emphasis upon program expansion is itself an expression of his "other worldliness." In contrast, the business-like leader bases his legitimacy upon his rationality and practicality. Therefore, the business-like leader must impress others with his matter-of-fact style, his ability to routinize activities, and his competence in obtaining the cooperation of his colleagues in carrying out plans.

The putative difference in expressive and rational styles of organizing and business-like leaders in parents associations implies consistent patterns of personal and social attributes. Organizing leaders, with their motivation elevated to a "calling," probably have more personality problems, more marital and family difficulties, and fewer competing interests than business-like leaders. In addition, the organizing leader is less likely to be of high socioeconomic and educational status, and more likely to be in a minority ethnic or religious group, and unlikely to be an active participant in the decision-making of the dominant economic and educational institutions of the community.

The difference in leadership style and abilities required for business-like leadership and organizing leadership are suggested by a study by Willie (1965) on the composition of boards of directors of health and welfare voluntary associations over a twenty-seven year period. In comparing the board members of a fund raising organization (Community Chest) with those of a health and welfare planning organization (Council of Social Agencies), Willie found that the fund raising group consisted of more males, businessmen (affiliated with manufacturing industries), and high ranking officers in business establishments (such as corporation presidents, vice-presidents, secretaries, and treasurers). The planning group had more women, professionals (especially social workers), managers and administrators. Willie concluded that the dominant leadership made the decisions regarding funding (and thereby the services that would be funded), while the subdominant leadership decided on the specific plans and policies (Willie, 1965). The lower socioeconomic status and the greater prevalence of women members suggest a greater emphasis upon mobilization of personnel and program expansion by the board of the service-planning agency than that of the fund raising agency. This difference also indicates the strategy whereby a business-like faction may attempt to control an organizing faction in an organization—by attempting to control the financial base and thereby restricting the kinds of programs which the organization may undertake.

References

[1]The alliance of the national unit with other agencies, foundations, and government bodies represents a mutual cooperation whereby "new elements are absorbed into the leadership or policy-determining structure of (the national organizations) as a means of averting threats to (their) stability of existence." Philip Selznick, *TVA and the Grass Roots*. New York: Harper Torchbooks, 1966, p. 13.

[2]See Gerth and C. Mills, *op. cit.*, pp. 297-301 and Roberto Michels, *Political Parties*. New York: Free Press, 1949.

[3]For a discussion of the various types of leadership in social movements, see Lewis Killian, "Social Movements," in Robert E. L. Faris, *Handbook of Modern Sociology*. New York: Rand-McNally.

FORTY-ONE

Major Issues Facing Associations for Retarded Children

NATIONAL ASSOCIATION FOR RETARDED CHILDREN

Can ARC's Divest Themselves of Services and Survive?

From the earliest days of NARC many local units have undertaken the direct operation of service functions. These have most commonly been in the nature of special education classrooms or sheltered workshops, but have also included pre-school services, diagnostic services, recreational programs and in a few instances comprehensive service centers. The justification for the undertaking of these programs by the units has usually been most compelling on the grounds either that "no one else is willing to do it so we must" or that "it is up to us to show the community the value and feasibility of the service." Both of these justifications are legitimate but each of them implies that the ultimate responsibility for service rests with the community through public or private agencies and that the undertakings of the ARC are in the nature of pilot or demonstration programs to be relinquished to the control of public agencies and duly constituted boards as soon as the community has reached the stage where this is possible.

Such relinquishment does not mean that the ARC and its members no longer have an interest in or an influence upon the service functions. To the contrary, the unit which has done its job well maintains a position of vital leadership as an established organization whose counsel in matters relating to the retarded is respected and sought. It will maintain a strong cooperative relationship with *all* the service agencies providing programs for the retarded, and is thus influential in the development and maintenance of a total program, not being harnessed to merely one segment of it. In addition, the ARC has a continuing responsibility to exercise its full influence in maintaining or improving the quality of services being provided and in procuring those additional services required to meet the needs of the retarded. Furthermore, the individual members will, if they have properly won the confidence of the community through effective leadership, serve on the governing boards and advisory committees for the various service functions along with other interested community leaders.

From "Background Papers for Group Discussion: 1967 Annual NARC Convention." Reprinted by permission of the National Association for Retarded Children, 1968.

The ultimate goal of community mental retardation programs is to provide a coordinated array of preventive, diagnostic, care, treatment and training services within reasonable access of every citizen. This will require careful advance planning, coordination and improvement of existing services and the initiation of needed new services. The changing patterns of service and methods of operation and support are exerting a profound influence on the role of local and state ARC's. NARC has attempted to respond to these changes by adopting a policy which states:

> Every effort shall be made at local, state and national levels, to obtain for the welfare of *all* the retarded a *total* program of necessary and desirable services, including the research efforts which underlie prevention and alleviation;
>
> That in working towards these ends, the primary responsibility of the Association at all levels, is to provide leadership, stimulation, and guidance to the public and private agencies which have the primary responsibility for providing, supporting, and operating the programs and services;
>
> That while Member Units of NARC may develop direct service projects for purposes of public education, they will provide such services only on a temporary, contingent, and demonstration basis which includes in its stated objectives the shift of operational responsibility to tax-supported agencies or private and independent boards as soon as practicable.

However, social change does not take place overnight.

Until recently many members of the helping professions have rejected the mentally retarded. Some parents, having experienced such rejection, naturally are concerned about the level of interest and the continuity of concern among professionals. Is professional care based solely on a profit motive? Will service agencies and their staff turn their back on the retarded once another group becomes "popular"? Cannot the ARC, with its intimate knowledge and concern about mental retardation, operate more effective programs than other community agencies?

A considerable number of local ARC units continue to maintain a tremendous financial and emotional investment in the operation of direct service programs. To relinquish control of these programs would radically alter the role of the organization. Can an ARC group continue to function as a healthy, vibrant organization after turning over operating responsibility for such a service function? Will the new goals and purposes of such an ARC group be as socially worthwhile and personally rewarding as operating a service program?

QUESTIONS FOR DISCUSSION

With the above discussion in mind, we need to consider the following questions:

1. To what extent is the ARC accountable to the community?
2. Should the ARC act primarily as a social organization or as a resource to parents and their retarded offspring?
3. If ARC's are to function as social groups, how can we facilitate the transition of service programs to other community agencies? What type(s) of community agencies?

4. How can an ARC unit be organized to function effectively as a social action agency?
5. If we are to play a broader role in mobilizing efforts to combat mental retardation, how can the ARC movement enlist new members from different segments of community life?

Can ARC's Effectively Reach the Underprivileged or Socially Disadvantaged?

The United States is the wealthiest nation on earth. Yet, paradoxically, poverty is one of the most pervasive problems facing our society. One out of every five American families has an annual income below $3,200, the poverty level established by the federal government. A minimum of twenty-seven million citizens and possibly as many as forty-two million live in daily deprivation. Between twenty and thirty percent of the nation's children are from poverty stricken homes.

Research studies suggest that ghetto neighborhoods provide a fertile breeding ground for mental retardation. The President's Panel on Mental Retardation stressed that the incidence of the condition is much higher among culturally and economically deprived segments of the population.

Generally, familial or cultural retardation is thought to have no neurological basis but to result from psychosocial, economic and education deprivation. Some experts, however, believe that a combination of minimal brain damage and adverse social, educational, and psychological factors cause this type of retardation. While the relationship between deprivation and retardation is not entirely clear, the evidence thus far suggests that the circumstances of poverty—poor nutrition and medical care and the stultifying effect on the brain of inadequate intellectual stimulation and emotional deprivation—frequently contribute to sub-normal functioning.

Familial retardation is particularly prevalent among deprived Negroes and other non-white groups living in city slums but is also frequently found among poor white families in Appalachia and other breeding grounds of poverty. The President's Panel suggested that the poor performance of slum area children is associated with four broad influences in their development:

1. *Lack of Motivation.* Raised in the surrounding of failure, the culturally deprived child fails to develop the cognitive processes and values common to middle and upper class children.
2. *Inadequate Home Environment.* A child from a home where the parents are socially dependent and emotionally crippled frequently fails to develop adequate methods of thinking and perceiving due to inadequate stimulation during the crucial early developmental period.
3. *Disorganized Family Life.* Frequently, children from poor families live in unhealthy home situations and fail to receive the attention, warmth, and affection necessary for proper development.
4. *Lack of Adequate Health, Education and Welfare Facilities.* Adequate health, educational, and social welfare facilities are generally lacking or seriously overcrowded and understaffed in slum neighborhoods.

Many mothers from low income families receive inadequate prenatal care, frequently do not deliver their babies in hospitals, do not receive an adequate diet and are ignorant of the proper spacing of children. Without prenatal care, a woman is about three times more likely to give birth to a premature baby and mental retardation occurs ten times more often in premature births.

Experience of the Office of Economic Opportunity and other federal and state agencies with programs devoted to the amelioration or elimination of poverty, suggest that there are no simple, pat solutions to the problem. On the contrary, a massive effort will be necessary to rescue economically deprived children from the inevitable cycle of poverty. Better housing, stable employment, improved health for all members of the family, and high grade educational programs must be provided as part of any effective program.

Do ARC's have a role to play in the battle against this major cause of mental retardation?

Since its inception, the goal of the ARC movement has been to serve all of the retarded regardless of their degree of disability, age, race, religion or economic status. Now the discovery of the relationship between poverty and retardation presents us with an immense challenge. If we truly accept this challenge of seeing that *all* of the retarded receive the types of services they require, we must, as a movement, uncover new methods of reaching out to persons from economically deprived backgrounds in an effort to prevent familial retardation and ameiorate its effects when it occurs. This effort will require the total cooperation and commitment of ARC units at the national, state, and local level.

QUESTIONS FOR DISCUSSION

In the light of the discussion above, we need to consider the following questions:

1 Can we effectively involve the poor and representatives of the poor within our local, state, and national ARC organizations? If so, how can we actively seek their involvement?

2. What special efforts to prevent retardation in poverty areas and aid the underprivileged retarded are being conducted within your community or state? What is the relationship of the local and state ARC to these efforts? How can the effectiveness and scope of these efforts be increased?

3. What is the most effective means of involving individuals from slum neighborhoods in activities on behalf of the mentally retarded—as members of established ARC groups or as a separate but affiliated group under the auspices of a community action agency? What techniques should be employed to launch such efforts?

4. What means can be used to stimulate parents of "high risk" children to have a greater awareness of mental retardation? What federal, state, and local agencies (public and private) can we cooperate with in an effort to achieve this objective?

5. What are the proper roles of the local, state, and national ARC units in a total effort to prevent familial retardation and aid poor families with a retarded child or adult? How can such activities be financed?

Can the Needs of the Mentally Retarded Be Met Through Generic Services or Will They Be Submerged and Neglected?

During the past five years we have witnessed a tremendous growth in community programs for the mentally retarded. However, we are still a long way from our goal of providing a continuous spectrum of services for all retarded persons. While particular elements of service have been developed in many communities, the disturbing fact remains that only a small percentage of the retarded presently have access to a truly comprehensive array of services. If we are to sustain the rate of program development achieved over the past few years, we must reevaluate our progress thus far and find the most effective ways of utilizing the human, financial and physical resources which will be available in the years ahead. In addition, we must take a hard look at the recent trends in public and private support for health, education, and welfare activities and their implications for community mental retardation programs.

Recently, heavy emphasis has been placed on initiating specialized services for the mentally retarded. Certainly, these services must play an integral part in any community's program. In fact, many more specialized programs need to be developed in communities throughout the United States.

Nonetheless, some experts feel that this concentration on specialized programs has tended to overshadow the development of adequate services for the retarded in generic community agencies.* They argue that most communities have untapped resources for serving the mentally retarded within existing agencies—e.g., orthopedic clinics, dentists, family physicians, special education programs in the public schools, vocational rehabilitation facilities, welfare departments, etc.

Frequently a generic service will have to be adapted to the particular needs of retarded individuals; specially trained personnel may have to be employed or training programs developed for existing personnel. In any case, advocates contend that an existing generic agency in the community, due to its superior expertise concerning the general problem, frequently will be able to extend and adapt its service to the retarded with a smaller investment of community resources (manpower, money, and physical facilities) than if an entirely new specialized service has to be established.

Proponents offer six reasons for increased use of generic community services:

1. *Limited Service Needs of Most Retarded Individuals.* Most retardates do not require complicated, specialized treatment in every situation throughout their lifetime. Many will be able to cope with the experiences of daily life if generic community agencies are adequately prepared to intervene on their behalf when they require assistance.

2. *Efficient Use of Scarce Manpower.* The rapid development of community pro-

---

*The definition of a "generic community agency" used here is any health, welfare, education, rehabilitation, or employment agency in the community whose exclusive mission is not service to the retarded but which offers a service of actual or potential value to retarded persons.

grams for the retarded is placing a severe strain on the nation's supply of trained manpower in all service disciplines. Therefore, it behooves all of us to search diligently for more efficient ways of using this scarce resource. Two means of accomplishing this goal are: (a) to increase the general level of knowledge concerning mental retardation among the staff of generic community agencies in order to institute more effective screening and referral services; and (b) to raise the level of competence and willingness to serve the retarded by placing a mental retardation specialist on the staff of each generic agency which comes in contact with a significant number of mentally retarded clients.

3. *Insufficient Financial Resources.* One of the chronic dilemmas of all public and private agencies at the national, state, and local level is the shortage of available funds to accomplish the seemingly limitless array of socially desirable goals. Those of us who are concerned with improving the welfare of the retarded must realize that only a limited amount of funds will be available for this purpose in the foreseeable future due to the endless demands on the public treasury and private philanthropy. Therefore, we must attempt to optimize the return on our investment in mental retardation activities. More effective use of generic services offer one means of stretching the mental retardation dollar.

4. *Trend Toward Non-Categorical Federal Grants.* Persistent complaints from state and local officials concerning the fragmented nature of federal programs and the difficulty of accomplishing program goals due to rigid federal restrictions is leading Congress to enact broader and more flexible federal assistance programs. Recent examples of this trend include the comprehensive health act of 1966 (PL 89-749), the "Model Cities" program (PL 89-754), and the pending consolidation of child health grants.

If, as seems likely, this trend continues, federal support for mental retardation activities in an increasing number of cases will be part of a broad non-categorical grant program. Mental retardation's chance of getting its fair share of support will be enhanced if services to the retarded are considered an integral part of the broad health, welfare, or education goals the assistance program is designed to meet.

5. *Wholistic Approach to Service.* Recent studies in the field of health and welfare suggest the need for an individual or agency which will maintain a continuing interest in the needs of the entire family unit in order to correct the present fragmentation resulting from over-specialization. Because of its proximity to the family, a generic agency can develop a deeper understanding of the retarded individual's abilities and disabilities, the total family situation, and the treatment resources available in the community. This information assists immeasurably in designing a treatment plan for the retardate and his family.

6. *Integration of Retarded Into Society.* The basic goal of any community mental retardation service should be to assist the retarded individual to become as much a part of everyday community life as his disability permits. As the President's Panel on Mental Retardation put it, "Even if there were no need for economy the conviction that the retarded must be viewed as a part *of* rather than *apart*

from their fellow citizens would be sufficient reason to advocate that wherever a general setting or service or a general law can properly and effectively embrace the retarded person, it should do so."

Too often, generic agencies have rejected mentally retarded clients because they were retarded. Instead, the individual is routinely referred to a specialized facility regardless of his actual needs.

Despite the many arguments in favor of using generic agencies, some parents and professionals favor continued emphasis on specialized services. They argue that:

1. *Some Retarded Persons Have Complex Needs.* Retardates with more complicated service needs will require treatment, care, and training in specialized facilities. Even a well developed network of generic services will have to be backed up by specialized programs. The number participating in these programs may be small relative to the total retarded population but their need for service will be extensive and prolonged.

2. *Specialization Leads to Increased Efficiency.* Since the turn of the century, American society has witnessed an exonerable trend toward specialization in all areas of human endeavor. This trend results from a need for efficient performance of increasingly complex tasks. The rising tide of specialization in mental retardation can be viewed as a healthy outgrowth of increased scientific interest and professional commitment to the field. As our knowledge concerning the etiology and treatment of mental retardation expands, an increasing number of professional and subprofessional categories of specialization are needed. This same pattern is familiar in innumerable other fields.

   A diagnostic or treatment clinic which specializes in serving retarded clients will develop more effective techniques for dealing with the retarded and their families than a health or welfare facility in which retardation is only part of the broader service mission. Specialization not only engenders more efficient diagnosis and treatment but avoids the wasted time and mental anguish associated with mis-referral and inadequate treatment.

3. *Generic Service Costs Are Often Understated.* Some generic service advocates tend to overstate the savings which can be realized. Barring the unlikely possibility that the agency is overstaffed or under utilized, an increased workload will necessitate the hiring of additional staff, obtaining more office and treatment space and increasing the operating budget. A physician cannot bandage a cut and counsel a distraught parent of a retarded child simultaneously. Considering the increased efficiency of specialization and cost of effective generic services, the actual savings in manpower, facilities, and money which can be achieved through the use of generic services is open to serious question.

4. *Specialization Results From the Neglect of Generic Agencies.* Some parents, who have experienced the frustration and heart-break of being shuffled from one agency to another in an effort to locate an adequate treatment program for their child, are understandably skeptical about the willingness and capability of ge-

neric agencies to serve the retarded. Past experience with such agencies provides scant reason for confidence in their future capacity to offer adequate mental retardation services.

5. *Frequently, Public Agencies Emphasize the Quantity Rather Than the Quality of Care.* Today, the success or failure of a public agency frequently is measured in terms of the number of cases it handled. When a premium is placed on the size of the generic agency's caseload, there is a tendency to favor the relatively simple cases which can be treated quickly and chalked up as another closed case.

Mental retardation is a chronic disability which is not susceptible to rapid treatment and recovery. There is a danger that the retarded—especially the more severely retarded—will be rejected by the generic agency in favor of clients who will assist in building an impressive statistical record. Evidence of this tendency can be seen in numerous cases throughout the country (e.g., local school boards which refuse to establish special classes for the retarded because of the additional expense, and state and local rehabilitation agencies which serve only the most mildly retarded due to the extended training period required by more severely disabled clients).

6. *Retardation Services May Get Lost in a Multi-Service Setting.* When we consider the broad unmet health, education, and welfare needs of the general population, the likelihood that the needs of the retarded will be overlooked within the context of a multi-purpose program cannot be passed off lightly. There is a legitimate reason to fear that the specialized needs of the "three percent" will get lost when they are buried in an agency whose primary concern is the problems of a much broader segment of the general population.

QUESTIONS FOR DISCUSSION:

In light of the discussion above, we should consider the following questions:

1. To what extent can generic community agencies provide effective services to mentally retarded clients? Are such agencies offering service in your community at the present time?
2. What are the advantages and disadvantages associated with specialized service facilities for the retarded?
3. Are there generic agencies in your community which should be providing service to the retarded but currently are not doing so? Are there others which are providing inadequate services?
4. What steps can a local ARC unit take to encourage appropriate generic agencies to offer new or improved service to retarded persons? How can NARC and state ARC's assist local units to accomplish this purpose?
5. How can state ARC's assure that the needs of the retarded receive proper attention when a mental retardation program is part of a large multi-purposed state agency?
6. How can we weld the various community mental retardation programs which are provided by generic and specialized agencies into a continuous spectrum of services? How is this goal being pursued in your community?

PART EIGHT

Provisions of Social Services for the Mentally Retarded and Their Families

Income and Social Services for the Mentally Retarded: A Specialized Task for Social Welfare

GUNNAR DYBWAD

There are many ways to assess the significance of the Report of the President's Panel on Mental Retardation, its findings and its recommendations. It has so comprehensive a coverage that it can hardly be judged on a unilateral basis; different agencies, different professions, different communities will see its value in different ways.

For the practitioner in the field of public welfare, a particular significance of the Panel's Report will lie in its emphasis on the major role played in the field of mental retardation by two programs—the Public Assistance program of Aid to the Permanently and Totally Disabled and the Social Security program of Old Age, Survivors, and Disability Insurance (OASDI).

There can be no doubt but that to many workers in social welfare and public health and even to seasoned practitioners in the field of mental retardation it came as a complete surprise to discover that these two programs alone paid out this year almost one hundred million dollars in federal funds to mentally retarded adults (as against only thirty million dollars for all service programs together).

If we consider that other public assistance programs, notably Aid to Dependent Children, include a considerable number of both mentally retarded adults and mentally retarded children (exact statistics are not yet available) and also add allowances paid to mentally retarded individuals under such programs as veterans' benefits and railroad retirement, it becomes strikingly evident that income maintenance is one of the most far-reaching program areas in the field of mental retardation. It is hoped that this presentation will point up the fact that income maintenance not only serves a very large number of retarded adults but indeed furnishes the essential underpinning for the effectiveness of many other programs.

How then can we explain that it took the Report of the President's Panel on Mental Retardation and a subsequently published excellent compilation of the U.S. Department of Health, Education, and Welfare, *Mental Retardation Program of the U.S. Department of Health, Education and Welfare, FY 1964,* to bring out these facts?

From Gunnar Dybwad, *Challenges in Mental Retardation* (New York, Columbia University Press, 1964), pp. 185-194. By permission of the author and Columbia University Press.

Here we need to remind ourselves that up to the most recent past and indeed right to the present time, the field of social work by and large followed the public's static view toward the retarded as a group of individuals segregated from the general stream of life and quite incapable of benefiting from the opportunities and services available to the rest of the population. If this sounds today like an unwarranted, far too broad generalization, let the record speak of the exclusion of the mentally retarded from a broad sweep of services such as child guidance clinics, public schooling, health services, and child welfare.

For many people both in the general public and in the field of social welfare, mental retardation meant eventual if not immediate institutionalization. The fact that less than 4 percent of the mentally retarded actually are residing in institutions merely underlines the extent of the misconception.

On the other hand, those actively engaged and considered knowledgeable in the field of mental retardation, whether as professional workers or volunteers, focused their attention on research, on prevention, and on organized services to the retarded in the fields of health, education, rehabilitation, and recreation, and on meeting the needs of the parents of the retarded for counseling and guidance.

A review of several dozens of major surveys and reports published during the past decade will bear this out.

Actually, the magnitude of at least the Old Age, Survivors, and Disability Insurance program in the field of mental retardation has been a matter of public record since 1958. We (and I am using this "we" advisedly) were just too preoccupied with the aforementioned service programs, with research and prevention, to give this aspect of our field proper consideration.

A brief reference to the available statistics is here in order. Of the total number of persons eligible in 1960 for the so-called Childhood Disability Benefits, 71 percent were found to be unable to engage in any substantial gainful activity owing to mental retardation. For 1961, this figure is 70 percent. The total number of mentally retarded persons receiving these benefits at the present time exceeds 100,000. Mental retardation therefore accounts for more than two thirds of all disability cases under this part of the program. All other types of physical and mental disabilities added together account for less than one third of the case load.

These figures alone bear out President Kennedy's statement to the Congress that mental retardation constitutes one of the nation's major health problems.

A further complication rests in the fact that many if not a majority of social workers still feel that mental retardation is essentially a problem for the mental health authorities. Administratively speaking, the activities of state mental health departments in this area have by and large been limited to providing institutional care. As was just pointed out, less than 4 percent of the mentally retarded are in institutions—and in quite a few states even these institutions are not within the state department of mental health.

On the other hand, community services, particularly those under the new Community Mental Health Services Programs, have by and large included only a token share of the retarded. Mental hygiene and child guidance clinics still largely reject the mentally retarded, and in any case most of their staffs are not experienced with this problem.

This by no means implies that the psychiatric profession and the allied professions active in these clinics have no significant contribution to make in this field. To the contrary, social workers in programs dealing with the adult retarded will find that many of these individuals will go through periods of severe stress when they face, as older adolescents and in subsequent years, community prejudices, situational pressures (such as in their place of employment), and personal conflicts (for instance, in trying to work out relationships with members of the opposite sex). Here the social worker will look for guidance from the psychiatrist if not for sustained support and treatment for the retarded client from a psychiatric clinic.

Unfortunately, the eagerness of the psychiatric profession to maintain control and direction of institutions for the retarded is not matched by a like interest in serving the adult retarded in the community. Indeed, it is practically impossible to gain acceptance for a referral of a retarded adult to a community psychiatric clinic. Here lies a large unmet need.

The question inevitably is raised: If the psychiatrists are not the ones to assume major responsibility for the problem of mental retardation, which discipline, which agency or professional field can be so designated?

The answer is quite clear. The problem of mental retardation is far too pervasive to be conveniently pigeon-holed in any one of the professional compartments. In some of its manifestations it is essentially a medical program; in others, one of training and rehabilitation. In one context we must approach it along with the major physical handicaps; in another context it appears as a major socioeconomic problem. Education plays a predominant role during the school years, while we must rely on public health nursing for significant services during infancy and early childhood.

The stratification of the field in terms of the new American Association on Mental Deficiency classification as between mildly, moderately, severely, and profoundly retarded could be the basis for another presentation of the involvement of disciplines and agencies.

The challenge that faces the field of public welfare is that through these major income maintenance programs it must relate itself to any and all of the agencies and disciplines whose services are needed.

A few examples must suffice. For a considerable time it has become obvious that the traditional institution maintained with state funds must be supplemented by other less formal, smaller, more community related residential facilities. Payments from the two programs here discussed offer us a tangible way to initiate these programs.

Vocational and other rehabilitation programs for the retarded have been slow to develop, in part because, in the case of the retarded, the program may require a facility for group living. Income maintenance programs can facilitate this.

The markedly increasing life-span of the mentally retarded has resulted in a reversal of survivorship; while formerly the parents were more likely to survive their retarded child, the opposite is true today, and income maintenance payments make it feasible to allow the surviving retarded adult to remain in the community either with relatives and friends of the family or in some type of boarding home placement.

OASDI payments have a very distinct effect on residential programs because enlightened institutions have used these funds to provide residents with opportunities for individualization and social growth, through purchase of personal belongings such as clothing, musical instruments, or even bicycles. These payments facilitate visits to the homes of relatives and friends and in many other ways have enriched the lives of these individuals and enhanced their personal and social development.

Under broader administrative interpretations following the 1962 Social Security Amendments, the public assistance programs of aid to the totally and permanently disabled likewise can play a more dynamic role in the field of mental retardation.

Manual material in general makes dreary reading, but I wish all of you could acquaint yourselves with the excellent sections pertaining to services for the mentally retarded contained in revisions of the Public Assistance Handbook released by the Bureau of Family Services of the Department of Health, Education, and Welfare in November of 1962 (State Letter 606). Many of the supporting services described there, including the involvement of volunteers, as initiated so successfully in public welfare programs for the aged, could of course be given by the public welfare departments in supplementation of the OASDI benefits, which are limited to the money payment itself.

Considerable interplay must occur not only with other public programs but with private agencies and the voluntary groups who can render significant supportive or adjunctive service.

It is obvious from the foregoing that the field of public welfare faces a most formidable task in fulfilling its share of responsibility as one of the major agencies serving the mentally retarded.

To what extent is actual practice catching up with these challenging demands? Considering the newness of these programs it is not surprising that little exact information is available. Indeed, hardly any articles have been written specifically on these programs and little is mentioned in published state reports.

In the preparation of this paper, it was possible to make informed inquiries in four states and one regional office of the Department of Health, Education, and Welfare. In general, it appears that the staff administering the OASDI programs are quite well in touch with developments of the Childhood Disability Benefit program as it affects mentally retarded individuals. There was clear recognition of some of the major problems in the choice of payees and also of the extensive need for auxiliary service programs for these adult retardates. With regard to the public assistance program of Aid to the Permanently and Totally Disabled, there was far less evidence of adequate understanding. Even the most essential state-wide statistics were described as "not available," and there was little indication that the excellent new provisions of the Public Assistance Handbook issued by the Department of Health, Education, and Welfare had been reviewed and put to a test. It is significant but not surprising that the situation looked distinctly more favorable in the one state out of these four where the public welfare department had a long-standing contact with the problem of mental retardation. In this state there was recognition of guardianship problems, of the many and varied services needed for the retarded, and of their individual need (such as to have the privilege of handling one's own money wherever feasible).

This poor showing may be disappointing but it certainly should surprise no one who is aware how long, for instance, it has taken the field of special education to move ahead. Granted that in several of our states we have not as yet specific mandatory legislation, the fact is that after fifty years of developing classes for the mentally retarded, we still have only one fourth of the retarded school-age children in public school and still have most drastic variations in the quality of these services from state to state. Obviously we must be prepared to engage in a major effort of intensive orientation for administrators, supervisory staff, and front-line public welfare workers if the great potential inherent in these two programs is to be fulfilled.

Social workers have in the past shown an overconcern with the emotional status of parents of retarded children and have tended to exaggerate the effect of this traumatic experience of the birth of a mentally defective child on the parents' capacity to fulfill their responsibility toward such children. Some excellent comments have been published in more recent years pointing out that in this regard workers have demonstrated a lopsided misinterpretation of what was essentially a normal reaction of grief.

What needs to be stressed is that a good share of the parental concern, or call it anxiety if you wish, has been related to the nagging fear of what will happen to their child after the parents' death. Without in any way detracting from the importance of parent education and parent counseling, programs which should be available to all parents of retarded children, it is quite appropriate to say that once the income maintenance programs together with the related supportive services have come to fullest development, parents will be able to think of the future of their retarded child with a much more positive outlook.

But this more positive outlook of the parent must be matched by a more positive climate for the mentally retarded in the community at large.

The seeming rapid shift in the public's appreciation and understanding of the problem of mental retardation in response to the President's inspiring and challenging statements should not deceive us. As yet, we are still facing considerable resistance toward the retarded in our communities; to have full support from the public welfare field in our efforts to overcome the prejudice and discrimination against our retarded citizens will move us forward on that front, too.

In this connection I would like to mention a particular aspect of prejudicial thinking about the retarded that can well be related to the otherwise quite descriptive designation "Childhood Disability Benefits." This can be a dangerously misleading expression. We are dealing here not with children but with adults. These adults are handicapped, mentally handicapped, and often are demonstrating besides this mental handicap a variety of physical disabilities. Their performance level may be very low and some of their behavior may strike us as very "childish," but a 23-year-old young woman with Mongolism who scored a Stanford-Binet I.Q. of 35 and a mental age of 5 ½ years is certainly vastly different from a 5 ½-year-old child, physically, mentally, and socially.

It is interesting—though certainly disheartening—how loose thinking about this concept of mental age has combined with and reinforced the sticky sentimentality of the popular saying that the mentally retarded are "eternal children." Even reputable psychological textbooks published in the 1960s continue to offer loose and unscientific generalizations about the concept of mental age, such as that a retarded person with a mental age of four will for his lifetime conduct himself like a four-year-old child.

In this respect, public welfare workers must be given an opportunity to become acquainted with the remarkable results that have been achieved in sheltered workshops and vocational training facilities for the retarded and in the more recently developed occupation day centers designed for retarded adolescents and adults too limited in their performance to qualify for admission to sheltered workshops.

The day-to-day performance in these rehabilitation facilities makes the psychological textbook writers look ridiculous indeed, a fate they could have avoided by acquainting themselves with the programs conducted in European countries, particularly England and Holland, which are considerably ahead of the United States in this regard.

I am making this point so emphatically because the success of the public welfare programs discussed here will depend on the degree to which those administering these services will embrace a dynamic view toward the mentally retarded as individuals distinctly capable of change, of growth, of self-expression and self-improvement.

This emphasis on a dynamic viewpoint has distinct and direct implications. For instance, whereas in areas of serious physical disability supportive services need to be rendered to prevent loss of capacity, in mental retardation the goal would be in many cases to provide such supportive services to further increase capacity of the retarded beneficiary or client.

In a recent paper, Neota Larson described several kinds and degrees of "incapability" the OASDI staff has observed among their beneficiaries, relating this in turn to varying degrees of independence allowed the totally disabled person in the handling of money. I predict that from year to year we will develop greater skill on our part in providing increasing freedom of choice and opportunity for growth for the mentally retarded.

And now a final observation: In view of the striking contribution social work is able to make to the field of mental retardation, the matter of appropriate training of social workers in this area takes on much significance.

Unfortunately all too little is done in the schools of social work—with a few noble exceptions—and all too frequently one gets the irritated comment: How do you expect us to crowd further courses in areas of speciality in our tightly packed curriculum?

This self-righteous defensive attitude on the part of so many graduate schools of social work falls far short of the mark. What is desired is not the addition to the crowded curriculum of the graduate schools of special courses on mental retardation. The problem lies in the opposite direction: the significant problem of mental retardation and its far-reaching effects on the lives of some twenty million people, namely the mentally retarded and their families, must no longer be ignored or at least practically passed over in the context of a large variety of present courses where it has pertinence. To put it bluntly, it is the ignorance of the present teaching staffs in the schools of social work which is at the core of this problem and which has led to the ignoring of the role of mental retardation as a major social and health problem as well as an area of serious family trauma.

Those of us who work full time in the field of mental retardation do not seek separate treatment of this subject matter. To the contrary, we want the social work student to recognize the pervasive nature of this problem in the context of many other phenomena in the life of the family, the community, and the nation.

In closing, may I quote the following from the Public Assistance Handbook, proof that a manual can be written in good, clear English prose:

> Public Welfare agencies carry a special responsibility to provide appropriate services, secure diagnostic services, and to evaluate the needs and potentials of their mentally retarded clientele. They are responsible for participating with the total community in developing diagnostic, treatment, training, and employment services for the mentally retarded, and for developing needed social services which support, encourage, and sustain the mentally retarded in areas of family and social functioning.

FORTY-THREE

Social Security Benefits for Retarded Children

BERNARD POPICK

Under social security's "childhood disability" provisions, lifetime monthly payments can go to a person age 18 or over who has been disabled by mental retardation—or other impairments—since childhood. Benefits can also go to the mother of the disabled child if he is in her care.

The Social Security Administration believes that some families with mentally retarded children who may be eligible for these benefits are not receiving them simply because they have not applied. All professional workers in the field, who are in touch with possible beneficiaries, are being asked to help in a program to get benefits to as many qualified persons as possible. Families that may qualify should be urged to get in touch with the nearest social security office. If a person finds it impossible to visit the social security office, arrangements can be made for a representative to take an application at that person's home.

Provisions for Retarded Children

Ordinarily, children can't get social security benefits after age 18 (or age 22, if they are attending school full-time). But a retarded youngster may be able to receive benefits almost indefinitely under special provisions in the law. If a mentally deficient child is so seriously handicapped as to be "disabled," he may be eligible for payments for the rest of his life.

What's more, the mother of a disabled child beneficiary can also receive monthly benefits for as long as the child is in her care, regardless of her age or her child's.

Amount of Benefits

The amount of the benefits depends on the average social security-covered earnings of the working parent. A family consisting of a worker, his wife, and a disabled son or daughter can receive as much as $271 each month. A child alone, with his parents dead, may be eligible for payments up to $102 a month. However, no bene-

Reprinted by permission from *Mental Retardation*, Vol. 4, No. 6 (December, 1966), pp. 28-29, a publication of the American Association on Mental Deficiency.

fits are payable to the child until the parent (covered under social security) on whom he is dependent retires, becomes disabled himself, or dies.

If a retarded child is unable to handle his own money, as is frequently the case, the Social Security Administration selects someone else to receive the checks on his behalf and take care of the money for him. Usually, this is one of his parents, or, if they are dead, some other close relative.

Who Qualifies?

To be eligible, a person must be so handicapped by a mental or physical condition that—in the words of the law—he is unable to engage in any type of substantial gainful activity. His impairment must have already lasted 12 months or else be expected to last that long and must have disabled him since before he reached age 18. The condition needs to be one that is determinable by physicians (a medical report will be required).

Sometimes an eligible youngster under 18 is already receiving social security benefits because a parent has retired, become disabled or died. So that payments will continue uninterrupted, he (or someone in his behalf) should apply at the local social security office for disability payments about three months before his 18th birthday.

Who Determines If a Child Is Disabled?

Disability decisions are made locally by an agency of the State in which the applicant lives. This agency, which is usually the vocational rehabilitation agency, works under a Federal-State agreement.

Each determination is made by an evaluation team consisting of a physician and a counselor skilled in vocational evaluation. Typically, the physician is a private practitioner serving the agency on a part-time basis. He reviews the medical, hospital, and laboratory reports, and, in conjunction with the vocational evaluator, determines whether a claimant's impairment prevents him from working.

The physician member of the team does not personally examine the applicant. Instead, he works from the written records sent in by treating and examining sources.

What Sort of Evidence Is Most Useful?

Mental retardation is a lifelong disorder characterized by below-average intellectual endowment as measured on standard IQ tests, and associated with impairment of learning, maturation, and/or social adjustment.

In evaluating the severity of such a condition from the written evidence, the State agency physician depends to a large extent on intelligence tests administered and interpreted by qualified psychiatrists or psychologists using such examinations as the Wechsler Adult Intelligence Scale, the Wechsler Intelligence Scale for Children, and the revised Stanford-Binet.

In communities where a qualified psychiatrist or psychologist is not readily available, an intelligence test administered by a vocational rehabilitation counselor or a specially trained person associated with the local school system can be accepted.

Tests should be administered when a person is age 16 or over, but a test taken at an earlier age may suffice to establish "disability" under the social security law if other evidence supports the conclusion that the condition is so severe that additional testing would serve no useful purpose.

Where the nature of the person's impairment is such that testing is precluded or cannot be obtained, the evaluating State agency physician needs specific information describing the level of intellectual, social, and physical functioning of the claimant. Reports from such objective sources as educational institutions, and welfare and social agencies are of value. The type of observation that proves most valuable in such reports deals with the individual's mental and social capacities as evidenced by his ability to care for his own personal needs (bathing, dressing, etc.); his capacity to understand the spoken word; his ability to avoid physical danger (as from fire or automobiles); his capacity to follow simple instructions; and his ability to speak, read, write, and do calculations.

Of course, there are some cases in which mental deficiency is not the only, or even the primary impairment. In such instances, a medical report covering the other condition should be submitted also. Often, the person may be obviously disabled on the basis of his other impairments (e.g., severe paralysis, severe *grand mal* epilepsy). In such cases, it is not necessary to provide extensive documentation of the degree of mental deficiency present.

Rehabilitation

Social Security is interested in seeing that, where possible, childhood disability beneficiaries are given an opportunity to obtain rehabilitation assistance in preparing for productive work (even though under special conditions or in sheltered workshops). The name of every disability applicant is automatically referred to his local Sate vocational rehabilitation agency for consideration for possible services.

What's more, social security trust fund monies can be used in certain instances to reimburse States for the services given to disability beneficiaries in order to increase the number of those rehabilitated. In the current fiscal year (which began last July), about 14 million dollars is available to the States for this purpose.

It may interest readers to know that in 1963, the U.S. Civil Service Commission established a program for the employment by federal agencies of mentally retarded persons certified by a State vocational rehabilitation agency. The Department of Health, Education, and Welfare—of which social security is a part—was the first federal agency to agree to participate in this program. Social Security hired its first mentally retarded person on April 27, 1964, and now employs about 25, most of whom have not only satisfactory but outstanding work records. In addition to the mentally retarded, social security has on duty about 2,000 other handicapped workers.

The Importance of the Disability Program

Most parents of retarded children find the protection afforded by the childhood disability program a source of relief from worry. It assures them that while their child may never become self-supporting, he will at least be receiving some income.

Currently, about 200,000 persons are receiving childhood disability benefits under the program. For more than 65 per cent of these, mental deficiency is a major or contributing cause of inability to work. The program is increasing in importance as more and more retarded people outlive the parents on whom they have always been dependent. Right now, about half of the childhood disability beneficiaries are over 35, and about 20 per cent of them are over 40.

If you know of any person who may qualify for benefits, suggest that he or his family get in touch with the nearest social security office. Your advice may lead to his receiving urgently needed funds.

Some Pointers for Professionals

LETHA L. PATTERSON

Of all life's problems, those presented by a handicapped child (and particularly a mentally handicapped child) require the utmost in teamwork within professions, among professions, and between professional and lay people, especially parents.

Through the National Association for Retarded Children we parents are attempting to assume responsibilities appropriate to the partnership through helping to define our separate roles and in heightening our communications in order to save other families from unnecessary trauma.

Dr. Martha M. Eliot, former Chief of the Children's Bureau has said:

"When officials of public agencies ask what kinds of services should be provided for retarded children, my advice is 'ask the parents' . . . [they] are often best qualified to say *what* help they need, though professional persons will have to provide the *hows.*"[1]

Thus, we laymen and professionals are indispensable to one another in our efforts to make up for past neglect of this serious medical, emotional, social, and educational problem.

Perhaps I can bring together for the readers of this journal for professionals some of the written and spoken insights which have come my way from both professional workers and parents. These, I feel, are relevant for those of you who find it your task to help families face this heartbreaking problem—whether you are physicians, psychologists, social workers, nurses, teachers, or administrators. On the basis of these and my own experience I urge:

1. Tell us the nature of our problem as soon as possible.

When I said this to a class of students of child psychiatry at the University of Minnesota Medical School, I was asked by an alert student, "But Mrs. Patterson, what can the physician do when he is not sure himself and doesn't want to worry the parents?"

From *Children*, Vol. 3, No. 1 (January-February, 1956), pp. 13-17. With permission of the author and The Children's Bureau.

"Just be honest with us," was my reply.

It takes great sensitivity and intuition to take a mother's couched remarks and detect that they spell "worry." Often we parents are concerned just as early as our practitioner, be we are reluctant to put our fears and worries into words. However, we give plenty of hints that we want our professional counselor to help us get them into words, to lead us on the proper course—whether that means waiting a while or consulting with specialists immediately. It is a wise counselor who knows when he does not have the answers and is willing to admit it.

One of my psychiatrist friends put it this way:

"When I am faced with a worried mother or father *I have got a problem.* Either there is something wrong with the child, or something wrong with the parents, or both. And if I can't identify the trouble, then I am obligated to get this family to someone who can."

2. *Always see both parents.*

Fathers are parents, too, and all professional workers need to be reminded of this. Both parents should be present whenever possible, and at least on first consultations regarding a child's handicap.

It is very difficult for a mother to go home and restate, interpret, and answer questions about a problem she does not clearly understand herself. Often the problem, with its fears, has brought about a lack of communication between mother and father. This is particularly true in a young marriage or when the retarded child is the first child. Establishing adequate communication is difficult in any marriage. Finding the words to support one another in *this* problem has been impossible for some of us. We have needed an objective person through whom to talk.

Unfortunately, all husbands (and wives) are not like the one who, when he learned that their little daughter would not progress like other children, said to his wife: "Honey, we don't know what lies ahead of us—but whatever it is, we can handle it because we are strong people."

Many of us can find this strength, however, if you will help us.

Another reason for seeing both parents is that both need to be pulled along together in their understanding and acceptance. I have seen too many mothers who realized the need for institutional care and were ready to "place" a child while the fathers trailed behind ignoring reality, not to recognize the great need for a common understanding. Sometimes it is the mother who will not admit that something is wrong and insists that her child stay in regular school classes when a special course of study is indicated, while the father suffers along in silence, afraid to precipitate the issue. If you but knew the isolation that can exist behind our four walls!

3. *Watch your language.*

Parents need to understand the implications of their problem, but too often we are given professional gobbledegook, or at the other extreme, plain talk of an obnoxious variety. Words like "idiot," "moron," and "feebleminded" used to be excellent and descriptive clinical terms but they no longer apply to our retarded children. Unimaginative writers and purveyors of so-called humor have polluted the meanings with connotations of social or moral deficiency in the mentally normal.

On the other hand, there was the doctor at a residential institution who wrote to two parents stating that their son was ill with "cervical lymphatic adenitis." The worried family did considerable research to find that the child simply had swollen glands of the neck.

The child psychiatrist, into whose capable hands my husband and I finally could put our problem, was very sensitive in his use of words. He avoided "moron," "feebleminded" and even "mental retardation" by encouraging us to evaluate our child's developmental status. And when he confirmed our findings, we felt quite pleased with ourselves. He always referred to our boy as "your son," "your lad," or "Stephen" with a voice filled with great compassion so that we started thinking more about Steve's problem and less about our own hurt egos.

4. *Help us to see that this is OUR problem.*

One way, of course, is by example—by not taking the problem over for us.

Too many well-meaning professional people in the past have thought they knew what was good for us and have recommended, even insisted on, institutionalization. We know, now, that denial of the existence of the child is not the solution for either child or parent, that abandonment is not the answer, and that it is psychiatrically unhealthy to rob parents of their responsibility for planning. Only as we parents are helped to work through our problems can we find any peace of mind. If we have not planned for our child ourselves, if someone else has made the decisions, we have not really made up our own minds and so must keep going over the ground again and again. We may never be at peace with the solution which was reached for us.

Administrators of institutions tell us that the best help for families in adjusting to their child's placement is the fact that the parents themselves have decided—with adequate professional guidance, of course—that placement is best for the child in relation to the total family welfare.

There is another reason for showing us that this is our problem. You have no idea how much unprofessional, unsolicited, and untried advice we get from well-meaning people—our neighbors, relatives, friends and even strangers standing on street corners. When, with your guidance and example, we realize that *this is our problem,* we can shut our ears to the static and rely on our own judgment. But we need your professional support in helping us to feel competent in making these decisions, your confidence that we will ultimately make the proper decision for care in our particular case, your assurance that there is no failure if we change our plan when circumstances change—life situations and retarded children present different problems at different times. You can help us explore the possibilities for meeting our problem; support us in adjusting to our decision; act as a continuing sounding board against which we can bounce our own thinking; and give us a good, sturdy shoulder on which to lean when we get dizzy going through the maze of decisions.

5. *Help us to understand our problem.*

Parents differ in the quantity and quality of information they can absorb during different phases of this problem. What they want and need depends greatly on the individual, but many of us have had to search for the knowledge we needed in order to understand our child.

In 1950, when I began my search, a severe scarcity existed in printed material on the subject of mental retardation. Today, there are many fine and helpful publications in this field.

Regardless of what we parents are able to read and absorb, we will always have questions to ask. We will continue to need support from someone, whether our child is at home or away—particularly in those days which follow the confirmation that mental retardation *is* our problem.

One medical counselor asks parents to come back several weeks after he has given them the bad news, knowing that they will have questions which could not come to the surface during the emotional strain of hearing the verdict. Moreover, he sees to it that the parents get to a social worker and he also urges them to join an association for retarded children.

Frequently he turns their names over to the local association's "parents counsel committee" requesting that some mature couple—a mother *and* a father—call on them. He has found that parents who have successfully faced their problems can offer a special kind of help to new families which transcends his professional services. Further, he has seen the therapeutic effects of parents working together in organizations to improve the lot of the retarded and their families. Incidentally, he was initially one of the "pros" who were afraid of this "lay" movement.

6. *Know your resources.*

In referring to services, Dr. Eliot has called the retarded child "nobody's baby." Certainly there is evidence in most States that services are disjointed and uncoordinated. Rarely is there any one place which can put parents in touch with the resources that *are* available.

In Minnesota, where the county social worker is the local resource for parents, a booklet, "You Are Not Alone," telling parents where and how to seek help, had been distributed to members of the State medical association, county welfare boards, clergymen of all faiths, family and welfare services, clinics, public-health nurses, associations for retarded children, and newspaper editors in the hopes that the booklet (or the information) will be passed along to parents. It was produced by the statewide Conference Committee on Mental Deficiency, a professional-lay body.

California has started meeting this problem with information centers for the parents of retarded children, set up in Los Angeles and San Francisco by the State department of mental hygiene. The psychiatric social workers assigned to this task have a variety of functions—counseling individual parents, putting them in touch with resources, providing information to public and private agencies, and serving as consultants in community planning.

Other States are developing a network of clinics with built-in social services for the sustaining help which is so necessary.

Anyone who has carried a handicapped child from one waiting room to the next in an effort to gather resources into one piece will appreciate the significance of these several efforts to avail parents of the services that do exist.

7. *Never put us on the defensive.*

All parents make mistakes in raising children. Those of us who have a retarded child are bound to make errors, but we should not be made to feel guilty about them.

One day I said to my medical counselor: "You know, of course, that I was angry at you for a good long time for 'confirming my diagnosis,' but never once have you put me on the defensive about it or any of the mistakes that we have made in relation to Steve."

"Why should I?" he countered. "How do I know I could have done any better than you, had I been in your circumstances?"

He went on to give this definition of "good parents":

"Parents are good parents, when to the best of their ability, understanding, and circumstances, they meet as adequately as possible the needs of their children."[2]

8. *Remember that parents of retarded children are just people.*

This has been *my* most amazing discovery. We are just people with a serious problem, a great sorrow—a living sorrow. We have the same strengths and weaknesses as others in the general population. We have the same problems, the same handicaps. But when the burden of mental retardation is heaped upon us, often these problems and defects are magnified and we, in turn, create problems for those of you who must deal with us. But *as a group,* I do not think we should be considered abnormal, particularly in view of the poor cultural attitude towards our problem, the lack of interest and services, and the fact that some parents have made great personal and family sacrifices to carry this "cause" to the public conscience.

You cannot generalize about parents of retarded children any more than you can generalize about retarded children. Gifted, average, or limited, any of us can find our problems complicated by our own emotional makeup. Professional people working with us must learn to appraise these variables in our intelligence and emotional stability.

Apropos of this are the technical articles which some of us read. Why do we *always* face such words as "anxieties, hostilities, frustrations, guilt-feelings," and other emotionally charged words to describe our reactions? Such pseudoscientific certainties merely serve to make parents feel even more inadequate, it seems to me.

You should take seriously the comment of a New Jersey parent: "... Is not what appears to be 'guilt feelings' to professionals, merely concern with the child's welfare, mingled with grief over his handicap?"[3]

"All parents experience some feelings of guilt about illness in their children ...," Dr. Julius B. Richmond, pediatrician, of Syracuse University has said. If outward manifestations of these feelings persist in us after you have assured us that "no act of omission or commission" on our part has been responsible for the condition of our child, perhaps our feelings might be more aptly described as "regret." We are bound to feel regret if we have rejected this child, if we have struck out at him and created problems for him. With this regret we very likely feel anger at not having had the proper guidance at the times we needed it.

Might not some of our hostility be nothing more than righteous indignation over the neglect of our problem? Actually, if some of the pioneers in the parent group movement had not become "mad" in the early days, our problem would still be largely ignored. Who can say, on the basis of present knowledge, when anxieties are neurotic overreactions, if parents must ask: "What will happen to this child after we are gone?" "How can we pay for expensive care outside our home?" "Where can we hire a sitter so that we can take a vacation?"

Whatever labels we use for these feelings, they have added up to a great determination—you might call it "compulsion"—for some of us to see to it that new parents coming along can walk a smoother path. And there is considerable evidence that many of these new parents are avoiding some of the emotional scars which some of us bear.

Dan Boyd, a New Jersey parent, has described three stages in the growth of a parent of a mentally retarded child: (1) Why did this happen to me? (Self pity.) (2) What can I do for my own child and family? (3) What can we do for others?[4]

These stages can be intermingled. The fact that a parent is working in an organization "to help all retarded children" does not necessarily mean that he has grown with his own problem. Some can be stage-3 leaders, without having graduated from stage 1. Such self-pitying parents are the hardest to help. It often takes a long wait and the greatest skill on the part of professional counselors and their parent counterparts to help them to begin to make realistic plans for their own child.

Most parents, however, mature quite rapidly under the stimulus of the group. Self-pity fades when they find that they are not alone. Soon they are seeking to learn from and emulate the parents who have met their problems successfully. And before they know it, they are experiencing the healing that goes with helping another family. Some move on to be eager for all parents to have access to the organization which has rescued them from desolation.

Even these mature stage-3 parents can slip back, temporarily, into stage 2, when a problem arises at home or when previous decisions must be reviewed. During these times we can be very difficult. Then you must support us, while feeling "nothing but plain, simple, humble reverence before the mystery of our misfortune," to use the words of John Cowper Powys.[5]

This means that you must look at your own feelings about us and our children. If you do not have a natural feeling of concern for the mentally retarded, if you feel indifferent to or repelled by children who are not mentally normal or by parents under great stress, then you should not be dealing with us at all.

9. *Remember that we are parents and that you are professionals.*

Some of us are becoming so well-informed in certain areas of this problem and we are associating with you in so many different pursuits that, at times, it must be difficult to remember that we *are* parents and, as such, will always be emotionally involved with our own problem and our own child, regardless of the "objectivity" we may have about the problem generally, or another family's problem, specifically. In communicating with us you must be clear as to whether you are speaking as counselor to client, adviser to organization member, coworker, or personal friend. In this we expect you to use professional judgment.

For example, don't in front of us: belittle or countermand the opinion of one of your professional partners; make critical remarks about other parents and their handling of their child; jump to conclusions about our case without adequate clinical study or knowledge of the facts. And, of course, don't try to do a job that is outside your professional discipline.

When we see so much that needs to be done, we have little time for professional jealousies, or for the individual who uses mental retardation as a ladder to personal success. It does not take long for us to pigeonhole a "problem professional" whose own emotional difficulties are getting in the way of our efforts.

10. *Remember the importance of your attitude towards us.*

Sometimes I think your colleagues place too much emphasis on "objectivity" and not enough on "loving kindness." Certainly we expect you to be objective about our problem. But about us? Never! A really gifted professional person cannot *help* feeling—being subjective, attempting to stand in our shoes and to look out at our problem through our eyes—in the process of helping us. Psychiatrists call this "empathy." It is only through empathy that you can divine the proper words and acts to help us.

There are greater depths and breadths in helping parents of retarded children than many of you have realized in your initial attempts. It has been as exciting for some of us parents to watch professionals grow as it has been rewarding for professionals to watch some of us parents grow. We can help each other become more effective people through our partnership.

You are obligated, it seems to me, to "feelingly persuade" us as Shakespeare said, to help us find "what we are." We have many strengths. If you can help us convert our problem into good for mankind, help us find the sweetness in the uses of our adversity, *you* will find a far more precious jewel in your professionalism than you ever thought existed.

And you will be professionals in the most noble and magnificent sense of the word.

References

¹Eliot, Martha M.: Unpublished address to the National Association for Retarded Children, Boston, 1954.

²Reynold Jensen, M.D.

³National Association for Retarded Children, New York. CHILDREN LIMITED, 4: 5, June 1955.

⁴Boyd, Dan: The three stages (in the growth of a parent of a mentally retarded child). Pamphlet. National Association for Retarded Children, New York, August 1953.

⁵Powys, John Cowper: *The Meaning of Culture.* New York: W. W. Norton & Co. 1929.

FORTY-FIVE

Chronic Sorrow: A Response to Having a Mentally Defective Child

SIMON OLSHANSKY

The purpose of this article is twofold: (1) to propose that most parents who have a mentally retarded child suffer from a pervasive psychological reaction, chronic sorrow, that has not always been recognized by the professional personnel —physicians, psychologists, and social workers—who attempt to help them; and (2) to suggest some of the implications of the phenomenon of chronic sorrow for the parent-counseling process. This discussion is based on the author's personal and professional experiences and on the experience of the Children's Developmental Clinic[1] staff in counseling parents of severely retarded children.

The Phenomenon of Chronic Sorrow

Most parents who have a mentally defective child suffer chronic sorrow throughout their lives regardless of whether the child is kept at home or is "put away." The intensity of this sorrow varies from time to time for the same person, from situation to situation, and from one family to another. The sorrow may be more intense for one parent than for the other in the same family. Many factors, such as a parent's personality, ethnic group, religion, and social class, influence the intensity of this sorrow. Some parents show their sorrow clearly; others attempt to conceal it, and sometimes they succeed. The need to keep a "stiff upper lip," especially outside the privacy of the home, is a common defense of parents. Anglo-Saxon parents in particular usually feel this need. Although chronic sorrow may be experienced by some parents of minimally retarded children, this reaction is probably more nearly universal among parents whose children are severely or moderately retarded—whose children would be considered retarded in any society and in any cultural group.

The helping professions have somewhat belabored the tendency of the parent to deny the reality of his child's mental deficiency. Few workers have reported what is probably a more frequent occurrence: the parent's tendency to deny his chronic sorrow. This tendency is often reinforced by the professional helper's habit of viewing

Reprinted from *Social Casework*, Vol. 43, No. 4 (April, 1962), pp. 190-913. By permission of the author and the Family Service Association of America.

chronic sorrow as a neurotic manifestation rather than as a natural and understandable response to a tragic fact. All the parental reactions reported in the literature, such as guilt, shame, and anger, may well be intertwined with chronic sorrow. Moreover, a parent's experiencing chronic sorrow does not preclude his deriving satisfaction and joy from his child's modest achievements in growth and development. It can also be assumed that the child's mental defectiveness has symbolic meaning, on an unconscious level, to some parents. The data that support this assumption, however, are rarely communicated by the parent except in deep psychotherapy.

The reality faced by the parent of a severely retarded child is such as to justify his chronic sorrow. When the parent is asked to "accept" mental deficiency, it is not clear just what he is being asked to do. The great stress professional workers tend to place on "acceptance" may suggest to the parent that he is expected to perceive his child from the point of view of the professional helper. This expectation may make him both resentful and resistant. In our clinical experience, we have seen relatively few parents so neurotic that they denied the fact that the child was mentally defective. We have seen relatively few parents who did not recover enough, after the initial shock of discovery, to mobilize their efforts in behalf of the child. It is understandable that some parents move slowly and erratically toward recognition of the mental defect and toward meeting the child's special needs. Some of them even "regress" to the point of denying, at certain times, the reality of the child's defectiveness. On other occasions they become unduly optimistic about the child's potentialities. In our view, such regression may help the parent to tolerate better the terrible reality that confronts him each day.

Why does the professional worker become so impatient with the parent's slowness or occasional regression, and why does he feel such a great sense of urgency to do something about it? After all, the parent has a lifetime in which to learn to deal with the needs and problems of a mentally defective child. In most cases one can ask what will be lost if the parent is unable for several years to view his child as mentally defective. The parents of one of our clinic patients have told us that their child was six or seven years old before they knew definitely that she was mentally defective. Although they had sensed that her development was slow, they had failed to act on their suspicions until her subnormality became self-evident. In what way had the parents been worse off in their "blissful ignorance"? In what way had the child been worse off, since she had had the capacity to meet the parents' expectations?

The parents of a normal child have to endure many woes, many trials, and many moments of despair. Almost all these parents know, however, that ultimately the child will become a self-sufficient adult. By contrast, the parents of a mentally defective child have little to look forward to; they will always be burdened by the child's unrelenting demands and unabated dependency. The woes, the trials, the moments of despair, will continue until either their own deaths or the child's death. Concern about what will happen to his child after he is dead may be a realistic concern for a parent, or it may be associated with death wishes, either for himself or for his child. Release from his chronic sorrow may be obtainable only through death.

The Counseling Process

What are some of the implications of the parent's chronic sorrow for the professional person who attempts to help him? First, the professional worker should abandon the simplistic and static concept of parental acceptance. Every parent—whether he has a normal or a mentally defective child—accepts his child and rejects his child at various times and in various situations. If both acceptance and rejection are universal parental responses, it is not clear just what the professional person is asking the parent of a mentally defective child to accept. Is the parent being asked to accept the fact that the child is defective? This the parent does, in general. Is he being asked to meet the child's needs realistically? This the parent tries to do, by and large. Is he being asked to abandon his chronic sorrow? This the parent wishes he could do but cannot. The permanent, day-by-day dependence of the child, the interminable frustrations resulting from the child's relative changelessness, the unaesthetic quality of mental defectiveness, the deep symbolism buried in the process of giving birth to a defective child—all these join together to produce the parent's chronic sorrow. That so many parents bear this sorrow stoically is rich testimony to parental courage and endurance. (One might ask, for example, how much progress would have been achieved in the field of rehabilitation if the issue of "acceptance" rather than the issue of managing the disability most efficiently through the use of prosthetic devices, had been made the primary focus of professional concern.)

Second, the professional person's perceptions of the parent will be different if he accepts the idea that chronic sorrow is a natural, rather than a neurotic, reaction. The worker's changed perceptions of the parent and his feelings may encourage the parent to discuss his chronic sorrow more openly and freely. There is a danger that some workers will become overinvolved and sentimental, so that they will serve as "wailing walls" rather than as helpers. This danger, however, is always present in any helping situation if a worker surrenders the discipline, restraint, and understanding he must have to fulfull his helping role. Although chronic sorrow is a natural, rather than a neurotic, response to a tragic fact, some parents do respond neurotically to their child's handicap and may require treatment for their neurosis. Judging from our experience, however, the number of neurotic parents is small. It is regrettable that this small number of people has received so much professional attention that the tragedy of having a mentally defective child has been viewed less as a tragedy than as a psychiatric problem.

The professional worker who learns to accept chronic sorrow as a normal psychological reaction will grant the parent a longer period of time than otherwise in which to adjust his feelings and organize his resources, both internal and external, to meet the child's needs. The worker will also plan to extend the length of the counseling process. He will alter the usual practice of telling the parent the facts about the child's mental defectiveness in as few as one to four interviews, since the worker will realize that the communication of facts is only one part of the counseling process and not necessarily the most important part. Some parents may require months, or even years, of counseling before they can muster and maintain the strength and stamina needed to live with the tragedy of having a mentally defective child. What the parent requires, beyond a knowledge of the facts, is an opportunity to ventilate and clarify his feelings and to receive support for the legitimacy of the feelings he is expressing. In some instances the parent will need to be given this opportunity at various times throughout his life.

In addition to providing more time during which the parent can learn to face his problem, and to offering counseling at a slower pace, the worker should also make himself accessible to the parent over a long period of time. No matter how effective the counseling is, many parents need to discuss their feelings and the problems associated with a defective child on many occasions. This need for repeated counseling is natural and should not be considered a sign of either regression or neurosis. The experience of our clinic has demonstrated the importance of accessibility—an "open door" policy—for the parents of mentally defective children. A parent may telephone a staff member again and again about a recurring problem, a new problem, an emerging crisis, or his own distress.

Finally, if the worker accepts the validity of the concept of chronic sorrow, his goal in counseling the parent will be to increase the parent's comfortableness in living with and managing his defective child. In addition to providing psychological help, the worker will emphasize, more than formerly, the help the mother needs in order to learn to manage such problems as how to feed, discipline, and toilet-train the child. The use of such facilities as preschool nurseries, special education classes, day care centers, and sheltered workshops should be made available when they can be used appropriately. Moreover, the mother should be given an opportunity to be away from the child at recurring intervals. Although some workers tend to discount the value of "baby-sitting" services, these services can make it possible for the mother to get much-needed relief and can enhance her sense of personal comfort. Greater comfortableness may help make her chronic sorrow more tolerable and may increase her effectiveness in meeting the child's continuing needs. Also, through increased comfortableness the parents may become more accessible to psychological help for themselves.

In summary, it has been suggested that the parent of a mentally defective child suffers from chronic sorrow. This sorrow is a natural response to a tragic fact. If the professional worker accepts chronic sorrow as a natural, rather than a neurotic, response, he can be more effective in helping the parent achieve the goal of increased comfort in living with and managing a mentally defective child.

References

[1]The Children's Developmental Clinic is supported by the U.S. Children's Bureau, the Massachusetts Department of Public Health, and the City of Cambridge.

The author is grateful to the following persons for their considerable help: Dr. Charles Hersch and Lillian Saltman, Cambridge Guidance Center; Dr. Samuel Grob, Massachusetts Association for Mental Health; Dr. Robert Flynn, Thelma Bloom, Gertrude Johnson, and Marjorie Kettell, Children's Developmental Clinic; Catherine Casey and Hilma Unterberger, Massachusetts Department of Public Health.

FORTY-SIX

Adapting Techniques

MICHAEL J. BEGAB

Social casework is defined as "a process used by certain human welfare agencies to help individuals to cope more effectively with their problems in social functioning." This goal is achieved through (1) a therapeutic relationship of worker and client that supports the client and enables him to understand his problem and its possible solutions and (2) opportunities or resources that ameliorate the stress situation or permit the client to use his personal resources toward more effective functioning.

The mildly retarded adolescent or young adult is particularly liable to the development of problems in his social behavior and relationships. Frequently he is exposed to damaging home conditions, his behavior violates the community standards and he learns to resent or distrust persons in authority. Unhappily, in many of these instances, even when the retarded individual can assess his problem, the tangible social, recreational and employment resources needed by him for recognition, status, and a sense of acceptance are not available.

Many of the retarded are unable to solve their problems because they do not understand them or have not developed skills in handling them. The mentally limited mother who is overwhelmed by the burdens of a large family and homemaking duties is one example. The adolescent girl who is denied companionship with boys because of parental fears and anxieties is another. Some of these mothers can be taught in the casework relationship what they did not know and provided, through training, with skills they did not possess. Similarly, interpretation can help the parents understand their adolescents' need for social relations, and guidance can help the adolescent to conduct herself appropriately.

For many of the mildly retarded who come to agency attention the problem is one of deep personality maladjustment of long duration. Their problems derive from unhealthy parent-child relationships, or uncompromising and hostile community attitudes. The outward symptoms of the disorder may range from mild situ-

From Michael J. Begab, *The Mentally Retarded Child: A Guide to Services of Social Agencies.* The Children's Bureau, U. S. Department of Health, Education and Welfare (Washington, U.S. Government Printing Office, 1963), pp. 70-79. By permission of the author and The Children's Bureau.

ational reactions to frank psychoses. Often the retarded is unaware of his inner feelings, behaving in an unpredictable and impulsive manner.

The problems outlined above are only a few of those common to the retarded which are subject to resolution by means of the casework process. Actually the adjustment problems of this group cover the total spectrum of social dysfunction. Whatever the nature or cause of the problem, however, its solution is generally accomplished through the medium of a meaningful casework relationship.

The essence of this relationship involves some interaction of feeling between worker and client, a joint concern for the client's problem and an atmosphere of trust, acceptance and helpfulness. It requires on the part of the client seeking help, a recognition of the worker's authority of knowledge and skill—a recognition which lends a feeling of security within the relationship and facilitates his use of guidance. On the part of the worker, the relationship requires a true appreciation of human dignity and integrity, a willingness to help, an expectation of the client's responsiveness toward a better social adjustment.

These elements are basic to all casework relationships, but their realization is frequently impeded when the client is retarded. For the most part, the retarded adolescent or adult seldom seeks help on his own initiative. Sometimes not only the retarded client, but his family as well, resent the intrusion of the agency's authority and are resistive to professional casework services. Some of these retarded individuals have come to regard all persons in authority as a source of punishment and persecution and are distrustful of interpersonal relationships.

Establishing rapport with these individuals is often difficult, but seldom impossible. Like his normal counterpart who has been traumatized in his striving for emotional acceptance and social interaction, the similarly deprived retarded person may demonstrate marked withdrawal symptoms and be hard to reach. Conversely some have had sufficient loving so that they continue to "reach out" for adult attention and affection. These individuals are quick to respond to a sympathetic and understanding attitude, sometimes to a point of fawnlike devotion that the worker may find embarrassing. Others will approach the caseworker with the same childlike innocence, trust and dependency they extend to all adults.

Whatever the initial capacities of the retarded person, the relationship develops as emotional experiences are shared and the worker demonstrates his identification with the problem and his competence to deal with it. Some of the retarded communicate their problems quite freely and simply, unembellished by elaborate rationalization and other ego defense mechanisms. Some blame their troubles completely on their mistreatment by parents, teachers or peers. And some do not disclose their problems, either from suspicion and distrust or from an inability to articulate their feelings. In each of these instances, as with intellectually normal clients, the verbal participation of the worker in the identification of the problem will vary. The likelihood is great, however, that with retarded clients, the worker will need to be more actively involved in setting forth the focus of the interviews and will need to rely more heavily on non-verbal skills in conveying an attitude of personal interest and acceptance. The worker's demeanor, facial expression, tone of voice, body movements and participation in activities with the client are often more effective than repeated words of assurance and support. Most important, the worker must convince his retarded client that he (the worker) is trustworthy and that he has trust in him. Only as the client is secure in the relationship and a sense of mutual trust exists can learning and behavioral change take place.

One of the major obstacles to effective casework with these clients is the difficulty encountered by some professional workers in applying the basic tenet of all social work practice, that every individual has intrinsic human value. Underlying feelings tend to emerge in the casework relationship and these workers cannot conceal their exasperation with the retarded client's uninhibited and impulsive behavior. Neither can they escape the impact of cultural attitudes toward low intelligence or the sense of revulsion aroused in themselves and in most people by the grosser forms of human defect. Some workers demonstrate this aversion by denying retardation in their clients and attempting to make their clients over, in their own self-image as it were. In this way they are able to free themselves emotionally to form a helping relationship. These reactions of some caseworkers—to which other professions are equally liable—impede the identification process which is essential for psychological helping. It is *relatively* easy for the worker to conceive of himself as blind, crippled, neurotic, economically deprived or socially maladjusted. Few however, can imagine themselves as truly retarded.

No magic formula exists whereby these attitudes toward retardation can be readily changed. In this as in other areas involving attitudes deeply rooted in our system of social values, the need for an objective self-examination of feelings is paramount. The worker should neither overestimate himself as an individual nor have distressing feelings of inadequacy or insecurity in dealing with the "unknown quantity" of his retarded client. He needs an especially generous allotment of kindness and sympathy to identify with these persons—often the least endowed of all his clients. More precise knowledge of the retarded and their potentialities, through formal educational processes or through self-learning activities, can also help. Perhaps the most effective approach in modifying attitudes is through a carefully supervised, successful work experience with a retarded client both on a student and practitioner level. With proper understanding of the "nature" of the client and convictions regarding his inherent worth and suitability for services, techniques can be properly adapted.

A fundamental principle in casework is the client's right to self-determination. Every individual, within the limits of reality, has the right to be master of his own destiny. While the validity of this concept is undenied, its application in work with the retarded is necessarily limited. For this group, the limits of reality are not defined solely by the external environment but must also include the incapacity of the retarded to choose between alternative courses of action and to make decisions in his best interests. The "right" to act in a given manner has no real value for the individual who is unable to exercise reason and judgment and who needs protection from his own imprudence.

This does not mean that the retarded client is completely unable to participate in the problem-solving process, for those who are so lacking are not appropriate candidates for the counseling aspect of casework services. It does suggest, however, that the retarded client may have a limited grasp of the facts that bear upon his problem, may not fully understand their significance and may be unable to apply them toward a resolution of his problem.

To promote greater understanding where only partial understanding is evident, the worker will need to devote more effort to interpretation, extended over a period of time. Language must be consistent with the client's level of comprehension and specific ideas or suggestions must be re-enforced in succeeding interviews to insure carry-over. It is wise, too, to test the client periodically for "feedback" to insure that communication has actually taken place. The retarded client, who is already burdened with a sense of his own inferiority, is apt to nod his understanding to preserve his self-esteem, when in fact the meaning of the worker's words has eluded him.

Even where the retarded client has or acquires some insight into the basis of his social difficulties, it cannot always be assumed these insights will be properly applied in future stress situations or important decisions. The objective of casework with the retarded individual is to promote his general adjustability, a highly feasible goal for most. But some of the retarded, while they are relatively *well-adjusted* or can be helped to become so, are not very *adjustable*. The well being of these individuals depends in large measure on a constantly favorable environment; they are apt to flounder under stress conditions. In these cases, the worker must rely more heavily on direct advice and guidance. He must act as the client's superego, imposing limits upon him which he cannot set for himself, and making decisions where he lacks the capacity to do so through his own powers.

Reliance on direct advice and guidance techniques is not confined to the intellectually limited person, though it may be used in greater degree here than with other groups. This places an additional burden on the worker to know the facts fully, to carefully appraise his clients' capacities and limitations and to be able to anticipate with some accuracy the consequences of a particular course of action. This is indeed a weighty responsibility and it presents special hazards to the casework relationship.

The danger is ever present that if he is very frequently advised on how a problem should be handled, the client may become overdependent on the caseworker and lose all initiative in handling new situations as they arise. There is the further danger that the advice proferred may not result in a successful resolution of the problem. This tends to place the caseworker in a potential scapegoat role and to relieve the client of responsibility for the outcome. Often this is less risky than when the retarded client makes the final choice with little knowledge about what the worker thinks is best. Much depends on the problem at hand. The retarded individual who plans to quit his job with no reasonable prospects for a new one may be a case in point. His dissatisfaction may stem from legitimate causes—low pay, lack of social contacts with fellow employees and demanding work schedules. His discontents, however, may arise from an unrealistic appraisal of his own potentialities, his improper placement within the plant or his own unfounded attitudes of suspicion and distrust. In either event, the retarded client's assessment of the facts may be inaccurate and his solution thereby faulty. Freedom of choice—to quit, in this illustration—may not get at the basic cause of dissatisfaction and may in fact greatly compound the client's adjustment difficulties. The client needs the protection of the worker's superior knowledge, and where the worker stands in a position of authority—as in cases on trial placement from the institution—it may be well to invoke this authority in the decision-making process.

While these hazards are undeniably real, a judicious use of this technique, involving the client's participation to the maximum extent possible, can minimize any negative effects. Supportive therapy with all clients—in the initial period at least—presupposes some dependency on the caseworker, a dependency designed in the long range view to strengthen rather than weaken the individual psychologically. With retarded persons this dependency may need to extend over a longer period of time, but the sensitive worker will know when the client is prepared to act on his own and will modify his participation in the problem-solving process accordingly.

When alternate solutions are possible, and particularly when the consequences of a wrong choice would not be seriously harmful to the client, independent action should be encouraged. Given the opportunity to make his own decisions, the retarded individual is less able to project blame on the caseworker. More important, should his judgment in a given situation prove effective, it will bolster his self-confidence and increase his adjustability. Even where his judgment is faulty, if the effects are not severe, valuable learning may occur and some long-range gains may ensue. In these instances, the casework relationship sustains the client and provides a setting in which previous errors can be analyzed and other methods of handling the problem identified without criticism by the worker or personal threat to the retarded client.

The caseworker should not approach every retarded client with the assumption that he is capable of only minimal participation in the problem-solving process. This capacity varies in all persons, even those with normal intelligence, depending on a complex of personality considerations. But this does not deny that, where other variables are equal, the individual of low mentality, poor judgment and impaired powers of reason, will need more direction in promoting proper social and emotional patterns of conduct.

The casework adage of "starting where the client is" has validity with retarded persons as with the normally intelligent, but is much more difficult to apply. Among the mildly retarded at least, the determination of "where the client is" is sometimes exceedingly complex. Often these individuals show a highly uneven rate of development in significant areas of growth. In the normal child, mental and chronological age coincide and are highly correlated with social and emotional development, though disparities are by no means uncommon. With the retarded these differences occur with greater frequency and are likely to be more marked.

Social workers are often puzzled as to the level on which to approach these youngsters and are further confused by parental reports of childlike interests, motivations and behavior. It is well to remember that in some cases, such interests and behavior are unwittingly fostered in the parent-child relationship and may not be a good index of actual growth patterns. For the most part, mental age is not a reliable guide to client readiness and casework techniques. The 16 year old child with a mental age of 10 is not like other 10 year olds. We cannot ignore the socializing effects of additional life experiences and the way in which family and community expectations influence the child's perception of himself and his range of interests. Social considerations embracing the whole range of the client's experiences, interests, motivations and capacitites, must be evaluated in assessing the proper approach to treatment.

Low intelligence affects the caseworker's approach in other ways, too. The verbal analysis and appeal to logic and reason that characterize certain aspects of the casework relationship has limited application with the retarded. These individuals cannot reason abstractly on a high level, grasp a complex idea, identify with a philosophy or ideal. They do, however, share the wide range of emotions to which all persons are subject. They can be quite responsive to the emotional components in a situation, including, as we have already noted, the attitudes of the worker. Where strong feelings of loyalty to family or friends exist, appeal to these emotions may change the retarded client's attitudes or guide his behavior.

Unfortunately, in some instances, these bonds of affection are with persons whose conduct and character are unwholesome. Sometimes it is desirable to work toward a severance of these emotional ties. If the client can be freed of these attachments, the conflicts between the values of his family and those of the worker—representing the larger society—may be dissipated. In these circumstances, the worker may come to be viewed by his retarded client as a parental figure, and as a "parent" he will be endowed with authority and looked to as a source of security and guidance. When this occurs—a not uncommon phenomenon in counseling with the retarded—some degree of character reeducation may take place.

The suggestibility of some retarded clients, when they are motivated toward the social values of the caseworker, can prove an asset in character reeducation. Sometimes the retarded individual, especially the culturally deprived, exhibits antisocial behavior patterns because the meaningful persons in his environment have failed to teach him otherwise. To be accepted and loved, he must emulate his parents and siblings and he feels little guilt about his conduct because he has not incorporated into his conscience the moral codes of the community. In other instances, the lack of love from his own family compels him to seek acceptance from outside sources. The emotionally vulnerable retarded boy is thus sometimes "led into trouble" because he seeks status, recognition and acceptance that is otherwise denied him. The retarded girl, for the same reasons, may engage in sexual behavior. Both are driven to follow the suggestions of others—at least partially—by virtue of their unfulfilled needs and wants in their family relationships.

The casework relationship can provide an emotional experience for the retarded client wherein his needs for acceptance and security may be fulfilled. To the degree that these needs are satisfied, the client may be freed to use his intelligence (most of the mildly retarded can distinguish "right" from "wrong") in assessing the inappropriateness of a specific course of action suggested to him. As the worker demonstrates his support and unwavering acceptance, the retarded individual may modify his behavior to gain or retain the worker's approval. Here the worker is able to exploit the client's suggestibility to good advantage, to create new desires and to control existing ones. In offering suggestions, as with direct advice and guidance, the worker should proceed with caution. He should be reasonably certain that the retarded client can act upon the suggestion and that it is an appropriate plan in the light of all the known circumstances. Properly used, this fairly common trait of the retarded need not be a social liability.

Another important consideration in casework with the mentally retarded is the need to stress their abilities, while at the same time they are helped to recognize their limitations. Most of the retarded who come to agency attention have been exposed to a constant dosage of "don'ts" and "cannots." Their inadequacies prompt admonitions in the family, school and neighborhood about the things they should not do, and they are frequently reminded of activities they cannot perform or goals they cannot undertake. As a consequence, they regard themselves as "bad" or inferior. Equally important, while they learn what they should not do, they are given little direction about what modes of conduct are proper in certain circumstances.

The caseworker cannot and should not avoid identifying the behavioral difficulties of the client, for only as these are realistically faced can motivation for change take place. Neither should he evade discussion of the client's mental limitations, for only as the client's aspirations are related to his capabilities can he be protected from unnecessary and further debilitating failures. Nor can the worker realistically fail to admonish the client when a repetition of his behavior will further aggravate his maladjustment. The problem lies not in the interpretation and discussion of these factors, but in how the interpretations are made and the extent to which these negatives are dwelt upon.

The guiding principle in these cases, as with intellectually normal clients, is to preserve or build up the retarded client's self-confidence and esteem and to avoid further ego threat. Most retarded persons are already aware of their learning deficiencies, but they may fail to relate these deficiencies to certain job requirements because they do not know what skills or education are needed to perform various tasks. Pointing these things out can be initially threatening, but the effects can be tempered by reference to the variations in the physical abilities of people and by acknowledging the accomplishments of the client, no matter how limited they may seem. Probably every retarded person has some small skill or talent. The worker is well-advised to identify these abilities, emphasize them in discussion, and build upon them by arranging for experiences in which these skills can be successfully applied.

The tendency to stress the "don'ts" in behavior when working with adolescents or young adults is probably most understandable. Unhappily, no list of "dont's" can safeguard the individual against every contingency. Neither can these young people be expected to exercise the controls such a list would entail in the absence of positive guidance, sex education, and adequate preparation for the channelization of behavior.

Many parents find the sex education of their retarded children beyond their comprehension. They fear the use to which such knowledge may be put or, like some parents of normal children, feel insecure in this area of child guidance. For related reasons, the schools, institutions and other training and rehabilitation facilities have also tended to overlook this basic educational need. As a result, the vulnerability of the retarded adolescent and young adult is heightened. He may not only lack inner controls and the opportunity for substitute outlets, but he is denied maximal use of his limited judgment because the "facts of life" have been withheld from him.

Sexual misconduct can be a serious source of social dysfunction and is in truth a major factor in the institutionalization of retarded girls above the age of 14. The caseworker can do much to safeguard these girls from exploitation by others and from their own uninhibited actions. Where the parents are the primary clients, the worker can help them decide what the retarded youngster can understand and what he should know about body functions, personal grooming and boy-girl relationships, and can encourage them to carry this educative function. If the parents cannot carry this function or there are no parents to do so, the social worker may help the retarded child with his knowledge and feelings about sex through the casework relationship.

In this process—whoever provides the instruction or treatment—discussion must be geared to the age and mental level of the individuals or groups involved. The subject should be approached casually and naturally, in discrete parts and with sufficient repetition to ensure understanding. To the extent possible, the discussion should be related to other aspects of the child's life, so that it does not arouse anxiety unnecessarily or focus undue attention on this phase of physiological and psychological behavior. For example, a general discussion of manners and consideration for others can lead to an exploration of proper conduct at dances, parties and social hours, of what it means to "go steady," of how to meet friends. Emphasis on personal grooming and hygiene can provide the initial approach to menstruation and a later discussion of anatomy, secondary sexual characteristics, and the reproductive process. When the objectives are primarily instructional and conducted on a group basis, the use of visual aids and demonstration is highly desirable. In all of these areas, the "do's" in behavior should be stressed.

The retarded boy or girl who is given an intellectual grasp of the principles of sex development and behavior has a better chance to exercise psychological restraints than one who is not so prepared. Knowledge alone, however, will not suffice for the youngster who misbehaves sexually because she is deprived in her affectional life or has identified herself with negative values in the home. These youngsters need help in finding other suitable outlets for their affectional needs and in developing a stronger moral conscience. Once rapport has been firmly established, a frank discussion of the problem may take place without fear of threat or personal rejection on the part of the retarded client. The consequences of such behavior must be realistically interpreted and limits set in terms of acceptable social norms. It is essential, however, that limits be reasonable and within the capacity of the client to abide by. Rigid controls destroy the retarded person's self-confidence and create the feeling that the caseworker has little trust in his capacity for self-regulation. The worker must recognize that for the retarded individual in the community, constant supervision is an impossibility.

This principle is often overlooked in the supervision of mildly retarded girls released from institutional care in family or work placement. Strict curfews, restrictions against dating and other social activities are often rigidly enforced, with return to the institution as an ever present and verbalized threat. While such regulations may have value early in placement and even contribute to the security of the girl who may fear her own acting-out impulses, their prolonged application is often self-defeating. In practice, many of these girls tend to rebel against restrictions in dating and resort to illicit contacts, which frequently arouse much anxiety in all concerned and aggravate the girls' social maladjustment. Conversely, where greater freedom is permitted, there is less need for "behind the back" activities and as a rule fewer community problems are engendered. These results can hardly be guaranteed, and in each case the individual's capacity for self-control must be determined. But we cannot expect the development of social maturity, independence and acceptable heterosexual relationships unless opportunity for the promotion of these skills is provided. Failure to educate and counsel retarded persons in this phase of life is apt to reap a host of social reprisals for him.

Adapting the Environment

The problem solving process in social casework, while it strives toward making the retarded client more adaptable to new and changing conditions, cannot rely entirely on this unilateral approach. Some clients can be helped to become reasonably adjusted, but with others, successful adjustment will depend on how much the environment can be "tailored" to their social capacities.

In this regard, the need to modify parental attitudes is often overlooked, particularly for children in foster family care or in the rehabilitation of the institutionalized retarded person. For the mildly retarded at least, family or community pathology—and generally both of these—is usually the underlying factor necessitating separation and placement. The value of the foster family experience or the institutional program, no matter how effective it may be in promoting social skills in the retarded individual, may be largely lost if he is returned to the same pathological environment that contributed to his maladjustment in the first place. If the conditions in the home are basically unalterable, return to the family is contraindicated. If the community from which he originally came is too intolerant, demanding, disadvantaged or complex, a more favorable community for placement must be found.

The importance of adapting the environment to the needs and capacities of the retarded client, and the consequences to the client when this is not done, are clearly illustrated in a study of population movement by Windle. Sixty-three percent of those returned from the institution to their own homes who failed in placement, failed because of antisocial behavior—crimes, sexual misconduct, pregnancy, minor antisocial actions. The reluctance of the family to seek professional intervention until "too late" and the less intensive responsibility of the social worker for individuals in the care of their own parents, partially explain these failures. But the most important considerations are the unchanging nature of the home, the lack of environmental supports, the inadequacies of parental supervision and guidance.

By contrast, placement failure in the moderately retarded stemmed largely from intolerable behavior—untidiness, temper outbursts, hyperactivity, destructiveness, etc.—or from medical problems requiring extensive care. The foster parents in whose homes these individuals were placed were often unequal to the tasks posed by the care of these children. In some instances, they were further handicapped by community objections or by interference from the child's natural parents.

Failures in vocational leave were due, for the most part, to poor work performance, difficulties in interpersonal relations and by voluntary departure from the work situation. Frequently these factors are interrelated, the anxieties and emotional problems of the individual being reflected in his work performance. With this group, partly because of the careful selection process preceding placement, antisocial behavior is far less frequently observed than in those returned to their own homes.

The need to modify parental attitudes and behavior and to improve home conditions before or while the retardate is in his own home is obvious. Satisfactory adjustment of the retarded in the regimented, controlled environment of the institution, does not guarantee similar behavior outside. Casework treatment therefore must be directed not only toward the retarded individual but toward his family as well. Sometimes the needed professional casework services to the family can be provided by the institutional staff; more often the family's distance from the institution and the worker's unfamiliarity with local conditions makes the assumption of this responsibility by local social agencies more feasible.

The difficulties encountered in the foster family placement of moderately retarded children further highlights the importance of adapting the environment to the special needs and capacities of the child. Foster parents of retarded children must be carefully selected and need to possess exceptional personal qualities. The community, too, must be reasonably accepting and provide at least minimal resources for social and recreation activities.

It can be seen from these brief illustrations, that the problem solving process may proceed in three major directions: (1) strengthening the retarded person's adaptability, (2) modifying the environment by effecting change in attitudes and expectations, and (3) carefully selecting an environment especially suited to the retarded individual's needs.

In the rehabilitation of the older adolescent, particularly those for whom social and vocational independence is the goal, the caseworker will often need to consider all three components. Though many of those identified in the school program as mentally retarded may not need casework help in the transition to adult life and the responsibility this entails, the socially maladjusted often do. Vocational training and guidance for these youngsters can provide the tools needed to compete in the labor market, earn a livelihood, gain in self-confidence and derive the emotional satisfactions of self-support. But before work skills can be effectively applied, retarded persons must learn how to get along with others, to accept authority, to be reliable and dependable and in other ways to adjust to the demands of the industrial setting. Some of these attributes can be acquired in the process of vocational training but frequently the factors contributing to social dysfunction must be resolved through casework and other therapeutic procedures.

Assuming that these ends have been achieved to a reasonable degree, the task is not yet complete. The mentally retarded cannot be expected to know what job opportunities are available, what kinds of work they can do, where they can seek help in job finding and how to apply. In these pursuits, they often need much guidance, direction and concrete assistance.

In some instances the real problem lies not in the personal or work inadequacies of the retarded, but in the attitudes of prospective employers. These individuals frequently underestimate the work skills of the mentally retarded and stereotype them unjustly as unreliable and untrustworthy. To ensure the retarded a proper chance to "make good" on the job, or indeed get a job at all, these attitudes need to be overcome. Public education through mass media and more direct, interpretative contacts with business and other employer associations, can appreciably alter attitudes and expand work opportunities for the retarded as a group. For the individual retarded person, however, the caseworker is often well advised to contact the prospective employer directly with the full knowledge of the client. This offers the opportunity to assess the work situation in relation to the client's skills, to explore the employer's feelings toward an understanding of the mentally retarded and to interpret the client's aptitudes and other considerations relative to his work performance. Equally important, an offer of continuing casework help, should adjustment problems arise, can often allay the employer's anxieties and encourage trial placement. The involvement of the employer as a partner in planning a productive work experience for the retarded client and the worker's shared responsibility for supervision and guidance in the area of interpersonal relationships, are vital elements in the placement process. In this way, the demands of the work situation, within the limits prescribed by the setting, can be adapted to the abilities of the retarded client.

Some settings—highly automated factories for example—may be too complex in organization and too demanding in technical skills, to be used as a placement resource for retarded persons. Similarly, industrialized metropolitan centers may present daily living problems and potentially undesirable influences that exceed the adjustment capacities of the less capable retarded individual. Other social institutions, too, cannot be readily adapted, modified or manipulated to accommodate them. In these instances, the environment in which they are to live must be inherently less complex and demanding.

Apparent differences are evident between rural and urban communities, though these differences are becoming less marked with the mechanization of farming and the gradual absorption of the small farm. Nevertheless, the expectations of a backwoods rural community are less exacting than those of a large metropolis. Many formerly well adjusted retarded children and adults who move from a rural to an urban setting become maladjusted in the large city. Standards for school achievement are higher, job requirements and qualifications more exacting, and the system of social relationship more complicated. The retarded individual of low marginal abilities, who must rely on his own resources for subsistence and otherwise independent functioning, is sorely taxed by the demands of urban living. The problem of fitting the environment to the retarded individual whatever the degree of handicap, is less crucial when acceptance, understanding and supervision from responsible adults are provided. Under these conditions, even the moderately retarded—as reported by Saenger—have adjusted surprisingly well in that most complex of urban settings, New York City.

Most of the retarded needing casework services to relieve problems of social maladjustment can be helped to achieve adequate solutions while living in their own homes, in foster family care, wage homes or independent living arrangements. For the few who lack impulse control and whose behavior is unmanageable and constitutes a threat to society and to themselves, however, the more controlled environment of the institution may be indicated. In this setting, a retarded person can be protected from the traumatic consequences of his antisocial behavior and can be freed to adopt a new orientation toward life. Here, he may be able to discard the values of his impoverished culture and establish a solid foundation of practical knowledge to prepare him for later return to the community. With the help of the caseworker and other therapists, he may once again learn to trust others and have confidence in his own capabilities. Properly applied, the institutional program of education, work training, recreation and group living, can complement the problem solving objectives of the casework process.

The caseworker in the institution is sometimes initially handicapped in his efforts at treatment by the retarded person's lack of preparation for separation from his family and community. These youngsters—usually mildly retarded and between the ages of 14 and 19—generally are institutionalized against their will. Their involuntary loss of freedom does not inspire trust in their strange surroundings and they regard the institutional personnel with hostility and fear. These reactions are sometimes further compounded by the court or caseworker's interpretation that he is being sent to the institution for more learning or specific job training with no reference to his behavioral conflicts. Many of these youngsters recognize these interpretations as half-truths. They tend to be resistive and disinterested in education in a "new school" when they have already attended school for many years and may, in the case of the older adolescents, have reached a stage of educational saturation or insensitization. They may also regard with suspicion an offer of job training when their parents, siblings and acquaintances have managed without such experiences. The indefiniteness of their commitment is looked upon as "unfair." Most important perhaps, the retarded youngster generally knows full well that his behavior is the primary basis for this placement. Failure to interpret his need to change his behavior patterns and for guidance in this area will be recognized as an evasion. It may heighten his sense of distrust, and perhaps minimize his feeling of "wrongdoing." Whether prompted by insecurity or by an unwillingness to be a bearer of sad tidings, the caseworker who avoids the reality factors resulting in the commitment can be guilty of a disservice to the client. The problem must be squarely faced, without punitiveness, if motivation for behavioral change is to result.

Ideally, treatment for these retarded youngsters starts on the day of arrival. The caseworker conveys an atmosphere of helpfulness and acknowledges and accepts the child's anxieties and possible resentment over separation from his family. The program of the institution is explained and concrete examples within the child's daily institutional experiences are used to make clear whàt is expected of him and thus protect him from exploitation by others or his own misconceptions. In this setting, as in other agency settings, the casework relationship places as much responsibility on the client as appropriate and tries to encourage a sense of independence in him. To the extent that the social worker formulates or contributes to policy development, efforts should be directed toward liberal "leave" regulations. These temporary visits to the community are vital elements in training for responsible independent living. Equally important, through such opportunities the child's hopes for reunion with his family or community placement are kept alive and he comes to view his institutional experience as something constructive rather than as confinement against his will.

The goals of social work in residential programs for the retarded are comprehensive and may include elements of staff development, administration and research, as well as group work and the more traditional casework functions with the retarded and their families. However extensive these functions may be, all are directed to the ultimate goal of enhancing the social functioning of the individual and his family. These activities are particularly pertinent to the mildly disturbed, "acting-out," retarded individual whose social deficiencies are the basis for his admission.

The remediation of these deficiencies cannot usually be accomplished solely by further education, work training, occupational therapy and similarly oriented programs. While it is essential that retarded persons acquire the practical skills of daily living that these programs try to instill, attitudes of resistance, low frustration tolerance, immaturity and other personality conflicts must be handled. Indeed, unless these barriers to learning and ego development can be overcome, the retarded individual is unlikely to profit from the formal program provided. Attempts at training before he is confident that others really want to help him may result in failure.

The social worker in the institution, having communicated his acceptance and understanding of his client's problem and a willingness to help him help himself, is then able to act as the retarded person's social conscience. It is the worker's task—shared in some measure by other staff members—to interpret society's demands and to insist that certain norms and standards be followed. Repeated explanations are often needed to make these standards clear and to convince the retarded client that conformity, not rebellion, is to his advantage. The sensitive worker will exploit his unique role as advisor, confidant and trusted partner in problem-solving. In the impersonal institution, he can be an island of security, the person to turn to when things go wrong and personal worries seem overwhelming. His work with the family and his liaison functions with the community—particularly in the placement program—represents to the retarded person an important link with his familiar past and somewhat uncertain future.

To make the future more hopeful, the worker needs to be readily available, not only through formal office interviews, but through many opportunely casual contacts, to deal with the retarded individual's misgivings, fears and helplessness. Punishment, when called for, must be geared to the personality of the offender, rather than administered routinely according to the severity or nature of the offense. Above all, the worker must be constantly supportive and not re-enforce the lesson learned by many retarded youngsters that the consequence of misbehavior is loss of love and assistance. In this way the retarded client may gain a better understanding of why he acts as he does and feel—perhaps for the first time—that he has been treated fairly.

The social worker must always keep in mind the treatment goals of the institution and the importance of motivating the retarded toward self-improvement. Segregation from community life, while it is sometimes necessary, frequently does not have the rehabilitative effects expected of it. If the environment is too rigid and regimented, if there is no responsibility for self-management, if demands are geared to the less capable residents of the institution, the retarded individual may downgrade himself in his own eyes and respond at a level beneath his potentials. These potential effects must be counteracted if he is to adjust eventually to the social demands of ordinary community life.

Casework with the retarded then, in whatever setting it may be applied, rests on the fundamental principles which govern casework with other clients and utilizes, with some modification, similar concepts and techniques. Unquestionably, intellectual factors impede the problem-solving process and complicate the retarded person's adjustment, but the total complex of personality factors—in the mildly retarded, at least—are the primary determinants of his fate. The personality of the retarded individual, as with other persons, evolves from the interaction of his constitutional endowment and the physical and social forces which surround him. The dynamics of this interaction can be altered through professional intervention. In this task, the social worker can contribute significantly by enabling the retarded person to become more adjustable or better adjusted and by "tailoring" the environment to his abilities as well as his limitations.

FORTY-SEVEN

Help to Parents of the Mentally Retarded Child: A Diagnostic Focus

HELEN HARRIS PERLMAN

"Social work and mental retardation" is the topic on which I agreed to speak tonight. The trouble with it is that there are so many facets in social work's relation to this problem—the work with families of mentally retarded children, with groups of children themselves, with other professional persons in inventing and developing and improving resources and services, with lay persons in interpreting needs and engaging support and participation—in all these aspects the profession of social work may validly be involved. If I were to try to touch on all of these the inevitable result would be considerable grandiosity on my part and a level of generalization that would only result in some agreeable feeling that social work does indeed have some relation to the problems of mental retardation.

I want to try to avoid talking big. I would like, rather, to take one part of what social work does in relation to mental retardation and examine it in a close-view way in the hope that this might offer some guidelines for action. The part I've carved out, then, is the help that social casework offers specifically to the parents of the mentally retarded child, and I've narrowed it even further, if you will permit that, to focus upon what it is that a caseworker needs to understand about these parents in order to give help as quickly and as therapeutically as possible. In its technical form, the question to which I address myself is: What do we need to diagnose in the parent of the mentally retarded child in order to design treatment that is appropriate, immediate, and effective?

The caseworker involved in problems of mental retardation needs to know everything that is basic to good casework practice, and then, some very special things. (And I must add, as I have reviewed the publications on problems, researches, and treatment means with the mentally retarded within the past five years alone, I am filled with respect and admiration for the exciting explosion of knowledge in this area of your specialty, and also for the new attitudes of openness and hope which have come to replace what was for so long a pall of silence and stoppage.) So there are many kinds of knowledge and know-how about the special physical, psycholog-

From a paper delivered at the Annual Conference of the Canadian Association for Retarded Children, Toronto, 1965. By permission of the author and the Association.

ical, and social problems of mental retardation that are in your area of expertness. These will underlie and give focus to your diagnostic thinking. I believe there is something about diagnosis in casework in general that has made us honor it more in words than in use. While we all give lip service to the dictum that diagnosis should design treatment, the fact is that we are not at all sure what the content of diagnosis for casework treatment consists of or should be. Sometimes we seem to think it must resemble a psychiatric diagnosis if it is to have respectability. Sometimes we just blunder along, hoping for some flash of diagnostic lightning to illuminate our case record. Examination of case records often shows complex and even keenly astute diagnoses of the personalities involved in a given problem; but these psychological dissections may give very little guidance to the caseworker's persistent problem which is the problem of what decisions to make, what action to take. Sometimes search for diagnostic understanding goes on so endlessly that while the caseworker fills in the pieces of a life history or life style, the real life client disappears.

The reasons for caseworkers' uneasy entente with diagnosis would make a paper in themselves. What I want to put forth here is that there is an important content in diagnosis which, I believe, we have not adequately recognized and used. It is a content that I believe is generic to any casework problem. Here I shall apply it specifically to problems of helping parents of mentally retarded children. It is a content that has particular relevance in brief-service cases, short-term cases, or intermittent service cases. It is contained in these questions: Why is it that the person who stands before me now needs my help? Why can't he cope with his problem on his own? Why can't he just take the information that the doctor or clinical team or his own intelligence conveys to him and go home and use it? What is it about this problem, or about himself in relation to this problem or about this point in his life history that makes it necessary for an outsider, a caseworker, to help him?

"Well," you say, "this is perfectly obvious. The problem is more or bigger than he can solve on his own." But I would persist and ask. "Why is this?" Because I assume that the person—any person—has been involved in coping with problems of one or another sort from the day he is born.

Every one of us copes with problems from the beginning of life. They begin with our being too warm, too cold, too hungry, too wet, too alone; and the constitution we're endowed with, combined with the mothering we get, determines from the first how confident or impotent we feel about mastering our problems. As we grow, our field of problems-to-be-solved widens. The table will not get out of the toddler's way, the spoon turned upside down will not hold food, one's mother says "wait" or "no" or "which do you like best?" There is a widening circle of people to be dealt with even when we are very young, not only parents to demand from and to please, but other children, too. Demands from above require that you act in certain ways—be "nice," "fair," "don't fight" or "hit back." Leaving home and going to school is a critical incident for many children—with problems to be solved even for those who look forward to it. And there follows—each of us can trace this throughout his own life history—an unending chain of challenges, obstacles, opportunities, problems, responsibilities for which you and I and every other human being must call on his inner and outer resources to adapt to, or compromise with, or overcome. In this sense, all living is an experience of problem-solving, some of it pleasurable, thank heaven!, and some difficult. So every person we encounter, every client, has had a history not only of what has happened to him but, even more important, of what he has done about it, how he has coped with happenings and circumstances and what he is doing now. What he has done about it has shaped his personality and his to-day's coping. It determines how effective or ineffective he is in the face of a new problem. But there are other factors that determine this, too. They are factors inherent in the intensity or size of the problem he encounters; in the support he can get from other persons and surrounding circumstances; and in the presence or absence in his environment of coping means and resources.

It has seemed to me that as one attempts in each case to find, not just what factors combine to make the problem, but also what factors combine to impede the person's own usual problem-solving work—one puts a fairly sure and quick finger on what the caseworker must do—what he must put in—to start the client's own stalled motor going again. To extend this figure of speech a bit, I'd say that our diagnosis question is not "what is this car made up of?" but rather, "why can't it negotiate this stretch of the road?"

But before I get too mechanized or theoretical, let me quickly turn back to human beings again and especially the human beings in whom your professional interest lies; the parents and families of children who are mentally defective. All of them have certain problems in common—and your literature has set these forth with eloquence. In general, it is like this:

Parenthood is a consuming role. It involves a person's deepest feelings, his fullest powers of understanding and planning. It involves interaction in relation to the other parent, to each individual child in the family and to the children as a group. Beyond this, being a parent involves not only what goes on privately between him and his child and his partner-parent, but also involves public—that is, societal—expectations, too. In our child-centered society there are fairly clearly defined cultural norms for what a parent and child are supposed to be like and act like at given times. Every parent is aware that behind the eyes of every person who looks at him and his child is an image or group of ideas as to what is to be expected. His mother, mother-in-law, neighbors, his child's teachers, playmates, even the corner grocer, all expect and make judgements about the attitudes and behaviors he and his child show commensurate with their age, their economic status, and so on. Taking on the role of a parent, in short, means undertaking certain expected behavior and feelings that show in the outside world along with spontaneous or self-directed changes in one's internal and personal life.

To take on the role of a parent is one thing. To become, or find one's self, the parent of a deviant child is something else. To normal parenting is added a number of additional burdens and from it is subtracted a number of gratifications. For reasons that you know so well, they need scarcely be mentioned, the parent of the defective child is affected in every part of his being. Old feelings of inferiority which every one of us trails with him in some degree from his past, rise up to prove themselves; old feelings of guilt, combined with new ones freshly created by his moments of rejection; even hate for his burden. Moreover, he and his child are the cynosure of all eyes. He sees in those eyes the emphatic pity of those who love him, the patronizing pity—or even disgust—of those who are strangers. He is burdened with physical care and child-tending long after parents of normal children have been released. He is realistically worried about what his child can look forward to; what sort of a social and economic future can be hoped for. What he is supposed to do, how he is supposed to act in relation to the child's best interest become problematic questions because he does not know norms nor even trust his natural feelings. After all, this is not a normal child or a natural situation. In short, into the role of this parent has been placed an extra load of emotional, social action-taking problems.

These are the common burdens of parents with defective or retarded children. Yet, as you know, the responses parents make to these common problems are different. All such parents do not need the same degree or even the kind of casework help. This is what diagnosis should design: differential treatment.

This question then must be answered: "Why is *this* person at *this* time unable to cope with *this* problem on his own?"

I believe there are three major reasons for such incapacity. Identifying which one is predominant in a given situation will provide a quick way of giving "first aid" of a psychological or material nature.

A person is unable to handle his problem on his own when there are:

1. Deficiencies or absence of the personal or environmental means and resources which are necessary in order to deal with the problem.
2. Disturbances in the emotional balance of the person which affect his motivation and capacity to think or act appropriately in relation to the problem.
3. Disruptions and misunderstandings of role interactions relationships between the person and the others who are involved in the problem.

These three categories of obstacles to coping are not mutually exclusive. Any one case at any one time may involve all three of these major causes for the parent's needing casework help. Yet in any case, one of them will be predominant. Our identification of which of these is *foremost* helps to identify the area of treatment concentration. Each of these reasons for a person's inability to cope needs further elaboration.

Deficiencies or absence of the means and resources for problem-solving may be of several sorts. They may be lack of actual, tangible things or services that the family itself cannot be expected to provide, that must be developed and supported by some part of the community. Or they may consist of lacks in the parent himself—physical and intellectual or cultural—that affect his ability to cope. Or there may be simple lack of knowledge in an otherwise adequate person. A person who does not know the facts of the problem he is trying to cope with simply doesn't know where to begin or end. A person who does not know the implications of those facts; what they mean, what they predict, what action they call for; will struggle futilely in the dark.

Probably nowhere more than in the area of the mentally defective child have so many parents known so little about the facts and implications of mental deficiency. Fortunately, the courageous work of many parents and of professional workers over the past decade or so has brought this subject out of the hushed, dark closet where it had been locked in for many years. It has become respectable to know about and talk about it. Nevertheless, there remain large numbers of parents of defective children who simply do not have the information or understanding on which to base their attempts to handle themselves or the child. I am not talking now about parents who do not *want* to know, those who have defensively thrust out of their eyes and ears any truths that have been proffered them. I am talking about those who have not been told by doctors what the trouble is, or who have been led to believe that the child will somehow, someday "catch up." (The term "retarded" itself carries that implication—it means held back, slowed up, but the promise of potential catching up is there.)

Then there are parents who have been given conflicting professional opinions; their doctor says the child has a very low IQ but an article in the *Reader's Digest* says that feeble-mindedness is due to glandular deficiencies and that certain experimental diets and medicines can cure all that. It is not unusual for parents to find a charlatan who will exploit that hope.

Perhaps one of the most important kinds of help a caseworker can give to the parents of a defective child is to learn from them exactly *what they know and understand* about the child's condition.

What the doctor has told them does not always carry the necessary implications with it. How do they interpret what he has said? What does it mean to them? What do they anticipate and expect? Then, if indeed a deficiency of knowledge is found to be basic to their faulty or futile efforts to cope with the problem, the supplying of necessary facts and their implications in the context of an emotionally supportive casework relationship is the first step towards re-establishing parental planning and action that is appropriate and productive. "In the context of an emotionally supportive casework relationship" is a vital clause here. It makes the difference between hearing facts and being able to take them in.

A secondary sort of deficiency that may make for difficulty in parental grasp and grappling with the problems of his mentally defective child is deficiency of intellectual or physical capacity in the parent, or a social deficiency which, for want of a better term, we may call "cultural poverty." If the parent himself is dull, one may find several responses. On the one hand he may not recognize his child's difficulty so readily, or be so readily threatened by it. But by the same token, he may not be able to use the means to help and bring out the child's best potentials either. In another parent, the lack of physical stamina—a mother's chronic illness, for example —may complicate and make most difficult the kind of body and clothing care and physical supervision that the defective child often needs for an extended time. The tensions of a psychological nature that rise to complicate such physical stress and debility are obvious. In instances such as these no amount of "talking out" or "talking over" these stresses can take the place of social work's provision of some part-time relief of the mother through auxiliary care arrangements for the child, or some household aid for the mother.

As for the deficiencies or emptinesses in people's lives caused by cultural impoverishment, we are only beginning to take account of what part these play in personal helplessness. Social workers have long known the economically poor. But our knowledgeable grasp of the social intelligence implications of economic deprivation that has been accompanied by long-time social, educational, and cultural poverty is only just developing. This cultural impoverishment shows itself in deficiences or absence of the means of communication—of reading, of talking together, of "talking out" in place of "acting out," of finding self-expression through various forms of sublimation. When these modes of self-expression and communication have been missing in the person's life development, his adaptive and creative capacities are dwarfed. This stunting or limiting of mental powers is increasingly coming to our attention in these children who are dubbed "dull" as they enter school, whose IQ's are low in standard tests but who, on examination, are found to have had none of the experiences with crayons and paper and picture books and words with which the middle class child is inevitably equipped. These may validly be called "retarded" children. Circumstances, not constitutional deficiencies, have held them back. Their parents are themselves suffering from these cultural deficiencies, from mental undernourishment. When this is diagnosed as a major reason for the parents' inability to cope with helping their retarded child, casework treatment will then require the most patient, laborious efforts to help these parents to say what they mean, to give them the words to talk with, to find with them and for them some ways—group association is one—to fill in their lives, and thence that of their child.

It is this group of economically and culturally deprived parents who bring most sharply to attention another kind of deficiency that hampers problem-solving. This is the deficiency of actual resources, means, opportunities which are needed but often missing in the community.

A parent may have fully digested the nature of his child's difficulty. He may be ready to take the necessary steps by which to mitigate it: institutionalization, a special school or special classes. But a community might offer none of these, or so few that they might as well be non-existent. Or the problem-mitigation (perhaps in these instances "solution" is too happy a word) might lie in some relief to the mother of constant care of the child—a few hours a week when she can put down her cross and be released from her constant supervision of the child. But such opportunities are often not available. This kind of deficiency—of resources—is too well known to you to need further comment.

The casework treatment implications are also well known. After the caseworker has fine-combed a community for the desired resource and not found it, he can sometimes invent it for an individual case. More often, he cannot because it takes concerted action, money, and planning to develop resources. But it remains the caseworker's responsibility to observe, record, and to convey to those whose function it is to plan and develop resources his appraisal of the crying needs-to-be-met. He may join in discussions with other social workers and/or with other professions interested in the same problem. His testimony as to deficiencies of community provisions as he encounters them case by case is the nucleus for communal planning and pilot projects.

Now to the second major category of reasons why people cannot cope unaided with their problems: the disturbances of emotional balance. When our emotions run high and intense, our ego capacity to see straight, and from there to act appropriately, is undermined. Among parents of defective children—and particularly at the times the caseworker is likely to be seeing them, when they are often facing up to the enormity and irreversibility of their problems—there is almost always high emotional upset or chronic conflict and depression about the problem.

I suppose that part of the daily meditation of every social worker who works with parents ought to be the exercise of putting himself imaginatively into the parental shoes. The birth of a wanted child is heralded by parents and a circle of relatives and friends as a major miracle. Parents glow with pride as if to say "Look at this remarkable thing I have done!"—and our culture supports this tremendously vital emotional spinal column we call self-esteem. Day-dreams begin early in mothers and fathers about what this new edition of themselves is going to be and to do, and even in the best of parents these dreams are tied not simply to how this tiny body and soul will fulfill itself, but how such fulfillment will add to parental stature and esteem. So one simply cannot underestimate the blow to such self-esteem when the child one has produced is in some way defective, in some way abnormal.

Thus, there is probably no situation of a parent and defective child where feelings about self and child, now and future, are not in high play. (Indeed, if there is no emotional reaction to such deviance something is radically wrong with the parental responses.) Such feelings will take different surface forms—Some parents will tuck them under a facade of frozen composure, some will turn them into the opposite of what they are, denying rejection of the child, recognizing only goodness is him; a few will be free to experience their swings of love and hate. But whatever form they take, high feelings or chronic emotional distress blur the clear and steady perception of the problem. This is how it is that so many parents do not see the defiance in their baby that everyone around them has long seen. When one does not see clearly, one cannot act appropriately. This is why so many parents wait for years before facing up to the child's backwardness or, in other instances, why they push and force and train the child beyond its tolerance.

The diagnostic question here is whether the emotional disturbance we see seems to be realistically called for and appropriate to the situation in which the parents find themselves embroiled. Or, does it seem to be excessive to the situation, to be an extension and intensification of long established emotional difficulties that have long hampered and obstructed the person's ability to cope effectively? In the first instance the caseworker's job is relatively easy with a hopeful outcome. That is to say, the outcome of casework help would be expected to be a lessening of acute distress through working over of the feelings that the problem creates, through supported thinking and planning, through compromises arrived at within the self in relation to the child, through the awareness of and acceptance of the child's limitations and of the means that have been devised to bring him to his fullest development. When I say this treatment job is "relatively easy" I mean that it is the kind of job we are professionally prepared and able to do in all sorts of cases: to help people in the various ways we know to release and then reconsider their feelings and to get hold of themselves in relation to the temporary breakdown in their functioning.

If, on the other hand, your exploration of the parent's feelings reveals that the disturbances of feeling and action in the parents are characterological, long established personality or character patterns, there is a more difficult task and a less hopeful outcome. These may be instances where the parents may need (if they can use) psychiatric as well as casework help. Or there may be instances where casework goals may need to be narrowly limited, where we may need to be satisfied with small readjustments of parental behavior in relation to the child. In such cases, we may need to plan on recurrent contacts with the parents at every point of change in the child's life.

Thus—and in much too brief summary—if one of the reasons for the parent's inability to cope lies heavily in disturbances of emotional balance, the caseworker's treatment focus must be upon releasing, relieving and reworking the feelings which obstruct or distort parental behavior. Short-term treatment may be anticipated when the feelings are appropriate and engendered by the child's condition and situation, or by the crisis of suddenly facing up to these. Long-term help and realistically limited goals may be anticipated when the emotional disturbances of the parents are seen to be chronic.

The third major group of reasons I have suggested for a person's inability to cope with his problems are the disruptions, conflicts, and uncertainties that are involved in carrying an unfamiliar role. Such disruptions and uncertainties may be those within the person's own interpretation of his role, or they may be the result of the interpretation and behavior of the other people involved in role interaction. That is to say, when a person is not sure or is in conflict about what a role requires of him and what his expectations can be of the other person who is in reciprocal action with him, the result is likely to be either conflict or confusion. This is what is involved in many marital and parent-child difficulties—that the persons involved have vague or cross-purpose ideas of what each one is supposed or expected to be and do in relation to the other. Feelings about unfulfilled expectations on both sides, then, rise high and complicate even further the interaction between the people involved.

I do not know that it would be correct to say that there is a special "role" of parent-of-mentally-defective-child. But I am sure that the usual expectations invested in parent-child interactions with all of the expected changes that occur as the child grows older are made different in many ways by mental deficiency in the child. And I am sure that at the crucial point where a parent faces up to the fact that his child is a deviate he experiences a great floundering about as to what he is going to be expected to be and do. He is going to have to learn what is involved in this different parent role. He is going to have to hold on to and revise his spontaneous acts and feelings and expectations. And then, since every role includes others

—the child himself, the other parent, other family members—they are all going to be involved in making the mental, physical, and emotional readjustments of their expectations of one another's actions and attitudes. Deviation creates dislocations, and unless there are agreements among family members as to what they are supposed to act like and be and expect in relation to their handicapped member, considerable confusion and conflict ensues.

There are, as you know, a number of "role-books" in print today that specify what expectations may be held of a normal child at given ages, and what the expectations are for parental interaction with him. We do not usually think of them as role prescriptions. We call them Dr. So and So's Baby Book, or The First Five Years of Life, or You and Your Child, and so on. They spell out what expectations of child development and behavior are supposed to be and what parental behavior is supposed to be in turn. Parents study these, and discuss them, and read dilutions of them in newspaper columns and try to apply them, and worry if their applications don't work. (If we live in a conformist society perhaps it is because from the moment of birth out, childhood behavior is shaped and judged by these ubiquitous systems of norms!)

Now, there has not been, until perhaps very recently, a "role-book" for the mentally defective child. Indeed, each such child needs to be examined for his own particular deviance. But the dilemma for his parents is that they are not sure about what they ought to expect of the child and of themselves. Or they may have very different ideas about this, one from the other, and pull and tug at one another and the child because of being misinformed and unsure about what they are supposed to do or not do, what the child is supposed to do or not. Neighbors and relatives are often full of advice about what's right and what's wrong about the child's behavior or the parental reactions. To be a mother to a defective child in a family of normal children requires that a different pattern of behavior and expectations be developed, and this requires high adaptability! Oh, of course, one would hope that mother-love and nurture would flow equally to every child in the family—although realistically we know this is more fable than fact. But the mother role involves more than affectional and physical nurture. It involves socialization too. And socialization—the teaching of expected behaviors—becomes very different with a deviate child.

A deviate family member can seriously upset a family's usual role relationships. For example, certain unspoken expectations hold about the defective child and his interaction with members of his family. And there are conflicts inherent in them. It is accepted, for example, that defectiveness is not the child's own fault. Yet there are parents and siblings who will at times hold him responsible for doing more than he can do, for responding further than he can respond. It is expected, since he is handicapped, that others in his family group will be tolerant and kind in the light of his defect. Yet an opposing expectation holds too: that he will not by his acts or even presence interfere with the normal life of the other children in the family. And so on.

What I am suggesting is that parents and a total family may be caught up in crises of conflict and turmoil because deviance disrupts usual taken-for-granted role relationships and often requires consciously managed modes of behavior. Conscious management that is effective and satisfying to several participants depends on clear ideas of what expectations of demand and reward can actually be. Conflicts or confusions about these in one family member or among several may create family disturbances. Certainly it undermines the capacity to cope with the deviant child's problems.

Thus, the third diagnostic grouping that explains why people cannot cope on their own, involves confusion and ambiguities inherent in unaccustomed or unaccepted roles.

Its treatment implications are that the caseworker must focus upon finding out and then discussing the ideas and expectations that family members bring to their interaction with the deviant member and in relation to one another about the deviant child. (By "family members" I mean those persons in the closest and most immediate relationship with the child.) This discussion, needless to say, would have to involve all the feelings that these expectations rouse and create. Behavior that is due, not to unconscious needs, but to not knowing "what to expect" may often yield and change in response to tempered, supportive clarifications with a caseworker. Role problems that are based upon conscious confusions may readily yield to a therapeutic-educational approach. If, on the other hand, we automatically assume that discord and conflict among family members always rises from intrapsychic needs, we undertake to deal with a far more formidable treatment problem. It is true, of course, that many expectations about roles rise out of our deep psychological needs. But it is also true that many arise and operate at a pre-conscious and conscious level. These are subject to conscious, rational reconsideration and change.

How can we know which is which? How can we know whether conflicts between and among family members are derivatives of long-running personality needs or are the products of faulty perceptions and misconceptions? Only by opening up the conflict for discussion and examination with the persons involved. That is the only way we can tell, too, whether the confusions or clashes are subject to change through conscious consideration of them promoted both by the caseworker's nurturing relationship and his more objective perceptions. This examination of "what it costs *him*"—these considerations, freighted with emotion, subject to degree of modification by release of feelings and discussion and compromise—is actually the content of "family diagnosis" and in large part is an assessment of the familial interactions involved in some problematic role. In your cases it is, typically, the role of parent-of-deviate-child.

In sum, what I have suggested here is that diagnosis for social casework treatment is rarely a simple thing. Without careful focus a caseworker may become so involved in "studying" and "diagnosing" and "understanding" that he substitutes viewing for doing. Particularly when circumstances decree that casework help must be given within narrow limits of time, there is the necessity to focus one's diagnostic thinking as sharply and pertinently as possible. The focus I have suggested is that of examining why the client's own usual problem-solving efforts have failed him at this time and in this particular situation. The underlying assumption here is that most people deal with their problems (with greater and lesser success) throughout their lifetimes; that if we can identify what obstruction or difficulties they now encounter, we may have a cogent entry point for help to them. By this diagnostic question we may find our immediate focus for treatment—to reinforce, to restore, or refashion the client's own problem-solving operations.

I have suggested that within this focus there are three major groupings of reasons for difficulty in coping with problems:

1.   Deficiencies of external means, or of knowledge, or of physical or mental capacities in the parents.

2.   Disturbances of emotion and undermining of capacity due to acute stress of the problem or to chronic internal stress.

3.   Conflicts and discrepancies in person-to-person interaction that are roused by the peculiar requirements and expectations of the problematic role which the person has undertaken or in our cases, has had thrust upon him.

These major reasons for inability to cope with a problem often overlap. I offer them as a way of possibly systematizing—and thereby hopefully simplifying—our diagnostic thinking-for-action. Hopefully then, we may be able to give quicker and more effective first aid treatment.

The question of why the person's own usual coping means have broken down, or are proving inadequate to the problem at hand, seems to me to have several further points to commend it. One is that it asks not "What are all the areas of problem and trouble I see?" but "What are those most closely associated with the immediate problem for which he needs help?" Secondly, and perhaps more important: it sets our sights in a certain way. It assumes that the client before us is there not because he's hopeless and helpless. It assumes that he is not at a complete standstill, waiting for an injection called "casework." Rather, it assumes that now, as in his past, he is trying to cope, to deal with, to master his problem. He is doing it unsuccessfully at this point. But his motor is still running, and it is to this running motor that casework treatment must attach.

FORTY-EIGHT

Counseling with Parents of Retarded Children Living at Home

SYLVIA SCHILD

In the light of the emergent philosophy and prevailing practice of encouraging home care of mentally retarded children, a re-examination of the casework counseling technique with parents is indicated. Until recent years, social workers in the field of mental retardation were primarily located in institutions and the focus of casework with families was usually geared around the problems of placement planning. With the advent of special clinics for early diagnosis and evaluation of retarded children, attention shifted to parental feelings and reactions and to ways of counseling parents more satisfactorily. The need for a sympathetic, supportive approach to the parents has been well established with the recognition that the impact of the retarded child is deeply disturbing to the ego-functioning of the parent.[1] The importance of having as complete a knowledge and evaluation of the child's problem as possible has been accepted as a necessary counterpart to being able to provide a meaningful explanation to the parents of the child's difficulty and to give consideration to the parental questions and emotional involvements related to having a retarded child.[2]

Social workers in specialized clinics and social agencies are now dealing not only with the areas of diagnosis and placement, but with the complex task of helping the family and child live together more comfortably in the home. The purpose of providing maximum benefit to the child needs to be interlocked with minimal stress to total parental needs and family functioning. Both the child and the family are faced with making adequate adjustments to and in the community in which they live. Unless these ends are achieved, maintenance of the child in the home serves little purpose.

Professional workers, in supporting a philosophy of home care for retarded children, must be keenly aware of the responsibility to know how to help families achieve this goal with maximum ease. This paper proposes to examine some aspects of counseling with parents of retarded children living at home that are characteristic of the problem and that may lead to a better understanding of how to work

Reprinted with permission of the author and the National Association of Social Workers from *Social Work,* Vol. 9, No. 1 (January, 1964), pp. 86-91.

with these families. These observations are drawn from experience in counseling with families receiving services in the Child Development Clinic at the Children's Hospital of Los Angeles. The clinic is a diagnostic and counseling center primarily for retarded children less than age 6. The observations thus are related to the early adjustment of the preschool child and his family, although they may be generic to the problems of the older retardate as well.

Ambivalence of Parents' Feelings

Enormous ambivalence of feeling is evoked in a parent when he learns that his child is retarded. Feelings of rejection, dejection, and disappointment collide with anxious hopefulness, doubt, anger, and self-pity. Strong emotions of guilt mix with protective parental reactions; resentment, confusion, and insecurity become pervasive. It is this ambivalence that characterizes initial work with families of retarded children. These conflicting emotions are never completely resolved, as the long-term aspect of the problem and the repeated crises that stem directly from the fact of the child's handicap stir up the ambivalence from time to time. To help the parent, it is necessary to ferret out the positive aspects of the ambivalence and help him to build on these so as to find some answers to the problem immediately at hand. Thus, ambivalence is dealt with in relation to the immediate crisis situation on a reality basis and by focusing on the areas that are conducive to meeting the needs of the family. The following cases illustrates this point:

> A young couple had just heard the diagnosis of retardation for the first time. In the hostile tirade the mother loosed on the social worker, she vehemently denied that this catastrophe could be true, attacked the doctors, blamed herself. Toward the end of the outburst, she cried out, "Nothing I ever do is perfect. How will I ever be able to raise this child?" In this plea for help the social worker recognized the mother's immediate fear and denial of the diagnosis as resulting from her shaken confidence in being able to successfully handle her mothering role with the defective child. The positive aspect of the ambivalence, underlying the fear of inadequacy, was her intense desire to be a good mother. This was an area that could be worked with realistically in counseling, since she was indeed performing successfully in her mothering role with her two older children. The husband's support to his wife was encouraged. With help and attitudinal change, this mother was enabled to depend again on her own inner strengths and resources in coping with the child; this in turn paved the way toward better understanding of the child's limitations and freed her to work on other aspects of the problem.

A factor accounting for sustained ambivalence toward a retarded child is that the parents are deprived of the opportunity to project any blame for the problem onto the child himself. It is too difficult in any rational way to blame the child for his own defect. This differs from situations in which, when social pathology exists and becomes reflected in disturbed parent-child relationships (for example, in emotional disturbance and delinquency), the parent realistically is able to hold the child partially responsible for a share of the problem. This serves to alleviate some parental guilt and lowers resistance to accepting help. In the area of mental retardation the self-accusatory parent, who feels that he alone is in some way accountable for his child's limitations, is very well known.

It is an accepted fact that part of the resistance of the person seeking help stems from his feeling of responsibility for the problem. When guilt is intensified, the resistance to help will be proportionately increased. Because of this, those endeavoring to help parents of retarded children must be aware that heightened resistance is usually due to the inwardly projected guilt of the parent. In counseling, this guilt needs to be alleviated and an emphatic understanding of the problem area imparted to lower the parent's resistance, freeing him to benefit from the offered help. Most parents hope to hear an authoritative and sympathetic endorsement of themselves, of their human and parental competence, and of their right to blame themselves for what has happened.[3]

One way of ameliorating the guilt of parents is to counsel them together in joint interviews. This helps to focus on the mutuality of feelings and responsibility shared by each parent and aids to shift away from individual parents the assumption of self-blame for the problem. The joint interview technique often may help to restore the marital balance around the mutual concern for the child so that the parents are better able to mobilize all their strengths to handle crisis situations.[4] Although mothers are generally entrusted with the major care of the child, management is a joint responsibility of both parents. Too often the father's role and share of responsibility are overlooked, especially when it is the mother who assumes the task of taking the child for his medical care and transmitting the medical information and advice to her husband. Joint interviewing frequently serves as a device to engage the father actively and to give due consideration to his concerns and attitudes, as well as to those of his wife. Counseling parents together is supportive and enables them to concentrate their energies, not as much on the fruitless searching for why this has happened to them, but more productively on how they can better perform in their parental roles in order to benefit their child.

Changes Required of Parents

The hard reality that needs to be faced is that with the presence of a retarded child the family is no longer the same and it cannot be reconstructed as it was before the arrival and impact of the defective child. Perhaps the area of greatest difficulty that needs to be resolved in the counseling process is the changes required on the part of the parents to meet the special needs of the retarded child. These often conflict with parental functioning that heretofore was considered satisfactory.

Often the management of the retarded child is perceived by the parents as being no different from their performance with their normal offspring. Counseling needs to be directed toward helping parents to see that their attitudes and feelings relative to mental retardation per se have indeed shifted their own parental behavior.

> One mother complained constantly of her child's temper tantrums. The disturbance the child was creating was upsetting to the entire household and the mother felt at her wit's end. The parents were beginning to feel that to keep the child in the home was almost impossible. The mother stated she was handling the problem behavior exactly as she had in the past coped with similar behavior in an older child.
> Closer examination revealed that in reality the mother, caught up in her disappointment and her attitude that a mentally retarded child was totally worthless, considered the

child not worth bothering to discipline. Also, the father was unsupportive, leaving all discipline to his wife. Hence, the mother responded to the tantrums with anger and helplessness, and was permitting herself to be manipulated by the child. The youngster, having no external controls put on his behavior, became increasingly infantile and difficult. This gave validation to the low value placed on him by his mother.

When the mother gained some insight and understanding that she was reacting differently to this child than to her normal offspring, she began to cope with the problem. Her self-esteem increased with her more effective management of the child. In addition, the father was helped to participate more meaningfully in the child's discipline, thereby giving his wife emotional support. As the child's behavior improved, the parents acquired a new appreciation of him. This in turn helped them to evaluate better the considerable potential latent in their mildly retarded son and to enjoy a more favorable relationship with him in the home situation.

The resistance and ambivalence of the parents in counseling are amplified also by the nature of the new stresses encountered merely by virtue of being the parent of a retarded child. The problem of keeping the retarded child at home is determined by a number of factors, such as sibling relationships, social status, family attitudes, the degree of deficiency in the child, and so on. These are all potential problem areas and the ability with which problems that might arise in these areas are handled and solved vary from family to family, situation to situation.

The new stresses arising from the presence of the family of a retarded child are not pathological as such, but should be viewed as a normal complement of problems for the situation that may affect the parent-child relationship and to which adjustments need to be made. When a pathological situation (i.e., divorce) is imposed on a family and is disruptive to family functioning, the focus in counseling must be directed toward the realistic problems that occur as a result of the pathology.[5] It has been pointed out that the presence of a retarded child in the home is often a precipitating factor in individual or family maladjustment or breakdown.[6] The family that is able to adjust satisfactorily to the impact on it of a retarded child has also to deal adequately with the many normal problems that occur in relation to the situation. Their attitudes, feelings, care and management of the child, and the like must all be taken into account.

These normal problems attending the presence of a retarded child in the home must be dealt with on a reality basis to permit the best possible solutions to be effected. Some of these problems are met often in other handicapping conditions of childhood: the increased dependence of the child on the parent, confusion and lack of finiteness in medical diagnosis, crumbling of parental aspirations for the child, rehabilitation and training problems, and the like. However, there are some conditions that occur uniquely in the case of the mentally retarded child and his parents.

One solution, which is culturally sanctioned, is often freely available to parents of the severely and moderately retarded. This is the opportunity to relinquish responsibility for care of the child to an institution if, considering the degree of his intellectual impairment, the child is eligible. Granted that placement holds the parents to a modicum of responsibility and is indeed an appropriate solution in many situations, there still is a need for recognition that this alternative presents conflict for the parents and may impair efforts to effect a successful adjustment in the home. From the time that parents are told that their child is eligible for institutionalization the ambivalence about the child and the problem increases. Again, this ambivalence needs to be handled in counseling, with the focus geared to the positive aspects inherent in the successful fulfillment of parental roles and responsibilities.

Counseling Should Be Spaced

One difficulty occurring in counseling with parents is that the resistance of the parent is sometimes insidiously supported by the behavior of the child himself. The parents may move well initially in shifting to more positive attitudes and methods of handling the child only to be thwarted by the slow movement of the child in responding to improved parental functioning. Although intellectually the parents can relate the slow pace to the child's mental limitations, they often become frustrated emotionally and can react by feeling that the counseling is unproductive. This can cause reversion to easier, more familiar patterns of behavior. The counselor, too, can become uneasy and impatient by the slow pace of the child's response and may fail to support the parents' efforts adequately or project blame on the parents for failure to utilize the counseling.

The most immediate help, consequently, occurs when the parents are having critical emotional distress and help can be directed toward easing their personal difficulty rather than being geared to change in the child himself. Casework for this latter goal, which is focused around the management and behavior of the child, can perhaps be best provided when spread out over proper and widely spaced intervals to give the child an opportunity to react and develop at his own speed.

A review of the reactions of forty parents to diagnosis and counseling emphasized that the parents needed time to take in the extent of their problem and solutions needed to be worked out step by step. Also, parental questions did not arise in an organized, crystallized fashion but gradually, as the child grew.[7] When the element of time is taken into consideration and work with the family is structured over appropriate intervals, the parents are able to bring into counseling some growth on the part of the child that might not otherwise have been apparent if counseling around the child had been sustained on an intensive basis. In other words, parents need intensive casework help at times of crisis situations but, in addition, they need a continued contact. The latter can be less intensive and made available to them over a longer period of time. Such counseling should be properly spaced and educationally focused, to help the parents with the practical problems of daily living with their retarded child. This help is often crucial in determining if the child can live in his own home and in strengthening and sustaining the mental health of the total family unit.

Counseling related to everyday living experiences with the retarded child helps to sustain the parents' motivation to continue in a program designed to improve the child's behavior and to develop his potential. Parents need to deal with concrete situations—the success they achieve in such common daily experiences tends to ameliorate the problems of living with a retarded child. For this kind of approach the caseworker must have a keen knowledge and awareness of normal growth and development. To help the parents understand their child's behavior, it is important to assist them in relating behavior to normal functioning and expectations of children as well as to comprehend the limitations in their own child and its implications.

Summary

In summary, this paper has discussed some aspects of helping parents who have retarded children living at home. The following points were suggested:

1. Professionals counseling parents to keep their retarded child at home assume an additonal responsibility to learn how to help the parents achieve this goal comfortably. This implies not only increased understanding of the problems faced by the parents, but also better awareness and skill in involving and sustaining parents more effectively in the counseling process itself.

2. The key factor to be dealt with in the counseling process is the ever present ambivalence of the parents about their retarded child. Movement toward satisfactory solution of problems is more easily attainable when the positive aspects of the ambivalence are used constructively to meet feelings and to free patterns for changes in attitudes.

3. Guilt feelings of the parents are enhanced by the fact that they cannot rationally project any responsibility of blame for the problem on the child himself. These guilt feelings heighten the resistance to meaningful participation in counseling. Involvement of both parents in joint counseling is one way of alleviating the inwardly directed guilt and of helping parents to focus on more rewarding functioning in their parental roles with the retarded child.

4. The presence of a retarded child changes the structure of existing family relationships. One area of great difficulty is that former parental functioning may prove to be inadequate in meeting the needs of a retarded child. Parents need help in seeing that their attitudes and feelings relevant to mental retardation per se affect their parental behavior.

5. There are many new stresses affecting families of retarded children that should be viewed as normal problems for the situation and that need to be dealt with on a reality level. Some of these, such as the easy access to shifting responsibility of the child through institutionalization and the slow reaction of the retarded child to parental teaching and management, are unique and may hamper counseling efforts.

6. Parents are best helped at times of crisis, but counseling geared to improvement of the child's behavior and to daily living can be structured over spaced intervals planned to compensate for the slow movement and the maturation of the child and to offer sustained support to the parents.

The importance of more and better knowledge about how to help these families has been best expressed by a parent who has written:

The greatest single need of parents of mentally retarded children is constructive professional counseling at various stages in the child's life which will enable the parents to find the answers to their own individual problems to a reasonably satisfactory degree. . . . We need guidance from someone who can help us to see that this thing which has happened to us, even though it may be a *life-shaking* experience, does not of necessity have to be a *life-breaking* one.[8]

References

[1]*See* Helen Beck, "Counseling Parents of Retarded Children," *Children*, Vol. 6, No. 6 (November-December 1959), pp. 225-230; and Alexander Hersh, "Casework with Parents of Retarded Children," *Social Work*, Vol. 6, No. 2 (April 1961), pp. 61-66.

[2]A. Wheeler Mandelbaum, M.D., "The Meaning of the Defective Child to Parents," *Social Casework*, Vol. 41, No. 7 (July 1960), pp. 360-367.

[3]L. Kanner, M.D., "Parents' Feelings about Retarded Children," *American Journal of Mental Deficiency*, Vol. 57 (1953), pp. 375-379.

[4]J. Geist and N. M. Gerber, "Joint Interviewing: A Treatment Technique with Marital Partners," *Social Casework*, Vol. 41, No. 2 (February 1960), pp. 76-83.

[5]H. Pannor and Sylvia Schild, "Impact of Divorce on Children," *Child Welfare*, Vol. 39, No. 2 (February 1960), pp. 6-10.

[6]Robert M. Nadal, "A Counseling Program for Parents of Severely Retarded Preschool Children," *Social Casework*, Vol. 42, No. 2 (February 1961), pp. 78-83.

[7]Charlotte H. Waskowitz, "The Parents of Retarded Children Speak for Themselves," *Pediatrics*, Vol. 54 (1959), p. 319.

[8]Mrs. Max A. Murray, "Needs of Parents of Mentally Retarded Children," *American Journal of Mental Deficiency*, Vol. 63, No. 6 (May 1959), p. 1084.

FORTY-NINE

Counseling Parents of Retarded Children

HELEN L. BECK

In all services directed at helping children, treatment necessarily includes, besides the child, another person who is directly responsible for the child and closely affected by his condition. This person is usually the mother, and though not a patient, is always a client of the agency. This is particularly true in clinics concerned with mental retardation. Treatment of mentally retarded children has to be primarily aimed at reduction of secondary difficulties and improvement in tolerance of the condition and in ability to handle it on the part of the persons carrying responsibility for the child. The problem of retardation is always a family problem, and diagnosis has therefore to be a family diagnosis focused on the total situation. Thus, parent counseling becomes one of the most effective treatment tools.

"Parent counseling" is used here primarily to describe a process of casework treatment, based on diagnostic findings and aimed at ego support and adjustment to reality. It is an enabling and helping process based on the understanding of the dynamics of personality and it uses relationship as a vehicle.

"Diagnosis" as used here will include medical, social, and psychological diagnosis of the child's condition, of the needs of the family as a unit, of the parents' personalities, and of their ability to use available services.

Many of the problems that occur in connection with mental retardation are common to families of handicapped children in general. The parents have to understand the nature and extent of the child's condition, face their own feelings of guilt and rebellion, and learn adequate modes of handling the afflicted child. In such families other children may be neglected and normal life experiences curtailed for either the healthy or the handicapped members, or both. Family breakdown may result from the parents' own withdrawal from normal activities. In the family with a mentally retarded child additional factors of social shame, embarrassment over the child's behavior, and bafflement over the child's uneven capacities, often must be dealt with.

In contrast to other medical conditions, treatment of the retarded child's condi-

From *Children*, Vol. VI, No. 6 (November-December, 1959), pp. 225-230. By permission of the author and The Children's Bureau.

tion rests primarily with the parents rather than with a professional worker, even if the youngster attends school or a day care center. It usually consists of helping the child to achieve optimal development and maximum use of his capacities. To do this effectively parents need help in working through their own feelings and adjustments as well as practical advice in regard to their everyday problems.

Relationship and Timing

Development of a good professional relationship is one of the main prerequisites for successful work with parents. Parents tend to reject painful information that comes from a seemingly uninterested or unfeeling source. If the diagnostic process in the clinic is an unhurried one, parents have time to understand step by step what the clinic personnel are attempting to do, to prepare themselves to accept the diagnosis and a treatment plan, and to develop a workable two-way relationship with the clinic personnel based on trust and respect. Much of the frantic "shopping around" in connection with chronic conditions may be caused by attempts on the part of clinicians to shortcut the diagnostic processes. The team approach in diagnosis gives the parent an opportunity to work through negative feelings that emerge in one or the other contact and to clarify interpretations. "Shopping around" can often be avoided by permitting parents to use the various team members for comparison of opinions.

Parents' previous experience with other facilities have to be dealt with directly at the time of first contact. If the new clinic does not want to be just one of a growing list of clinics in the parents' experience, client and workers must clearly understand the reasons for dissatisfaction with the previous agencies and what the client's present expectations are.

At the Mental Retardation Unit of St. Christopher's Hospital for Children the diagnosis may extend over several weeks. The clinic is staffed by a team representing a variety of professional disciplines. Cases are screened for admission by the pediatrician and most of the team members are involved in the diagnostic work-up. This is terminated by a team conference in which plans are worked out with full consideration of the child's needs, family wishes, and available facilities. The team delegates discussion of such plans with the family and who will have to carry the main responsibility for helping them carry out or modify the suggested plans. This is frequently the social caseworker.

In regard to mental retardation there is sometimes a strange notion that establishing diagnosis is identical with giving treatment. The parents' expectancy and readiness for help is necessarily being aroused during the diagnostic process. If this is not followed up promptly with an actual treatment plan, their readiness to involve themselves in a treatment process may be lost.

The parents' most crucial need for service occurs at the time when they first learn of the diagnosis. It is then that they need support in handling their emotions, help in clearly understanding the diagnosis and its implications, and assistance in planning for their child.

Considerable anxiety is usually aroused by a diagnosis of mental retardation. If this is not handled properly, parents may develop rigid defenses which are not easily amenable to change. A caseworker can help parents set up the kind of defenses that will cushion reality adjustment rather than paralyze functioning. Even the most stable parents have to cope with a certain amount of personality disorganization in reaction to severe stress and shock. Professional casework services at this point work as a "catalyst" for helping parents to recognize their thoughts and reestablish ability to function.

Casework Approach

The parents who come to a mental retardation clinic are as a rule quite aware of the fact that they have a problem. They may, however, deny its nature. Parents should clearly understand the findings of the clinicians in regard to their child's difficulty. However, they need not accept these findings immediately and fully in order to work toward relief of their problem. Diagnosis of mental retardation is not likely to change, and the parents' acceptance may come gradually as a result of treatment.

If a parent persists in calling his child "slow" instead of retarded, the worker may do the same. If the parent continues to express conviction that the child will eventually "catch up," or does not belong in this "terrible" special class, the worker need not contradict him but can patiently help him face the truth. Parents can be helped gradually to see the diagnosis not as a "dead end" verdict, but as a starting point from which to approach much of the problem.

Parents often spend considerable effort in trying to prove to the worker that the child is normal. If they really believed this, they would not continue with the clinic. They often try to push the worker into an argument in order to convince themselves. The worker does well not to be drawn into such an argument. In time the parents draw their own conclusions.

We found most of the parents seen at our clinic very eager to find and use services. Many cooperate far beyond their own need and show good grasp of the value of their contributions to the understanding of the problem. However, as in any clinic setting, some parents withhold information or try to manipulate clinic personnel and time. Such behavior has to be discussed quite directly with the clients and limits should be set.

Service cannot be effective without the full and voluntary participation of parents. The parent who cannot respond to efforts to help him and who continues to try to manipulate the clinic will manipulate treatment goals. Neither he nor the child will in the end profit from treatment. However, the amount of responsibility for initiation and continuation of contact that can and should be put on the client should be determined on the basis of the psychosocial diagnosis rather than on rigidly established clinic procedures.

Through social-casework counseling, parents of retarded children can be helped to develop:

1. Some understanding of the meaning of the term "retarded" as it applies to their child.

2. Understanding of the degree of their child's handicap and what this will mean in the future.

3. Ability to understand their child's assets, his needs, and his difficulties.

4. Appreciation of the effect the presence of a handicapped child has on family life in general, on their other children, and on themselves as parents, and on adjustment of the family within the neighborhood.

5. Understanding of the fact that the child's retardation and his behavior are separate entities and that behavior can be influenced at least to a degree by educational approaches.

6. Ability to judge whether neighborhood reactions are caused by the child's behavior, appearance, or mental ability.

7. Techniques to use such understanding constructively in order to help the handicapped child, the entire family, and the community.

8. Knowledge of available resources relating to their own situation and to the problem of retardation in general.

While needs differ, time for consideration of these areas has to be provided in planning. The "one shot" approach is rarely helpful.

Patterns in Counseling

In spite of the uniqueness of each case, definite patterns emerge that may serve to guide program planning. Contacts fall roughly into four phases: (1) *the initial period*, encompassing the diagnostic process, clarification of the situation and needs, establishment of treatment goals, and selection of treatment methods; (2) *treatment*, consisting of more or less intensive counseling, individually or in groups; (3) *tapering off*, a time when goals being achieved, contact becomes less frequent and is eventually stopped; (4) *followup*, consisting of occasional contact either as needs arise or as children are brought to the clinic for other appointments.

INITIAL PERIOD.

It is neither feasible nor necessary to offer counseling services to all parents who come to a clinic for diagnosis of their child. By the end of the diagnostic period it should be possible to estimate fairly accurately the parents' need for counseling services, their amenability to this type of service, and the feasibility of intermediate as well as long-range goals.

Selection of appropriate treatment methods should be made after consideration of a number of factors:

1. *Ego strength*—the parents' maturity; emotional stability; capacity to accept their roles as parents, as marital partners, as members of their community; their intellectual endowment and the use they make of it.

2. *Family strength*—the quality of interrelationships between the different members of the family, and the kind of emotional and practical support parents can count on from other family members.

3. *Environmental and cultural influences*—the presence or absence of other irritants in the home or in the neighborhood and the influence of cultural and religious factors on the family's acceptance or rejection of the problem.

4. *Degree of handicap* and the parent's understanding of it. It is considerably more difficult for the parents of a moderately retarded child who is physically healthy and attractive to accept the diagnosis than to see him as plain stubborn, lazy, or spoiled. The parent of a severely retarded child with external stigmata is less able to avoid the problem.

TREATMENT GOALS.

In mental retardation, treatment is aimed at increased comfort of all people concerned with a trying situation.

Problems have to be analyzed so that partial solutions can be found as the need arises. Tension and frustration in parent and child may be reduced by cathartic experiences for the parents, and by help with practical problems such as learning ways of handling unacceptable behavior, and planning for school or other types of placement. If problems are met as they occur, many retarded children can live happily within their own family groups and make their contributions to family living, at least during their childhood years. Where placement away from home is indicated, the parents can be helped to see that this has advantages for the handicapped child as well as for the rest of the family.

LEVEL OF TREATMENT.

In general, the level of treatment remains in the area of reality adjustment, ego reintegration, and development of techniques for daily living. Intensity and depth of treatment vary greatly within the range of clinic function. If the parents have prominent personality disturbances or many problems in addition to their child's retardation, they may have to be referred to more appropriate agencies.

TREATMENT TECHNIQUES.

Treatment techniques most often used are clarification, supportive counseling, and environmental reorganization. This does not preclude the use of insight therapy, but where such therapy is of paramount importance, referral becomes necessary. Though the counseling focuses on the problem of mental retardation, parents may be enabled by treatment to translate the help they get for one problem to others as needed. This happened in the case of the A family.

> The A's were referred by their family physician, who was struck by the intensity of the negative parent-child relationships. The oldest child, Tim, retarded because of an organic condition, was extremely hyperactive and lacked concentration. The parents' severity in trying to control his behavior had led to violent negativism on his part. The younger brother, Don, considerably brighter than Tim, got vicarious enjoyment out of teasing his older brother into temper outbursts resulting in actions for which Tim eventually was punished.
>
> During the contact here, explanation as to the organic basis of some of Tim's behavior was given to both parents. They were helped to evaluate their own approach to the chil-

dren, to consider the differences of their children's needs, and to try ways of meeting these needs.

The parents became aware of the teasing of the younger child and of the effect on both children of their own impatience and high standards. They also became aware of their own strained relationships and how these resulted in their undercutting each other's effectiveness with the children. Gradually the whole family situation calmed down. When a new baby was born, both parents were able to avoid many of the mistakes they had made at Don's birth which had created such intense jealousy and difficulties between the boys.

TREATMENT METHODS.

The caseworker may counsel either in individual contact or in groups. It has been hoped that the development of group techniques might prove more economical of the worker's time than individual contacts. This has hardly been the case as far as economics of time and professional efforts are concerned. The economy lies in the fact that the more appropriate treatment is the more effective one.

Individual Counseling

At the St. Christopher's clinic individual counseling has been offered to the parent with highly individualized needs, strong emotional dependency, intense masochism with certain types of passive-aggressive adjustment, or clearly psychotic tendencies. We found such parents poor group risks, since they tend to be disruptive to group processes because of their urgent need for attention, the intensity of their relationships, or their need to act out. In individual contact the worker can adjust the process to the individual and can control the gratification of his particular needs. This was the method used in the B case.

> The B's had accepted the diagnosis of their only child's retardation before coming to the clinic, but they felt strongly resentful of the doctor who had given the diagnosis. They interpreted his statements as meaning that no limits could be set for the boy's behavior. They joined a parents' organization and used the group to project their anxiety about their own problem.
>
> In individual contact, the B's were brought back again and again to their own problem of handling their child's behavior. They were helped to face their misinterpretations of what they had been told. They also came to realize how much they acted out their own discouragement by proving time and again that they were not able to set limits for their child, while other people were able to do so. As it became necessary, the caseworker allowed them to forego discussion of the child and his problem and focus on their general discouragement and disappointment, of which the child was only one factor.
>
> The caseworker saw the parents in separate interviews and helped them work through some of their rivalry in their positions within the family so that a common approach could be established.

Group Counseling

In group counseling we are not concerned with intensive group therapy, but with casework counseling in groups. Goals are: personality reintegration and adjustment to reality. Group processes and teaching methods are combined to afford the individual relief from tension, understanding of children's behavior, and techniques for handling specific problems.

Group processes are helpful to basically mature parents whose functioning is temporarily impaired by the overwhelming nature of their problem; to parents with a tendency toward projection and intellectualization; to parents with pronounced though well-controlled feelings of hostility, who can find relief through limited acting out; and to parents with dependency needs which may be met through group identification and support.

In selecting members for groups at St. Christopher's we have not found it particularly necessary to strive toward homogeneity of social strata, intellectual capacity, personality makeup, or degree of defect in the members' children.

Groups soon develop a homogeneity of their own, the members becoming quite supportive of one another.

The case of Mrs. C. illustrates several of these points.

> Mrs. C. was unable to make effective use of individual contact when it was offered. She covered up her intense feelings of hostility by complete denial and adopted an attitude of submissiveness. In the group she quickly assumed a certain amount of leadership, which the group kept from going beyond bounds. She used the group constructively to gain better understanding of her own problems, to learn from other parents techniques of handling situations, and to get gratification for her need to dominate. After the series of group sessions ended, a second attempt at individual counseling, made at Mrs. C's request, was no more effective than the first. But in another series of group sessions she again used the group experience constructively.

Length of Contact

Length of time necessary to achieve intermediary or long-range goals varies greatly, depending on the kind of emotional or reality problems to be worked out and the complications encountered in the process. Length of contact may be in inverse ratio to the severity of the actual handicap. An obviously severe handicap often allows for clearer diagnosis, less parental resistance, and fewer alternatives. On the other hand, parents of a more salvageable child may be in need of longer periods of service to achieve an acceptance of the retardation and evaluate a variety of possibilities for the child.

At the St. Christopher's clinic cases that receive *short-term services* only fall roughly into three groups.

Group 1 includes parents who during the diagnostic process or previously have learned to understand and accept their problem and are basically able to handle it on their own. Usually only one interview following the diagnostic period is needed to clarify that the clinic stands ready to help them whenever necessary. Such parents use the clinic as need arises.

Group 2 includes parents who are not accessible to continued treatment even if they are in need of it. They either have not accepted the diagnosis or are unable to mobilize themselves sufficiently to involve themselves in treatment. The caseworker alerts other team members to these problems so that the parents may receive some help when they bring the child in for followup visits to the physician or the psychologist and may be referred to the case worker at a later date if feasible. In the interim the caseworker seeks opportunities for casual contact with the parents in the clinics.

Group 3 includes parents already known to community agencies, which usually continue service to the family, often in collaboration with clinic personnel.

Intensive casework treatment over a longer period is offered parents with complex problems either of their own personalities, environmental situations, or difficulties with the child. We have found it most economical and helpful to offer intensive, frequent interviews at the very beginning of the treatment period and then to gradually decrease contacts as parents become able to manage on their own.

Recently we have begun to experiment with a more extensive than intensive approach consisting of a cooperative effort between the public health nurse and the social worker. Two groups of parents have been included in this program: (1) basically stable parents whose problems of child management are caused by the child's severe handicap; (2) immature, anxious parents who have management problems with their children caused at least in part by their own insecurity. No attempts are being made with either group toward too strong involvement in the parents' own problems. Explanations are given for the child's behavior and new approaches to handling are suggested. The public health nurse visits the more immature parents to demonstrate ways of handling the child. It is too early to say how helpful such an approach may be. However, considerable relief of upset has been achieved in a few of the families in this experiment.

All tapering off of long-term treatment should be on a planned basis. Unplanned "fizzling out" devaluates the treatment received and may leave the parents with a feeling of dissatisfaction. As treatment goals are gradually realized, parents themselves usually begin to express a lessened need for contact. Increase in problems and anxiety may occur as wider spacing of interviews begins. If the caseworker permits the parents to set their own pace, the frequency of contacts will decrease.

One advantage of casework at a clinic is that cases can be followed over extended periods of time without maintaining intensive or regular contact. Parents often use scheduled followup visits to the pediatrician, psychologist, or speech pathologist as opportunity to bring the caseworker up to date with their present stage of affairs. The caseworker also may schedule followup interviews at certain stages in the child's life, for example when he is getting ready for a nursery school experience, camp experience, or school placement.

Parents' Organizations

Parents' organizations such as the Association for Retarded Children should be used as a resource in planning with parents of mentally retarded children. These organizations provide such parents with strong emotional support and valuable outlets for the constructive channeling of their anxieties, frustrations, and tensions.

However, referrals to such groups should be made on the basis of diagnostic considerations, and should include preparation of the client and the organization as in
any agency referral.

The timing of such a referral is important. These organizations properly expect
their members to promote understanding of the problem of mental retardation. To
do this effectively and without harm to themselves parents have really to understand and accept the nature of their own problem and they have to be ready to identify with a large group. Otherwise they may use activity in the organization to
avoid facing their own problems and working through their own anxieties and
difficulties. We have found that parents who have joined large organizations of
parents without preparation often accept mental retardation as a community problem, but do not really acknowledge their own problems in relation to their own
mentally retarded child.

Parents who are well prepared for group membership can offer a great deal to
these organizations in their work to spread understanding of the needs of the mentally retarded.

However, this type of activity cannot substitute for the emotional and practical
help needed by parents at crucial points to maintain their own and family stability
in facing the problems presented by the fact of their child's retardation. In offering
such help, the goal of casework counseling, whether to individuals, or groups, is to
help parents achieve their optimum functioning to meet their own responsibility for
the treatment of their child.

FIFTY

Continuing Treatment of Parents with Congenitally Defective Infants

LAWRENCE GOODMAN

The birth of a congenitally defective infant transforms a joyously awaited experience into one of catastrophe and profound psychological threat. The apprehension of failure that is a normal part of the psychic anticipation of parenthood turns into reality—and the family find itself in crisis. A demonstration treatment program sponsored by the New York State Department of Mental Hygiene provided an opportunity to see clinically 140 families in the process of adjusting to the birth of a mongoloid infant. All had sought state institutionalization, although about forty withdrew their applications following casework contact. Families from the regular clinic case load, who never openly considered placement, did not appear to differ greatly in the extent of their disturbance and in their use of counseling. The study population is, therefore, considered to be reasonably representative of families confronting the crisis of a congenitally handicapped child. Selected cases will be presented throughout this paper to illustrate how the offer of help was responded to in terms of each family's adaptation to crisis and their patterns of coping with it.

Initial Parental Reaction

Greta Bibring considers the entire period of gestation as one of strain and enhanced narcissism for the mother. Significant endocrine and general somatic, as well as psychological, changes occur. The pressures continue after delivery and disappear gradually in reciprocity with the child's development.[1] Thus, the natural course of discharge of tension, as the mother responds to her normal child and achieves the emotional satisfaction of experiencing expected maturation milestones with him, is denied the parent of a child with severe birth defect. The heightened emotionality of the father—as a result of his own anxiety and in response to his wife's needs—is also denied its normal release.

Grief, mourning, and planning for the future must be lived through simultane-

Reprinted with permission of the author and the National Association of Social Workers from *Social Work,* Vol. 9, No. 1 (January, 1964), pp. 92-97.

ously and can be overwhelming in their impact. Engel describes "uncomplicated grief" as running a consistent course, modified mainly by the abruptness of the loss and the nature of the preparation for the event.

> It generally includes an initial phase of shock and disbelief—followed by a stage of developing awareness of the loss, characterized by feelings of sadness, guilt, helplessness, etc. Finally there is a prolonged phase of recovery during which the work of mourning is carried on and the trauma of the loss is overcome.[2]

Grief faced by parents of a defective child is much more complex.

Solnit and Stark define the parents' experience as one of loss of the wished-for, expected baby at the same time as the birth of a feared, threatening, anger-provoking child. There is no time for working through the loss of the desired child before there is the demand to invest the new and handicapped child as a love object—attempts to withdraw libido from the lost normal child are disrupted by the demands of the living blighted child.[3]

Parents search within themselves for nonexistent answers to "Why has this happened to me?" "How did it happen?" "What have I done?" Previously worked-out feelings of self-doubt and inadequacy may be reactivated as they view the damaged child as an extension of themselves. It is as though their flawed self-image has taken form and shape and can no longer be concealed. Marital disruption can occur if the child is seen as a symbol of underlying failure in the marriage. Conscious or unconscious death wishes toward the child intensify the anxiety.

This is not to imply that there must inevitably be a pathological reaction. Sorrow and a sense of crisis are natural responses to a tragic experience. During such periods, however, the balance in personality integration usually goes through a phase of disorganization. In helping families at this point of turmoil the social worker faces both an especially difficult challenge and a unique opportunity. As Gerald Caplan points out, during an important life crisis pathogenic sequences can originate or become aggravated but there can also be a sudden acceleration of personality maturation.[4] The necessity for treatment as soon as possible to help the family move toward healthy solutions becomes crucial.

Much has been written about the importance of the initial informing of parents, usually by the physician.[5] In retrospect parents are often critical of the doctor's failure to discuss developmental and prognostic implications frankly and realistically. They frequently report a callous, perfunctory attitude that intensifies their disturbed reaction to the diagnosis. In such instances, the physician may feel a sense of having failed the family and may be attempting to deny his own emotional involvement. While the most thoughtful and sensitive early handling can only mitigate the impact of what has occurred, it can help establish a framework for the family to engage the healthier part of their ego in the first vital stages of crisis response.

The role of the physician takes on a more lasting effect if his desire to rid the family and himself of this symbol of failure results in a premature recommendation that the child be institutionalized. At this time of strain and regression the doctor can be viewed as an omnipotent figure. The family may feel compelled to move toward an emotionally self-destructive decision to place the child before they have the opportunity to face the crisis on a reality level. Even when parents appear to have rejected the child completely, their underlying guilt, denial, and struggle make it imperative for them to have appropriate counseling before determining their course.

There have been attempts to systematize patterns of family crisis response and ways of adapting.[6] Such frames of reference, which can help an understanding of family dynamics immeasurably, are of little immediate use to the physician and social worker who must act at the height of the parents' emotional intensity. Recognizing the existence of a crisis and the normal reactions of grief and sorrow following a calamitous event, the worker must still individualize the family's strengths, weaknesses, and potentials. This includes an assessment of the family's ability to respond to crisis in terms of (1) the damage to the ego caused by having produced a defective child, (2) the almost infinite variations of guilt, (3) facing the prospect of a lifetime of concern for the needs of a handicapped person and continuing emotional reaction to it, (4) capacity to recognize anger, resentment, and intense frustration, and (5) social, economic, ethnic, and possible genetic influences and implications.

Clinic Program

The program of the clinic has utilized individual counseling, group counseling and therapy (for couples), and home counseling. Individual treatment has given parents the opportunity to ventilate emotions freely and to be given support in the expression of hostility and bitterness. They have been accepted as parents of a living child, one worthy of love and attention. The workers have attempted to relate them to specific content for an understanding of mongolism and mental retardation and to face the distortions in their conception of the child so that the decision to institutionalize—if it is followed through—will be reality based. If it becomes clear that deeply pathological response is being dealt with, the goal may be to motivate for intensive psychotherapy. However, this is rarely feasible.

Frequently what appears to be a psychotic reaction may be a transitory phase in parents with borderline personalities. Denial, isolation, projection (including ideas of reference) may be used to an extreme degree. Disowning the child totally, claiming that the nurse has "switched babies," or insisting that everyone is conspiring to mislabel an obviously normal child are not completely uncommon. Yet as such parents are held to reality they can often be helped to re-establish what probably at best have been tenuous controls.

Group counseling has obvious advantages for parents who feel themselves suddenly cut off from the mainstream of the uncomplicated and conventional life around them. They are given the opportunity to meet with other families struggling with the same trauma. In structuring the groups it is, of course, ideal to include one or two couples who are willing, under the direction of the group leader, to help other families incorporate their own healthy solutions. It has also been found of value to set up the groups so that there will be some balance between families who already are moving toward a decision for home care and those who will go ahead with placement. This introduces dynamic conflict, which the leader uses to point out that there is no single solution—that each family must come to terms with its own reality.[7]

Counseling in the Home

The home counseling activity has been a practical response to the needs of part of the patient group. It has been an attempt to cut through the self-destructive pattern of withdrawal and isolation by reaching out aggressively for the client. The mongoloid child can be viewed as an outcast. Through the parents' association with him, which reactivates early feelings of separateness and not belonging, they, too, feel shunned and closed off from the rest of society. In addition, the intensity of the emotional reaction may be so immobilizing that it is not possible for the parents to reach out for desperately needed help. The following shows how home counseling was able to help one family feel the necessity for constructive action.

> Mrs. E is the 34-year-old mother of a 10-month-old mongoloid child. She is an unsophisticated, dependent, somewhat limited woman who has been depressed and partially immobilized since the birth of her son. She is obese and suffers frequent petit mal seizures. Mr. E. is vaguely supportive and passive, one of the few fathers in the project to be involved only minimally. It was with great effort that Mrs. E was able to bring the boy to the clinic for evaluation. She has rarely left the house since his birth and lives a considerable distance from the clinic. The needs of her two normal children were being denied as she became more and more involved with Louis—a low-functioning child with severe somatic involvement, who needed constant supervision. Although placement in this case was clinically indicated, Mrs. E was wavering in her decision.
>
> Weekly interviews in the home were set up with Mrs. E. At home she appeared overburdened and poorly organized, but was warmly affectionate to all the children. With increasing trust in the worker she was able to discuss her ambivalence around placement but as the time for separation approached she regressed further. With much support and encouragement she was able to relate her severe separation anxiety to her own feelings of abandonment as a child when she was hospitalized for epileptic attacks. She could also express her fears that her child's defect was related to her own handicap and that she had failed her husband. With continuing intensive support and bolstering, and with much reiteration of the necessity for placement in this case, Mrs. E was able to follow through.
>
> Home visits continued as Mrs. E was helped to handle her fears that the child was being neglected, that he might go into "shock" from loneliness, that he might die soon, alone. Later there was guilt over feeling relieved of the constant burden of his care. The working-through of grief continued.
>
> With much nurturing from the caseworker, a functioning level of adjustment and independence was re-established. Mrs. E was able to use the worker's support to propel herself toward constructive action in all areas of functioning—for ventilation of feelings of guilt, inadequacy, and separation panic, and for the development of sufficient insight to enable her, after a prolonged crisis period, to face her mongoloid child realistically and free of disabling conflict.

Rejection of Casework

Contact may be rejected completely by those families responding to the situation by immobilization or avoidance. There is an inability to seek clarifying information about the diagnosis or to strive for understanding the social and psychological implications of the condition. There is little examination of feelings of guilt, anxiety, or shame, in spite of the obvious underlying tension. The following cases illustrate this orientation.

> Mr. and Mrs. A are a bright and sophisticated couple who showed frequent hostility and sarcasm during the intake interview. Their 2-month-old child had been in a private infants' home since birth, pending admission to the state school. They made it clear early in the interview that the child will remain there. "We only came to the clinic to hear what you have to say—if you promise us that you can change her physical appearance or raise her intellectual level, we will bring her in for study." Both parents had been informed at birth of the diagnosis and decided immediately, with little awareness about mongolism, not to take the child home.

In this case, the parents were too defensive to permit an expression of feeling other than generalized, displaced hostility to emerge. The future detrimental effect of the unresolved conflict that was being closed out can only be speculated on.

> Mr. and Mrs. B placed their child in a private infants' home as soon as they learned the diagnosis. Everyone has been told that the child is dead, and Mr. and Mrs. B obviously are trying to view her this way. In the course of the interview it was clear that they knew nothing about mongolism and did not care to know anything about it. They seem to have built a defensive wall between themselves and their child in an attempt to preserve their vulnerable intactness.

> Mr. and Mrs. C presented a similar veneer, but as a result of the worker's persistence (and a breaking into awareness of their conflict) agreed to attend a parents' counseling group after their child was placed in the state school. Mr. C assumed a didactic role in the first meeting. In an emotionally detached way he insisted that placement of his child had been right and that the other parents in the group were being misled into considering alternatives. He insisted that he was attending the session to help others now that his problems were solved.

> Mrs. C went along with her husband during the first meeting. In the second session, however, she revealed some of her confusion and despair at having produced a mongoloid infant, which she viewed as a punishment. In the third meeting she broke into anguished weeping, saying, "The way I act is a front. I have tried to keep my feelings on ice because I couldn't bear to look at my suffering, but it's there."

> Mr. C could not risk exposure of his own wavering adjustment and withdrew from the group, but was seen in a few individual sessions to help him restructure his defenses. Mrs. C entered one of the other clinic groups for mothers alone, and has been helped to greatly increased self-awareness and understanding of the dynamics of placement.

Optimal Adjustment

Families at the other extreme, who participate most readily, are those with an awareness of deeply conflicted feeling, a willingness to use their accelerated energy in a search for information and new sources of inner strength, and the ability to focus on the problem.

> Mr. and Mrs. D learned immediately after the birth of their child that he was a mongoloid. Following the strong urging of their obstetrician, who insisted that the child would develop better if he were placed immediately, they planned to arrange for placement as soon as possible. It was only after the intervention of the hospital social worker that they decided to disobey the physician's instructions and see the child. They found him not to be a monster at all, and began to experience a strong attachment toward him. He remained in the hospital for three weeks while the D's investigated placement facilities and, as they put it, tried to regain some perspective in their thinking. None of the private nurseries they visited seemed satisfactory, and it was decided to take the boy home while awaiting state school placement.
>
> The D's accepted the clinic's offer of evaluation and services eagerly and asked many questions about mongoloids—what could be anticipated developmentally, what kinds of educational and social programs were available, and so on. They requested pamphlets and asked the clinic to recommend readings. They were affectionate and relaxed with the child, and during their participation in a parents' counseling group withdrew their application with the state Department of Mental Hygiene.
>
> Pride in their son's progress became possible while their expectations remained realistic. As they have learned to feel more at ease with the boy, friends, relatives, and their two older children have also been able to show warmth and acceptance of him. There is no shame or reticence in discussing him with anyone. They admit to discouragement at times when they contemplate his future, but are obviously able to handle their anxiety. They verbalized their appreciation for the clinic's support and for the opportunity of meeting and sharing the experience with other couples faced with the same problem. They suggested that the clinic could be of further help if it set up supplementary parent education groups to discuss specific problems of management.

In this case what is dealt with are intact and resilient parents who are not likely to be encountered in treatment agencies unless they have produced a handicapped child. Yet even they went through a period of impaired judgment and regression. It is impossible for them now to conceptionalize their willingness to follow the doctor's suggestion and attempt to dissociate themselves completely from their child. Had they followed through, much guilt and self-recrimination obviously would have resulted later.

Summary

Families of congenitally defective infants have had a tragic occurrence fatefully thrust upon them, and a crisis situation suddenly exists. Even parents with a high level of intactness go through an initial phase of regression and disorganization. It is vital that counseling begin as soon as possible so that the family can be helped to mobilize its strengths for combating threat on many levels. The family's self-concept is shaken, social position and mobility are endangered, individual adjustment patterns may be permanently damaged.

The decision to institutionalize without the opportunity to face anger, guilt, and conflict can be particularly destructive. At this time, the family looks primarily to the physician for guidance and direction. Since he, however, cannot be expected to assume the required casework function, the hospital social worker must intervene. In planning programs of continuing treatment the value of home counseling, in situations characterized by withdrawal and avoidance, should not be overlooked. Group counseling, for those able to participate, has obvious and unique advantages for parents of the handicapped.

References

[1]"Some Considerations of the Psychological Processes in Pregnancy," in *Psychoanalytic Study of the Child,* Vol. XIV (New York: International Universities Press, 1959), pp. 113-121.

[2]G. L. Engel, "Is Grief a Disease?" *Psychosomatic Medicine,* Vol. 23, No. 1 (January 1961), pp. 18-22.

[3]A. J. Solnit and M. H. Stark, "Mourning and the Birth of a Defective Child," in *Psychoanalytic Study of the Child,* Vol. XVI (New York: International Universities Press, 1961), pp. 523-537.

[4]"Patterns of the Parental Response to the Crisis of Premature Birth," *Psychiatry,* Vol. 23, No. 4 (September 1960), pp. 365-374.

[5]*See* especially Israel Zwerling, "Initial Counseling of Parents with Mentally Retarded Children," *Journal of Pediatrics,* Vol. 44, No. 4 (April 1954), pp. 469-479; M. J. Giannini and Lawrence Goodman, "Counseling Families During the Crisis Reaction to Mongolism," *American Journal of Mental Deficiency,* Vol. 67, No. 5 (March 1963), pp. 740-747; and Richard Koch, *et al.,* "Attitude Studies of Parents with Mentally Retarded Children," *Pediatrics,* Vol. 23, No. 3 (March 1959), pp. 583-584.

[6]*See* for example, Howard J. Parad and Gerald Caplan, "A Framework for Studying Families in Crisis," *Social Work,* Vol. 5, No. 3 (July 1960), pp. 3-15; and Caplan, "Patterns of the Parental Response to the Crisis of Premature Birth," *op. cit.*

FIFTY-ONE

Group Processes With Parents of Retarded Children

ARTHUR MANDELBAUM*

The Loneliness and Isolation of the Parents of the Retarded Child

A parent who is confronted with the tragedy of having a retarded child suffers deeply, and enters into a period of mourning and grief accompanied by emotional isolation and loneliness. He feels himself in exile and uniquely alien in a world which has turned suddenly cruel and harsh in an unexpected way. Such feelings of loneliness and exile, tinged with vague, obscure and little understood feelings of guilt and shame, tend to lead to silence. This causes further withdrawal from others, a sinking into self and communication is unbearably difficult. Thomas Mann stated that the "experience of a man who lives alone and in silence are both vaguer and more penetrating than those of people in society; his thoughts are heavier, more odd, and touched always with melancholy."[1]

Because of these reactions to tragedy, there is even further isolation. The human spirit, however, with its vast capacities to endure tension and stress, evolves defenses and methods to deal with sorrows. Some of these efforts become valuable parts of our culture and institutions, adding to our humanity and enriching our civilization. An attribute of the human condition is its restlessness, its refusal to be complacent and content with the word. "Content is a word unknown to life; it is also a word unknown to man."[2]

One method parents have evolved to express their discontentment, their wish for creative action, is by joining together in an Association of Parents of Retarded Children, whose purpose is to sustain and strengthen individuals who are dealing with a mutual concern, thus halting the unbearable feelings of being alone and isolated. By joining together, parents not only meet important universal needs but use their collective strengths to help their retarded children. They organize and build Day Class and Training Centers, urge special classes in the school systems, raise money

*The author is indebted to the Topeka Association for Retarded Children for its sponsorship of this project and to the encouragement and support it gave to all participants.
From a paper delivered at the 1967 Annual Meeting of the American Association on Mental Deficiency. By permission of the author.

for research and persuade legislatures to improve state institutions. The helping professions of social work, psychology and psychiatry have been sympathetic and supportive of the group efforts of parents to evolve independent and creative ways of dealing with the problems of the retarded child. These are external methods. But what of the interior life, the inner feelings. The great French physiologist Barnard once said, "the stability of the interior environment is the condition of free life."[3] This maxim, so well recognized for human psychology, must lead us to consider ways of helping troubled parents find a stability and freedom for their inner selves.

One special method of help, which the professional disciplines can offer in addition to such specialized services as evaluation and diagnostic studies, psychiatric treatment, educational and institutional care, is to bring together small groups of parents for the purpose of having a mutual experience of educational, social and emotional benefit to each individual in the group. It is my purpose in this presentation to describe and analyze a series of group processes with parents of retarded children, and draw out of them further knowledge and experience which might be helpful in our work with retarded children and their parents.

My presentation is based on the experience of working with a number of selected groups of parents of retarded children beginning in 1960. The first groups were with mothers and fathers, meeting once a week, for one-and-a-half hours each session, and ran from six to twelve weeks consecutively. Several of the later groups were with mothers only, meeting over a period of several months, with the groups themselves determining how long they needed to continue.

The groups were formed around a common purpose, the concern for the retarded child in the family. The parents applied to join the group, after reading a notice of intent to form such a group in the Newsletter of the Association. Each couple was interviewed in advance to explain the purpose of the group, to evaluate their interest and wish to participate, to get a grasp of the ways they view the problem of the retarded child, and to sense the expectations they might have from such a group experience. The terms of the "contract" were stated, and their thoughts and feelings explored as to whether these terms could be met. They were as follows: to give their time and attend every meeting; to participate by giving their thoughts and feelings; to expect some anxiety and discouragement because not all sessions would be easy and profitable, but their continued presence and efforts would be essential. The worker explained that these sessions would not consist of didactic lectures, but that their thoughts, ideas, feelings, would be the essential content, with his occasional comments and guidance.

The failure to state the terms clearly under which the group process will proceed may often bring it to a halt and lead to its close. The way the worker sets the structure, obeys the time rules (beginning and ending the sessions promptly), and conducts all of the weekly sessions regularly, places an obligation on the individuals against which they may struggle and their doubts and anxieties be discussed and recognized. But if there is no clarity to the structure, and doubts and misgivings are not clarified early, then the worker has no basis on which to help the group evaluate the experience and their concerns about it.

The Purpose of the Group Process

It is the purpose of a group process to assist each member to bring forth concerns, angers, and thoughts so that gradually the strengths of each individual come to the forefront, and these strengths are utilized more creatively and independently around the social and emotional problems with the retarded child. If it is possible for the group, which has a core concern, to express both positive and negative feelings, and to do this with a worker who is critical, hostile, authoritative or judgmental, and whose skillful intervention facilitates communication, then the voyage the group embarks on will be a growth oriented experience for all. As each member gradually expresses his concerns, he gains more knowledge of himself and the others in the group, and there is a greater freedom and spontaneity to express himself.

He learns about feelings in his wife, which he did not know existed, in her or in himself. He learns about the feelings which he thought existed only uniquely in himself, but now he hears and sees others possess as well. He begins the difficult and arduous task of listening to others, their inner selves, and not only his own. He listens to ideas expressed in a continuous evolving process, and experiences how ideas and thoughts slowly dredge downwards until he realizes how little or nothing he knew of the intense feelings which are beneath the surface. He may come to understand some of the sources of his angry feelings, sense their irrational roots, his disillusioned expectations, the failure of intense fantasies. It was the famous psychologist Groddeck who stated, "We have to reckon with what exists, and dreams, daydreams, too, are also facts; if anyone really wants to investigate realities, he cannot do better than to start with such as these. If he neglects them, he will learn little or nothing of the world of life."[4] But perhaps most central to a group process is the opportunity it gives the parent to experience the further resolution of grief and mourning, a resolution which is necessary before the retarded child can be seen with all of the parental capacities for profound understanding. Solnit and Stark state that "coping with the outer reality of a child with a congenital defect and the inner reality of feeling, the loss of a desired normal child requires a great deal of mental work. Such psychic work is slow and emotionally painful, and it proceeds through the gradual and repeated discharge of intense feelings and memories. These mental and emotional reactions enable the parent to recognize and adapt to the reality of the retarded child."[5]

For many parents, still comparatively young, with a major portion of their lives and the lives of their children still ahead of them, the freshness of the trauma of the birth of the retarded child is yet a raw, unhealed wound, vivid and throbbing with pain.

CASE EXAMPLE: FROM A THIRD SESSION WITH A GROUP OF YOUNG MOTHERS.

Mrs. Arnold, in a dramatic way, spoke of a dream which had occurred to her several months prior to the birth of her child. In the dream, she had been holding a baby, and then she climbed up to a balcony and dropped the baby down, and there she saw him on the floor, shattered. There were gasps from the group. Several mothers quickly stated they had premonitions also. Mrs. Benjamin stated that while pregnant, she had seen the TV program "The Defenders" concerning the mercy killing of a Mongoloid baby. She vividly remembers being disturbed and thinking "how dreadful if this would happen to me." Then it did happen. "I was in shock, I couldn't think."

Mrs. Clark spoke of the curious lack of enthusiasm she had inside of her about having a first child; she felt cold about it, did not think about preparations. It was not until the very last minute that she made preparations for buying diapers, a crib; there was no anticipation, no enjoyment.

Mrs. Dennis wondered whether all mothers were not fearful in the same way and had dreadful thoughts about something that might go wrong. This was denied. No, these warnings were strong and particularly strange. There was a great deal of discussion then that some of them had not known soon after the birth of the child that things were wrong. The doctors suspected, but had not shared their knowledge. It was easier for the mother who knew right away. There was no uncertainty then.

Mrs. Clark recalled the neurologist telling her that her son was not only blind, which she had known previously, but that he was also severely retarded and should be placed in an institution. There were again some expressions of shock and momentary silence. Mrs. Ewen told of an experience of her sister-in-law in Washington, where the doctor was impersonal and busy. He threw over his shoulder, as he left the hospital room, "You have a retarded child."

Again, there was a shocked silence. Mrs. Franklin stated softly, "I imagine it must be hard for the doctors also." After some moments of further discussion, *the worker wondered why the group thought it was hard for the doctor to tell them about the retarded child.*

With great intensity, Mrs. Benjamin spoke of the shock, the wish not to see the baby, not to have anyone else see her, the wish to die. Mrs. Arnold recalled how cute she thought her baby looked, "like a Chinese baby." She had not known nor heard of a Mongoloid child. She thought God had given her something special. She said this through tears of irony, bitterness, self-mockery at her naivete. Her husband had not been able to express his feelings. He had gone to the library and looked up the subject, and when his teacher had asked why he had written a term paper on this, did he have a special interest in the subject, her husband denied any special interest. It had not been possible to talk with him about this. She had been desperate for someone to talk with at that time. There was no one. She had not known of the Association or even that other people might have children like this. She shook her head in disbelief.

Mrs. Benjamin spoke of her feelings of not wanting to talk to anyone then. She feared visitors, could not face them. She could not stand pity. That is one thing she could not stand. Her friends came anyway. Now she is glad, looking back at it, she is glad they came.

Mrs. Gould described how her doctor tried to tell her a little every day, warn her. She guessed he was afraid she might not be able to take it. He was a good personal friend. Finally one day she told him, "For goodness sake tell me the truth!" He then told her. Her husband, who already knew, went to the library and brought her home some books. It was the wrong thing to do. Her husband meant well, but the books, some of them, contained the wrong information.

Mrs. Benjamin described how she read also, the sentimental books, the phony ones, but "I did learn a little about the subject."

Mrs. Clark stated, with a shrug, "I was in shock, but I got over it right away." Mrs. Gould laughed at Mrs. Clark in a challenging, anxious, skeptical way. Mrs. Clark stated quickly, "But I did. I realized it was not too bad to have a blind child, because they can do so many things for a blind child. I didn't know then he was also retarded."

Mrs. Dennis stated that for a long time her doctor did not know, "Doctors don't know many things yet."

Mrs. Ewen spoke of not knowing too much about her daughter's condition, but it is her own feelings which keep her from taking her daughter outside. Her daughter is delighted when she goes with her mother shopping; she is so friendly with everyone; but people stare at her daughter for she has an unusually large head and this makes Mrs. Ewen angry. She wants to shout, "If you want to take a look, then take a good hard look." Mrs. Clark spoke bitterly and angrily of an old woman who kept peering into the carriage when she would wheel her son outside. Mrs. Benjamin spoke of taking her son everywhere; she is not ashamed of what other people see or say. Mrs. Ewen stated her feelings were due to her vanity, and then Mrs. Gould spoke of her tears when she had to tell her mother. As she related this, tears appeared, and she recalled how her mother wept. This led into thoughts of how the retarded child cried, and the need to keep a faith in God.

There was a discussion of the fear of having more children, and Mrs. Arnold said that when she sees other couples having healthy babies, she cannot enjoy this; a pain occurs in her; she thinks she is jealous. Mrs. Benjamin stated she is jealous, too. It is wrong to have such feelings. The discussion then turned to parents who have normal children, who complain about them or abuse them; they do not know how lucky they are.

Universal Themes

There are themes universal to all parent groups of retarded children and these emerge with insistent force as the group process begins: feelings of isolation, loneliness, inability to communicate are quickly recalled and expressed. Many parents recall the time it became possible to speak after the initial shock of discovery. Then it seemed there was no one available to listen, at least no one capable of understanding. Professional people could not understand. In one sense, professional people seemed *like* the parents, human, fragile, fearful, lacking the courage to face the problem, to speak about it, to talk to the parents honestly, directly, kindly. *Unlike* the parents, professional people are outsiders and cannot genuinely understand. There is an awareness of angry feelings, wishes that such a tragedy would befall others, outsiders, professional people, *then* they would understand. These feelings, however, are forbidden, dreadful and produce guilt. They must be concealed, controlled, denied. Perhaps these angry feelings, within ourselves (parents) have had magical power, existed a long time and caused damage during conception, or impaired the fetus during pregnancy; or they came out of past acts of an aggressive sinful nature, and for which the parents now suffer retribution. Thoughts come to the fore, that in some ways, not understood, God punishes because of these thoughts; or perhaps the parents are not sinful and God has blessed and rewarded them by creating children who symbolize innocence, purity, and are holy objects. This last is always stated tentatively, with awe of mysterious forces which seem ir-

rational and there is an accompanying bitterness, irony, doubt. The question per-
severes, "What did I do in my lifetime to have had this happen to me?"

Feelings emerge toward the children as grotesque, to be hidden from public view
and concealed from friends and relatives alike. As these feelings unfold, they become attached to feelings of self-esteem and adequacy. A sense of being inwardly
grotesque themselves, fearful of being viewed as tainted, genetically imperfect, contaminated, and inextricably identified with the damaged child, becomes a frequent
theme. The child is a reflection of everything they believe to be imperfect in themselves.

CASE EXAMPLE:

Mrs. Zale described her mother-in-law as boasting of the pure stock in her family.
Before the retarded child was born, her mother-in-law used to boast about the family and
the 14 grandchildren; that there was "not one crooked finger among them." With a
laugh she described how some of her children have the Simian line and blunted fingers.
She guessed there was a little of the Mongoloid in all of her children. After the birth of
the retarded child, her mother-in-law did not go near the retarded child, did not look at
him, did not pick him up. Mrs. Zale angrily spoke of the mother-in-law's comment about
the 14 grandchildren, and not "one crooked finger among them." How angry she had
been with the mother-in-law about these comments, even before giving birth to the damaged child. Afterward, the mother-in-law had wanted them to place the child, and was
disappointed when they took the child back into their home after a period of hospitalization due to a serious illness. Once when the father was going to visit a relative, his mother
urged him to take the normal child along also, so that "they could see you are capable of
having normal children."

As the parents describe the cruelty of others and the outside world, glimpses are
caught of their own severely harsh and punitive views of themselves, modified and
made more benign by the gentle, kind insights and judgement offered by the group.

CASE EXAMPLE:

Mrs. Stephens spoke angrily of taking her daughter Betty to a party. She briefly left
her side, and Betty accused her mother of trying to abandon her. Betty said this in a loud
voice so all could hear her.

Mrs. Jason spoke of her embarrasment when her son had a haircut, and he tried to talk
with the barber in his poor, jumbled speech.

Mrs. Voss described her son running into the living room when they have had company, speaking so excitedly that his speech was incoherent, and then trying to calm him
down, finally sending him to the basement.

Mr. and Mrs. Franklin confessed they never take their daughter anywhere. She was
so obviously a retarded child, and embarrassed them.

Mrs. Stephens spoke of impulses to shout, "She's a retarded child." She has to master
the feeling and control it with all of her effort. There was a shocked, numbed pause.

*I said they all talked about these feelings of embarrassment, uncomfortableness, what
understanding, what thoughts did they have about it.*

Mrs. Franklin said it was a feeling of shame and humiliation. Mr. Voss said it was
also resentment and anger for having such a child. Mrs. Franklin said she felt like hurl-
ing it right back at them, that is, those who look at the child, those who thought she was

different; she wanted to attack them and defend her child. Mrs. Ewing said, "Yes, I want to say to them, 'Well, what are you looking at!' " Mrs. Tingram said, excitedly, "I used to do that, think that, I used to look but now I avert my eyes." Mr. Franklin said, "I do, too. I was guilty of that. Inside you feel inferior, ashamed." Mr. Tingram said they had left their daughter Betty at a party tonight with great apprehension. They have never left her before. "My mind is there while I am talking. The people we leave Betty with, when we come here, are out of town. Betty, talks, talks, talks. It is more important to come here, we have never talked with anyone else before, never even with relatives or friends." Mr. Franklin said, "We come here for the child as well as the parents." Mr. Ewen wondered whether all these feelings we are talking about are not due to the hurt inside. The child does not hurt as much as the parents. Mr. Tingram said, "Yes, this is true, when they look at you, it is because you feel there is something wrong with you, that you should have a retarded child." Mrs. Franklin spoke of knowing a 19-year-old retarded boy whose parents take him everywhere. "Maybe it is our fault, and the child picks up our feelings about him."

As the group enters a period of mutual mourning and solace, themes of loss and the dangers of death alternate with themes of how gentle and lovable retarded children are, and what solace they offer the family. The fears of the children possibly dying are based on serious reality factors, for many have a wide-range of congenital disorders which make their care arduous, and days and nights are filled with apprehension. The members praise each other's children and amidst the positive feelings, slowly dare to venture to speak of their angers, the persistent intrusion of death wishes, and fright over their persistence and intensity. "It's like a death, it's worse, at least you can get over a death, but this is never behind you, it never goes into the past. I will have to live with it the rest of my life."

When the group becomes aware of the intensity of this theme, they move away from it, and there are many expressions of not wanting to see that far ahead, not wanting to look. The group is extraordinarily free from false assurances, and platitudes are quickly challenged or produce silences. The child is living, a reality which cannot be escaped. The future is feared for the child must surely fail then; his faults and defects are magnified by growth. There are wishes the child might remain young, an infantile love object to be cuddled, pampered, and not too much, if anything at all, demanded of him. The converse of this is, that as an infant, quite retarded and slow in development, the child is a burden, tyrannical in the need for attention and care, enslaving in his demands. Each parent fears that the other will be drawn to the child with such force, that all others in the family will be deprived, neglected. Thus angers alternate with guilts in a repetitive cycle. Concern about what to tell families in the community, what to tell relatives and friends, how much to tell the other children in the family, also screen doubts and misgivings about how much to lift the walls of silence between their innermost thoughts in the group. There are frequent expressions of relief about their ability to do so, wonderment that they have been able to talk about things, "I have never been able to tell my husband or best friends." Such expressions, albeit positive, herald further doubts and fears of revealing deeper thoughts, and stand as an opposing force against their pressure to emerge.

So great is the need to protect self-esteem and self-concept, that the group may subtly divide into those whose children are not too damaged and severely retarded versus those who have Mongoloid children, and are obviously retarded and damaged as additionally reflected in their physical appearance. Here again is another genesis for discrimination, for dividing into superior and inferior categories, but this is so flimsy a defense that it hardly suffices to withstand the assault of despairing thoughts.

Strengths of the Group

Defeats are there, yes, for each member of the group, but they believe there are pieces of victory that the outside world, a vast engima, is not equipped to understand. Often, the thought is expressed, "Our children are different, we can shed a tear together. We are alert to, and take pride in, every sign of small improvement in our children. Every step forward, imperceptible in our normal youngsters, is a major triumph in the handicapped child."

The identifications each member of the group forms with the others is intense and binding. Since their children are different and "unique," they are unique also and belong together, sometimes united against the outside world, against the leader of the group, a representative of that outside world.

CASE EXAMPLE:

Mrs. Thomas stated that for two years she wouldn't admit to herself that her child was retarded. She knew of the Association but did not want to come near it. She recalled the first doctor she had seen. She hated him. Mrs. Noon pointed out that perhaps it was because he was the first to tell her about her child's retardation. Mrs. Thomas agreed and thought this was true. The discussion then became heated and intense as they spoke of doctors, how they were told, needing someone to talk with. For the first time, two or three parents were speaking at once. *I raised my voice slightly in order to be heard and I stated that it seemed to me they were saying three important things. The first was the failure of the doctor to help them in the way they wanted at a time when they felt shocked and hurt. The extent of his help had not gone as far as they had expected out of their intense need. Secondly, the doctor by giving them the diagnosis had hurt; thirdly, that they had found consolation in talking with others through the Association; others who had shared the problem with them. Outsiders did not understand and therefore could not help them.*

They agreed to this, with Mr. Peters picking up the point, saying he thought it was very important. *I, then, stated that several times previously I had tried to get into the discussion, and they had been so intent in getting their points made and expressed that I had not been able to get into the discussion, and I wondered whether they were aware of this, and if so, could they understand why.*

Quickly Mr. Peters said, "you are an outsider, too." *I said, "I thought this was important."* Mrs. Thomas, as if emboldened, spoke of the fact that one of the "professionals" in the Association was supposed to attend a meeting of the School Board but was too busy. If he was a parent of a retarded child, he would have gone. Professionals are not invested in the same way as parents. Mrs. Noon stated it had nothing to do with being a professional; even some parents had to be pushed. It was valuable to be in the Association. Mr. Noon said that at the first meeting of the Association he had attended he felt strange and uncomfortable. Would it have not been better to have a small session like we're having tonight? Mrs. Noon enthusiastically agreed. When the group session ended, the group remained outside as I drove away. Mrs. Stephens said, waving goodbye, "You see, we are going to continue outside in the cold."

As the process enters into the hidden labyrinth of these feelings, there is an attempt to find values that are right for them, which will sustain and nourish. The members give support to one another, bring out their feelings to be scrutinized by the group, question irrational ideas, point out the inefficiences and dubious values of certain behavior and gradually raise the level of ability of each individual in the group to look at the realities of the retarded child. The worker must have faith in the inherent ability of individuals in the group to do this, to grope towards integrative, mature ways of viewing behavior, and to release their inherent capacities previously blocked by angers, conflicts, and fantasies. If he does not have the faith in the individuals of the group to accomplish this, he will intervene hastily, become authoritative and didactic, causing his activity to become more that of a lecturer, thus diluting the emotional intensity of the experience.

  CASE EXAMPLE: OF GROUP QUESTIONING AN UNREAL POINT OF VIEW.
Mrs. Clark began the third group hour by reporting a conversation she had had with a practical nurse living on her street. This nurse, to her annoyance, began talking about the fact that it was better to have a retarded child than a handicapped child. The handicapped child would always sense his difference from other children, and be hurt and ashamed of it. The retarded child would never know. This thought had never occurred to her. Mrs. Masson disagreed with this. There were many handicapped children she knew who did marvelous things, and became very skilled adults. But the retarded child would always be that way, their minds were affected and they could not improve beyond a certain point. Mrs. Vass agreed. The nurse was wrong. Retardation was a handicap also, but a more severe one. Retarded children also realized their difference from other children, unless they were very, very badly retarded, and could not recognize anyone. There were nods of agreement from a major number of the group.

  CASE EXAMPLE: ONE GROUP MEMBER MAKES AN IMPORTANT INTERPRETATION
  TO ANOTHER.
Mrs. Ewing began to talk of her child in the institution and how she was being given medication. She was concerned about the child's care there, her poor appearance when she visited, the poor care of the clothing, the guilt she experienced when on one visit she criticized everything in front of the child herself, and the aides. She really had a temper tantrum. Mrs. Ingram said, "I guess when you left the aides must have said, 'thank goodness, that child is living here instead of living at home with that awful kind of mother.' " The whole group laughed, with Mrs. Ewing joining in, and saying this was certainly true.

The Group Process and the Worker

The group process of work with parents is increasingly being used as another of the major tools in clinical practice. The worker who attempts the process must be skilled in dealing with individuals in the one-to-one interview situation, *preferably prior* to his attempts to deal with the group process.

If he should choose to work with groups because he is discontent and disgruntled with the one-to-one method of helping individuals, he takes on a task of greater complexity in which many more variables are present; in which there must be not only an understanding of the dynamics of individual behavior, both normal and sick, but an understanding of the behavior of groups. If the worker should be discontent with the slow, cautious progress of the one-to-one process, he will be disillusioned if he expects to go at a greater pace with groups. For no matter what you will, the worker must have respect *for* and knowledge *of* the repetitive aspects of the mourning and grief process in parents of retarded children, of the adhesive quality of conflict, of the fact that confidence and trust are only won after repeated trial and error, of the fact that each individual in the group must choose his own pace to grow.

As his frame of reference, the worker must have a comprehensive knowledge of personality, growth and development, of parent/child relationships, of family interaction, of the interaction of each member of the group with all the others, and of the nature of the relationship of each individual *and* the group with the worker. He must have a knowledge of the techniques of treatment, how the relationship may be used to cause change and growth. He must know which comments are ego-supportive, which will lead to emotional insights, and when purposeful intervention is necessary.

It is tempting to use the group process to teach about mental retardation, to answer the worried questions of the parents about their children, to discuss at length the reasons for paralyzing, slow development growth. Only too quickly, will listening and observation show that many of the individual members of the group are exceptionally well-read, and, indeed, some have become quite scholarly on various facets of the problem; far more masters of its content than the worker. Rather the worker utilizes, as his frame of reference, his knowledge that sorrows can be borne if you put them into words, or tell a story about them. Sorrows can be absorbed and dissolved if they can be expressed in words to those who suffer somewhat like you, who have the same immediate and inescapable social reality, and who wish to examine that reality as it interacts with their innerselves. The process weaves back-and-forth between the reality as seen and felt by the individual members, and how and what they understand about their world, themselves, and each other.

As this occurs, relationships develop between the members, the worker becomes a representation of the outside world, with a host of feelings directed toward him, tempered by the group, their reality considered, tested and examined. Harsh judgments about oneself, particularly, for angry, destructive wishes toward the retarded child become less severe, and with a growth of confidence, some forbidden thoughts tentatively emerge to be dealt with by the group, with a diminution of depression and anxiety.

The worker guides the group toward the examination of the ways they utilize the process, their fears and resistances towards venturing themselves, their own inherent strengths in eventually grappling with a seemingly insoluble problem, and eventually their ability to catch a glimpse of the truth, no matter how frightening. Each individual in the group protects and risks himself according to his own need, and learns and takes from others. The respect for the emergence of strength symbolized by the attitude of the worker through his patience, through his steadfastness, through his calm certainty, that despite the arduousness of the struggle and pain, growth will occur, moves each member towards an increase of trust and confidence in themselves.

The worker is an outsider of the group, a permanent exile. As the group speaks of professional people not understanding, of treating parents abruptly and harshly, of not helping to the deepest measure of their wishes and expectations, the worker must exercise, to the fullest extent of his disciplined self, control of his angers at being an outsider, of being viewed as helpless to do very much, of being a person who cannot truly understand the feelings of the group because he has not undergone the same tragic experience.

The worker is a screen against which are projected feelings toward all outsiders as critical, uncaring, judgmental, punitive. He is a representative of all parental, authoritative figures, who have failed them, failed to protect them, permitted the irrational and malignant to happen, will not give answers, forces them to think for themselves. He forces them to work, to search out their feelings. "Will no one give us answers to our grief, will no one hear us?" is their silent cry, soon becoming heard more and more in the process. The language of the group is "phatic" to use Malinowski's term. It concerns itself with the commonplace of experience, suddenly and sometimes without warning, slipping into expressiveness or expressions that shock with portending awareness.

"Do you ever get over it, the depression, I mean?"

"I felt that being around friends who were pregnant was like some curse."

"What did I do in my lifetime to have had this happen to me?"

"Sometimes, I wish he would have died at birth, the doctor should have killed him and not told me."

"When I did bring the baby into the store, the clerks all admired her and cooed. I wonder whether they knew she was retarded, and they did that just to please me. Then when I didn't bring the baby they asked about her. I felt guilty wondering whether I had left her at home because I was angry. Maybe the fact is, I'm too sensitive."

The dialogue is sometimes drab, superficially mundane, gropes apparently to convey information, but searches restlessly for contact, for empathy, for an explanation of those outside myths, theories, beliefs, conflicts which might illuminate their lives. In this search, fear is expressed that the worker will view them as damaged, inferior and ill, not see their strengths. Then, of course, how much it is safe to see and understand.

There is anger that the group process means they are to devote their lives, their dreams, their torments only to the retarded child, and neglect others as well as themselves. Are they in bondage? Will the worker let them go? And if members express the full measure of their thoughts, their angers, will they be able to control the emergence of these feelings after they leave the hour, during the times between when they do not have each other for support? And will the worker, as a result of the intensity of their concerns and angers, become overburdened and ill? Is the worker like all other men, in that he becomes preoccupied with his work, too professional, too insensitive, too unobservant as to how they really feel? When there are interruptions in the group process because the worker has to be away, where does he go, and to whom does he give his portentous words of wisdom, which are denied to the group? How shall the group contain him, make him do their bidding, and gain mastery over him, so that he can be of greater gratification?

These and other questions are stated, more or less simply in terms of the retarded child, in terms of family life, and their lives outside the group. But there are incrustated layers of meaning, of deep significance which the group slowly unfolds until drabness and cliche yield to the richness of new insights that their words refer to many things, hitherto undreamed of in their world.

Time and time again, there are surprised expressions concerning their former narrow views, now so utterly changing about other people, members of their families, societal institutions, what needs to be done and some hope as to what and how they may do the tasks ahead of them.

The end of these processes is like the termination of a voyage. The passengers have come together, talked, laughed, cried, struggled to share feelings, struggled to achieve deeper, wider understanding. Now it is the time to say goodbye. During the process a wider circle of social interaction has occurred, and close friendships have been established. There is sadness that the group cannot continue and must disperse, at least in its present form. There is always the fear of letting go of something which has been helpful and of being alone again. Each group, however, is surrounded by the larger structure of the Parents Association for Retarded Children, and within that institutional arrangement there are goals to be formulated, further social tasks which will require the finest group efforts. For the time of the group process, each individual focused on himself and on others in a series of interactions in which he both gained and lost something of his exclusive preoccupation and self-interest, and turned inward and outward towards others. "The more inward we are, the more we may undertake outward activities; the less inward, the more we should refrain from doing good."[6]

This easier trespass between inner and outer, between thought and action expressed in the process, teaches that no individual needs to feel loneliness or isolation again to the same extent as in the past. If the group process has gone well, each individual experiences a combination of knowledge fused with empathy, and when this happens, there is a new feeling of harmony and peace of the inner self. Surely this is at one and the same time a modest and momentous goal.

References

EISELEY, LOREN. *The Immense Journey.* Time, Incorporated, 1962.

FALCK, HANS S. "The use of Groups in the Practice of Social Work," *Social Casework,* February, 1963.

HUXLEY, ALDOUS. *The Devils of Loudun.* Harper and Brothers, 1953.

MANN, THOMAS. *"Death in Venice," The Thomas Mann Reader.* Alfred A. Knopf, 1950.

JARRELL, RANDALL. *A Sad Heart at the Supermarket.* Atheneum, 1962.

SOLNIT, ALBERT J. and STARK, MARY H. "Mourning and the Birth of a Defective Child," *The Psychoanalytic Study of the Child,* Vol. 16, 1962. International Universities Press.

Notes

[1]Mann, Thomas. *Death in Venice.*
[2]Eiseley, Loren. *The Immense Journey,* p. 31.
[3]*Ibid.,* p. 30.
[4]Jarrel, Randall. *A Sad Heart at the Supermarket,* p. 211.
[5]Solnit and Stark. "Mourning and the Birth of a Defective Child," *Psychoanalytic Study of the Child,* Vol. 16, p. 533.
[6]Huxley, Aldous. *The Devils of Loudun,* p. 87.

FIFTY-TWO

A Women's Club for Deprived Mothers

JUNE L. TRIPLETT

The interrelated problems of familial retardations and poverty are familiar to public health nurses everywhere. Nurses, social workers, and others have tried to help these deprived people, but have often met with failure and frustration. Public health nurses who are interested in working more effectively with such families might gain some clues from a longitudinal study known as the Pine School Project.

This project was designed to study children with endogenous or familial mental retardation and their families. Provisions were made to record the effects of altering the environment in a variety of ways in an attempt to counteract the environmental deprivation thought to be a part of their poor functioning. Each child accepted for the study met the following criteria: (1) came from a family of lower socio-economic class; (2) had at least one sibling or parent who was mentally retarded; (3) had an IQ between 50 and 80 on the Stanford Binet Test; (4) had no known or presumed "organic" cause for the mental retardation; and (5) was between the ages of three and six on admission to Pine School.

The school program was planned to alter the environment of these children by providing more stimulation and social experiences than they usually received in their own homes, thus preparing them more effectively for public school experience. At the same time the preschool children were attending Pine School, the multidiscipline team, including a pediatrician, social worker, public health nurse, special educator, psychologist, and home economist collected data and gave direct service, in accordance with their respective skills to the families.

The Mothers' Group Is Begun

At the end of the second year, a tremendous amount of data were collected, and the potential of a multidiscipline approach had been demonstrated. The project staff continued to offer a variety of services to these families. Only one of these will be described here—the group work with the mothers of children enrolled in Pine School. Several staff members had described these women as lonely and socially iso-

Reprinted, with permission, from *Nursing Outlook,* Vol. 13 (January, 1965), pp. 33-36.

lated. This observation led to the formation of a "women's club" which has met approximately twice each month for over five years. Meetings are held in the various homes, with another club member assisting with refreshments.

During the first two years of the project, the home economist worked with each hostess before the meeting to help her plan for the occasion. Very few households had sufficient cups of coffee, or silverware and plates, if needed, for dessert. Chairs frequently needed to be borrowed, also. One woman, whose home was almost unbelievably dirty and inadequate, asked if she could be the last one to entertain the group. With the assistance of the home economist, this woman then painted her living room walls and made curtains for the bedroom windows. The women had many ideas as to what they wanted to learn at the meetings, and a small portion of each meeting is still devoted to a formal presentation or activity.

The topics selected suggested a desire for more knowledge about homemaking skills, ranging from planning low cost meals to home beautification. The mothers also wanted to know more about child rearing practices. The actual topics or activities selected depended, in part, on the professional staff assisting with the project— their own interests and abilities. The home economist had primary responsibility, during the two years she was employed, with the public health nurse assisting in some activities. Later, the public health nurse had the help of the county extension worker who emphasized family nutrition and the use of surplus foods. For the past two years, the public health nurse has used the group meetings as a learning experience for students in public health nursing. Programs presented by the students have included a series of meetings on first aid, weight control, normal growth and development, and a few craft activities, such as making simple newspaper bags, painting weeds or the cups from egg cartons.

Effectiveness of Group Approach

Unfortunately, change had not been measured and there are no data which can be used to demonstrate the effectiveness of this group approach in helping multiproblem families. There have been changes, however, which at least give some clues to how this approach might be studied more scientifically. To describe these changes, it is necessary to first describe some of the common characteristics of these women as they appeared early in the project. These might be categorized as: (1) poor concept of self; (2) lack of skills; (3) loneliness; (4) lack of concern for others; and (5) a desire to improve.

The first characteristic, poor concept of self, was demonstrated early in the project by their consistently poor grooming and inappropriate selection of clothing. Three of the women had many open sores on their arms and legs which were self-inflicted. Although several women talked about wanting to lose weight, none of them took meaningful action. Lack of confidence made it difficult, if not impossible, for them to shop in department stores. Perhaps the best illustration of this lack of confidence was an observation made at the first meeting. They were to paint weeds for winter bouquets, but none of the women could proceed without asking: "Is this the way you want me to do it?" "Does this color go all right with this one?" "Will this look okay in my living room?" Their lack of self-confidence was closely related to the second characteristic, their lack of skills.

Many of them came from broken homes, foster homes, or institutional backgrounds. They did not know how to welcome guests to their homes nor even how to respond to common courtesies. For example, in leaving one home, the staff members thanked the hostess for the nice time and, in each instance, she replied: "Yes." Only a few of the women knew how to do simple mending or had the equipment in their homes to do it. Housekeeping skills were often negligible, and one woman needed help in using the recipe books she had. Washing clothes was made more difficult because they tended to wash and rinse too many clothes in too little water, or because of insufficient hot water and equipment.

As mentioned earlier, the women were essentially lonely. Few of the families attended church or sent their children to Sunday school. They did not attend PTA meetings or community functions, nor did they do much visiting, other than with relatives. They were suspicious and fearful of professional workers in the community.

The fourth characteristic, lack of concern for others, was demonstrated in many ways. Most of the families depended on used clothing from welfare and church groups. They tended to hoard these clothes in large boxes whether or not they fit any member of the family. When clothing was brought to a meeting, they tended to grab as much as they could—without considering the needs of others. It was rare, at first, to hear one woman offer to help another, and this was even more obvious when it involved transportation to the meetings. Although staff members furnished transportation early in the project, a few of the women did drive. They never thought to offer a ride to a neighbor, but would do so if asked by a staff member.

The fifth common characteristic, wanting to improve, can best be illustrated by describing some of the observed changes.

Observed Changes

There has been a marked improvement in grooming in most of the women, evidencing more pride in their appearance, even though several women are without teeth or dentures, or have badly decayed teeth which detracts from their appearance. There is talk at the meetings of hair styling and of giving each other home permanents. Two of the women lost from 20 to 30 pounds of weight in one year, and others have cut down on waist, bust, and hip measurements, even though actual weight loss has been minimal. One of these women remarked, "I feel better, now that I'm losing weight. I know I'm not pretty, but I *feel* prettier, and that's what counts." The other woman commented that her husband has begun to "notice me again since I lost weight." A specific example of an increase in self-confidence was first noticed about two years after the weed painting incident. The women were painting the cups from egg cartons to make Christmas decorations. No one in the group asked how the staff wanted it done, or which colors to use. Instead, they were holding things up to admire them, and get praise for what they had accomplished.

Knowledge and skill have also increased demonstrably. Some of the women learned to do some sewing early in the project, and others have expressed a need for similar classes. They use a wider variety of foods and have a good working knowledge of normal nutrition. Their attention span has increased considerably, and they are becoming more adept to discussion. Early attempts to discuss less tangible subjects such as discipline were unsuccessful, but now most of the women freely express their feelings, beliefs, and questions about child-rearing practices. However, they still want concrete facts or suggestions, rather than principles.

With more self-confidence, knowledge, and skills, several things have happened which have alleviated some of the loneliness and demonstrated an increasing concern for others. Almost all of the women now bring the used clothing which they cannot use. Some women now look out for the needs of others as they sort clothing, and they have even found ways of controlling one member who continues to grab more than her share. There is planning within the group for transportation to meetings, and there are times when the staff do not have to provide transportation for any of them.

Several people have brought guests to the meetings, and, within the group, there is a great deal more socializing between meetings. Four years after the group began, they asked if they could "do something for the poor people at the county home." They made all arrangements with the personnel at the home, furnished the cookies, helped with the hostessing and, apparently, gained a great deal of satisfaction from this venture. This past year, there has been more evidence of reaching out to become a part of the community. Several women have expressed an interest in attending—and possibly joining—the local association for retarded children. Two women are helping to form a new women's group in a low-income housing area on the edge of the city. With major changes imminent in the Pine School project, the women are giving thought as to how they can continue their group when they no longer have the nucleus of Pine School. Very few of the women can express, directly, what it has meant to them to be a part of the project or even the mother's group. The intangible gains must be inferred from changes in behavior and from their concern that their friends have similar opportunities.

Results of the Project

Not only have the families benefited from participation in the Pine School project, but the staff have learned a great deal as well. This knowledge needs to be applied to other groups to determine the validity of the approach. Some of the generalizations which need closer study are the following:

1. Women from low income groups tend not to participate in organized community activities, but will attend functions at which they feel comfortable.

2. Not only do these women have emotional problems which interfere with their effectiveness, but many lack the necessary knowledge and skills to be good homemakers.

3. Most women will need help with becoming group members—listening, staying on the subject, and allowing all members to be heard.

4. The women will demand specific answers to problems, rather than working from principles and generalizations.

5. Considerable adaptation of content may be necessary to make it useful to families of limited circumstances.

6. The amount and rate of change will vary from one woman to another, but it will be slow, with both setbacks and plateaus observable.

7. Since, to some of these people, life is a series of crises, many of them will need individual services from a variety of disciplines, in addition to the group experiences.

Just what, in all of this, are the implications for public health nurses? There aren't many such "ready-made" groups available with which the nurse can assist. It might be possible, however, to invite a few women with common problems to meet over a cup of coffee and talk with the nurse. As they talk informally, the nurse can learn a great deal about their values, concerns, and strengths, gradually adapt her teaching, and select meaningful ways of motivating these people toward more positive health. With this knowledge, the public health nurse could help bridge the communication gap which exists between families in the lower social classes and the middle class community.

An incident which occurred early in the life of the Pine School project can best illustrate this gap. The teacher at Pine School showed the children a picture and asked them to tell a story about it. The picture showed a well-dressed woman with a book in her hand, and two children in pajamas sitting beneath a floor lamp. The children were unable to respond to this picture, and the teacher was mystified. The observer watching this incident later explained the reason. The Pine School children did not wear pajamas and were not familiar with them; most of them did not have floor lamps, but depended on an overhead droplight; there were no books in most homes, and none of the children was accustomed to having stories read to them at bedtime!

There are many such gaps which, in themselves, seem almost insignificant, but, nonetheless, make the children from culturally deprived families stand out as "different." The differences are perpetuated by lack of understanding and poor communication between the social classes and the professional people who serve both groups. If this cycle is to be broken, new approaches to old problems must be found. The Pine School project has demonstrated a multidiscipline group, using a variety of methods, can effect positive changes in a limited number of multi-problem families.

It is proposed that public health nurses, working in conjunction with other disciplines in a community, could work more effectively with similar families by strengthening *existing* nursing services to them and by adding group experiences for the socially isolated family members. Such an approach will not eliminate the familiar frustrations, but it will provide increased opportunities for achieving satisfactions which come from contributing to more positive physical and emotional health.

References

McCANDLESS, B. R. *Children and Adolescents.* New York, Holt, Rinehart and Winston, 1961, pp. 449-485.

PARSONS, MABEL H. Home economist in service to families with mental retardation. *Children* 7:184-189, Sept.-Oct. 1960.

ROLL, M. H. A study of retarded young children. In *Social Work Practice, 1962.* Selected papers from the 89th annual forum of the National Conference on Social Welfare, New York, May 27-June 1, 1962. New York, Columbia University Press, 1962, pp. 146-157.

SCHOLZ, B. W. Medicine in the slums. *Clin-Proc. Child. Hosp.* (Wash.) 18:345-353, Dec. 1962.

WARNER, W. L., AND OTHERS. *Social Class in America.* Gloucester, Mass., Peter Smith, 1957.

FIFTY-THREE

Siblings of the Retarded: A Guided Group Experience

MEYER SCHREIBER AND MARY FEELEY

In the course of providing group work services to retarded children during the past decade, the staff of the Association for the Help of Retarded Children in New York became impressed by the frequent references made by parents to problems these children created for their normal adolescent brothers and sisters, and vice versa. Parents expressed concern, for example, over the normal child's feelings of being overburdened by the care of the retarded sibling, of his overt expressions of hostility and resentment toward the retarded sibling, of responsibility for the retardation, of obligation to make up to the parents for what the mentally retarded brother or sister could not give them, and of guilt for being the normal child.

At the same time, the staff became impressed by the large number of normal adolescents who were taking their retarded brothers or sisters to social group meetings and to special events, and by other indications these young people gave of being able to cope with the fact of their sibling's retardation. Many of them obviously had been able to work out their feelings about their retarded brothers or sisters with no major intrapsychic, interpersonal, or intrafamilial strains, by developing healthy defenses and using compensatory mechanisms.

Thus with evidence both of need and strength in the normal adolescent siblings of retarded children, the staff began considering what the agency could do to include such young people in its total efforts to strengthen family life in the families of retarded children.

Consequently, with agreement from the appropriate lay committee, composed in part of parents of the retarded and the agency's board of directors, the decision was made to establish a demonstration program of guided group discussion for selected normal adolescents, through which they could examine, clarify, and understand more clearly a dynamic aspect of their life situation—their role as siblings of a retarded child. The experience in such a group, it was anticipated, would help these young people to become more effective and assured in their intrafamily relationships and responsibilities, and so would enrich the total family life.

Reprinted from *Children*, Vol. XII, No. 6 (November-December, 1965), pp. 221-229. By permission of the authors and The Children's Bureau.

More specifically, the aims of the demonstration were delineated as:

1. To assist the individual and the group to identify the nature of their reactions to having a mentally retarded brother or sister—stress, strain, mixtures of affection and antagonism—and the effects of these reactions upon their relationships with their parents, brothers and sisters, peers, and their entire life situation.

2. To help the individual and the group to examine and to clarify strategies for understanding and dealing with their siblings, their parents and peers, and the problems of daily living related to their status as the brother or sister of a retarded child—strategies which would be helpful not only to them but also to others in similar circumstances.

3. To throw light upon the extent to which the concern and reactions of such adolescents represent strength as well as intrapsychic, interpersonal, and intrafamilial strains, and to determine whether their defenses are similar to or different from those of adolescents with no retarded siblings.

Since expressions of interest in the program came from all parts of the city, it was decided to conduct the group sessions at the association's office, which was centrally located. To qualify for admission to the group, an adolescent had to be between 13 and 17 years of age, and be willing to participate in the group sessions every 2 weeks to discuss his problems and feelings in relation to his retarded brother or sister and his life situation.

Twenty-eight adolescents met this criteria. Obstacles to attendance, such as the day, time, and travel involved, reduced the number selected to participate to 10. Twenty other young people were interviewed by staff members and helped to see why they could not be included in the group. These included several who were "pushed" by domineering parents to apply because "this is good for you," others whose parents expected the group to provide a therapeutic experience, and a few whose needs were basically social. For many of these young people, the group experience might have been too anxiety-provoking or otherwise inappropriate. Unfortunately, shortage of staff members prevented followup of those who seemed in need of individual counseling.

The 10 young people who formed the group included 5 boys and 5 girls, mostly from lower middle-class backgrounds. The age spread was from 14 through 17, with the boys generally 1 to 2 years younger than the girls. Six of the participants were in junior high school and four in high school. Judging from their own comments about school, seven could be considered above average in academic ability and three as average students; and seven were involved in extracurricular activities at school. All participants indicated a real desire to participate in this new experience.

All the retarded siblings of these young people were living at home. Some were mildly, some moderately, and some severely retarded. Half were younger and half older than the normal brother or sister.

The Group Process

The group, which its members called the Brother-Sister Group, met every 2

weeks from October 1962 through May 1963, under the leadership of a professional group worker. The first session was devoted to a consideration of the voluntary
nature of the group and what the group hoped to accomplish. The adolescents
agreed on their own accord to come regularly, and to share their problems and experiences in order to help not only each other but also other teenagers in similar
circumstances.

At the end of each session the group agreed upon the focus of the next. In the beginning, the group worker took an active role in suggesting possible subjects for
discussion, and such as "How do you tell your friends about your retarded brother
or sister?" However, as the members became better acquainted and more comfortable with each other and the worker, they began to bring up spontaneously the concerns they wanted to talk about. These included such questions as: "Does the fact
that our family has a retarded member lessen our chances of marriage?" "How can
we deal with the feelings we get when our friends show us pictures of their brothers
and sisters and brag about their accomplishments?"

The participants offered little resistance to telling the group about their experiences with their brothers and sisters, families, and friends.

The worker helped the group look at different aspects of the material under discussion, adding information as needed, or raising questions and suggesting alternative courses of individual and group action. The worker also dealt with problems
of individual needs and intragroup relationships. At the same time, she helped the
group hold to its aims and special function. She filled a variety of "roles"—confidant, leader, counselor, resource person, agency representative, and even parent—
as the situation demanded and the group progressed.

By the fifth session a cohesive group had emerged, held together by a common
bond and meaningful relationships between the members and between members
and group worker. From that point on, the group was largely self-directed, taking
major responsibility for the content of the meetings and for individual participation. The group worker became largely a resource person, who provided clarification of points, support for individual participants, and information to indicate alternative courses of action.

Each session lasted an hour and a half, and included a period of light refreshments provided by the agency. At the end of each, the worker summarized the progress made, emphasizing the positive, the constructive, and the realistic aspects. She
encouraged the members to share their findings with parents, other normal siblings
in the family, and friends; and to feed back significant reactions from them to the
group. Such reporting back was frequent.

The group usually stuck with an issue until it reached a termination point.
Completion of a subject of discussion sometimes took as many as three sessions.
The group worker's attitude of constant acceptance provided a safe climate for the
expression of concern and the ventilation of feelings whether these were of hostility,
hate, or love. The participants also found support and recognition of the right to be
different from their peers. They learned a method of analyzing life situations which
was not only appropriate to the current scene but which could be used in dealing

with future problems as well. Attendance at sessions over the 8-month period averaged 92 percent.

Concerns and Feelings

What were some of the common problems which emerged? The following list was prepared by members and group worker together. The illustrative material comes from the group records.

1. How do you tell your friends about your retarded brother or sister, especially friends of the opposite sex?

> At this point, Bonnie turned to Susan and said, "Should I ask the question?" Both girls giggled, and Susan encouraged Bonnie to ask it. The question was: "How do you tell a boy that you have a retarded sister?"
>
> Mark responded immediately by telling about his experience in telling a girl about his sister. The girls listened attentively, but then Susan said, "It's different telling someone that you really care about."
>
> Susan is "going steady" and she hopes Stanley will never find out about her retarded sister, Gail. Could she tell why? She feels ashamed and embarrassed.
>
> Kenneth said he knows how Susan feels, but he has been trying to help himself by asking whether he would be ashamed if his sister had no arm or no leg. He said knowing about this should have no effect on a person who had nothing to do with it, and if the boy really cares about you, this won't change him.
>
> Kenneth told us that a few weeks ago a girl asked about his sister and he did not tell the exact truth. He felt ashamed about the way he acted and made up his mind to tell the truth the next time he saw this girl, but he just couldn't get himself to do it. He knows that it was wrong but he couldn't help himself.

2. How do you deal with your parents who have not discussed the problems of mental retardation in the family and their implications for you?

3. How do you deal with friends and people in school when you are hurt by their talk of the retarded as nutty and crazy?

4. Are these meetings really helpful or are we betraying our families' confidences?

5. Are our parents' expectations concerning our role and their role in continued care of our brothers and sisters, real and fair to all involved?

6. What should be our responsibility toward our retarded brother or sister in the event of our parents' deaths?

> Even before the meeting began the teenagers were discussing among themselves the requests made by their parents for the care of the retarded sibling if anything ever happened to the parents. Regina and Diane have promised never to send their retarded siblings to an institution. Bonnie promised to visit her sister Barbara regularly in the institution. She would definitely not care for her if her mother were unable to do so. The other girls laughed at this and told Bonnie that she was "just talking" again, and that she would be the first one to object to having her sister placed in an institution.

7. What are we to do when our parents do not really feel affection for our retarded brother or sister?

8. How can we deal with our feelings when our friends show off their brothers' and sisters' pictures and talk about their accomplishments?

Bonnie broke in here and said:

"It is hard when you hear the other girls boasting how smart their sisters are, and the things they do, and you can't say anything about your sister. In fact, very often I do not admit that I have a sister at all. Some of the girls in school think I am an only child and others want to know if I have a brother or sister since I never talk about mine. . . ."

9. Does retardation in our family lessen our chances of marriage, and is it hereditary?

10. How can our parents help us with our problems?

11. What can you do together with your retarded brother or sister in the home or in the community?

12. How does a teenager really accept a problem that he will face the rest of his life?

13. How can a teenager plan for his adult life?

14. What are our hopes for the future?

At this point Kenneth asked why Susan had such feelings about her sister. He thinks that they should all be very happy that they are living now when so much is being done for retarded children. Years ago people would hide retarded children, and nothing was done for them.

Bonnie said that was easy to say but the fact remained that the situation was hard to face. She says that she has heard all these things before. You are supposed to feel good because the President of the United States, who is very smart, has a retarded sister.

Other feelings expressed by participants in the group were: a feeling of not being loved as much as the retarded child; jealousy, resentment, and hostility toward the retarded child; denial of the severity of the retarded child's condition; and guilt about having negative feelings toward the retarded child. Such feelings, however, were not characteristic of the group, and their intensity in the individuals who held them was often repressed. The worker recognized their significance but did not delve deeper or bring them into focus before the group in view of the anxiety that would be evoked. Rather, she held to the group's educational focus, leaving the resolution of deep and involved feelings as the function of individual therapy.

As part of the group's activity, the worker suggested, after about 18 sessions, that the participants might want to consider ways and means of helping other young people who had a retarded brother or sister. This resulted in a group project, the writing of a pamphelt directed to other teenagers.[1]

Some Observations

Over the 8-month period, the experience with these young people led members of the agency staff to make a number of observations. We present them as hypotheses which need further testing with a larger number of retardates' siblings—young adults as well as adolescents:

ABOUT THE NORMAL ADOLESCENT

1. It was not the degree or kind of retardation in his sibling which seemed to affect the adolescent's life or happiness as much as the way he felt about himself and his retarded brother or sister, and the way in which he learned to live with the fact of having a retarded sibling.

2. What the normal adolescents really needed and wanted was accurate, up-to-date information, in language and concepts which they understood, about mental retardation and what they could do to help their families and their retarded siblings. They wanted to know how to manage *now* and what they could look forward to.

3. The young people's attitudes were not consistent at all times.

4. Almost every adolescent in the group brought up the question: "*Why* did it have to happen in my family, to us, to me?"

> He said the question of "Why did this have to happen to me?" comes to him often. I told him this was a natural question, but said I wondered what it meant in the way of his making friends, or in school. . . . He said that it hadn't meant much up to this point but wondered what would happen when he has to tell a girl about his sister. I pondered that question too. (Kenneth is unable to use the word "retarded.") He said he would just say his sister was different.
> Kenneth mused that everyone has something in their family. One of his friends doesn't have a father—parents are divorced. He can see this as a real problem. I asked him if this friend might also ask himself, "Why did this have to happen to me?" and he admitted that this might be so.

5. The sessions helped the teenagers see some of the strengths, as well as limitations, in their brother's or sister's functioning, and in the family.

6 The importance of good communication and feeling between parents and adolescent depended on the existence of the kind of relationship which encouraged the adolescent to go to his parents whenever he felt the need.

7. The teenagers seemed to be helped by the very fact of knowing that the agency was interested in them as well as in their parents and their retarded siblings.

8. The group worker to be helpful had to look at life as far as possible through the adolescents' eyes, show her care and respect for them, and treat them with dignity and understanding. She had to be careful not to generalize and assume that the problems and feelings of all the siblings of retarded children are the same.

9. The group worker found it important not to underestimate the strength of adolescents or to expect too little of them. It was clear that the young people wanted their parents to involve them in planning for the total family.

ABOUT THE GROUP AND THE GROUP WORKER

1. The experience was appropriate for the adolescents in the group. They were

able to express spontaneous feelings, to invest themselves in the experience, and to extract positive help and strength from their contacts with others who are in similar circumstances. For other adolescents such an experience may be anxiety-provoking to the point that the youngster is not able to handle his feelings appropriately. In some instances, such as when family relationships and parental roles were discussed, an adolescent's group experience carried a potential threat to his parents.

2. The meetings had meaning for the group not only in giving the young people help during a period of hardship, but also in helping them to maintain and build healthy family relationships.

3. The support of others—their peers and the worker—was helpful to these young people.

4. The size of the group was important. Ten members seemed about right for providing good opportunities for exchanging experiences and sharing the worker with each other.

5. Timing the meetings in relation to the many pressures on teenagers—school work, social life, family obligations, and work—was important.

Conclusions

Thus we concluded that this short-term group experience was useful to the teenagers involved. The spread of time helped the young people, at an age when it is difficult to put feelings into words, to open up problems, to delve into certain aspects of relationships, to pull together and integrate what had been accomplished, and to begin to think more realistically about the future.

The sessions did not always contribute to modification or change of basic attitudes, but they enabled the participants to know that others knew and experienced similar problems and that it was all right to feel the way they did. Although their problems and feelings could not always be resolved since some were "bottled up" inside, for the most part these adolescents gradually became able to express their feelings more fully as meetings progressed and to become more realistic in their appraisal of them. This seemed to result in their being better prepared to see the next steps necessary in their planning. As time went on, they seemed to be able to look at the broader implications of mental retardation not only for themselves but for others who also had retarded brothers and sisters.

Many parents of retarded children are panicked into the belief that their retarded child will adversely affect his normal brothers and sisters. However, in some families where the parents have dealt with the situation constructively, such young people have developed greater maturity, tolerance, patience, and responsibility than is common among children of their age. Our experience suggests that the young person with positive family relationships is often capable of enduring the emotional hurt and anxiety of having a retarded sibling without severe disruption of his family and social life. He needs reassurance and support, but more often his primary requirements are educational. The more clearly normal siblings of the mentally retarded can see the realities of their particular situation, the better position they are in to cope with them. This is the point of a group experience.

As the young people wrote in their pamphlet:

> . . . We helped each other. We learned how to "talk" about retardation and felt free to discuss our problems. We helped each other to be better prepared for any unexpected behavior of our brothers and sisters. We knew that we were not alone.[1]

Reference

[1] Brother-Sister Groups, Association for the Help of Retarded Children, New York City Chapter: It's tough to live with your retarded brother or sister. New York. 1964.

FIFTY-FOUR

The Challenging Opportunity for Social Workers in Genetics

SYLVIA SCHILD

New and dramatic advances in technology and knowledge in the field of genetics have produced a recent upsurge of public and professional interest in the field. This interest has been expressed in a demand for expansion of genetic centers to foster further research and to offer genetic counseling services. This trend reflects a reawakened concern with hereditary disorders and other genetic defects as related to family planning, from the personal concern of the affected individual or family to the broader troubling problem of a world confronted with an exploding population. Those best endowed genetically are at premium value in a nuclear-age society that requires higher levels of educational, technical, and scientific achievement and in which the complexities of social adaptation are ever increasing. These societal demands and expectations complicate the problems of those members less fortunately constituted and have helped to foster the growing interest in the application of genetic knowledge through genetic counseling.

Unfortunately much ambiguity has become attached to the practical application of genetic information. Semantic confusion occurs around what is meant by genetic used interchangeably to impart the same or different processes. There has been relatively little analysis of what goes into genetic counseling and what comes out of it. There is fuzziness about goals to be achieved or about understanding of the consequential events that result from the fact of and the kind of specific counseling intervention. Geneticists who are traditionally academicians and researchers rarely have experience or training in dealing with personal and interpersonal relationships of clients. Physicians, while obviously experienced and better prepared for the personal interaction, have expertise in matters of medicine and health and not, generally, in problems of a social or psychological nature. Social workers, who have the professional training to help people in stressful psychosocial situations, have a rare opportunity to provide valued service but as yet have barely tapped the surface in making their potential contributions felt.

Reprinted with permission of the author and the National Association of Social Workers from *Social Work*, Vol. 11, No. 2 (April, 1966), pp. 22-28.

The Population Explosion

Some geneticists have postulated that genetic counseling will one day be applied universally to provide a solution to the population explosion whereby societal sanction will be given to the selection of those of the best genetic strains for childbearing.

Goodman has enunciated well the issues related to the population explosion which must one day be resolved.[1] He has pointed out that answers will need to be found to the quantitative problem stemming from the breakdown of natural selection factors through advancements in medical science and health care, and to the qualitative problem stemming from the increasing number of mutant and abnormal genes in a larger population unchecked by natural selection.

Indeed, there can be little if any dispute about these vital issues. It may well be that moral, ethical, and religious values will need to be reshaped to find workable, rational solutions to the dilemmas of the growth of population. Perhaps, indeed, a eugenic approach may one day be needed to determine selectively who shall be fruitful and who shall not. In terms of our present state of knowledge and empirical evidence, answers to these formidable questions are a long way off. At best, these questions can be acknowledged as important philosophical and practical concerns that must be reckoned with in time in the context of the total evolutionary process of man in his mastery of his biophysical and sociological existence on earth.

Dr. Constantine Doxiadis, noted architect, planner, and the father of ekistics (the science of human settlements), has estimated that, barring war, and even if birth control is decided upon now, by the end of the next century there may be an average of some thirty-five billion people in the population. He has stated:

> By then, because of the limits of the habitat, the rate of increase will be curbed either as it occurs in other animals—by the operation of biological self-controls—or by conscious decisions on birth control, whose nature may not be genetic, but which are social decisions as a part of the overall biological process.[2]

Doxiadis postulates that, since there is no agreement among experts as to whether we should interfere with genetic processes or, if we do, how to do it and what might ensue, for all practical purposes we shall probably be dealing with the same man, genetically speaking, for the next few generations before society will sanction mass intervention in man's genetic forces.

Family Planning

This is not to state unequivocally that nothing can be done now in regard to the population explosion. Certainly efforts to control the population through family planning must be made. However, in its broadest sense, family planning should be viewed as an approach to population control defined in terms of the values of our social structure. The major goal is not on the qualitative genetic improvement of the race. The broad objective is directly related to the needs of the family to control its size so that the family can better provide its members with the benefits of society in all spheres: economically, socially, educationally, physiologically, psychologically. In this sense, man is seeking to modify his environment for his social betterment, and family planning is not dictated by value judgment based on who is genetically best suited to reproduce.

It is not yet possible to define family planning as a broad-based method for resolving the qualitative aspects of the population problem. Knowledge in this area is still too limited. We do not yet have an electromicroscope with powers of resolution great enough to identify the genetic structures of each mating partner, nor the electronic computers that can predict with accuracy the genetic composition of a fertilized cell. It is not yet known if some genetic adaptations or mutations will in time prove to have compensatory advantages for the affected person. For example, it may be that experience will show that a phenylketonuric who is treated from birth will also have an inborn resistance to carcinomatous diseases, so that his genetic defect may provide him with a compensatory benefit relatively greater than the loss of freedom he has in not eating what he likes. How do we know what the treated galactosemic individual will be like as an adult? For all we know, his genetic aberration may be minor compared to a better genetic adaptation to other deleterious influences in the environment of this nuclear age. If such speculation seems very farfetched or facetious, attention should be paid to the fact that the noted Nobel Peace Prize winner in medicine, Dr. Peter Medawar, has pointed out that the aberration causing sickle-cell anemia has also an inborn resistance to malaria, a disease which in our day and age is responsible for an astounding number of deaths yearly.[3]

However, family planning related to the quantitative control of population, based on a nonjudgmental view of genesis of the individual but concerned with helping people and society to resolve health and welfare problems, is of another order.

Genetic Counseling

The point here, perhaps more simply stated, is that it is an error to identify family planning with genetic counseling or to consider them to be synonymous. The latter is one approach in family planning and, while it might be trite, the following truism needs to be stated: *Genetic counseling must be confined to those families who have identifiable or known genetic defects.* Here there is a need to assume value judgments in trying to impose some controls on human reproduction in order to achieve qualitative improvement of the race. Genetic counseling dictates the assumption of cautious and judicious responsibility for family planning within the limits of our present state of knowledge with regard to each specific genetic disorder.

Doctor Medawar has eloquently responded to the fears related to the increase of genetic mutations in the population. In commenting about the well-founded fear of building up in the human population a huge and increasing genetic liability, he has this to say:

I, myself, am not dismayed by this prospect, and I see no very good reason why anybody else should be dismayed. The point is that the rate of genetic deterioration . . . is extremely slow. The unit of the time scale of evolution is a generation, and the order of the length of time one is thinking of when one speaks of genetic deterioration is not tens of years but hundreds of years. During these future years, solutions will be found to cope with these difficulties. If you will forgive my comparing two obviously uncommensurable quantities, the rate of accession of knowledge and so the rate of increase of our power to cope with these difficulties of this kind is enormously greater than the rate of evolutionary change. The point I want to make is that we must not at this time arrogate to ourselves the task of trying to provide solutions for all the problems that may afflict mankind in the future. I think the time will certainly come when our present-day medicine seems to future generations as inept as Galen's seems to us, and we are not yet qualified to prescribe for the medical welfare of our great-grandchildren. In a slogan, I should say that present skills are sufficient for present ills.[4]

The last statement of Doctor Medawar contains a significant implication for social workers: ". . . present skills are sufficient for present ills." The psychosocial problems engendered for families with the diagnosis and identification of genetic disorders are not at all alien to the social work profession. Social work expertise in dealing with the adaptive functioning of individuals and families reacting to stress and in crisis is as applicable to the area of genetic problems as it is in other areas of health and welfare concerns. Nevertheless, although an estimated seven million persons in the United States have visible genetic aberrations, the impact of the new scientific discoveries in the biophysical sciences have not been reflected in social work education or practice.[5]

It is only in recent years, with new discoveries in chromosomal and genetic functions at the molecular level, that attention has been focused on a better definition of genetic counseling. The geneticist has in the past traditionally confined his counseling role to that of supplying risk figures, having little, if any, direct contact with the families. Tips and his co-workers have made a considerable contribution in defining modern genetic counseling as the clinical approach to family problems arising from the genetic implications of disease. They define genetic counseling as:

Clinical procedures whereby the patient with genetic disease is evaluated in terms of his relationships and management in the scope of his family environment. The opportunity for such family units to participate in a therapeutic program, which creates an atmosphere conducive to the exploration of over-all family problems, distinguishes this from the traditional, stereotyped mathematical probability approach.[6]

Genetic counseling, viewed in this context, clearly offers much opportunity for the application of casework services. Supplying the client with genetic information meets only part of his needs. Neser and Sudderth have recently pointed out that the social worker's chief contribution is to individualize the meaning of genetic information for the client, and this differentiates the social worker's task from that of the geneticist.[7] Tips and colleagues in their work have found that a wide spectrum of psychopathology is found in the psychosocial conflicts precipitated in affected families.[8] They report a demonstrated cessation of childbearing among extended family members following the birth and diagnosis of an affected offspring. Multiple emotional stresses frequently occur, leading to the disruption of family stability and to conflicts with extended family members. Furthermore, it has been the experience of these investigators that through "empathetic communication with the family, genetic counseling promotes reasonable acceptance and realistic adjustment plus a measurable effect on reproductive performances of female kindred."[9]

Social Work Role

Doctor Stanley Wright of the School of Medicine of the University of California at Los Angeles visualizes the social worker's role in genetics as discussing the implications of genetic counseling with the family and as assisting in field services to the family, particularly in the unique role of enlisting co-operation for their participation in research activity where little promise for direct service benefit can be made.[10] He states that he is "most impressed that what is called genetic counseling amount to about 5 to 10% genetics, and the remaining time is spent in counseling the parents regarding psychological difficulties, sociological problems, possibilities of adoption, referral to other agencies for additional information, etc."

In fact, there are no new skills in practice to be identified as specific to genetics; there is, of course, the need for acquisition of some specialized knowledge and information about genetics in order to apply social work skills. But is not this the case whenever the social worker moves into a specific setting or into a specialized area of practice? However, there is a new contribution that can be made through a heightened role participation and involvement in genetic programs. Social workers will have a rich opportunity to identify some of the psychosocial dynamics that occur as a result of the presence of genetic aberrations in the family. It will be the social worker's responsibility, not only to provide service, but to conceptualize and make visible the nature and kind of problems that occur and the ways in which professional services can best be provided to assist the families in coping with genetic problems. This can perhaps be illustrated best by the following rumination: Olshansky, not long ago, described the chronic sorrow syndrome as a normal manifestation in parents reacting to the impact of learning that they have a mentally defective child.[11] By so doing, he gave new depth to our understanding of how families may be expected to react at the time of diagnosis and a new dimension to the formulation by the professional of how to perceive the parental behavior in proper perspective to pathological versus normal response to the stress situation.

One dynamic that operates with families having genetic disorders might, for lack of a better title, be termed the "shattered self-adequacy syndrome." The knowledge that one possesses a defective gene causes a momentous insult to the ego structure of the affected individual. Self-esteem is especially vulnerable; expressions of inadequacy become very manifest. Intense feelings of stigma and shame are evoked. This is borne out by the evidence, previously mentioned, that there is a decrease in subsequent childbearing, not only in affected individuals but in kindred as well. It is as if the individual in fact feels he is the result and bearer of a bad seed. It has been noted in social work with parents who are heterozygotes (carriers of the defective gene for phenylketonuria) that they display excessive inadequacy in their parental roles and experience considerable difficulty in their child-rearing practices.[12] In part, at least, this inadequate parental functioning may reflect the shattered self-adequacy syndrome.

The recognition of this dynamic helps to focus service with the client in that it identifies the imperative need for casework at the time of diagnosis or provision of genetic information, to permit the exploration of feelings related to the loss of self-esteem, to provide for a catharsis of feelings of shame, inadequacy, and insecurity, and to permit an opportunity for the resolution of old conflicts reopened by the new information. Understanding of this dynamic supports the use of casework help philosophically based on supportive ego psychology.

Case Study

The following recent case illustrates the syndrome of shattered self-adequacy:

The C's are a Catholic, Mexican-American family composed of ten living children ranging in age from infancy to 20 years. They came to clinic for evaluation of their 18-month-old mongoloid (Down's Syndrome) infant, who was one of a set of twins, the other having died in infancy. The normal 6½-year-old was similarly the survivor of a set of twins. When it was learned that the 10-year-old daughter was also a mongoloid child with severe mental retardation, chromosomal analysis was done on the entire family. For obvious reasons, priority was given to the testing of children of childbearing ages. The resulting karyotypes showed that the mother, Mrs. C, the eldest daughter, Margo, age 20, the 15-year-old son, Juan, and the 9-year-old daughter, Elena, were all carriers for Down's Syndrome (translocation type). The maternal grandmother was also a carrier. She had given birth to about fourteen children, but except for Mrs. C and her living sister the others had all died at birth or infancy. Mrs. C's sister is married and has several children, all described as "slow."

The social worker saw the family on numerous occasions—in whole family sessions, in individual interviews, and in joint interviews with selected family members. When given the genetic information, the family responded with tremendous shock and grief and with inability to verbalize feelings, except for Mrs. C, who cried pathetically, "Why didn't they tell me long ago?" She had not wanted children following the birth of the first mongoloid child, but Mr. C had objected to sterilization or contraception on the basis of his religion. However, following the birth of the second affected child, the mother had her tubes tied with the consent of her priest.

Mrs. C, in subsequent interviews, blamed everyone, including her mother, her husband, and the church, until she could at last intellectualize and understand that from the outset any one of the children could have had the defect. She realized that her mother was ignorant of her own carrier state. This seemed to free Margo to express her own angry and resentful feelings about Mrs. C and enabled her to lift the depression she had experienced following the genetic diagnosis (her depression was so extensive that she could scarcely function in school). Margo talked a great deal about her sense of inadequacy, about being a damaged human being. "How could anyone want to marry me?" After a while she talked with the social worker about practical, realistic ways to meet her needs, for example, adoption. Margo also struggled with her conflict as to whether to "confess" to the priest. Eventually the social worker helped her to believe that neither she, her mother, nor her grandmother had "sinned," but perhaps she could counsel with an informed priest regarding family planning with the medical documentation being made available as needed.

The family's closeness and sensitivity for each other was a great help in the situation. The parents assured the children that the two mongoloid siblings were not their ultimate responsibility and they would begin to make plans for them. Juan was helpful in his emotional support to his sister. After several months Margo began to date a boy regularly; she told her social worker that she thought it was best that she knew the true condition, although her first reaction had been otherwise.[13]

This is a thumbnail sketch of what was a tragic, critical situation—one in which the sensitive, skillful work of the social worker can be seen in shoring up the weakened egos of the daughter and mother and in which they are able to emerge with a reconstructed sense of self-adequacy as human beings.

Conclusions

In conclusion, several implications that present challenges and opportunity to social workers for creative professional endeavors are as follows:

1. The profession as a whole needs to be vitally concerned with the broad social problems posed by the population explosion and to participate in developing programs that will ameliorate the present situation realistically within the framework of our present knowledge and abilities.

2. Family planning is broadly concerned with the health and welfare of the family and conceptually ensures that "full freedom is extended to all population groups for the selection and use of such methods for the regulation of family size as are consistent with the creed and mores of the individuals concerned."[14] The social work profession has shouldered this responsibility in principle, and needs to expand its support and actual participation in family planning programs, particularly in the health fields of practice.

3. Social workers have a significant role to play in the area of genetic counseling. Recent biochemical and medical advances have created social problems for those identified as affected individuals or as carriers of genetic defects—social problems that often pose more conflict and pathologic disturbance than the genetic defect itself. The social worker has the over-all skills to handle many of the problems involved in providing genetic information. Social workers have a specific contribution to make in team efforts with geneticists and physicians in enabling families to cope with the genetic problems and in coming to grips with value judgments that might interfere with normal needs to bear children. Furthermore, they have a challenging opportunity to identify and conceptualize the operative psychosocial dynamics and

to apply professional skills creatively in their helping endeavors with these families. On every level in social work education, in the development and administration of programs, and in practice social workers need to be concerned more and more with the area of genetics.

4. Social workers must make their contributions highly visible, particularly in the health field where they are not in a primary social service setting and where they need to work interrelatedly with many other professional disciplines. Although some genetic centers employ social workers, it was startling to note that at several well-known large medical centers there are no social workers included as intrinsic staff of their genetic centers.[15] If social workers are ever to attain equal status as members of genetic teams, if the social work profession is to be included in the planning of services and programs in which social work should be a valued part, if social work is indeed to recruit the interest of many to become social workers, social workers need to make their work highly visible. They need to write, to think, to take part in research, and to be action-oriented to social problems. Without this visibility, social workers will not be asked to take this appropriate role and will not be able to serve the very clientele they most eagerly wish to help. No longer can the practicing social worker be bound in isolation in his individual work with his client. Every social worker must assume a broader stance and value his professional contribution highly enough so that others can appreciate its worth. The practitioners in the public health and medical fields particularly have a rare opportunity through the expanding new areas of services such as genetic counseling and family planning to demonstrate this newer professional posture.

References

[1] Harold O. Goodman, MD, "Let Them Be Fruitful and Multiply?" Paper presented at Annual Meeting of Medical and Social Consultants in Public Health and Medical Care Programs, Atlantic City, New Jersey, May 21, 1965.

[2] C. A. Doxiadis, "On the Measure of Man," *Mayo Clinic Proceedings*, Vol 40, No. 1 (January 1965), pp. 71-89.

[3] P. B. Medawar, MD, "Do Advances in Medicine Lead to Genetic Deterioration?" *Mayo Clinic Proceedings*, Vol. 40, No. 1 (January 1965), pp. 23-34.

[4] *Ibid.*, p. 33.

[5] W. B. Neser and G. B. Sudderth, "Genetics and Casework," *Social Casework*, Vol. 46, No. 1 (January 1965), pp. 22-25.

[6] R. L. Tips, D. L. Meyer, and A. L. Perkins, "The Dynamics of Genetic Counseling," *Eugenics Quarterly*, Vol. 9, No. 4 (December 1962), pp. 237-240.

[7] Neser and Sudderth, *op. cit.*

[8] R. L. Tips, H. T. Lynch, and C. W. McNutt, "Genetic Counseling," *Texas State Journal of Medicine*, Vol. 60 (August 1964), pp. 650-663.

[9] R. L. Tips, MD, and H. T. Lynch, MD, "The Impact of Genetic Counseling Upon the Family Milieu," *The Journal of the American Medical Association*, Vol. 184 (April 20, 1963), p. 183.

[10] Personal correspondence with Stanley W. Wright, MD, April 21, 1965.

[11] Samuel Olshansky, "Chronic Sorrow. A Response to Having a Mentally Defective Child," *Social Casework*, Vol. 43, No. 4 (April 1962), pp. 190-193.

[12] Sylvia Schild, "Parents of Children with Phenylketonuria," *Children*, Vol. 11, No. 3 (May-June 1964), pp. 92-96.

[13]Herbert H. Rock, Child Development Clinic, Children's Hospital, Los Angeles, casework summary.

[14]"Policy Statement: The Population Problem," *American Journal of Public Health,* Vol. 49, No. 12 (December 1959), pp. 1703-1704; "Text of Resolution Adopted by the NASW Delegate Assembly, Cleveland, December 13, 1962" (New York: Planned Parenthood Federation of America, 1962). (Mimeographed.)

[15]Children's Hospital, Los Angeles, University of California at Los Angeles Medical Center, and Baylor University Medical Center.

Planning for Retarded Children

MICHAEL J. BEGAB

Planning for the care and training of retarded children occurs at various periods of developmental crises—when the handicap is first recognized or diagnosed, when family stability is threatened or disrupted, when the child enters school, when behavioral problems arise, when he approaches adolescence and its attendant problems, when he enters adulthood with its implications for economic and social self-sufficiency. And the family has its own crises too: the birth of additional children, financial hardship, marital dissension, parental disability or old age. In many families, the problem is not one of acute crises, but of constant adjustment and readjustment.

Each family brings to the crises posed by the retarded child a different set of prior life experiences, perspectives, material and psychological resources. Likewise, each child presents a unique syndrome of problems, needs and potentialities. The interaction of these many variables can and does result in an infinite combination of problems.

The development of a single set of guidelines, therefore, for a population as heterogeneous as the mentally retarded and their families is virtually impossible. Criteria would need to be so broad and general in nature as to provide little direction in their application. The needs of the mildly retarded, culturally deprived child, for example, whose behavior is a source of irritation to the community are quite unlike those of the severely handicapped, organically impaired child whose prolonged and total dependency is largely a family problem. Furthermore, community attitudes and tolerances toward the two groups differ, and these in turn influence the child's concept of himself and how he is perceived by others. This often bears directly on the nature of the parent-child relationship. Clearly, planning for the former group involves considerations that are not pertinent to the latter, at least not in like degree.

Whatever subcategories are used to differentiate among the retarded—organic,

From Michael J. Begab, *The Mentally Retarded Child: A Guide to Services of Social Agencies*. The Children's Bureau, U.S. Department of Health, Education and Welfare (Washington, U.S. Government Printing Office, 1963), pp. 109-123. By permission of the author and The Children's Bureau.

non-organic, mild, moderate, severe—in the final analysis each situation must be carefully individualized. Yet guidelines, while they must be adapted to individual cases, must be established according to the common characteristics and needs of groups. Such guides will not apply to all the retarded children in a specific category all of the time, but they may well be true for most of the retarded, most of the time.

Home Care Versus Institutional Care

The kinds of care children need vary at different stages of child development. What may be necessary and appropriate for the teenager may be quite damaging to the infant and young child. Since the formative years of development are generally the most crucial in an individual's total life experience it may be well to begin where the child himself begins—in infancy—and consider his needs and the criteria to be applied in planning for him.

The parents of a severely retarded infant are faced with a serious dilemma in deciding on the best plan of care. When the condition is diagnosed at birth, they may be advised to place the child in institutional care directly from the hospital and "try to forget him." Should they follow this course of action, they may be severely condemned by relatives for their "heartlessness" or suffer from gnawing doubts about the hastiness of their decision. Actually there are relatively few instances in which a decision regarding placement is of extreme urgency. Most parents want to keep their children at home and need every opportunity to fulfill their sense of parental responsibility. Only as they are convinced that the welfare of the child and other members of the family is best served through placement, can they reach this decision without needless anxiety and guilt.

For the retarded child, as for other children, there is no substitute for an adequate family environment. Numerous studies have demonstrated again and again that children deprived of maternal affection and proper environmental stimulation may be retarded in their intellectual, social and emotional development. Children reared from early childhood in institutions that are overcrowded and understaffed get little fondling and individual attention. As noted earlier, they lag behind in their development in every dimension—in their language abilities because they are seldom spoken to, in their mental performance because they are neither motivated nor stimulated, in their social skills because of regimentation and lack of normal opportunity for social intercourse.

In a sense, handicapped children need the advantages of family life even more than the normal child, who has a greater inherent capacity to rise above his surroundings. This point may be illustrated simply. Consider two children with *potential* IQ's of 40 and 75, who because of environmental deprivation actually function at IQ levels of 30 and 65. Each has lost 10 points. As a result the first child is now ineligible for special class instruction in many school systems. The second child is now retarded by legal definition in many States and can be admitted for institutional care should his behavior constitute a problem.

Admittedly, quantitative measurements in one area of performance are a poor index for the assessment of environmental impact on development. Yet this highly oversimplified mathematical approach to child development does illustrate what actually can happen to retarded children who fail to realize their full potentials. Abhor as we may, a system that determines a child's future status on the basis of a test score, we cannot ignore the reality of current practice, nor can we minimize the significance of a reduced level of performance.

In planning for the young retarded child, we can say without equivocation that a *satisfactory* family living experience can best meet the child's developmental needs and should be our immediate goal. For most retarded children, early institutionalization is undesirable. Tizard in a summarization of English studies is most outspoken on this point:

> ... institutional children are particularly retarded in all aspects of language and speech, and in verbal intelligence as compared with similar mentally handicapped children who live at home. The older the children the greater becomes the discrepancy between their achievements and abilities and those of comparable children brought up in their own homes. The same is true of their personal independence. . . . Observation also shows them to be extremely backward socially and emotionally; and it is clear that in these and in other ways insititutional care today warps and stunts the development of already seriously handicapped children.

Does this mean that all retarded children—at least for the first few years of life—should remain in their own homes? Is there merit in the current practices of many State institutions that limit admissions to children of four or more years of age? Can institutions for the very young retarded child be eliminated together?

The temptation is great to answer all of these questions with a resounding, Yes! But to do so would be to ignore the principle of individualization and to overlook completely the interests of the family. We know that some profoundly retarded children—the progressive hydrocephalic, the severe convulsive disorder, the spastic quadriplegic—may have extensive medical and nursing needs that are beyond the mother's physical energies or the family's financial capacity to provide. Other children—perhaps less retarded—may be so aggressive, hyperactive and destructive that even the highest degree of parental patience and tolerance is insufficient and family stability is threatened. Still others may be so emotionally unresponsive that they offer few gratifications to parents and are potentially destructive to a healthy parent-child relationship.

Maintaining the child in his home at the cost of severe family disruption is not warranted, but the task is first to determine whether such effects are inevitable or are subject to change with professional services. This can only be determined by a thorough interdisciplinary evaluation of the child and a careful psychosocial evaluation of the total family and the many variables affecting its adjustment and adjustability.

The *interaction* of these factors precludes their application in checklist fashion as a means of predicting what course of action a family may or should take. The factors, however, do suggest certain predispositions which the professional counselor must understand and offer clues regarding the type of plan that certain families would find most acceptable. With this kind of knowledge, we can be more objective about parental motivations, needs and capacities, and be of greater assistance in helping parents decide on the best plan for their retarded child and the other members of the family.

In brief, though we must subscribe to the general principle that the developmental needs of the young retarded child are most likely to be met in his own home, we must also recognize that exceptions occur. In truth, the family that cannot adapt its living patterns to embrace the needs of its retarded member—no matter how adequate it may be adjudged by ordinary standards—should consider placement. A substitute home or even group care may be less damaging than a home characterized by marital tensions and general family disorganization.

As the retarded child grows older and his sphere of activity extends outside the home, community concerns play an increasingly important role in planning. Adolescence is a troublesome period for many youngsters and it is difficult to change the behavior patterns of that small proportion of retarded children who have been exposed to an atmosphere of immorality and antisocial behavior.

In families where this occurs, therapy with the child while he is in his own home is not likely to be effective, unless parental attitudes and behavior can be properly modified. If they cannot, plans for separation may need to be considered. In some instances—particularly when the youngster's behavior is a serious threat to the community or himself—institutional care may be the best available plan. Some retarded adolescents, despite an extremely negative home environment, are strongly identified with their parents and siblings and would be unaccepting of substitute foster family care. Conversely, foster parents who are willing and able to care for such youngsters are few in number.

An important factor in planning for these youngsters is the nature of their behavior and the degree of protection and supervision they require. A community has greater tolerance for certain types of misconduct than for others. Illegitimacy, for example, is a matter of grave concern to society and the sexually promiscuous girl of retarded intellect may sometimes need to be temporarily segregated until, through a process of character reeducation and supportive therapy, she is able to establish better inner controls over her behavior. Similarly, assaultive behavior may be looked upon as a greater menace than crimes against property. Here too, the protection of the retarded youngster and society may warrant the consideration of institutional placement. Hopefully, these will be regarded as temporary measures and the individual will be returned to community life when he—and his family, if he is going back to them—have been successfully rehabilitated.

Foster Family Care

Institutional care is not the only alternative available to families who lack the essential resources for home care, nor is it usually the most preferred. For the years of early childhood at least, the needs of the retarded child for basic child care are not unlike those of normal children in most instances. Foster parents can frequently provide this kind of care and individual attention.

Unfortunately, foster family placements as treatment resources are used sparingly for retarded children with organic damage, except as a stopgap pending admission to an institution. A primary factor in this is the defeatist attitude some social workers and their supervisors have toward locating foster homes willing to accept such children. Many communities have demonstrated that, with sincere effort, homes for these youngsters can be recruited. More foster parents indeed, are willing to accept such children than agencies are to place them!

What are some of the special considerations in foster family care of retarded children? Who are the children most likely to benefit from such care? What criteria can be applied in the selection of foster parents?

Several broad considerations regarding the suitability of children for foster family care can be identified. They relate to his physical condition, mental abilities, behavior, and capacity for interpersonal relationships.

The child who requires close medical supervision or special therapies—and the medical needs of some of the severely handicapped are legion—is more likely to receive this care in a well-staffed residential facility than through the ministrations of foster parents or periodic clinic visits. Furthermore, foster parents should not be expected to assume this kind of responsibility, particularly when there are other children in the home. In these circumstances, demands, which exceed the capacities of natural parents may also be beyond the capacities of foster parents.

Similar considerations apply in lesser degree to the child's behavior. Although the behavior of these children frequently has an organic basis, there is often a functional component as well. Foster parents are less involved emotionally than true parents and, where a more favorable adult-child relationship can be provided, the behavior of brain damaged children sometimes shows marked improvement. These effects are difficult to predict, but unless there are strong indications to the contrary, and management seems highly unfeasible, a trial period in foster care is warranted. Sometimes improvement is considerable and institutional care becomes unnecessary; in other instances the social experiences within the family enable the child to make more constructive use of institutional life, should it be indicated later.

The child's lack of capacity to respond to adult affection and attention, while it may not disqualify him for consideration for foster family care, cannot be ignored. Many foster parents—whatever their motivation for this kind of work—derive gratification from the achievements and responsiveness of the children entrusted to their care. When these are denied them and when they cannot accept limited goals, they are ill-equipped to stimulate the child's development or contribute to his sense of security. The sad truth is that parental adequacy toward normal children does not guarantee adequacy in the case of retarded children. Yet there are some foster parents who, through many long years of experience in the care of "problem" children, have acquired a degree of "semi-professionalism" in meeting the special needs of handicapped children. These parents would have much to offer the relatively unresponsive child.

Foster parents of retarded children need all the personal qualifications—understanding, warmth, consideration of others, emotional stability, security—that all foster parents require, plus some additional qualities. These special characteristics relate not only to the child's mental limitations and its concomitants, but to the wide range of behavior and needs these children present. For this reason, a single, precise profile of the qualifications needed by foster parents of retarded children is unfeasible, though certain generalizations can be meaningful and practical.

Because the retarded child generally lacks the compensatory skills that even many physically handicapped children possess, foster parents must first of all be able to understand and accept the limited capacities of these children. They need a great deal of patience and tolerance in adjusting to a slow rate of maturation and learning, must recognize the need for intellectual stimulation and accept routine and repetition as a necessary teaching technique. Above all, foster parents must be able to accept prolonged and sometimes extreme dependency, and yet at the same time give the child every chance to grow and become responsible. Firmness in discipline, a capacity to guide rather than control, and flexibility in differentiating the retarded child from the normal children in the home are also important characteristics. Equally important is the ability to give of themselves unselfishly and to find emotional gratifications in minor achievements and sometimes a minimum of responsiveness.

Community attitudes also pose problems for the foster parents of these "different" children. To withstand the pressures that can arise, especially in response to "acting-out" children, these parents need a great deal of stability, secure relationships with their neighbors, and a strong conviction of the innate worth of handicapped children.

The identification of these characteristics in foster parents requires careful evaluation. Some of the background and personality factors to be explored are suggested in a study by Fanshel. Foster fathers, for example, are more successful with aggressive foster children when they have experienced relatively little deprivation in their own childhoods. Some foster families are effective in caring for several types of handicapped children—physical, mental and emotional—and infants with colic as well, all of whom share the essential element of dependency. Most of these successful parents have had the experience of caring for their own children before becoming foster parents. In addition, many come from large, closely knit families, which Fanshel conjectured may provide added social supports to the parents or contribute to the understanding that *all* family members are to be valued. Another important observation, in view of the long term foster care required by some retarded children, was that the foster parents of handicapped children were more strongly identified with the foster parent role than those caring for normal children.

In selecting a foster home, some thought also needs to be given to the community and its available resources. Are there suitable educational facilities, social and recreation opportunities? Are the social expectations complex or relatively less demanding?

Even when foster parents possess the qualifications outlined above, they cannot be expected to have full knowledge of mental retardation nor to escape the many anxieties that arise. Therefore, the foster parents must be persons who can work in close cooperation with and accept supervision by the agency worker and who are sufficiently secure to seek help as the need arises. Only through a close partnership can full understanding of the special needs of the retarded be approximated.

The careful placement of retarded children in foster family care may have preventive as well as treatment values. With mental stimulation and better cultural opportunities, the deprived retarded child can frequently progress beyond the defective range of intelligence. The organically damaged child may be protected against secondary, but often equally disabling, emotional disturbances. And the older child, whose behavior is marginally acceptable but who needs to learn new way of adaptation, is more apt to find good models for identification in foster parents than in institutional personnel.

Small Group Homes

The use of small agency homes (generally 7-12 persons) as a resource for retarded children has particular promise for mildly disturbed adolescents and for those needing a transitional, supervised experience to bridge the gap between institutional and community life. These homes offer greater opportunity for individual attention than do large residential facilities and have some of the qualities of interpersonal relationship that characterize family life. In these settings there is less need for regimentation and greater chance for developing social skills through the "parental" guidance of the adult supervisors. Equally important, small group foster homes permit a more selective placement of children according to age, behavior, nature of handicap, special needs and other vital considerations.

When the child's behavior does not exceed community tolerance but his own home is damaging to his welfare and substitute foster family care is unacceptable or unfeasible, the small group home might be most appropriate. Much depends on whether he needs special training and what prospects exist for early return to his own family or independent placement. Treatment needs may be even more crucial. Does the child have sufficient self-control over his behavior and impulses? Does he need intensive therapy and is it available in the community? Can he profit from a close relationship with adults and intimate living conditions with his peers?

When these questions can be answered affirmatively, the small group home has many advantages as a placement resource for individual retarded children. The adjustment from his own home to this setting is much less complicated than to the strange and artificial environment of the institution. The stigma of commitment to a State institution for retarded persons is avoided. The individual maintains his role as an integrated member of the community and learns new skills in the natural environment in which he must eventually apply them. Furthermore, family contacts with the retarded youngster are more easily maintained (where this is desirable) and professional services more readily coordinated than when social services to the retarded and his family are provided by different agencies or from a distantly located institution.

The "half-way house" is not readily distinguished from the agency operated group home, although it has been used traditionally for individuals released from institutional care rather than as a substitute for institutionalization. While such resources are extremely limited, the need for an intermediate living experience for selected retarded children appears widely accepted. The older adolescent who has been away from the community for years often requires a period of acclimation under continuing supportive help. Adjusting to a new job, finding suitable living arrangements, making friends and learning to use leisure time, is too great a responsibility for some of the retarded to assume all at once. The "half-way house" provides companionship, adult guidance and protection, and reduces the initial task of adjustment to manageable proportions. In time, the retarded individual becomes more independent, extends his scope of activities and personal relationships and is gradually assimilated into the larger community. When this stage of independent living is reached, the semi-protective climate of the "half-way house" is no longer necessary.

Agency-operated group homes and "half-way houses" are new forms of foster care being developed by child welfare agencies and institutions for various groups of children. The stimulus for these developments comes from a better awareness of the differential needs of children and the limitations of traditional methods of care in meeting these needs. Gradually elements of intake, staffing, program and other considerations in the administration of these facilities are being identified and defined.

Adoption

The advantages to the retarded child of a family living experience may be found not only in his own or a foster home, but in adoptive homes as well. For many years, child placing agencies followed a policy of withholding from adoption infants born out of wedlock to mothers of inferior mental status. Because they believed that these infants were likely to be retarded, or because the child appeared to be slow in his development, they felt that they should hold the child until his mental normality could be established in order to protect the prospective parents. Frequently these infants were placed in emotionally sterile group homes pending later evaluation. Subjected to the depressing forces noted earlier, these children often failed to realize their full potentials and so seemed to support the wisdom of this agency policy.

On the basis of current knowledge that infant psychological testing has questionable value in predicting a child's future potentials and that environmental experiences are important factors in mental growth, this policy is changing. Today, in the absence of gross neuropathology or severe defect, children are placed in adoption as early as possible. This practice is not without its risks, but the greater risk lies in allowing them to remain in culturally deprived environments or denying them individual attention and love. For some, adoptive placement may spell the difference between a lifetime of marginal dependence and social usefulness. As for the prospective parent, there is reason to believe that many parents are willing to accept "less than perfect" children.

While adoption practices are most applicable to the retarded child without pathology, other groups should not be excluded from consideration. Many cases are known of foster mothers or relatives who wish to adopt retarded children who have been placed in their care. If there is full knowledge and acceptance of the child's handicap and the prospective parents are able to provide the child with a suitable home, adoption appears warranted. Sometimes, foster parents are motivated by neurotic needs of their own, but if these patterns are well established and "fit" the child's needs, they are not necessarily harmful. In all of these cases, the social worker and the agency have a weighty responsibility to evaluate the capacities of the prospective parents. And in all cases, the adoptive placement of retarded children should be guided by the same principles, protections and legal safeguards that govern the placement of normal children.

Supplementing Parental Care

Planning for the retarded child and his family, then, starts early in life and rests on the fundamental principle that wherever possible he should be maintained in his natural, substitute or adoptive home. Parents of retarded children are no more able than parents of normal children to meet the needs of their children for education, recreation, socialization and religious guidance—especially since these services are not routinely extended or available to the retarded in many communities. The added responsibility and burden this places on parents cannot be carried by them alone. If the gains to be derived from family living are not to be lost or jeopardized, parental capacities must be supplemented and the child's environment enriched by experiences outside the home.

The stress of caring for the school age retarded child at home is alleviated to some degree when the child is eligible for schooling. Where he is not eligible other programs are needed, including day care, homemaker services, temporary residential care, recreation and even babysitting. Some of these programs are aimed primarily at relieving parents of the overwhelming and sometimes disabling burdens of care and supervision. Others have as their primary objective improving the child's social competency through group learning and interaction. Actually the goals are interrelated, for as the parents are made more adequate and the child's social needs are met, his overall development is enhanced. These programs are effective methods for preserving family unity.

Whatever plan is proposed for a specific child it must be related to his particular needs and level of readiness. This is especially important in determining whether the service should be provided within the home environment, through family day care, or through an outside group.

DAY CARE

Among the various services that can be used to supplement parental care, care outside the home—for part of the day—is probably the most useful for the largest number of retarded children. The objectives of a day care program are to give care and protection to children whose parents are unable to provide adequate parental supervision. For the large majority of normal children, the lack of parental supervision stems from the employment of the mother. But many other factors too, while they are not easily assessed quantitatively, interfere with parental capacities to meet the developmental needs of their children. Children may need day care because of illness in the home, the presence of more young children than the mother can find time for, immature parents, behavior problems in the children, and handicapping conditions.

Not the least of these is the last, for the handicapped child—including the mentally retarded—often sorely taxes the physical and emotional energies of the mother to care for him. Even relief from the need for constant supervision of the child for several hours during the day, enabling the mother to organize her household chores, shop, or just rest, can serve as a stabilizing force in family life. Yet this is not the only, or perhaps even the most important, consideration in day care for retarded children. The retarded child, because so few opportunities for peer relationships are available to him and because he is so vulnerable to overprotective or overdemanding attitudes in the home, is particularly in need of developmental and socializing experiences.

The terms "care and protection" in their most literal meaning, actually do not connote the comprehensiveness of day care programs and goals. These have been more clearly expressed in the report of a national conference on day care (61): "it is more than an educational program, more than safety from physical harm, more than health and sanitation, and embodies the whole child and his family situation. . . ."

These observations suggest that day care is not universally applicable to all children or to all retarded children, and that in each instance, the needs and interests of the child and his parents must be carefully assessed. There are also implications in these remarks for program content, staffing and standards—factors which must be given full consideration if goals are to be met.

Perhaps because of the newness and predominantly private sponsorship of day care centers for the retarded, much remains to be done in identifying the kinds of developmental experiences most appropriate to this group, desirable qualifications of personnel, ratio of staff to children, eligibility criteria, and many other considerations embodied in standard setting and licensing procedures. The beginning trend toward the assumption of public responsibility for this program (eight States now provide some public funds for this purpose) has spurred greater activity in this area and promises improved programs.

At the present time, however, there are strong indications in many day care programs that parental needs dominate and sometimes supersede the child's needs.

This shows up most clearly in the inadequacy of intake procedures and the almost complete lack of exclusion criteria. The retarded child who is ineligible for public school attendance is not perforce a suitable candidate for group day care. Some of these children are so frail physically, subject to such severe convulsive disorders, or so aggressive, that their welfare or the safety of others would be endangered in a group setting. Others are too emotionally immature to share the love and affection they need with others, and require so much individual adult attention that their presence in the group tends to deprive others and disrupt the program.

There is widespread acceptance of the principle that most normal children under three years of age are not ready for group day care. The point is hardly debatable for retarded children, since those who are identifiable at this age are generally severely handicapped, have limited communication skills, and function at a one year to eighteen months level, mentally, socially, and emotionally. For these children, if care outside the home is desirable, family day care is a more appropriate plan. Here, too, the home must be selected for a specific child, taking into account the personality and needs of the natural mother and the capabilities of the daytime mother to care for and relate to the child.

Group day care is generally thought to have less widespread application for normal children over 12 years of age, many of whom are capable of looking after themselves. It can, however, serve a highly useful purpose for the adolescent retarded child of severe disability who cannot attend school and is unsuited for occupational training, but who can profit from a recreational, socially-oriented program geared to the promotion of self-care skills and higher social functioning.

In contrast to seriously retarded children, many of the mildly retarded can fit into day care programs for normal children and profit from the relationships thus fostered. The often expressed concern that they will be rejected by the other children or will require an undue amount of supervision, is not borne out by experience. Young children in general do not share adult respect for high intelligence and are relatively free of social prejudices. The likelihood is great that the mildly retarded child will be an accepted member of his group and find greater opportunity for speech and social development than he would if he were placed with others of similar or lesser abilities. The normal child, too, may profit from an appreciation of individual differences and the satisfaction of helping other children less capable than himself. How many retarded children can be absorbed in such groups is still a matter for experimentation, but a ratio of one to five would not seem to present any special stress for either the children or their adult supervisors.

The concepts and principles underlying day care standards for normal children apply to the retarded as well, though some of the standards themselves may need to be modified. For example, day care programs for retarded children usually involve some pre-academic training, but for this group the ratio of children to teachers might need to be smaller than for normal children. The associated physical defects of these children (some requiring daily medication) may require special attention to health standards, personnel skilled in health supervision or more frequent medical consultation. Some adaptation of play equipment may be necessary for children with difficulties in sensori-motor coordination. Special safety measures may be needed for children especially oblivious to common dangers. Six or eight hours in day care may be too much for retarded children. Children who cannot walk need less outdoor play space per child. And so on. The development of new standards for this group of children, or the adaptation of existing standards, requires the combined experience, knowledge and training of people in many professional fields.

One additional factor that must be emphasized in day care for retarded children is the importance of casework with their parents. While all such parents do not require this service, the proportion of those who do is large for reasons already stated. The day care program provides, for many retarded children, a whole new range of experiences, some initially frightening and others uplifting. The child is often subjected to different forms of discipline and training than encountered at home and to group pressures he is unaccustomed to. Sometimes this creates inconsistencies in training that confuse the child and further complicate his adjustment. Casework services to the family can prevent such confusion and facilitate continuity between the home and day care center, which will reenforce the learning of desirable habits and skills. Moreover, and equally important, through this service, parents can be helped to resolve feelings and attitudes about the child that hamper his growth potentials.

HOMEMAKER SERVICES

Sometimes it is more feasible to bring services to the child in his own home than to provide them elsewhere, as a means of supplementing parental care and maintaining family unity. Homemaker service is one of the tools social workers and health agencies can use when a retarded child threatens this unity. Unfortunately, this service has not yet achieved the status it deserves and is in very short supply throughout most of the nation. Its application on behalf of retarded children is even more limited.

Considering the many stresses to family life occasioned by a retarded child or stemming from parental inadequacies, the value of homemaker services to these families seems self-evident. Crises such as illness or hospitalization of the mother, the birth of a new child, or the mother's death, are often cause for serious family disorganization and institutionalization of the child. In these cases, relatives or friends may be reluctant to provide temporary care for a retarded child and short term foster family care may be unavailable. Furthermore, the parents, knowing full well the problems of care involved, may not feel comfortable about placing their retarded child in a strange environment and depriving him of the security of being with his father and siblings. Bringing the homemaker into the home in these emergencies can insure proper care of the retarded child and enable a mother to devote full-time to her new-born infant. Or it may allow a surviving father and the agency the time needed to work out a satisfactory placement plan or other arrangements. Even where the mother is not ill but needs occasional relief to avoid becoming so, the homemaker can be very helpful. The same is true for families with difficult-to-manage retarded children who cannot be placed in an institution because of long waiting lists.

The homemaker as teacher is no less valuable a tool in strengthening family life. Most parents of retarded children are socioeconomically deprived and some are of limited mentality. Nevertheless, there are often real strengths and warm relationships in these families that can be preserved and put to more effective use. Usually these parents want to give proper care to their children, but they lack the maturity, know-how and, often, the resources to do so. The homemaker, with the supportive help of the caseworker, can teach these parents how to budget, plan meals, market, keep house and care for their children better. With this kind of help, community pressures are reduced and fewer families are broken up because of unintentional child neglect.

The two major functions described briefly above are not mutually exclusive, but each have primary use with different kinds of family situations commonly encountered in work with retarded children. Administratively, providing for both may be the only way to sustain a homemaker program, especially in rural areas.

Other Services

In discussing guidelines in planning for retarded children, only those services have been considered that are traditionally provided by social agencies. Obviously many other resources can be utilized which the social worker must know about, make referral to, and help interpret the need for. These include maternal and child health care, social and recreation facilities, occupational training centers, sheltered employment, religious guidance and, of course, special education. All of these contribute ultimately to social functioning and are therefore appropriate resources to be explored by the social worker in helping the retarded child and his family. In some instances, the worker plays a significant role in determining the usefulness of a specific resource for a specific child; in others, the decision rests primarily with another discipline or agency.

Maternal and child health care resources can be particularly helpful to social workers in providing a diagnostic evaluation of the child and recommendation for treatment, particularly in cases involving pathological defect and special medical problems. Without a full understanding of the "whole" child—of which physiological components are an indispensable part—social work treatment goals are apt to prove ineffective. The special clinics for mentally retarded children which have been recently established in almost every State but which are still limited in number, are especially well equipped to contribute to this understanding and to other aspects of interdisciplinary evaluation.

Among the other services noted, the importance of special education is obvious. Probably no other service has more to contribute to the largest number of retarded children than the public school system. But here too, the social worker has much to contribute.

The retarded child—even when he is part of a special class program—is a "different" child in the eyes of the larger student body and the "different" child is often, though not always, a "troubled" child. In the school setting, a mental handicap is apt to set a child apart from other students and create problems of adjustment. Should these conditions prevail unabated, school may become a source of dissatisfaction and truancy, and delinquency or early dropouts may result.

The social worker, in cooperation with the teacher and other school personnel, can contribute to the broad educational and social objectives of the school program. He can make individualization of the child truly meaningful by interpreting to the teacher the emotional climate in the home, the child rearing practices employed, the family's attitudes toward achievement, the cultural values of the community, and many other areas essential to a full understanding of the child's problems. And he can explain to parents the methods which have proven successful in school in matters of discipline, training and management. Through these liaison functions and counseling services to parents, he may be able to improve the family situation or refer the parents to other appropriate community resources for help.

To carry this responsibility, the social worker must understand the school organization, its structure and policies and its delegation of authority. He should know, too, the laws relating to child education and have a fundamental understanding of the curriculum and its objectives. Fortified by this knowledge, the social worker is better able to pool his resources and skills with the teacher toward enabling the child to use his school experiences to achieve the maximum measure of independence and happiness.

Planning for retarded children is not an exact science. More research and experimentation are needed, diagnostic skills must be sharpened and instruments for evaluation and measurement, refined. The major problem, however, is the lack of resources and facilities and the shortage of skilled professional personnel. Nevertheless, as criteria for meeting individual needs are clarified, we can begin to formulate goals for community action and move toward their achievement.

FIFTY-SIX

John-John

NORMA MANUEL

John-John came to us on Friday, August 26, 1966 in the middle of the morning. I was quite uneasy at the time, waiting for his arrival, as it was my first experience with a Mongoloid child. I had heard of these children but had seen only one or two, and then only from a distance and for a brief time. I don't know why I was so apprehensive. I think it was a fear of being inadequate in my ability to care for him. I thought he would be demanding of my time and my energy because of his handicap. I also feared the body deformations would be such that I could not love him and care for or about him like a normal child. When he arrived, my first impression of his physical appearance was that he wasn't as bad as I had anticipated. His head was large, but not extremely out of proportion, but his little arms and legs were so thin and his color was pale and he seemed almost transparent.

Almost immediately after his arrival he started fussing . . . his social worker said he was fussing for a bottle. I immediately put on one of the bottles which had been brought with him. She held him while the bottle was heating, and he fussed and wriggled so that even she was having a hard time holding on to him. I thought to myself that with all her experience, if she was having trouble what would it be like for me?

When the bottle was heated I gave it to the baby. I know if he had been a normal baby I was taking in I would have most likely picked him up and held him myself. The social worker suggested that I should hold him, and I took him. It seemed very awkward to hold him, and I took him. He seemed all arms and legs. He held his own bottle and curved his little back rigid, which I realize now was to push his little tummy up to help support his bottle.

The social worker left and I was alone, and almost a feeling of panic struck me and my thought was, "Dear God, I hope I didn't bite off more than I can chew. Well, all I can do is try, and if it proves to be too much I'll just have to say so and ask the state to move him elsewhere."

John (he was John then; he is affectionately John-John now) finished his bottle, I

Reprinted from *Foster Parent News,* Winter, 1966 (Boston, Division of Child Guardianship, Massachusetts Department of Public Welfare). By permission of the author and the Division.

burped him and figured I'd better change him before I put him in his crib. I was shocked when I removed his diaper to see he was only a few inches wide through the hips and his penis and testicles were very, very minute. His little bottom was all broken out and quite raw and sore looking, and his bowel movement was round, hard little balls. I put only one diaper on him, folded quite small. I put him in the little crib we had for him, with some of his toys that came with him, and stood looking down at him. I started to cry. He was so pathetic and frail looking, I felt God would have done him a favor if He had taken him from birth. I cried not only out of sympathy for this poor, innocent little thing, but I cried in gratitude that I had my own four children just the way they were, even though my oldest boy is hard of hearing and my own baby boy (now four) is profoundly deaf. I cried with the realization that it could be so much worse for them, but wasn't.

I went about my work after that, but worrying how my husband and children were going to react to this poor, pathetic little thing. The children, I felt, would accept him as he was just because he was a baby, but I feared my husband's first reactions. My husband is very soft-hearted and his heart breaks for anything or anyone like John-John, but his surface reactions are usually anger. I knew the first reaction would be, as it was, anger at me for bringing this child into our home. Angry that he and his children had to be exposed to face the fact that these pathetic little creatures do exist; after all, even though you know it, if you don't come in contact with it you don't have to think about it. Just the same way as you don't really think about war until you read the paper, watch T.V. or it somehow touches you personally through a loved one.

When John-John started to fuss about 3:30 (it had been about 5 hours since his morning bottle) I figured it was really too late for dinner but too early for supper, so I diluted some of his S...... with water so it would satisfy him for a short time, and I could give him a solid meal between 5:00 and 6:00. His social worker had left his schedule and said he was fed four or five times a day. I believe a child should be put on a three-meal-a-day schedule as soon as possible, and with five other children to care for (we have another foster child who has been with us since she was two weeks old), a husband to feed and love, and a little small house to try to keep clean, I just couldn't imagine myself being able to find four or five ½-1 hour periods a day to feed John-John, so I proceeded to start him over to the three meals.

I changed John-John's diapers before I gave him his bottle. I was surprised that even though he only had one diaper on, and it had been several hours, he wasn't very wet. This was true for the next few days, also. He did not seem to pass much urine.

About 5:30, I mixed eight ounces of warm S... with cereal to make a mixture a little thicker than paste. This filled a bottle to the very top (about nine ounces). I made an extra large hole in a nipple. John-John by this time was ready to eat, and having fussed for 15 or 20 minutes was hungry enough not to care what was inside the bottle. He finished the complete bottle, burped, and was quite contented. I changed him for bed at 6:30 and by 7:00 he was sound asleep, until 7:00 the next morning. I put him on three meals that day, breakfast and supper being the same and lunch being a meat dinner combination, a jar of fruit and enough milk and cereal to make it nine ounces of thick but easy flowing mixture. If the mixture is too thin, he drools a lot of it out of the sides of his mouth. If it's thicker, he has to suck it and is able to swallow it as he can.

By the next day most of my fears of his care were gone and the feeling of a kind of embarrassment at being seen with him was almost completely gone, and we took John-John visiting with us, although I'll have to admit I was careful to dress him in long pants and long sleeved shirt so his thin arms and legs wouldn't be so conspicuous, thus feeling he wouldn't be noticed as Mongoloid quite so easily.

By Monday his bottom was well on the road to being healed. I had to start putting two diapers at a time on him, as he was urinating in larger quantities or more frequently. His bowel movements were softer—about normal. He moved less frantically and uncomfortably, and became more interested in playing rather than squirming.

He has been with us four weeks now. He has gained five pounds. His skin is pink, and though still thin is much less transparent. He lies on his belly and supports his upper body with his arms. He seems to try to creep and crawl, but his legs aren't strong enough yet. He sleeps on his stomach more, although not always, and he's happy and contented all the time except when he might have a little bubble. He sat yesterday in a walker for about 45 minutes, quite contented to sit and play with the toys on the walker. He reaches and grabs for things, and seems to be getting a little inquisitive about things close to him, like feeling my nose and mouth and eyes. When I hold him over my shoulder he grabs hold of my neck and lays his head on my shoulder. Before, he wriggled and strained against being held, although he still does not like being held for long periods of time. He is much more contented to be in the play pen, busy rolling and moving and playing, but his motions now have a purpose where, in the beginning they seemed like they were uncontrolled. He is no longer on S....; he's on whole milk and in those four weeks we had only one setback.

He's lovable and sweet, and although we still feel it's a shame for him to be as he is, he's not the pathetic little creature we received four weeks ago. Now he's John-John, our little foster son and brother, and we call him one of "God's angels" because he can do no wrong.

He seems to respond to my voice when I say "Hi, John-John." Whether it's my voice or his name, I'm not sure but he does turn around to look at me when I speak to him. He's made a lot of progress in four weeks, and this book will record his progress for as long as he's with us.

Saturday, 9/7/66

John-John's little world of just himself and his play pen is expanding. I sat him in the jumper chair today on the kitchen counter. He was propped with a blanket and small pillow. I'd squeeze one of his toys at him and he laughed and grabbed for it with both hands. When I stopped playing and began working around the kitchen, he watched every move I made. I moved him, chair and all, into the living room.

He sat and played by himself for 1/2 to 3/4 of an hour before he began to fuss. He is also making much more noise than he did before, not groans and grunts as in the beginning but a form of talking and sounds of word formations. The only recognizable one at present is da-da-da, but it's a beginning. I talk to him every time I go by, and the children talk to him. With a constant stream of words going at him, he's bound to pick up more sounds which, if they register, he may start to mimic. I don't expect that he's going to be talking, but from a little experience with speech in the case of the deaf, I know even different sounds like da-m-oe, etc., are a good beginning with the deaf and I imagine it would be the same with the retarded.

Monday, 9/19/66

Sunday John-John started putting his feet on the floor and pushing himself while in the jumper chair just a little, but today he was really bouncing himself so hard the chair was moving on the floor. Yesterday, I also noticed he was holding his bottle up in the air, whereas he always held it against his stomach for support. His sounds are increasing from da to ya - na - ah - usually one sound at a time, repeated several times. He has developed a slight runny nose, and seems to be getting a cold in his right eye.

John-John seems to recognize the kitchen counter, because I just start to lay him down and he cries. This is where I wash and change him. He is putting his arm and feet in his sleeves and pant legs. He either recognizes the shirt and overalls or just knows it's the next step. He knows when I'm going to clean his nose or ears, and fights before I start.

The foregoing is an exact copy of a portion of Mrs. Manuel's Diary, as found in foster parents publication in one of the district offices of the Division of Child Guardianship. She maintains a diary in order to record her feelings and the development and progress of the children placed in her care by the Division. Learning of the Diary's existence, we asked Mrs. Manuel for permission to publish part of the recorded material in this first issue of F. P. News. The Diary has enabled Mrs. Manuel to share her experiences and feelings around John-John in a thorough and truly meaningful way. Isn't the diary a wonderful idea?

FIFTY-SEVEN

Foster Homes for Retarded Children

MABEL RICH

There has been a trend in recent years for the proportion of mentally retarded children remaining in the care of child welfare agencies to increase. These children present a problem in placement and supervision, since community resources in most areas are inadequate either in number or in scope. Institution care is unavailable for most of these children and inappropriate in many cases if good foster family care with enough good community facilities could be found. Faced with this problem, the staff of the Children's Aid Society of Metropolitan Toronto became very discouraged because of our inability to help this group of children. In order to do anything, one question urgently needed to be answered: Where could we find foster homes for these children? Should they be looked for among the present foster homes or should they be looked for elsewhere?

Comparison Between Foster Homes for "Ordinary" and Retarded Children

A study was made of some of the foster homes considered "good" by the agency. A group of ten foster homes used for boarding retarded children over 3 years of age (Group R) was compared with a group of 22 foster homes boarding "ordinary" children, also over 3 years of age (Group O). No firm conclusions could be drawn since both samples were small and the criteria for selecting the two groups were not exactly the same, but the study did reveal some data that are worth considering.

The two groups of foster parents were similar in many respects. When they applied to board, most of them were already a well-settled family unit, not young couples striving to become established. The family income had about reached its peak; the majority of foster fathers earned about $4000 and none more than $6000. Their employment was fairly steady, most of them being skilled or semi-skilled workers. The foster mothers tended to have had slightly more education than their husbands, but few had gone beyond the tenth grade. About a third of the foster mothers had worked as domestics or as "mothers' helpers" before marriage. About

From *Child Welfare*, Vol. XLIV, No. 7 (July, 1965), pp. 392-394. With special permission of the author and The Child Welfare League of America.

half of the families were known to have supplemented their incomes by renting rooms, growing vegetables, etc., before applying to the agency. Most of these foster homes were located on the outskirts of or outside the city.

Even though all of the foster parents or both groups enjoyed spending much of their time at home with their families, the majority of them were well accepted in the communities in which they lived. They encouraged the foster children to mix with neighbors and to join in the local activities, and they talked with their neighbors about the agency's work and on occasion interpreted the foster children's behavior to them. These people seemed to be successful with every kind of child—ordinary, disturbed, or retarded.

DIFFERENCES

As anticipated, we found some differences between the two groups. Most of the foster parents in Group O were in their 30's when they started boarding children, whereas most of the foster parents in Group R were slightly older, i.e., in their late 30's or 40's. All of the foster families in Group O had children of their own living with them, but only eight of the ten foster families in Group R had children of their own living with them. Nearly all of the foster parents in Group O had children who were of school age when application was made. In Group R, however, the natural children were in their teens or grown up when the parents started to board.

Some of the older, more experienced foster parents had moved from boarding "ordinary" children to boarding retarded children when their own children were older. All of the families in Group R had applied to us originally to board ordinary children, and two-thirds wanted to board babies or toddlers. When the Group O families had first applied to us, however, only one-quarter of them had stated that they had any interest in taking a child under 3 years of age. In other words, we found that we could look to our homes boarding infants to supply many of the placements for retarded children at some future time. The foster parents boarding retarded children were found to have altered their family routines to meet the needs of the children more than had the foster parents of the ordinary children.

Motivation

The reasons given for boarding by the foster families were examined in detail and compared with each other. The motivations given at the telephone intake level, on the application form, and to the homefinder, as well as the homefinder's own recorded assessment, were all examined. In addition, each foster parent was asked at the time of the study why he had started boarding. All gave different reasons, with many inconsistencies. We concluded, therefore, that no single statement of motivation is very meaningful.

An interesting fact, however, was noticed that probably has some bearing on motivation. In about three-quarters of the homes, at least one foster parent had had a personal experience of not having been able to live with both natural parents as a child, or had lived with a close relative who had this experience. Interestingly, only one of these people gave this as a reason for wanting to board. A third of the group boarding retarded children had a handicapped child of their own, but none of the other group did.

We can deduce that some foster mothers in applying to board were looking for a way to supplement their family income, which had about reached its peak. Most lived some distance from possible employment outside their homes, and only about a third had a readily employable skill such as typing or hairdressing. Thus, although they could not hope to make nearly so much money from boarding as from employment outside the home, they chose boarding. Also, some foster mothers may have felt a degree of frustration because they were not working to capacity and may have wanted something further to occupy them. Since working in the home and rearing children was the occupation they most enjoyed, they chose foster care.

These factors suggest that these people feel that their life fulfillment can be better accomplished through their relationships with people than through competition for material prosperity. They are more interested in their families and homes than in the outside world, and we can surmise that they place human relationships higher on their scale of values than money and material goods. Through their life experience, they have gained a positive identification with children who have no parent or parents of their own. This means that foster parents are particularly vulnerable if their foster children do not reward them by responding to their affection. Hence, workers must "pay" them with some evidence of agency approval, e.g., verbal recognition when they have completed a difficult, unrewarding task.

Concluding Comments

The study showed that our agency could hope to recruit many of its foster homes for retarded children from the ranks of its present foster parents. If the foster parents have shown a preference for boarding babies, they may become interested in the more challenging task of boarding retarded children as their own children reach adulthood. We also found that the majority of good foster homes are on the outskirts of the city or in the country. Unfortunately, at present, schooling and other community facilities are usually less adequate for retarded children in these locations than in the center of a city.

FIFTY-EIGHT

The Adoption of Mentally Retarded Children

URSULA M. GALLAGHER

In the past, both professional people and the public considered the mentally retarded child as unadoptable. Rarely did social agencies give thought to whether the degree of retardation could make a difference, and rarely indeed did they search for couples who might accept such a child. Adoption was for the "perfect child" and the "perfect family." The mentally retarded child was often hidden in an institution, a cause of shame to his family. Now, the picture is changing. Aware of the benefits of adoption and of the great progress recently made in the field of mental retardation, agencies are broadening their definition of "adoptability" and are seriously considering adoption for the mentally retarded child. They are increasing their efforts to find homes for these "special" children and are making their requirements concerning age, income, employment status of prospective adoptive mothers, and other aspects more flexible.

What Kind of Child?

Retarded children cannot be placed as readily as normal children, of course. Most agencies have far more hard-to-place children, including physically, psychologically, or mentally handicapped children, awaiting placement than applicants who will consider them. Yet couples *do* come to agencies expressing interest in adopting handicapped children; many others become interested in adopting mentally retarded children when they are encouraged by the agency.

In speaking of adoption for mentally retarded children, I am speaking only of the *mildly* retarded child, that is, the child who is capable of completing the sixth grade, who can be guided toward acceptable social behavior, and who can acquire the social and vocational skill necessary for minimum self-support. Most of the retarded people in the United States are only *mildly* retarded. Children who are profoundly retarded, severely retarded, or moderately retarded—the categories into which other retarded children fall—are not usually adoptable because their handi-

Reprinted from *Children*, Vol. 15, No. 1 (January-February, 1968), pp. 17-21. By permission of the author and The Children's Bureau.

caps are too great for most couples to handle. The *profoundly* retarded child, characterized by gross mental impairment and, often, physical handicaps, needs constant supervision and nursing care. The *severely* retarded child has poor motor and speech development and can take care of himself only minimally. And although he can learn to communicate, the *moderately* retarded child has poor social awareness and motor development and will always require a sheltered environment.

In considering the potentials of mildly retarded children who need permanent homes, we must look for certain general characteristics. Though they vary in ability to learn and to function, and there are differences between them and normal children, these differences do not negate basic similarities. An agency's chief questions, then, in determining adoptability include these: Can the child fit into family life? Can he accept love? Can he have a relationship with parents? Can he identify himself with a parent? Is he trainable for employment?

The feelings and attitude of the social worker toward mental retardation are important influences in the adoption of retarded children. Sometimes a worker assumes that because he would not want a retarded child no one else would. He may arbitrarily decide that a child not acceptable to him would not be acceptable to others. Such a possibility points up the need for supervisors or caseworkers to expand their knowledge and examine their conceptions of mental retardation. They have a grave responsibility to help caseworkers progress in their thinking and to help them make valid, individual evaluations of every child in their caseloads.

Who Should Adopt Them?

We have so little experience with the adoption of mentally retarded children, and what we have is so scattered, that our knowledge of the characteristics of successful adoptive couples is slight. Certainly, the foster parents of a retarded child who later adopt him have had opportunity to acquire understanding of his limitations and needs and, therefore, willingly take on a lifelong responsibility. Perhaps more foster parents would be willing to adopt their retarded foster children if caseworkers would explore the possibility with them without applying pressure.

To my knowledge, no one has yet delineated the qualifications of couples who successfully or unsuccessfully adopt mentally retarded children. Although many of the basic qualities of other adoptive parents are no doubt important, certain other qualities are also necessary. On the basis of the needs of most mentally retarded children, I would expect to find the qualities listed below in couples who successfully adopt such children.

1. They emphasize *giving* to a child rather than *receiving* from him. They want to reach out to help the child who most needs help. Many are moved by religion and a desire to make a special effort to "love their neighbor."

2. They have a healthy attitude toward mental retardation based on sound information. They are not unduly afraid of the problems it may bring.

3. They do not want to adopt a child as an "extension of self." Frequently, they will already have natural or adopted children with whom they have good relationships.

4. They expect no more of the child in school or on a job than he can achieve. They will not be embarrassed or frustrated by a child who requires special education or is near the bottom of his class. His social adjustment will mean far more to them than his academic or professional success. They will not expect him to become a physician or a lawyer or a schoolteacher.

5. They feel secure in accepting a child with limitations and can cope with the questions of relatives, neighbors, and friends.

6. They are able and willing to accept a child who is more than normally dependent on them, but they will encourage the child to develop his ability to help himself.

7. They have patience beyond that of most parents. They are satisfied with small, slow gains and rejoice at gradual improvements. They have high tolerance to frustration.

8. They are flexible and can change both their short- and long-term plans for the child.

Could highly educated, intellectual couples successfully adopt a mentally retarded child? Some could, particularly if they have children of their own. If they have raised a child of their own who was an "achiever," they may not need an "achiever" as an adopted child. However, because a retarded child is likely to be "different" from natural children, an agency must determine the degree to which a couple will accept this difference. Social agencies must be openminded and prepared to consider those families whose own unusual needs may equip them to meet the needs of special children.[1]

Should a single person be allowed to adopt a mentally retarded child? The same principle would apply here as with the normal child. Safeguards are necessary, but such a placement should certainly be seriously considered if the alternative is no permanent home.

The selection of a particular family for a child is based on an evaluation of the needs and strength of each. The child will require warm, understanding parents; a normal home; educational opportunities geared to his capacity; and never-ending encouragement. Ability that might go unnoticed in the normal child must be unearthed and cultivated in the retarded. Adoptive parents must be able to do this.

The child must be allowed to be dependent while being given every opportunity to develop his ability to its maximum. The social worker is responsible for helping the adoptive parents strike a balance.

What Are His Potentials?

As in the adoption of any child, caseworkers must help the parents realize that responsibility for child rearing will rest on them for a long time. In considering the adoption of a mentally retarded child, adoptive parents will want to know the characteristics of the child and his potential for socialization. For many children, mental retardation is a dynamic rather than a static condition,[2] subject to change as the environment changes. The adoptive parents must understand this and be ready to make the most of an opportunity to raise the level of the child's performance. Let me give two examples from case records of State welfare departments of how this can be done.

Maggie came into boarding care at 14 months of age in 1962 as a referral from a juvenile court because of neglect by her parents, both of whom were considered retarded. Though she was pretty, Maggie had no animation and little expression; she was infantile and quiet and did not respond to stimulation. Her first foster parents loved her and allowed her to move at her own pace. A year after placement, however, they had to move out of the State and Maggie was placed in her present foster home. From good care in that year, Maggie had improved, but she still was not walking or talking and was not toilet trained. Her new foster parents gave her the same care required by an infant, although she was over 2 years old by this time. They loved her and treated her as a member of the family. They met her physical and emotional needs, and a very strong relationship was formed between them. The foster parents accepted her limitations and were proud of every improvement she made. Her dependence on them increased their love for her, and, in accepting her, they began to think of her as their own child. In fact, they often told the caseworker they did not believe they could ever let Maggie go. Maggie improved in their home. She began to say "Mama" and "Daddy" and started to walk.

On later visits by the caseworker, the foster parents spoke of their interest in adopting Maggie. In October 1965, the agency described its efforts to make Maggie legally available for adoption and let them know that their love for Maggie was recognized. Maggie's natural mother was reached in November 1966, and in December she surrendered her parental rights to the State department of public welfare. Every effort to locate the father was futile. After considerable effort, the State agency obtained termination of his parental rights through its legal services section. After a study of Maggie's foster parents and their home for her possible adoptive placement, the home was approved last year.

Maggie now walks normally and can run well. She can say several more words and even small phrases—"Mama, wash dishes," "Daddy gone." She is able to carry out simple instructions and expresses her understanding in words and gestures. The foster parents are permissive, stimulating, and encouraging. They seldom scold or punish. They are patient with her and understand her needs. To Maggie, this is her home and she loves her "Mama" and "Daddy." The foster parents want Maggie to develop fully and will see that she gets special schooling or any other service that will help her. They now regard her as their own child and are looking forward to adopting her as soon as the legal process is complete. With them, Maggie has the advantages of a permanent home where she has an opportunity for a good life.

Timmy was born in April 1962 to an unmarried woman who was later committed to an institution for the mentally retarded. The child was placed in an approved foster home shortly after birth, where he remained until June 1963. At that time, after evaluation, he was placed in an institution for the mentally retarded. He was found to have a profound neuro-sensory impairment and has been given intensive auditory training. In 1965, the agency decided that, as an institution for the mentally retarded was not the right place for Timmy because he needed constant individual love and care, consistent understanding, and firm control on a one-to-one basis, he should be placed in a foster home and given schooling at the State school for the deaf.

A childless couple interested in helping a child like Timmy was found. They were told of his hearing handicap, but they accepted him anyway because they wanted to help develop his potential and to make him happy. The agency felt that they should first take Timmy as a foster child; if all went well, they could adopt him later. The couple agreed that a "trial period" would be good, and they faced squarely the possibility that adopting him might not be best for Timmy or for them. They did not anticipate failure but accepted the difficulties Timmy brought. A warm, understanding couple, they completely accepted Timmy and gave him a great deal of stimulation. He progressed in their home. They have since adopted Timmy, and have expressed an interest in taking another child like him because they have acquired insight and knowledge from their experience.

These cases argue against regarding the mentally retarded child as "hopeless" and for encouraging adoptive parents to help the child develop fully.

What of Heredity?

Several research studies report that children with low IQ's categorized as retarded tested within normal range after exposure to a stimulating educational environment.[3, 4] Another study reports that children who were born to mentally inferior mothers but who were placed in adoptive homes before they were 2 years old reached educational, social, and occupational attainments consistent with that of their adoptive parents. Moreover, the study also found, their own children have scored at average or above on intelligence tests.[5] These findings are particularly significant because of the kinds of questions applicants for adoptive children ask about the heredity of children who might be placed with them. Still another study reports that after a group of mentally retarded children were transferred from an orphanage to an institution for mentally retarded persons where retarded women developed close mother-child relationships with them, their intellectual growth picked up to the point where they could be placed for adoption as normal children.[5]

It is clear from such studies and from individual experience that relationships with parents and the environment can profoundly affect the retarded child's course of development. An agency should stress this point in talking with applicants who fear that delinquency, impulsive sexual behavior, or other problems may occur as the child grows up. Some mentally retarded children may as adolescents engage in sexual misconduct, for instance, but there is little evidence to show that their retardation is the cause. Education and supervision, provided according to the child's needs, are usually adequate safeguards against such conduct. Without a doubt, many mentally retarded children, given the love and stimulation they need to achieve to capacity, adjust to jobs suited to them, make good marriages, and successfully raise children of their own.

What Other Considerations?

Proper selection of an adoptive home for a particular child is essential in the adoptive process. The caseworker must be ready to give continuous supportive supervision for some time after placement. As with the normal child, incidents will surprise, puzzle, or produce anxiety in the parents. Even the best prepared, most understanding parents may have such reactions and may need support and reassurance. Integration of the child into the family is the goal, but reaching it may be slow. The adoptive parents need to know that the agency is not expecting good adjustment instantaneously and that the caseworker will help parents and child adjust to their new lives after the placement for as long as they require help. The filing of the adoptive petition should be timed to the need for support in the particular family, not automatically tagged to the end of the waiting period required by law.

Some couples learn after they have adopted a child that he is not normal. Their original motive for adopting the child and the expectations they have will affect how they respond. Their first reaction (a common reaction among both natural and adoptive parents) may be to deny that a handicap exists because denial protects them from pain. They will "explain away" the differences, make excuses, blame others for their own reactions to the child's handicap, or go from physician to physician in a vain attempt to get the diagnosis they want to hear. In time, however, their ambition for the child will be thwarted, their pride injured, and their hope for raising the child as an extension of themselves destroyed.

Adoptive parents, however, are not likely to feel guilt as often as natural parents. Whether the reason for the child's handicap is genetic or environmental, adoptive parents are usually more objective, but they may blame the social agency or other source of the placement for "duping" them. However, both adoptive and natural parents face many similar situations. Although mentally retarded children are often as lovable as normal children, most couples prefer to adopt children who can develop into capable adults. Out of disappointment, some adoptive parents withdraw from social contacts when they realize the child is retarded. This is the point at which they need counseling and reassurance the most. The agency can help them understand the child's handicap, can explain the meaning of "mild" or "severe" retardation in terms of their own home life, can help them see what they can look forward to. The parents will also need help in understanding the state of their own feelings: Do they truly want to keep the child? Can they make the deep commitment necessary and find satisfaction in doing so? An understanding social worker can do much to help the parents adjust to the new circumstances and make the best decisions for the child and for them.

Another case illustration from the records of a State welfare department comes to mind.

Mr. and Mrs. W, a young couple, after learning that they could not have children of their own, decided to adopt a baby. After careful study, a social agency placed 10-day-old *Jimmy* in their home. The adoption was completed within a year. Jimmy seemed slightly behind other children in ability to hold up his head, grasp, sit up, crawl, walk, and talk. Soon, relatives began to ask questions about his "slowness." At first the parents denied that there were any problems. But by the time Jimmy was 2, the parents could no longer ignore the truth. Mrs. W called the social worker and asked for a clinical evaluation of Jimmy's condition.

In the interviews that followed, both the mother and father were anxious but gave no sign that they wanted Jimmy removed. The evaluation resulted in a diagnosis of "mental retardation, cause uncertain." The social worker secured additional information on the prognosis, explored with the parents their feelings about the child as he was and was likely to be and their ability to cope with the attitude of relatives, and discussed resources that would be available to the child. As a result of intense counseling, the parents felt that they could accept Jimmy's limitations, were comfortable about being the parents of a retarded child, and were able to face the community. They decided on their own to keep Jimmy.

If, however, after a series of interviews in which their feelings are fully explored, the adoptive parents do decide they should not keep the child, both for his and their own sake, the agency should be ready to help make other plans for him.

What Is Required?

According to Michael Begab, " [mentally retarded children] are in some measure dependent on persons in their environment—at the very least for their maximum well-being, and at the very most for their ultimate survival. In our societal structure the fulfillment of dependency needs rests primarily with the family . . . ."[6] And he also says: "In the total life experience of retarded persons, no force is more vital than the family itself."[2] In these words, he expresses well, I believe, the great value of finding homes for retarded children needing adoption. The retarded child needs a mother and a father who will accept him despite his limitations and, at the same time, will encourage and stimulate him to develop to his maximum potential.[7] To accomplish this objective will require a good diagnostic study of the child and an accurate evaluation of the characteristics of the applicants—their ability to face reality, their expectations, their patience and tolerance, and a primary interest in giving rather than in receiving. At the same time the child's special needs are met, the special needs of the parents may be satisfied. There *are* such people in the world, and we must find them for the retarded children who need them.

References

[1]Watson, Kenneth: Adoption philosophy and practice. The Chicago Child Care Society, Chicago, Ill. July 1967.

[2]Begab, Michael: Sociocultural deprivation and mental retardation. *In* Report of Institute on Mental Retardation, June 22-26, 1966. School of Social Service, St. Louis University, St. Louis, Mo. 1966.

[3]Kirk, Samuel A.: Early education of the mentally retarded. University of Illinois Press, Urbana, 1958.

[4]Smilansky, Sarah: Progress report: Henrietta Szold Institute, Jerusalem, Israel. 1964.

[5]Skeels, Harold M.: Effects of adoption on children from institutions. *Children,* January-February 1965.

[6]Begab, Michael: Mental retardation and family stress. *In* Report of Institute on Mental Retardation, June 22-26, 1966. School of Social Service, St. Louis University, St. Louis, Mo. 1966.

[7]Beaven, Paul W.: The adoption of retarded children. *Child Welfare,* April 1956.

FIFTY-NINE

Homemaker Services to Families with Young Retarded Children

IRENE L. ARNOLD AND LAWRENCE GOODMAN

In an effort to bring together two social trends which have been slow to meet—the growing concern for the retarded in our population and the increasing recognition of homemaker services in helping families cope with situations of stress —two voluntary agencies in New York City recently carried out a 3-year project to demonstrate the potential contribution of homemakers and other home helpers toward preserving families of the retarded. Its results may suggest guidelines for the most effective, economical, and efficient utilization of such services in community plans for the retarded.

Established to examine systematically the effectiveness of homemaker and other home-help services to families with retarded children under 5 years old, the project was cooperatively conducted by the Retarded Infants Services, Inc. (RIS), and the Association for Homemaker Service, Inc. (AHS), with support from the Federal Children's Bureau.[1] Behind its establishment was the conviction that such services, perhaps with various levels of integration with casework services, have an important place in the chain of services required by families of the retarded at the various times in the retarded person's life.

How parents respond initially to the fact of their child's retardation will determine to a great degree the quality of their lifelong reaction to their child, whether or not he remains with the family. The shock of learning that their child will not develop normally may cause them so much inner turmoil—characterized by ambivalent feelings of guilt, sorrow, and disappointment—that they may want to cut themselves off from the offending object by immediately placing the child in an institution or by withdrawing from him emotionally. New and more lasting problems can be created in such a futile effort to regain a semblance of normality.[2] If the child is to be placed away from home, the effect of an insufficiently considered decision can result in later self-blame and other manifestations of unresolved inner conflict. Providing the parents with help at the crucial period following their confrontation

From *Children*, Vol. 13, No. 4 (July-August, 1966), pp. 149-152. By permission of the authors and The Children's Bureau.

with the fact of their child's retardation must be the first phase of any broad program for the retarded.

In planning to help families at such a time, the first concern, of course, must be with the accessibility of comprehensive medical and psychological evaluation of the child and of whatever treatment may be indicated. At the same time the provision of skilled casework counseling to the parents can mean for many of them the difference between workable solutions and destructive ones. But also of vital importance are the associated services which may be able to relieve parents of the overwhelming sense of burden sufficiently to permit utilization of other kinds of help. Here is where homemaker services may play a key role. Our purpose was to demonstrate how.

Procedures

The project focused on 35 families. All were drawn from new referrals to RIS. Twenty-four had been referred from general hospital clinics, six from the New York State Department of Mental Hygiene, three from clinics for the retarded, two from private physicians. The intake social worker's determination that the family needed homemaker service was the basis of selecting the family for participation in the project. The only criteria were that the family have a mentally retarded child under 5 years of age and appear able to benefit from the presence of a helper in the home.

Of these 35 families, 9 were referred to AHS for a conventional homemaker service in which a caseworker and a homemaker, both on the staff of the agency, work closely together as a team; and 20 remained with RIS for service, which included the help of domestic workers called home aides recruited for the family by the agency and some limited casework treatment. A control group of six families received no service but were put on the waiting list for future service.

A clarification of the two terms, "homemaker" and "home aide," seems pertinent. According to the standards suggested by the Child Welfare League of America: "The distinctive elements of homemaker service are (a) placement in the home of a trained homemaker employed as an agency staff member, who works together with a caseworker in carrying out a casework plan to help restore and strengthen parental functioning, or otherwise assure that the child has the care he needs; and (b) use of casework as an integral part of the service. . . ."[3] Homemaker service, as thus described, is closely interwoven with casework.

Home aids, as used by RIS, also are assigned and supervised by caseworkers, but the emphasis is placed on their ability to do light cleaning and cooking and their experience in caring for children, rather than on working consciously with the caseworker to help restore parental functioning. The family may concurrently receive some casework treatment focused on helping the parents reach the best plan for the child's care.

Experienced homemakers from the staff of AHS who were selected for the project participated with the casework staff in a seven-session orientation program. These sessions focused on the condition of mental retardation; the differences and similarities between retarded children and normal children; and the kinds of parental responses they could expect.

Most of the home aides who took part in the project had had previous experience with RIS. Each was carefully prepared by the caseworker to be aware of the general dynamics of each case situation.

In each case the particular homemakers and home aides assigned to the families were selected on the basis of the caseworker's professional judgment.

The two treatment conditions were not set up for the purpose of measuring the efficacy of one service over the other, but rather to seek further understanding of the impact on families of direct assistance in meeting the burdens of the family's daily routines, whether or not this assistance is interwoven with continuing casework treatment. If improvement were possible without the close caseworker-homemaker teamwork, this would seem to suggest that homemaker services for families of the retarded might be offered at different levels of casework involvement, depending on the families' need, capacity, and readiness to use total services.

Instruments created for the study included a "family rating form" for measuring the quality of interaction within the family; and a "decision-making form" for evaluating the character and adequacy of the parent's decision about the retarded child at the close of treatment. At the end of the period of service, all participating families were seen by a social worker in a followup interview. In this the interviewer attempted to view objectively the carry-over effect of the treatment received.

Findings

Both the data secured from testing the case material with the measuring instruments and the data from the clinical followup showed improved functioning in the families served by either homemakers or home aides, in contrast to the families which received no service.

The family rating forms indicated that, in contrast to the control group, families served by AHS made important gains in their intrafamily relations as did families served by RIS, though there were some subtle differences between the two groups in the types of changes which occurred. For example, the AHS group showed a greater increase in friendliness among family members than the RIS group, but the RIS group showed greater development in rationality of conduct.

The decision-making forms indicated that families in both serviced groups rated much higher than those in the nontreatment control group in the quality of plans made for the retarded child. Little difference existed between the AHS and RIS groups.

Similarly, the clinical followup of cases indicated a high degree of sustained gain in families which had received service, regardless of which agency had served them. Some parents who had become involved in relatively intensive casework were able to face openly some of their basic conflicts about their child. However, even families in which the parents regarded the casework they had received as superfluous, but who had a high regard for the help they had received from the homemaker or home aide, improved in intrafamily interaction. Also, the families who had had only occasional encounters with a caseworker focused on specific problems showed sustained improvement.

Thus the findings suggest that, in families confronted with the reality of retardation, help from a homemaker or home aide, selected and supported by a casework agency, can in itself be salutory.

The following two cases illustrate how this may be so at different levels of casework involvement.

The A Family

Mr. and Mrs. A were referred to RIS by a diagnostic clinic. At the time of referral, their retarded child Amy was 4 years of age. Her brother James, age 9, had normal intelligence. Mr. A was unemployed because of a strike. Mrs. A said she was at the breaking point because Amy was completely unmanageable, could not be left alone at any time, and had proved to be a tremendous burden to James, who was charged with some of her care.

Both parents seemed immature, demanding, and manipulative. A severe marital problem had developed out of conflict around Amy. The mother was particularly anxious, describing herself as confused, forgetful, and fearful of harming Amy. Mr. A and his parents were pressing her to send Amy to an institution; Mrs. A was not yet ready to do so.

RIS referred the case to AHS, which sent a homemaker into the home. She was trained not only to assist the mother in carrying the burden of household management and child care, but also to observe changes in behavior and attitudes. Part of her role was to help find out whether or not Amy was educable.

Under the regular supervision of the AHS caseworker, the homemaker assumed a nurturing, maternal role with both the children and parents, but she was careful not to encourage lingering dependency. Amy responded well to her special attention and soon began to show remarkable improvement. Mrs. A apparently had been too tense to handle her in a way that could bring out her potentials.

James, too, showed improvement. He had not only been relieved of Amy's care, but was also getting more attention from his parents. Soon he seemed less withdrawn and behaved in a more forthright and appropriately aggressive manner.

Mrs. A seemed more relaxed, since for the first time in years she had some time for her own needs. The tension between the parents also relaxed a little, and both seemed to have less need to reject Amy.

The AHS caseworker kept in regular touch with the staff of the referring diagnostic clinic who soon reported that the homemaker services had helped clarify the condition of the child and the dynamics of the family situation. It was then agreed that the AHS caseworker would take over the family counseling role from the clinic and would attempt to bring about better relations between the parents by helping them both to a better understanding of the needs of their retarded child, of their normal child, and of each other. As a result, it became possible to enter Amy into a special day class for the retarded instead of into an institution.

This case exemplifies homemaker service in its complete sense. The steadying influence of the homemaker, working in close partnership with the caseworker, expanded the understanding on which a diagnosis could be made, thus making possible more appropriate recommendations for the child's management and care.

As is common with organically damaged children, Amy had responded negatively and with hyperactivity to the anxiety-ridden, erratic handling she had been getting from her parents, and thus her true functioning ability had been obscured. The consistent, well-planned approach of the homemaker helped the child function less destructively and on a higher intellectual level. The resulting decrease of tension in the home increased the parents' ability to make use of casework help. Thus, an institutionalization, likely to be harmful to both the child and the parents, was avoided.

The M Family

The following case illustrates the provision of home help chiefly to relieve harried parents while they are mobilizing themselves to adjust to a severe emotional blow.

> Mr. and Mrs. M were first known to RIS in 1962 after they learned that their 2-year-old daughter Ruth was severely brain damaged and hopelessly retarded. With the assistance of the agency the child had been placed in an institution. Recently the tragedy was re-enacted. RIS received a call from Mr. M, who was crying hysterically. His wife was in a hospital having an operation and he had just been informed by the family's pediatrician that his 7-month-old son John was also severely retarded. Mr. M seemed to be at the breaking point.

> The RIS social caseworker made a home visit the next morning and immediately arranged for a home aide to go into the home to assist Mr. M in the care of both the retarded baby and the family's 5-year-old normal child. Within a few days, Mr. M had recovered sufficiently to go back to work.

> After Mrs. M returned from the hospital, the home aide, a person of much warmth and sensitivity, remained in the home to help out while Mrs. M recovered from her physical weakness as well as from the emotional shock of the baby's retardation. At the same time, the social worker and the family pediatrician worked closely together to help both parents accept the diagnosis and again prepare for placing a child in an institution. Mrs. M also received help from the social worker in explaining the baby's condition to the 5-year-old.

Throughout our analysis of the project cases, the effectiveness of the help given by the homemakers appeared most clearly when, as in this case, it was extended to families in the early stages of their response to a crisis. By providing instant help with the burdens of daily existence, the home helper often made it possible for parents to begin to regain enough psychic balance to be able to use casework counseling and help with planning for their child's future.

Some Conclusions

The nature of parents' early reaction to their child's retardation—often with the need to deny reality and to isolate all feeling—can block parents from entering into a therapeutic relationship with a social caseworker, as well as from being able to encourage their child's progress or create the kind of emotional atmosphere that can stimulate development. While not all parents respond to a crisis in the same way or experience trauma with the same intensity or duration, many do remain fixed in a state of emotional turmoil for long periods of time. Suppressed anger toward the retarded child, and toward fate in general, becomes internalized and thrust upon the self.

When such psychic turmoil is taking place, the introduction of a homemaker or home aide, who offers warmth and support and provides direct evidence of the community's desire to share their misfortune, can cut through some of the sense of hopelessness. Freed sufficiently to deal with the needs of other family members and to resume activity outside the home, the parents may then be able to perceive the retarded child with sufficient objectivity to consider alternatives in planning and to participate in the kind of continuing casework treatment that can build up the strength in the family. Thus the dynamic potentials of homemaker services go far beyond the practical assistance offered.

We found in the project that most families were enabled to maintain the child at home until a reasoned, reality-based decision about his future had been made. But even when parents proceeded with inadequate planning, the home helper's assumption of many of the responsibilities of the retarded child's care tended to mitigate their guilt and anxiety regarding their child.

Because existing homemaker agencies can obviously play a major role in helping retarded children and their families to a better life, community plans for comprehensive care for the retarded should incorporate such agencies into the overall design and goals of their programing. Ideally, these agencies should be able to provide home help flexibly, according to the varying needs of families of the retarded. Some families can benefit by home help which is not so closely interwoven with casework treatment as is required to help other families. Where such flexibility is not possible, home aide services might appropriately be offered by specialized agencies for the retarded.

While the project described here focused on the needs of families with young children, homemaker service should not be regarded solely as an emergency resource. Actually it is badly needed by many families on a long-range basis. The demands of a severely or moderately retarded child can be so consuming that at least part-time home help may be needed as long as the child remains in the home.

The complex needs of retarded children and their families require bold new planning that includes the creative use and adaptation of existing approaches to families in trouble. Agencies which specialize in service to the retarded must provide the direction that will encourage others to open up a variety of previously unobtainable services to families of the retarded.

References

[1] U.S. Department of Health, Education, and Welfare, Welfare Administration, Children's Bureau: The value of homemaker service in the family with the mentally retarded child under five. Child Welfare Demonstration Project No. D-66. 1965.

[2]Begab, Michael: The mentally retarded child: a guide to services of social agencies. U.S. Department of Health, Education, and Welfare, Welfare Administration, Children's Bureau. CB Publication No. 404. Reprinted 1965.

[3]Child Welfare League of America: Standards for homemaker service for children. New York. 1959.

DIAGNOSTIC, EVALUATION AND TREATMENT CLINICS

SIXTY

The Social Worker's Role in Clinics for the Retarded

LAWRENCE GOODMAN

Although they were almost nonexistent as early as 1950, interdisciplinary clinics for the retarded are now an integral part of the community's basic service structure. An awareness of the retarded and their glaring unmet needs for multiple services at significant points in their lifetimes has finally emerged. The negative cultural stereotype, which implies rejection and devaluation of the retarded at all levels of planning, is no longer discouraging efforts to confront the problem actively and search for ways of helping.

Social workers are also products of their society and must be influenced by it value judgments and attitudes. Concepts about the retarded have been so at variance with the social worker's basic philosophy of the dignity and worth of all individuals that group defensive reactions have resulted. The social work view of the problem has too often been characterized by oversimplification. Misunderstanding the true nature of most institutions for the mentally retarded and failure to evaluate the long-range effect on families of premature institutionalization have led many social workers to make immediate, often ill-considered, recommendations of placement. Until recently, social workers have failed to recognize that, although mental retardation can be understood only as a medical, psychological, and social entity, it becomes primarily a chronic social disability. The handicap presents problems for the family, for school and recreation facilities, and for all community services. The retardate will be disadvantaged in whatever social role he enters and will require specialized planning in each new status.

Identifying the Problem

Thus, the social worker's role in clinics for the retarded becomes of the utmost significance. It begins with an evaluation of the family unit and continues with responsibility for treatment of the family. Every member will be affected by the presence of a child who carries a threat to the family's self-perception and equilibrium.

Reprinted by special permission of the author and The Child Welfare League of America from *Child Welfare*, Vol. XLIV, No. 4 (April, 1965), pp. 214-218.

When diagnosis is established early, as with the mongoloid child, there is an immediate crisis reaction. Even parents with a high degree of intactness go through an initial phase of regression and disorganization. It is imperative that counseling begin as soon as possible so that parents can be helped to mobilize strengths to combat this many-leveled challenge to the family's adjustment pattern.[1] Help with working through initial feelings of guilt, disappointment, and anguish will facilitate their capacity to meet and handle the later demands.

When the condition cannot be immediately detected or verified, parents experience a delayed crisis reaction. They are disturbed by the infant's lack of response, and they may assume that, in some way, they have failed their child. Anger at his continuing erratic progress increases guilt and confusion, and leads to frantic, random searching for new ways of encouraging growth. Further tension is created, and the child's pace of development may be handicapped even more. Parents can despair completely; adopt strong defenses of denial, avoidance, and isolation of feeling; or give up the struggle and attempt to deny their rejection by fostering a lingering dependency beyond that imposed by the child's handicap.

These parents are especially vulnerable and in need of counseling at the point at which confirmation of the diagnosis makes a reality of their gravest anxieties and creates fear of the future and doubt about their capacity to continue to face and react to the specialness of this kind of parenthood. At this time, help in resolving the conflict lays the foundation for an acceptance of the retardation that assumes limitations, but permits latitude for recognizing achievement and success within the framework of circumscribed goals.

School

School presents the next major hurdle. Special classes mean public acknowledgement of the problem. Rejection by peers, with further damage to the child's self-image, must be faced. The sensitive parent empathizes with the child's pain and is often propelled to try to compensate through over-protection. Other parents try again to deny the extent of the child's limitations by developing an excessive level of expectation. Both reactions damage the child's already weak ego development. The parents' own feeling of separateness and inadequacy may become intensified or reactivated through overidentification with the child. The family can become hypersensitive and hostile toward the community, which they view as not offering sufficient support or understanding. Thus, the initial tendency to retreat can re-emerge.

Adolescence

Even assuming a relatively satisfactory handling of the latency phase, the adolescence of the retardate poses new threats to parents. Anxiety about the future intensifies with emerging adulthood. Vocational planning brings up problems in accepting the child's limited potential in still another major life area. Realistic concern about sexual acting out adds to the pressure. Parents must be helped to find the delicate balance between permissiveness and maintaining closer supervision and concern than would be appropriate with the nonretarded adolescent. New answers and solutions must be sought at each major point of development.

Social Work Role

Within the overall clinical structure, the social worker generally has responsibility for intake selection; social diagnostic evaluation of families; individual and group counseling; participation in interdisciplinary case planning, training, and research; and community organization. His function is similar to that in other interdisciplinary settings, but is broadened to include the expanded team of pediatrician, neurologist, public health nurse, educator, speech pathologist, and others. Working productively with less familiar disciplines carries new challenges and calls for mutual professional readjustments. The complexity and scope of the problem of mental retardation require experimentation with new team combinations to deal most effectively with a particular problem at a particular time.

In carrying out the social work role in this relatively new area of practice, it is helpful to identify specific knowledge and methods that go beyond generic professional preparation. The setting is neither psychiatric nor medical, but a fusion of both; it is both rehabilitative and habilitative; it deals with a chronicity that has unique social inferences that engage all of the traditional skills of the social worker.

Within our center, which has for several years trained social workers for clinical specialization in mental retardation, as well as providing field instruction for social work students, we have found that, in order to work successfully with this patient group and to carry out effective social work practice, supplementation of knowledge was essential in the following areas:

Recognizing etiologic and prognostic factors and treatment implications of both common and rarely seen diagnostic categories.

Interpreting psychological data that evaluate intellectual, social, and emotional functioning and the relationship of these data to habilitative, educational, and therapeutic intervention with the child and the parents. The intellectual evaluation is viewed in terms of potential for growth and improved adaptability rather than as a symbol of limitation and restriction.

Understanding atypical growth and developmental patterns of children at various functioning levels—similarities, differences, and realistic expectations.

Increasing awareness of reactive and functional emotional disturbances and their applicability to the retarded. Of even greater importance is developing understanding of the nondynamically determined motivational behavior of children with organic and endocrine disturbances.

Interpreting social, economic, and environmental influences; fostering awareness of differences in attitude, acceptance, and handling of the retarded within socioeconomic, ethnic, and religious sub-groups, and investigating the etiology and extent of cultural and academic deprivation and the implications of these for preventive action.

First Contact

Families seeking help from a specialized agency have the right to anticipate expertness from all of the professional staff. The social worker will usually have the first opportunity to set the tone for the family's response to the clinic. Significant contact begins with the initial, anxious, hesitant phone call asking for help, which is usually not immediately available. Handling the disappointment or anger that parents feel when we are forced to speak of waiting lists is the first step in establishing a relationship with the family.

Recognizing how anxiety-provoking the waiting period is for families, especially when contacting the clinic seems to concretize their suppressed fears about their child's slow development, we have set up a policy of seeing new applicants immediately, usually in intake groups. The intake worker, with an adequate foundation of knowledge of all aspects of mental retardation, is able to make a tentative judgment of the appropriateness of the referral. Often the children have not been previously diagnosed. Through this procedure, as many nonretarded children as possible are screened from the waiting list. Such cases include the emotionally disturbed slow learner who is not retarded, the obviously psychotic child, and the physically handicapped youngster without intellectual impairment. Referrals are then made to the proper agency.

The worker must also be alert to emergency situations that require immediate attention—the possibly hypothyroid or phenylketonuric child for example, whose retardation could be reversed, or the rare case in which emergency surgical intervention is indicated. Medical consultation is, of course, available to the intake worker. Throughout the clinic contact with parents, a thorough knowledge of the characteristics and prognosis of each diagnosed condition is vital. Some parents will read everything available on the subject and will test out the worker's expertness before relating comfortably. Intellectual defenses cannot be effectively challenged unless the worker can meet the client within a framework of authority.

Atypical Development

A thorough understanding of atypical growth and development patterns and methods of encouraging optimal progress is more than advisable academic background. Many parents, as they struggle to maintain their psychic balance, are unable to examine feelings that inhibit the emergence of satisfactory adjustment patterns. Although they may reject the initial exploration of their feelings, they may readily respond to help focused on dealing with the concrete problems of daily living with a retarded child. When, with direction and encouragement, parents are able to view some small beginnings of progress and experience minor successes, the feeling of futility and hopelessness may be diminished.

We can anticipate that, during the course of atypical development, retarded children will emerge with behavioral and trait disturbances that approximate in appearance, if not in depth, the neurotic patterns of the child with normal intelligence. The worker must go beyond this, however, and possess a broad grasp of the behavior patterns that accompany many forms of organic and endocrine damage. A child with such injury can present parents with overwhelmingly complex management problems. Limited attention span, hyperactivity and destructiveness, poor conceptualization, and perseveration combine to form a behavioral syndrome that can exist in a child within the most stable family. The constant assault of the child threatens the family's integration and strains the most positive existing relationships. In no other area, perhaps, does a greater need exist for informed counseling. Families need help in learning how to cope with this most provocative behavior through specific ways of setting up an adequate structure and consistent controls. It is only then that we can deal with attitudes, feelings, and planning for the future.

Social Factors

Social science theory is playing an increasingly important part in generic education for social workers. In the area of mental retardation, too, additional dimensions of individual understanding are possible through more inclusive examination of sociological data. Studies within the clinic have shown, for example, that many more middle-class parents than lower-class parents institutionalize retarded infants. This reflects many factors—including the physician's identification with his middle-class patients and the more frequent and intense recommendation of placement. The family's perception of the child is a blow to their prestige and social mobility, and their high aspiration levels for their child is mocked by the presence of retardation. Families of lower socioeconomic status seem to react to a retarded infant with less sense of crisis.

It is the culturally, socially, and academically deprived child, however, who offers social work the greatest challenge for the future. Aggressive social planning and movement into the community to attempt to attack the problem at its source offer a great potential for prevention. A large proportion of the higher level mildly retarded could benefit especially. Few are seen within special diagnostic and treatment centers, whose programs are generally geared toward the moderately and severely retarded and are too often middle-class focused. Much of the total social problem of retardation, therefore, is not being met and requires daring, forceful action. Social workers within community clinics have a particular responsibility to stimulate planning and programing for this still-neglected group.

Casework with the Retarded

Direct casework with the retarded recognizes the existence of slower intellectual and physical development and the diffuse, undifferentiated ego structure of many retarded children and adolescents. Individual treatment requires flexibility and limited, but specific, goals, Insight therapy can rarely be achieved. The use of nonverbal techniques and the ability to communicate acceptance and concern are requisites for the therapist. Genuine warmth and an interest that does not gloss over pain and resentment can be a new and corrective experience. Treatment will be ego building and supportive, encouraging the retardate to hold back impulses when necessary, but at the same time encouraging him to recognize and express negative feelings. Through the relationship, identification with the therapist proceeds, and more appropriate controls begin to develop.

Stella Chess points out that the first lesson to be learned by a therapist planning to work with the retarded is to estimate a reasonable goal and to be aware that this goal will almost always fall far short of complete elimination of symptoms.[2] Assuming that results might be optimal, the question of carryover to life situations is of even more significance than with the nonretarded child and is more difficult to solve.

Familiarity with the child's environment takes on new importance. Working with the family, the school, recreation centers, and rehabilitative agencies elicits all possible forces to reinforce the therapeutic goals, to help minimize the effect of additional traumatic experiences, and to encourage testing out of new behavior in a supportive atmosphere.

Concluding Comments

The broad, still evolving role of the social worker within a multidisciplinary clinic for the retarded and their families has been briefly discussed. Some of the content beyond generic education required by the social worker in such a setting has been identified. There are strong indications for the necessity of additional specialized training for those planning to work comprehensively with the retarded. It is important to stress, however, that much can be achieved within nonspecialized child welfare agencies, where the majority of the retarded will continue to be seen. Needs of families resulting from handicapping conditions, whether physical, social, or intellectual, share a wide common ground within the traditional skills of the social worker. Where further diagnostic understanding is required, specialized services should be used collaboratively.

References

[1]Lawrence Goodman, "Continuing Treatment of Parents with Congenitally Defective Infants," *Social Work,* IX, No. 1 (1964), 92-97.

[2]Stella Chess, "Social and Rehabilitative Aspects of Mental Retardation," *Proceedings, Institute on Social Work and Rehabilitation* (New York: New York University, 1963).

SIXTY-ONE

Riding with Batman, Superman, and the Green Hornet: Experiences in a Very Special Group

PAUL ABELS

Batman looked at the large plastic globe that separated him from Superman. He fingered it lightly at first, then began to smash at it with his fist. He then started to kick it, and it began to crack.

"He's breaking your globe," the Green Hornet yelled at Superman, who turned just in time to see his globe crack into three large pieces.

"I'll kill you, kill you," Superman screamed at Batman. "I'll kill you, kill you ... I'm going to tell your father on you."

The worker-driver pulled the station wagon into the nearest parking lot, stopped, and turned to the boys.

"Why did you do that to Don's globe?" he asked Ed, who was looking around not knowing what to expect.

Don was yelling, "I'm going to tell your father and he will take care of you." The words were coming hard from between large sobs.

The other boys sat silently, concerned about the incident that they had just been partners to.

"He shouldn't have done that," Lou stuttered.

For the first time the others listened to his entire sentence even though it took him 30 seconds to say it. Some of the boys nodded in agreement. Ed, although quiet, sat with a large grin on his face, as if to say, "It really doesn't matter."

The driver, the social worker with the group, trying to make sense out of the experience, turned and said: "We had better talk about this right now. Is this what we want to happen to our club?"

The "Club"

The "club" was formed by the Mental Development Center in order to provide a therapeutic group experience for boys 8 through 11 years old with mental development problems. The Center traditionally served as an outpatient clinic and information center concerned with problems of "slow mental development." In addition

Reprinted by permission from *Mental Retardation*, Vol. 7, No. 1 (February, 1969), pp. 37-40, a publication of the American Association on Mental Deficiency.

to counseling, the Center provides evaluation services and a preschool program for educable mentally retarded children, and carries out research and serves as a community information resource.

This group, one of the first specifically established at the Center to focus on the use of the group to help, was led by a professionally-trained social group worker.

None of the eight boys in the group had shown any signs of brain damage. They were all educable, and some were in regular classes in school. Three of the boys were being seen regularly by caseworkers. In six cases, the parents were being seen. In two instances, neither the parents nor children were receiving individual counseling.

The large plastic globe had been given to Don by two workmen at the "Metals Center" which they had left about ten minutes before. He was extremely excited about the globe, as were the other boys. It was going to be a flying saucer or a sled. Three of the boys (Ed, Tim, and Andy) had been fairly upset that there had been only one globe and that they hadn't gotten one as well. Ed was the most upset. As they climbed into the car for the return trip, the group climate began to change, and some rumbling and "sniping" directed at Don by Ed was picked up by some of the older boys. The worker could see that the other boys were very envious of Don because of the globe, but he did not pick up with the group. He took it for granted that the return car ride and lack of opportunity to play with the globe would "cool out" some of the upset the other boys felt. Unfortunately, the plastic globe, about three feet round and a foot deep, was placed between the rear and middle seats of the wagon. It was a little cramped in the car.

The return trip seemed to be going well, when suddenly Ed attacked the globe. None of the other boys said anything until the first crack appeared. This was the group's first major crisis.

For two months, the group of eight boys, a worker, and an assistant had met weekly on Saturday mornings for about two hours. One of the major difficulties was that there was no place for the boys to meet at the Center. This necessitated taking weekly trips to various points of interest, such as museums, playgrounds, parks, and frequent visits to McDonald's for a snack. In a way, the mandatory trips had helped to create an extraordinary situation. Not only was the group an activity therapy group, but it evolved into a small club held captive by the demands of the car. The boys were also drawn together by the common interest of having a club, "just like other boys," and in working on some of the problems that were bothering them. The confines of the car, the "behavior setting" and the "trip time" created a strong catalyst for verbal communication.[1] The only other major activity that could be carried out comfortably within the confines of the car was "controlling."

"Controlling" was the name of the game, although no one ever named it. "Controlling" was played by being Superman, Batman, Mr. Terrific, Green Hornet, or Kato. "Controlling" meant that the station wagon was Batmobile or a magic carpet which could transport a boy from an unfriendly home situation, where none of the other children wanted to play with you or would scapegoat you, to a club, where you had friends and even fights just like in all clubs.

"Controlling" made you feel that you were strong and people had to listen, even if in real life you were in a special class and people called you dumb. It meant that those two big guys who worked with the club (the workers) did things that you wanted to do. They didn't yell too much, never pushed you around, and acted like you really had something important to say. You could even "control" them because you had a chance to plan what you wanted to do at meetings.

The boys are continually struggling to control their own destinies, a struggle in which the odds against success are overwhelming.

The Search for Autonomy

This search for control, so that you can control and not continually be controlled by others, is not too different from the search that all men carry out as they strive for independence, maturity, self-actualization or interpersonal competence.[2] It is the quest for autonomy. It is simply to be able to control your environment so that you have the kind of things happen to you that you want, to be able to do the things in your life that will get you the rewards you want from others, and to make your own decisions and know that these decisions may be implemented.

This lack of autonomy or feeling of inability to control one's own existence is often the source of people's search for help in solving problems. For these boys, their quest led them into a group. This quest led their parents to come to the Mental Development Center for help. The parents sought help in obtaining the rewards for themselves and their children that they wanted and needed. The group was offered as an additional way of working on these concerns. Some of the parents were "working" by meeting regularly with the casework staff of the agency. Some of the children were being seen as well, but the children's brief encounter with an adult was not sufficient to get at some of the conflicts they were facing as they attempted to solve their difficulties in learning to deal with others in their environment.

This search for autonomy is one of the common goals that the worker in the group shares with the members. He is one of the people who has been placed in the position of helping the member in his quest. The other members can share and, in fact, must help each member in his quest if the group is to survive and fulfill its purpose.

The worker with the group has three major goals in his encounters in the group during its existence:

The major goal is to enable the member to solve the problems he came to the group to work on. In some cases this may mean helping him focus on the problem when it is not clear to him, or to help him partialize the problem in order to select a piece of it that he can work on. This can often be done during the initial phases of the life of the group, when the worker and the group come to some agreement as to some of the problems that they are there to work on; i.e., the purpose of their existence together. In addition, the worker attempts to spell out with the group some of the ways they, as a group, may accomplish their purposes. This "contracting" period serves to establish the group's purpose, some of the means of achieving its goals, and the rules of the game. The group contract is a dynamic, frequently changing and modified understanding, which group and worker continually negotiate together. It is seen as the dynamic agreements between the worker and the client system in which the problems to be worked, the goals, and the activities (means) by which the goals are to be accomplished are negotiated.

The second goal, which becomes a crucial ongoing task for the group, is for the group to maintain itself as a working unit long enough to achieve its purposes for being. This is the group maintenance aspect of the task.

The third goal of the worker and the group is to insure, nurture, and enhance each individual's quest for autonomy. The realization of this goal requires that there be some carryover from the experience of the helping situation within the confines of the group to increase competence of the individual in the course of his life in other parts of his existence as well. Somehow the problem solver must be able to come to terms with his environment; i.e., with the "real" world outside the mutual-help group.

For the boys in the club, this meant not only learning how to get along with some of the other boys in the group, but hopefully with children in the neighborhoods where they lived, as well as with the teachers in their schools. The systemic interrelationships among individual members, the group, their parents and their schools would lead us to believe that changes for the better in school, for example, would lessen some of the pressure on the boy and the parent, and would result in less stress reactive behavior in all the areas of his life space.

The Power of Interaction

The continuation of the trip home which followed the breaking of the globe was charged and intense. For the first time there was very little screaming. Tim was not making animal noises, and Jim was not starting fights with the boys next to him. Don was repeating over and over, "I will tell your father, he will give it to you, he'll beat you, I'm going to tell." Ed was calling him a squealer. The boys were silent.

Then Lou said, "You shouldn't have done that."

This was voiced by a few of the other boys and repeated by Don.

Sam said, "He shouldn't be in the club."

Andy said, "Yeah, kick him out Mr. B."

"I don't think that is up to me, couldn't you guys have stopped him?"

Don said, "Kick him out, he broke my saucer."

Lou yelled, "He shouldn't be in the club. He knows he isn't supposed to do that."

Andy concurred: "The group is for fun and getting along together."

Ed was feeling the anger of the group, and for the first time the smile left his face. The worker asked Ed if he would like to say something about what happened. Ed said that he was sorry. Don wasn't satisfied and said he should be out of the group.

Ed told him that he could rip his hat and offered it to him. He grabbed it and was going to rip it. The worker told him not to, and said he couldn't let him rip it, and that he didn't think it would solve anything.

"Did anyone else have any other ideas?" He returned the hat.

Ed said he wanted to be in the club and that he wouldn't do it again. The boys looked at Don. He was the key. . . .

Don was always threatening to kill or beat up on the boys, but he never did. He would wrestle with the worker or box with the other boys with the large stuffed bears as go-betweens, but had never hit any of them. He was frequently frightened. In the Terminal Tower he was not able to look out the window, and following the trip he dreamt of falling from the Tower. Spiders terrified him, and on trips he was fearful when riding over bridges that they would crack. His father was in prison, his mother didn't want to take care of him, and he lived with his grandparents. His grandmother was a very large woman who loved and cared for him, but would not be engaged with casework help. She overwhelmed the small grandfather, who faithfully brought Don to the meeting each week. He didn't know why, except that something there was attracting the boy, and that was good enough for him.

It's hard to say what it was that enabled Don to shift through the hurt and anger of the broken globe. Perhaps some understanding of the meaning the club held for him and, therefore, the other boys allowed him to say, "I think we should give Ed another chance."

"Yes," the boys seemed to say in unison, "another chance."

"Another chance," Lou echoed in his stuttering way.

The worker looked at Don for a second, and said he thought that it was a hard decision for him to make, but a good one, and that he was glad Don had been able to make it. Don said he still was going to tell Ed's father. Ed began making up a number of excuses as to why he had broken the globe—whether for the club's benefit or as a rehearsal for his father, it was hard to say. The boys didn't really care any more; they were back to talking about other things, such things as where they would go next week and when it would be warm enough to go to the zoo.

Ed sat back and thought quietly. He was no longer in control of the group, but he was in control of himself. He had been able to muster the strength to come to terms with the group. Perhaps he was thinking of the close call he had just come through. He had only missed one meeting since the group began, and his caseworker had uncovered the importance of this group to him. Ed was able to tell her that these were "my friends."

He was a stepchild who had faced a number of rejections from his stepmother. She was now pregnant, worried about holding onto the pregnancy, and she had told Ed that when the new baby came, he might have to go. This was a hard time for him. Although he was ten, he couldn't read, but he could remember everybody's order at the McDonald's drive-in. When he was happy, he lit up the entire "Center" with his smile. When he was unhappy, you had your hands full.

As they drove into the parking lot of the Development Center, Don ran out, saying he was going to tell Ed's father. Ed walked from the car, holding the worker's hand; it tightened as his father approached, but Don had not spoken to him. Ed and his father walked to their car, talking.

The worker found Don hiding in the room, sitting in the corner . . . alone.

"I know how badly you feel about that saucer. I'm sorry it got broken."

"I really wanted it, Mr. B. Why did he break it?"

The worker sat with his arm around Superman. The pain was for real.

References

[1]The settings in which groups meet can play a vital role in determining the group's activities as well as its "life style." For an interesting approach to the study of "behavior settings," see Roger G. Barker, "Ecology and Motivation," in *Nebraska Symposium on Motivation, 1960* (Lincoln: University of Nebraska Press, 1960). Barker defines a behavior setting as ". . . a place where most of the inhabitants satisfy a number of personal motives where they can achieve multiple satisfactions," p. 25.

[2]On self-actualization as the essential and basic drive see: Kurt Goldstein, *Human Nature in the Light of Psychopathology* (New York: Shocken Books, 1963). p. 143. See also: Robert W. White, "Motivation Reconsidered," *Psychological Review,* Vol. 66, No. 5 (1959) and *The Study of Lives* (Atherton Press, 1963).

Casework with Mentally Retarded Adolescents and Young Adults, and Their Families

TWO PAPERS BY JEROME NITZBERG

The Setting and the Client

The observations made in these two papers are based principally upon an experience of several years duration in a sheltered workshop and training center. At this writing some 130 mentally retarded adolescents and young adults—most of them in their early twenties—spend approximately thirty hours per week in the Shop performing simple production and service tasks for which they are paid. Most sit at long tables performing assembly and disassembly, pasting, lacing, insertion, banding operations, which involve no tools. A few use a hammer or a screw driver. A sizable number receive training as messengers and travel through the community on foot and by bus and subway. A sizable number work in the Shop cafeteria as counter workers, bus workers, kitchen helpers. Others function as floor workers, freight handlers, inside messengers, shoe shiners. Many wrap and pack.

In addition to learning simple skills, they learn appropriate work habits. There is a network of "off-the-shop-floor" activities in which the trainees are involved. They attend shop meetings, elect a trainees' council, put out a biweekly newspaper, attend an art class, enjoy a musicale, sing in a choral group. Many receive individual and group counseling. Some are treated by a neuropsychiatrist. Almost all are tested by a psychologist. In the main each trainee relates to a shop supervisor who teaches him work skills and work habits and makes certain his work is adequate, and with whom he spends most of his time, and to a social worker who uses the interview and the group meeting to develop a treatment relationship intended to help him make optimal use of the agency.

Actually there are two agencies in one. One, the Workshop, which encompasses half the trainees, is a permanent facility. The trainees are here indefinitely. In the main, but not entirely, they tend to be older, less mature, with lower I.Q.'s, than their fellows in the Training Center. Workshop trainees have I.Q.'s largely in the fifties. Training Center trainees, who are with the agency for periods of up to one

Presented at an Institute on Casework in Mental Retardation, University of Connecticut School of Social Work, 1962. By permission of the author.

year, have I.Q.'s mainly in the sixties. For them employment in a competitive or less sheltered setting is the goal.

The shop supervisors are not professionals but persons drawn from many walks of life who are interested in being helpful to retarded people through the medium of work instruction and supervision. Counseling is provided principally by social workers. A psychologist is responsible for testing, for research and performs some counseling. A rehabilitation counselor is responsible for job placement and performs some counseling related specifically to developing competence and security in seeking and holding regular employment. A large staff of students and volunteers, called Shop Aides, provides much of the instructional program, e.g., instruction in travel, grooming, work-related academic subjects.

All of the trainees live in the community, almost entirely with families. Except for three or four, all have learned to travel between the Shop and their homes. Most live with intact families which are essentially stable, of low to middle income. There is evidence of brain damage for most of the trainees. Almost all attended special classes for retarded people in the public school system. Almost all came to the agency because they had failed to make a vocational adjustment after leaving school. Many come with important emotional, physical and situational handicaps in addition to the intellectual. Thus they are not simply retarded people but retarded people with important social and personal problems.

Casework with Retarded Adolescents and Adults

On a recent Sunday three of our staff members attended the wedding of a former client whom we will call Florence, who had been a trainee at our Shop for four years prior to obtaining a job in 1961. During those four years this woman, now 30 years of age, with an I.Q. of 64[1], had received work training, intensive individual and group counseling, had been a member of several activity groups, and had had the benefit of the overall Shop community. She had been an extremely anxious, self-conscious woman, constantly expecting failure and rejection, never really, reconciled to her deficiency. New demands upon her became crises which she met with whining complaints and gloomy foreboding. Striking a match terrified her until the age of 28, by which time many hours had been spent with her to enable her to light a gas stove so that she could prepare simple meals. Her mother had died several years before and her father was an indifferent homemaker. Staff shared this travail by eating her experimental puddings and spreads. Finally, when she had mastered the match, she applied her new skill for the first time to the lighting of candles for a candlelight dinner she had prepared for her friend—now her husband. The dinner came out of tin cans, which we had taught her to open, and frozen food packages. It was a tender and happy moment symbolizing many achievements—the mastery of simple skills we take for granted, a genuine romance, and even some poetry.

After the wedding ceremony, when the guests had taken their places at the dinner tables, the accordion player called upon Florence and her husband to dance to first waltz alone, as is the custom. I felt a surge of anxiety as I thought of this clumsy and self-conscious couple attempting to be graceful on an acre of dance floor, the center of fifty pairs of eyes. The couple, tense but controlled, made their way down from the dais, and as the accordion played the waltz, they gravely walked their dance in slow, leaden circles, but did it with dignity and courage. After a tense moment, universally shared, smiles wreathed the room and applause recognized their achievement. As she had told us in many counseling sessions, Florence said afterward that she had been scared to death and had two left feet but what had to be done had to be done, and with a grin, added that a new girdle had not helped. Florence and her husband melted into the assemblage of ordinary people and it would have taken some careful looking to have noted the differences between them and the others, which certainly did exist. Even with the knowledge that the future would present new crises, this was a time of gratification.

KINDS OF PROBLEMS

In increasing numbers the Florences will be showing up in our caseloads as public attention is directed to the three percent of the population considered to be mentally retarded, and particularly to that ninety-seven percent of the retarded who are thought capable of remaining out of the institution if given proper help.

What kinds of problems are we likely to encounter as we meet our retarded adolescents and young adults? In our Shop, of course, the problems to which we are especially alert are those related to vocational habilitation. However, these are not entirely specific to our setting and they are likely to be encountered elsewhere.

We completed a study of 101 temporary clients who stayed with us for periods of up to one year. Three-fourths of these persons showed seriously deficient motivation for employment. Employment frightened them or was alien to their self-expectation, a sign of their immaturity. Some have explained in counseling what they feared "on the outside":

I won't make friends (on a regular job). (Age 27, I.Q. 59)

They push you too much. (Age 21, I.Q. 65)

They may say my work is lousy. I won't stick it out. (Age 20, I.Q. 50)

They yell at you if you're late. (Age 20, I.Q. 62)

Because of our vocational function, the incidence of this problem among our clients is probably greater than it would be in the general population of retardates, but the likelihood is that it will constitute an important problem in any setting.

Well over half of our clients showed problems in their choice of job objectives. They selected jobs for which they had inadequate ability or jobs so severely circumscribed as to be virtually impossible to find. Some wanted to be scientists, business men, teachers, social workers, doctors, astronomists. One young man scoffed that he could easily be a social worker since all that social workers did was to sit behind a desk and talk. Some would work only within walking distance of their home, at certain hours, in a very special setting. Underneath this problem often lay resistance to work, immaturity, ignorance of the workaday world, rejection of their handicap, and anxiety over adulthood.

Just over half showed problems in relating to authority figures, carrying over into our setting a lifetime of experience with parents, neighbors, teachers, and other adults. Many reacted badly to correction and criticism, no matter how gently given. Many feared to ask for help with their work. Some balked at shop regulations. Many resisted doing work they disliked even to a small degree.

Over half of our clients presented serious travel problems which ranged from acute to mild anxiety over traveling anywhere alone by bus and subway. "When you're lost," explained one woman (Age 26, I.Q. 59), "you're in a wilderness." And said a young man (Age 28, I.Q. 50), describing the kind of response he expected should he ask a stranger for directions, "What's the matter, boy? Can't you read the signs? So I blush and feel bad. Getting lost is wanting to cry like a kid." In a large city like ours, the ability to travel alone is a mark of adulthood. It often is a revelation to frightened, overprotective parents and to the retardate himself. It is a blow struck for freedom for the retardate and his parents from one another for a few precious hours. And it is a very important means of achieving a more stimulating social and cultural life. The movie house around the corner turns out not to be the sole repository of the nation's culture.

About a third of our clients showed important defects in grooming, personal hygiene and appearance. They may be unshaven and the women not know how to use cosmetics properly. Clothing is often tasteless, ill-fitting and shabby. Offensive body odors and unclean skin are not unusual. Sometimes this is the result of parental deemphasis on attractiveness possibly originating in a fear of sexual attraction. We suspect it is also a product of insufficient social interaction, of a self-image of unworthiness, of a lack of interest in or hope for heterosexual relationships. Possibly it is related to the failure to integrate adult self-expectations and to a general intolerance for disciplined behavior as is characteristic of immature people.

Almost one in five persons manifested problematic peer relationships which forebode trouble in employment. However, since an isolate can do well on a job, his isolation may not constitute a vocational problem although it may be a personal problem. Thus we did not consider as problematic in our setting a large number of inadequate peer relationships. Perhaps a better indicator of the extent of problem is the statistic on friendships. Of 67 persons for whom we had reliable intake data in this area, three-fifths reported having no friends at all. By far the reason usually given for coming to the Shop—next to having something interesting to do—is the desire for friendships. There are many problems in heterosexual relationships. Social workers on staff spend a good deal of their time with clients who feel ignored or rejected by the other sex, and who are frightened about losing a boyfriend or a girlfriend to a rival. One woman was depressed by her "ugliness" which presaged a life without marriage. Some yearn for the normalcy implicit in marriage but are frightened by its demands, including childbirth. Some would be content with a long term stable relationship with a person of the other sex which provides affection, acceptance, recognition and sexual pleasure, but which may never culminate in marriage. There is a good deal of confusion and ignorance about appropriate behavior between the sexes, and about the sex act. In recent issues of our Shop newspaper, there was an angry clash of opinions over whether retarded women should go out with non-retarded men. One trainee wrote (actually dictated to a volunteer):

> In case you meet a boy and he's not retarded and you are, it wouldn't be good. He would be asking questions you wouldn't know how to answer. I'd rather be with the ones that are retarded. . . . If a boy asked you where you worked, I would have to tell them where and then they would have nothing to do with me. (Age 30, I.Q. 61)

To this another young woman wrote an irritable reply:

> If a girl wants to go out with a normal boy, they could. I do and I at least consider myself as normal. I don't tell everyone where I worked before or tell them what class I went to before. When I go out I dress neat and clean and talk about whatever he talks about. You don't have to announce your whole life story to people that you just meet. If you dress neat, clean and talk sensibly, they won't know unless you act silly or talk nonsense that you don't know what you are saying or make scenes.
>
> . . . If you trainees, some of you, want to be called that, you go right to it, but then you will first lose friends. . . . No one is going to get me to say I am retarded because I never considered it and I never will.
>
> If I see another trainee writing these things again that a normal person doesn't go with others like yourselves, I will personally come to the shop meeting and tell you a few things, that you wouldn't like to hear. . . . (Age 30, I.Q. 64)

Of course, an important area of problem occurs within the family, in the relationships between retarded grown children and their parents, principally along the axes of independence-dependence, overprotection-overexpectation, and acceptance-rejection. Sibling relationships are frequently seriously strained and it is commonplace for the normal brother or sister to want to conceal the existence of the retarded member of the family out of a fear that prospects of marriage would be dimmed. Often the parents actively assist such siblings, benevolently perhaps by going to the movies with the retardate the night of the date, less benevolently by banishing him to his room during the visit, or exiling him to an institution during the courtship years of the normal sib.

PSYCHOLOGICAL CHARACTERISTICS

Underlying the manifest problems which our clients present, apart from plain ignorance of social conventions and expectations, are certain recurrent psychological characteristics. Without listing them in any order of importance, they are:

1. Feelings of general inadequacy, causing high expectations of failure. Our client has failed his parents many times over by the time he comes to us. He walked, talked and achieved toilet training later than the neighbors' children. He failed in school, failed to keep friends, failed to date, failed to hold a job, failed to marry, failed to have children.

2. A high expectation of rejection, depreciation and disinterest. His past probably echoes with cries of "stupid" and the irritated dismissals of busy adults.

3. A low tolerance for interpersonal tensions and environmental discomfort. At the voting age of 21, he may still become enraged when someone pokes out his tongue at him, and whine when asked to carry a small parcel, or be deeply hurt when someone fails to greet him with "good morning."

4. A passive waiting for things to happen to him. He is likely to sit back and expect others to shape his life, without any particular guilt or shame. Past necessity and discouragement may have made this a fairly inflexible posture.

5. A strong proclivity for minimizing or denying psychological problems generally. Minimization and denial have long served their purpose of keeping out of sight overwhelming problems and it is likely that a deficient intellect makes denial and its consequent contradictions quite tolerable.

6. A low tolerance for hostility leading to an avoidance of overt conflict and a preference for covert resistance and pseudosubmissiveness. Persons working with retarded people often feel very satisfied with their achievement only to discover later that the plans ostensibly accepted by their client were promptly forgotten or ignored.

7. A preoccupation with one's own needs and desires and an insensitivity to the needs and desires of others. Unabashed and unadorned selfishness characterizes many of our young adults, side by side with a strident self-righteousness, reminiscent of the child who seeks to conceal his real self beneath an ill-fitting cloak of non-integrated adult ethics.

8. A preoccupation with the present and an inadequate consideration of the future. Appeals to the future consequences of present actions often fall on deaf ears. At best the future is very nebulous and a rather tiresome monster which countless adults have invoked in futile efforts to beat some sense into someone's uncaring head.

9. An expectation of indefinite dependence upon others with little guilt or shame. Despite the protestations to the contrary and the facility for rendering homilies on one's obligations to one's parents—and even these are not encountered too often—our clients tend to be quite comfortable about envisaging long vistas of dependence upon their parents or parent-substitutes.

Of course, it would be a serious error to believe that all retardates demonstrate all these traits or even most of these traits. All that is meant is that in this agency's experience, we have found a high incidence of such characteristics among our retarded clients. We suspect that they will be found among other retarded people appearing as clients in other settings.

COUNSELING CHARACTERISTICS

There are certain characteristics as counseling clients which our retardates have manifested which need to be reckoned with.

Not only do they generally lack a future-orientation which is so useful in counseling, but they also often demonstrate a very weak expectation that one day they, too, will play adult roles. The implicit assumption in much of counseling that the client might want to protect his future and to realize adult aspirations cannot be safely made with this client.

Language is a serious problem. Our retardate has a poor comprehension of even ordinary abstractions. Convenient terms like "independent," "mature," "responsibile," "hostile," "guilt," and so on, often cannot be used by the caseworker as a convenient psychological shorthand, and he finds himself struggling to communicate such difficult concepts with grade 1 or 2 or grade 3 language.

Verbal productions are often difficult to follow and understand. Much is repeated. The client rambles. Irrelevancies, abrupt transitions, contradictions, illogicalities abound in his speech. Often he mouthes concepts he has heard countless times but does not comprehend. He often does not use words in the same manner as the counselor. I once anticipated with a certain satisfaction telling the trainees at a Shop meeting that the agency would make a sizable contribution to their Christmas party. To my bewilderment, the news was greeted with silent disappointment. Trainees explained that they understood themselves to be the agency and it was hardly good news to learn that they would be expected to make a sizable contribution to their party.

The production of personal history tends to be meagre with most clients. Material on relationships with parents, whether in the past or the present, is often hard to obtain, probably because of anxiety and guilt.

Workers accustomed to viewing their clients as active collaborators and coequals on a treatment team, will find much less of this in working with retarded people than in working with intellectual normals. These clients are less likely than intellectual normals to objectify a helping process. The analysis of transference, countertransference and of the shifting client-work relationship is sketchy at best. Seeking the roots of present behavior in past experience produces some material but not much. The isolation of patterns of behavior and the establishment of causal connections between manifest behavior and underlying thinking and feeling are difficult operations. Our retardate often cannot comprehend the concept of a therapeutic person but is more likely to see him as a dear friend—a bright, competent, kind, helping and interested authority figure—an idealized parent such as he had never had. Our lower level clients sometimes call us "mother" and "father" albeit with sufficient embarrassment to suggest that they know we really are not their parents although they might wish we were.

Both impressive and exasperating is the tenacity with which so many of our clients will deny problem in the face of its obvious existence. It is particularly difficult for them to grasp the notions that *feelings* may change as a consequence of counseling, although they grasp readily that the ability to *do* things may change. The widespread notion among lay people that one can alter the behavior of retarded persons simply by requesting them to change it often enough because they are so suggestible has not been our experience if such change involves change in thought and feeling and if it creates anxiety or other distress.

Typical, too, of so many of our retarded clients, especially at the outset of their counseling experience, is their tendency to view the sessions as discrete experiences rather than as interconnected events flowing in a certain direction.

However, for all of these characteristics, many of our clients do change their behavior and attitudes. Motivation for employment has increased and job goals have become more realistic. Security in seeking work is achieved. A better acceptance of authority figures and a more comfortable association with peers often occur. Improvement is noted in appearance, in tolerance of hostility and physical discomfort. We have seen a greater assumption of responsibility for one's own behavior, better self-control, greater planfulness. Frequently staff comments that a client "is opening up," becoming more sociable, more assertive, more responsive. Parents often marvel at the new interest their sons and daughters take in living. Instead of lying in bed until noon, they are up with the sun, wash and dress without having to be prodded, even make their own breakfast, and rush out of the house "like other working people." Perhaps most important, there is a growth in self-respect and a less troubled acceptance of their retardation.

While many of our clients undergo such changes without counseling, in response to the impact of the total shop community, others seem unable to advance without counseling.

For all of their differences from intellectual normals, retardates are more like us than unlike us. They do experience real distress in their life situation. Many do wish to be different for all of their denials. Many are aware of how they feel and how they function with others. In their yearning for a positive relationship with another person, many will attempt new kinds of behavior if only at first to obtain the worker's respect. In time they do it to obtain the respect of others and of themselves, and find that the new experiences, for all of their fearsome qualities, yield profound satisfactions, and new ways of coping with the world and of enjoying it become integrated. Perhaps what they seek in us most is affectionate respect and concern. One client said, "Staff are really my favorite people and trust me as a person as I said once before and that is why I'm so happy in the workshop." (Age 28, I.Q. 64)

THE SOUND OF RETARDATION IN COUNSELING

How do these clients sound in counseling relationships? What do they say: Their definitions of mental retardation are meaningful, felt and often projections of their self-image. For example:

Retarded means you're stubborn like a mule. You can't take no. You can't read, you think slow. (Age 21, I.Q. 63)

They can't help each other. They can't do things at school. They need help like they can't write or do things. (Age 19, I.Q. 64)

Needs help with everything. (Age 18, I.Q. 64)

You're slow in getting things out and thinking. (Age 21, I.Q. 68)

That's me! Something in my head makes it hard for me to learn, like a 12-year old kid. (Age 18, I.Q. 48)

You're back in everything, in work. Sometimes I feel, sometimes I feel I'm not. (Age 19, I.Q. 48)

The mind don't function so good. You can't have friends like everybody else. (Age 19, I.Q. 48)

It is often better to be "slow" than "retarded." Being retarded is often interpreted as being "very slow" and sometimes as being "crazy." For some it has the implication of a completely immutable condition. Some prefer to see themselves as "disturbed," a more popular term of late. Some focus on a physical disability in preference to the intellectual deficit. Like the rest of us, many take comfort in being better off than others. "Like my mother says, we should thank God we are not the worst. I feel sorry for them," one boy solemnly said. (Age 18, I.Q. 64) Some find compensations. ". . . but I can read real good!" (Age 18 I.Q. 70) "Man! My reading is bad, but I can drive a team of horses!" exclaimed an alumnus of Letchworth Village. (Age 17, I.Q. 63)

While some prefer to see themselves injured at birth, others prefer to blame themselves. "I could be smart. Maybe go to college. I didn't study or do homework like other kids. I don't pick up so good but I shoulda studied. If I studied, I coulda been a cop or a detective or an engineer or a drummer." (Age 18, I.Q. 68) And some blame bad luck. "Boy! You have to have luck in this world. They didn't work and go through (school) and I worked and didn't." (Age 20, I.Q. 61)

Retardation hurts. Retardation is not good to have. A lot of people don't understand what it means. You go around feeling that people don't want you around because you are retarded . . . . We have to live with it all our lives. We shouldn't be like this but what can we do? It wasn't our fault that we had it—just Nature's way. (Age 18, I.Q. 53)

Anger and bitterness are often expressed:

What do I need money for? I got nothing to spend it on, no girl, no car, no place to go. Nothing. (Age 20, I.Q. 80)
I'm a flop. I'm alone—me, myself and I. . . . When you're hurt, you don't trust anyone. I believe half of what I see and nothing that I hear. . . . I'm like that typewriter when I am hurt. I click like it does and the whole thing moves all of a sudden (the worker had depressed the tabulator key sending the carriage flying). When I'm angry, I think only of bad. I forget that good things happen to me also. (Age 18, I.Q. 64)

There is wistfulness as well as bitterness:

I want to be like other people. I want to marry, have kids, have money. . . . I don't want to sit home and just sleep and eat and walk. . . . If you don't get some money, you're a nobody. I can't go out with friends without money. I like nice clothes. I want to be like other people. (Age 18, I.Q. 48)

[When I worked] it was like paradise, working for a change like a regular, normal person and getting out to meet other people." (Age 28, I.Q. 64)

I know I am a little slow. But it was nice dancing at the Y with boys like all other boys. It was not like dancing with Frank (a trainee). I don't know. It was different. It was nice. (Age 24, I.Q. 54)

There is an awareness of the feelings which rise when "the outside" is contemplated, and an awareness of ambivalence:

I felt half for and half against trying to make out. . . . I want work but the thought of leaving made me put on five pounds already. (Age 28, I.Q. 64)

It's like walking on a pier to the end and falling off. (Age 17, I.Q. 74)

Some of us are nervous when we think about going for a job so maybe we can talk about it and get over it a little. (Age 27, I.Q. 59)

A client denounced a staff member for not moving swiftly enough to get her a job once she had mobilized herself to seek one:

I want to inform you that I have given you enough time for you to get me something— you can't say that I don't want to go on any places if you don't work on it. . . . I don't like to call you a gunif which means a fiber. (Age 28, I.Q. 64)

The same client, contrite after an angry session with the social worker, left a note on his desk which read in part:

I want to apologize if I made you angry with me if you were, I don't know why I do these things, or to complain too much, maybe it's because I want a attention like a child, in which I'm not. I know I acted like one yesterday and I am sorry I picked on a couple of persons yesterday.

I found out why I complained so much about everything. Because I like to have my own way, about a few things, like for instance, when you sometimes break your appointment to see someone else, I get upset.

If our client is unlikely to anticipate the helping process, he often understands that something has happened to him as he looks back over the many weeks and months of sessions:

They [the group meetings] gave me courage. I was scared to see Mr. B. [the 'job man']. But I saw other people knock at his door and go in. They said it was okey. So I went to see him. It gave me courage. It hurt me a little when Mr. N. [the social worker] told me my work wasn't so good. I felt like two cents. But then I got over it. I knew it was to help me. So I am doing better. You have to face the facts. (Age 21, I.Q. 60)

At the beginning I was scared. As each day and each month came I knew I can do it, I can get a job. I am not so scared. Put my mind to it and I can do it. If I can do it, all of you around the table can do it. (Age 29, I.Q. 61)

I am getting out of the habit of being shy. I'm not afraid of people any more. I used to be afraid to talk up. I'm not so nervous with people. . . . Talking helps you look for jobs. I am less nervous in the group now. (Age 21, I.Q. 77)

I feel now I have to work. I didn't feel like that before. (Age 28, I.Q. 64)

THE WORKER'S EXPECTATIONS FOR HIMSELF

The social worker expecting to counsel the retardate should expect to use a certain style and certain methods of work. He should also expect to experience certain troublesome feelings within himself as he relates to this kind of client.

Working with the retarded client can be exhausting. As has been noted elsewhere the worker is constantly searching for simple language. Given the likelihood that he is accustomed to using language in its most polysyllabic form and dealing with ideas with great ease, it is rather disconcerting suddenly to find oneself unable to communicate.

The caseworker must expect to be very active. Generally, he cannot sit back while his client ventilates. He must be directive. He must help his client grope for words. He encourages, restates, recalls, suggests, speculates. He proposes alternate formulations in the hope that one will be understood. He teaches his client how to be a client. The degree to which the worker must be active presents a problem for, with or without his awareness, he is in constant danger of imposing his will on this client. He can suggest in ways which deny to the retardate a freedom to find his own response. The agony of pursuing a client through his labyrinth of tortuous thinking tempts the worker to cut through the maze with interpretations which seem logical if not applicable to this specific person. A good deal of tension can be generated between the two as communication breaks down and the client, wanting to spare himself and even his worker, learns to say the "right" thing in an appropriate manner, which gratifies the worker and rescues the client momentarily even though it does not advance the case.

If the intellectual components of the helping process are less significant in counseling the mentally retarded than the intellectually normal, the emotional components are more significant. It is likely that the retardate responds more to affect than to words much of the time and since affect is more likely than words to open a window onto the worker's real attitude toward his client—for language is more easily controlled and, therefore, misleading—the worker who is inadequately concerned for his client is readily betrayed. For the retarded the dynamics of change provide little excitement per se while the personality of the worker becomes more important. This puts a considerable burden on the worker. His interest must truly be genuine for if it is not, his technical skills and verbal facility are not likely to be of much use.

The importance of nonverbal communication also puts a premium on spontaneity in the worker and this in turn necessitates substantial security in his role as well as an adequate range and ease of expression.

The reduced verbal content sometimes necessitates other forms of interaction between client and worker as the latter seeks a medium in which to develop a treatment relationship. Oftimes the worker must be prepared to do relatively unorthodox things with this client. He may have to find adult hobbies or games for them to do together. He may want to tutor his client in reading or writing or arithmetic, show him how to travel, to go to department stores with him. The worker may have to learn to free himself of his office. His desk may become a work table at which both he and the client sit on the same side.

Because the client is often ignorant of social conventions and procedures, the worker may become a teacher and advisor. Writing a letter, planning purchases, working out a budget, finding a movie, may become session content with this adult.

Because this client often moves so slowly, experiences so many regressions, is sometimes so exasperatingly forgetful, and so often seems to approach old counseling territory as if for the first time, the worker is hard put to it to be patient. He finds himself in the same predicament as the retardate's parents and like them, is apt to clutch his head in despair, to flee his client, and to punish him.

Because this client finds it so difficult to explore his past and to probe his preconscious and unconscious feelings, the worker who feels that nothing is happening until the sessions are rich with the memories of past experiences and with the revelation of repressed conflicts and desires, will experience endless frustration.

Most of us are oriented toward ending cases. We often think of beginning, middle and concluding phases. Our basic objective, we have learned time and again, is to help the client separate from the worker in a manner which permits the former to function more competently and with more satisfaction without further dependence upon the latter. The worker writes his closing summary with an inner "well done!" Unfortunately, our retarded client, whose basic intellectual equipment is irreparably damaged, does not share the closing summary. He often returns. Our culture offers him little peace so that life for him is apt to be a series of crises. In his case, success may have to be measured in terms of how far in advance of crisis he seeks help, of the ease with which he seeks help, of the kind he manages to survive without help. He may never have a closing summary. His return to the agency can strike a note of despair in the worker. "How have I failed?" For the agency, beset with long waiting lists, and needing to present its donor public with statistics of successful outcomes, the reapplication of the retardate poses administrative and psychological problems. Shall he be put back on a waiting list with the almost certain knowledge that the crisis will indeed shatter him before he is reached, or is he to receive service ahead of the many who have waited for so long and who have never been seen? And for how many years shall he be permitted to return? This is a depressing and bewildering prospect for those oriented toward the closing summary.

In vocational rehabilitation, some agencies count the days on which the client remains employed, and when the magic thirtieth day arrives, triumphantly close the case as successful, file it away hurriedly with a sigh of relief, and do not think of what may happen on the thirty-first or thirty-second day. Were time differently ordered, they might report fewer successful outcomes.

Because of the nature of his personality problems and the cultural context in which they occur—a context shared by the worker—our retardate makes us vulnerable in certain psychological areas. We must try to be on guard against our feelings in such areas.

Since our retardate is likely to be a flagrantly self-centered person, violating cultural expectations that he show concern for others, he is likely to create within us anger against him as he seeks to monopolize us and to make relentless demands upon us.

Our retardate often copes with the world in ways which we associate with children. Much value is attached in our culture to "acting your age." We may well have trouble with our own hostile feelings toward the twenty-year old who fails to "act his age," who whines, cries, sulks, pouts, attacks irrationally, pokes out his tongue at others, and cries petulantly in eternal defense of his behavior, "I don't like it."

Our retardate is usually too timid to differ with us openly or to attack or to assert himself. Instead, he is apt to resort to subterfuge and covert resistance. Our culture values open difference and self-expression so that we are in constant danger of reacting with scorn to the client who lies, feigns innocence, and pretends cooperation while sabotaging our most brilliant plans behind our backs.

Our retardate resists self-reliance, flying in the face of the cultural imperative of standing on one's own two feet, earning one's own living, making one's own way, etc. He is in no hurry to relieve his parents of the burden of supporting him, or the worker of having to make decisions for him, so that we may find ourselves resenting him for draining us of time and energy and frustrating us in achieving a basic objective of our profession: independence.

Our retardate often presents himself as a sweet, likeable, cuddlesome and helpless young person, quick to show affection and admiration if treated well. For those of us who enjoy the role of the strong, giving authority figure, and who have a special need for affection and adoration, such a trainee may encourage overprotection and inappropriate physical demonstrations of affection. To such a worker this trainee seems to have no problems at all.

Our retardate often has bizarre mannerisms and acts in ways associated with mental illness. He may have epileptic seizures. He may be palsied. He, therefore, is apt to arouse in us feelings of awe, dread, anxiety, helplessness and panic.

Our retardate is a difficult person to help because of his many personality, intellectual, physical and situational problems. Concomitant with his intellectual problem, for example, is often an array of speech, hearing, and visual defects, of problems in coordination, cardiac complications, and so on. He can frustrate in us the culturally-induced need to be rewarded for our pains and to succeed as quickly as possible. At times he moves like a tortoise and having moved forward one step, slips back two. Echoing his parents we are likely to exclaim inwardly, "We try so hard for you—and what do you do? Nothing!" We feel guilty in finding relief in expletives of "crazy" and "stupid" because these, after all, are his chief symptoms. Instead we devastate him with the judgment, "hopeless!" The extent and complexity of the problem, the seeming eternity of time and infinity of patience required, and the lilliputian dimensions of change as well as its uncertainty, conspire together to nudge the worker choosing more successful prospects, labeling the others as poor counseling clients—often, however, with a nagging trace of guilt.

In our culture our client is often less respected albeit not less a sympathetic figure than anyone else. The terms "moron," "idiot," "imbecile," are terms of opprobrium. Periodically we search for new terms to shed old derogatory associations. The worker must become alert to the possible existence of his own unconscious hostility and disrespect toward this kind of client. He must pause to consider whether his goals for such a client—so modest in our culture—may not make him feel unworthy in such work.

Our retardate may never fly a rocket ship to the moon but he may learn to polish it, which is also necessary. He can be helped to find this a truly satisfying activity and the worker who helps him may find deep personal and professional gratification in this retarded person's achievement and appreciation.

Working with the Parents of the Mentally Retarded

In our setting, the major objectives in working with the parents are:

1. To help the parents perceive the retardate neither as a child nor as a normal adult, but as he is—an adolescent or young adult with intellectual and probably emotional handicaps;

2. To help the parents develop a more realistic appraisal of the retardate's capacities;

3. To develop a balance between dependence and independence in the retardate's relationship with his parents, which recognizes both his healthy separation tendencies, and a permanent residue of dependence upon the parents or parent substitutes;

4. To help the parents relate to the retardate with as little guilt and anguish as possible; and

5. To enable the parent to engage in rational planning for the future when he is no longer alive or able to care for the retardate, should he want such help.

At the beginning of our work with parents we usually find them deeply grateful for our interest. We offer some hope for the future and a certain amount of freedom from the retardate during the day. It is later, as we seek to come to grips with the problems almost always present in family relationships, that we find that we do not have a client in the parent. We have found it difficult to involve parents in true counseling relationships, so that they constitute another hard to reach category of client. These are not only parents living in marginal and disorganized homes and who tend to pursue peripheral roles with all of their children. These are often fairly sophisticated persons, responsibile in their parental roles, who have good relationships with their normal children, and head fairly stable families. In the main, our parents strike us as tired, wanting relief after twenty years of struggle and disappointment, and by no means willing to struggle more in order to scrutinize their relationships with their retarded offspring and to find new ways of living with them.

Given a society which makes rigorous demands upon its members without providing them adequately with the means for fulfilling such demands, it is little wonder that many retarded people experience a lifetime of maladjustments which deeply trouble their parents and siblings. In general, we find the parents either too protective, seeking to avoid anxiety and disappointment for themselves and the children, or too demanding, unwilling or unable to surrender goals appropriate for normals. While it is true that beneath such behavior may lie long term and unconscious needs to control, to reject, to infantilize, to succeed, and so on, and while it is true that the existence of a retarded person in the family may lay bare the most vulnerable layers of the parents' personalities, it is also true that the retardate is a most difficult person to live with in our culture. He is a real problem and finding ways of living with him is truly bewildering. The parent may be quite normal emotionally and intellectually and experience hostile and rejecting feelings toward his retarded child. A basic counseling goal is the reduction of the guilt such a parent feels, and the parent who denies such feeling is suspect.

The social agency must expect to set for itself the goal of helping the parent to perceive the retardate somewhat differently. We hold a family interview during the intake process, for example, in which the worker wants the parent to view him speaking simply but without condescension to the retarded son or daughter, speaking seriously to him, listening to him, soliciting his opinions honestly, if possible acting on his statements, yet not pushing or humiliating him if he remains silent. Later, the parent should be able to witness the retardate venturing into new areas of behavior which he thought forever closed to him. Our parent is often startled with pleasure to discover that junior can tolerate a work day, can bring home a few dollars, can take the floor at a meeting, think out a letter to the newspaper, and manage to survive the subway rush hour. It is a revelation that junior can navigate the labyrinth at Union Square or Grand Central stations. When the worker solemnly awards a travel or employability certificate to a trainee at a shop meeting, he is also holding it up for the parents at home to see as documentation of what might be possible in more mature behavior.

In the early days we urged the parent to help the trainee to travel, to accompany him to employment interviews, to teach him to light a match, or do other difficult things with him. In time we found that with most of our parents, this encouragement might be in error because these lessons could not be learned in this way. Many parents could not tolerate their own anxiety and frustration and anger sufficiently to teach. The teaching process would be contaminated with tension. The retardate was better off with someone not related to him and our maximum expectation of most parents in this area now is that they permit and support our efforts rather than undertake them themselves.

Many of our parents create more problems in choosing vocational goals than do the trainees. For some parents the choice of a job brings to a head their feelings about mental retardation. If one's employment is the family's face to the community, how does one face the community with a job such as that of a porter or a busworker in a cafeteria or a shoe shiner? Some parents content themselves with unskilled jobs if they occur in hospital settings as if association with doctors and nurses to some degree compensates for the shame of the kitchen. The parents of many of our women clients hope against hope to snatch something from the debacle by getting their daughter some kind of office work—*any* kind of office work. For some white families who suffer from racial prejudice, there is a shock in learning that the unskilled jobs their children would have to do are precisely the jobs which many Negro and Puerto Rican persons are forced to do for social reasons, and that their children would have to associate with Negro and Puerto Rican workers. For some, going to club meetings, visiting the homes of other retarded people, going to work, brings to the fore strong anxieties always just beneath the surface. The messenger who works outdoors is certain to catch pneumonia in inclement weather or be struck by a car. The daughter will surely be a masher's victim on the crowded subway train, or be seduced or raped.

Other obstacles appear as the worker helps the retarded client toward more mature fuctioning. While we are busy helping the trainee develop a more adult self-image, quite the opposite is occurring at home. There he is often treated as a child. We go to much trouble to provide him with pay which we put into a real pay envelope on Friday afternoon, but when he goes home, he promptly hands it unopened to his mother, or puts its contents into a piggy bank. He is something of a wage-earner now but every morning his parent doles out to him transportation tokens and lunch money. Nothing new has happened for all of his having become a working person.

One trainee complained bitterly that while she was expected to seek work by her parents, she was not allowed to stay out after dark. When she had to go to an employment agency for the first time, she consciously punished her mother by forcing her to come along. In another case, a newly employed young woman fulfilled an old ambition by buying scores of movie magazines and comic books with part of her newly earned wage, creating dismay in her intellectual parents who could not bear to see such publications resting side by side with the *Saturday Review* and *The New York Times*. They had to be helped to understand and control their own reactions.

In counseling much is made of the retarded person's making decisions concerning the spending of his earnings or his allowance, his choice of clothing, of hobbies, of recreation, of friends, of TV and radio programs. Yet often nothing new occurs at home in these areas. Or while we are busy structuring limitations and responsibilities for him at the Shop, at home he continues to experience the same overindulgence and permissiveness as before.

For all his stated desire to see the retardate "grow up," once he is actually on the threshold of such an era, the parent may draw back in fear. Actually dependency and sheltered living for all the bad feeling they gave the parent, had been less frightening than the vistas now opening up. Perhaps unconsciously the parents all along had been protecting themselves from such fears. Often we find parents sabotaging job referrals and club referrals after having given their permission to the worker to help the retarded client develop motivation and security precisely to attain such goals. Sometimes parents are so casual and indifferent about some new venture in order to demonstrate their love for the retardate no matter whether he succeeds or fails, that the retarded person himself becomes indifferent toward achievement, or yields to his own anxieties, and fails

We have found that some parents, consciously or unconsciously, had molded a role for the retardate within the household which precludes movement toward optimal maturity. The retardate may provide valuable service as a housekeeper or baby sitter or companion in one's old age. One parent, a widow, would not stop accompanying the retarded daughter to the agency for an entire year even though the latter was able to travel alone and wanted to do so. It was not fear that motivated the mother but her own insatiable need to have the daughter near her. It was easy to mask her own need with the socially acceptable and even admirable explanation that she did this in order to protect her daughter.

How much freedom should a retarded person have? Should the girl be allowed out after dark? Should the retarded person be married? Have children? There are no universal answers to these questions. How can one know without knowing many other things about this retarded person and his parents? One would want to know something of the retardate's judgment, psychological needs, social competence, capacity for sustained, intimate relationship with the other sex, the extent to which parental supervision might be necessary and if necessary, available. What would the financial and housing arrangements be? What sort of person is the spouse and what are the expectations, attitudes and availability for supervision of the spouse's parents? The very posing of the questions implies that a worker must be prepared to work in such a case for some time and in some depth.

Of course, for many parents growing up and becoming self-sufficient constitute signposts to marriage and this generates much feeling. The possibility of out of wedlock children is often a nightmare. Helping the parents discuss their attitudes toward sex, helping them take a close and individualized look at their children to see whether such problems really do exist, and helping them consider sterilization, are important kinds of help the worker can offer. For some parents and for some retardates, if marriage could occur without offspring, it would be manageable and even welcome. Parents with grown children usually want to feel free of daily child care and it is disheartening to them to envisage having to take care of grandchildren —as parents and not as grandparents—after having raised their own for two or more decades. For some parents, a childless marriage for their retarded children is a way of achieving their own freedom without having to institutionalize the retarded person.

It is difficult to confine oneself to the parents of the retarded trainee only in terms of their relationship with the retardate. The worker has to be ready at times to consider other relationships within the family although he certainly should not shoulder himself into such areas if he is unwanted there. Often the entire family needs help. The marital relationship may have suffered because of the presence of the retardate. It is commonplace for parents to differ sharply on such matters as how much freedom to grant the retardate, what kind of schooling to obtain for him, how much responsibility to demand of him, whether he should stay home or enter an institution. These can be charged issues. It is not unusual for the retarded person to be a pawn or ally in the marital conflict. On another level, the retardate may have crystallized strong feelings of guilt and hostility in the parents vis a vis one another. If marital counseling is not within the ken of the worker or the function of the agency, the worker at least may have to help the parents to identify the problem areas and to seek help with them elsewhere.

There is also an important problem with siblings who find the retardate a threat and burden. The parent is hard put to it to know what to do about such conflicts. Perhaps the agency might work with the siblings as well. Perhaps groups of normal brothers and sisters of retarded people could be formed.

There needs to be a large didactic element in working with parents as with their offspring. Adequate parent-child relationships usually do not suffice to solve management problems although they certainly create a climate which is necessary for their solution. The worker must be prepared to help parents with immediate everyday problems, such as how to budget the retarded trainee's earnings, how to find friends, to organize his social activities, to utilize money to develop economic interests, to find within the operation of the household ways of helping the retardate develop a more mature self-image. Ordinary details of living which normals may absorb through observation or imitation or communication or doing often escape retardates. To expect the parents to be able to teach such things unaided to such difficult pupils, especially when they must also carry the load of troubled feeling, is to expect something which often baffles more objective experts.

A basic problem, of course, is what to do about the retarded person when his parents die or cannot care for him any longer. This depressing prospect haunts many parents, probably most parents. We hope that the day will come soon when the retarded people can live in professional supervised urban residences while they work in the community in regular jobs or sheltered workshops, possibly with supplementary public assistance. Were such facilities presently available, an enormous weight would be lifted from the shoulders of both the parents and their retarded children, and both would be freer to help the latter strive for more independent living. Preparation for adult living is more meaningful if it contains the promise of continuity.

However, since very few such residences exist, the worker should be able to create a relationship with the parent which frees him to discuss the future. This is likely to include a discussion of institutionalization. The worker cannot achieve this if he himself dreads separation, if he feels guilty about helping a family divide, and if he himself sees the institution as a nightmare. Sometimes it is highly desirable for the retarded person to experience new adults. Institutionalization may be a godsend for the retarded person and his parents long before the latter are too old to care for him. At certain times in the history of a family, separation may be the best plan. The worker's role would be to help the principals consider institutionalization with as little guilt and mutual accusation and anguish as possible. Sometimes the recognition that institutionalization might be only a temporary interlude, is helpful. The principals might be helped to appreciate that whatever security and social competence the retardate has mastered can be of great use in this new setting. The worker may have to be ready to arrange for both the parents and the retardate to visit the institution and possibly to accompany them on such a visit. I recall one such visit during which the retarded person was able to find parallels with her Shop experience and could anticipate being helpful to the cottage parent in ways similar to those she had worked out with her shop supervisor. One of our trainees ran back to the institution in order to escape his parents.

Because of the likelihood that problems in the relationship of the parent and his retarded child are likely to recur down through the years, the agency must be prepared to work with them many times over a very long period. The parents' case cannot be closed any more than that of the retardate.

Many of us have strong feelings about parents who reject their children. These we absorb from the culture and our identification with the person who is helpless—the child—is probably strengthened by whatever inner forces moved us into social work in the first place. There is too often a quickness to condemn the parent who is hostile to his retarded son or daughter and sometimes our condemnation takes the form of our concentrating our energy on the parent's personality. The parent is made to run the gauntlet of self-analysis in search of hidden sources of his rejection. The more aggressive and secure parent sooner or later gets fed up with this and tells the worker, "Look, *you* never had to raise a retarded child. I did!" The worker's first impulse then may be to say inwardly, "Ah-ha! More resistance!" He might do well to control this impulse and take time to ponder. He really has not raised a retarded child whereas the parent had. The parent may well have personality problems and they are likely to contribute to the problem or to have been aggravated by this handicapped child. However, a rule of thumb should be that the worker should view the retardate as a serious problem for *anyone* to raise in our culture, that negative reactions to him may be healthy ones, that primary objectives may be the management and amelioration of problems, and that concern about the parents' personality disturbance should become central only as evidence for it accumulates.

Parent group meetings are particularly helpful in reducing guilt about hostile feelings toward retarded children and can become useful means for the exchange of management devices. Parents have every right to know what to *do* with the retarded. If the experts are puzzled, why should we expect more of the parents? Sometimes the worker himself is puzzled and takes refuge, unconsciously, in doing what he knows best to do—helping the parent analyze his own behavior.

In summary, the immediate casework goal often is less one of helping the parent to be a more loving parent than to become a less guilty and a more competent one. His retarded child is truly difficult. We should not consider as inadequate necessarily this hostile, dejected, harassed and bewildered parent who has been so badly treated by society and fate. He may remain unable and unwilling to exercise fully his parental role so that the worker may have to share it with him, or even help him surrender it in part to an institution. Our retardate often seeks out the worker as a parent substitute and it would be well for the worker to see this as intuitive wisdom which may be beyond change, and to refrain from judging the parent who has found this role an impossible one.

References

[1] All I.Q.'s were obtained on the Wechsler Adult Intelligence Scale.

SIXTY-THREE

"Tell Him . . ."

GERDA CORVIN

This is an article about counseling. Whenever a trainee starts in the Shop, a counselor is assigned to him and to his family and the main job of the counselor is to use certain skills and methods to help the trainee and his family to make the best possible use of the Shop so that the trainee can become as good a worker as possible, perhaps good enough to work "on the outside," and to become as happy and as stable and as capable a person as possible, and to help him get along as well as possible at home. Some trainees and a few parents have weekly or even semi-weekly sessions with the counselor for weeks, months and even years. Sometimes the sessions continue after the trainee leaves the Shop. Most trainees have meetings with the counselor on an as-needed basis. This is true of some parents. All Training Center trainees and their parents see the counselor at least every second or third month during the review of the trainee's evaluation and program. During most sessions what mainly happens is an exchange between the counselor and the other person—an exchange of talk and an exchange of feeling and some of the feeling is expressed not in talk but in a look, the expression on one's face, the way one holds one's hands, how one sits. With some trainees talk may be accompanied by doing things, such as painting, or shopping for an article of clothing in a nearby store, or traveling on the subway or walking on the street, or figuring out a budget, or doing arithmetic or writing or reading together. When these exchanges occur privately just between the counselor and the other person, we call it individual counseling. When these exchanges take place on a regularly scheduled basis, we call it intensive counseling if the appointments occur at least once a week. When these exchanges occur among a counselor and several people during a session, we call it group counseling.

The counselors who do this work are specially trained people who receive graduate level training in social work, rehabilitation counseling or psychology. When they are employed at our Shop, their training continues. For their first two years they must have intensive conferences with a counselor supervisor at least once a

Reprinted from *Parent-Staff Exchange*, Vol. 1, No. 8 (January, 1968), pp. 1-6. By permission of the author and the New York City Association for the Help of Retarded Children.

week and usually more often. They are evaluated frankly. Throughout their stay with us they must attend learning seminars every Friday afternoon. Thus, their training never ends.

Time and again, exasperated parents, overwhelmed by frustration over their trainee's persistent, inappropriate behavior will turn to the counselor with the plea, *"You* tell him; maybe he'll listen to an outsider." The tone is one of helpless anger or utter desperation; often there are tears or clenched fists. There is sometimes the implication that the trainee will be withdrawn from our program and institutionalized if he refuses to listen.

The counselor can sympathize with the parent's exasperation—there are limits to tolerance and it is not easy to put up with immature, irrational, self-indulgent, possibly destructive behavior day after day, for some twenty years or more. Parents have stated repeatedly that they are getting more and more irritable and, therefore, less able to cope with unacceptable behavior as they and their retarded children grow older. Some parents, in the interest of self-preservation, adopt attitudes of weary resignation; they attempt to detach themselves from their child, to ignore the intolerable. At the opposite end, there are those parents who are fiercely determined to accomplish basic (and often unrealistic) changes in their trainee to have him fulfill whatever expectation they may have of him. Among these parents are the ones who keep on saying that they know the trainee could change "if he just wanted to." Therefore, they figure, "telling him" might be helpful; it could be the way to achieve the miracle that they have been waiting for all these long years.

Unfortunately, there are no miracles.

Retardation cannot be undone. While damaged brain cells do not prevent change, they make it more difficult and put a ceiling on how much can be accomplished. Exactly where the ceiling rests, of course, is not known, and it is in this ignorance that lie hope and frustration, an incentive for striving and the lure of unrealistic ambition. The poor judgment that goes hand in hand with mental retardation is hard to undo but it can be modified.

The thing that can be done, however, is to help the retarded person function at his highest potential—something that he and his family (and staff at times, too)— often underestimate. Recognizing that there are serious limitations, the aforementioned ceiling, this is the goal of anyone who works with the retarded.

Not What You Should Be—But Who Are You?

It has been demonstrated abundantly that in most cases "telling him" is not enough to reach that goal. Most of our trainees come to us with lifelong histories of having been told what to do and what not to do, endlessly, by their families, teachers and other interested persons. And the telling has not always been harsh or without sensitivity or without feeling, although some of it has been all these things and worse. It is not the counselor's job to perpetuate these histories. It is the counselor's job to help trainees change certain attitudes and behavior patterns that interfere with interpersonal ralationships including those that get in the way of work.

Often the counselor can cause such changes to come about if he can uncover the source of the trouble, if he can understand the purpose of the troublesome symptom —and then share this understanding with the trainee. The way to do this is not by "telling him" or by "talking *to* him"—which only too often takes the form of talking *at* him—but by "talking *with* him." Talking *with* a person is more than just carrying on a conversation. It means responding to the *feelings* that words often cover up. It means that consistent efforts are made to understand such feelings and, when it is appropriate, to point them out. This is not anything the counselor can do on his own. While his training and experience and intuition may enable him to take an educated guess at feelings, he cannot do the job properly unless the other person —the trainee, in this case—is willing to cooperate, to share material that may be embarrassing and painful, including details which may seem insignificant.

A trainee may have heard a thousand times that he should earn a living but he sabotages job referrals. He says the train was delayed or he could not find the office or the neighborhood was tough. But sometimes, after many weeks and months of counseling sessions—sometimes never—he is able to admit that he had sabotaged the job referral and to understand that he did so because he really did not want the job and that he did not want the job because he really does not want to be grown up or he hates being nagged to work or he feels terrified that someone will discover he is retarded or he is frightened of failure or he cannot give up his dream to be a doctor or a mechanic or a secretary and just will not settle for cleaning toilets or carrying messages or washing dishes.

Talking with retarded people is essentially not very different from talking with other troubled persons. The main difference is probably that retardates generally are not able to express ideas and feelings as well as normals, who don't do too well either when the ideas and feelings are painful. Therefore, the counselor must depend a good deal upon his observation. He must learn to communicate with the retarded person in simple language which is not childish, in facial expressions and gestures which are readily understood, and sometimes in ways other than words. He may have to form a relationship by playing adult games with him or going on walks or shopping trips with him or teaching him how to shave or to budget or to take dictation from him for a letter to the shop newspaper. He may teach him to travel in the subway.

Trust Is Basic

Like most people, trainees have been raised on the dictum that it is most important to create a good impression, and most do. The majority are reasonably poised, polite and cooperative. By and large they are dressed neatly and appropriately. At first glance, only a few will give any indication that they are different from other young people. Our trainees have been taught to keep tight control over "bad" feelings such as anger, hostility, jealousy, rivalry, rebelliousness, and so on, and in many cases the teaching has been so successful that they tend to deny the existence of such feelings altogether, to lie and to evade questions about them.

Some insist and believe that they love their parents and their brothers and sisters and staff members but actually they may be full of anger against all of us. They must be helped to say what they feel—and actually to try to find out what they feel —without fear of condemnation or reprisal. These are things like, "Yes, I *am* lying; I do enjoy fooling you normals; I am frightened to death of a job and of growing up; I do want to be taken care of; I am retarded and hate it; I am jealous of you for being smart while I am stupid; I do have sexual feelings and I don't know what to do with them; I do want to have my own way." And so on.

And he should be able to say these things just as we may have to tell a doctor, "I have a pain in my head; I feel dizzy; I get hot flashes; I pass blood in my urine."

In both cases the person is talking about his symptoms, about what ails him. The doctor has to *know* his patient's physical feelings to help cure him. A counselor needs to *know* his client's emotional feelings in order to help him change. In both cases the feelings and the ideas are symptoms. In both cases something needs to be treated or changed. Neither person can be helped if he conceals what is significant.

There is a difference between these two kinds of symptoms. It is not a "bad" thing to have a headache. Therefore, it is easier to mention. But we are taught that it is a "bad" thing to admit you do not want to support yourself and prefer that your parents take care of you for the rest of your life. Admitting that is extremely difficult.

Probably the first lesson the trainee has to learn is that his counselor knows of the possible existence of these feelings and of their power over him. He also has to learn that the counselor does not see these feelings as "good" or "bad" in a moral sense. Feelings are not seen by the counselor as moral or immoral, demeaning or exalting. Feelings are experienced as pleasurable or painful or both. They are not judged ethically. In time the counselor and the trainee have to figure out together whether the feelings finally admitted by the trainee help or hinder him and how to strengthen those which help him and to weaken those which hinder him.

The counselor can make it clear to a trainee in time that he does not think the way he is behaving is helpful to the trainee or to others or is appropriate but in all instances, however, he must make it clear that he is interested in the feeling behind the behavior and that he respects these feelings and is prepared to discuss them in a nonjudgmental manner.

However, the trainee will not permit this to happen unless he can trust the counselor. The counselor must try to win the trainee's confidence and this is a formidable job, especially with people who have learned that "silence is the best policy" and "what you don't know won't hurt me," who have had a long history of rejection, and thus have become suspicious and fearful that whatever they say may be used against them sooner or later.

Trainees must learn in time that it is in the nature of the counselor's job that they will be asked questions that are personal and may create pain. However, the counselor is not asking them out of personal curiosity or because he wants to hurt, condemn or praise. He needs the answers to the questions in order to be truly helpful. At times, the counselor's questions or comments may be designed primarily to stimulate thinking on the part of the client as to why he does or does not do certain things. For the majority of our trainees, as indeed for most of us, this is a new and often unpleasant experience. Few people rarely, if ever, bother to explain to themselves or to others the reasons for their behavior. If they do it, they will try to do it in the most superficial way in order to avoid facing underlying feelings which may be classified as "bad" and thus create for themselves the extremely uncomfortable state of guilt.

Truth Can Liberate

In a good counseling relationship, the client ought to be able to experience after a while—which may be a very long while, weeks, months and even years—the exhilarating, liberating sensation of being able to discuss practically anything that goes on within him without shame or embarrassment, in the sure knowledge that he will be carefully listened to, that the counselor is *with* him at all times, is genuinely interested, truly sympathetic and sharply alert.

Such an experience is quite unique. In any event it is particularly unique for retarded people who have grown accustomed to being either ignored or else being chided for their "childishness," "laziness," "stupidity," and so on, without anyone taking the trouble to find out what may be underneath all of this. Almost without exception, trainees enjoy and benefit from their relationship with the counselor. Eventually, they come to see him variously as their "friend," "lawyer," "doctor," as parent substitute, or all of these, depending upon their need and situation. Of course, there is always a hard core of people who remain inaccessible regardless of intense efforts to reach them, but fortunately, they are a minority.

As is true of almost all developments in our Shop, evolving a counseling relationship becomes a learning experience—not only for the trainee but for his counselor as well. As we get to know each other fairly well, we discover our strengths and weaknesses and learn to own up to the latter. Thus, when a counselor makes an error, as he will, it is beneficial to the relationship if he can acknowledge it freely to the trainee and discuss it with him, taking care to recognize openly the feelings of pain or discomfort he may have created with this error. This is only one way of demonstrating to the client that in a mature relationship each partner must carry responsibility for his behavior and also that such a relationship does not fall apart just because someone makes a mistake.

It is our hope that the trainee will one day integrate—make a normal part of himself—the sense of self-esteem and the new values derived from counseling and will transfer them to the world outside of the counseling relationship. Hopefully he will find that this makes him a happier person who gets along more easily with others (since he finds it easier to get along with himself). Hopefully he will be more willing to take risks by experimenting in untried areas since he has learned that he will not be shattered by failure. We hope he will learn to assume responsibility for himself, for his actions and their consequences. We hope that he will make sufficient peace with his retardation and other handicaps to find a happy place in the world.

We do not expect miracles. We know that there will be periods of going backward, depression, rebellion, overwhelming anxiety, when acting-out in a destructive way becomes an almost irresistible temptation. This is the reason why counselors remain available to all of our trainees, even after they leave the Shop—if necessary for the rest of their lives. Troubled people cannot become completely and permanently untroubled within the limited time they spend with us, especially in a society which does create so many real problems for them. But many of them develop enough confidence and self- awareness to be able to pick up a telephone, even after months and years of no contact, to say, "I'd like an appointment. I have a problem." They will be given an appointment as quickly as possible and attempts will be made to iron out problems in one or more sessions.

The Parents

Often parents are uneasy about the trainee's relationship with the counselor. There can be a sense of rivalry, the understandable resentment against an outsider "butting in," a feeling of working at cross-purposes. One parent once told a counselor with a great deal of anger, "What's the sense of my trying to tell her to control her temper when you encourage her to scream her head off?" There was a misunderstanding. The Counselor, who was aware of the trainee's inability to cope with any kind of frustration had told the trainee that she could come to the counselor's office and "scream her head off" if she needed to but it was not correct to do so on the Shop floor where it might irritate and disturb others and disrupt work. The trainee, who was quite mature, quickly picked up the suggestion but then misused it in arguments with her parent.

It was helpful to the counselor to have gotten this information from the parent and to be able to discuss it with the trainee, pointing out to her the tendency to manipulate people and distort statements, that had gotten her into trouble before. There were no anger and recriminations—it was an honest discussion between two adults concerned about the future of one of them. It took many such discussions before the trainee was helped to understand that her behavior was really caused by an insatiable need for attention and the conviction that she could get this only by creating conflict, which was the pattern of her entire family.

A number of parents, such as the one mentioned above, experience feelings of guilt which are more or less vague and they warn the trainee against revealing "too much." The result of this is that the trainees, given their immaturity and dependency, find themselves in an endless conflict and flounder about, not knowing what to say, whom to trust. In such cases—and they are by no means the only ones—the counselor may ask parents to come in for individual interviews to explore *their* feelings and attitudes. It is interesting that so very few parents are willing to become involved either in individual or in group counseling.

The parents are a vital part of the treatment team. Not only does the counselor need their help to understand the trainee but the parents need to understand the changes they begin to see often in the trainees' behavior at home. Often they have to know how to act differently toward this one childlike person now changing into a somewhat unrecognizable adult. The retarded person begins to want freedom to move about the city alone, wants control over his earnings, goes out with girls and talks about marriage and children. Such developments can create intense anxiety in parents who like so many of us, may need help with their own feelings. In some uncertain way, some begin to sense that they really did not want the retarded person to grow up and go away even though they had been honestly and firmly convinced that this had been their goal. Such parents, understandably, may become so anxious (and angry) that they want to withdraw the trainee from counseling and even from the Shop entirely. It would be better if they could ask the counselor for an appointment instead in order to discuss their own feelings and the new situation in which they find themselves with their retarded sons and daughters. The counselor is as available to the parents as he is to the trainee.

To Summarize

Trainees are assigned to counselors because we are aware that most of them are troubled by personal and family problems which affect their work habits and other social adjustments. The counselor is a treatment person. He treats their problematic attitudes, feelings, thoughts and actions. It is his job to help trainees understand their motives for their behavior and to help them change it if they can. If they cannot do so, they will not be penalized by rejection or other forms of personal retribution. However, since the counselor acts as a representative of a social agency which involves many people, it is a part of his job to alert trainees to possible consequences of inappropriate "acting out." It is not part of his job to "tell him," to nag, plead, cajole, lecture, threaten, argue, preach. Most of our trainees have had more than enough of that. It is the counselor's goal to reduce excessive anxiety, insecurity, depressiveness and rebelliousness, to help trainees to become more self-reliant and self-aware.

As part of his job of helping the trainee realize that he has a true—if objective —ally in him, the counselor must always keep pace with his client. This may mean, often, that he will have to move at a very slow pace which may be alien to him— that he will have to endlessly remind, restate, reformulate fragments of previous discussions.

It also means that much of what the trainee tells the counselor cannot be repeated to the parent without the trainee's permission, something which can be upsetting to the parent. Similarly, much of what a parent confides in a counselor will also not be shared with the trainee without the parent's permission.

The counselor cannot accomplish his aims without cooperation. Because so many of our clients are as immature and dependent as they are, it is often necessary to enlist the cooperation of the parents. The more cooperation counselors can get, the more effective they will be. It would be good if the parents can encourage the trainee to be as free as possible with the counselor even if this means criticizing and opposing the parents. It would be good if the parents can try to avoid trying to force the counselor to "make" the trainee become different. The parent who finds himself unable to tolerate and understand the counselor's methods, is unable to agree with the counselor, unable to alter his ways of dealing with the trainee, who is feeling angry and anxious and confused about what is happening in the Shop, is unable to develop a good feeling toward the counselor, should make a real effort to discuss the situation with the counselor. He will be most welcome at the Shop. If he calls the counselor for an appointment, he will find the counselor very eager to see him as soon as possible.

The trainee has to be helped to tell himself what he needs to do that is different, and he needs to believe it, and he needs intensive and long term help in achieving this. *Telling him* doesn't work. He has been told before—a thousand times.

Material Prepared by the Florida State Department of Public Welfare for Consideration in the Development of the Florida Comprehensive Mental Retardation Plan

Child Care

I. FAMILY COUNSELING

Family counseling is a crucial service in maintaining or promoting family stability in any situation which places unusual stress on parent-child relationships. This service has long been provided by the State Department of Public Welfare with emphasis upon children who have been or are being neglected, and casework is geared toward strengthening the child's own home.

Family counseling needs of the parents of a mentally retarded child are many and these change and may be very intensive at points of crisis as a child grows older and his developmental needs change. Counseling may be provided by a variety of disciplines, particularly at these points of crisis.

The State Department of Public Welfare staff, in daily contact with thousands of families, has an opportunity to contribute toward this service to the mentally retarded child and his parents. This may involve casework service geared toward making it possible for the child to remain in his own home, providing guidance in improvement of health conditions, providing guidance in developing homemaking and child caring skills in order to strengthen the home for the mentally retarded child, helping parents and child with feelings around separation when this is in the child's best interests.

Recommendation: It is recommended that the State Department of Public Welfare strengthen its program of service to children in their own homes in order to make this service available to all parents and children who need it. This would include service to parents of a mentally retarded child in his own home, in foster care, in one of the Sunland Training Centers when it is determined that the child could benefit from return to his own home, placement with relatives, or placement in the Department's foster care. It is further recommended that funds be made available for staff training to enhance the effectiveness of Department's service to the mentally retarded child and his parents.

Reprinted by permission of the Florida Department of Public Welfare, 1965.

II. HOMEMAKER SERVICE

Homemaker service is provided by people who are regularly employed by the agency providing the service. Housekeeper service is provided by people who are employed for a specific period in a specific family situation.

Both homemaker and housekeeper service provide care for children in their own home when parents are either unable to care for them or need help in providing adequate care. This service is in recognition of the value to a child of remaining with his own family and of preserving and strengthening the home whenever possible.

The State Department of Public Welfare has provided this service in situations in which parents are unable to care for their children due to hospitalization, imprisonment, desertion or death, or when, because of illness, emotional disturbance, inability to cope with overwhelming responsibilities they need help in providing adequate care.

The Department has a pilot program of homemaker service in Tampa where two homemakers are regularly employed staff members. The Department has housekeeper service available on a statewide basis. (Approximately three hundred children are kept in their own homes each month through this service.)

Homemaker service, on a part time basis—i.e. one or two days per week, to a family with a mentally retarded child could be of invaluable help in making it possible for the child to remain in his own home by providing relief for the parent when physical and emotional energies would otherwise be excessively drained. Homemaker service, on a part time basis, could also be beneficial to the parent who is limited in knowledge and care of the retarded child.

Recommendation: It is recommended that the Department's homemaker service program be expanded on a statewide basis and that it include provision for part time homemaker service to the family with the retarded child when this service is needed and it is determined that it is in the best interest of the child and his family. It is further recommended that funds be made available for training of homemakers and for professional staff training in order to make this service truly effective.

III. DAY CARE

Day care is seen as another service which should be given to supplement the capabilities of parents to care for their children.

While day care has generally been developed as a means of providing care for the children of working mothers it is recognized that this is a concrete service which can be very beneficial to the mentally retarded child and his family.

The full value of day care for the retarded child can be realized only when the service goes beyond providing care to include basic socialization training for the child and when it provides an opportunity for parents to better understand the problems related to their retarded child.

The Department of Public Welfare does not operate a day care program but has carried responsibility for licensing day care facilities in three counties since 1945. In eleven counties licensing is done by the Board of Health. One county has its own licensing board. The remaining 52 counties are not covered by any licensing law.

The Day Care Advisory Committee for the Department is currently advising the Department with regard to the study of day care facilities including those for retarded children, and ways by which the Department may cooperate in offering training to the staff of these facilities and by which it may otherwise help in improving the quality of care offered.

Recommendation: It is recommended that a day care program for mentally retarded be developed; that case work service be an integral part of the day care program.

It is further recommended that a statewide licensing law be passed thereby assuring uniform standards in day care facilities.

IV.   FOSTER HOME CARE

For the child who can not remain with his own parents or relatives, and for whom adoption may not be considered, placement with warm, understanding foster parents is the form of care which can best nurture his emotional and physical needs and promote his healthy growth. For the retarded child, as for other children, there is no adequate substitute for family life—the only exception would be the child who is profoundly retarded, lacking in emotional response and unable to benefit from interpersonal relationships.

Foster home planning for the mentally retarded child may be used as follows:

a. When parents, adequate to meet the needs of their normal children, are not able to withstand the stress of caring for the retarded child.

b. When parents are so disadvantaged as to be incapable of promoting the child's healthy growth and development.

c. For some children who will ultimately require placement in an institution. This would include children who could benefit from this interim care as well as children who are awaiting admission to one of the Sunland Training Centers.

d. For some children, now in one of the Sunland Training Centers, when it is determined that they can benefit from such planning.

The State Department of Public Welfare currently provides foster home care for 3,200 children, including mentally retarded children. Some need institutional care and approximately 80 are on the waiting list for Sunland Training Centers. Limitations of funds and available staff make it impossible to provide foster home care for all children who need it.

The Department's District #9 in Miami has a small unit of service devoted exclusively to serving mentally retarded children and their families. Service is currently being given to 25 children in their own homes, 2 in the home of relatives and 80 in foster home care. Excellent medical and diagnostic services are available in the community. The staff has had remarkable success in recruiting and maintaining good foster homes.

Recommendations:

1. That the foster home program of the State Department of Public Welfare be strengthened and made truly statewide—that foster home care be made regularly

available for all mentally retarded children for whom such care is appropriate.

2. That funds be made available for such expansion and strengthening of service including funds for the necessary additional staff and for staff training purposes.

3. That other units of service to mentally retarded children, similar to the Department's unit in Miami, be developed in other large cities in the state.

V.   GROUP LIVING ARRANGEMENTS

Such planning would require careful study, selection and supervision of foster parents, preliminary and continuing work with public and/or trade schools, employment resources, recreation leaders and other community resource people who need to work together to provide the retarded with an opportunity to develop and function to the maximum of his capacity.

a. This form of care could offer much for mentally retarded children who cannot remain in their own home or with relatives and for whom neither institutional placement nor regular foster home placement is appropriate—children who cannot take on the close personal relationship of foster parents of their own yet who need the degree of interpersonal relationships present in a group care family setting where more individual attention is given than in the institutions, where there is more opportunity to develop social skills through organized recreation and play activity with other children in the community, where there is less need for the regimentation of the institution.

b. This form of care would have much to offer many older retarded who (1) do not need to remain in an institution or (2) who do not need to be placed in an institution, but who are not ready to be on their own and require a form of control and supervision in various personal, social, and economic areas of living. As the individual gains more security in these areas he can be given more and more responsibility until he is ready to be on his own in the community if this is indicated.

Recommendation: It is recommended that group care homes be established on an experimental basis to see what can be done for a small select group of retarded children, adolescents, and adults who have the capacity to benefit from this type of care.

VI.   ADOPTION

For some mildly retarded children who, for one reason or another, can not grow up with their own parents or with relatives adoption placement planning can be accomplished. This has been demonstrated by the State Department of Public Welfare's unit of service to mentally retarded children in Miami and by other agencies in Florida and elsewhere.

The Department's adoption placement program is relatively new, having been started in October 1963. Because of the many problems inherent in planning and developing a new program of service the number of children served since the beginning of the program is small.

The Department is now beginning a study to determine the number of older children in our boarding care population of approximately 3,200 for whom adoption placement might be appropriate either through our Department or one of the licensed child placing agencies. These would be children whose parents have demonstrated no interest in re-establishing a home, contributing to support or visiting.

While it is not realistic at this stage in the development of the Department's adoption placement program to anticipate that the service of adoption can be offered to any appreciable extent to the mildly retarded child, this is certainly an area which, in time, could be developed even though the numbers served would be very small.

Recommendation: It is therefore recommended that, as the Department's adoption program develops, consideration be given to making this service available to the mildly retarded child who can use adoption.

Public Assistance

I. AID TO THE DISABLED

This is one segment of public assistance categorical program of aid to the aged, blind and disabled, commonly called the adult category.

In order to be eligible a person must be permanently and totally disabled which means in effect that there must be a major physical or mental condition or combination of such conditions of a permanent nature which prevents work or training for work. To be eligible a person must be over 18 years of age and under 65. (After 65 the recipient receives Aid to Aged—maximum grant remains the same.) The maximum grant allowed is $70 per month.

In addition there is limited financial assistance for basic and special needs to include home nursing care, housekeeping service, prescribed medicine, medical supplies.

Size of the Aid to Disabled Program and Extent of Mental Retardation. There are approximately 16,000 people currently receiving Aid to the Disabled. According to a previous study approximately 13% of this particular group are mentally retarded. This would be a total of 2,080 mentally retarded people being assisted by this part of the Public Assistance Program.

There is a general lack of readily available facilities for diagnosis, evaluation and treatment; there are problems in relation to finding a willing and suitable guardian and there are many unmet needs of the disabled related to the limitations of the maximum grant.

II. AID TO FAMILIES WITH DEPENDENT CHILDREN

This category of public assistance is available to families in which there is established need and in which children are deprived of parental support.

The maximum aid which can be received is $32 for a family with one child, $55 for a family with two children, $78 for a family with three children and $81 for a family with four or more children. The limitations of this assistance obviously creates many problems.

As of December 1, 1964 there were 28,009 families with 85,741 children receiving this assistance.

The Department is currently attempting to identify in every AFDC case the needs of each child with respect to lack in day to day supervision and any unmet health or educational needs. Through this process the Department hopes to identify the special needs of retarded children which are not being met.

The Department anticipates revision in policy which may make it possible to provide more specific services to such children and their families. This might include such things as an item for housekeeper or homemaker service in order to relieve the mother of some responsibility. Day care costs are now recognized when the parent is employed. The Department already has a policy which provides recognition of the cost of special educational experiences for these children but unfortunately there are no funds with which to make direct payment for such services. Limited medical care through vendor payments for hospitalization only is available.

As is indicated the limitations of the AFDC grants poses a real hardship. There are also limitations of diagnostic and treatment facilities for children in the majority of counties and there is a lack of special resources.

WHAT IS NEEDED IN PUBLIC ASSISTANCE?

1. An increase in the maximum grants in the adult and children's categories to more adequately cover actual need.

2. Provision for more adequately meeting cost of nursing home care.

3. A more workable and valid statewide legal procedure to determine competence and for the appointment of a guardian.

4. The availability of comprehensive medical services for the indigent with special emphasis on local facilities for diagnosis, evaluation and treatment.

SPECIFIC RECOMMENDATIONS:

1. The establishment of a more realistic maximum grant in the adult and children's categories. (LEGISLATIVE ACTION)

2. Increased vendor payments for nursing home care. (LEGISLATIVE ACTION)

3. Improved guardianship laws. (LEGISLATIVE ACTION)

4. An increase in all medical services for the medically indigent through a more comprehensive utilization of the Federal Kerr-Mills laws (LEGISLATIVE ACTION); the full implementation of the Hospital Service for the Indigent Act (LEGISLATIVE AND LOCAL ACTION); the development of local medical resources through provision of the Economic Opportunity Act of 1964 (STATE AND LOCAL ACTION); independent local development of medical facilities for the indigent to take care of gaps in service. (CITY AND COUNTY ACTION)

SIXTY-FIVE

Public Welfare Serves the Mentally Retarded Child

ADELINE BRAIK

The child who walked down the hall of the agency was obviously different. Her legs were braced, and crutches supported her body, which was so heavy that ambulation was difficult. Sandy is a victim of the rare medical disease of Calcinosis, which means that her body muscles and tissues are gradually hardening. Although Sandy physically is quite mature at 14, her mentality has not grown correspondingly. She is called "retarded." Sandy, along with many others, has been spared unnecessary premature institutional care through the efforts of the Services to Retarded Children Unit, Child Welfare Division, of the Florida State Department of Public Welfare in Miami, Florida.

The unit had its beginning in January, 1959, following a 1957 survey in Dade County by the Welfare Planning Council of the needs and resources available for retarded children in this community. It was discovered that the only existing service to this group was custodial placement in one of the six local, residential homes at a total cost to the county of $13,500 to $15,000 per month. As of April, 1957, 146 children were so placed; 25 had been in care for more than six years, and 72 more than two years. Most important, however, the survey revealed that there was no provision for professional differential diagnosis, treatment, or reevaluation of the child's condition and progress during these long periods of time. Therefore, the Welfare Planning Council recommended that a program of care for retarded children include essential services for sound, long-range planning, such as medical, social and psychological evaluations on all retarded children placed, continuing supervision of the child, periodic reevaluations, and continued contacts with parents regarding the placement and ultimate planning for the child.

After full consideration of the need for such a program and the way in which it could be developed, a cooperative working agreement was reached between the Florida State Department of Public Welfare in Miami, and the Dade County Department of Public Welfare.

From *Public Welfare*, Vol. XXV, No. 2 (April, 1967), pp. 110-115. By permission of the author and the American Public Welfare Association.

Initial Study of Each Mentally Retarded Child

The Florida State Department of Public Welfare agreed to be responsible for the initial study of each mentally retarded child referred to it. Included in the study would be a psycho-social evaluation of the child and his family to determine whether his needs could best be met by placement in a custodial setting, an institution, a local residential facility or a foster home. The Dade County agency agreed to assume financial responsibility for all foster care costs for retarded children, and to continue to plan for those youngsters whose needs could best be met by placement other than foster care. The Florida State Department of Public Welfare assumed responsibility for providing casework service to families of retarded children needing foster care, as well as those who might remain in their own homes, and for all administrative costs involved in carrying out this responsibility.

Thus, the first year of operation of Services to Retarded Children Unit began in January, 1959, when we were uniquely created as the fourth unit of the Child Welfare Section, which already included emergency shelter care, regular foster care and a program of special services. With one experienced social worker as supervisor and one caseworker, neither of whom had worked previously with retarded persons, there was much to learn! Both supervisor and worker equally were busy with caseloads and the development of the program. Foster homes had to be developed and licensed, and the community resources had to be explored which would serve retarded children.

We began operation with an allocation of county funds in the amount of $13,500 to care for approximately 15 children for a period of nine months (until October, 1959, when a new fiscal year would begin). It was presumed that it would cost $100 a month to care for a retarded child—twice the amount of the department's usual board rate. We found, however, that we were able to operate more economically than planned, and care was extended for 22 children instead of 15, because many parents were quite willing and able to pay some of the placement costs. Also, we learned that only in exceptional cases did retarded children require a higher board rate than did the normal child. The average cost per child of $67 per month was much less than that of institutional care, which was approximately $200 per month.

Our understanding of the many facets of retardation and its effect on families and communities was enlarged by reading available books and professional publications, and by our many contacts with the Developmental Evaluation Clinic, which was pioneering in research and service in this field. (This is a demonstration diagnostic clinic set up under the State Board of Health and financed by the Children's Bureau.) Our firsthand experiences, however, began to teach us the reality factors of retardation and its effect on families and communities.

Referrals Began to Come

As the community became aware of the creation of the unit, referrals began to come from pediatricians, school psychologists, lawyers, public health nurses, Developmental Evaluation Clinic, hospital clinics and from parents themselves. In each individual case, we found ourselves looking carefully at social factors in the child's environment, as well as his current psychological functioning. For example, were the needs of the child being met in his own home? How was his presence there affecting his siblings? Was the mother able to equally distribute her time to the other children, or did the retarded one consume the major portion? Were the parents basically rejecting or overprotective of the child? What was the meaning of the defective child to his parents? Could the family be helped to be more accepting and to participate in a stimulation program at home that would help the child develop to his fullest extent? Was there evidence of stability of the parents and togetherness in their understanding of the needs of the retarded one? Were other family pressures entering into the request for placement away from home?

One of the most important areas of learning in our experience was that through casework help to the family, a retarded child might be able to remain at home. Parents need not only an acceptance of their child's ability and limitations, but also encouragement to work with him day by day in an effective way for maximum development. Relief from their parental tensions and anxieties, help with realistic planning, adjustment to a way of life that includes the retarded child, and guidance to other resources must be a part of the goal-directed interviews with parents to enable them to make appropriate decisions for their retarded child.

> Mr. and Mrs. A, ages 35 and 32, had seven children under 15 years of age. The youngest was a nine-month-old Mongoloid baby girl with a heart murmur. They came to the agency asking for placement of the child in a custodial situation. Study of the social factors indicated intelligent, interested parents. Their marriage had existed 16 years and this couple had weathered many stressful periods. The children seemed well adjusted. The baby was loved by his siblings and did not require more of the mother's time than a normal infant might. The mother's anxiety seemed to be whether her child would live any appreciable length of time. We found that there were many financial pressures due to Mr. A's asthmatic attacks and loss of employment for several days at a time.
>
> The caseworker, in exploring this family's feelings about the Mongoloid baby, became aware that placement did not seem to be what was really desired. The direction of her work with this family was to help Mr. A. get into an allergy clinic, where his doctor prescribed medication to control the asthma. Thereafter, Mr. A's earning power increased. Free lunches were provided for the five school-age children. The mother was helped to place the baby under care at the Cardiac Hospital, where specialists made a thorough evaluation of the child's heart condition and freed the mother's mind of this over-shadowing anxiety.
>
> Through a succession of interviews, the parents came to understand more fully their Mongoloid child and her problem of retardation. They learned how to stimulate her development at home, to love her yet at the same time realistically face the fact that some day institutional placement might be needed. Emotional support from the caseworker to this mother has continued over a period of months, both by home visits and telephone contacts; and the family seems relieved that their baby can remain with them at home.

Realizing that parents with retarded children are frequently troubled people, harassed, uncertain and frustrated, we learned very early that it was extremely important to help families who keep their child at home to get direct services and the supportive help needed on a continuing basis. This can help previously immobilized parents to function again. The caseworker enters the process of turmoil with the family to the extent that there is a sense of "togetherness" in the goal of helping the retarded child in the family setting. As counselor, the caseworker—gentle, understanding, yet firm—can help the parents work out their disappointment, conflicts, and guilt feelings, and can guide them to appropriate medical and educational resources available in the community. She shares their moments of joy and despair as together they appreciate the child's slow gains; yet she must keep an eagle eye on the reality factors involved so that future plans for the child can be made on a realistic basis.

Studied Each Individual Situation

As we studied each individual situation, there were many instances, of course, in which it seemed best for the retarded child to be placed away from the family. An example is that of Ann, whose parents came to the agency to ask for placement when she was eight years old, by which time the family conflict was deep-seated.

Ann was the third of seven children born to Mr. and Mrs. B, ages 36 and 33. Both parents were high school graduates with good intelligence and an unusual degree of ambition for their children.

Mr. B. held an important position and Mrs. B, through practical economy, had given the children a well-ordered home and the cultural advantages that the parents considered necessary. Petite, attractive, but fragile appearing, this ambitious mother was worn by the stressful years she had gone through since learning that Ann, at nine months of age, was diagnosed as being a dwarf of genetic origin and that she would be mentally retarded.

History revealed the usual nonacceptance of the diagnosis, the visits to various pediatricians and nationally known clinics, and the parental despair at the final confirmation of the diagnosis. Body disproportion, strange facial features, slow development, and—greatest of all—mental retardation, were just intolerable in a family which held such high expectations for each child.

Although the parents had cared for the child for eight years before they finally asked for placement, family discord was very apparent. Tensions were high, parents were openly hostile to each other and also to Ann because they considered her as "different," odd looking, and not able to fit into their parental ambitions. Ann's siblings were ashamed of her, and they avoided bringing their friends home. Ann hindered the family's normal social outlets and her mother openly acknowledged that she found it hard to love her. The father, who was normally a rigid person, intolerant of misbehavior, could not tolerate Ann's "silly laughing, pranks and incorrigibility" and lack of judgment.

Ann, feeling rejected at home, and in her search for love, would run into neighborhood homes and engage adults in conversation; that is, before the neighbors began locking their doors! Then she began to seek attention by being a show-off, by kicking, spitting, and slapping, as her temper demanded. She seemed quite unwelcome at home and whatever she accomplished was not sufficient for such demanding parents.

We began to ask ourselves: Could we, through foster care, offer retarded children a substitute family and an environment of love and concern where the demands made upon them were within the realm of accomplishment, where they would be protected from situations dangerous to their welfare, yet not over-protected to the point that dependency is unnecessarily prolonged? We would want the child to develop his potential as fully as possible, increase his feelings of self-worth, and ultimately be helped to be a productive member of society. Should institutionalization eventually become necessary, could the child not adjust better by having had this period of living and learning in a family group?

Their Concern Must Go Beyond Sympathy

We began to realize the utmost necessity of finding foster parents who could help us achieve our goals for retarded children. They had to be people who could give an unusual amount of love to these youngsters with special needs. Their concern must go beyond sympathy and reach deeply into mature feelings and understanding of the child. Calmness, warmth, gentleness, and patience would be required, along with an ability to receive satisfaction from helping a retarded child develop his utmost potential. It is common knowledge that many retarded children have associated physical handicaps. Foster parents would have to help us achieve the goal of procuring medical care. They would have to help prepare the child for clinic visits and surgical procedures when, for example, there were cleft palates and harelips to be repaired, muscles to be lengthened or clubbed feet to be straightened. Eyes and ears would have to be checked too, as any impairment in vision or hearing would, of course, limit the child's development of his ability. Foster parents must also be aware that there would be special reading clinics, speech evaluations, and therapy.

We also began wondering if we could help foster parents understand and work with problems the retarded child would bring into their homes. Could they accept his need for his natural family and understand why he could not be with them? Could they appreciate the family tensions and conflicts from which he came and see his behavior in terms of its meaning for him in light of his former experiences? Could they be helped to accept his shyness, or defiance, or apathy; to deal delicately with nervous mannerisms, mumbling, hyperactivity, enuresis, untidiness, and the myriad problems which had irritated others? Could they motivate him to please and accomplish, and to find means of self-expression in acceptable ways? Were we really asking the impossible?

One of our most important discoveries during the first year of our unit operation was that such parents could be found. In fact, some of them became so challenged and enthused with caring for retarded children that they asked to take only these into their homes. Underlying their various motivations of being foster parents was always a warm concern for mentally handicapped and a great pride in their role of loving, nourishing, and healing children who were not their own. Truly their desire to help retarded children has been amazing; our replacement rate has been extremely low, in spite of the numerous medical problems that have been encountered with many of these children. During the first 21 months of the program we were giving casework services to 20 children in their own homes and 44 retarded children in licensed foster homes, including 15 Mongoloids, three hydrocephalics (either arrested or with shunting operations), two spina bifidas, one arthrogryposis, one Calcinosis, and several others with varying degrees of retardation and emotional disturbance. All of these children were managed well in foster care with the exception of the spina bifida victim, whom we found could best be cared for in a custodial setting.

Reciprocal Value

Some foster homes which also provided care to the child of normal intelligence were used on a selective basis. In fact, one of our more important areas of learning was the reciprocal value of this. The normal child provided more stimulation to the retarded child, who imitated the normal one and thereby improved his own performance. On the other hand, the normal youngster learned a very important lesson—that there were many less fortunate than he.

Our first placement into foster care was a nine-month-old Mongoloid boy, abandoned at birth by his unmarried mother. We took him from the custodial setting where he was placed originally and placed him with a normal family with three children.

> At the time of placement, Reggie was expressionless and unresponsive. Within two weeks after placement with children in a foster home he was smiling, showing interest in his environment and in the other children, learning that his foster mother loved him, and he was becoming aware of strangers. This child has remained in the same foster home for the past five years.
>
> Reggie's responsiveness has endeared him to his foster family. With their help he has developed a degree of real sociability, and has been participating in family activities and routines. He has learned to feed himself, and has even learned toileting. His speech is quite limited, but he has found other ways of making his wants known. Now at six years of age, he is ready to go into a state institution for the retarded, where he can more successfully compete with others his own age and thereby maintain the ego strength he has developed in foster care.
>
> He has gained much happiness and pleasure from the ordinary things of life and much self-respect from the menial tasks he has learned to perform in the home. Certainly, he will adjust better within the institutional setting by having had these meaningful experiences in foster care.

Another important lesson in our experience in the Services to Retarded Children Unit was that widows, carefully selected, can be very effective as foster parents for retarded children. In fact, they seemed to have more time to spend with the child in the stimulation process than did the average busy housewife. A widow, age 59, has been extremely helpful in a case involving a child whose father continued his contacts with her.

Mr. and Mrs. Y were referred to the office by the Cerebral Palsy Clinic to discuss placement of their three-and-a-half-year-old retarded daughter, Starr. The mother, aged 33, who had been previously under care of a psychiatrist, was again entering a depression because of her inability to cope with her many problems and feelings about herself and her situation. She seemed irritated at a world that gave her so little and demanded so much. Recognizing herself as a "deprived child," she resented social agencies. She had failed to find happiness in her marriage which was childless for eight years. Starr is the younger of two children born just 15 months apart.

Mr. Y, although a good provider, was not a strong, masculine person from whom his wife could derive much emotional support. Unfortunately, he was away from home when, at six weeks of age, Starr's congenitally damaged heart suddenly stopped and she suffered cerebral anoxia before being revived at the nearest hospital.

Both parents blamed themselves, and each other; estrangement was obvious.

Mr. Y, because of his feeling of guilt, tried to be an exceptionally good father to Starr, pampering and spoiling her to the point that Mary, the older child, grew extremely jealous, resented Starr, voiced her feeling of being unloved, and showed signs of physical illness such as "heart pains." Starr's reaction to her sibling's jealousy and her mother's frustration was to be very destructive with toys and to fight constantly. She refused to be toilet-trained and would not eat. Also, daily she broke out in skin rash which the pediatrician called an emotional allergy. It seemed that removal of the child from this hostile environment was indicated. Agreeing to Starr's placement in foster care was difficult for the mother, for it reinforced her feelings of inadequacy as a parent. However, in due time she was able to accept the situation and Starr was placed in a foster home. In an atmosphere free of tension, filled with love and praise, Starr responded. Within a week she was eating and sleeping without difficulty, was toilet-trained, and her morning allergy was completely cleared without medication. Her destructiveness disappeared as it lost its value as a weapon of offense against a hostile sister. Color books, crayons, and phonograph records enlarged her world. She developed in ego strength and blossomed as praise was given her for her every accomplishment.

Family adjustments at home improved as family and child accepted each other at a distance. The father remained active in the child's life, seeing her weekly—the mother and sister much less frequently. Starr has now been in this home for five years, has learned to talk, and is attending classes for trainable children in the public schools.

Importance of a Home Stimulation Program

In working with retarded children we have learned the importance of a home stimulation program. One of the most dramatic cases of improvement of a retarded child in foster care and one which emphasized the tremendous value of such a program is that of Danny, placed at age four in July, 1961, in one of our most stimulating homes for retarded foster children.

Danny had come from a severely deprived background. His parents, unmarried, were both alcoholics. There was indication of severe neglect and physical abuse of the child. At the time of placement at age four, Danny would not talk, feed himself, or be toilet trained. He seemed an odd, frightened little boy. His natural parents separated soon after he was legally removed from them. He had numerous medical problems, including some Mongoloid stigmata, so that he was accepted for study by the Developmental Evaluation Clinic, as he was a diagnostic problem.

The foster mother worked daily with this child to encourage speech, help him feel secure in her home, and increase his feeling of self-worth. At her own expense, he attended a nearby kindergarten for socialization. Picture books, stories, and weekly speech stimulation classes helped.

Within a nine month period, Danny was carrying on a conversation. Fortunately, he has remained in this home for four years, is repeating the first grade due to his immaturity. It is planned, however, that he be allowed to try regular second grade at the next school term.

At the time of placement, it was thought that Danny was so retarded that he needed to be institutionalized. Through use of community resources, such as the Developmental Evaluation Clinic, with its team approach; Jackson Memorial Hospital Clinic; our own agency; and the love and stimulation of the foster family; this child is making exceptional progress and has been spared an early, inappropriate institutional placement.

Several other foster children have improved in foster care to the extent that though formerly labeled retarded, subsequent testing has placed them in the average range of intelligence. Three such children have been adopted and two others have been referred to child placing units for adoption when the right parents can be found.

One of our most delightful areas of learning has been that of helping parents of children with Down's syndrome to later accept the child into their hearts and homes. Generally, Mongoloids come into placement directly from the hospital where distraught parents have been advised by doctors, religious counselors, or well-meaning friends and relatives not to take their child home. Parental reactions have varied from weeping, nausea, and hysteria, to suicidal thoughts. It is usually impossible to change their preconceived ideas immediately. For example:

Mary Ann, newborn, was placed in a foster home upon the insistence of the parents and their pediatrician. She was born into an intelligent family of good financial means, and was the youngest of four children. At the time of her birth, the father considered pretending that the child had died, as he felt the mother would probably suffer a nervous collapse upon learning that Mary Ann was retarded. Fortunately, he came to the agency to ask for help with the problem. Mary Ann was placed in foster care while the family could be given time to learn about Down's syndrome, and to consider the effect the child would have on their family life.

Through many interviews, this couple was gradually helped to accept themselves without any feeling of guilt, as parents of a mentally deficient child. They began to accept the child "at a distance," through gifts and visits. The siblings accepted Mary Ann most wholesomely and, within a two-year period, all accepted the child into their home, feeling assured that the future would not be as bleak as they had feared.

They are prepared for her eventual institutionalization. Mary Ann, now five years old, is attending a neighborhood kindergarten. She is loved devotedly by her family. The father and mother have come to accept the fact that their parental ambitions will have to be realized in their other children. But they also feel that Mary Ann has contributed to their parental satisfaction as they have watched her develop her own abilities at her own rate. They take great delight in her every new accomplishment.

As of February, 1967, we have in our care 143 retarded children with IQ's of between 25 and 75, of whom 123 are in foster homes and 20 are in their own homes. Sixty-six foster homes are serving these 123 children. Casework staff in the Services to Retarded Children Unit has increased to three workers as the demand for services has grown. An average caseload of 45 children keeps a caseworker extremely busy. The caseworker must deal with the emotional trauma of the retarded child, must work intensively with both the natural parents and the foster parents, and must keep steady surveillance on the medical involvement of the children.

The Lack of Certain Services

In our work in Services to Retarded Children Unit, we have felt poignantly the lack of certain services for certain children. How helpful it would be to have nursery schools, kindergartens, and day care facilities available to the retarded child, as well as vocational opportunities for the older youngster who can remain in the community. There is need for psychiatric help for the emotionally disturbed retarded child, but this is seldom available even for the child who can verbalize and relate well.

In the work of Services to Retarded Children Unit, we are not curing retardation. We are merely providing, through our care, an atmosphere of love and concern, motivation and stimulation of the child to develop his every potential as fully as possible. In addition, we have tried to relieve any accompanying physical limitations which will impede his development. Fortunately, there are many community agencies which have been helpful with this problem. As a liaison between the foster parents, the school, and the clinic, work for the child is coordinated in such a way that each agency is aware of its respective role and does its utmost to help the child. A bond seems to grow between the foster mother and the social worker, built on mutual respect and real interest in the retarded child's development. To the foster parent the social worker lends her knowledge, her warm support and her ever-listening ear, sharing moments of exciting progress, or discouragement and frustration. To the child she lends her identification and understanding, and to the public she offers a conviction that these children deserve recognition, intelligent help, and the services offered to any child.

SIXTY-SIX

Services to the Retarded in His Own Home

ROSEMARY ANDREWS

In our work at the Public Welfare Department we often work with the mentally retarded individual and his family. In many instances more than one person, including a parent or parents, has this handicap. Regardless of whether the individual is eventually placed in an institution or other plans outside the home are made, this individual is always seen first as a member of the family unit and it is our purpose to help the individual remain in the family unit if this is possible. More and more the trend is toward providing case work services, which in some cases falls into the category of protective services, in an ever increasing number of ways to help this individual to remain in his own home. Two examples of this are Homemaker Service and Day Care for pre-school children accompanied by intensive counseling with the parents. The ultimate goal of case work services to the retarded in his own home is to help the individual attain the optimum physical, emotional, social and mental development which is possible.

Attaining this goal is much more of a problem in some families than in others. Many of the families with whom our department comes in contact are in the low socio-economic group. Often this means the family is culturally deprived and can offer little or nothing in the way of intellectual and social stimulation and guidance unless they receive a great deal of help from our agency.

Our first step is diagnosis. Although we receive referrals for service from medical clinics, relatives, schools and other agencies, or a request for help from the parents themselves, often the caseworker is the person who first suspects retardation. From examining report cards of children, observing the person's ability to comprehend explanations or follow through with instructions and function from day to day, and from talking with school personnel, we are guided to make psychological referrals. Testing then clarifies the picture and gives us both general and specific guidelines to follow. From this, we can better evaluate and re-evaluate a person's ability to understand and function in a specific situation or situations. This continuing process of evaluation is interwoven with counseling around the situation. Often this coun-

From a collection of papers presented at the Interdisciplinary-Interagency Conference on Mental Retardation under the auspices of the Mental Retardation Institute, University of North Carolina, 1965. Reprinted by permission of the author, the Durham County Welfare Department, and the Institute.

seling involves not only other members of the immediate family, but also members of the extended family.

Providing needed case work services involves referral to one, or oftentimes, many agencies and joint planning. Supportive, and in most cases, aggressive, case work is necessary to carry out a previously recognized need. At times a retarded parent has so many problems which need immediate attention in order to properly function as an individual and as a parent to a retarded child, that the worker is subject to the pitfall of spending so much time with the retarded parents that not enough attention is given at the time of the earliest need of the retarded child for help.

To some degree this has been the situation with the family we wish to bring to your attention today. This multi-problem family has been described by some individuals as "hopeless" and is known to many agencies and groups here as one presenting many problems, which fact is borne out by its presentation a year ago to the Child Case Conference sponsored by the Community Planning Council. Our agency considers this family as a great challenge and is grateful for the past and continuing joint planning, cooperation, and support of all involved.

This family consists of parents who are severely mentally retarded and six children ranging in age from nine years to ten months. The three oldest children are retarded to some degree. The three youngest have as yet not been psychologically tested. Although some of Mr. C's family feel these children need to be taken from the parents, we hope to be able to help these parents assume their responsibility to their children in such a way that it will not be necessary to ask for custody of the children.

The family consists of Mr. C—age 33, Mrs. C—age 32, Harry—age 9, Tommy —age 8, Randolph—age 6½, Aurella—age 3, Maxine—age 2, and Bobby—age 10 months. Our first contact with the family was in November, 1960, when Mr. T, a close friend of Mr. C for at least half of Mr. C's life and who has played the role of father-figure, helped the parents apply for assistance for their three children. It should be noted that after the completion of the application, this family has had only two caseworkers, with the exception of about five months, in spite of factors that ordinarily would have resulted in a change of caseworkers more often. This has helped to provide continuity of case work services.

Mr. C came from a culturally deprived home in which alcoholism, neglect, illness and poor educational opportunity are factors. He was psychologically tested during the application for assistance as medicals completed by the clinic indicated he was able to do full-time work. The revised Stanford-Binet Intelligence Scale Form L revealed Mr. C's I.Q. to be 36. On the verbal scale of the Wechsler-Bellevue Intelligence Test Mr. C's I.Q. was 50. The psychologist felt his emotional condition was more serious than his mental condition. He exhibited depression, distrust of his ability to do anything, nervousness, over-anxiety, and inability to concentrate. The psychologist felt him unable to assume any adult responsibilities.

Mrs. C also came from a culturally deprived family. Mr. T says she is the brightest one in the family. She was psychologically tested about a year and a half after the family applied for assistance and rated an I.Q. of 56 on the verbal scale of the

Wechsler-Bellevue Intelligence Scale. She was better in vocabulary than any other ability, showing an I.Q. of 63 on the Binet Vocabulary Test.

There was no evidence of excessively disturbed emotions. She had difficulty in situations requiring ability to concentrate and appeared to have ability to do low fourth-grade work. Her arithmetic is poor and she counts incorrectly on her fingers. She uses her limited intelligence apparently better than one would think.

There are three problems which have taken, to this point, more time than any other. These are family planning, money management, and Tommy. Also important are the problems of each of the other children, adequate housing and cleanliness, the emotional problems of Mr. C and the parents' ability to give adequate and constant supervision to their children.

The first problem with which we were involved was that of family planning, which need was pointed out at the Intake interview by Mr. T who felt Mrs. C should be sterilized as they did not need any more children. At this point, we wish to say that we recognize that the situation has at times broken down as we have not been able to work concentratedly on the plans which were made, although we had regular, and oftentimes, frequent contacts with the family. At our next contact with Mr. T sterilization was discussed and Mr. T offered to discuss this with Mr. C, saying he could get him to agree to an operation much quicker than the worker could. On our first home visit Mr. C brought up the subject, but his wife was stunned by this as he had not discussed this with her. She was reluctant to discuss this as she was afraid she wouldn't be any good anymore if she had this operation, in spite of the fact that her husband assured her that it wouldn't affect their family life in any way. Mr. T, it should be noted, was always able to discuss this with Mr. C and work well with him along these lines, but he could not talk with Mrs. C about this.

We continued to discuss sterilization with the C's for over a year with Mrs. C giving various reasons why she did not want the operation. As she was having trouble using a diaphragm given her by the hospital, she was urged to go to the Health Department for instructions and possibly other methods of birth control. She again became pregnant. By this time Mr. T had overcome Mr. C's apprehensions about having the operation and Consent forms were signed by both.

Aurella was born early in July. Much planning was necessary to help Mr. C care for the children while his wife was in the hospital. For instance, Mr. T did find a lady to help with the children but she couldn't stay there because the children were "so bad." Mrs. C was urged to go to the Family Planning Clinic for help until arrangements could be made for Mr. C to have the operation. The operation was performed in October, 1962, but by this time Mrs. C was again pregnant. Maxine was subsequently born in June, 1963.

Later we learned Mr. C's family felt his operation was a method of catching her. At this time worker was helping the family with several problems, including an attempt to untangle the complicated relationship between Mr. C, his family, and Mr. T. Mrs. C again became pregnant and told worker she felt it all right to go elsewhere as she was not satisfied with their sex relationship since Mr. C's operation.

Mr. T told Mr. C his operation did not work as it was felt Mr. C would do violence to someone if he knew the truth.

At the Child Case Conference we learned Mrs. C was talking against the sterilization operation for herself to everyone but the caseworker, which she continued to do until coordinated planning, including an explanation by the Duke doctor of the value of a vaginal hysterectomy over a tubal ligation, resulted in both signing the Consent forms.

Detailed planning was necessary with Mr. and Mrs. C and Mr. T to help Mr. C care for the five children while Mrs. C was in the hospital to have the baby. Mr. T obtained someone to help with the children; the worker obtained money to pay her from a church. Several slip-ups occurred which normally a person takes care of themselves. For example, there was no crib for the baby the day before he came home; a member of a Sunday School Class gave theirs.

Mrs. C was then followed closely with worker meeting her at the Health Department Family Planning Clinic the day after her six-week checkup for the purpose of making sure that Mrs. C followed through on her expressed intention of having the intrauterine device inserted. The Eugenics Board approved the sterilization of Mrs. C and plans for the operation were made and carried out with many difficulties. For example, an interested Sunday School Class contributed money to pay a housekeeper to help Mr. C care for the five oldest children while Mrs. C was in the hospital. Arrangements were made for Mr. C's sister to keep the baby. The housekeeper hired by Mr. C walked off the job one morning and worker that day had to find someone to stay the rest of the time with Mr. C and the children.

Although the problem of family planning has been resolved, the problem of money management continues to be with us although progress has been made. The assistance check was originally in Mr. C's name as he managed the money with Mr. T helping him. We were then told that Mr. C managed the money himself, although we knew Mr. T continued to help somewhat. Mr. C can only write his name, can count hesitatingly to 100, and do simple addition. Mrs. C has always wanted to manage the money and brought to the attention of Mr. C's step-mother that her husband and Mr. T did not give her money for clothes for the children or enough food. This was in 1963 and was the first time we knew Mr. C had a living father and that his family was trying to help them.

We discussed appointing a personal representative with Mr. C and Mr. T and Mr. T did not wish to be that person. A personal representative can be appointed before the Clerk of Superior Court to help a person manage his money if he is unable to manage it properly or does not manage it properly. Although Mr. C did not want his step-mother to manage the money, he eventually turned to her after using up the entire check one month about two days after its arrival. She and his father helped for two months, but gave this up because of his behavior.

Then the worker tried to help them manage the money, as they wished very much to take this responsibility themselves, by planning with them and doing the arithmetic. This did not work and Mr. T was finally appointed personal representative. He now goes shopping with Mr. C once a week instead of twice a month.

Actually, shopping is needed twice a week as often they consume the food purchased before the end of the week. One Health Nurse worked closely with Mrs. C around menu planning and buying habits and made some progress. For example, the egg consumption of the family was reduced from several dozen a week to a more proportionate amount, they bought oleo instead of butter, and they learned to use meat substitutes some of the time. This family needs continued help with this now and points up the need for Homemaker Service.

Tommy, now age 8, is the child who has had the most attention given to his needs in the way of services from this and other agencies. Tommy's behavior has and continues to be a problem to his family. He was referred to Duke Clinic in October, 1962, because of enuresis and behavioral difficulties. He was seen in Pediatrics and referred for ENT, speech, and psychiatric evaluation. ENT recommended certain procedures, speech therapy was recommended as general intelligibility was poor, and the general observation from psychiatry was that the child appeared to be severely disturbed. Arrangements were made for this child to have psychometric testing and to be referred to the Child Guidance Clinic. Child Guidance felt, however, that the psychometric testing should be completed before they could determine if they could help. The preliminary impression was questionable slight mental retardation. Tommy was approved for speech therapy under the Crippled Children's Program. We were later notified the authorization was cancelled as the mother failed to bring him back after four sessions. At this point the worker did not follow closely Tommy's progress due to other problems of the family.

We later learned the school referred him to the Edgemont Community Center a few weeks after he entered first grade because of his behavior and immaturity. His behavior improved but because he did not learn, his mother stopped bringing him.

Early in the summer of 1964 there was consideration of a Murdoch School application. The Duke Clinic was contacted and we were later advised that his psychological testing places him in the dull normal range and he would be ineligible. Then coordinated planning resulted in Tommy's enrollment in a pre-school readiness class. He was again a disruptive factor in the classroom and was asked not to attend unless his behavior improved. After a conference with the Health Nurse, she again began working with Tommy's problems with the idea of a Child Guidance referral. Subsequently, additional testing was begun and the case was presented to the Child Case Conference mainly for planning for Tommy.

Because of Tommy's behavior problems which disrupt the family and take much more than his share of the family's time and emotional strength, and because of their inability to discipline him properly and in a consistent manner, the Welfare Department expressed, and continues to express, an interest in a trial Murdoch School placement. It has since been proven that other persons can discipline him and that he finally made a satisfactory behavioral adjustment in school last year. At the Child Case Conference it was learned that Mrs. C had not kept the necessary appointments for testing and no recommendation could be made at this time. The plan was made that the Health Nurse would plan closely with this mother to complete these tests.

Recently the Health Nurse checked the Duke records and found that they indicated Child Guidance or Murdoch. We were advised that the Duke records revealed his I.Q. to be 77, but recent testing shows an I.Q. of 70.2. A letter of a month ago recommended special education, however, based on the I.Q. of 77. A joint conference is now needed for more planning and in order that a coordinated approach might be formulated.

Time does not permit us to discuss provision of case work services for the other problems previously mentioned. Hopefully this presentation has re-emphasized the value of a coordinated approach and pointed up some of the unmet needs of the community.

Getting Ready to Go Out: The Use of Social Group Work to Prepare Residents for Community Placement

JANET T. FERGUSON

Introduction

Six moderately and mildly retarded women residents of Fort Custer State Home (Michigan) were prepared for community placement through the use of Social Group Work treatment. This paper will describe the treatment experience. The problem-solving techniques developed by these women through their group participation and the behavior modification subsequently achieved will be discussed in some depth. A composite diagnostic picture of group members will be presented as well as a brief summary of the social group worker's observations of the effect of the institutional milieu on these specific residents.

Social Group Work was introduced at Fort Custer State Home to broaden the variety of techniques available for individual social work treatment. The social work staff had been concerned that the retardate's meager verbal and conceptual skills often limited the effectiveness of casework intervention. Some residents could use casework; many could not. Perhaps some residents could more effectively be served through a treatment which offered repeated practice of new roles and new behavior in concrete situations, with on-the-spot discussions of what the resident was doing and feeling, and where conceptualizing and verbalizing were less necessary. This is what Group Work could provide. The group worker could work with the resident in both verbal and non-verbal ways—both talking and doing together —and could vary the emphasis according to client need.

At Fort Custer, Social Group Work has been used primarily to prepare residents for community placement. This purpose has been both indicated and made possible by the current emphasis on community rehabilitation in the mental retardation field. Many of our moderately and mildly retarded adult residents have been institutionalized far beyond the point of maximum training. The Michigan Department of Mental Health and local communities have been developing half-way houses, sheltered workshops, recreation programs, and other resources available to our res-

Presented at the 1967 Annual Meeting of the American Association on Mental Deficiency. Reprinted by permission of the author.

idents placed in the community. Thus the time was right for this particular use of Group Work.

The following will be presented in three sections: (1) a description of the client, (2) a discussion of the method, process, and results of Group Work with one group of women, and (3) a summary of the group workers observations about the resident in the institution milieu.

The Client

Pulling together the most common elements we found in the strengths and problems of our group participants, the following is a composite picture of the moderately or mildly retarded institutionalized woman as we learned to know her through Social Group Work.[1] This is the group worker's client.

Clearly, she has certain *strengths*: her pleasant appearance and sociable manner; certain well-learned skills at job tasks, personal care, and leisure activities; her usual honesty and dependability; her simple verbal and conceptual skills; often some ability to read and write; and her real desire to learn, to "improve herself," and to be a useful person outside the institution. But her *problems* are many:

She is deeply confused about her own identity. She knows her age. But she is basically unsure of what she is—adult or child. Her role has changed little since childhood except that she may work harder. She is unsure of her female role—is she girl or woman? She is anxious about the whole area of her sexuality. She tends to feel she should be "neuter" to be a "good patient." She confuses the meanings of "mentally retarded" and "mentally ill." At times, when her controls of emotion or behavior break down, she may fear she is "losing her mind."

Her appearance and dress reflect her confusion about self. Her hair and clothing are often worn in outdated styles appropriate to a girl much younger than she. She has noticeably poor posture and enlarged stomach and hips. She has never worn girdle, hose, or heels.

She feels rejected by the "outside" world, including her family. She feels "outsiders" would "look down on" her or "slam" her if she returned to the community, that they identify her with the profoundly and severely retarded residents of whom she is ashamed.

She feels anxious and frightened of her emotions. She believes they are bad. She tries to deny and repress them, occasionally is not successful and becomes "upset," is terrified of the results. She feels she has no control over the "pandora box" of her own feelings once they are let loose.

She feels she is unlovable and unloved, unwanted, unsuccessful, unskillful, and at times bad. She has no protective cushion of self-esteem. Words, or behavior of others reinforce feelings about herself just enough to make them immediately intolerable, to unsettle the tenuous balance of peace she keeps with herself. She must say or do something to reclaim minimal self-respect. But her repertoire is very limited.

Often she can only express anguish, frustration, and desperation. It comes out in crying, screaming, swearing, hitting. And this inadequate cry for help or recognition gets punished. A ward-mate's package or visitor means to her, "I didn't get the attention—I am less loved." This is the meaning of the frequent "upsets" in which she becomes involved and which are reported as happening "for no apparent reason."

She lives a lonely parallel existence with other women residents. Her interactions with peers are superficial—brief talking, listening to radio or television together—except in moments of conflict. She is jealously rivalrous for attention from personnel. She craves the acceptance and giving inherent in a friendship, but does not know how to form or maintain friendships. (Or she is jealously attached to one "friend," cannot share that friend with others.) She feels her controls threatened by the presence of the few severely disturbed or acting-out residents on the ward. In her way, she has repeatedly asked protection from them. ("She should see a psychologist.") But she feels no one hears or understands, that the disturbed ones more often "run things" on the ward, that they are less disciplined by attendants than she, and that she is more likely to get blamed for disturbances. She often misunderstands "upset" behavior of peers, sees it as aimed at hurting her. Without help, she tends to see peers as a threat—rivals for scraps of attention and affection, possessors of their own "pandora boxes" of emotions that can "get her in trouble," make her lose control of herself.

She is vaguely aware of her unused potential. She feels she can do more than is allowed here but cannot say what. These feelings make her guilty, seem to conflict with being a "good patient." She is often depressed or angry, feels she should repress this too. She wants to be a giving person, but she needs assurance that her urge to give will "not get anyone in trouble." She has not learned to give to peers.

Her talk of leaving the institution is laden with ambivalence. She feels her need to stretch and grow. But she is both eager and terrified of the "outside." She suggests grandiose plans for her life (her own apartment, bank account, job, marriage, family) at the same time she feels she can do nothing.

This has been the typical group participant. The problem confronting the group worker has been *to change the resident with these problems and concerns to an adult who can function, according to her own capacity, outside the institution.*[2]

Our first group (which will be discussed here[3]) consisted of women chosen by the Social Service staff as the most likely candidates for community placement. On the surface these women appeared fairly similar—six "working residents" who lived in the same ward and who had been institutionalized most of their lives. They were referred to the group worker with various individual problems noted: *Elizabeth,* (Liz) age 57, IQ 66, was a compulsive housecleaner, a perfectionist, a loner, tended to dress in bizarre fashion, was "nervous" and was known for her temper. *Doris,* age 44, IQ 63, was known to lie and steal occasionally, was a loner, and tended to be sloppy in her personal care. *Sylvia,* age 33, IQ 68, was attractive, was considered by personnel as too bright and "normal" for the institution, but had real difficulty making decisions or judgments. *Nancy*, age 39, IQ 42, was loud and awkward, often sloppy in personal care, and was easily involved in conflict with other residents. *Hazel*, age 59, IQ 70, was considered a pleasant fumbling older woman, was easily confused, and was sometimes poor at personal grooming. *Leila*, age 43, IQ 39, was neat and attractive, was having frequent temper outbursts on the ward, and was easily involved in her sister's conflicts with others. All were considered excellent workers in their work assignments.

This superficial picture reflects the limited extent to which these women were known as individuals by institution staff. Therefore, as Group Work treatment began, it was also necessary to continue working for a clearer diagnostic understanding of each woman. What emerged were six individual variations of the institutionalized woman described above.

The Method

Social Group Work was the treatment of choice for these women. This group was seen in weekly one-and-one-half-hour sessions for fifteen months. During these sessions the focus was always problem-solving and the goal was individual behavior change. In addition to group sessions, the group worker freely used individual interviews.[4]

It has been pointed out that "group experience" for any one of us "is an important part of our lives" . . . "through group experience we find acceptance . . . develop our self-image, . . . learn and practice reality testing, . . . become social beings." We learn how to deal with other people. For the institution resident the group is "a laboratory where the tasks of social living can be experienced or learned." "In the ideal group, the (resident) is provided with a tolerable level of frustration, with pleasure, with relief from anxiety, with opportunity for growth, and with experience in problem-solving."[5]

THE TREATMENT CONTRACT

With this group, the understanding between group worker and client about why the individual was in the group varied for each woman and related to the foremost problem about which each was concerned. For example: Liz saw being in the group as a way of learning to control her temper and "get over her nervousness." Sylvia understood that in group she could learn to make decisions for herself. As a group, they understood that they were "getting ready to go out." This was further specified to include: learning to understand themselves, to know and use their own feelings and strengths, to live with their limitations, and to know the "outside" well enough to handle themselves in the community easily and without fear.[6]

THE TREATMENT GOALS

Based on the developing diagnostic picture of each group participant, the group worker planned treatment goals for each. Work done with Liz illustrates goals and how they were implemented.

Liz had lived for fifty-three years in institutions and bitterly expected to die here. Heavy make-up, mismatched clothes, and constant anger gave her a bizarre appearance. She housecleaned compulsively and with a vengeance. She criticized the cleanliness standards of others, and when they did not see fit to improve, she cleaned for them. At best, her relationship with peers was distant. Intensely fearful of revealing her limitations, she refused to participate in ward or recreation activities. Although eager for community contact, she refused bus rides because the bus displayed the institution insignia and "outsiders" would think her "a fool." Her "nervousness" clearly involved fear of failure and anxiety about her ability to control her anger and behavior. When confronted with a problem—such as new opportunity or sudden change—she often did lose control and project angry invective at the confronting person. The group worker, aware of these problems, formulated treatment goals for Liz that included: (1) Helping her achieve self-satisfaction and a more acceptable self-image by discovering strengths she was not aware of, developing and using new skills and interests, and successfully taking new adult roles in the group. (Short-range goals used to accomplish this were: improving her dress and appearance, broadening her interests and skills beyond housecleaning to include hobbies (crafts), and use of community resources (YWCA); (2) Helping her strengthen her controls and reduce the impact of her fears and anxieties (through practice in verbalizing and understanding her fears and her angers, through coping with stressful situations (sudden change, meeting "outsiders," etc.) with the support of group and group worker; (3) Assisting her to become a helping person and to find satisfaction in peer relationships (through sharing with the group her verbal skills in problem-solving and her skill in crafts.)

Group treatment goals were a composite of such goals for individual members. In essence,[7] they involved self-awareness, behavior change, and the development of new skills that would enable these women to move out of the role of "good patient" —the bland, non-assertive, dependent behavior expected of any non-individualized person under care in a residential institution—toward an ability to successfully perform some of the many roles available to a self-determining adult woman.

The group worker discussed with the women the group purpose and how the group would function and then reinforced the message with non-verbal activity or objects. For example, matches provided for use during early group sessions helped to concretely establish the ground rules. Seldom before in their institution life had these women been invited to regularly light their own cigarettes. The gesture said to them: You are trusted and expected to be responsible adults. Group sessions will be different from anything else you have experienced here and you will be allowed to be different.

Process and Results

In the course of fifteen months, these women did, in varying degrees, reach the treatment goals set for them. Basically they did move beyond the confines of the "good patient" role toward some self-determination, self-awareness, control of their own behavior, and ability to behave appropriately in community settings. Each clearly proved to herself and to us that she had far more potential for growth and successful handling of adult roles than anyone had hoped.

This was accomplished through the use of group and individual discussion sessions, group program activities, and a variety of institution and community resources. Focus was on the total person and her total life situation.

GROUP STRUCTURE AND PROCESSES

In Social Group Work, the group itself is used as a tool in the treatment of each member as well as the place of treatment. In helping these women, the group worker needed to be aware of and use the variety of group structures and processes that are a part of any group life.[8] An example of this is the use of *roles*, which played an important part of the group work process.

It was important that roles be clearly structured—both the role of the group worker and the role of the group participant. The *role of the group worker* involved intervention in many ways: questioning, demonstrating, modeling, limiting, reflecting and clarifying expressed feelings, and always attempting to keep the awareness of both group worker and group focused on the problem-solving and, at any given time, the degree of group achievement of treatment goals. The *role of group participant* was new, strange, and anxietous for each woman as she entered the group. Since the focus of the treatment goals was self-determination, the group worker could not allow the women to play the "good patient" role during group sessions. For many being a "good patient" was their best and only social skill. At times they would rather stay within its confines. It was familiar and required no growth or problem-solving. But it was strictly superficial role-playing, and, created as it was for the benefit of the institution structure, it had little to do with their individual needs. Its limitations were the source of much of these residents' frustration and anger. Group activities and discussions were structured to pose problems for which the "good patient" role was inadequate, problems which required the trial of new adult roles.

For example, the group worker helped Liz successfully try several roles within the group which later carried over into her total life and clearly replaced her need for the "good patient" role. From the first group discussion, she took on the role of leader in digging and fighting her way through problems, often clarifying feelings for the others. As her pleasure and skill in craft activities developed, the group began to accept her and she proudly saw herself as their craft expert. And with the self-satisfaction she found in these roles, she could then be encouraged to take the role of a helping person in group. She could share her skills in problem-solving and crafts with others. Eventually she continued the role outside of the group. For Liz, whose peer relationships had been sparse and irritated, this was dramatic change. A year after she started in Group Work, a younger ward-mate was heard to gratefully call Liz "the most understanding woman in the world." She spoke frequently of each person having a "gift" to find and use and this became a kind of group motto. With her new sense of self worth established through these roles, she began to be willing to work on ways of living with her limitations.

The use of roles in Social Group Work treatment can only be glimpsed here. The group worker helped Liz and each of the others find and develop roles within the group for which they had potential ability. Through trial of these roles, each was helped to achieve specific determined behavior change. And the new roles of each became, together, a system of roles useful for achieving group goals.

GROUP WORK TECHNIQUES USED

(1) *Discussion:* The women were introduced to group work through *group discussion.* At first this consisted largely of individual ventilation of feelings directed at the group worker with others chiming in. Most came into group initially because they wanted to talk about themselves. Encouraged by the group worker, they expressed anger, resentment, hurt, frustration, uncertainty, excitement, eagerness to learn and be master of oneself, and desire to give to and help others. They talked about ward conflicts, uncertainty about their own controls, their uncomfortable image of themselves compared with "outsiders," their distorted image of life "outside," their feelings of rejection by relatives and the entire "outside" world, and their confusion about why they were in the institution. Through every early group discussion ran the underlying theme of confusion about their own identity (including age and sex.)

In this group (and most succeeding groups) ward conflict and "getting upset" was their first concern. It was an area of tense anxiety. How they functioned in the ward group directly reflected to them their only concept of success or failure as individuals. They repeatedly wanted to talk about the behavior of one severely disturbed ward-mate. The discussion always reflected their concern about the threatening effect of her behavior on their own controls. ("Sadie makes me nervous"— "I'm afraid I will get in trouble and lose my chance.")[9] A major treatment goal for each group participant was for her to learn to understand the meaning of these "upsets" both for herself and for the others whose "upsets" bothered her. As she did so, the specter of an "upset" became less threatening. And acceptably expressing her own feelings and controlling of her own behavior became increasingly possible. In these discussions they were encouraged to suggest and try new ways of controlling themselves and of influencing situations with peers. They then evaluated the new behavior at later sessions.

As the women began learning to listen, talk to, support, and argue with each other, they could increasingly be led through discussion into new understanding and toward successful new behavior. The following record excerpt shows group discussion used to help the group reach new understanding of themselves.

The group worker felt that, in helping the women develop self-respect, their sense of worthlessness as they saw it in their rejection by relatives had to be dealt with. With the worker's encouragement, several told of open rejections (such as waiting with bags packed for relatives who invited but did not come for them). Liz felt that "my relatives look down on me." Doris said the behavior of relatives was "just mean." Leila asked, "Why do they do that?" Sylvia added that relatives may still think of them as they were before commitment. This allowed the group worker to involve them in thinking how each had changed since that time. The group recognized, too, the strangeness some people feel about visiting an institution. They related this to the strangeness they themselves feel about going "out." The group worker asked then, "What about friends? Do they understand you?" This led to eager discussion of volunteer and staff friends (they had not yet learned to form peer friendships) who understand more than relatives and with whom they feel more comfortable. As the worker summarized that they seemed to be deciding that relatives may not intend to be mean but rather were not comfortable with them because they did not understand them, Sylvia smilingly said, "yes, but they could try!" The laughing agreement showed apparent relief.

One such discussion did not solve the problems. But group worker and group went back over ideas expressed until the women had learned new skills in understanding and verbalizing feelings and new perspective upon which to base new behavior. Here the goal was for the women to begin understanding that there is not necessarily something wrong with them because their relatives ignore them, to break dependency ties with non-functioning relatives, and to begin trying more successful ways of fulfilling relationship needs that relatives do not fulfill. This led into learning to form and take part in friendships which was a major treatment goal for this group.

(2) *Program Activity*: In addition to discussion, many activities were used. For each group participant, these allowed spontaneous acting out and on-the-spot handling of problem behavior. Group activity enabled trial of new roles and new behavior, with the support of group worker and group, based on newly acquired understanding of self. Although these women came into group with an urgency to talk, their need to understand in concrete terms made it important for the group to *do* as well as *talk*. The talking did not stop. Some of the best discussions took place traveling to town, over coffee in a restuarant, or cooking dinner in the kitchen. But also, some of the real new growth in self-awareness came for each in finding she could cook a roast "like an outsider," sew for the local Cancer Society and have her efforts needed and appreciated, visit with ease in the home of an "outsider"—or that she *could not* count and handle money well enough to avoid embarrassment. Each activity was structured to offer a set of problems that could be solved only by using initiative, self-assertion, and decision-making. Each experience provided each woman a clearer understanding of her strengths and limitations. The women excitedly understood this and rose to the challenge. Each problem-solving gave them new skills with which to tackle the next experience and its set of problems.

Successful *doing*, as it increased their awareness of personal ability and their self-respect, decreased their need to avoid looking realistically at their limitations. This seemed to work like a see-saw—the higher the self-esteem on one side, the deeper they were willing to dig into problem areas on the other. Whether gaining in understanding of self or in specific skills, the group was guided in continually building on success.

But the job of preparing these women for community placement could not be done effectively by the group worker and group *alone*. In addition to the treatment techniques described above the group worker made use of a *variety of resources* both in the institution and in the community.

(3) *Use of Institution Resources:* In the institution, cooperation between group worker and ward personnel was essential. A portion of the group workers time was allotted to interpreting the group work program, sharing information, and exchanging observations and insights about group participants with ward attendants. When a good team relationship between group worker and attendant was established, growth gained in group sessions was reinforced on the ward. In addition, the group worker gained awareness of the resident's specific behavior in ward situations that enabled a sharper focus on problems during group sessions.

As individual strengths, limitations, and need for further training became apparent through group sessions, the group worker and staff in other departments planned cooperatively. The Education Department set up a Home Living Class to teach community living skills such as cooking, sewing, familiarity with stores and shopping, and planning and eating together family style. The Recreation Department made available classes in leisure time skills, with focus on community living, to which we referred group participants as interests and needs arose. The Vocational Officer considered changing needs and skills of which the group worker became aware in adjusting work placement. The Business Office set up a special fund with which indigent group participants learned to buy girdles, hose, and dress shoes (and so to dress appropriately as adults when visiting the community).

(4) *Use of Community Resources:* In time, community resources were used extensively. Volunteers (particularly the Red Cross Grey Ladies), church groups (such as the Catholic Legion of Mary), and the YWCA were major resources. The two YWCAs in our nearby cities were most cooperative. The group was first taken to "Y" activities and programs for casual contact with "outside" women; later the group exchanged several visits with a "Y" club (whose members were largely culturally deprived women and with whom this group shared similar social adjustment problems); finally, several group participants became "Y" members and regularly attended a club or activity.

(5) *Use of Volunteers:* The volunteer was used to go with the individual resident into the community. She was supervised by, and closely cooperated with, the group worker. Her assignment was to model various adult roles, including that of "friend." She learned to guide the resident through behavior appropriate to these roles. With her help, the resident began learning to function in peer relationships with "outsiders." As the role of "friend" allowed, the volunteer also freely said what she thought. For most this was the first experience with an adult social response (as opposed to a professional response) to their behavior. It greatly enhanced self-awareness. The volunteer provided invaluable observations of behavior that enabled the group worker to more precisely assess current individual progress toward treatment goals. With her, the women learned to comfortably use community resources, meet and make friends with a number of her acquaintances, and be-

have appropriately in a casual social situation. Occasionally they had a trial run at home living, with the volunteer as model, when they spent a day in her home. The volunteer was thus utilized as an important auxiliary staff person.[10]

RESULTS

These women are now in community placement. Group work has not been a panacea to solve all their problems. Nor did we expect it to be. They still live with limitations inherent in their mental retardation. At times they are overwhelmed by confusing situations. They are still somewhat dependent, need guidance in non-task areas of living. But as a result of group work with them, we know their individual strengths and limitations in many living situations and can place them accordingly. They know them too and have learned ways of living with both. When necessary, pressures and changes in the placement have been weathered with obvious help of behavior, self-control, and self-respect learned during their group participation. Growth patterns appear to be continuing. We are increasingly aware that good placement simply begins a new stage in problem solving in the life of each resident. *The focus of our institution group work program must be preparing them to cope with this new set of problems.*

Some Observations About the Traditional Institution Milieu

One additional aspect of Social Group Work in the institution is the opportunity it offers to observe the cause-effect relationship between the institution milieu and the social-emotional problems of the resident. It is the group worker's job to know the individual group participant and her problems. This inevitably leads the group worker into increasing awareness of *what the institution says and does to the resident.*

The resident continually receives certain "messages" about herself from the institution milieu. The perception of, and response to, these "messages" appeared often in the content of Group Work sessions. Briefly, the resident clearly "gets the message" *that she is not worth respect and has no rights as an individual;* she is steadily pressured by the milieu to *repress and ignore her emotions and sexual feelings;* and she learns well that to "stay out of trouble," to be a "good patient," and to receive real approval, she must strive to become emotionally bland and sexually neuter. (Since this is usually a losing battle for her, she is continually reminded, by the stirrings of her own feelings, of the "badness" within her.)

Although the retardation was certainly part of the picture, *most* of the problems of our group participants appear to have been shaped and reinforced by daily life in the institution—by this kind of *"message" from the milieu.* The ineptness at handling adult roles and peer relationships, the unclear concept of self as adult and feminine, the intense guilt about emotion and ignorance of acceptable emotional expression, and the inability to form an opinion or a decision—*these* problems, and not the residents' mild or moderate retardation per se, were blocking the successful return of these women to the community.

We used Social Group Work to treat these problems for a few residents. A decision to revise the milieu—*to change the "message"*—would have been far more effective.

Conclusion

In our experience of the past three years, we have found Social Group Work to be a valuable method for problem-solving and behavior modification in the institution. We have found among our moderately and mildly retarded residents a group who have a basic desire to understand themselves and others and to change their problem behavior. The Group Work method with this group has provided the following:

1. An excellent diagnostic method.

2. An excellent method for behavior modification, through change in understanding of self, including specific trial of newly understood potential ability and new roles.

3. A specific practical method for emotional and social problem-solving with the retardate, who is best at concrete tasks but needs to use and strengthen what abstract and conceptual skills he has as tools for coping with change, the unfamiliar, and the world outside the institution.

4. Opportunity to observe the cause-effect relationship between the milieu and the social-emotional problems of the resident.

Group Work individualizes. Through it we have known our residents as institution residents have seldom been known. It allows the resident a new self-awareness. Seemingly this combination can produce a degree of individual growth and change new to the state institution.

But in the light of total need, Group Work is slow. Much of the growth from "patient role" toward adult self-determination could happen in the milieu with well-planned goals, good staff team-work, and a supplementary treatment-focused Group Work program. Thus use of Group Work leads inevitably to consideration of the milieu and the possibilities of milieu therapy. Today, with new focus on community placement of older residents, and the use of the institution as a short-term training center for young retardates, we have compelling reasons to know our residents as individual personalities. In general, we do not know them now. The institutionalized retardate, like any of social work's clients, needs to have his social worker develop a working relationship with him based on respect for his individuality and enough understanding of him to truly "start where the client is"—not where, from our front office notion, we *think* he is. We need to learn to communicate *with* him as well as *about* him. Sometimes, in his way, he can tell or show us better than anyone what he needs.

Appendix

Treatment goals for this group included the following:

1. Learning to know and comfortably accept themselves as individuals. This in-

cluded: (a) becoming acquainted with and learning to successfully integrate their own feelings into their daily living. (When they recognized their own feelings they could better understand and get along with others.); (b) each becoming acquainted with her own strengths and limitations. (Through reinforcing and increasing strengths, self-respect was developed. With sufficient self-respect established, limitations could be frankly and comfortably faced. Each could then begin to plan and practice her life to use strengths and work around, or protect herself in, the areas of her limitations.); (c) gaining perspective about themselves in relation to others, both inside and outside the institution. (A first step was learning to see themselves separate from the severely retarded residents); (d) learning to take an appropriate age and sex role—i.e., adult women.

2. Learning to control and understand their own behavior.

3. Learning to improve and maintain manners and appearance at an average level of acceptability in the outside community.

4. Learning to form and sustain friendship relationships with peers.

5. Learning to plan, make decisions, and handle privileges and responsibilities, both individually and as a group, i.e., taking responsibility for beginning to plan one's own life.

6. Learning to handle new experience, unexpected change, and to cope with situations that are socially or intellectually confusing.

7. Learning a socially acceptable role in relation to the opposite sex.

8. Gaining familiarity with the outside community environment and community living, including: (a) ability to get around, find one's way; (b) use of community facilities; (c) establishing contact and sense of belonging, with friends, community institutions, etc.; (d) gaining some familiarity and ease with home and family living.

References

[1]These problems brought to group sessions by women were the same ones revealed in every succeeding adult group with which we have worked.

[2]Women are discussed here, but the same pattern has emerged as we have worked with preplacement groups of men. Age also, has not seemed to greatly change the picture except in emphasis. The teen-age and young adult groups are more openly concerned with relationships to the opposite sex.

[3]Since January 1964, the Group Work Program at Fort Custer State Home has expanded to serve both male and female residents. In this period, four Social Group Workers and four Group Work students from the University of Michigan School of Social Work have worked with fourteen groups of mildly and moderately retarded children, adolescents, and adults. The treatment focus has always been problem-solving and behavior change, although with younger groups community placement has been seen as a long range rather than an immediate goal.

[4]Our concept of Social Group Work with all our group participants is that of a total Social Work function in which the worker draws upon whichever of the variety of Social Work techniques seems to most appropriately serve client needs at the moment.

[5]Sallie R. Churchill and Paul H. Glasser, "Small Groups In the Hospital Community," (Michigan Department of Mental Health, Lansing, Michigan, 1965), p. 47.

[6]In the first group, early emphasis on "getting ready to go out" seemed to reinforce the ever-present anxiety about where and when they would go. This happened to the point of sometimes blocking problem-solving. In later groups we stressed the second part of this understanding instead.

[7]See Appendix A for detailed group treatment goals.

[8]This would include such group phenomena as interaction between group members, friendship ties, individual roles, ranking order, and subgroupings that formed as the group worked together.

[9]Anxious group talk often revealed how, without staff awareness of what is happening dynamically within the ward group, the ward tends to be controlled by the most assertive and often the most disturbed. It showed the lack of protection for those who may be struggling to maintain their frail self-control in the presence of the ward-mate who is skillfully seducing others into "upsets" and "bad behavior."

[10]The writer would like to give special recognition to Mrs. Lucylle Bidelman of Battle Creek, Michigan, whose enthusiasm, and insight were indispensible to our developing this role for the volunteer. We later taught other volunteers to do many of the tasks she developed.

SIXTY-EIGHT

The Security of Institutional Care Without Institutionalization

BARBARA A. MARLOWE AND HERBERT A. SILVERMAN

This paper concerns a service being offered to a small group of patients of The Rosewood State Hospital, Owings Mills, Maryland. This group is unlike the great majority of our patients. They have never stayed at the hospital overnight and have never had a meal there. They have, in fact, never been on the wards of the hospital. Briefly and simply, the paper describes the reasons for and procedures by which certain retarded individuals are legally admitted to our hospital, but are placed in our Foster Care Program immediately rather than in the hospital itself.

We believe this practice is certainly uncommon if not unique in the care of retarded persons. A search of the A.A.M.D. journals of the past 15 years has not revealed anything exactly like it.

Miss Beryl Bishop in "Family Care: The Patients," *American Journal of Mental Deficiency,* January, 1957, suggests a trend which may have led to something similar to our program. It is not clear from the publication whether it ever did.

Mr. H. O. Wildenskov in his article "The Care of Mental Defectives in Denmark," *American Journal of Mental Deficiency,* July, 1948, when describing the State supervision of the retarded in Denmark writes of a system which, in actual practice, can be taken as similar, in some respects, to what we have initiated. However, it operates against a social and political background quite different from that of the United States. We believe that what we have done is compatible with the common practices of caring for the retarded in the United States. We believe, also, it is applicable for and easily adaptable in those states where the state institutions for the retarded are autonomously operated with respect to other services for children.

Most of those working in the field of mental retardation have realized for some number of years that family life is often the most appropriate plan for meeting the needs of many retarded persons, at least for various portions of their lives. With this recognition came the right of the retarded individual to have this plan as indicated. Out of this right grew the need for providing this to retarded persons having

Reprinted by permission of the authors. From a paper presented at the 1965 Annual Meeting of the American Association on Mental Deficiency.

no families able or willing to accept them, and unable to find another family setting for them which held a reasonable amount of stability or, even, adequacy.

For some years we at Rosewood have looked seriously at the need for this individualized care for the retarded. We have attempted to meet this need in several ways. First, we found that skilled counseling offered in our Pre-admission Service altered attitudes and feelings of some natural parents to the point that they found themselves able and wanting to provide home care for their retarded child. Secondly, we attempted to have community agencies in our State of Maryland, especially Department of Public Welfare, offer their foster care services to retarded children. In this area we were less successful. While these agencies are providing homes for some children currently testing at a retarded level, their policy is that the retarded do not fall within the realm of their responsibility. This policy is not in conflict with Maryland law.

Despite our efforts, retarded persons were admitted to Rosewood who would have benefited by family care. We hope to observe these persons, "work them up" quickly, and place them back in the community in our own expanding Foster Care Program. In reality, a number of these persons became submerged and "lost" for a period of time before they went back to the community, if, indeed, they did so at all. Such admissions ran the risk of social regression and the development of problems not present prior to institutionalization. Thus, by the time the person was "found" again, foster care was often contraindicated.

There was a growing awareness on the part of the Staff of what was likely to happen and, indeed, was happening to these persons after admission. Also, there was concern about the trauma of institutionalization which seemed an unnecessary thing for these persons to have to experience. Often, they already had histories of frequent moves from home to hospital, to foster home, to other institutions, etcetera. Nor were we without concern for the families of these individuals and what all of this meant to them.

Perhaps the establishment of a waiting list with no beds to meet the needs of those who really needed the full services of our hospital, or the very practical side of this, caused us to look even more closely at this other group.

These individuals needed personal care, physically and emotionally, which is, of course, not available in an institutional setting. Concurrent with this were needs for periodic re-evaluation, counseling, and support of both the retarded persons and those caring for them. Parents, or other responsible relatives, needed the assurance that adequate care was being provided for their charges with professional persons able to plan future changes as needed with them or without them.

It was believed that maintenance of family and community care, as long as possible, in these cases would provide these retarded individuals with the best opportunity for development physically, intellectually, and emotionally. For some, this would hopefully mean, especially with developing community resources, a lifetime of community living. Others, it was clearly recognized, would have to experience actual institutional care at sometime in their lives. However, it was hoped that individual care, as long as possible, would enable them to lead a more satisfying and productive life in the hospital and have a better chance for return to the community.

It was decided we would attempt to meet the present needs of these people by having our Pre-admission, Admission, and Foster Care units work more closely together, with the result that patients as described above are now placed in Foster Care the day of their admission. In some cases they do not even come to the hospital on that particular day.

While the number of cases handled in this manner since the inception of this program in April, 1961, has been small (14 cases), the service is increasing with our growing experience. Of note is the fact that to date we have had no need to change the initial living arrangements made for any person offered this service.

Such a program presupposes the existence within the hospital of a thorough Preadmission Service and a soundly structured Foster Care Service.

In our hospital the process works like this. Pre-admission Service is offered the applicant and his family. At a Pre-admission Staff Meeting headed by our Clinical Director, the psychologist reports the results he has obtained on psychometric and, often, projective testing. The physician gives the physical condition of the applicant. The social worker who has assembled history information and spoken with the family, and the applicant when that is possible, reports his findings to the Staff. Included in these are the current problem. There is an assessment of the resources within the family, of other community agencies, and of Rosewood, with which to alleviate the problem and meet the applicant's needs.

At this Staff recommendations are made which are taken by the social worker back to the family or legal guardian. In the even that family care is recommended, the social worker's first emphasis becomes that of reviewing the possibility of care by the natural family. If this is not available, the area of admission to the hospital and direct placement into foster care is opened for exploration. While this is often more painful for families than institutionalization itself, as it may cause more guilt, with skill this aspect can be handled. In the long run they usually feel better for being asked to consider and participate in what is believed to be a more advantageous plan for their relatives.

The family is helped to understand that legal admission to the hospital will take place, and that the retarded individual and his family will be entitled to any service of the institution that may be of value to them, including the patient's care within the hospital if needed. The parents, or legal guardian, are introduced to the foster care supervisor and the social worker who will be home finding and supervising the placement. The questions they have about foster care are answered. The details of the relationship to each other of those involved (the retarded person, his relatives, the foster parents, and the hospital) are clarified. Depending upon circumstances families may take little or no part or interest in their relative's new home or may be very active, visiting the prospective home with the social worker, etcetera. Questions of fees, provision of clothing, visiting, and other similar matters, are worked out.

In addition to admissions effected at the request of parents or legal guardians, we do have court commitments. For a long time the hospital has tried very hard to encourage the courts' use of our pre-admission service before committing a person to Rosewood. We have been successful in this in many areas of the State, particularly in Baltimore City from where we receive our greatest number of patients. The Baltimore City Juvenile Court learned of our new program through a case for whom they had requested pre-admission service. Now this Court will refer certain children to us with the specific request that they be considered for this plan. Time is given for the necessary procedures, so that on the day one of these children is committed to our hospital, he can be taken by one of our social workers directly to the foster home from the Court hearing.

Once the retarded person is legally admitted, Rosewood can use its boarding care funds to provide in whole or part the financial support of the patient in the community when necessary. Our supervisory services insure that the person's needs are met. The visiting caseworker helps the foster parents to understand the retarded person's limitations and how to best help him. The hospital offers to the family and to the foster parents the security and stability of involvement with a responsible agency.

It should be stressed that the hospital's involvement does not eliminate the patient's family from the picture. On the contrary, the institution tries to keep the families actively involved in planning for their retarded relatives, in the hope that, someday, some of these patients can return to their own families.

While there are no definite limits in regard to the types of retarded persons for whom this service is available, it is most often used for infants in an effort to prevent maternal deprivation, children for whom neither the family nor foster care services are available but who are able to benefit by family living, and, often, public schools, and older persons who have lived in the community all their lives but whose relatives are no longer able to offer them care.

Steven is a mongoloid. He is now 20 months old. At the age of four months, he was referred for admission to Rosewood. He had two older siblings, one of whom had a history of emotional disturbance antedating Steven's birth. It was felt that the amount of time the mother was giving to Steven would cause a setback in the older sibling. An appointment was arranged to give Steven a thorough evaluation to determine whether any medical problems existed and from this information to determine what range of planning possibilities existed for him.

The evaluation showed that Steven had no other complications aside from the basic mongolism. It was felt he could benefit from a home environment. The family was clear in wanting him out of the home. They showed signs of guilt, shame, and rejection, as well as concern for the older sibling. When the possibility of foster care through our new procedure was suggested, it was at first rejected. The attitude behind this rejection seemed to be, "if another family can care for our child why can't we?" and, on the part of the mother, "if another woman can take care of my child, it means I am inadequate."

The benefits of home-like care were discussed with the parents. After much struggle and further consultation with their private pediatrician, the family consented to foster care for Steven.

He was placed in a loving foster home which was well prepared and motivated for receiving him. By that time, he was eleven months old. He was unable to sit alone. Within four months in the foster home, Steven was able to pull himself into a standing position. He has continued to make excellent progress and the physician following Steven in the community is very impressed with the progress he has shown.

The natural parents visit him in the foster home. They take him out for rides. However, they seem to have the need to disparage the very real progress he has been making. This hurts the foster mother. Social work help is being given in an effort to change this situation.

Martha was placed in a private foster home by her father when her mother had to be admitted to a mental hospital. Pre-admission evaluation revealed that the foster home was a warm accepting one for this appealing eight-year-old with an I.Q. of 33 which was thought to be potentially higher, although certainly within the defective range. The lowered functioning was believed to be the result of lack of stimulation in the past and emotional disturbance caused by her earlier experience in her own home. The foster mother needed help in planning for Martha and assurance that, should the father who frequently left town not pay the board bill, someone would.

The child was referred to us by Juvenile Court, to whose attention she had come because of the aspects of dependency and neglect. Our findings were presented to the Court and she was committed to Rosewood. The Court gave permission for the placement that very day, however, with the same foster mother under the supervision of our Foster Care Program.

Martha has been a patient of ours for two years. At this time she attends school. Her academic progress is slow. She presents no behavior problems at home, in the school, or in the community, and plays well with the younger children in the neighborhood. She cares for her own needs well.

Iris is a 71-year-old woman. She was living with her 77-year-old step-mother and her 57-year-old brother. When her brother died suddenly, the step-mother found she was unable to carry the burdens of maintaining a home and supervising Iris. The step-mother began to plan for her own entrance into an old-age home and turned to Rosewood as a placement for Iris for the remainder of her life.

Pre-admission evaluation showed that Iris had an I.Q. of 59. She was capable of caring for all of her personal needs, with occasional supervision. She was used to privacy and obtained her chief amusements by listening to the radio, watching television, and looking at pictures in magazines and newspapers. It was felt that Iris could be regarded as a person who showed as many characteristics in keeping with her age as of retardation. Little value was seen in admitting her to Rosewood and it was felt that a placement approximating her accustomed mode of living would make Iris' adjustment to change easier. Accordingly, she was placed in a boarding home. Her Social Security payments supplemented by Rosewood boarding funds provide for her support.

On the first day of placement, Iris cried. However, it appears that she acclimated herself rapidly. Her careholder, who has had other placements from Rosewood, is very understanding of Iris. She seems able to provide an atmosphere where Iris is comfortable and happy, and, at the same time, more involved in household activities than she ever was at home.

That the program just described can be successful seems to have been demonstrated. The development of such program is not without problems and questions certainly. One problem on which we are working at present concerns the fee that parents of patients using this service should be charged. In Maryland, families pay at the rate of from nothing up to $166 monthly dependent upon income, dependents, et cetera. This is reduced to one-fourth of the maximum after the retarded person has been in the institution 30 months if, indeed, the family can pay that fourth. We have been asking the family to pay as much of the board rate (approximately $60 monthly) as possible and provide clothing and other miscellaneous items. We have been providing the difference if there is one. We have also been providing the services of the foster care worker, the services of others who may aid in planning for this retarded person, and other often unthought-of items such as the gasoline used in visiting the foster home. We are looking at this closely as this service increases, for one day such a program may well take the time and salary of not one but two or more social workers and the accompanying expenses mentioned above.

Another problem is the fact that with overcrowded conditions, waiting lists, and the touching appeals of families in need of help, there is a temptation to use the paper admission procedures as a valve to relieve some of the pressures on the hospital for those who would probably most appropriately need hospital care at least for a time. We have found the best antidote for this is to hold firm to the conceptions, purposes, and practices of a professional administered Foster Care Program.

Last, but certainly not least, is our question about the appropriateness of our agency offering this service, especially to retarded *children*. It seems to us that the needs of these individuals, again especially children, while certainly different from those of the average child in foster care under public welfare auspices, can be met with few, if any, modifications in the present programs of these agencies.

The question then remains, are we by assuming this responsibility encouraging the singling out of the retarded? Are we fostering the prevalent thought by community agencies that retarded persons as a group are so different they can be helped only by specialized services?

Our conclusion is that as long as institutionalization remains an alternative to public welfare foster care, our refusal to offer such a service would be of little value in the development of this service in the community itself.

We will certainly continue to work toward the establishment of services to the retarded by community agencies. We will continue to strive for closer working relationships and sounder planning between these agencies and ourselves. We will participate in planning for such things as sound guardianship plans for the retarded. At the same time we plan to continue on our current course because it is a fact that we are dealing with human lives whose future cannot conveniently await the resolution of issues.

SIXTY-NINE

Improving an Institution's Services for the Retarded

OWEN E. FRANKLIN AND DONALD J. BAKER

Public institutions for the mentally retarded have long been handicapped by shortages of professional workers, limited funds, overcrowding, long waiting lists, and isolation from the mainstream of society. Paradoxically, they have been constantly pressed to admit more patients and at the same time to improve their services. Confronted with these problems and with the growing public interest in the quality of programs for the mentally retarded, many such institutions have been searching for solutions which would help them not only to improve their intramural services, but also to integrate them with an overall community program for the retarded. Woodward State Hospital-School at Woodward, Iowa, is among them.

Woodward is one of Iowa's two State institutions for the mentally retarded. Five years ago, the institution was so overcrowded that in some of the wards beds were lined along the wall flush with each other with no space between. A long waiting list was growing steadily as individuals and communities vied for priority for their candidates. Numerous, often conflicting, calls about particular children awaiting admission created confusion in admission practices. Community-based services for the mentally retarded were sparse and uncoordinated.

Sadly lacking in the institutional program were: (1) sufficient attention to differential planning and programing for the patients on the basis of individual diagnoses; (2) clear admission and release policies; (3) planned pre-admission and after-care services; (4) strong ties with the outside community; (5) sufficient professional personnel of all types. For example, the institution's seven-month social service department included only two persons with master's degrees in social work—the director and the social service supervisor.

In 1961, the institution began a unified effort to improve the quality of its services, reduce both the patient load and the waiting list, and become an integral part of a many faceted State and community program for the retarded. In this effort, it had the backing of the Iowa State Board of Control of State Institutions which had recommended that the institutions for the mentally retarded adopt a 4-point program to (1) transform the two institutions to specialized treatment, and care cen-

From *Children*, Vol. 13, No. 2 (March-April, 1966), pp. 49-54. By permission of the authors and The Children's Bureau.

ters; (2) cooperate in the development of adequate extramural services; (3) develop inservice training for all types of staff; and (4) encourage research into clinical and administrative practices.

Involving the entire staff, the institution's effort to revitalize its program proceeded through two main lines of attack: (1) devising methods for the more effective use of professional and auxiliary staffs; and (2) keeping the staff, and hence the institution and its patients, in closer touch with the outside community. Today, the institution has about 1,000 resident patients as compared with nearly 1,700 5 years ago, and its waiting list has been abolished. What is more important, its patients, both inside and outside the institution, are receiving more of the kind of attention they need to help them function at their best.

This article will focus on the role of the social service department in these developments. However, since this role was closely integrated with the entire revitalization program, a brief description of the framework in which it has been carried out is pertinent.

At the beginning, the administration decided that the institution, which consisted of 37 buildings, including 13 residences for patients, would be divided into 4 administrative areas and that an interdisciplinary team would be set up to serve the residents in each area. Each team would consist of a physician, a psychologist, a social worker, an educator (academic or vocational depending upon the ages and needs of the residents in the area), a chaplain, a recreation worker, a ward attendant, and a representative from Nursing Attendant Service. Previously, the professional members of the staff had their offices in a central administration building, far removed from the residential buildings. Now each team office would be located within the area of the institution for which the team was responsible, thus putting the clinical staff in regular touch with the residents and so providing more opportunities for interaction between them.

The plan was for the teams to begin to work immediately on a "crash" program of evaluating the functioning level and potential of each resident and to follow each evaluation with habilitation services according to individual needs. One of the purposes was to determine which residents had needs that could best be met in their home communities and which needed further training or care within the institution.

While this program got under way, the new administration assigned staff members to a preadmission evaluation clinic and named the director of the hospital's social service department as chairman. Other staff members of the clinic included a physician, a psychologist, a director of nursing, the director of the institution's education and training department, the registrar, the chaplain, and the social service supervisor. The purpose of this clinic, which replaced the institution's previous diagnostic clinic, was to provide the kind of selective admission process which would enable the institution to furnish a specialized program of training and education to its residents.

In order to carry out this overall plan, the administration set up a clear-cut salary budget for each department designed to attract more professional workers to the institution and to reduce staff turnover.

Social Service Priorities

At the time of this reorganization, the administration delegated to the social service department several specific responsibilities: major responsibility for determining who is admitted; strengthening ties with communities; arranging for the return of patients to their own communities on the basis of a decision by the area team; and participating in the intramural team staffing arrangement. This meant new and greatly increased responsibilities for a department which had heretofore largely confined its efforts to interviewing parents of the patients, writing case histories, corresponding with relatives, and finding jobs in the community for some of the higher functioning res·.ents. The department would now have to address itself to two broad objectives:

1. Offering individual services to deal with the social, emotional, and environmental problems of patients and their families, before, during, and after the patient has been placed within the institution.
2. Fostering and maintaining a constructive relationship between the institution and the community to help the community bring about more nearly adequate social services for the retarded.

Obviously, making the best use of all available staff members would be the key to the department's effectiveness, and in this effort the clear-cut salary budget would be a great help.

As a basis for a logical consideration of its personnel needs and uses, the department established the following specific goals, in order of priority:

1. Participate in the evaluation of all the residents.
2. Contribute to strengthening the preadmission evaluation process.
3. Recruit additional persons for the staff.
4. Initiate a series of meetings with the county board of supervisors in each county served by the institution, as the Code of Iowa places administrative and financial responsibilities on this body for the care of the mentally retarded at the county level.
5. Promote an organized release and aftercare program.
6. Improve social services within the institution.
7. Provide inservice training and other means of development for the department's staff.
8. Conduct service-related research.

The department then initiated an intensive recruitment program to secure the type of manpower commensurate with these goals—social service representatives to work full time outside the institution as community consultants and social service representatives to work in the institution on the professional teams. Simultaneously, the department intitiated communication with the county boards of supervisors to pave the way for future meetings between representatives of the institution and the boards to discuss ways in which the institution and the county boards could work together in the interests of the mentally retarded. At these meetings, the institution offered its consultation service to the counties.

The needs of patients, the institution's budgetary limitations, and the shortage of graduate social workers, considered together, resulted in a plan to have two levels of social service staff—persons with graduate degrees in social service and persons with bachelor's degrees only. This plan emphasized the importance of having a good and continuous staff development program.

Research activities, it was decided, would have to be developed later and directed primarily toward the study of factors bearing upon the development of the community services program.

Assessment of Client Needs

The next step was to determine the deployment of the department's staff to provide the best social service coverage possible within its means. This meant defining the tasks involved and determining which required the skills of a graduate social worker and which could be performed under professional supervision by a person without formal social work education. To do this, it was essential to determine the needs of the department's many types of clients. These included (1) the communities of 48 counties; (2) the retarded people in their populations; (3) the various agencies which could serve the retarded; (4) the institution's residents and their families; and (5) the professional teams.

In the communities, local agencies, such as the county welfare department, the public health nursing service, the schools, the courts, and the associations of parents of retarded children, needed a helpful relationship with someone who had knowledge of mental retardation, the State and national resources for dealing with the problems, and the roles of the family, the institution, and the community in meeting the needs of the mentally retarded. They needed to know that the institution's policies in relation to their county would be based on an individual assessment of the county's resources. They needed an opportunity to express freely their attitudes toward the institution, its program, and its policies. And they needed someone to help stimulate more effective cooperation among social, educational, medical, and citizen groups and the agencies in the locality.

The patient, on his admission, needed at least someone to help acclimate him to a strange, large, relatively impersonal institution—someone to tell him about what might happen to him, help prepare him for its programs and services, and help him feel accepted. Above all, he needed emotional support and assurance that his family or someone still cared for him and about what happened to him. Later, if he were to leave the institution for home, temporarily or permanently, or to be placed in another community facility, he would need preparation for the change.

The parents of the patient needed someone to help them deal with the many problems they would face during the admission process and to keep them informed of their child's progress in the institution. They needed assurance that the institution was interested in the family and was willing to help them maintain contact with their child, and they needed to be drawn into the planning for the aftercare of their child.

The professional teams, with responsibility for the specialized treatment, training, and care of the residents in their respective areas of the institution, needed to be kept aware of developments within each patient's family and the resources available to him in the community. They needed to know the kind of family conditions or substitute care to which the patient would go, if recommended for release.

After thus analyzing the needs of its clients, the department assigned the community work to its staff members with graduate social work degrees, because functioning effectively as a community consultant implies a high degree of autonomy and requires a variety of social work skills. Staff members with bachelor's degrees only were assigned as social workers on the institution's area teams to work under the close supervision of the social service supervisor and were provided with a continuing program of inservice training.

The Community Worker

The three community consultants each spent about 3 months in the institution to become oriented to its programs and objectives. They attended the area team meetings and participated in regular discussions with the administrative staff about their community responsibilities.

The social service director then arranged with the county boards of supervisors for an introductory visit from the consultants to be assigned to their counties. At the conclusion of each of these initial meetings, the county board was requested to designate a county employee to provide liaison with the institutional community consultant in planning for the mentally retarded. This they did, and the person so designated, usually the director of the county welfare department, came to be known as the "county designate" and became the focal point for merging community and institutional interests in the mentally retarded. From then on, the community consultants worked through the county designate's office to involve the health, education, and social agencies of the community in individual case planning and in community program development. The community consultant offered help in case planning whether or not institutionalization was being considered.

Each community consultant lives within the group of counties he serves. His office is his home.

Among the consultant's specific activities are:

Establishing a working relationship with the county boards of supervisors and their designates, and with other community leaders as necessary, to coordinate case-by-case planning for the mentally retarded both in and out of the institution.

Helping county designates understand the needs of retarded people and the implications of specific methods for meeting them.

Helping the county designates and other interested persons understand the emotional factors associated with mental retardation.

Demonstrating methods of dealing with such emotional factors in specific cases.

Studying local communities to find resources for the mentally retarded; suggesting ways of using them more effectively; and stimulating the development of new programs.

Stimulating a cooperative approach to problems at the community level.

From the beginning, the department recognized that the community consultant might be exposed to resistance, misunderstanding, and outright antagonism. Some of these negative reactions would be based on actual past experiences with the institution; some, on a preference for local, as opposed to State, programing; some others, on resistance to the new pre-admission and release policies; and still others, on a reluctance to develop new services at a time of high cost. Hence, an opportunity was provided for staff members, "on the firing line" in communities, to spend at least 2 days a month within the institution to consult with the administrative staff and team members individually and in meetings. They were also brought into the institution at intervals to substitute for the social service supervisor or the director of social service in order to help them maintain their identity with the institution and to develop professional versatility. While working in their communities, the consultants were encouraged to telephone the social service department whenever they felt the need. They sent in regular narrative reports of their activities, findings, and impressions. Further, they were encouraged to attend various professional meetings in the State, and each year one consultant was selected to attend an out-of-State meeting on a topic related to the institution's work.

Area Team Social Workers

As vacancies occurred rather quickly among the nongraduate social workers who were already on the staff, their positions were filled by recent college graduates interested in careers in social work. These recruits were selected for their apparent warmth and concern for people, their interest in mental retardation, and their flexibility.

The new team social workers spent the first months or so in an orientation program in the administration building, which included instruction and job assignments under the close supervision of the social service department. During this on-the-job training, they attended meetings with the teams to which they were to be assigned as well as with other teams. Thus, theory was immediately combined with practice.

After their assignment to their area teams, they remained under the supervision of the social service supervisor and continued to attend staff meetings with the social service staff, the community consultants, and the administrative staff. They had ready access to the social service supervisor or the director for assistance in handling their work assignments.

As a member of the professional team, the team social worker contributes information about the resident, his family, and the community to the other team members. In addition, he carries out the team's recommendations related to the social service department's responsibilities. Some examples of other tasks performed by team social workers are:

Interviewing parents, other relatives, and guardians in regard to the resident's progress, referral to other agencies, and tangible needs such as money and clothing.

Serving as liaison regarding specific patients between the team and local agencies, parents, and other interested persons.

Serving as liaison between the team and the social service department.

Conducting individual tours of the institution for parents of prospective patients.

Helping prepare new residents for their stay at the institution, providing them with a supportive relationship while they are there, or preparing them for release to their own homes or to community facilities.

These tasks were assigned to college graduates without social work training. The contacts with patients and families they involved were brief and concerned only with tangible needs. The department realized that many patients and their families needed intensive social casework of a kind the team workers were not able to supply. However, the tangible services of the team social workers were important to both residents and their families. The addition of more intensive service remains a goal for the future for the institution.

In addition to having an "open door" policy for the team social worker, the social service supervisor scheduled weekly conferences with each one. After the new program got well under way, the department initiated a series of bimonthly seminars to introduce social work knowledge, attitudes, and skills. Subjects discussed in the seminars included principles of interviewing, recording, social work methods, human growth and development, professional development, and public welfare. Lectures on mental retardation by staff members of other departments were also included in the seminars. The team social workers were encouraged to use the new professional library being developed within the institution and to attend social welfare meetings held by various organizations within the State.

Some Results

In the 5 years since the inauguration of Woodward's unified effort to improve its services, and the resultant expansion and reorganization of its social service department, the institution has experienced a noticeable acceleration of turnover in its residential population—an important indication that it has been accomplishing at least some of its objectives. For example, only 34 patients had been admitted in 1960, because space was not available for more. In 1964, the number of admissions had quadrupled to 136. Yet, in spite of a steady increase in admissions, the number of residents was reduced to 1,010 by July 1, 1965, as compared with 1,648 on July 1, 1961. Full discharges increased from 153 for 1960 to 204 for 1964. The residents on leave within various community facilities—own homes, foster homes, group custodial homes, and nursing homes—increased from 192 in 1960 to 596 by July 1, 1965. And, as already mentioned, the waiting list for admission has been eliminated. Nevertheless, all plans for admission or release have been worked out on an individualized basis involving parents and community agencies.

Behind these developments lay hour upon hour of ponderous effort by the institutional staff in working, case by case, with local agencies (which were sometimes suspicious of the institution because of past experiences) and with parents who often viewed their child's institutionalization as the "end of the line."

Undoubtedly, one of the most important results of this effort is the partnership formed between the institution and community agencies for developing local services for the mentally retarded and their families. Because the original three community consultants are still on the staff, the relationships between institution and the outside world have retained continuity—relationships which are born of mutual involvement with local people in connection with real cases and with the needs of the community.

The social service staff development and supervisory arrangements have not only helped hold staff members with graduate degrees in social work but have also helped enlist recent college graduates into social work. There has, however, been a complete turnover of staff members with bachelor's degrees only, although all who have left have expressed satisfaction with their experience in the institution. Of the first five who left permanently, three went on to graduate training in social work; one took other employment in a hospital social service department in her home town; another left to get a master's degree in a related field, special education. Another worker left to attend a school of social work on a stipend provided by the institution and since graduating has returned to the institution to work.

Reduction of the institution's population was as important as increase in staff in improving professional services, for this reduction also brought about a better staff-resident ratio. Residents are now evaluated thoroughly twice each year for the adequacy of their programs or needed change. The fluidity of movement of patients to and from the institution makes it possible for the institution to provide its patients with a truly dynamic program of training, treatment, and habilitation.

These efforts to improve Iowa's services for the mentally retarded may have much broader significance than the accomplishments in the program for which they were devised. They were a conscious attempt to try out ideas which have been discussed widely in recent years among persons concerned with services to the retarded, for example: to use two educational levels of social service staff in different ways; the deliberate plan for making the institution a part of a continuum of resources for comprehensive care, through the provision of the community consultants; the use of the mental retardation specialist to help the generalist—and again through the community consultants working with the employees of local health, education, and welfare agencies; and the establishment of a referral point in each locality for problems concerning mental retardation—the county designate backed up with consultation and service from the community consultant.

Above all, the institution's experience demonstrates the effectiveness of a give-and-take attitude on the part of all concerned in bringing about greater coordination and development, both in quantity and quality, of services for the mentally retarded and their families.

SEVENTY

Separation Used to Help Parents Promote Growth of Their Retarded Child

WILLIAM C. ADAMSON, DOROTHY F. OHRENSTEIN,
DOLORES LAKE, AND ALEXANDER HERSH

In the majority of cases parents of a young retarded child find it difficult to sustain their relationship to their child in a meaningful way.[1] "Meaingful" in this context refers to the process by which parents feel a sense of fulfillment in a primary function of parenthood—that is, that their actions and attitudes promote and contribute to the growth of their child.[2] In contrast to normal children who grow in an energetic manner appropriate to their age, a retarded child's growth is slow, and at times virtually imperceptible. Under these circumstances parents have a difficult time dealing with their own frustrations, and need specific help in knowing in what ways they can contribute to their child's growth.

This paper describes a philosophy and method by which help is given to parents of mentally subnormal children enrolled in a private residential school.[3] It represents an arrangement of the "essentials," as it were, of a theoretical framework of helping developed by the authors and found to be suited effectively to the needs of parents of young handicapped children.

The population on which the paper is based consisted of a residential unit serving twenty-six children in a nursery school and readiness-for-learning program. The children, of both sexes, ranged in age from 3 to 9 years; their mental ages ranged from 18 months to 5 years. All these children functioned at mentally subnormal levels, and many entered the school without a previously established diagnosis. They were children with multiple problems of central nervous system dysfunction, with various degrees of associated ego insufficiency. In descriptive terms, they had social, mental, and emotional problems and were functioning at the borderline educable or high-trainable levels of habilitation. For the majority the potential for habilitation and return to their family and community or to a semicontrolled environment was quite good, provided special classes were available for them in public or private schools in the community.

Recurrent observations were made and the method on which this paper is based elaborated over a five-year period. It was noted that in this population the decision

Reprinted by permission of the authors and the National Association of Social Workers from *Social Work,* Vol. 9, No. 4 (October, 1964), pp. 60-67.

to enroll the child in a residential setting represented the outcome of stress in family relationships. As stated in an earlier paper drawn from this setting, the authors believe that the decision to enroll represents a constructive move by parents to obtain help for their child, as well as for themselves.[4]

Philosophy of the Helping Process

It is the authors' contention that the entire issue about parental "acceptance" of retardation is a wasted and overstated one.[5] The real issue for the helping professions is how to help parents understand their child and find ways of promoting his growth in every phase of living. This process is a gradual, ever changing one and represents a creative blending of parents' awareness of themselves and their own needs in relation to the emerging and changing needs of their child. The residential experience offers an opportunity for a full-dimensional approach to understanding and helping the child and his family.

Though separation from the retarded child does indeed strip the parent of the conventional expressions of parenthood, i.e., feeding, dressing, and physically caring for the child, this situation facilitates the helping process. It allows the staff of the institution, as helpers, to concentrate on the critical area of parent-child interaction, for the goal of the residential experience is to unify parents and child emotionally. As the retarded child is observed in a "neutral" environment, apart from his parents, his severe handicap in "relating for growth" is made evident. The child seems to lack the drive and autonomy to relate through his needs, save in a "do-it-for-me" manner. Unlike the normal child who uses relationships to build his own individual growth pattern, the retarded child's manner of relating, by virtue of his innate insufficiencies, often results in distortions in interpersonal relationships.

Therefore, if help to families of retarded children is to be truly effective, it must be available to them early in their lives together. Otherwise, as time goes by, early distortions pyramid into greater distortions leading to lack of a meaningful connection between the parents and the child. Through such a lack of connection comes misunderstanding, mistrust, hurt, anger, and a lack of fulfillment in the relationship. What appears later to be a drifting away or rejection can often be traced back to these earlier distortions. Parents cannot be expected to withstand this kind of severe frustration too long, so that often parents are seen who have insulated and defended themselves against this type of repetitive, hurtful relationship. Without help in the early years the distortions become immutable and parental lack of belief in involvement with the child becomes a way of life.

The term "subnormal child" is not only diagnostic but descriptive of the child's problem. He simply does not, because of his insufficient endowment, fit into normal society without special management. For this reason his removal from the community almost always (in this setting, at least) results in some demonstrable rise in his functioning, as measured by the Vineland Social Maturity Scale, which is administered within the first two months of placement and then again a year later. With the exception of the most troubled, the children the authors have known have shown considerable personality stabilization and organization within a year of enrollment. The children experience a sense of relief from the pressures spoken of earlier and freedom from the circular, interlocking, and sometimes stereotyped relationships in which they are trapped. As the child relates to those not previously engaged in the unhealthy, unsupporting relationships, he grows, becoming more available to the "positive side" of family feelings.

Yet this relief, which is the dynamic of the separation, can be a major pitfall, for it is altogether too easy to be satisfied with relief as the sole achievement of the separation. The relief provides the respite needed by weary families in order for them to surge on, to strive for and to achieve a deeper level of unity. The relief is in actuality a beginning. But in families having retarded children, the community, often including a large segment of the professional community, culturally acts to support the relief as an end rather than a means. The professional duty is to counteract this trend, to provide leadership for a goal greater than custodial, a goal that is not satisfied with the achievement of less than each child's fullest potential endowment.

Methods of Preparation

An important principle underlying this effort should be stated here: the parent-child relationship is a sustaining force. Even though separation of a retarded child may eventuate in lifetime care, placement of the child must be effected through conviction and in a manner that does not preclude this principle. The child belongs, in every sense, to his family, and his relationships in a residential school, though warm and loving, are, nevertheless, not as permanent as those of his family.

As the parent thinks of separation for his child he needs to feel the weight and importance of his own decision, its meaning to himself, his family, and to the child. Parents are helped as much as possible to deal with the separation in terms of its purpose, its timing, and what it can bring to the child and to the remainder of the family. Parents benefit from gaining from the caseworker a belief in separation as representing something different, a new experience for themselves, which they can then transmit to their child.

In the setting described, a preadmission evaluation is done with each child and his family, following receipt of medical, psychiatric, educational, psychological, and speech reports. The first step in the preadmission process is evaluation of the child by a child psychiatrist and by other professional disciplines when indicated. At the same time, the parents are interviewed by the caseworker. The purpose of the preadmission evaluation is primarily threefold:

1. To understand the general nature of the child's needs.

2. To determine whether those needs can be met by the staff and program, and

3. To determine the readiness of the child for separation and the readiness of the parents to support that separation.

A beginning understanding of the family dynamics is evolved from the preadmission process, with the focus on salient factors relating to separation. From the child psychiatrist's clinical impression that the child has the capacity to live through and handle the separation, the parents are able to move toward their role in preparing the child for the separation experience.

The casework process helps parents to define the child's need for special help in a residential setting and to be able to feel that the separation offers him the best chance for growth. The parent also needs help in trusting his child's strength to deal with the separation. With communication as the keynote of the preparation, as indeed it is of all relationships, the following methods were conceptualized on two levels: verbal and experiential.

Verbal Preparation

As we know, the parent holds the right to plan for the child, but the child has a right to participate and deal with the separation on his own terms. The parents with whom this paper is concerned are those who have reached a stalemate with their children. They often minimize or deny the child's participation, his right, and his strength to deal with the separation. They are apt to want to deal minimally with the separation out of defense against involvement. Parents often try to "sell" the school to the child by telling him "You'll have a lot of fun at this school," or asking "Don't you want to have children to play with?" They may ask the child if he would like to go to the school. Yet, if met with conviction and support as to the importance of preparing the child, most parents can rise to the occasion.

Though many children in this setting cannot fully comprehend the meaning of the words, they seem to be able to relate to the tone and seriousness of the words and their parents' manners. It is important, therefore, not to err on the side that the child does not understand content, for he almost always understands intent. Parental sanction and encouragement are the "green light" for the child to accept the school. The parents' own feelings of ambivalence, conflict, and guilt may also be conveyed to the child, but can be offset by their growing sense of trust in the school and the caseworker's support for the separation. The parent must speak from his awareness of his child's need for the special help he can get in the school and his own trust in the people with whom the child will come in contact. The parent must free the child to move to new relationships with the staff. The child needs to feel a quality of conviction in his parents' actions, for only in this way will he be able to mobilize his own strength to meet what he feels to be the inevitable.

Parents need to be helped to value the child's right to protest, for this protest— which to the professional person signifies the child's healthy will and involvement —is frightening and guilt provoking to the unsure parents. Children protest in various ways, some of them quite subtle, especially with nonverbal children, yet parents can deal with these if they have some idea of what to expect.

Time and again, it has been observed that as parents have felt trust in the staff, because of their conviction, they were enabled to borrow on the staff's strength, to participate in preparing the child for the separation. In the stalemate that has led to the separation, parents have often lost the sense of what their child was feeling, so that at the anxious time of actually separating from their child they feel even less sure of what he may be experiencing. This provides further opportunity for helping them to "tune in" on their child's needs. The actual parting from the child is a culmination of the whole separation process, and a painful experience for most parents. Therefore, it is not surprising that large numbers in the group described sought to avoid this difficult task. Although parents should not be forced to participate, the authors' conviction is that this is important to the child. It serves also to enable the parents to give the child final assurance that they will be back. In both these climactic moves parents put some of the guilt they have about leaving the child into useful action, thereby reducing their inevitable feelings of emptiness and guilt.

Experiential Preparation

Since we are dealing with children many of whom are perceptually, mentally, and emotionally handicapped, the medium of verbal communication presents severe gaps and limitations. Therefore visual components of experience must necessarily be highlighted to supplement the child's understanding of the meaning of the separation. They also provide parents with further means of communicating to the child, in concrete ways, the meaning of separation. An especially valuable aid that has been used is to have parents take pictures of the exterior and interior of the building in which the child will live. Pictures of his room, his bed, his housemother, his teacher, and some of his new playmates, made into a booklet, give him a chance to place himself visually in his new environment in a way that reduces the very thing he fears the most—the unknown.

To help families move to and through this separation at least two stages are involved. The first occurs at the time of the preadmission evaluation. Following the evaluation itself, the caseworker takes the parents and child to visit the child's unit, which includes dormitory and living areas as well as educational and recreational facilities. This is done informally, with the focus on enabling the parents to begin to connect with the person in charge of the program and through her with the housemother, teacher, and others, and it also serves to give the child a sense of what is to come.

The child's sense of time is often not well developed, so although some interval between the evaluation and enrollment is necessary for parents and child to digest, decide, and prepare, this should not be an extended interval. The child and parent, too, lose the impact and decisiveness of the experience, and some innate tendencies toward resistance and procrastination inevitably appear.

The next step should involve a planned visit to the school, usually occurring not more than seven days before the admission. This is carefully worked out with the parents ahead of time so that they know what will take place and feel comfortable with the plan. In general, the parents arrive with the child in the morning at the building where the evaluation took place, to help the child connect with the setting. They then go to the child's unit, where the supervisor takes responsibility for guiding the visit. The child is prepared ahead of time by the parents for the visit, which includes having lunch at his "new school." After walking through the dormitory, dining room, and classroom, the parents leave the child, usually in the classroom he will be joining. They may or may not join him for lunch with the staff and the other children. This decision is made by the parents. While the child is visiting, the parents speak with the caseworker, the focus of the session being placed on the coming separation. They also meet with the supervisor of the unit for the purpose of sharing with him their special concerns about their child's habits and to discuss further the program the child will soon be entering. Before the visit ends, the parents again accompany the child through the setting. Experientially this is the highlight of the visit for the family, because at this time they go through the residential unit, showing the child all the things that will be his to use in his new life experience: his bed, his table in the dining room, and his classroom. Following this visit parents can verbally reinforce the experiences they have had together in the visit.

The visit also enables the staff to know better where the child and his family are in relation to the separation and to help them accordingly. In certain instances, the child psychiatrist sees the child before the visit itself. In other cases, a visit ahead of time is not possible because of distance. What is then recommended is a visit to the school on the day before admission, the child staying overnight in the area with his parents.

Ongoing Counseling

Once the separation is in motion the residential school offers the handicapped child an experience much apart from his family. This affords the staff the opportunity to see him apart from the attitudes, relationships, expectations, and pressures normally associated with family and community living. Though the residential setting is not, in actuality, a neutral setting, for the purposes of the child it offers him a clean slate on which to make his mark. From the outset, the parents see the staff as experts who will know best how to bring out the child's true nature and how to deal with him effectively as well as therapeutically. Obviously, many factors affect the degree to which this is so, but for the most part, the child can be dealt with without the biases associated with a historically troubled relationship. This clearer, more objective view tells the staff much about the child's patterns of relating to others and the numerous pitfalls into which parents may have fallen in their efforts to support his growth.

Parental counseling from this point on deals extensively with these gleaned insights woven into the fabric of the total family dynamics. Certain key concepts and patterns in the manner of working with families are given here:

1. All parents need, for the sake of the helping process, *a relationship of their own*. As Mandelbaum and Wheeler have said of parents of retarded children:

> Their rigid and hostile defenses often give way under the consistent warmth and empathy of the worker. Through warmth and understanding, the parents come to feel that not only they, but they and their child, are loved. Their need, therefore, to defend both him

and themselves is no longer so intensively felt. They can then apply themselves in a more constructive manner to the task of securing necessary help for themselves, and the total family.[6]

The authors believe that parents of retarded children are not as neurotically involved in the origin of their child's difficulty as are parents of emotionally disturbed children, though their own personality organization and especially their own needs and emotional conflicts may be highlighted in relations to the child. We are dealing largely, therefore, with a group of people reacting to a critical life circumstance and chronic stress in their own personal and family lives in response to having an exceptional child. This group to a large extent feels lonely and different. Often they are isolated to the degree that they feel apart from others and not understood. The existence of a large, stabilized facility for exceptional children, with the prestige of a national reputation, suggests to them that here is a place where they need not feel apart, but rather where they can gain a sense of belonging, where they can afford to risk their feelings and be understood and accepted. Further, they can venture that this residential setting, apart from the community, may at last be able to provide for them a set of norms for child rearing that they have been seeking unsuccessfully.[7]

2. Parents need *honest reassurance that their choice to enroll their child in the school is the right and timely one*, that it has hurt neither the child nor family, and that the staff will have the integrity to let them know if the enrollment jeopardizes the child and therefore should be terminated.

3. Usually in the beginning parents need much *reassurance that the child's potential for growth actually exists*. Once parents see clear evidence of the growth process and their own anxiety is reduced, they often become impatient for more rapid progress or even allow themselves the fantasy that the child may yet become completely normal. They then need a new kind of reassurance to deal with the child's appropriate pace of development, the irreversible nature of the handicap, and the meaning of this in personal and social life terms. The careful guiding of parents to a balanced perspective calls for a dedicated belief in the meaning a handicapped child holds for his family as a primary goal, rather than that of prognostication or determination of the child's objective usefulness to society.

This approach calls for a strong dedication to the notion that parents of young children can derive the greatest pleasure from their children by living in the present. Preoccupation with the future outcome seems to lead to reinforcement of guilt for the child's condition and status, a fervent hope for unrealistic accomplishments, and an interruption of parental availability and support to the entire family as it moves through its normal cycles of development. The more the parent can understand his child, contribute to his child's growth, and share in his life, the more apt he is to feel fulfillment in the essence of parenthood. From this feeling of fulfillment he will move to a more realistic appraisal and expectation of his child.

4. Parents need *to be included in a psychologically and physically active participatory role in the growth process of the child*. Most parents have a high level of concern and anxiety about the child and his future. Yet the separation can act to

reinforce existent ambivalence about the importance of their role as parents, causing them to wish to abnegate this role. Therefore, each visit—and these are most productive when structured on a regular basis (usually monthly in the setting described)—is a critical test of parents' motivation for continued involvement and the school's sensitivity and willingness to engage them in a meaningful partnership.[8]

Logically, the early visits are especially critical. Since relationships have been intense by virtue of the stalemate, the first month following separation is equally intense in its separating quality. Parents bring to the initial visit a sense of their own loss so that they are laden with anxiety and concern about how the child has fared. They also are concerned about how much the child has changed, particularly how he will react to seeing them. Parents, therefore, need help in reconnecting with their child in a way that now takes into account their new and unfamiliar role of parents of a child apart from them. From the outset, and then step-by-step, parents need to know as definitively as possible what use the child is making of the school experience, its meaning in terms of the special nature of his needs and handicaps, and how best to support him in his further use of the various relationships available to him in the school. Creative ways for including the parents and helping them to sustain the child's enrollment include the following:

a. Understanding the child in a general way as representing certain distinct behavior characteristics is useful as a foundation on which parents can grow, but these must become sensitively specific to the individual child and his family in order that the family become "tuned in" to his needs. For example, there is general agreement on common characteristics of brain injury, such as disinhibition, perseveration, hyperactivity, weak ego formation, short attention span, perceptual and conceptual difficulties. Interpreting this picture to parents serves to alleviate their anxiety as well as guilt for their feeling of helplessness in relation to their child.

b. However, pieces of behavior must be analyzed in terms of specific meaning to a child in given instances so that parents can see in dramatized terms how they can learn to intervene successfully in a difficult situation or, better yet, how they can structure the child's situation within reason to insure even and acceptable behavior. This leads to a new understanding of the child, which if successful usually indicates that parents have a more realistic expectation of the child, or a fresh appreciation of what he may be able to do with proper stimulation, support, and understanding of his needs by the adults in his environment.

c. Visits are carefully structured in all dimensions (time, space, and activity) to create conditions favorable for success and gratification in the relationship. Depending on an understanding of the child's needs, the readiness of the parents to deal with the child, and the meaning of the visit to the child, the visiting plan must be studiously shaped so as not to create a situation that can lead to a reliving of earlier problems. The philosophy underlying visits is that they should be built up gradually with emphasis on the positive aspects of the relationships, new skills that the child develops, and new abilities on the part of the parents to understand the child and to deal with special problems he presents. Skill and ability to partialize effectively the parent-child interaction throughout the visits are the factors determining the achievement of the desired outcome of family unity by which parents can feel they are contributing to the growth of their child.

d. Invariably there are differences in the way parents perceive and react to the child and his handicap. These, plus the fact that the young handicapped child responds best to an uncomplicated environment, has led the staff to assess how they can best utilize differential strengths in relationships. For example, individual rather than total family visits at pivotal points in the child's ego development prove useful in furthering his growth and change.

e. By nature the counseling process is a human and subjective one. Therefore, to enhance this process and to insure that neither the parent nor the school becomes lost or detoured in this subjectively satisfying experience, both need some guideposts outside themselves. The psychological evaluation, usually on a yearly basis following the baseline study, is a means by which a child's social, emotional, and intellectual development might be seen in quantified terms. Later, academic achievement also provides quantified landmarks.

f. In addition, periodic psychiatric evaluations by the child psychiatrist serve to gauge, in depth, the child's growth in relationship to the hierarchy of adults in the residence, his feelings about himself, and the quality of his relationships to his peer group. Clinical judgment is also made as to the kind of personality pattern and affective (feeling) life organization the child is building. This is described in terms of the way he appears to handle both comfortable and stressful situations in the interview and in the residential milieu, the nature of his intrapsychic conflicts as they are revealed within the psychiatric evaluation, and the kinds of psychological coping patterns he seems to be bringing into both his life-space experiences in residence and into the evaluation hours with the child psychiatrist. Understanding of the child's development gained from these evaluations may then be seen to have special worth in defining his areas of deficit and endowment. This information is technical and usually alien to parents, so that careful explanation brings a new and deeper understanding to them, thereby reducing the degree of their unsureness. The ensuing assimilation or digestion of this new knowledge and the use to which it may be put in relationship to their child become vital functions of the careful month-by-month counseling process.

g. The monthly interviews (and visits) should also flow into periodic large conferences with other staff members in a smooth, uninterrupted fashion. These conferences, which are designed to give parents authoritative reviews of the child's status, provide them with continuity of experience as well as renewed opportunity to feel the harmony and strength of the full effort of staff relationships in which they can put their trust. Because of the irreversibility of their child's handicap, the continuous acceptance and support of the staff helps parents to deal not only with their anxiety but their heavy burden as well.

A balanced approach is carefully planned by the clinical team in terms of both the timing for the larger team conference and the specific content to be shared with the parents by members of the team. Much of the content of the conference centers around parental concern about the nature of the neurologic or medical impairment suffered by the child. Every effort is made by the staff to be clear and articulate within the limits of medical knowledge today. It is recognized that vagueness or medical uncertainty heightens parental uncertainty and leads to parental distortions in how they view their child in the present and the future. The ever present concern for prognosis and outcome is discussed within this frame of reference. The conference is in effect a group process in which parents can discuss their feelings openly with others who share their burdens and concerns; once again, it represents the ultimate in a subculture formed for the purpose of dealing with the problems of care and planning for the handicapped child, thereby reducing parental loneliness and assembling for them, for the purposes of child rearing, a set of norms by which they may be guided.

Summary

This paper has described a philosophy and method by which help is given to parents in promoting the growth of their young mentally subnormal children enrolled in a private residential school. Detailed methods found to be effective in the process of preparing for enrollment were conceptualized on two levels: verbal and experiential. Key concepts and patterns in working with families in sustaining counseling process were also enumerated, as were adjunctive methods.

References

[1]Arthur Mandelbaum and Mary Ella Wheeler, "The Meaning of a Defective Child to Parents," *Social Casework*, Vol. 41, No. 7 (July 1960), pp. 360-367.

[2]Otto Pollak, "A Family Diagnosis Model," *Social Service Review*, Vol. 34, No. 1 (March 1960), pp. 19-31.

[3]The terms "mentally subnormal" and "mentally retarded" are used interchangeably in this paper.

[4]Alexander Hersh, "Casework with Parents of Retarded Children," *Social Work*, Vol. 6, No. 2 (April 1961), pp. 61-66.

[5]Simon Olshansky, "Chronic Sorrow: A Response to Having a Mentally Defective Child," *Social Casework*, Vol. 43, No. 4 (April 1962), pp. 190-193.

[6]*Op. cit.*

[7]Bernard Farber, "Family Organization and Crisis: Maintenance of Integration in Families with a Severely Mentally Retarded Child," *Monograph of the Society for Research in Child Development*, Serial No. 75, Vol. 25, No. 1 (Lafayette, Ind.: Purdue University, 1960).

[8]Letha L. Patterson, "Some Pointers for Professionals," *Children* (January-February 1956).

Mentally Retarded Teenagers in a Social Group

SIDNEY GERSHENSON AND MEYER SCHREIBER

Children learn to live with others only through experience. However, the retarded child is often caught in a vicious spiral that is negative and limiting to his social development. The lack of social experiences leads to social retardation and ineptness in chronologically appropriate social skills, accompanied by emotional difficulties arising from feelings of rejection and deprivation; and the lack of social skills further limits the opportunities the retardate has of participating in social experiences.

Mentally retarded children must be taught many things which normal children learn spontaneously or incidentally. Often they must be taught to play and to be helped in developing creative qualities that give them fun and pleasure. When this has been achieved the retardate can gain the same satisfactions from participating in social activities as other people. These satisfactions derive from: (a) being recognized and accepted in the group situation; (b) a sense of accomplishment in activities in which he is successfully interacting with his peers; (c) the experience of self-expression, especially when making positive contributions to the group's activities; (d) the enhancement of self-esteem; (e) and the feeling of "belonging."

To give young retardates these opportunities, the New York City Chapter, Association for the Help of Retarded Children has conducted a group work, recreation, and camping program for mentally retarded children, teenagers and young adults for the past 11 years. At first the program was directed by a social caseworker, but for the past 5 years it has been the responsibility of a professional social group worker who spends full time on the job.

The program was developed on a decentralized basis in whatever facilities were available in neighborhoods throughout New York City—churches, synagogues, schools, park buildings, housing projects, and veterans and union halls. It includes groups of elementary school-age children, teenagers, and young adults. In placing individuals in the groups, chronological age, previous social experiences, and social adequacy and functioning are considered together. Trained group workers are used

From *Children*, Vol. 10, No. 3 (May-June, 1963), pp. 104-108. By permission of the authors and The Children's Bureau.

as group leaders, assisted by a nonprofessional person of the opposite sex who may be a staff member or a volunteer.

The purpose of the program is to provide:

1. A medium of enjoyment for mentally retarded children and youth.

2. A setting which will aid them in social adjustment—one which provides a small, intimate, face-to-face experience with others of the same age, including members of the opposite sex.

3. Experiences to help them develop simple, useful skills that they can carry over to the home, to the community, and perhaps to employment.

4. Experiences to help them accept themselves and the limitations imposed by their retardation, as well as to utilize their capacities to increase their feelings of self-worth.

5. A means of freeing parents for a few hours weekly of the supervision of the retardate and of helping them to carry over into the home and community attitudes that will promote increased independence in their children.

One of these groups is the Queen's Teens—a coed social club of adolescent retardates 12 to 15 years of age, one of 12 such groups throughout the city. The group meets each Wednesday evening from 7:30 to 9:30 p.m. in the basement recreation room of a large cooperative housing project in a middle-class neighborhood in the borough of Queens. The location of the meeting place is far from ideal—neither having the facilities of a community center nor offering potential contact with other children, but it is adequate.

The membership of the Queen's Teens reflects the socioeconomic character of the middle-class neighborhood.

The New York City Chapter, Association for the Help of Retarded Children provided the overall program structure, supervision, and administration, which in this instance included the paid male leader, special interest and holiday programs, and program supplies. A women's auxiliary affiliated with the New York City Chapter supplied two female volunteers a week, refreshments, and occasional special program needs.

Composition of Group

Members were referred to the group by the New York City Chapter after their application had been processed through intake. The intake process included an interview by the director of group work services with the young person and one or both parents at the office of the Association. Before the interview, information about the child's development and his family situation was obtained from school records, clinic material, and other sources. Criteria for membership in the Queen's Teens were: (a) membership of the parents in the Association for the Help of Retarded Children; (b) chronological age, 12 to 15; (c) the ability to participate at the level of the group; (d) the capacity to derive benefit from the group experience. Eligibility in relation to the last two criteria was determined only after the teenager had participated in several group meetings. The final decision was made by the

Chapter's director of group work services, the leader of the group, the parent, and the teenager himself to the extent of his ability to understand.

Within the 8-month period on which the observations in this paper were based, a total of 19 teenagers were referred to the group. While the aforementioned criteria identified this as a "formed" group, it contained some elements of a "natural" group in that its members referred to it some of their classmates from school. (Most of the young people attend special public school classes for the retarded.) The group became stabilized at 10 members, with an average attendance of 8 or 9 youngsters at each meeting. Of those who did not continue: one was found by the leader to be functioning at a higher level than the group; another chose not to come because he himself felt the group was too young for him; one child had no means of transportation; three teenagers never attended because their mothers were not interested in the group after visiting the meetings; one youngster was asked not to come because his attendance was irregular, averaging less than once a month, and his behavior when present was disruptive to the group.

The teenagers who remained in the group came regularly to meetings not only because of interest in the group and the program, but also because the parents assumed the responsibility for bringing them. Only two of the members lived within walking distance, the others being scattered in a 5-mile area.

The children's IQ's ranged from the forties to the seventies. This information, however, was found to be of little use in planning recreational activities for the group, for it did not give any indication of the young people's ability to function in a social group. What was of greater importance in program planning was the youngsters' ability to relate to adults and peers, to work and play with others, and to use program materials. At present there is no meaningful measure of this type of ability available.

A scale rating the children on the nature and extent of their social functioning and adequacy would be of great help in the selection and placement of individuals in social groups. There appears to be a distinct difference in the individual's intellectual level, his chronological age, and his social functioning. We found that the child who had previous positive social experiences functioned better in the group, regardless of his intellectual level.

Program Structure and Content

In programing for the "QT's" the emphasis was on the provision of both social and learning experiences which to the participants would be regarded as exciting, satisfying, and full of fun. The group worker and the volunteers worked with the youngsters in an uncritical and supportive manner in regard to their participation while attempting to further their development in the areas of self-care, use of program activities and materials, interaction with their peers and adults, and self-expression.

The group was called a "club" on the assumption that the term would have status significance to the adolescents. The group worker took the responsibility for planning a program and modifying it to both the group's and the individual's readiness at the time of the meeting.

The activities relied upon were the kinds common to recreational groups—loosely organized games, square and folk dancing, singing, arts and crafts. In addition, activities involving the retardate in learning a functional task related to everyday living were included and were especially popular. These activities included (1) short trips in and around the immediate community; and (2) preparation of refreshments. The trips included shopping in the supermarket, buying sodas and cakes in a local cafeteria, walking to the park, riding the subway, and eating lunch in the automat. The supermarket and cafeteria trips provided the basis for later role playing as waiters, clerks, and customers.

The volunteers were responsible for selecting and bringing refreshments that the children could prepare for themselves. They started with caramel apples and popping corn and moved to chocolate and tapioca puddings, pizza pies, vegetable salads, hot dogs, and stuffed celery. The parents were especially impressed by the skill their children developed in these activities.

Special projects—puppet making, mad-hatters ball, birthday parties, and celebration of holidays—were also successful.

Each 2-hour meeting was planned to allow for individual participation both in choosing and leading activities. The breakdown and approximate time involved in each session were as follows:

1. Premeeting (15 minutes). While the group was gathering for the evening, the teens moved about the room playing with various games and equipment. During the period of initial development these were set up before the young people arrived. Later the young people helped the worker to get the room ready for the evening.

2. Meeting (15 minutes). The group worker would call the members to come and be seated around a table. The "meeting" opened with a set of seated circle games used regularly from week to week. After this opening the group worker asked the members to tell about their individual experiences during the week and encouraged them to talk about their other interests, with the purpose of engaging the individuals in informal conversation, allowing for and stimulating interaction between the members themselves and the adults. In addition, the evening's activities were planned at this time.

3. Major activity (30 to 45 minutes). The theme of the evening was developed and carried out during this period—parties, walks in the snow, games, or arts and crafts.

4. Refreshment period (30 to 45 minutes). While the members ate the refreshments which they had helped prepare, the group worker and volunteers engaged them in individual informal conversations. Afterwards the members helped in cleaning up.

5. Closing period (30 minutes). The program ended with singing, dancing, or a game or two. Then the group worker made an announcement about the following week. Before going home the young people helped to put away the program equipment and made a game of folding and stacking chairs. The group worker and volunteers always greeted the parents as they arrived to pick up their youngsters.

Some Observations

From the experience with Queen's Teens one could draw some general observations on group work with the retarded:

1. *Retardates, like other individuals, can be expected to react differentially to group experiences.*

Contrary to a common belief that retardates tend to be passive and overconforming, the group worker found evidence among the Queen's Teens of a normal range of behavior. For example:

> Mary, Jane and Alice can be counted on to do whatever the group wants to do or what the leader suggests. They always vote as the others and never do anything on their own or in disagreement with the others. They seem too insecure to express their own wishes. Yet, when a decision was left up to the three of them and nobody else, one of them came forth with a suggestion that the others followed.

> In contrast, Bob, Jim, Dick, and Lottie act completely independently, participating in the group activities only when they want to. They seem to regard the meeting as an opportunity for individual expression. Jim, for example, entered the room one evening saying, "Leave me alone tonight; I don't want to play." He then moved away from everyone and began walking around the room by himself. When he got tired of doing things by himself, he came back into the group and participated in activities with the others for the rest of the meeting.

Thus, some of these young retardates found in the group experience a chance not only to do things with the others but also to express their individuality by choosing when and where they would participate. As long as an individual's expression of independence was not disturbing or limiting to the others in the group activity, it was respected and encouraged by the leaders.

2. *The individual's needs take precedence over the group's needs.*

The group worker found that often the actions of an individual were more important to deal with than to keep the group activity going—for example, when Larry threw a tantrum because he was not allowed to dominate the group in playing a game; or when Bob kept running around screaming.

However, in such instances, after the group worker stopped the group's activity in order to deal with the individual he would involve the entire group in the discussion of the situation. In that way the problem of the individual was woven into the program of the group.

Often independent actions were expressive of creative urges or moods rather than the acting-out of hostility or anxiety. Thus, Bob rushed to the piano and banged away loudly while the group was singing *She'll be Coming 'Round the Mountain*, and at another time Jim listened quietly to a phonograph record while the group played tag.

At such times, the group worker adapted the group's activity to involve the independent individual in a positive and encouraging manner: With Bob—"Let's join him at the piano and sing while he plays," applauding his efforts when the song ended. And with Jim—"Jim, will you help us play musical chairs by turning the record on and off while we play?"

In both these instances the individual moved with the group into the next activity after such an approach.

When it was not possible to adapt the group's program to an individual's independent behavior, the individualist was asked to stop what he was doing but with the condition that later on he could come back to finish what he had started. In essence the group worker was saying that he thought the individual was as important as the group.

3. Program is planned to provide individuals with opportunities to experience success.

It was assumed that a successful experience in participating in the group's program would loosen the individual's inhibitions and give him the security to participate in the program more fully. Therefore, games were modified so as to give everyone a chance to win. Arts and crafts projects were always admired if the individual himself liked what he produced. The group worker made a practice of informing each parent—in front of the child—that their child had done quite well that night in the group.

In playing "choosing" games sufficient control was provided by the group leaders to assure each teenager a chance to be both chooser and chosen.

4. Expectations of the level of an individual's performance must vary in relation to the intellectual, social, and emotional aspects of behavior.

Among the Queen's Teens the group worker assumed an uncritical role in relation to a child's intellectual performance. However, when it came to cleaning up, putting on coats and hats, getting chairs, he was more demanding. The level of expectation of course differed for each child, according to the child's physical and motor coordination. When the child did not respond as expected, the issue was dropped and taken up at a later time when the child seemed more cooperative. For example:

> Laura who is almost blind was given a record to place upon the phonograph. (Her mother had mentioned earlier that she had never done this at home.) Because of a spastic condition, Laura had very poor motor coordination, but she was able to get herself to the record player, place the disk on the turntable, and almost get the needle in the right groove. She exhibited great pride in this accomplishment.

> Alfred, an obese and overprotected child, was afraid of going out into the snow. He said he would catch cold or he would slip and break a leg. It was a difficult task to get him outdoors—one which involved seeing him through three tantrums—but after this was accomplished, he became more amenable to other trips away from the building.

5. Group activities must be carefully selected to suit the functioning level of the group.

For the Queen's Teens the group worker chose familiar games which the young people knew and liked. New games were also introduced but modified to suit the group and allow for successful play. Among them was a clapping rhythm game that is popular with adolescents generally. It took 3 months for the group to learn this game, but they did learn it and liked to play it so well that they made it part of the opening portion of each meeting. Regardless of the type of activity, the presentation was always geared to the level of the group members in order to minimize frustration and provide for satisfying participation.

Group Worker, Individual, and Group

While the retardate benefits from experience in a social group, he evidences a slower than normal development in social skills. It is up to the group worker to remain "enthusiastically patient" during the long, slow process of gradual improvement. While enthusiasm and warmth are important factors in work with any group, they are even more important in work with retardates. Parents and teachers of retardates, because of the demanding nature of their responsibilities, may at times have their enthusiasm worn thin. Yet, like everyone else, the retardate needs people around him who are stimulating and enthusiastic.

In spite of the necessity to suit the activities to the group, it is not necessary to "talk down" to the retarded. The leader talks to them in the same manner as he would to other adolescents.

On the other hand, because the retardate is limited in social experience, it is necessary for the leader to have a highly structured program plan that remains similar from week to week. As the participant becomes more accustomed to the pattern, he begins to anticipate what will come next, deriving much satisfaction from this accomplishment.

Experience with the Queen's Teens, and other groups of mentally retarded formed by the Association, indicate that while individuals change within the group, there is some group movement toward higher levels of activity. Individuals, however, do learn to participate in activities with their peers, and in social adequacy to move closer to the social expectations of their chronological age.

The Queen's Teens is now in its third year of existence. In this third year we have noted some movement toward subordinating individual needs to that of the group; in the ability of the group to carry out a short "business" meeting; in the individual's ability to take on more responsiblity for his own behavior and for planning together with the other members; and in the ability of the group leader to lessen the active nature of his role in the knowledge that the group could take more responsibility in regard to simple activities.

The Association, in extending its program to serve additional groups in different parts of New York City, has found that variables such as previous group experience, religion, culture, and socioeconomic and minority group status have an impact upon a group experience for the retarded adolescent, although there are still many unknowns in this regard. In some families of low socioeconomic status, retardation of a child may be only one of the many other serious problems affecting the family and is not therefore always perceived as a crisis situation, as it is apt to be in middle-class families. Many retarded adolescents in such families, who are in the higher functioning range of retardation, seem to have much in common with their normal contemporaries and to have acquired some social skills in the process of daily living. Barring gross stigmata, their intellectual deficit or perceptual difficulties are the most obvious signs of their retardation to the group worker.

In the group situation, these young people need a great deal of help in planning and following through on responsibility for program development, as did the Queen's Teens, and again structured program is helpful. However, relationships are formed more readily between the members who are of the same socioeconomic or cultural background in view of their having similar experiences in school and in the neighborhood. The members also relate more easily than those in such groups as the Queen's Teens to other young people who use the group service agency, as they generally share a similar background. These young retardates also seem to have greater interest in energetic activities, especially athletics, and less fear of risking injury. They have had more exposure to group experiences with their peers, both retarded and normal. This is probably due to less maternal overprotection.

As additional experiences are accumulated with such groups and analyzed, the findings may not only help to refine social group work method with the mentally retarded, but bring to light additional information about social development patterns and the use of leisure time and about what kind of interaction patterns occur between retarded and normal individuals as well as between retardates.

SEVENTY-TWO

Integrating Mental Retardates in Normal Groups

MORTIMER GOODMAN AND RICHARD GOLDBAUM

"Mom, I shot a basket tonight," shouted Harvey several times as he ran into the house and upstairs. Harvey's mother was thrilled as she listened patiently to her 19-year-old son's awkward explanation of what had happened. Harvey is good-looking, has considerable poise and self-control, but is mentally retarded and stutters severely. He is now an accepted member of the Spartans Club, thanks to social work diagnosis and intervention.

Bill, age 16, has been a member of the Panthers for two years. Bill is much less retarded than Harvey, but Bill has a visual limitation and physical one-sidedness; however, Bill has gradually been accepted into team sports and has been afforded compensatory kinds of recognition—elected secretary by his club, assigned to be manager of the basketball team and in other ways. Both Bill and Harvey have gained a realistic awareness of their limitations in getting dates for occasional club parties. Reuben, on the other hand, who is also 16 years old and mentally retarded, experienced his first coed party late, after asking and receiving advice from his club advisor on apparel and manner. Reuben was integrated into the Trojans Club eighteen months ago.

The Jewish Community Centers Association of St. Louis has assisted 30 mental retardates ranging from age 6 to 19 during the past year. Each has been placed individually in clubs, classes and camp groups after careful selection of a group that seemed to be compatible with the total profile of each selectee. This new approach is based on the assumption that personal traits, handicaps and limitations are as important as the retardate's I.Q. level, and that these factors can be studied in order to gauge a person's ultimate social potential. According to the United States Government, "Classification in terms of gross achieved scores of intelligence has never served as an adequate gauge of potentiality nor as a good basis for grouping, planning or training."[1]

Reprinted from *Jewish Center Program Aids,* Vol. 26, No. 1 (Winter, 1964-65), pp. 1-3. By permission of the authors and the National Jewish Welfare Board.

Three Percent Are Retarded

Current interest and research in the entire problem of mental retardation have brought into focus the challenging figure of 3 percent of any given population. Selection of these youngsters for special placement by Center workers is relatively simple because their principal symptom, a limitation of learning capacity, is usually detected early in their school careers, with separate placement in school as educable mental retardate ("EMR"). A second symptom, however—the limitation of social competence—has been given insufficient attention by educators and clinicians.

"The normal adolescent can satisfy his gregarious tendencies through . . . various forms of group experiences. The retarded, however, frequently sense their own inferiority and are either rejected by their peers or feel so uncomfortable in their presence that they hesitate to seek group companionship. Thus they are denied maturational experiences. Their characteristic immaturity cannot be attributed solely to limited mental development."[2]

There is no body of observed data to indicate mental retardates' potential for personal and social skills. Some of these personal traits are: Capacity for good grooming, self control and clarity of speech. Other personal factors that are assessed clinically, such as hand-eye coordination, attention span and space-and-depth perception, also need to be tested and measured in (normal) social groups. When all types of factors (unmeasured personal traits, clinically measured personal factors, *in addition* to I.Q. scores) are observed and evaluated in normal group interaction, integration of retarded youngsters within the give-and-take of normal group experiences can serve to guide them into adulthood more creatively than is currently the case.

Centers Provide Wide Range of Groups

Jewish Community Centers provide a wide range of groups wherein, by means of adult intervention, EMR children can be individually placed in order to interact with normal peers. In this way they can be helped to gain more insight into the dynamics of group acceptance and the permeability of small groups. This approach has equal merit for both small and large Centers since the key to it is individualization rather than the forming of separate and "special" groups.

When this concept was taken to the Children's Committee and the Board of Directors in the fall of 1962, not only was sanction given, but much interest was also expressed in the beneficial effect on normal peers who absorb the "different" child into their midst. This aspect is one of the five advantages of integrating retardates (see below), and the social effect on normal peers, their parents and siblings will be an important aspect of the total study of this demonstration next year.

Five Basic Advantages

Individualized (integrated) placement has five basic advantages over separate groupings of mental retardates:

1. Integration exposes the total EMR "self" to public view, automatically enabling him to develop a realistic self-image. It helps to free the subject from the self-perpetuating cycle of social failure, guilt and withdrawal. The EMR child usually spends two-thirds of the school day in a special class in the company of his retarded classmates. He has, therefore, few chances to discover how he talks, how he hears, how he sees, how he appears and how he responds, in relation to normal boys and girls. Here is an example from the Center's case records: Harold was a 10-year-old, but he was placed by the Center in a winter season boys' sports club for 8- and 9-year-olds. The first week nobody knew his name, but the leader observed that in the second weekly session one boy called to him by name in order to throw the ball to him; by the fourth week, he was "in the game," although it was only the adult leader who congratulated him for shooting two baskets that particular afternoon.

2. The integrated approach gives the retardate the chance to compensate for his mental weakness in the context of everyday (although protected) peer competition. He must draw upon every faculty at his command in order to meet the test of group activity. Very often, this demand helps his parents to overcome the middle-class habit of over-protection. Following is another example:

> D. J., a 9-year-old boy, was able to enjoy nature walks in the science club. His conceptual ability was obviously limited and his participation slightly limited. His reaction one day to a demonstration of the microscope was to make a proud "speech," telling how his brother received one as a Chanukah present.

3. Individualized integration gives those who are selected many new opportunities to receive and gain the respect of normal people, even while they conform to the rules of the normal and share in their decisions and judgments. As Kirk and Johnson have spelled it out: "The program for the mentally handicapped should stress:

1. occupational adequacy
2. social competence
3. personal adequacy"[3]

Ten-year-old H. C. had been in summer day camp for two seasons. He was classified as EMR and his mother was finding it very difficult to accept the judgment of the school. He adjusted poorly in summer day camp. His mother placed him in Pee Wee basketball. In conference with physical education workers, a sharp contrast between his adjustment here and in day camp was realized. In Pee Wee basketball he showed good control and coordination and under the eye of a worker he participated in practice routines as well as elementary team-play, showing an ability with normal boys that could not have been inferred from his erratic and uncontrolled behavior in day camp groups.

4. Integration also makes it possible for the parents to better evaluate their child's growth and adjustment in real-life situations. This plus-factor can never be attained as long as the child is *only* interacting with other mental retardates. One example of parental reaction to placement follows:

Mrs. L. came in with her 4½-year-old boy last spring to register him for summer play camp. She explained how he had been tested at age 2 by a private psychologist and was found to be EMR. She was wondering how he would get along now in his first group experience. He was placed in play camp and did very well. He was observed to adjust to routine and to get along with other children in a normal manner. The observations were shared with the mother who had him retested in the fall. His retest I.Q. was 111.

5.   Finally, it helps normal people who become exposed to the EMR in their midst to accept him and to help him. This is a social derivative of no small importance in a world of stereotypes and scapegoats.

Professional Steps Involved

Five professional steps are involved in the St. Louis experiment:

1.   *Case Finding*—Many of the children in this project were spotted by the Center's professional staff before a formalized approach to their integration was initiated. From these core cases was seen the need for the present demonstration. Once the community was made aware that the Center was prepared to help the EMR, referrals started to come in from pediatricians, child guidance clinics, the special school districts, the Association for Retarded Children and from parents who were told of the service by other parents. Finding the EMR child has not been the Center's problem, but rather staff time to adequately serve the 25 children already in the program and finding groups for those who are just now seeking the services.

2.   *Selection*—Each child is interviewed by a social worker who also has some training in the education of the mentally retarded. The parents are interviewed. Selection is then based upon these individual contacts with a diagnosis of potential adjustment to a group situation. This diagnosis is based upon the verbal skills of the child, interest level, physical ability, the potential sociability and educational level. It has been found that most of the "trainable" children are not suitable for this type of program. Therefore, the project has confined itself primarily to the educable mental retardate, although some very interesting borderline cases showing group adjustment potential make themselves evident.

3.   *Placement*—Once the above selection has been considered favorable, the next step is to determine which group will best suit the EMR, and whether or not the EMR child will fit into the group. Some factors determining this decision are: a) the group's level of interest, b) size of group, c) degree of group structure, d) activities of the group, and e) the group leader's capabilities. There has been a conscious effort not to place more than one EMR in a group. The reasons for this are: 1) this eliminates a tendency for the EMRs to rely on each other for support, thereby hindering the EMR integration process; 2) this allows the leader and the group a better chance to accommodate themselves to him. The experience to date has been that after proper diagnosis of individuals and groups, these EMR children become accepted in varying degrees in a variety of different types of groups: friendship clubs; special-interest clubs; classes such as arts-and-crafts, cooking, woodworking; sports, clubs and leagues, and the gameroom setting.

4. *Supervision*—Of these five steps, that of supervision of leaders is probably of utmost interest to Center workers.

Each group leader is required to complete a group record form. This record is written by all the group leaders whether they have an EMR in their group or not. In addition to the group record, the leader with an EMR child in his group must complete an individual record on this child every two weeks.

The individual record gives the supervisor a descriptive analysis of the EMR's functioning within the group. These descriptions are the child's relationship with the leader, his relationship and interaction with new members of the group, the members' reaction to this child, the EMR's functioning in planning and participating in the group's activities (focus on skill development) and dependency patterns demonstrated when coming to the group or within the group. The individual report form and group record are the basis for supervisory discussions about the EMR.

Supervision of Leaders

The supervision of the leaders with EMR children is shared by all the professional staff of the Children's Department. The staff person directly responsible for the integrating project in the Children's Department is used as a consultant by the other professionals, besides supervising some of these leaders himself. The individual report form was assembled in such a way as to facilitate the making of a carbon copy.

The part-time leaders who are working with these EMR children raised some very basic questions about what the Center is trying to do with retarded children and voiced some concern about wanting to know more about retardation, its characteristics and what it meant. A booklet was written for these leaders to give them answers to the questions raised and direction and guidelines in assisting their work with these handicapped children. The booklet was also distributed to members of the board and lay committees to help them better understand the purposes and focus of the work the Center is doing with retarded children in the community.

Supplementing the individual supervisory conferences, a few group supervisory sessions were set up at which time leaders were encouraged to raise questions and discuss problems they were facing with the EMR in their groups. All the staff supervisors were present at these meetings. These group meetings have given the leaders an opportunity to discuss common problems and share ideas of how to cope with them.

A major aspect in the supervision of these leaders, both in individual and group conferences, is the handling of personal feelings about the retarded child. Leaders have to be helped to see how important their own feelings are in helping the EMR group member. They have to be shown that if they feel uncomfortable with the handicapped child the others in the group will sense this feeling, and this would hinder the child in integrating fully into the group. The leaders also have to see that over-protection could be just as bad as no protection. They have to learn that independence is a major goal for the retarded, but that it has to be fostered and mastered slowly with guidance and patience.

Supervision of these leaders is close and intensive. These are highly competent people, but because this is a new and experimental field, only through experience and sharing can more be learned in order to help more. Supervision, record writing, and group discussions are all used as learning tools.

5. *Individual or Group Counseling*—Each parent has been assisted in some way, either individually or in a group, to better understand and sometimes further accept the limited capabilities of his or her retarded child.

Individually, the parents have been periodically informed of their particular child's progress and his level of functioning within the groups. Through these individual interviews, common problems are raised by the parents, although existing staff loads prohibit monthly interviews with all the parents.

Some of the parents are now seen on a group counselling basis and one series of five sessions, involving eight families, has been completed. The modification of attitudes, development of realistic goals for their (limited) children and the handling of denial and their own self-image continue to be the general goals of the Center's work with the families, whether on an individual or group basis. Evaluation of these beginning efforts has yet to be done. As Anderson has pointed out:

> "Unless the family is helped, factors contributing to the child's problems remain unchanged. When parents are helped through group discussion or individual casework treatment or both, much can be done to relieve the effect of retardation and help the child to develop to his full potential."[4]

By means of this process, some very positive results have been achieved. Teen clubs exhibit self control in responding to the frequent slow verbal responses of an EMR member. These EMR members, over a period of time, begin to be emotionally involved in the decision-making process in girls' clubs and in boys' clubs. Some EMR day campers are able to transfer specific skills gained at summer day camp to their daily life, such as clearing the table, or baking biscuits, a skill learned in JCCA Cooking Class. The responses of family members to the opportunity for integrated placement has grown steadily so that the Center has had to limit case-finding until special demonstration funds are obtained.

Meanwhile, the professional staff of the Center is alert to special requests and continues to process new selectees whenever possible. Also, the staff continues to work with the parents group on a monthly basis and with most of the parents on an individual basis. It is hoped that additional resources will be developed in order to expand this unique group service approach for this particular handicap.

References

[1]*Mental Retardation: Activities of the United States Government,* Department of Health, Education and Welfare, p. 9 (May 1962).

[2]Begab, Michael J., "Factors in Counseling Parents of Retarded Children," *American Journal of Mental Deficiency,* No. 60 (January 1956) pp. 515-524.

[3]Kirk, Samuel and Johnson, O. G., *Educating the Retarded Child* (Houghton Mifflin Co., Boston, Mass., 1951), p. 117.

[4]Anderson, Alice V., "Orienting Parents to a Clinic for the Retarded," *Children* (Sept.-Oct. 1962) p. 182.

SEVENTY-THREE

Day Camping for Mentally Retarded

ROSE STOCKHAMMER

We are all aware, but it bears repetition, that recognition of the need of the mentally retarded to be regarded first as people and only secondarily as people with a disability has gained considerable impetus during the past 15 years. The emphasis has shifted to how much the retarded person can do, rather than how little. More and more, community planning has reflected interest and effort in his behalf and in that of his family.

A greater number of the traditional welfare and social agencies are now extending their services to the mentally retarded. Studies and experience reaffirm that when understanding and knowledge are adequate, progress is possible. Thus slowly, but increasingly, the trend is toward easing the isolation and loneliness that have made the retarded person's life difficult.

It is worth noting that a few group service agencies have, for a long time, responded to the particular needs of the retarded. Bronx House is one of the agencies that has pioneered in this area. Through its day camp service, it has affirmed the principle that retarded children need as much as we can give of our skills and interests. It hopes to further their social growth, strengthen their sense of self-care, and provide them with opportunities to learn skills and new experiences in the out-of-doors. An obvious value of the day camp for parents is to free them from the close supervision of their children for a substantial part of the day. Also, it involves more frequent contact with the parents on the part of staff and opportunity to help them modify their attitudes toward retarded children. Of particular concern were parents who found it difficult to relax the overprotective attitudes that tend to prevent their children from growing. It was felt, therefore, that the more intimate group experience which camp offers would help make the parent's job of guiding and freeing such children far easier.

Obviously, the all-day nature of day camp life demands careful and sensitive consideration of aspects that can provide the child with a particularly potent group experience. I would like to consider three areas that are central to the service and at the same time are of concern to us who have elected to serve the retarded. These

From *Rehabilitation Record*, Vol. 5, No. 1 (January-February, 1964), pp. 32-34. By permission of the author and the Vocational Rehabilitation Administration.

concerns deal with selection, training, and supervision of staff; program and some of its dimensions; and work with families.

In considering staff, we know that the key to a positive group experience lies in the ability of the counselor to unlock the potentialities of each person so that both the individual and the group of which he is an integral part will grow. Frequently we have our best success with group leaders from our year-round program. However, after one or two summers such promising individuals may be "pirated" by other camps for supervisory jobs, so that we go through a never-ending process of recruiting and training counselors. Personal warmth, maturity, insight, empathy for the individual's inadequacies, an ability to relate to the retardate's slow-growing and slow-moving pace are qualities we look for in a counselor. It is desirable that he also have knowledge of outdoor living.

As part of our supervisory task, we assume the training necessary to work with the mentally retarded. The precamp orientation period includes preparation for service to the retarded so that all staff members may be sensitized to them and their special needs. At this time, very often counselors with other group assignments begin to evidence a new appreciation for the worth of the handicapped individual. However, the effort to increase other staff members' understanding of the handicap and help them relate to it is an on-going process.

Counselors involved in direct contact with the retarded meet as a group during this period for discussions regarding the causes and kinds of retardation, the role of the counselor, techniques of working with this group, and consideration of program. Referral summaries and intake material on each individual serve as a guide for the counselors. Obviously, such records can be helpful in planning for the individual and group and on program formation, including grouping of campers.

Staff meetings, as well, can provide training on the job. The periodic evaluations of the program for the retarded do much to clarify and establish principles of work and guide its further development. Another element in staff training is the use of resource material. Suggested reading lists, books, and pamphlets can help him grow on the job.

Furthermore, through the supervisory process, the counselor can see himself as the enabler of the camper's growth. Considering the nature of the retarded child as a member of a group, it is important that the counselor be helped to relate himself to the child's lack of self-worth, his deep need for adult approval, his excessive demand for the adult's attention, his short interest span, and his impulsive behavior. Generally, too, his physical coordination, especially in small muscle activity, is poorer than in other children. All this suggests that the counselor must affect the experiences of individuals in a way that will help each member of the group relate to his peers and develop his own individual skills and abilities. What is of considerable help to the counselor is a real knowledge of the specifics of the retarded and of a group of retarded individuals.

In a camp setting, everything that happens may be considered program—the planned or unplanned activities, the group contacts, and individual contacts. With regard to the mentally retarded, program must basically reflect our understanding that they have a potential for social development and a continuing capacity to learn, grow, and change. A day camp that utilizes woodland facilities provides rich opportunity for living close to nature, more than is possible in an urban setting. Living in the out-of-doors, even preparing for cookouts or an overnight, is part of fun and at the same time teaches new skills that contribute to a sense of self-worth. Learning not to damage trees and to conserve plant and animal life leads to respect for life. These are individual and social needs which the camp can serve.

It is through other activities too, such as group games, singing, dancing, boating, and swimming, that many of the children begin to derive a sense of self-worth.

It stands to reason that we must be sensitive to the potentials of an activity or experience in which we involve the mentally retarded. A sense of trust in what they are able to do needs to be effectively communicated. Their fear of risk tends to be acute and the reaction may be either a passive one or a direct negative response. The major task, then, is to be aware of limitations and move the children toward experiences that will make appropriate demands on them.

Some program activities can bring groups into contact with average or normal groups. For instance, practical service projects which contribute to the total camp's needs bring about a feeling of giving, belonging, being useful, and receiving recognition. Such experiences include assistance with blazing of an essential trail, helping with building a bridge across a stream which is used by all groups, assuming responsibility for the care and maintenance of the camp's "farm." Also, contributions to the nature museum are generally met with considerable appreciation.

Another level of involvement can be use of the group's skill in singing as a contribution to the program. Still another approach can be to move individuals out of their own groups from time to time. Some can be charged with responsibilities in the supply area where communication with other campers is frequent; some can participate in hobby groups that include music and cooking.

Working with parents is essential. We cannot, either in theory or practice, separate the helping process for the children from the one for parents. Working with parents of the mentally retarded is especially important. Since society exalts the "quick mind," it is more difficult for parents to accept a mentally retarded child than one with a physical handicap. Our referral material and intake interviews reflect varying degrees of parents' feelings and attitudes toward their child and his disability. Some parents are able to discuss mental retardation realistically; they realize and accept the child's need for both independence and dependence and can communicate understanding to him. Many are overwhelmed and bewildered by the difficulties; they are unable to free themselves from self-blame but are able to express concern and have the strength to make use of help. Others have isolated the child through avoidance of communication or have withdrawn from close association with people and, in defense, deny the need for help.

The difficulties of many of these parents are so deep-seated as to interfere with the effectiveness of working with the child. They have so infantilized their child that he cannot function independently of the parent. We recognize that problems such as these are usual for the parents of retarded children and that these parents need some help.

In many group services agencies, the mentally retarded, like other children, are registered on a family membership basis. It implies a commitment to provide definitive services to the family. Both in the year-round programs and in day camps, parents are encouraged to participate in a broad program of family activities. Fund-raising projects, special family holiday events, outings, and programs dealing with discussions on childrearing are planned. Parents also meet in small groups to discuss children's group experiences, achievements, and carry over to home activities. This is aimed at strengthening parent-child relationships.

In addition, parent-child programs involve joint participation in games, group singing, dancing, and supper parties. Staff members are also available for parent consultation. However, periods of freedom from the routine of everyday life and from the role of parenthood must also be made available to the adult. Parents need to realize their potentials and to rediscover old skills and interests. They, therefore, have available to them the gamut of agency activities for adults. Some are active in art programs, dance, and music. They serve on agency-wide committees and often become leaders. It should be noted that when the need is indicated, families are helped to use community resources. In all, the agency's service reflects a total effort toward moving the family into the mainstream of community life.

In concluding, the following should be highlighted:

1. Serving mentally retarded children in a normal day camp setting demands an awareness that capacities differ according to each retarded person, just as they do with average children. The emphasis should be on trying various approaches to find out just what each individual is capable of and at what level the group can function.

2. Essential ingredients in working with a mentally retarded group include: (a) experience with groups; (b) acceptance of individuals for what they are and at their present level of performance; and (c) constant experimentation with different activities. The richer the program and the more varied the opportunities for different individuals at different times, the more helpful it will be.

3. Our major objective is to help the mentally retarded become as capable and independent as possible. We will be able to achieve this only through staff members who have deep regard and the greatest understanding of the retardate. The mentally retarded children demand a great deal more time and energy than do other children served in the program. The responsibility requires a most patient and most sensitive counselor.

4. A nonjudgmental attitude towards parents is basic, so that they will not become defensive. At the same time, we must maintain an honesty aimed at not destroying their hopes but rather helping them to look at reality.

A group service agency, through its day camp program, renders an important and needed service to the individual retardate and his family.

Prevention of Mental Retardation: The Contribution of Social Work in Maternal and Infant Care Programs

MIRIAM F. MEDNICK

In this paper, I want to discuss the contribution which social work can make to the prevention of mental retardation within the structure of federally funded public health Maternal and Infant Care Programs. These programs are designed to provide maternal and infant care to the members of our population who most frequently lack preventive health services; namely, poor people. Social work can play a role in the primary prevention of problems during the pregnancy and in secondary prevention after the birth of the baby by early identification of and help in the utilization of medical care for hazardous health and social conditions.

Study after study has shown that there is a connection between poverty and prematurity and between prematurity and mental retardation. Low birth weight has been called a disease of poverty. Premature birth is now considered by many primarily a social rather than a medical problem. The World Health Organization Expert Committe on Maternal and Child Health[1] stated "The unfavorable conditions associated with low birth weight will vary in degree and substance throughout the world, but will include a variety of unfavorable factors which may affect adversely the health and general efficiency of the mother, including malnutrition, infections, fatigue and overwork, bad housing, inadequate educational and health services. There is also evidence that these conditions, unfortunately, are a type that do not occur singly. For example, the poorly nourished woman is often the one who gets or seeks little care during her pregnancy, lives in poor circumstances, ignores signs of impending obstetrical difficulties, has had many previous and closely spaced pregnancies, has many family problems, knows little of simple sanitation and hygiene and is, in general, too ignorant and poorly motivated to care for herself."

In her paper on Social Class and Premature Birth,[2] Helen Wortis points out that "Of the pathogenic circumstances of pregnancy, parturition, and early infancy that play a major role in causing cerebral defect and mental retardation, premature birth is one of the most important. About 8 percent of all births in this country are

From a paper delivered at the 1968 Annual Meeting, American Association on Mental Deficiency. By permission of the author and the Department of Public Health, Maternal and Infant Care Project, City of Philadelphia.

premature: that is, the infant's weight at birth is less than five and a half pounds. Premature birth is the largest single cause of infant deaths, and a large proportion of the babies with very low birth weights die within the first week of life. Among those who survive, prematurity has a deleterious effect, and, in some studies up to 50 percent of these infants have handicaps ranging from minimal neurologic damage to severe mental deficiency. About one third of the children with cerebral palsy have been born prematurely. Even if children born prematurely have no obvious defect, their I.Q. scores are, generally, lower than those of their siblings of normal birth weight."

Dr. Edwin M. Gold,[3] who has written extensively on maternity care, called attention to "the unevenness of progress between the less and more advantaged groups of the population between white and non-white groups" in terms of improvement in maternal death rates, infant death rates and incidence of prematurity. He quotes extensively to support his statement that the incidence of prematurity is intimately associated with the quality of prenatal care.

It is always a shock to have figures quoted which puncture our pride in the United States. Most Americans find it incredible to be told that the U. S. ranks only 11th in comparative rates of infant mortality. In 1966 the national average was 23 infant deaths per 1000 births. It isn't surprising that western European countries such as Sweden and England do better. But what about Russia, Japan, and even Thailand? We should be able to do better by our babies than Thailand.

The Panel on Mental Retardation convened by President Kennedy focused on the problem of excessive low birth weight rates in the low income families and the accompanying relationship to brain damage. The Panel therefore recommended the authorization of a Maternity and Infant Care Program to provide necessary funding to state and local health departments. The major purpose stated in the January 1963 Maternal and Child Health and Mental Retardation amendment to the Social Security Act is "to help reduce the incidence of mental retardation caused by complications associated with child bearing." This was to be accomplished by providing comprehensive health care to women in low-income families "who have, or are likely to have, conditions associated with childbearing which increase the hazards to the health of the mothers and their infants."

As a result, there are now 54 Maternal and Infant Care Projects in the country. It is even more significant that President Johnson's budget message of 1968 included an increase in funds for Maternal and Child Health at the same time that so many other domestic welfare funds were cut back sharply in order to finance the war in Vietnam.

These federal funds permit expansion and improvement in standards of obstetrical care for women in the high risk group we are so worried about. When a woman appears early enough in her pregnancy, high risk conditions such as diabetes, syphilis, placental insufficiency and RH incompatability can be diagnosed and treated. The pregnant woman can, with proper medical management and adequate treatment, have a greater opportunity to be delivered of a healthy, full-term baby.

The problem is to get women to begin prenatal care early in their pregnancy.

The reason women seek early prenatal care is not because they identify the care with producing a healthy baby but because they are concerned about their own bodies, their own health, in fact, themselves. There is a vast difference between a woman's perception of herself as "pregnant" and as "having a baby." The baby is not perceived as a separate being until the last trimester of pregnancy or sometimes not until after the birth has separated the fetus from the mother.

If we accept the premise that coming for early prenatal care depends on the woman's feeling about herself, then it follows that the woman who has a poor self-image, no hope for the future, and little faith that she can exercise choice, sees no point in coming for early prenatal care. This attitude is a result of living in poverty. Deprivation suffered by this group leads directly to their failure to secure the prenatal care which would help to insure the delivery of a full-term healthy baby and thus lower the incidence of mental retardation. As Colvin and Adams[4] state in their paper "The Deprivation Hypothesis: Its Application to the Functions of Child Welfare Services in Meeting the Needs of the Mentally Retarded," "In America today between 15 and 20 million children live in the detrimental environment of chronic and severe poverty. This sub-culture is characterized by several or all of the following disruptive conditions—chaotic family life styles, single parent families, overcrowded housing, apathetic (and not infrequently mentally ill) adult figures, and a general sense of alienation from the prevailing norms of society. Within this social milieu...the young child is likely to be deprived of satisfaction of physical and psychological needs, of sensory stimulation and reinforcement." When one adds to this bill of indictment the risks imposed by prematurity, it is easy to see the enormous importance in the prevention of mental retardation of facilitating prenatal care.

We tend to think of deprivation as a chronic condition which pervades the lives of poor people. Crisis theory proposes that the professional wait until the crisis erupts before the social worker's intervention is acceptable to the client and help is utilized to change the condition which the crisis has made unbearable. I would like to suggest that the deprivation is *itself* the crisis; that the alienation from normal sources of satisfaction and standards of living creates a feeling of living in a continual state of crisis. Pregnancy exacerbates the crisis of deprivation by adding the physical and emotional burden of the developing fetus.

How exactly can social workers within a Maternal and Infant Care Project meet the crisis or attack the depriving circumstances which weight the scales so heavily against adequacy of prenatal care? I believe very strongly that the best way to do so is to assume that the entire patient population is the social worker's caseload. As I have said, for many women in the low socio-economic group whose life is a constant struggle against overwhelming environmental and emotional deprivation, the fact of pregnancy, whether planned or unplanned, is a crisis situation. The woman who was working now has to turn to public assistance; the woman who thought she had a man she could depend on emotionally and financially is faced with his desertion; the woman who had achieved an uneasy balance between family pressures and her physical stamina has to reassess her ability. I submit that unless the social worker can offer an initial interview to the entire patient population, she will not be able to offer preventive and ameliorative action before the manifest crisis becomes so acute that the only action possible is to help the client pick up the pieces. From experience with such client groups we can assume that the vast majority will not voluntarily seek assistance before the time an acute problem erupts for a variety of reasons; unwillingness to admit to inadequacy, previous bad experiences, passive acceptance of life's blows or ignorance that help is available. Only by universal screening will the social worker be able to reach all the patients. Those who need help can be identified in time to make help available as a preventive measure.

In order to implement universal screening and insure its maximal utilization, it is important that the social worker employ techniques which are efficient and effective in the first interview. There are four basic elements, not one of which can be omitted, if the interview is to be successful.

1. The social worker must identify herself as a social worker whose focus is on helping with economic and emotional problems and interpretation and implementation of medical recommendations. She must establish herself in the unique role of one who is concerned about the patient as a person and who offers help in all the non-medical areas of her situation. This carries with it the implication that the social worker does not do the job of a financial rating clerk by securing information about income and expenses nor does she do the clerical job of "filling out" the basic identifying information. By the time the patient sees the social worker she has probably given this information more than once. Not only is it annoying to have to repeat the facts about oneself, not only is it time-wasting to do so, but more important, the social worker loses the opportunity to be perceived as a professional helper.

2. The social worker must find out what the reality factors are in the patient's present and future plans for herself during her pregnancy and after the baby's birth, and what intervention or support may be needed. Does she have enough money? Is her housing adequate? Is she interested in birth control? If she is the mother of many children, has she considered tubal ligation? Can the baby come home? If not, is help needed to plan toward relinquishing him for adoption or toward foster care?

3. The social worker must establish what plans have been considered for the care of older children during the mother's hospital stay for delivery. She must evaluate with the mother whether the plans the family has made are realistic and dependable. She must offer her the opportunity to consider homemaker service and decide whether it would be preferable to having her husband take a week off without pay or the price of a bus ticket to bring her mother up from Alabama. She must leave the door open in case the present plans break down. If no adequate plans exist, she must help to provide homemaker services or temporary placement.

4. The social worker must learn whether any emotional problems have been created or exacerbated by this pregnancy. If she is a married woman, how stable is her situation? Is marital counselling indicated? If she is a young, illegitimately pregnant girl, what is her relationship with the father of the baby? What is her re-

lationship with her parents? If she is of school age, does she want to complete her education? What direction does she want her life to take?

When the social worker includes these four areas in her initial interview, she will have established a relationship with her client and have the specific knowledge of her problems which will enable her to mobilize preventive action. Certainly, there will be patients who will not need or will not accept help. But this is the only technique I know which will insure maximum early identification of problems in the crisis situation of pregnancy. It is equally essential to provide continuity of social service to avoid the fragmentation which is a further deterrent to comprehensive service.

If we are to give good service to this patient population, we cannot stop with the baby's birth. Again I quote from Colvin and Adams[5] "the primary need of the retarded child is early identification of the problem . . . either in its manifest form or as a potential threat because of the adverse features in the environment . . . A necessary sequel to early identification is prompt intervention." This is a primary goal of the federally funded children and youth programs. Early identification in a Maternal and Infant Care Project is possible through the provision of follow-up service for the infant.

In the Philadelphia program in which I work, we have instituted an "At-Risk Infant Registry and Follow-Up Program." The At-Risk Infant is one who has an acute or chronic medical condition at birth, such as prematurity, anoxia, cardiac disease, congenital anomalies, etc; who develops a problem in the neo-natal period such as respiratory distress syndrome or hyperbilirubinemia or who is born into a family with a pathologic social situation. All such infants are registered for social work follow-up and adequacy of their medical care is investigated repeatedly. The basic intent is to assure that each infant will receive adequate medical care during the first year of life and that no baby will fall between the cracks of service provision.

The Maternal and Infant Care Project social worker visits all the homes where the family is not following through with medical care. Our experience thus far has shown that there is an indissoluble connection between the family's social problems and their ability to follow through with medical care for their infant. In order to get the baby back to the doctor, the social worker must first explore and deal with the social problems which have prevented the mother's return for medical supervision and treatment.

In her doctoral dissertation, "Patterns of Infant Care and Their Association with Conditions of Living in Poverty,"[6] Mary Susan Brubaker demonstrated that those families whose pattern of care was negligent and depriving to the infant, all had in common an income level of less than $14.00 per week per individual family member. It didn't matter about the family composition or the emotional problems of the mother; if there was insufficient money, the care of the infant deteriorated. Our experience goes along with Dr. Brubaker's findings.

The early identification of the at risk problem enables the social worker to perform a bridging function. Current organization within hospitals of the delivery of medical care recognizes the existence of the patient when he is physically present in the institution. There is very little reaching out to the patients who break appointments. Hospital social workers traditionally do not make home visits. It is only within recent years that hospitals are reorganizing services to make them more accessible to patients and are expressing concern about the patients who break appointments. The social worker who makes a home visit and motivates the mother to return to clinic is thus performing a job that has been neglected.

In the care of babies with at risk conditions which could lead to mental retardation, medical treatment and supervision during the first year of life is of enormous importance. The aftermath of conditions such as anoxia, neonatal infections, borderline abnormal neurological findings, respiratory distress syndrome or low Apgar scores needs continuous evaluation. Those babies who live in the marginal families which have been identified as socially pathological can benefit if the social work help to the family prevents the occurrence of socio-cultural retardation.

In summary, the social worker makes her contribution toward prevention of mental retardation in both the prenatal period and after the birth of the baby. Prenatally, primary prevention of mental retardation is fostered when she makes it possible for the patient to utilize medical care by the identification of and help with social problems through universal screening of the patient population.

In a short, focused initial interview the social worker includes the four basic elements: (1) identifies herself as a professional person uniquely qualified to help with social problems, (2) evaluates the reality factors in the patient's present and future plans, (3) investigates plans for care of older children during the mother's delivery, and (4) explores the emotional problems related to the pregnancy. This enables patient and social worker to cope more adequately with the acute crisis situation of pregnancy in a socially deprived population.

Postnatally, secondary prevention is made possible by the social worker facilitating early identification and prompt remedial treatment of at risk conditions. Such action can ameliorate mental retardation sequelae or hopefully lead to prevention of socio-cultural retardation. Social work and medicine must, of course, work closely together to achieve success.

I want to tell you about a patient whose story confirms the value of the point of view I have presented here. She was thirty-eight, very poor, had a diagnosis of epilepsy, had been married for sixteen years and was pregnant for the first time: obviously a patient at high-risk. She broke several appointments after her initial examination and didn't respond to follow-up letters. The social worker made a home visit. At first the patient was silent and guarded in her responses. She seemed intellectually limited, but she listened to the social worker's expression of concern for her and finally she said, "No one has ever talked to me like you." Her story was that she had not felt the baby move, so she decided she wasn't really pregnant and stopped coming to clinic. Imagine the burden of anxiety she must have carried; her feeling that pregnancy was too good to happen so it couldn't be true. She agreed to keep her next appointment. When the social worker got up to go, she walked her to the bus. It was a bad neighborhood and she wanted to give something to the social worker who had come to give her the gift of hope.

References

[1]Public Health Aspects of Low Birth Weight, World Health Organization Series No. 217, World Health Organization, Geneva, 1961.

[2]Helen Wortis, "Social Class and Premature Birth," *Social Casework,* November, 1964.

[3]Edwin M. Gold, M. D., "A Broad View of Maternity Care," *Children,* March-April, 1962.

[4]Ralph W. Colvin and Margaret E. Adams, "The Deprivation Hypothesis: Its Application to the Functions of Child Welfare Services in Meeting the Needs of the Mentally Retarded." Paper presented at the First Congress of the International Association for the Scientific Study of Mental Deficiency at Montpellier, France, September 15, 1967.

[5]*Ibid.,* p. 4.

[6]Mary Susan Brubaker, "Patterns of Infant Care and Their Association with Conditions of Living in Poverty," Bryn Mawr College, April, 1967.

Parents Counseling Other Parents of Retarded Children

JOSEPH T. WEINGOLD

The problem of mental retardation is extremely complex. Many factors contribute to its complicated and deep personal, social and economic impact. For one, it is the single largest permanent disability of childhood, affecting more children than all the other permanent disabling conditions combined. Its complexity from an individual point of view is attested by the innumerable and still unsuccessful attempts at classification. As we learn more medically, we discover more and more medical reasons for this condition until now we have more than 90 known medical causes, and individual variations in all of them as to intellectual, motor and other functioning.

Its economic impact on the family and society is enormous. Just two new institutions being built in New York State to house about 4,000 retarded will cost almost $80,000,000. It costs the state about $2,000 per year per patient just for upkeep and services in the state schools, without capital construction. The general population increase has resulted in a greater influx into the state schools. Last year, for example, there were 1,100 more new admissions than discharges, an additional cost of over $2,000,000 a year—for how many years? The extended life expectancy of the retarded raises additional problems.

And overlaying all this has been society's attitude of stigmatization and repulsion. Happily there are signs that this is abating, but who can tell in what neighborhood this still exists.

In the midst of all this is the retarded child and with him, his lifeline to society and the great world around him, his family. How can he be helped? What reinforcement would he need to survive adequately, realize his potentials, be able to contribute according to his ability? What reinforcement does the family need? And how can this be provided?

It is a truism today that no child stands alone; that he and his family must be considered together. Perhaps, in many respects, it may be even more important to concentrate initially on the family. In commenting on this, wrote Sheimo, "It seems important not to underestimate the intense repressed forces which become mobi-

Presented at the New York State Welfare Conference, 1960. By permission of the author.

lized in parents who have mentally defective and/or handicapped children. At such time to center one's attention on the defective child rather than towards the parental conflict, might be attempting to deal with the least relevant factor in the total situation."

The principle of counseling is, of course, as old as troubles. Even in biblical times, persons in trouble sought, and frequently were offered unsolicited, advice. Job, of course, is a classical example. People have been offered crying towels and soft shoulders from time immemorial. The theory, long recognized in practice, before it became formalized in modern psychology, that it is good for persons in trouble to talk things out is reflected in our cliches. For example, two heads are better than one in order to solve something. A friend in need is a friend indeed, and so on ad infinitum.

This panel is a recognition of this custom, but certainly is not motivated by the desire to point out the obvious. Some new element must have been added to this age old procedure to bring it to the attention of so professional a body as this, many of whose members devote so much time to counseling. This element is that counseling of one segment of the population with troubles by another with similar troubles has apparently achieved positive results; furthermore, as this kind of counseling becomes more wide spread it is beginning to achieve a qualitative change and perhaps even assuming a quasi-professional aspect by becoming organized with recognizable objectives.

I see on the program that your body has recognized its efficacy with alcoholics. I note more and more that this procedure is being followed by people with other troubles. Recently it was called to my attention that "single" parents have organized and are now engaging in counseling each other. "Single" parents, I might add, are those who are divorced or separated from their spouses. I note, however, that all these people with troubles who are trying to advise and counsel each other consist of groups which are distinguishable in one major respect from the parents of the mentally retarded. Whereas the persons counseling each other in the other groups are themselves affected in their own persons, in the case of the parents of the mentally retarded the trouble, although personal in a very deep sense, does not affect the person of the counseling body or those being counseled. It is one step removed in that their children are the mentally retarded. I note, too, that whereas the topic assigned to me is "Parents of Mentally Retarded Counseling Other Parents of Mentally Retarded," the other part of the panel dealing with lay counseling says "People Counseling Alcoholics" rather than "Alcoholics Counseling Other Alcoholics." This has given me some pause. There may be a very simple explanation for this, but I think it points up a very important difference between the parents of retarded children and some groups. In the case of other disabilities, such as alcoholism, it becomes evident that those who are going to counsel the alcoholics, if they are themselves alcoholics, must have overcome this handicap. In the case of the parents of mentally retarded children, however, in a very real sense, this handicap is never overcome, although of course, the parents can become adjusted in some degree to their child's disability and assume, which all of us deeply desire, a more positive attitude.

It is interesting to note that this phenomonon of parents of retarded children counseling other parents of the mentally retarded did not become significant until the organization of formal parents groups. In a sense, this was the first counseling of parents by other parents. By this time, most of us are aware of the reasons for the organization of such groups, the great lack of services for the mentally retarded, the attitudes and rejection by society, the helplessness of professionals in the face of this handicap and the utter despair of the parents when faced with these frustrations. Frequently, if not invariably, the parent who first finds that his child is diagnosed as mentally retarded feels himself utterly alone in the world, knows of no other such parents and, until the organization of parents groups, probably never heard of other people in the same fix. I very distinctly remember the first general meeting of the Association for the Help of Retarded Children here in New York City. Present at that meeting were about 250 parents, but also a number of professionals who had heard of this meeting, many of them school people who attended, not only out of curiosity, but out of apprehension at what may come out of such a meeting. At that meeting were parents of all kinds of mentally retarded children, high-grade, low-grade, middle-grade, young ones and adults, those in state institutions, those in public schools, and those whose children had absolutely nothing and were living at home with them. All were motivated by a deep desire to do something, at that time not quite specified, for their children. The first counseling, if you will, then was an organization where these frustrations could be channeled into some kind of positive action. "These parents," wrote Sarason in 1952, "by virtue of becoming a group, have done more for their own happiness and stability than the professional or specialist have ever done for them."[1]

Each of these parents had, during the lifetime of his child, received all kinds of advice and counseling. It varied from put your child away and forget about him, which was considered good pediatric practice in the case of newly born retarded children whose retardation was fairly evident early, such as the mongoloid, to go home and love your child and accept him in the family. Very seldom, indeed, was any of this advice accompanied by any specific solutions for immediate or long-range problems. I have had parents over and over again say to me if only someone had helped me in toilet training my child, for example; or, if only someone had told me what to do about teaching him how to eat; or, if only someone had advised me about the vocational rehabilitation possibilities in the community for the mentally retarded, and so forth right through the gamut of needs of the mentally retarded. And this situation was further complicated by the extreme rejection of the whole problem by society, the social stigma attached to mental retardation, and the consequent desire of most parents to avoid this label through latching on to another label more palatable to them and to the public, such as schizophrenia, emotionally disturbed, brain-injured, autistic, aphasic, neurologically impaired, neurophrenic, etc., etc.

In brief, all such advice and friendly counseling that went before the advent of parents groups had little if any permanent affect because it was not accompanied by a suggested short term or long term solution and the parents returned always to the climate of social rejection if not hostility. And, indeed, how were such solutions possible at that time with the almost complete absence of many services or even possibility of such services within the forseeable future. The parent of the mentally retarded child in 1950 did not have a single specialized clinic to turn to. The family agencies, with their long waiting lists and overcrowded schedules, could do very little to help such a parent. The public schools were extremely selective in whom they accepted and frequently put out the youngster at 17, the age when, perhaps, he needed the most training. There were almost no vocational rehabilitation or training facilities for the youngster outside of school. There were no pre-school or nursery groups. And above all, there was no organized attempt to achieve any of these things to give the parent the hope of something yet to come. The organization of the parents groups changed materially this picture and made counseling, whether it be by parents of other parents or by professionals who understand what is going on and the dynamics of the parent movement, much more meaningful and productive.

Parents of retarded children counseling other parents of the mentally retarded has proceeded along certain developmental lines. Initially, of course, parents just got together and talked things over. If a professional was present he was there to have his brains beaten in with questions which he was in no position to answer. Some of this still continues in newly organized groups, but has advanced to a considerable degree beyond this initial and, although productive, rather chaotic state. Today, the parents help others in a number of ways. In its simplest form, there is the committee which goes to visit the parent who first approaches the association or the committee or individual parents who go to the parent who is thinking of committing the child to a state school or who has just done so and is going through a very traumatic experience. On a more advanced or formal level, there are the parents of children in various facilities acting as specialized parents groups, such as the parents who are taking their children to the clinics or the parents who have their children in special classes or in a sheltered workshop or recreation groups, scouts, etc. In addition, there is the more formalized preparation of the parents for such counseling through parent education courses given by professionals in the various disciplines, with question and answer periods. Another method is a school for mothers where a group of mothers with children of the same age and same level of development get together to discuss their problems under the leadership of a professional and finally there are the group therapy sessions psychiatrically oriented with an accomplished group leader such as we have at the Shield of David Institute for Retarded Children in the Bronx.

You will note that this runs through the whole spectrum of parents counseling other parents up to and including the utilization by professionals of parents to counsel other parents in a guided program. We must, however, be extremely aware of certain elements whose presence is absolutely necessary if we are to achieve positive results. We must also be keenly aware of the dangers in this type of counseling.

The elements that must be present are (1) that those doing the counseling must have achieved some accommodation to if not solution of their problem. This means a number of things on different levels. It may mean that they have adjusted to their own situation and accepted their child for what he is and are now looking for more positive solutions on a day-to-day and long-range basis. It may mean that they have found a service for their child which helps them to live with the problem at this time. It may be very simply that they have achieved a great faith in the organization to which they belong and that the future looks much better to them because of research efforts and the promises of more services to come.

(2) There must be some means of ameliorating the condition. In other words, whether it be the absolute necessity of institutionalization, or whether it be the need for schooling or training, vocational rehabilitation, temporary residence, recreation, or even temporary relief of the mother for a short period of time, there must be the means for achieving this either immediately or in a fairly short time. "It seems axiomatic," I wrote in 1953, "that successful group guidance depends on at least two factors, both of which are necessary, i.e. a group to be guided and somewhere to guide them."[2]

A complicating factor is that mental retardation, except for a few instances, is at present incurable and irreversible. To accompany this, however, we must recognize also that enormous advances are being made in the field of research and that already at least two forms of mental retardation can be detected in early childhood and retardation prevented. Furthermore, recent discoveries in the field of genetics, such as the extra chromosome in a mongoloid child that may help us predict whether the parents can have another such child, gives us a great springboard for counseling and hope for many parents.

We might say, then, that the development of parents counseling other parents has gone through a number of phases. The first of this was hope through the organization of parents groups. The second that affected the quality of the counseling and its results was the establishment of services that did not previously exist. The third step was experience in counseling and in predicting the possibility of services for individual children and finally, the advent of sophisticated professionals who could utilize the parents groups in counseling each other and refine it down to smaller groups with more definite objectives.

We must always remember, however, that there are a number of dangers present in all counseling, certainly in parents counseling other parents. One of these dangers is that the parents of mentally retarded children who are doing the counseling frequently find themselves in a rather exalted state through having achieved acceptance of their children and may be impatient with other parents. Another danger is that although there are facilities now available, there are long waiting lists and many hopes may be raised through parent counseling sessions only to be dashed to the ground again. I clearly recall an incident which occurred in the very beginning of our existence in our school for mothers. After about ten or twelve very interesting sessions in which the mothers learned all about mental retardation and had a free opportunity to discuss the problems of their own children and what to do about them they finally came up with the combined chorus: we want a nursery for our children where they can go and get the training which everyone says they need. It was a very troublesome time for the organization and for these poor parents when the money was not available immediately for the establishment of such a facility.

Another difficulty is how to contain the hopes of the parents for cures when exploring the limited amount of research and some of the limited successes that have already occurred. And, of course, perhaps the greatest difficulty still is society's attitude to the mentally retarded. The parents may achieve acceptance of the child when dealing with other parents, but continually faced with the reality of his neighbors, agencies, school systems, hospitals, physicians, and many others who to him are the breakers outside of the lagoon of his parent session, but among whom he must live, venture, and find help.

On the whole, however, we must remember that the continued planning and creation of more facilities is forcing us to deal with the problems of mental retardation as they exist in their natural setting, the community. More and more we are faced with the retarded individual as a person living in a family group and who will continue to do so for sometime to come if not for his or her whole life. Thus, the first element in society that the retarded comes in contact with is the family group, where the parents, of course, are the protagonists. If they do not act positively the child is doomed. This perhaps final challenge the parents are meeting. They have and are making a valiant effort at self help. It is clear to me, after more than ten years of intimate contact with this movement, that one of the most valuable contributions parents have made has been in the area of counseling and supporting each other, at first, and still today, in many instances, with hope, but also with noble example and daring to make a new and better life for their children.

Perhaps we have discovered a new professional discipline, parents.

Bibliography

1. SARASON, SEYMOUR. "The Psychology of the Exceptional Child, Proceedings of the Annual Conference on Education and the Exceptional Child." The Woods School, Langhorne, Pa., May 1952, 16-20.
2. WEINGOLD, JOSEPH T. "Parents Groups and the Problems of Mental Retardation." *American Journal on Mental Deficiency*, 1952, 56, 484-492.

SEVENTY-SIX

The Development of Professional Social Work Within the Framework of a Parents' Association

HENNY ROTHSCHILD

When I first came to work for Israeli Association for Rehabilitation of the Mentally Retarded in 1956, the association consisted of only a few groups of parents, who had come together to find some solution to their own problems. Today, AKIM membership consists of about 2500 parents, individual volunteers as well as volunteer groups (i.e. Bnai Brith, Lions' Clubs) who help us, and last and not least, a group of teachers, nurses, doctors, lawyers, psychologists, etc., who also volunteer their services.

I had both the honour and difficult task of being the first professional worker in this volunteer association, a challenge in itself. Nine years ago, when I came to AKIM, all "professional" work was done by non-professionals on a voluntary basis (although some were, of course, "professionals" in their own fields). I found that before I could start with the ordinary work at hand, I had to convince a great number of parents that they needed professional and systematic help. However, I was greatly helped by the chairman of the association, who was the initiator of introducing professional work into the voluntary frame. Later on I heard that he had quite a job convincing his colleagues of the need for such work.

Though the parents finally agreed to have me employed, they did not quite know what I was supposed to do for them, and neither did I. We grew together. In the beginning I tried to consult some of my colleagues, and gather information on the nature of my proposed new work, but could not find even one who was employed by any voluntary group, and in fact, I was somewhat looked upon not quite seriously for working in a non-professional frame. Many of my colleagues were critical of my accepting work in a voluntary and non-professional agency. I found myself, consequently, fighting on various fronts:

1. It was hard to convince my employers that I had to have a free hand in planning my work;

2. I had difficulties in convincing my fellow professionals that they should take this voluntary association seriously, and look upon us as equals;

Reprinted from *International Child Welfare Review*, Vol. XIX, No. 4 (1965), pp. 157-163. By permission of the author and the International Child Welfare Union.

3. We had to convince the Ministry of Social Welfare, responsible for the work with the retarded, that we were not competitors, and were only trying to help, with the cooperation of the parents, by more clearly defining the nature of the problems, by supplementing and not *duplicating* the existing services. We faced the same problems again with the Ministers of Education and Labour.

4. Finally, professionally I had to undergo an inner conflict. As it was hard to gain the confidence of the parents in the beginning, on purely professional lines, I sometimes had to "forget" some of my training and apply unconventional means of approach, thus deviating from professional techniques. Some of "my parents" believed that I was just their employee and felt I should only carry out their instructions.

I found that my first job was to learn and understand all the personal problems of the committee members, who seemed unable to detach themselves from their own personal problems and look upon my professional efforts at face-value. I managed to win them over and enlist their help, first by aiding them personally with their individual problems, even though it meant going against my professional upbringing. I learned very quickly that I could not force my professionality on them. Although I tried to get the parents who were members of the committee to see the over all problems of our Association, in some cases I found I could win their confidence only after relating to and "arranging" their own child, thus solving their own problem first. This was a frequent conflict for me, but I could not find another technique for recruiting the services of certain intelligent and valuable parents for the organization. Many of these are still active members of AKIM, but some became active only after their own child was properly placed with the help of our services.

In this organization, and as its very first employee, I found that I needed to be especially perceptive in order to break the ice and get on with my job. Planning my actual work, I had first to learn the parents' attitude towards their children, in order to be able to tackle their problems.

Finding the Cases

When I began the job, I had very little information and practically no contact with the existing services and facilities for the retarded in Israel. Our counselling service was primarily aimed at case finding and helping parents out of their desperation and loneliness. Knowing that in Israel educational facilities for the retarded were then very poor and few, I surmised that the moment we advertised our new counselling services, my waiting-room would be over-crowded. I found out that the contrary was true. Many days passed and only very few people turned up, so I decided to find out why people did not come to our office, although it was clear to me that there was great need of our service.

My first reference place was the Tel-Aviv welfare agency, where I asked for addresses of parents of retarded children, who had applied once and never returned. I must say that my colleagues "appreciated" my efforts, but I had the feeling that the moment I left the room they mocked the crazy social worker who had just left. The first visits to very lonely and destitute parents were in fact the corner-stone to a growing contact and professional relationship with the parents. I had the feeling that they were waiting for me. They were ready to talk over their problems as long as I came as a friend who wanted to understand them. At my first visit, I announced myself as a member of the new parents association, because of my feeling that they would reject everything connected with social work. There were some who refused to talk to me at all, but I left the office's address everywhere and some of them appeared later. This showed me that although the first reaction was complete rejection, after thinking the problem through, parents realized that AKIM, being a parents' association, would be able to understand and help them. I found myself in odd situations. Sometimes I spoke with both parents, many times only one appeared without the knowledge of the other, and sometimes brothers or neighbours came to inform us about a certain case but forbade me to mention the source of information. Shame, a deep feeling of guilt and the impulse to run away from the fact, prevented many of the parents from turning to us. They were also afraid that being a member of AKIM would put a label on the whole family. There were parents who consulted me and were willing to talk freely about their problems, under the condition that I would not open a file.

It is through these parents that I first came into contact with professional or semi-professional existing services, hitherto unknown to me. I managed to interest in our work such persons who had, at one time or another, dealt with the problems of, or the services for the retarded. It is through my contact with parents that I learned of other associations such as ours abroad, of existing medical and educational experiments in Israel and elsewhere. In fact, the parents proved through their own individual experiences in search of solutions to be an invaluable source of information.

Bridging the Gap Between Families and Agencies

At that time, there was no special department in the Ministry of Welfare which dealt with the problems of retardation, and we could therefore not apply to them for information. Existing local welfare agencies dealt mainly with the financial aspects of placing a child in an institution. They did not develop educational and rehabilitation services. People of the middle class, not being welfare cases, had no address to turn to and found in our counselling the badly needed guidance, help and understanding. These parents were especially sensitive about everything connected with their child's problem, but would not appeal to any of the other existing services, lest they be considered "social cases." AKIM gradually became the intermediate link between families and the social agencies, where governmental or institutional help was needed. Many a parent preferred to go without help rather than be considered a "social case." As a result of constant contacts with various government bodies, and social educational agencies, AKIM became a well-known and recognized factor in the field of mental retardation. Furthermore, being aware of AKIM's work and professional services, many social agencies referred to AKIM cases known to them already, for counselling. AKIM's social workers in the meantime had the opportunity to become more specialized, dealing only with the problems of mental retardation, than their colleagues in other agencies which accepted work with all kinds of social problems.

As our case load grew and our contact established with various government and municipal bodies became more regular, we felt ready to use the data collected, in order to plan AKIM services. Our principle in planning was to establish demonstration projects in cooperation with local and national bodies.

The First Task: A Sheltered Workshop

Due to the lack of any service for older adolescents (with the exception of the small weaving workshop started in 1954 by the Jerusalem Branch) AKIM's first priority was to put up a sheltered workshop in Tel-Aviv, a combined project with the Tel-Aviv Municipality and the Ministry of Labour. This was the first time the Ministry of Labour recognized the training capacity of the mentally retarded and the function of a sheltered workshop as a formal vocational training centre, a recognition which was of a tremendous importance to us, certainly not less than the material help it accorded.

Life in our workshop naturally brought closer contact with parents of trainees and in addition to individual counselling, regular parents' meetings started taking place. Parent education became an integral part of our work. This was an instance where we reached parents through their children, and not vice-versa.

The workshop became our show-piece and enabled us to launch a publicity campaign, even though on a narrow scale. This campaign brought forth financial help, as well as the awareness of more parents and cooperation of professional workers, who had hitherto not known much about rehabilitation possibilities in mental retardation. The sheltered workshop, being situated in the middle of town, helped our neighbours to get to know us. We, on the other hand, had to teach them how to treat us. We went so far as visiting neighbouring schools, trying to make both the normal children and their teachers understand our specific problems. This also gave us the push to start a country-wide public education campaign, starting with a short 3-minute film on the workshop and counselling services of AKIM. With the increase of members throughout the country, we opened new branches, and with the continuing generous contribution of *Malben*, the Israeli agency of the American Joint Distribution Committee, who have followed our work with consistent interest, we were able to employ more social workers, thus expanding our social work staff. These new social workers discovered new cases and new needs and fought for improved and new services. Under pressure from our new branches (at present there are 9) we opened more training workshops and a kindergarten, which after two years was officially recognized by the Ministry of Education.

Our most recent enterprise is a new day center for preschool children in Jerusalem, a joint project of AKIM, the Henrietta Szold Research Institute, the Jerusalem Municipality and the Hadassah Medical Centre.

All children benefiting from AKIM facilities are carefully screened by screening committees, headed by AKIM social workers, and attended by at least a doctor, psychologist and social worker of the local agency.

It is interesting to note that, by participation in the screening committees, these specialists become involved with the problems of our daily work, thus enlarging the circle of our professional friends so badly needed.

A specific Israeli problem is the retarded child in the kibbutz, due to the special and unique setting of its social structure. Despite excellent educational services extended by the kibbutz for its children, a retarded child in this setting can be a more difficult problem to handle than the one in an ordinary family setting. For this reason, the kibbutz health and education services make great efforts in the field of mental retardation and were gratified to be able to take advantage of our services.

AKIM's National Role

The increase in members and the success of rehabilitation projects have established AKIM as a well-known and respected organization. AKIM has achieved the status of a body to be accounted with, and in some cases we even managed to be received by parliamentary bodies for special hearings preceding general debates. We use this status in order to promote legislation and safeguard the rights of the retardates and their families. It is through the social workers that the management of AKIM obtained specific data on shortcomings and special needs of services for the retarded, and because of a need for cooperation among the various Ministries, AKIM pressed for the establishment of the National Council for the Mentally Retarded. In this coordinating body are represented the Ministries of Social Welfare, Justice, Labour, Education and Health, and also AKIM, and through its functioning we hope to fill in the gaps existing today in the programme for the retarded.

In fact, a great many of AKIM's projects have been initiated by its social workers, who have strongly influenced the organization's policy. This influence is felt not only within our organization, but also in every new project erected for the benefit of the retarded, by municipal or government agencies. All public agencies include AKIM's social workers in their planning committees and there exist today various sheltered workshops or other institutions in Israel, which were initiated by AKIM and later on taken over by local official bodies. This is our aim, although we do not succeed in turning over our projects to the responsible public bodies in every case. Thanks to high professional standards, AKIM succeeded in establishing contacts with the U.S. Vocational Rehabilitation Administration in Washington, and was awarded a grant for a research project on rehabilitation of low-grade retardates in agriculture.

Today, we are six social workers in the services of AKIM, although the expansion of our activities requires more social service. However, I am confident that none of us, no matter how hard is the work under constant stress and lack of facilities, would dream of changing our job for an easier one. Not being bound by "red tape" and being allowed to use our own initiative and imagination, as well as the personal contact with the parents, children and governing bodies of AKIM, makes the social worker who is employed by a parents' association like AKIM feel an integral part of its growth and achievements. This feeling of constant constructive building is the most gratifying reward and gives us strength to overcome many difficult situations and obstacles, as well as incentive to carry on with our task.

Guardianship for the Mentally Retarded

MICHAEL J. BEGAB AND HARRIET L. GOLDBERG

Parents of normal children generally can look forward to the time when their children will achieve some measure of financial security and social prestige. For many of the retarded, however, in spite of the considerable expansion of educational and training resources that has taken place in recent years, there are still unattainable goals. For those among the retarded who are chronically dependent or semidependent persons, a lifetime plan of guidance, care, and supervision is needed.

The trend toward keeping mentally retarded children in their own homes and integrating them wherever possible into community programs and functions has focused attention on the need for long-range planning for them. Many parents have demonstrated remarkable ingenuity and adaptability in meeting the immediate needs of such children. Yet even among the most adequate parents, today's successes are often marred by tomorrow's uncertainties. "Who will look after my retarded child's interests when I am gone and can no longer do so myself?"

The deep concern and anxiety reflected in this oft repeated question is well founded. Parents of retarded children—perhaps better than anyone else—fully realize the self-sacrifice and dedication often entailed in their care. When because of parental effort, the retarded child is happy, content, well-adjusted, and in many ways a contributing member to family and community life, the parents are apt to be reluctant to accept institutional care as the ultimate living arrangement for him. They cannot expect, nor indeed are many willing, to burden other members of the family with the often trying responsibilities of caring for and supervising a retarded adult. They hesitate to seek the assistance of friends for this purpose and fear that strangers may lack understanding of what their children need and how these needs may be fulfilled.

With advances in the medical sciences, the survival rate of damaged infants has been increased and their life expectancy prolonged. More and more, parents are faced with the likelihood that their retarded children will survive them. With ma-

From *Children*, Vol. 9, No. 1 (January-February, 1962), pp. 21-25. By permission Michael J. Begab and The Children's Bureau.

chines displacing men from jobs and many families moving from one community to another, life in our society has become more complex. These changes sorely tax the capacities of the handicapped adult for independent functioning and social usefulness.

These developments have brought into sharp focus the need to re-examine existing measures for safeguarding and promoting the welfare of the retarded in case of parental death, disablement, or inadequacy.

Sometimes the need for guardianship stems not only from the incapacities of the retarded person, but from the inadequacies of his parents who are still living. In some cases, parents are unable to meet the physical, emotional, or behavioral problems of their retarded child and are unresponsive to professional efforts to help them. Where these conditions prevail, society, through its established agencies and social institutions, has a responsibility to protect the child's interests and rights and to provide opportunities wherein he may develop to his fullest potentialities. Though the legal rights of children may vary within States, this fundamental value in our culture is an inherent part of our social system as it is expressed in our customs and in our laws.

Current practice in relation to guardianship and the concepts and philosophy underlying these practices vary greatly. A few States encourage guardianship arrangements under public welfare departments for all retarded persons, whatever the family's status and capacities and the individual's living arrangements. Most widespread, however, is the practice of vesting legal custody and sometimes guardianship responsibilities for the retarded in the superintendents of State institutions, but only for those persons who have been admitted to the institutions—approximately 4 percent of the mentally retarded population. Unfortunately, many families with retarded children at home, who do not plan for institutional placement, do not recognize the need for future guardianship arrangements.

Complexities in the present systems of guardianship are thus formidable obstacles in the long range planning many retarded persons need. Happily, the National Association for Retarded Children and its State and local affiliates are actively exploring different ways of planning for the future of the retarded. It has already launched upon a group insurance program. Among other techniques being considered are arrangements for guardianship.

Forms of Guardianship

The needs of the mentally retarded for protection have long been recognized in the legal systems of many countries and in all the States of the United States, and various methods have been developed to safeguard their welfare and protect their financial and personal interests. Traditionally they have been grouped with the mentally ill and with minors as being mentally incompetent to conduct their own affairs or to perform adult functions such as making wills or conducting litigation.

Various forms of guardianship have been utilized in efforts to promote their interests. These are of four kinds: guardians of the person; guardians of the property; general guardians (of person and property); and guardians *ad litem*, appointed solely in connection with court actions.[1]

In the main, there are relatively few instances of considerable property belonging to the mentally retarded just as there are in the population at large. Usually, the need for guardianship exists more in the area of personal concern and interest in their well-being than in relation to property. Therefore, the appointment of general guardians should probably be made more frequently than separate guardians of the person and of the property for the same individuals. A general guardian could well exercise the necessary fiscal care of moderate amounts of property and at the same time evince the degree of personal interest and concern which is so vital to the welfare of the mentally retarded. In any event, the capacities of the mentally retarded person's natural guardians for this role should be considered paramount. Others should not be substituted for natural guardians during the natural guardians' lifetime unless they are unable to fulfill the responsibilities inherent in guardianship.

Parents are recognized as the natural guardians of their minor children and of their mentally retarded children who reach the age of adulthood and have been *adjudged* incompetent. However, the existence of mental defect in an adult, no matter how apparent, does not automatically confer guardianship responsibilities on his parents. Although in many instances, controversial issues regarding the management of the retarded adult or his estate are not apt to arise, it may be a wise precaution for parents to seek an adjudication of their child's incompetence while they are living. In this way arrangements for future guardianship can be expedited and continuous protection of the child assured.

This concept of the need for a continuation of the natural guardianship functions for the adult retarded child is expressed in provisions of revenue laws concerning dependency exemptions, in social security legislation, particularly regarding eligibility of handicapped dependents for social insurance benefits, and in decisions regarding medical and other forms of care.

Individual Need

Mentally retarded persons—by definition—lack the intelligence and social competency to manage their own affairs with ordinary prudence and judgment. Within this broad definition, however, the range of incapacity is great. A fairly large proportion of the mentally retarded are only identifiable as such and actually function on a defective level only during their school-age years when the expectations and demands of a normal life exceed their abilities. At the age of majority, many of them become self-supporting, and need guidance and supervision only when confronted with situations of serious social stress. For these persons, guardianship may not be necessary.

However, the more severely handicapped or the less socially adequate, lacking the capacity to act for themselves, need someone who can act in their behalf. Whatever their chronological age, they cannot be expected to behave responsibly in certain situations, to negotiate contracts, or to be liable for their misdeeds—especially in instances where they lack the intelligence to distinguish right from wrong. Even as adults they need social and legal protection against exploitation and also personal guidance toward social adjustment and training.

Retarded persons whose intellectual deficits stem primarily from social and cultural factors often differ markedly from persons who are retarded from other causes in many respects and have a greater capacity for self-direction and self-maintenance as adults. Hence the need for guardianship provisions in these cases is not always apparent. The need should be determined by careful interdisciplinary evaluation and subjected to periodic review, not only of the retarded person's capacity for self-reliance but of the environmental circumstances which may have dictated the need for guardianship in the first place.

Functions and Responsibilities

Much confusion exists in the public mind regarding the functions and responsibilities of legal guardians and how they differ from those of parents. For this reason, some parents hesitate to plan for such arrangements, and at times persons who could be potential guardians are somewhat reluctant to act in this capacity.

In many respects, guardianship and parenthood carry similar responsibilities.[1] Like the parent, the guardian becomes responsible for the care, custody, and control of the child. He is entrusted with authority to make important decisions regarding the well-being of his ward that may affect the individual's whole life. These decisions may involve medical care, employment, consent to marriage, and entry into the armed forces—all of which may be considerations for many of the retarded and problems about which they cannot be expected to exercise sound judgment.

Judicially appointed guardians, on the other hand, are subject to certain limitations to which parents are not subject. These stem from various legal aspects of guardianship. Guardianship—where minority is the basis for appointment—automatically terminates when the child attains his majority. This does not apply in cases based upon mental incompetency. In any case, while the guardianship is in force, the relationship is subject to continuing supervision and review by the court. The wide discretionary powers of the guardian are, in contrast to those of parents, exercised under court direction—at least in theory.

Aids in Planning

Planning for care, education, and treatment, or regulating behavior of the mentally retarded is often complicated by lack of resources and facilities, negative social attitudes, or limited opportunities. In many other instances, the most suitable plan for a retarded ward cannot be carried out because of very limited or totally unavailable financial assets. The guardian has no duty to support and educate the ward except from the ward's own estate, nor does he have any right to the ward's earnings and services.

Guardians cannot always be expected to have the special knowledge to handle effectively the sometimes complex situations involved in the care of a handicapped person. However, they can be helped to discharge their responsibilities toward a retarded ward more effectively when the supervision of the court is supplemented with skilled social services, competent advice, adequate safeguards of the ward's interest, and a plan suited to his special needs.

State laws generally define the conditions relating to the value and kind of property under which a guardian of property must be appointed to hold a fiduciary relationship to the ward. At times, the same person is appointed to act as guardian of the person and estate and is thus called a general guardian. Though this is often a highly desirable practice, where the property involved is not extensive, clarification is essential as to the respective powers and duties of each office. The guardian of the property's activities are confined primarily to the "prudent and economical management" of the estate entrusted to him and these activities are subject to court direction and periodic accounting to the court.

As fiscal responsibilities are better understood, especially as social insurance programs are expanded with wider coverage and larger benefits, parents may become more conscious of the various alternatives available to them in long-range planning for their retarded child. Already, as noted earlier, extensive efforts have been undertaken by parents' associations to familarize their membership with group life insurance plans and other techniques for the future care and support of their retarded offspring.

Guardianship of mentally retarded children and adults then, particularly in the assumption of certain parental functions, is a weighty responsibility. It is incumbent upon the courts therefore, and upon the parents who may designate their choice of guardians through last will and testament, to use the best judgment in their selections. Equally important, such appointments call for the availability of skilled social services to the court and guardian.

What happens when both parents die and no provision has been made for guardianship? Much will depend on the age and capacities of the retarded person himself. However, even the obviously retarded person who needs someone to protect his interests is not likely to come to court attention unless an action for dependency or institutional commitment or probate of an estate is initiated. These actions do not ensure that a guardian of the person will be appointed. Therefore, when a retarded person is bereft of his parents it is important that relatives, friends, neighbors, or others concerned with his welfare petition the court to appoint a guardian who will have responsibility for him. Where the welfare of the retarded person is in jeopardy, the public welfare agency has a responsibility for initiating the necessary protective measures, of which guardianship may be a crucial component.

Properly used, the guardian-ward relationship can serve to establish an atmosphere of affection, security, and recognition for the retarded person and contribute to his social growth and development.

Institutional Guardians

As already mentioned, in certain sections of the country it has become customary to replace natural guardians of the mentally retarded with institutional superintendents appointed to serve as guardians for those persons who are involuntarily committed by courts to institutions. Even in many instances of voluntary admissions, such guardians are appointed. The rationale behind such appointments, or the appointment of State welfare directors as guardians of noninstitutionalized persons, is that the appointees can make necessary decisions and promote the interests of their wards.

In practice these systems of public guardianship tend to become routine and stereotyped. The individual is easily lost sight of in these large-scale guardianship systems which are apt to become bookkeeping arrangements rather than socially significant efforts to aid the mentally retarded. Where a single guardian is responsible for hundreds or thousands of retarded persons, he cannot be expected to keep abreast of the individual's changing circumstances and needs. Often whatever action is taken is in response to emergencies or situations of stress, rather than to a positive plan for meeting anticipated needs. Furthermore, complicated legal and supervisory problems may arise when the retarded person is transferred from the institution to some other facility or is returned to the community on family or work placement. These are additional arguments for a one-to-one guardianship arrangement.

Moreover, the appointment of guardians, when parents would like to continue exercising their full responsibility and have demonstrated capacity to do so, is often a disservice to the retarded persons and to the parents themselves. In effect, the parents of children with institutional or State guardians are, or can be, precluded from manifesting a substantial interest in the welfare of these children in regard to many areas of life planning—placement in and release from foster care, special medical service, marriage. This exclusion of the parent militates against a strengthening of the natural ties between institutionalized persons and their families. Such an involuntary estrangement can weaken family relationships and impede the ultimate return of the mentally retarded person into family living. Hence the guardianship can result in a prolongation of the very problems the court action sought to alleviate.

Then too, when public guardians are appointed society is lulled into the belief that all the interests of the retarded are being protected, whereas in reality in many cases only a modicum of protection is afforded.

One of the objectives of guardianship for persons in institutional care, whether this be undertaken by a public guardian or a private citizen, is to facilitate their rehabilitation and return to community life. This objective is interfered with when commitment is accompanied by real or presumed loss of the retarded person's civil rights.

Recruitment and Termination

Guardians for the mentally retarded can be recruited by utilizing the specific interests of various groups of people. One of the principal sources might well be organizations of parents of the retarded where there is a common concern and background of meaningful experience in dealing with the mentally retarded. Many of the members might be encouraged to function productively as guardians. Such parents, particularly those who have resolved their personal conflicts about having a retarded child, possess a unique understanding, sympathy, and feeling for the mentally retarded. Consequently, they could bring to bear a sympathetic interest which could not be duplicated easily by others.

Local bar associations might be another source of recruitment. The legal training and experience of members of the bar would be a valuable asset in a guardian. Moreover, having bar association members act in this capacity should enhance the interest of these organizations in the retarded.

Another recruitment source might be service groups—men's clubs, women's clubs, civic organizations, and the like. Many such groups are already actively engaged in volunteer work with the retarded and in the sponsorship of social and recreational programs.

An essential component in the productive functioning of guardians appointed from such sources would be cooperation beween them and social service agencies within the community. By pooling their understanding of the mentally retarded, by joint planning, by interpretation of special problems and needs, they could accomplish much for the welfare not only of the mentally retarded but of the entire community. Local social agencies would seem to have a particular obligation to help recruit such guardians and to give them guidance and stimulus in their efforts.

Sometimes guardians appointed for the mentally retarded continue on long after the need for such guardianship has disappeared, as , for example, when the retarded person has achieved a degree of social competency where he can reasonably manage his own affairs. Thought should be given to arranging for a periodic review of guardianships in relation to individual circumstances and with regard to the manner in which the duties are carried out. As soon as it is shown that a person can function adequately without guardianship, the arrangement should be terminated. Where the responsibilities of guardianship are not being competently discharged, a successor guardian should be appointed. Generally, courts are required to supervise the activities of judicially appointed guardians. However, the extent to which supervision is exercised and the methods employed vary considerably. There is reason to believe that in practice there is more supervision of guardians of property than of guardians of the person. The vital role of the latter warrants greater community effort and concern in promoting the best possible safeguards.

Legislative Suggestions

It is perhaps time for States to review their laws and administrative practices regarding guardianship and other provisions for the mentally retarded. This can be done by the use of statewide citizens' committees charged with specific responsibilities for both study and report to the State legislature. Many statutory provisions need reexamination in the light of modern developments in psychology, social services, medicine, and other fields.

In such reviews special attention should be given to the clarification of judicial and administrative functions in respect to the mentally retarded and to the provision of services and legal protections which will improve the condition of mentally retarded individuals and promote their well-being.

Reference

[1]Weissman, Irving (in association with Laura Stolzenberg, Harry S. Moore, Jr., and Robbie W. Patterson): Guardianship; a way of fulfilling public responsibility for children. Federal Security Agency, Social Security Administration, Children's Bureau. C.B. Pub. No. 330. 1949.

SEVENTY-EIGHT

The Need for Protective Services for the Mentally Retarded and Others with Serious Long-Term Disabilities

ELIZABETH M. BOGGS

Since the Middle Ages, "fools" and "idiots," as well as children, have been entitled to the special protection of the king and his successors in government. One is inclined to conclude, however, that there has been little progress, either in concept or practice, in the last 800 years. Indeed, the rise of the ideal of individual rights with its resultant limitations on the authority of government to intervene in personal and family affairs has probably impeded the proper implementation of the principle of "parens patriae" in the case of those who do not have the capacity to bespeak their own cause and to seek their own best interests.

In the first century of the American republic little attention was given to this issue as it affects children, and even less to "fools and idiots." Indeed provisions affecting the mentally disabled were directed more toward "protection" of the public than of the person disabled. A "cause celebre" of child abuse in 1875 became the point of origin of today's child protective services in the United States. It is significant that its first development took the form of delegation of police powers to private agencies, which were thus more fully franchised than public child welfare agencies in the affected states, a situation which persists today in New Jersey and a few other eastern jurisdictions.

In the modern idiom, protective services are social services directed toward the welfare of individuals who are not fully able to act for themselves, by an organized social agency which has the capacity to invoke legal sanctions to reinforce its efforts on behalf of the client. These concepts are currently most often discussed either in relation to children or in relation to older people. Child protective services today are most likely to focus on protecting children from neglect or abuse by their parents; the legal sanction needed relates to the right to intervene in the parent-child relationship, a relationship privileged under most laws. Discussions of protective services for older people focus on intervention in the presumptive right of the adult to self determination. The increase in the number of older people and the changes in conditions of life for the "extended family" have created more extensive prob-

Reprinted from *Proceedings, Conference on Protective Supervision and Services for the Handicapped* (New York, United Cerebral Palsy Associations of America, 1966), pp. 17-23. By permission of the author and the Associations.

lems of protection for persons with failing mental and physical capacities, problems which are increasingly a legitimate subject of social concern.

Mentally retarded and handicapped children may need protective services for the same reasons as other children, and protective legislation which is sound for other children will usually be sound for them also, even though the specific service needs may be different. Disabled adults and especially mentally retarded adults, on the other hand, present problems more like those of the elderly, problems which are much discussed but far from resolved in social welfare circles today. Social disability may be mild, requiring support and good counsel, but scarcely warranting legal differentiation, or it may be serious, in which case failure to intervene may itself constitute social neglect, or it may be in the perplexing intermediate area which invites an attitude of laissez faire—until a crisis arises.

Recently the New Jersey Association for Retarded Children was advised by the county prosecutor's office of such a crisis, involving a young woman we shall call Ann Brown. Nine years ago at the age of 12 she had been placed by the state child welfare agency with foster parents, Mr. and Mrs. Smith, in a rural area. She is known to be mentally retarded, and since leaving school had been working at a sheltered workshop for the handicapped in her county. A few months ago Sid Jones, a man in his mid seventies, of dubious reputation in the area, began paying Ann unwanted attentions, Mrs. Smith reported to the police when, on a recent Sunday while the Smiths were attending church, Jones came to their house and took Ann with him to his trailer in a trailer camp some miles away. Approaches to Jones' trailer had met with threats from him based on his right to privacy and to freedom from intrusion into his dwelling, claims which the police felt bound to respect.

The State Bureau of Children's Services, which had placed Ann with the Smiths, was notified. They apologized for their own oversight in not having terminated service on Ann's 21st birthday, announced that they had no jurisdiction, would drop Ann from their roles and discontinue payments to Mrs. Smith.

NJARC, through counsel, was forced to inform the chief of detectives that, not being a protective agency, they were powerless to act and could only advise the Smiths (who had expressed an interest in continuing to care for the young woman) that they might institute proceedings to have her declared incompetent and placed under their guardianship. This process (even if it had succeeded) would have cost several hundred dollars and a lot of red tape, not to mention a physical examination of the subject, which could not be obtained under the circumstance.

The State Division of Mental Retardation considered itself powerless to take any steps since mental retardation has not yet been formally established. They did make it clear that, once the incident was over, they would entertain an application from Ann (or her guardian if one were appointed) for admission to their services, which could include a family care placement with the Smiths.

Clearly, in this case, protection for an adult retardate is presumtively needed and is not forthcoming, although New Jersey's laws, had they been invoked earlier, might have provided a basis for action. If Ann had been receiving services from the Division before the incident, there would have been an administrative determination as to whether as an adult she should be considered capable of making her own decisions (in which case her present situation would be the same as that of any other young woman) or whether she should be considered "mentally deficient," i.e. in need of further supervision because of lack of capacity to manage her own life in her own interest. In the latter case she would have been eligible for "guardianship services" from the Division, who thereby would have retained a right and obligation to regain custody. Such rescue action, if taken, would constitute exercise of a protective service.

It is easy to be misled from the main issues by the specifics of this case. For example, sexual exploitation may seem the issue, yet the young adult retardate is vulnerable to other kinds of exploitation. Instead of BCS, let us imagine that the state employment agency had secured the girl a job as a live-in domestic and that the employer overworked and underpaid her. Being retarded, she might well not have known how to quit or secure redress. Similarly it is easy to blame the BCS for not coordinating with the Division of Mental Retardation, but how many natural parents with retarded adult children at home have taken the necessary steps to have their need for protection formally established before an adverse event precipitates a crisis? No protective agency can intervene on behalf of one who has not been clearly identified as a member of its target group.

What powers and duties should be assigned to a protective agency for disabled adults, including those who are mentally incompetent, in fact if not in law?

Basically such an agency should be authorized and professionally staffed to:

1. offer continuous advice and counsel on a casework basis to its primary clients and those who immediately affect the lives of these clients (relatives, employers, landladies, insurance agents, federal social security personnel, local police and firemen, visiting nurses, etc.)

2. engage in active case management including mobilization of community resources, (engage the homemaker, find and call the doctor, file the social security application, locate a more suitable apartment, enlist the "friendly visitor," arrange transportation to the social group, secure an attorney, etc. etc.—all of which can be accomplished with the acquiescence of a legally competent client as well as for a ward).

3. maintain continuing case contact and case records, under provisions for confidentiality which protect the interest of the client.

4. seek any necessary legal sanctions (apply for an order of commitment, or for legal custody, initiate an incompetency proceeding, petition for the recall of an inadequate guardian, etc.)

5. assume and conscientiously exercise the functions of a legal surrogate or personal guardian when so designated by a court or as otherwise provided by law.

In order to perform its functions effectively the protective agency must have authority to inspect and license or approve institutions, boarding homes, foster homes, family care homes and day care facilities which serve its clientele within the state, under any auspices, or be supported by another agency with such an authority. It should also have fairly broad authority to petition the court for redress of any wrong to any of its clients even though the agency itself may not be the guardian or attorney for the client.

As a rule the protective agency should be administratively separate from agencies rendering direct care and treatment services.

Although in theory the enumerated functions and powers could be granted by law to private voluntary agencies, history in the child welfare field suggests that, in the last analysis, such authority must be vested at least concurrently, if not exclusively, in a public agency or state wide network of agencies accountable to the State. This does not preclude active collaboration by voluntary and private organizations. Their services should be among the community resources which the protective agency may seek to mobilize for its clients. But since the private agency by its very nature must reserve the right to limit its clientele, ultimate legal responsibility for seeing that service is rendered and interests protected should be vested where accountability can be insisted upon. It is significant that one of the most promising supplementary protective activities of a voluntary nature, the MARC Retardate Trust, specifically excludes the assumption of guardianship or direct legal responsibility for the individual client or "participant." It wisely does not attempt to assume a role beyond its resources or powers.

The majority of state child welfare agencies now have protective authority which covers most, if not all, these points in relation to children. Few states have agencies which approach these objectives for the aged or mentally retarded or other disabled adults except for those who have been committed to mental institutions, and to a partial extent, for the blind. Thereby hangs our dilemma in the modern world of "community services" for the mentally retarded and neurologically disabled.

Manning such agencies for the adult disabled is and will remain difficult but we have some idea of where to begin. Obtaining the general legal authority to act aggressively on behalf of the client in the absence of some sort of legally established guardianship relationship may be more difficult. Public guardianship or supervision of those with no more than modest funds and without suitable private guardians can be made acceptable as a concept, especially where it can be interpreted as providing supervision without the cost of full institutionalization, formerly the only alternative. Nevertheless we are still hung up on the issue of how much "due process" we should require ourselves to invoke before assuming major control over the life of another adult American citizen who is in fact not able to assert his own rights even in opposition to our own presumably benign direction.

Some states, however, rely quite heavily on the "no protest" principle; as long as the adult does not fight back, he can be bossed around, told where to live and what to eat, paid less than a minimum wage, and required to save whatever he may have earned. This can happen, for example, when a child, accepted for care in a center, or residential institution, without ceremony, is continued under care, custody and control (whether in residence or in community placement) until he dies of old age. He has, in effect, been placed under guardianship without benefit of "due process." Other states observe some distasteful formalities of "court commitment" to institutions, and hence to custody of the superintendent, but they are simple, perfunctory and speedy procedures indeed as compared with what is required to go in the front door to establish guardianship of the person.

The general problem of placing a person who is, in fact, incapable of self direction in the legal position where we can treat him, manage him, control him and protect him without his informed consent and yet avoid overwhelming our courts with the lengthy and costly proceedings which they now demand in connection with "guardianship" is one with which leaders in the welfare field generally (and particularly those working with the aging) have become increasingly concerned in the recent years. The study on *Guardianship and Protective Services for Older People* published by the National Council on Aging is commended as a succinct review of the dilemmas. The issue has been brought to a head in part by the extension of the Social Security system and by the large number of elderly or incompetent people who have become entitled to small but regular monetary benefits of one sort or another.

To avoid the cumbersome business of having guardians appointed, procedures for agency selection of "representative payees" were established by the Veteran's Administration and the Social Security Administration. This in turn has led to misgivings about depriving beneficiaries of property without "due process." By contrast the states administering federally aided public assistance programs to the aged or adult disabled could (until '65) make payments on behalf of a client to another person only if that person had been "judicially appointed...as legal representative of such individual for the purpose of receiving and managing such payments (whether or not he is such individual's legal representative for other purposes)..." (Section 1111 of the Social Security Act). To comply with this requirement some states have enacted special "quickie" one-purpose guardianship laws which put the stamp of pro forma judicial approval on agency determinations.

Such special "guardianship" provisions are unsatisfactory for at least three reasons. First they can result in several people who are appointed independently each having a small piece of responsibility for the incapacitated person. Second the procedure itself, while fulfilling the formal requirements of "due process," actually mocks it; the court, of practical necessity, must go along with the agency in most cases, yet it is the court rather than the agency that accepts responsibility. Thirdly, even such perfunctory proceedings clutter up a court calendar.

Accordingly still another approach was attempted in the 1965 "Medicare" act. All public assistance titles were amended to specify other conditions under which "protective payments" may be made to someone "who is interested and concerned with the welfare of the needy individual" when the recipient is unable to manage his funds. These conditions include:

1. determination by the State agency administering the public assistance that payments directly to the needy individual would be contrary to his welfare
2. opportunity for a fair hearing on such determination
3. periodic review of the need for protective payments with resort to formal court

appointment of a guardian or legal representative if this more nearly serves the interests of the recipient

4. continuing efforts to bring the recipient to a point where he can manage his own assistance payments.

The language paraphrased above (from Sections 406, 1006, 1406, and 1606 of the Social Security Act) has obviously been designed to provide the minimum formality which is consistent with Constitutional guarantees of "due process." It parallels the precedents set in recent years by many regulatory agencies where administrative decisions by review panels and boards after a hearing are considered to respect "due process" and to have the force and effect of a judicial finding unless appealed to a court.

Perhaps this provides us with a precedent for resolving the dilemma of "due process" in connection with the designation of private individuals or protective agencies to perform guardianship functions for incapacitated adults. An expert panel of three, say (perhaps with one or more having backgrounds in the law and social work or psychology) charged with responsibility to review independently evidence offered by a suitable evaluation team might well provide better de facto protection than any now available through the courts.

By affording an opportunity to all interested parties to appear and be heard with a right of appeal to an appropriate court, these cases could be handled in situ more expeditiously, more economically, and more perceptively than under present traditional methods. It should be possible for applications to be made on behalf of the incapacitated adult by an interested person, without cost to the applicant; it should be the duty of the protective agency to apply when one of their clients or prospective clients requires it. Each state must shortly conform to some such procedure with respect to the incapacitated aged and adult disabled if the state is to retain full federal aid under the categorical assistance titles. Professionalizing this service and extending it to those needing protective services for reasons other than eligibility for public assistance may prove both practical and just.

Determination of disability in adults as a basis for eligibility for services or for income maintenance is assuming increasing importance. It is not reasonable to permit a multiplicity of agencies each to establish its own machinery and criteria and bring them each to bear independently on the same unhappy people. There are at least three functional levels at which disability is significant in establishing the rights of the individual or his need for protection. Inability to manage a large estate may justify appointment of a conservator or guardian of the property without control over the person. Inability to engage in substantial gainful employment as a result of disability may entitle the individual to social security benefits and/or disability assistance payments, and there is talk of income tax exemption for this group also. Inability to manage the money needed for one's day to day expenses represents a more serious degree of disability which is closely related to need for protective services for the person, since the individual or agency who controls the spending of money for daily living does, in fact, control the choice of "living space" for the incapacitated person.

It is suggested that, for various practical reasons, traditional guardianship procedures be retained with respect to the management of capital funds requiring investment, or large incomes,—say in excess of $5,000 annually. Persons in this position should be eligible for public or private guardianship of their persons, if needed, but the management of their property should be vested in suitable private fiduciaries.

For the large and increasing number of disabled persons for whom more modest sums can be made available, whether from social security, public assistance, pensions, trust income, insurance benefits or public or private sources, it is suggested that a consolidated publicly administered system of determination of disability or incapacity be developed, based on the general principles now proposed for public assistance for the permanently and totally disabled. This already involves among other things, coordination with determination of eligibility for vocational rehabilitation where the issue is ability to work. The same review board which would determine inability to work should also have responsibility for making a separate determination as to the need for protective supervision—i.e. protective payments expressly combined with a degree of control over the critical decisions which must be made on behalf of the individual as to living arrangements, medical care, daily activity, etc. As part of this process of determination the review body should also determine in each case whether protective supervision, if needed, should be exercised by a designated private individual or by an agency through a case worker. The proposed review board would be classed as an administrative agency with the duty of clarifying the entitlements and status of individuals under any one of several public income maintenance, protective or other special service programs. As such it would serve the agencies as well as their clients but it would be directly accountable to no one of them. Each agency would have the responsibility to present information bearing on the needs and rights of its clients for assessment by the board.

The situation is fluid at present because states are still adjusting to the 1965 federal amendments and will shortly be faced with new concepts based on the proposals of the National Advisory Council on Public Welfare, which have just been released. The voluntary organizations concerned with the total well being of the disabled obviously have a responsibility to view the various federal, state, and private roles and programs in relation to one another and to propose intelligent well integrated solutions.

The development of two distinct but related public functions is proposed:

1. a consolidated system for review and determination of the rights of disabled individuals, and
2. state systems of protective services for those with long term disabilities which are socially incapacitating.

These appear to be timely objectives for combined action by appropriate national voluntary health and welfare organizations, such as United Cerebral Palsy and the National Association for Retarded Children.

Introducing Institutionalized Retardates to the Community

JOSEPH J. PARNICKY AND LEONARD N. BROWN

The period of transition from institutional to community living has long been recognized by practitioners in the field of mental retardation as a time of special stress and adjustment. The incidence of and reasons for readmission have pointed up the institutionalized retardate's need for social competence and community acceptance. These impressions from practice have been affirmed in follow-up research. In a comprehensive survey of studies reported on by Windle, Stewart, and Brown, the chief reason for community failure of subnormals released from institutions was given as difficulties of interpersonal relationship.[1] Gunzburg further substantiates the need to prepare the retardate more adequately in social skills, stating they may need more help in this area than in vocational training.[2]

The impressions at the Johnstone Training and Research Center, Bordentown, New Jersey, drawn from individual case reviews and surveys of students returning from community placement, point up similar needs and difficulties. Cohen reported that for the most part the reasons for students' return to institutions were social rather than vocational. These included lack of judgment with regard to social norms, poor attitude on the job, lack of readiness for employment or difficulty in adjustment, and severe problems at home. Besides these factors, it was also noted that the stigma-rejection pattern in the community toward the institutionalized retardate presented barriers to acceptance that intensified the problems of adjustment.[3]

In a recent statement by the Vocational Rehabilitation Administration recognition is given to such findings, especially in its statement of the goal in rehabilitation of the mentally retarded as

> . . . to provide conditions and circumstances that permit the retarded person to perform the activities of daily life and to learn how to behave socially and vocationally in such a manner that he may compete successfully within that segment of his milieu that is within normal limits.[4]

Reprinted by permission of the authors and the National Association of Social Workers from *Social Work*, Vol. 9, No. 4 (January, 1964), pp. 79-85.

Providing Introductory Experiences

In order to achieve this goal institutional programs provide introductory experiences within the community, experiences with which the retardate can cope successfully and that are part of a progression leading to independent living off the institution grounds. One of the aspects of community life for which the retardate needs preparation is the varying degree of acceptance he may experience, including possible rejection and hostility. Disabilities are variously defined culturally and, since our society places a high premium on normality, retardation is unacceptable to many.

This is evident even within the social welfare services. In response to the handicap, the community may react by restricting the availability of community resources, which in turn may contribute further to the social disability of the retardate. When community services exist, they are often more segregated than is necessary and limit the handicapped person's interaction with the more normal population.[5]

From the point of view of the residential program, what is needed is a program of community reintegration *during* institutionalization so that the retardate can begin to develop positive community experiences with some planning according to his needs. The best place to develop and reinforce competence in social skills is within the community rather than the institution alone.[6] This can often best be accomplished through use of small groups. Collective group support can offer additional protection during the period of transition to the community. Current residential treatment programs are so focused on the individual that they may not deal with his group-related needs within and without the institution. Polsky, in analyzing an institution for adolescents with emotional problems, states:

> If the goal of therapy is re-integration of the individual into a rational cooperative human community, then we must concentrate on the social relationships in which the resident is integrated as well as on individual psychopathology.[7]

While the concept of using group service agencies for institutionalized retardates is new, these services have long been used successfully for released patients of psychiatric hospitals. Reporting on a resocialization project in Kansas, Morgan noted various gains in healthy functioning, including use of judgment, decision-making, and planning.[8] At the Fellowship Club in San Francisco—a therapeutic club for post-hospitalized psychiatric patients—meetings were held in a community center because it was felt that social integration could be more easily effected in a social rather than a clinical setting.[9] Individuals can test out a variety of roles in the group. This opportunity to find and restore social roles is consistent with Parsons' description of the therapeutic process. According to him, "The therapeutic process must always have as one dimension the restoration of capacity to play social roles in a normal way."[10]

Use of Community Group Services

As the Social Service Department of the Johnstone Center began to revise and extend its social rehabilitation program in response to the literature and clinical impressions, one development was to initiate co-operative relationships with community group service agencies so that groups of students might actually use community facilities during the period of their institutionalization. This kind of agency is associated with normality and in some measure represents community values. It was believed that through the feeling of belonging and acceptance within the semi-protection of the agency, which provides a means of identification with the community, it would be possible for the institutionalized retardate to reach out even further to less protected community experiences. The social group work method was utilized for this purpose, with the focus set on more healthy ego functioning.

Actually, the center has begun using community resources as a progression toward greater social participation in the community. Starting with selected community experiences for supervised groups of younger, less mature adolescents the program ultimately provides students with opportunities to visit the social agencies on their own. Those presently offered the latter experience are usually day workers in the community. Selection is made jointly by the social service and vocational staffs.

The center staff has been conscious that such experimentation requires frequent review and evaluation to provide information for further modifications and improvements. The development of this program was also perceived as an opportunity to add to the knowledge available from previous studies.

One facet of community experience essentially missing from the data reported in the literature is the first-hand reaction of the retardate to the experience of moving from the institution to the community. Believing this to be of critical import to postinstitutional adjustment, the center initiated an exploratory study with a focus on the question: "What are the perceptions expressed by institutionalized retardates as they face introductory experiences in the community?"

Procedure of the Study

Selected for this study, which was conducted during the summer of 1962, were eight young men ranging from 18 to 20. Intellectually they were in the mildly retarded or educable category. Years of institutionalization varied from five to eleven. All were in the final phase of residential training and were conscious that community placement was under consideration. Only one had previously been placed in the community and returned.

Data were gathered from group discussions held in eight weekly meetings at a local "Y." The students had earned their membership through a series of work projects or had paid for it out of earnings. The weekly visit to the "Y" included eating at the cafeteria, swimming, playing pool or ping-pong, and use of the gym. The last part of the evening was the group discussion, which was tape recorded and focused on their immediate reactions and adjustments to the agency and community.

The students were living through similar events, sharing their impressions, and using the social worker and the group in the process of working out adjustments to community living. An essential characteristic of the study is that reactions of the retardates were gathered during a phase of their adjustment to the community, rather than in retrospect or from secondary sources.

Since this was a preliminary, exploratory study, a rather simple approach was taken toward analysis of the content of the discussions. Topics that appeared with sufficient frequency to warrant tabulation are (1) the local YMCA, (2) job placements, (3) the community, (4) the residential institution, (5) the group as a whole or an individual member, and (6) themselves.

The range of topics approximated the authors' projections. There were, however, certain omissions, such as the topic of girls. Although the boys had typically adolescent interest in girls, they evidently did not think the subject was relative to the purpose of the group sessions. This suggests that although they were instructed that any topic of interest to them could be covered, they apparently did have some unstated conception of primary purpose. The topics indicated covered well over nine-tenths of the content of the discussions.

The verbatim recordings were reviewed and comments made pertaining to each topic were abstracted and listed as separate items. Each item was then judged on a three-point scale: positive, neutral, or negative.

Findings

A total of 267 comments were identified in the sessions pertaining to the topics listed. The most frequent topic was the group itself, which accounted for slightly over a third of the items. The frequency order of the other topics was self, YMCA, institution, job, and community. The last accounted for less than 7 percent of the comments. When the concentration of discussion topics was examined meeting by meeting, it was noted that the first session was focused primarily on the experience in the "Y." From then on the meetings centered most heavily on discussion related to the group itself.

With respect to the relative incidence of negative and positive comments, 67 percent were on the plus side. The most strongly positive topic was the "Y," which had a response of 90 percent. Next came self, rated as 75 percent positive. Comments about the community and the group were two-thirds positive. Falling below the mean were the job and the institution, with the latter having only 38 percent positive comments.

When the percentages of positive comments during the first four sessions were compared with those in the last four, differences were found according to topics. The comments relative to two topics became more positive: the "Y" from 84 percent to 100 percent and work from 50 percent to 71 percent. Positive comments about the "Y" were concentrated especially in the last session. Comments about the group itself became less positive during the latter half of the discussion, from 80 percent to 69 percent. There was no appreciable shift in comments about the community, the institution, or the self.

The statistical distributions of the subjects discussed are not the most critical findings of this study. The figures on frequency and the proportion of positive to negative expressions are not in any way to be construed as typical of what other institutionalized adolescents express under similar circumstances. To assure that such import would not be ascribed to these figures, the statistical analysis was purposely kept elementary, with no mathematical tests of significance applied.

The data obtained were based on a small, selected group. The staff of the center had reviewed the individuals carefully and had selected those who showed considerable "readiness" for community experiences. Moreover, the introductory work and social experiences were carefully planned and executed. Personnel at the "Y" and the job placements were well oriented to the nature of the individuals involved in the project, all of which undoubtedly tended to influence the positive results attained.

This must be weighed when the highly positive reactions of the group members are noted. There was an absence of any devastating community experiences such as are at times evident in the reports of individuals returning to institutions after placement. Moreover, there was little evidence of strongly negative attitudes toward any aspect of the community. Yet it is safe to say that more negative feelings toward community living (and the other topics) are present within the institution's population. It is reasonable to assume that greater differentiations may be obtained if the number of subjects is increased and the conditions are broadened. This should also afford an opportunity to test out hypothetical questions and predictive conditions in relation to successful community placement arising from practice and available studies.

Make Community Life Desirable

One set of hypotheses is suggested by the comparative reactions toward community and institution expressed by the group in this study. These results appear to have some relationship to experiences at the Johnstone Center, which are not unique to this setting. At times follow-up workers have commented that a student in the community *wants* to come back to the center. The preference for institutional life over community life on the part of some poses a programmatic problem for the field.

The authors believe the central solution lies in making community life more desirable (and desired) than institutional life, not in making the institution an undesirable, unhappy experience. The problem is how to help the residential student realize that life in the community can be rewarding, satisfying, and enjoyable even more than life under institutional conditions. There is a need to reduce the student's ignorance, fears, and anxieties about life in the community.

The exploratory study undertaken suggests that it may be possible to develop an index of readiness for community placement, or at least one aspect of such an index. This might enable testing of such hypotheses as "Readiness for community placement is achieved when reactions of individuals are more strongly positive toward off-campus living than on-campus living," and "Success in community placement is facilitated as positive attitudes toward community living are relatively stronger than those toward residential living."

In the present study, the reactions of the participating group were more frequently positive toward the community than the center. The quality of the reactions become evident when comments about the institution are examined for content. Negative feelings were on the order of "If you don't know something, they'll yell at you," and "They think we need someone to watch over us." This group, moreover, had an appreciation of the major objectives of the habilitation program of the center, as expressed in statements like, "The gold card is a way of training you," and "You learn about good manners in the dining room, the cottage, in class, in work [meaning vocational training]." Although this still needs validation, the authors would like to believe that this evidences a rather favorable state of readiness for placement—an appreciation of both negative and positive aspects of the residential program without finding it necessary to tear it down to make life in the community appear attractive.

Students' Comments

One topic not included in the earlier analysis was mental retardation. Actually this term was discussed only in the very first session. When the topic was raised the primary remark made by the boys was, "I was wondering what they thought about me." The group then concerned itself with whether or not they appeared mentally retarded to people in the community, and more particularly to others in the "Y." The conclusion was : "I don't think they thought we were mentally retarded because we certainly didn't show it." However, this was not said with great assurance. Actually, in this session the group *did* stand out considerably in the agency—in dress, manner, behavior, and compliance with procedures.

The basis on which they reassured themselves is contained in the following quotes from the session: "If we were mentally retarded we would be jumping around crazy." "A retarded person is someone who you can't trust." "If we were retarded they would always be watching us and standing around to see that we won't hurt ourselves."

From the position of assuring themselves that they could not possibly be so extremely deviant, they considered in later sessions two other points that had meaning in the process of becoming accustomed to community experiences: they examined how people behave in the community and they considered their own degree of competence. Their observations about persons in the community ranged from such generalities as "Everybody in the world makes a mistake," (IV)[11] to more specific identification of deficiencies, such as "There are plenty of people in this world that can't count money." (IV)

As for their own competence, the following remarks illustrate some of the changes: "I got excellent manners." (II) "They can't fire me, I'm a good worker." (II) "At least I prove to people I joined something [the "Y"] that's got some sense to it." (VII)

By the final session of this series they were no longer comparing themselves with the community at large. The content strongly affirmed that they were perceiving themselves as a part of the world outside the institution. In this regard they showed both an urge to move in wider circles as well as some appreciation of difficulties they might experience when placed in the community. The desire to go out further varied from a limited suggestion like, "We know the prices at the ["Y"] cafeteria. Let's try some new places," (V) to "Why can't we all get together ourselves and go to Atlantic City?" (V) As for their perception of what living on one's own could mean, here are two samples from the third session: "One problem I'm going to have is living in a room and paying money." "My trouble is going to be facing different people and getting to know them."

Another emphasis obvious from the content of the discussions was the value of the group to the participants. For one, the members were very much conscious of each other's adjustments and behavior. At first they turned to the group leader for direction and correction, but once they realized that this responsibility was theirs, they accepted it with considerable vigor, as evident in the following comments made about each other in the sixth session: "You act like a fool." "He wants everybody to baby him." "He should be big enough to stand up for what he thinks is right." "He will never go out until he gets a good report." Similar comments from a staff person might well have enraged the boy singled out, but getting this barrage from his peers made it acceptable as shown by this comment in the next meeting: "I really feel good about it [the group]. Even though we have had a couple of arguments, I still feel good about it. As long as the boys try to help you when you make a mistake."

Summary

Follow-up studies and impressions of practitioners who are concerned with habilitating individuals in institutional programs identify the period when residents move from institutional to community living as especially stressful. Available results are largely based on retrospective data. Little published material is based on information derived from individuals as they undergo the transition into the community. The project reported sampled the reactions of eight educable, late-adolescent males who were being introduced to work and social experiences in the community while remaining in residence at the center preparatory to placement. Based on the preliminary findings, the field is urged to undertake more extensive study of how retarded individuals feel, think, and cope with extrainstitutional experiences.

References

[1]C. D. Windle, E. Stewart, and S. J. Brown, "Reasons for Community Failure of Released Patients," *American Journal of Mental Deficiency,* Vol. 66 (1961), pp. 213-217. Studies on which the authors reported, all published in the *American Journal of Mental Deficiency,* were: D. L. Brown, "The Working Convalescent Care Program for Female Patients at the Rome State School," Vol. 56 (1952), pp. 643-654; R. D. Collmann and D. Newlyn, "Employment Success of Educationally Subnormal Ex-pupils in England," Vol. 60 (1956), pp. 733-744; M. Craft, "Withdrawals from License in Mental Deficiency," Vol. 63 (1958), pp. 47-49; and G. Tarjan and F. Benson, "Report on the Pilot Study at

Pacific Colony," Vol. 57 (1953), pp. 453-462. Others, variously published, were: W. E. Fernald, "After-Care Study of the Patients Discharged from Waverly for a Period of Twenty-five Years," *Ungraded*, Vol. 5 (1919), pp. 25-31; N. O'Connor, "The Successful Employment of the Mentally Handicapped," in L. T. Hilliard and B. H. Kirman, eds., *Mental Deficiency* (London, England: Churchill, 1957), pp. 448-480; H. W. Potter and C. L. McCollister, "A Resume of Parole Work at Letchworth Village," *Proceedings of the American Association for Study of the Feeble-minded*, Vol. 31 (1926), pp. 165-188; G. De M. Rudolph, "Improvement in Mental Defectives in Colonies," *Journal of Mental Science*, Vol. 96 (1950), pp. 272-275; and R. J. Stanley and H. C. Gunzburg, "A Survey of Residential Licenses from a Mental Deficiency Hospital," *International Journal of Social Psychiatry*, Vol. 2 (1956), pp. 207-213.

[2]H. C. Gunzburg, "The Place of Further Education in the Rehabilitation of the Adult Subnormal," *Proceedings of the London Conference on the Scientific Study of Mental Deficiency*, Vol. 1 (1960), pp. 251-257.

[3]J. S. Cohen, "An Analysis of Vocational Failures of Mental Retardates Placed in the Community After a Period of Institutionalization," *American Journal of Mental Deficiency*, Vol. 62 (1960), pp. 371-375.

[4]M. A. Seidenfeld, *Mental Retardation: A Further Assessment of the Problem*, Rehabilitation Service Series No. 63-62 (Washington, D.C.: U.S. Department of Health, Education, and Welfare, Vocational Rehabilitation Administration, 1962).

[5]Melvin Herman, "Reintegration of Handicapped Persons in the Community," in *New Perspectives on Services to Groups: Theory, Organization, Practice* (New York: National Association of Social Workers, 1961), pp. 70-78.

[6]Gunzburg, *op. cit.*, p. 253.

[7]H. W. Polsky, *Cottage Six* (New York: Russell Sage Foundation, 1962), p. 41.

[8]Patricia M. Morgan, "A Project on Resocialization of Patients in a Mental Hospital: Use of Group Work Techniques," *Social Casework*, Vol. 42, No. 2 (February 1961), pp. 60-65.

[9]Dorothea Cudaback and R. Daniel Kahn, "A Therapeutic Social Club for Post-hospitalized Psychiatric Patients," *Social Work with Groups 1959* (New York: National Association of Social Workers, 1959), pp. 52-65.

[10]Talcott Parsons, "Illness and the Role of the Physician: A Sociological Perspective," *American Journal of Orthopsychiatry*, Vol. 21 (1951), p. 453.

[11]Roman numerals refer to the session in which the comments were made.

EIGHTY

Reintegration of Handicapped Persons in the Community

MELVIN HERMAN

The purpose of this paper is to examine the problem of reintegrating into community life individuals who are handicapped by physical, mental, or emotional disabilities. We shall consider first some of the factors that tend to prevent reintegration. Whatever the type of disability, these factors are essentially the same and therefore have similar consequences for the individual. We shall then describe one agency's effort to utilize group services in the solution of this problem.

The Problem

There are, of course, individuals whose impairments are so severe that they will continue to require services that can be provided only by certain specialized social institutions. However, there is a much larger number of handicapped persons who, after a period of treatment, might be expected to fulfill the major social roles required of all others in society. Of course, the restoration of the handicapped to normal life is or should be the goal of any treatment program. Unfortunately, too few of those who possess the capacity to return to normal life have achieved this goal.

Evidence of this discouraging pattern is constantly before us in the reports of follow-up studies. In the field of physical rehabilitation, for example, a significantly high proportion of discharged patients not only do not maintain the performance levels they held at point of discharge but deteriorate and eventually require rehospitalization.[1] Similar experiences are reported in the treatment of mental illness and delinquency.

The existence of an impairment by itself cannot explain why a given individual is unable to participate effectively with others who have no major limitation. In order to understand the reasons for these failures, we must first review some of the forces that influence the outcome of treatment efforts.

From a paper delivered at the National Conference on Social Welfare, 1961. By permission of the author.

The Community Defines Disability

Use of the terms "disabled" and "handicapped" presupposes not only an appraisal of the degree to which an individual is deviant from the norm but also a definition by the community of how its members shall respond to this deviance.[2] Once this definition has been invoked, it will produce two types of consequences. First, it will serve to restrict the availability of community resources for handicapped persons, and secondly, through such restriction it will tend to produce *social* disability in the individual.

As an illustration, consider a personal example. The author, as a young boy, wished to play the catcher's position of his neighborhood baseball team but found his left-handedness a problem. He soon learned that this position, according to the folkways of baseball, must be filled by a right-hander. He did not have to undertake a systematic analysis of community attitudes to discover this definition. It came through to him quite clearly when he found that no manufacturer produced a left-handed catcher's glove. Psychoanalytically oriented readers can probably assess the degree of trauma that ensued and culminated in his decision to become a pitcher.

In this illustration, the boy was barred from his goal by the nature of the definition rather than by his difference. This barrier no longer exists; today a left-handed boy can find a suitable catcher's glove. Unfortunately, the barriers that interfere with the integration of handicapped persons into the community have not been significantly reduced. Like the would-be catcher, these people are frustrated by the nature of the definition rather than the nature of their disability.

Let us consider an example from the field of physical rehabilitation. An average boy of 10 attends a regular elementary school, plays with friends on his street, participates in the after-school program of a neighborhood community center, and attends the summer camp operated by that center. He is suddenly struck with polio, which requires hospitalization during the acute phase of the illness and a longer period of inpatient care for rehabilitation. During this period of treatment—which of course we recognize as necessary—the child begins to face the fact of his difference. He is physically removed from his community and confined with others of similar disability.

In the rehabilitation center he is assured that he will be able to resume his major activities when treatment is completed. At discharge, he is able to walk slowly with the use of double long-leg braces and crutches. He has made a good recovery, although it is unlikely that he will ever be able to run, jump, or get about without the aid of his appliances. He has no other residual disability.

Upon his return home, he is faced with a new set of circumstances. The community, because of its prior definition of those who cannot walk unaided, has determined that this child may use only certain restricted community services. He is informed that he may not return to the elementary school around the corner (although he can walk there). Rather, he is transported to a school several miles from his home where there is a special class for handicapped children. He also learns that the community center does not feel that he can be served in a group of normal children. His mother, in her anxiety to provide recreational opportunities, arranges to enroll him in an after-school program restricted to handicapped children. When summer comes around, the normal camps feel that they cannot cope with him and he is enrolled in a camp for handicapped children.

Effect of Segregated Programs

Thus far in this example we can see that the community's definition of disability, through its limitation of the services the child may use, has set in motion a series of events which are destined to result in his acceptance of a deviant role.

The segregated programs, which are a manifestation of existing community attitudes, limit the boy's interaction with those who are not disabled and thus decrease his opportunities to acquire the social skills required for future full participation in the community. But perhaps of even greater importance: as he becomes increasingly aware of the community's definition he will begin to internalize it, with the result that his level of aspiration and functioning will be reduced.[3] In effect he will become what he is defined to be. He may begin to realize that he is not considered an object of service by those agencies which presumably have been established to serve the entire community.

We can anticipate the possible course of his future adjustment. As he grows older, the opportunities for heterosexual experiences are likely to be limited to handicapped girls. His marital partner is likely to be handicapped. We can also expect his occupational aspirations will be negatively affected, as he becomes aware of the limitations of employment opportunities for handicapped people. He may well spend his working years in sheltered employment.

Thus, as a result of the community's definition of the person with a handicap, deviance is established, reinforced, and internalized. This problem has long been with us. A review of the development of welfare services in the United States offers ample testimony to the community's ability to create excellent separate facilities for those who face special problems of adjustment. We have expended great amounts of time, money, and professional effort in establishing institutions for the treatment of the blind, the deaf, the retarded, the physically handicapped, and the mentally ill. Many of these are residential facilities, while others exist in the open community.

Except for those few which are entirely custodial, these institutions agree that their primary purpose is to facilitate the handicapped person's return to maximal functioning in the general community. However, it is evident that, despite the excellence of many of these institutions, they cannot alone achieve the goal of reintegration. The general community, not the specialized treatment agency, will ultimately determine the success or failure of treatment efforts. In order to fulfill such roles as husband, father, student, and wage-earner, the individual must have not only motivation and skills but also opportunity to perform these roles. Treatment programs, if successful, can help the individual to develop motivation and also some required skills. However, unless the opportunity to perform is made available to him, treatment must inevitably fail, with the result that he loses both the motivation and the skills he has previously acquired.

Segregated educational, recreational, or vocational programs, however excellent, cannot reverse this process; they can only strengthen it. Indeed, many treatment facilities actually tend to reinforce deviance through the structure of their services, which limit the handicapped person's interaction to others who themselves are deviant. A patient recovered from mental illness, for example, cannot be reintegrated into activities with those who have not suffered mental illness unless he is provided with the opportunity for participation in such activities. A blind person cannot learn to live successfully in a sighted world if he is confined to participation with other blind persons.

It would seem that an approach toward overcoming the "disabling" portion of disability requires effort on two fronts. On the technological front, the picture is encouraging. Great strides have been made in both prevention and treatment. Electronic devices are helping the blind to see and the deaf to hear. New materials make braces lighter and more maneuverable. Improvements in artificial limbs make possible great freedom of movement. Drugs are now available to control epileptic seizures and also reduce disabling anxiety and fear. Even greater scientific and technical achievements cannot be far off.

On the community front, however, the picture is not nearly so bright. We have not yet been able to reduce the barriers to reintegration and provide the social opportunities that will make it possible.

Dr. Richard A. Cloward has identified the central problem cogently in discussing the high rates of recidivism in juvenile correctional institutions. He points out that "various types of social resources must be made available to the deviant if he is to negotiate the transition to a conforming status. . . . The problem of the released boy is, in short, one of gaining re-entry into the society which only recently expelled him."[4]

Role of Group Services

While it is unfortunately true that social work agencies possess limited ability to create housing, employment, and educational opportunities for handicapped persons, group service agencies do have the resources to provide the opportunity for handicapped and nonhandicapped persons to participate jointly in leisure-time activities.[5]

We know that in every community there are many handicapped children and adults. However, it is a discouraging fact that they are rarely served by the traditional agency. Some agencies have permitted groups of handicapped persons to use their facilities on a segregated basis. There are a number of such programs for the cerebral palsied, the retarded, and the mentally ill. These are essentially housing arrangements; the agency's function is limited to providing a meeting room and certain other physical facilities. The intent of these programs is doubtless laudable, but their contribution to reintegration is minimal. It has been suggested that such segregated experiences are a necessary prerequisite to integration, and also that the mere physical presence of these segregated groups in the agency helps to provide a bridge to participation with nonhandicapped members. No convincing evidence has been presented for either of these assertions. (Few would argue, for example, that segregation is a necessary and desirable step in facilitating the integration of Negroes and whites. Nor would this argument be seriously advanced in the entire field of intergroup relations.)

From time to time some agencies have permitted a handicapped person to join one of their groups, usually in response to great pressure from a parent or another social agency. Rarely has an agency taken a public position indicating both its willingness and its desire to serve handicapped individuals.

If we can assume that many handicapped persons possess the motivation and ability to participate in "normal" groups, perhaps it would be appropriate to discuss briefly some of the factors that might explain their absence from agencies offering services to groups.

1. *Definition of function*. Agencies have increasingly tended to restrict their definition of eligibility for service. Members are sought and accepted who already conform to agency norms and consequently require little modification of program.

2. *Fear of deviance*. Like all people, lay boards and professionals fear what they do not know. Gross stereotypes exist in many agencies. For example, in spite of efforts at community education, many still view the child with polio as highly fragile, the retarded as incapable of learning, the emotionally disturbed as dangerous to others, and the cerebral palsied as possessing a contagious disease. The continued existence of such stereotypes precludes an objective judgment regarding the individual's ability to participate in program.

3. *Inadequacy of physical facilities*. The facilities of most group service agencies have been designed to be used by those without physical disabilities. This is unfortunately true of many public buildings as well. The use of meeting rooms and play areas usually requires the climbing of many steps. Few agencies have elevators. Many physically handicapped individuals could effectively participate in club groups and special-interest groups if it were possible to overcome the problem of poor building design.

4. *Fear of negative consequences*. Some professional workers have expressed the fear that the inclusion of handicapped individuals would result in the withdrawal of nonhandicapped members from their program. Although this fear would probably not be borne out in fact, its very existence serves to justify the exclusion of those with disabilities.

5. *Lack of demand for service*. Some agencies have indicated a willingness to serve handicapped persons but report no request for such service. They apparently are not aware that, for the reasons cited earlier, the individual with a disability may not perceive himself as eligible and consequently makes no request. From the standpoint of the individual and the agency, this may be regarded as an example of self-fulfilling prophecy.[6]

6. *The role of special disability groups*. The agencies currently offering services to special disability groups have not pursued an active program designed to achieve integration. The reasons for this lack of exertion are undoubtedly complex, but part of the explanation may be found in their own structure as social institutions. Many

are preoccupied with their own needs for fund-raising, membership, public visibility, and self-preservation. They feel that offering direct services to their own groups under their own auspices is a requirement for survival. We can understand, but should not condone, their reluctance to preside at the liquidation of their own empires.

What Can Be Done?

The experience of the author's agency in New York City suggests that significant gains can be achieved. In 1960 the New York Service for Orthopedically Handicapped launched a program designed to integrate orthopedically handicapped children into neighborhood community centers. Originally limited to the Lower East Side of Manhattan, the program has since been extended to Brooklyn and will soon be extended to the Bronx. Through professionally trained group workers, the agency has offered the following services:

1. *Case-finding.* Workers contacted clinics, hospitals, and special schools to locate handicapped children.

2. *Screening and preparation.* In home visits, workers assessed each child's ability to profit from an integrated program. They also tried to help child and parent to overcome their fears of the child's participation in such a program.

3. *Agency contact.* Once the child had been located, a worker tried to enlist the co-operation of a neighborhood community center or other group program, such as the Scouts, by means of education, persuasion, or even appeals to guilt feelings. The worker assessed the physical facilities and program to determine its suitability for the particular child. After the agency's co-operation was secured, the worker discussed the child's needs, abilities, and limitations with the program supervisor.

4. *Referral.* The worker returned to the child and prepared him for referral by explaining the agency's program and discussing some of the problems the child might face.

5. *Intake.* The final decision regarding the child's acceptance into a program was made by that agency's staff. The New York Service assisted by supplying referral information and suggesting possible assignment to a group.

6. *Transportation.* Where required, the service arranged and paid for transportation to the center.

7. *Additional staff.* If the child's disability was so severe as to require an additional adult in the group, the service supplied the funds to hire an assistant leader.

8. *Follow-up.* After placement, a worker maintained contact with the agency and the child to assist in the solution of problems.

It is not yet possible to evaluate the effectiveness of this program fully, but certain facts and impressions can be reported. Seventy-five handicapped children have been placed in 17 agencies. Most of these children have been in after-school programs two or three times a week, but 18 were in a five-day summer day camp. The major diagnostic categories were post-polio, cerebral palsy, and muscular dystrophy. Many of the children used braces and crutches. Several were confined to wheelchairs. Most were in segregated classes in schools.

In interviews with the handicapped children, their parents, and the agencies a group of graduate students found that placement was successful in approximately 70 percent of the cases.[7] We do not yet know the determinants of success or failure. However, it appears that severity of disability was not a critical variable.

Conclusions

Treatment agencies cannot by themselves achieve the goal of reintegrating the handicapped into the community. Segregated groups are sometimes necessary; however, it would be most unfortunate if we were to transform this necessity into a virtue. Community agencies have the responsibility to provide the opportunity for the handicapped person to use his motivation and skill. They may find it necessary to re-examine their definitions of whom they will serve. As social welfare institutions, they cannot be satisfied with policies and programs that tend to exclude individuals who most require community intervention in meeting their needs.

We must seek more effective ways of overcoming the resistance we find in many traditional agencies. Additional experimentation should be undertaken to evaluate both the determinants and the results of differing approaches to integration. If we are successful in developing integrated services, our efforts may well have important unintended consequences. Not only will we have the satisfaction of knowing that we are making a significant contribution to the happiness of disadvantaged individuals; we may recapture the sense of dedication and urgency which all too often has been absent from traditional group service agencies. We may also find that the problems associated with integrated services require the full range of competence and skill possessed by professional group workers. This in turn might reduce the need of some of our fellow professionals to seek fulfillment in the special settings.

Not long ago, in our own country, we saw dramatic evidence that in space travel the critical problem of re-entry has been solved. Would it not be an at least equally important achievement if the same problem could be solved in relationships among people?

References

[1]See *inter alia* Georgia F. McCoy and Howard A. Rusk, *An Evaluation of Rehabilitation* (New York: Institute of Physical Medicine and Rehabilitation, 1953).

[2]H. D. Rawls, "Social Factors in Disability," *New Outlook for the Blind*, Vol. 51, No. 6 (June 1957).

[3]Hans Von Hentig, "Physical Disability, Mental Conflict and Social Crisis," *Journal of Social Issues*, Vol. 4, No. 4 (Fall 1948).

[4]Richard A. Cloward, "Conformity, Deviance and Opportunity," New York School of Social Work, 1961. (Mimeographed.)

[5]For a discussion of the importance of contact in the modification of attitudes, *see* H. H. Remmers, "Social Attitudes," in D. H. Fryer and E. R. Henry, *Handbook of Applied Psychology* (New York: Rinehart & Company, 1950), pp. 10-13.

[6]Robert K. Merton, *Social Theory and Social Structure* (Glencoe, Ill.: Free Press, 1957), Chap. 11.

[7]Herbert Barrish *et al.*, "The Integration of Physically Handicapped Children into Group Service Agencies." Unpublished M.A. thesis, New York School of Social Work, 1961.

PART NINE

Utilization of Paraprofessionals and Professionals in Delivery of Services

EIGHTY-ONE

Social Forces and Manpower

LOUIS H. ORZACK

The purpose of this paper is to assess some of the relations between social forces and the recruiting of manpower and its training, use, and retention. In the area of mental retardation these are especially difficult problems, problems for which many solutions have been offered. And as one sees the current and prospective increases in the number and kinds of organizational and community programs for the retarded, one readily imagines that the many problems already associated with manpower will multiply. Thus, it may be helpful to those in the field of mental retardation to look at the discussions and appraisals of economists and sociologists of current trends in the field and of what may be in store.

First, we will turn to a brief discussion of manpower in the organizational settings where services are provided to the residential retarded[1], and consider the manners in which behavior patterns of staff members are structured in these institutions. Second, we will review the impact or probable impact of broader social forces and trends on manpower recruitment and utilization in the field of mental retardation.

Concerning organizational settings, two major points stand out as striking to a sociologist. The first is that in the residential institutions, there is a good deal of role conflict. This means something fairly simply, namely that the ways in which staff members organize and pattern their daily rounds of task performance bring them into conflict with each other. The physicians, psychologists, psychiatrists, social workers, nurses, teachers, counselors, rehabilitators, physical and occupational therapists, do not agree and probably cannot be expected to agree in their conceptions of the nature of mental retardation, in their views of the developmental prospects of the residents, or in their assessments of the worth of each others' work and capabilities. By virtue of their diverse educational backgrounds and by virtue of the significant differences in the kinds of work experience that often precede their involvement in the field of retardation, staff members approach their work with wide-

Reprinted from "Manpower and the Expanding Mental Retardation Programs" (Bordentown, N. J., The Edward R. Johnson Training and Research Center, 1965), pp. 4-11. By permission of the author and the Center.

ly varied notions of what they are supposed to do and how they are supposed to act.[2]

This conflict has historic roots and is often quite independent of the psychological make-up of the persons engaged in conflict. It goes back to the manner in which institutions for the retarded have developed in the United States and to the degree of priority that work with the retarded has had in the various professions and occupations. This may be put in the form of a general proposition that the residential centers for the retarded have historically not had a high social priority in the allocation of scarce economic and social resources. Both governmental and private support, while occasionally lavish for particular institutions or in selected regions, has been less than that which would provide professionally satisfactory care and treatment. A reflection of this may be seen in the (now disappearing) belief that the centers should be economically self-sufficient and should be located in out-of-the-way places which are both salubrious and invisible. This was based of course on the view that the colonies were necessary to prevent both the retardate and society from harming one another, coupled with the belief that retardates were a necessary burden.[3]

This meant having a low priority in the claim on society's resources, and these resources include manpower. Primarily the dedicated, who were perhaps by chance the competent, accepted assignments in these centers. In any event, the systematic patterning and organization of the tasks for their assignments or roles was also largely neglected by the established organized professions. This in part was due to the then existing state of knowledge concerning retardation and of course the then existing body of attitudes, beliefs, and stereotypes concerning retardates. Whatever the origin of this neglect, the effect was that the established, organized professions did not encourage their members to select retardation as a field, and did not provide those who did make that choice with ready-made and useful guidelines to behavior.[4]

This suggests that the role-defined patterns of behavior have had to be developed by local improvisation, and that these patterns have not been evaluated, codified, and extended systematically through the sanctioned channels that exist in the various professions. Three processes have contributed to this: (1) Insufficient scientific study and research has been supported in the field of retardation. (2) The men and women who have worked in retardation have not received adequate guidelines for their work from the organized health, welfare, and education professions or from the leaders of these professions. (3) An extensive, informed, and interested set of representatives of the professions has not been a characteristic feature of the field of retardation.

As a consequence of these factors, professionals and non-professionals who have worked in this field have largely been on their own. Within the residential centers we have seen the extensive development of what sociologists call work groups, and these seem to have been the dominant feature of the kind of social organization that has developed there.[5] In these kinds of settings, improvisation has dominated rather than innovation informed by a clear-cut set of professional imperatives. Programs have developed, but these have been adaptive to immediate problems, and have represented solutions very often worked out on a trial and error basis. We have not seen these overtaken by thoughtful, scientifically based, and professionally supported norms such as might be assumed to be associated with the conceptions of professionals who constitute an interested colleague group. This suggests that there has been a rather gigantic failure on the part of the professions which have neglected, ignored, and therefore not coped with the manifold problems of the mentally retarded.

The individual professionals and non-professional staff members have imported into the residential facilities conceptions of their work and views of the mentally retarded that largely seem to be vestiges and partial mis-applications of ideas and perceptions acquired in other training and work contexts. Little general agreement seems to exist concerning the nature of retardation, the problems of the retardate, his family and community, and how best either to conceptualize or to handle the situation. The result is often a focused attention on factors of care which are common to most institutions: mere physical survival, maintenance of clean wards and play rooms, and reduction of per capita costs. In some cases, these become the goals; in all cases they directly influence a sizeable proportion of money spent and manpower used. (In Massachusetts, these costs for the retarded average about 25 % of expenditures for the care of emotionally disturbed children.)

The individual professionals and staff members vary widely in their views and activities. Very many occasions arise in the daily care, management, and treatment of the retarded in which conflicts occur. Such conflicts may range from such relatively minor matters as the appropriate timing for classes and training programs to questions of large theoretical import, such as the extent to which learning reinforcement programs that stress social learning and development can either intrude on nursing care time or can be incorporated into the roles of nurses and attendants. Such conflicts might occur over whether experimental and demonstration programs for a limited number of residents ought to be developed and continued perhaps temporarily by volunteers or students at the cost of bypassing and possibly offending the regular attendant and nursing personnel. Other examples of conflict may be found in the manner in which newly-funded programs for rehabilitation, education, and research may seem to contravene the authority, competence, and worth of the regular staff, or in the introduction of nursery school programs and teachers into a nursery area previously controlled without question or threat by physicians and nursing staff.[6]

Role conflicts of this sort can, I believe, be found in very many residential centers, although the specific illustrations I have provided can undoubtedly be altered to accommodate differing situations. The implications of such conflict are important in assessing the structure of residential centers and point to another important feature: the relative lack of well-supported guidelines as to the way in which authority should be exercised. Do we yet know if these centers are to be called hospitals, schools (in the academic sense), training centers, or rehabilitation facilities; should we employ primarily physicians and nurses, teachers and educators, child development specialists and social workers, or psychologists and social workers? Do we know how and when to integrate these organizations with other existing community centers and facilities; do we place them close to centers of population and in proximity to university research centers and other schools? On what basis do we encourage staff members of the residential institution to be flexible, adaptive, and supportive in their relationships with the children, so that, for example, they *can* be willing and ready to spend much time in helping an individual child to learn how to dress or eat, perhaps at the cost of slowing down the dressing or the eating of other children on the ward, and perhaps interfering with the daily routines of housekeepers and porters, of cooks and laundry personnel?

It strikes me that our state of knowledge about mental retardation and about mental retardates, as well as the management techniques we employ, are relatively primitive, and that there is a great gap between the problems that residential staff members confront when they provide care and the theoretical principles of the various helping professions. The model that has been followed in the past in operating residential retardate centers is largely what might be called a physical care model. A general set of principles concerning how they are to be integrated seems to be missing, and ways in which their combination may be translated into the resources of staff abilities, staff assignments and time, space, and equipment that are found within these settings are generally absent. This is my second point about organizations.

There are, of course, many ways in which guidelines are acquired by the staff when professional or institutional rules are either absent or in conflict. These are unofficial, but known to any one who has confronted daily problems at work. One may ask the old guard or the residents, apply one's former experiences to any new situation, or perhaps simply muddle through. Indeed, "do what you can," may be the reply to a question addressed to a supervisor by an attendant, and as long as the resident is not abused or maltreated in a public way, some kind of care will be provided. Solutions will somehow be found to work-a-day problems in this fashion, but clearly the role obligations into which solutions of this kind must be translated are likely to have limited usefulness. The main reason for the wide variety of role obligations of manpower in the mental retardation field is, it seems to me, found in this very process. Roles have not been secured to a widely-known and accepted body of professional principles from which they derive.

The role of attendants, nurses, training school teachers, physicians, and other care personnel have developed in helter-skelter fashion from principles, to be sure, but the principles have often been rather distorted and constricted. One principle for determining the responsibilities of aides and attendants may be "what worked in the last place I was at," and that place might have been a general hospital, a prison, a school, or a clinic, fields having many criteria different from those of retardation.

This format for establishing and justifying the roles and obligations of professional and sub-professional staff permits too many degrees of freedom to the staff members of particular residential centers, and encourages, I submit, the tendency toward looking only for common denominators in treatment mentioned earlier. New approaches to control, institutional renovation, innovations, and experimentation in care and treatment programs—any of these may be introduced to these centers only to confront staff resistance at any level of responsibility, often at all levels. But this is not a simple personally-based antagonism to change of any kind. Change is tolerated in our society. The resistance and antagonism derive, it seems to me, from the simpler fact that in the residential centers for the retarded, the sources of control, authority, and change behavior that are considered legitimate by the staff have been largely internal to each institution. And efforts toward change that have been begun by qualified professionals and by interested non-professionals —by parents, volunteers, and others—have not been mounted on a broad enough scale over a long enough period of time on more than a demonstration basis to sustain the impact of momentary changes.

Whether the changes proposed have been sufficiently imaginative and creative, I cannot of course say with finality. But I would suggest that the necessity for imagination and creativity in both the formation of service orientations and goals and in the ways of implementing these goals is daily becoming more essential. For we are slowly and somewhat awkwardly moving toward a society of increased abundance, toward a Great Society, to be sure, but one in which categorical handicaps and social stigma may nevertheless still be associated.

Newer social, psychological, and medical techniques give promise of prevention of at least certain types of mental retardation and of the reduction of disabilities associated with them. Community facilities are being enhanced and these may provide greater opportunities for a fuller participation by the mentally retarded in society. Whether sufficient numbers of prepared personnel will be provided for the pattern of services that will be desirable is, however, problematical. Several factors account for putting this as a question. The first is the probable multiplication of the numbers of personnel in this field that an expansion of services may well require.[7] Second, we are seeing almost everywhere in the arena of social welfare services predictions of great increases in manpower demand, and this means that competition for recruits to the fields in question will intensify.[8] Third, we may continue to see, although possibly in different forms, continuance of the social ambivalence toward the retarded that exists at present, and this may continue to discourage recruitment.[9]

The ambivalence toward the retarded that seems a part of our culture, and the hostility that may be part of that ambivalence, does not appear to rest on an economic base. The retarded may be excluded from all sorts of social and civic opportunities, but not as a result of a threat they pose to the achievement of others. The mentally retarded do not seem to prevent other people from getting ahead, from acquiring desired roles in our occupational, social, religious, educational, recreational, or familial institutions. It seems to me that the source of the culturally perceived threat comes from the other end of the continuum, from the very fact that the retarded either cannot or are prevented from, but in any case, are not, competing with others. They are dependent, some totally so, and their sustenance requires a commitment of resources and time that historically and culturally we may ordinarily be ready to give to anyone who competes effectively for these resources.

It may be true that we are becoming an affluent society, but ours is also a society with deprivation and a structured lack of opportunity; it is also a society where achievement is the norm, one in which the possession of the right kind of educational certificates increasingly comes to mean almost guaranteed access to positions that carry prestige and other rewards; it can surprisingly be moving toward a tighter social structure, with categories of status set off by age, by education, and by sex; it may be a society where the residues of mis-treatment of generations of human beings on the basis of mental retardation may continue for a very long time.

The parallels between Negroes and the mentally retarded may be worth investigation, for learning from either group about the treatment and the prospects of the other. After all, categorical assessment of the individual, institutionalized deprivation, and the loss of hope seem to be weapons common to society's attack on both groups. Discriminatory practices, neglect, and the like may in fact have positive consequences for those who practice them whether directed at racial groups or at the mentally retarded. The residential institutions for the retarded, and the schools, welfare agencies, courts, and other screening and treating facilities may depend in part on systematic techniques for discrimination against the mentally retarded that are sanctioned and supported by a complex body of traditions.

The change of programming by the centers and institutions will undoubtedly be vast; the shift in role-patterned duties of professionals and others will be extensive, the additional numbers of personnel required will be large. It remains to be seen whether this kind of challenge can be met through planning or through enhanced educational and training programs, or whether entirely new facilities may have to come into being.

Dr. Leonard Duhl has recently been quoted as suggesting "a whole new concept of institutional and semi-institutional care." He proposes the establishment of whole communities dedicated to the care, education, and training of persons such as the retarded. A most interesting part of Senator Kennedy's summary of this, which appeared in the October-November 1965 *Children's Limited*, is the obvious extensive reliance on the vast resources of selected towns and cities restructured as service communities. The Senator referred to all employers, bus drivers, salesgirls, policemen and housewives, teachers and students, as potential contributors to the large effort described.

For this and other changes to come about, possibly we may find our problem magnified, but its solution is a simple one, and I prefer to put it this way: more people with more varied skills may work with the retarded in the future. Following Duhl's point, their contacts will be closer to the usual round of their day's labor and leisure than at present with less separation and isolation of the retarded from the community at large. Increased professionalization and standardization of services with improved levels of care, treatment, and rehabilitation will be necessary to provide a greater integration of work rules than exists at present.

References

[1] The 135 public residential institutions for the mentally retarded in the United States in 1965 housed approximately 192,000 individuals. American Association on Mental Deficiency, *Directory of Residential Facilities for the Mentally Retarded* (Willimantic, Conn.: 1965), p. iv.

[2] Goode, William J., "Encroachment, Charlatanism, and the Emerging Profession: Psychology, Sociology, and Medicine," *American Sociological Review*, Vol. 25, Number 6, December 1960, pp. 902-914.

[3] Dybwad, Gunnar, *Challenges in Mental Retardation* (New York: Columbia University Press, 1964); and Kanner, Leo, *A History of the Care and Study of the Mentally Retarded* (Springfield: Charles C. Thomas, 1964).

[4] Wilensky, Harold, "The Professionalization of Everyone?" *The American Journal of Sociology*, Vol. LXX, Number 2, September 1964, pp. 137-158; and Lynn, Kenneth S., editor, *The Professions in America* (Boston: Houghton Mifflin Company, 1965).

[5] Gross, Edward, *Work and Society* (New York: Thomas Crowell Company, 1958).

[6] Dykens, James W., Hyde, Robert W., Orzack, Louis H., and York, Richard H., *Strategies of Mental Hospital Change* (Boston: Massachusetts Department of Mental Health, 1964).

[7] Clague, Ewan, "Economic Manpower and Social Welfare," Presented at Symposium on Manpower for Social Welfare: Goals for 1975, University of Chicago, April 1965.

[8] Orzack, Louis H., "Social Change, Social Policy, and Manpower: A Social Welfare Fantasy," in Edward L. Schwartz, editor, *Research Approaches to Manpower Problems* (New York: National Association of Social Workers, 1966); and Orzack, Louis H., "The Function of Sociological Research for Planning Treatment Programs for the Residential Retarded" (New York: National Association for Retarded Children, mimeographed, 1965).

[9] Richardson, Stephen A., Goodman, Norman, Hastorf, Albert H., and Dornbusch, Sanford, "Cultural Uniformity in Reaction to Physical Disabilities," *American Sociological Review*, Vol. 26, Number 2, April 1961, pp. 241-247.

EIGHTY-TWO

Training and Utilization of Nonprofessional Personnel in Services for the Retarded

LAWRENCE GOODMAN AND IRENE ARNOLD

Creative participation of nonprofessionals, already demonstrated in action programs to combat the social destructiveness of poverty, can have a similarly significant impact in the drive to expand and add depth to services for the mentally retarded. Effective recruiting and training of nonprofessional aides and experimentation in their utilization in programming is not, of course, the solution to crucial manpower problems in mental retardation and other areas of health and welfare. Yet in face of so massive a challenge, we would be shortsighted indeed to hold rigidly to a conventional, idealized treatment structure with narrowly defined paradigms of professional domain.

While it is unquestionable that many services can be provided only by fully trained professionals; others by semi or subprofessionals; there are additional ancillary, less complex, more concrete, or still unspecified needs of the retarded and their families which can be dealt with by assisting, supportive individuals working in conjunction with professional staff. The experience of Retarded Infants Services, for example, in evaluating the role of homemakers and home aides with families of the retarded illustrated both the direct therapeutic effect of the homemaker and the high quality of observation shared with the caseworker. This, in turn, added immeasurably to understanding of the child and his impact on the family (Arnold & Goodman, 1966).

Further reflection and enthusiasm over the potential use of nonprofessional personnel as a major element in overcoming the continuing lag in services for the retarded led to development of a demonstration project, supported by the Children's Bureau, to explore methods of training and placing unskilled personnel to function in a variety of roles in retardation facilities. The project is under the direction of Retarded Infant's Services, which maintains responsibility for recruitment and placement, in cooperation with Flower-Fifth Avenue Hospitals, New York Medical College. Training is provided within the hospital's interdisciplinary Graduate and Post-Graduate Training Center in Mental Retardation.

Reprinted by permission from *Mental Retardation*, Vol. 5, No. 6 (December, 1967), pp. 11-14, a publication of the American Association on Mental Deficiency.

It is our contention that nonprofessional workers can serve a potentially important function in a broad span of programs in the following ways: (1) assisting the professional directly, (2) providing service apart from the professional relationship but enhancing treatment goals, (3) carrying out important forms of help that the professional cannot offer.

A by-product of the project, which daily takes on increasing significance, is the creation of job opportunities for untrained and unskilled personnel. As facilities continue to multiply and widescope action programs for the culturally retarded develop, a primary source of satisfying permanent employment will be opened to staff members who are products of the same deprived community.

Recruitment

The program has trained three groups of 15 members each, for four-hour daily sessions over successive three-month periods. Trainees received allowances of $45 a week. Criteria for selection were minimal in order to approximate as closely as possible the group composition of future ongoing programs in urban communities.

Applicants were obtained from the New York State Employment Service, guidance counselors, community agencies and anti-poverty programs. A screening interview focused on such qualities as alertness, quality of relating, flexibility, and capacity for developing warmth with patients. Eliminated were those applicants with obvious personality pathology, the educationally over-qualified, those with highly unstable work histories, and those who appeared to be too involved emotionally with the problem of mental retardation.

The ethnic composition of the groups consisted of approximately 70 per cent Negroes, 20 per cent Puerto Ricans, and 10 per cent whites. The age ranged from 18 to 53. The younger members, who had had limited work experience were primarily from agencies concerned with school dropouts. The majority of the older women had been employed with varying regularity as domestics. A few had been hospital attendants.

Motivation for entering the program did not reflect an articulated or inner urge to work with the mentally retarded or "to serve humanity." The disadvantages of their collective background with lifelong struggle for personal survival and identity had permitted little latitude for the development of strong empathic feeling for the physically and mentally handicapped. The trainees saw the program as a means of improving future employability and providing an opportunity to move into a vocational area of higher status.

Curriculum Development

The content of the curriculum and the methodology of training must have both immediacy and future pertinence. It is of necessity related to the experiences, attitudes and life style of the trainees. At the same time our aim has been to stimulate interest in the retarded, job identification, and, finally, some sense of commitment to service.

Studies of characteristics of low income culture refer frequently to an orientation that is "...physical and visual rather than aural...problem centered rather than abstract centered...with words used in relation to action, rather than word-bound" (Riessman, 1962). Haggstrom (1964) speaks of the "keen sense of the personal and the concrete, with interest typically restricted to the self and the family. There is pessimism and fatalism over the ability to affect one's own situation."

In our program we found, in general, that the participants were activity-focused with a limited framework for conceptualization. Their composite self-image was tenuous and deficient. There was a strong underlying sense of futility which exhibited itself through a weather-beaten facade and "show-me" attitude.

In developing a training curriculum it is of primary importance to highlight repeatedly the significance of the program, the value placed on it by professional staff (as evidenced by their direct participation), and the contribution that the trainees alone can make. Didactic material should be presented in a pragmatic context. The advantage of visual impact can be utilized through direct observation of retardates, field trips, and the careful use of selected films. The material presented must be alive, focused and exciting.

Structurally, the training groups are conducted by an experienced social worker who plans programming, organizes materials, and becomes the constant stabilizing figure to whom the trainees relate during the training period. In addition to her role as teacher, she remains consistently aware of the individual functioning of the trainees, their relationship to the goals of the program, and the effect on each member of other group members and of the group as a whole.

The specialized data included in the training course seems to us to be less important than method and process. Content has included: definitions of mental retardation, some picture of historical development, family factors, the question of institutionalization vs. home care, demonstration of clinical types, general content from pediatrics, social work, psychology, rehabilitation, nursing factors including first aid and home training, language development, therapeutic approaches, and the uses of recreation.

Opportunity for field observation was provided through trips to a private residential nursery, state institutions, "model" day centers, sheltered workshops, and special public school classes. Films proved most valuable in helping trainees concretize some of their thinking, and in encouraging class discussion.

The participation of guest lecturers gave the program increased status and stature in the eyes of the trainees. Selected to represent major disciplines concerned with the retarded, individual speakers should be determined by the ability to humanize their presentation without condescension, to avoid professional jargon, and to stress the utility of their material. Case illustrations and problems from practice are especially useful in stimulating involvement. After the lecture, with its discussion, the class reacted further with the group instructor. She attempted to give the new material further meaning both in terms of specific job roles and of the trainees' emerging awareness of themselves as helpers.

The Group Process

The negative attitude of low income people toward authority has been mentioned by many investigators (Saltzman, 1965; Christman, 1965; Gans, 1962). At the same time there may be discomfort and lack of experience with the much valued middle-class concept of group equalitarianism. There is initial distrust of the instructor, and her interest in them, and constriction in class interaction.

What Haggstrom (1964) has noted as "envy and hostility toward those who prosper" can be detected in the initial classroom atmosphere. The first sessions have been structured with activity and shared response in order to engage the trainees as soon as possible in an interacting process with the leader and with one another. The leader shows her genuine interest in them, her deep concern for the retarded, and projects her recognition of the important roles that trainees can fill. At the same time she maintains control that is fair, nonauthoritarian and respectful. This enables the trainees to begin to view the experience as a new situation that may offer internal as well as concrete rewards.

As with any organized small group, dynamic interplay arises which must be understood and handled by the leader. The group can threaten or support, encourage or stifle spontaneity, facilitate or interfere with learning. Although clearly not set up as treatment groups, in skilled hands the power of the group action can be used as a unique framework for expanded identification and growth, for cutting through stereotyped and inner-directed thinking, and for the beginning development of a more positive concept of the self.

Once the trainees functioned as a group it was no longer necessary to limit their expressed attitudes toward the retarded to acceptable cliches. In the first group some of the trainees could verbalize what several were thinking, "Is retardation really so bad when families are fairly well off?" This developed into an outpouring discussion of their own deprivation and sense of being handicapped. As they were encouraged to understand their own feelings of alienation and not belonging, identification with other handicaps became the basis for the release of object feeling for the retarded and the beginning of empathic awareness. Each of the groups has, in its own way, reached a similar critical point.

On another day, following a lecture on "The Role of the Homemaker" much hostility came to the surface. The trainees had overlooked most of the positive aspects of the homemaker function and fixed on those areas that suggested a menial work role. One member stated, "Are we in class for three months in order to scrub floors again?" In a later meeting the question of the high proportion of middle-class families using services was raised with the implication that low-income families were not considered as important to agencies. This led to expression of their sensitivity around their own status—that they are, in the words of the trainees themselves, "lower class" people and that middle or upper-class parents might look down on them.

The field placements that were about to begin brought out the fears of those going into homes that they would be rejected because they were Negro or Puerto

Rican, or would be used entirely as domestics. The class was quite tense as these feelings came to the surface, obviously anxious over the leader's reaction. This is indeed substantive material which provides a rich opportunity for utilizing group expression as a method for self-development. The instructor's acceptance of their right to express negatives, her recognition of the reality basis for their concern, and her constructive handling of the issue led to verbalization by the class of the meaning to them of being able to discuss these feelings, openly, to "clear the air" and to discover that the leader (representing the community) could understand, accept and care about them.

Field Work

A major aspect of training has been a two-week field experience which permits trainees to test out concepts and to view themselves in a work role within a functioning program. Their shared reactions broaden the knowledge base of all the trainees.

Eliciting the cooperation of agencies involves interpretation of the program; handling of uncertainty over the readiness of trainees to be participant observers; and the nature of their potential contribution. An extensive program of community education is involved. The success of this effort can perhaps be suggested by the large number of trainees who were later hired by the field agencies. Placements were arranged at a residential nursery, a rehabilitation hospital working with the multiple-handicapped, children's day centers, sheltered workshops, an agency working with the blind retarded, and mental retardation clinical centers. A numbers of trainees were assigned as home clinic assistants to families known to the Flower-Fifth Avenue Clinic.

At the close of the field experience, trainees were asked to write their impressions. What emerges most strikingly in reviewing their statements is the high level of enthusiasm, feeling and perceptiveness. The following are a few typical excerpts: From a residential nursery—"I felt that some of the children were ready for a kindergarten of some kind...they had the ability to be trained if it were my decision. I must say I really enjoyed caring for the retarded children, it was one of my greatest experiences. I gained a lot as a person." From the adult training center—"For the future there should be more day-training schools, more workshops, day camps for vacations, and for those whose parents are dead, a residence like a half-way house instead of institutions. I liked my two weeks there very much. I also learned how to string beads and do ceramic work which I just loved." From a nursery school program—"The children are from high-income, middle-income and low-income families. They are treated alike. The center is just the kind of work that I would enjoy."

The following recording, in its entirety, by one of the trainees who spent her field period in an assigned home, gives some indication of how the nonprofessionals' knowledge of family interaction can influence the total treatment plan as it shifts and modifies in relationship to additional disgnostic understanding.

The cause of Fernando's mental retardation is meningitis. The mother believes that the boy will be normal again. This is founded on her religious beliefs. She used to be Catholic, but, after the boy's illness, she changed to Pentecostal.

The mother thinks that the boy's mental retardation is part of God's way of showing her the right way to choose the true religion. She told me of having dreams in which God appears to her and shows the boy with new brains, walking, talking and playing like a normal child of his age. She told me of calling her social worker and asking her about her son's x-rays. She is under the impression that they show that his brain is clear of damage. Then, she asked me if I knew of any school where she could send the boy so that they could teach him and train him.

The mother does not like to put the boy on the floor with his brothers or by himself because he might get hurt. It seems that she doesn't make much of an effort to train him. After feeding him, she puts him in his crib. He doesn't have toys to play with. Mostly what she does is to try to have him say "mama." They talk to him in Spanish, Engish and baby talk. The child has no schedule for eating or sleeping. The boy tries to reach for plates or cups from the table but the mother stops him. When I went to the house, she was feeding Fernando baby foods or soft foods. I tried to feed him solids—cereal, meats, vegetables—and he liked them. He particularly liked milk, and did not care very much for juice or water. While I was there, he started to walk by himself, and, if he fell, would crawl to the nearest piece of furniture, and pull himself up so that he could walk again. When taken from the floor and put into a crib he would cry.

Fernando is very friendly, but he does not know the difference between parents and friends. He does not seem to understand anything, or understands very little. When I called him by his name or made some kind of sound next to him, he did not respond (or didn't hear). He did not cry or show any signs of discomfort when wet. It appears as if he is attracted to bright colors. He keeps his thumb in his mouth. When he sees something that attracts his attention, he will not grab for it with his hands, but will try to get it with his mouth. The mother told me while I was there that the boy had convulsions, and she told me that she did not have any medication for the convulsions, so that she prayed that he would be well again.

In this case the clinic assistant, who provided an avenue of direct communication with a previously unresponsive parent, furthered the clinic's treatment plan in several ways: (1) Additional diagnostic data was made available. (2) The assistant became an extension of the clinic's service, offering general support to a parent who felt freer in talking with someone from whom she felt less social distance. The assistant, after conferring with the caseworker, was later able to begin to encourage the mother to give up some of her infantilization of the child. (3) She served in effect as a bridge between a "hard-to-reach" parent and available service—including vital medical help—that was not being utilized.

Placement and Utilization

All the trainees available for employment have been placed in services for the retarded and multiple-handicapped representing many specialized agencies in the New York City area. Several jobs have been created on an experimental basis, with or without consultation from the project, to define a new job title and test methods of employing additional levels of help to the retarded. Graduates are being used, for example, as teacher assistants in special classes, case aides and field assistants in mental retardation clinics, recreation aides in programs for the blind retarded, rehabilitation aides, and nursery school "stimulators."

Agencies willing to reach out for low-income families within existing programs and to plan realistic community services for the culturally retarded may find trained nonprofessionals assuming a focal role in bringing help to those who do not readily move toward structured health services.

Rein and Riessman (1966) term nonprofessional staff aides "expediters" who "facilitate the delivery of service by playing a variety of roles including those of intervener, interpreter, helper, negotiator, escort, and baby sitter." The expediter is often able to achieve through active involvement what the most efficient intake services cannot hope to approach. Our own initial experience in using aides in this way has only begun to suggest the enormous potentials for broadening services thru the imaginative use of trained assistants.

Where graduates have filled job vacancies in existing and traditional positions an initial follow-up indicates a higher level of job readiness and relatedness than agencies generally find in personnel at this level. Following the training experience, the participants appear to be freer in their use of themselves; better able to express feelings of warmth and concern; and with the capacity to view themselves as fulfilling a meaningful and specific role within a therapeutic structure that they now understand. Hopefully, their function has come to imply something more than a low-paying job. A source of gratification and individual fulfillment may emerge as well as improved care for the mentally retarded.

References

ARNOLD, I. AND GOODMAN, L. Homemaker Services to Families with Young Retarded Children. *Children,* July-August, 1966.

CHRISTMAS, J. J. Group Methods in Training and Practice: Non Professional Mental Health Personnel in a Deprived Community. Paper presented at the American Orthopsychiatric Association Conference, New York, 1965.

GANS, H. The Urban Villagers. New York: The Free Press, 1962.

HAGGSTROM, W. C. The Power of the Poor, In *Mental Health of the Poor,* F. Riessman, J. Cohen, and A. Pearl, Editors. New York: The Free Press, 1964.

REIN. M. AND RIESSMAN, F. A Strategy for Anti-poverty Community Action Programs. *Social Work,* 1966, *11*, 2, April.

RIESSMAN, F. The Culturally Deprived Child. New York: Harper and Row, 1962.

SALTZMAN, H. The Poor and the Schools. In *New Careers for the Poor,* A. Pearl, and F. Riessman, Editors. New York: The Free Press, 1965.

EIGHTY-THREE

Adolescents Who Want to Help: Some Experiences With Teen Volunteers in a Group Work Setting

MEYER SCHREIBER AND STEPHEN H. BROMFIELD

Major changes are taking place in an old established American institution: the volunteer. A volunteer is a person who of his own accord, and without pay, assumes certain obligations. Recent innovations have been shown in new uses of volunteers in "person-to-person" settings serving those less fortunate than themselves.

One such change is that volunteering is no longer the privilege of a wealthy few, nor is it limited to adults with considerable leisure time at their disposal. In the past, and even today, professionalization of the helping professions, as well as specialization, have tended to diminish the volunteer's function or have eliminated him entirely.

Today, however, unlimited opportunities for volunteer service have been revealed in the many areas of human need and endeavor which exist in hospitals, camps, clinics, schools, low-income neighborhoods, community centers and in a host of other societal institutions. If we believe that the person in need is not an inferior person, and by our very approach strengthen his and his family's belief in society's concern for individual dignity and worth, then the concerted effort of the volunteer and professional can help to achieve democratic goals and values.

Responsible participation by the adolescent in the major institutions of society has often been denied him or discouraged at the moment when his interest in the world has been poignantly awakened. However, when opportunities have been offered them, these adolescents have shown a no-nonsense attitude toward their volunteer efforts. These participants are motivated, committed, serious, chairedge sitters and doers who seek to develop understanding about themselves, others and the community, and to take appropriate social action in these spheres of human concern. Through their volunteer activities, young Americans are finding a new and significant leisure-time avocation—that of aiding the rejected, the neglected, the deprived and the excluded, or the "superfluous" person in our midst, such as the retardate, the aged, the mentally ill and the disadvantaged minority group member.

Reprinted by permission from *Mental Retardation*, Vol. 4, No. 6 (December, 1966), pp. 13-19, a publication of the American Association on Mental Deficiency.

In programs dealing with mentally retarded persons it is only lately, within the past decade, that meaningful opportunities for volunteer effort have developed in the community proper in addition to those of the residential school or hospital setting. Among the significant gains made in our total efforts to maximize the development of the retarded person through purposive contacts with normal persons have been the programs developed to include the adolescent volunteer.

The new effort and thrust by these young people is being carried on in many fronts. There are programs in community centers serving the retarded child, adolescent and young adult; in parent-sponsored associations dealing with the needs of retarded persons; in state schools and institutions; in day and resident camps for such handicapped children and even in clinics and hospital settings geared to meet some of the other pressing needs of the retarded child.

Most of these efforts have provided little attention and recognition for the volunteer—the normal adolescent. But even less recognition has been given to the fact that this volunteer participation is not simply a "vacation" from real life to be taken by a few of the young, but has broader implications for development of new career interests through explorations and exposure to new ideas and many people. One particularly productive program using adolescent volunteers was sponsored by the Association for the Help of Retarded Children, New York City Chapter.

The Agency Setting

Started in 1949 by the efforts of a parent seeking service for her child, the Association for the Help of Retarded Children (AHRC), New York City Chapter, has since developed into an organization of parents, professionals and friends of the retarded. Its program encompasses a broad array of health, education and social welfare services for retarded persons of all ages and levels and their families. Several professional disciplines are utilized to provide such services.

Unique in its philosophy is the continuous effort to demonstrate what retarded young people can accomplish in the community under conditions conducive to their potential as family members, workers, friends and community residents.

Aims of the Program

As a social agency, interested in stimulating and innovating change in community patterns of service, the Association's lay and professional leadership looked at and faced the question of how normal adolescents could be utilized in an existing group work program. Conditions were sought which would be appropriate and conducive to the best utilization of professional staff in serving the mentally retarded, and yet would serve to uncover new and creative sources of available volunteer help to carry out vital services. The group of adolescents in the community who wished to give freely and fully of their time and skills appeared to be such a reservoir of help. There was never a question of *if* or *could* the teenager be used, the inquiry was *yes, but how?* The act of volunteering seemed less important than the "how" and "why" of it.

Staff and lay persons felt that the group of normal adolescents represented an important resource to be tapped for volunteers to serve the large group of clients needing help in developing social skills through relationships with a variety of people like and unlike themselves, in utilizing community resources, in developing competencies such as in' bowling and swimming and in acquiring improved self-images through contact with others.

Accordingly when the program for the "Group Work Aide" started in the fall of 1960, the original aims included:

To integrate for the adolescent volunteer an educational experience usually not found in school or at home with strong element of personal service to handicapped individuals.

To develop within the adolescent volunteer a more mature understanding of human needs and problems and variations in people—as seen with the mentally retarded—together with some awareness about himself as part of this society.

To generate a group of aware adolescents, with new perceptions, gained through their own experiences who could bring such new insights regarding mental retardation as a major social problem into their schools, communities, as well as to share such understandings with their friends and families.

To give the adolescent a feeling of being useful to his fellowmen in less fortunate circumstances, and to the community.

To develop actual volunteer work experiences for teenagers, umder supervision of professionally trained social workers, in serving mentally retarded persons of varying chronological ages.

To devise and test ways of recruiting, training and retaining such highly motivated adolescent volunteers.

To open up vistas of career opportunities in social work, teaching and other helping professions permitting those interested to probe without feeling pressure that might be exerted by parents to pursue a particular career or thing

The First Year's Program

The staff and lay people wanted adolescent volunteers who would want to be volunteers more than they would want to play Beatle records or dance. This does not mean that the agency or the teenagers themselves looked down upon such pursuits or even the individuals who pursued them. It just meant that to them, at least, they would want what the agency offered more than they wanted to do some other things available to them.

To initiate the program a cooperative relationship was developed with Wel-Met Camps, a non-profit social agency camp. For a number of years this agency had conducted a teenage careers program for adolescent girls. This relationship provided a supply of interested volunteers that could be tapped without involving the AHRC staff in time-consuming recruitment activities in the community. The savings in staff time and effort were put into developing the other aspects of the volunteer program. Hence use of existing community resources, which are numerous and are typified by this camp, was a basic ingredient in the recruitment process.

To be eligible as volunteers the girls had to be in high school at least at the 10th-year level and 13 years, or more, of age by July 1. This minimum age was developed to permit young and generally inexperienced persons to come into and develop within the program. Teenagers were expected to discuss the activity and its implications (e.g., work with retardates who might be chronologically older, travel, evening meetings, regularity and giving up time that could be devoted to school work or family activities) with their parents and secure a letter of approval.

In addition, two letters of recommendation were requested from persons such as teachers, physicians, ministers, employers, and others in the community, to indicate the applicant's reliability, maturity and relationships with people. A commitment to participate in training was part of the requirements. A health examination and chest x-ray were required of all volunteers. A personal statement including the young person's reasons for applying to the program was included to ascertain her interest in such activity, her level of maturity and understanding of what was involved. Working papers were required for volunteers under 18 years of age as part of the state legal provisions. Finally, emotional stability, although difficult to determine, along with a high degree of motivation and desire to work with children were looked for in each young person. Each applicant was interviewed by the director of group work, a trained social worker.

Because the staff desired to use a small group, one that was manageable in terms of providing training, supervision and development, three girls were selected for the first year. These girls were referred to as "Group Work Aides." Their assignments included work within a social club or friendship group made up solely of retardates.

"Matching" a volunteer with a group or an individual was a difficult job and at best represented a series of risks for all concerned. As these girls were young (average age was 15 years) and had little experience in work with people, the retarded individuals to whom they related were selected carefully and included relatively uncomplicated cases who needed such relationships and/or help in skill development such as crafts, bowling or social dancing. Deciding upon the group to be assigned to the volunteer involved considerations such as the group worker's skill in dealing with such a young person, the age level of the group (to avoid its being made up of much older retardates who might perceive the aide in unusual ways) and finally, the needs of the group and its members for the additional program content. The amount of travel involved, the adolescent's availability and her own interests were additional factors considered in making assignments.

In each group there was a trained social worker and a college student assistant, in addition to the aide. The aide assisted in work with the group and with the individual by providing companionship and participating in the program. These activities included helping with crafts, outdoor games, making trips in the community, managing and working with an individual child to assist him in self-care areas such as dress and toileting.

The aides worked with different age groups. One girl assisted with a group of severely retarded young adults, another with a mildly retarded children's group and the third with a group of moderately retarded children. Each girl had about an hour's travel to and from home, exclusive of the two-hour group session. The aides also proved to be quite generously available for planning before and after the meeting, special events and other similar activities. It was clearly indicated in the orientation and agreed to by the aides that they were performing a community service to less fortunate individuals and that promptness and regularity of attendance were extremely important in giving the retarded a feeling of acceptance.

An agency does not find or get the services of the volunteer simply because it finds teens ripe for plucking. A volunteer may have been involved even though she did not have any special skills. There must be clear-cut job expectations about the job these volunteers are to do, in relation to their ability. To get the volunteer in a position to do the job, a training program was set up. The AHRC expected the volunteer to be willing to learn and to take part in this training program, while the volunteer counted upon the Association to provide instruction and supportive help as she went along. "Teachableness" is an attractive and priceless quality when found in a teenage volunteer.

During the September to June program, the aides participated in monthly training sessions conducted by the director of group work. The first was an all-day session held before the aides began meeting with their groups and dealt with what the retarded individuals were like (focusing upon the person, not upon the disability, the dynamic nature of retardation, the levels of retardation); how to begin with a group (establishing rapport and relationship, use of program, communication); what the third worker or aide meant to the group, to the leaders and to the aide herself (role identity and avoidance of role strain or confusion); and administrative information regarding AHRC (its services, where to go for supplies and materials, its history, and a perspective in relation to the total agency operation). She was helped on a beginning basis to see where she fitted into the agency setting.

The small group of three girls started out with lots of enthusiasm and determination to help but lacked self-confidence and needed much supervision and "spelling out" of tasks in the beginning. Suggestions were given on how to communicate with a retarded person, about methods of partializing the program and about developing concrete content in activities.

Thereafter, the aides met one evening a month, at a supper meeting, and covered two specific areas of content: (1) work with a group of retardates; and (2) program skills. The first content area included needs of the retardates, what needs arise from dysfunction of the individual, how to use program media and activities, how to work with the individual and the group, what values underlie AHRC's way of serving people, and how to set realistic goals. Considerable opportunities were given the volunteers to discuss their own experiences and ideas.

Program skill development included instruction in songs, games, social and folk dances, and crafts—all aimed at increasing the aide's ability to know the program media and to use it appropriately.

Direct supervision was provided by the trained social group worker who spent an hour with the aide every two weeks to review the aide's progress and problems and to assist her in doing a better job. This supervision, as it was developed by experienced workers, served to provide opportunities for the aide to learn how to work with the individual and the group; planning programs to use the aide's skills and relationships; and evaluation of the aide's helping role with the individual and the group. Such tutorial help was made available in a supportive, non-threatening way, always concrete in content, and respectful of the teenager's background and maturity. The conferences were usually held after the group meeting.

In actual experience the teens' ideas blossomed under the careful supervision of the professionals with whom they worked. The aide's ability to take on increased and more complicated tasks and relationships reflected her heightened capacity for giving help.

Aides were held to expectations regarding their responsibilities. They were told, "You're expected to turn up just as if you were paid." They were required to provide sufficient preparation for the group's activities, to dress properly, and spend sufficient time after the meeting with the group leaders or with parents and siblings.

Firmness was required in recognizing that lines had to be drawn between what the volunteer could do and what the professional could do, if unfortunate results were to be avoided. A specific illustration—that of attempting to "compete" with the professional for child's affection—was utilized.

First Year's Evaluation

In evaluating the first year's program, the aides reported that they had been exposed to a new world, one which gave them considerable satisfaction. They indicated that such satisfactions included being of service to others; gaining a new and enhanced image of themselves as responsible persons; identification with the agency and its staff of social workers; and finding new friends among parents, retardates and other aides. In fact, before the program season ended, 10 unsolicited applications came from other adolescents, friends of the volunteers, who wanted to be a part of the program.

While the teenagers realized that no dramatic changes had been effected in the lives, abilities or outlooks of the retarded persons with whom they worked, they also saw that these relationships and activities had brought to the retarded and their families a sense of renewed interest by the community. The aides also learned that it takes time to learn, to make responsible decisions, to know one's place in the program and to get to know the agency and its function in order to do the jobs needing to be done.

The teenage volunteer found that it took courage to stand up to friends and families who were not so convinced about their need to assist, and who also made demands of the aide, and that it took courage to deal with the professional. It took faith for the adolescent to believe in the worthwhileness of her own contribution even though immediate results might not seem to be commensurate with the time and effort spent in training, thinking, and doing, required by volunteering.

When pressures of examinations, friendship and family sometimes created less enthusiasm as the volunteer was finishing her assignment, the AHRC stepped in with solid recognition of the good job she had done with the group or individual retardate in order to counteract the murmurs on the home, school or friendship front. Sound recognition was part of agency responsibility. Volunteers were not only told that they were helping "somebody," but the agency also developed a system of recognition based on sound achievement, not at inflated or low levels, which may consist only of a certificate at an end of the season party.

More than adding to the volume of services, teen volunteers brought special qualities of value: inquiring minds; a willingness to shift efforts and acquire new learnings when needs change; a capacity to plan and a willingness to say yes; and probably most important—commitment.

There were times when wanting to serve, being able to do something or being willing to try, endearing as these qualities may be, were not enough, *per se*, to give the teen volunteer the willpower to withstand the impact of the retardate and the problems he presented. Teenagers and staff agreed that motivation, conviction, commitment and dedication to purpose were also essential.

Their volunteer experience was viewed as a real learning experience by the participating teenagers, and as a good reference for future use with employer or a college.

Second Year's Experience

After careful evaluation of the first year's experiences by the professional group work staff, by the lay members of the Group Work Committee, and by the group work aides themselves, it was agreed that a meaningful pattern and base had been established for the program and that no major changes were required at the beginning of the second year.

A relationship was established with the community service club of a girl's high school, Hunter College High School. This group, in contrast to the previous social agency which the AHRC staff had sought out, initiated this contact on its own after making a survey of several social problem areas. The cooperative relationship with an established school group buttressed the program's objectives. The involvement of such community groups provided feedback of volunteers' experiences into a larger audience made up of teachers, social workers, parents, fellow students and friends.

Fifteen aides were accepted in 1961 and included two boys for the first time. The entire first year's group returned. Thirty adolescents were processed. Several applicants were friends of the three original aides. While letters from parents and other persons, and the teen's application itself were helpful, the major screening instrument was the interview with the director of group work. In an informal and relaxed setting, the teenager had an opportunity to discuss his or her interests while the social worker was able to explain what being a volunteer meant, and what the agency offered and looked for. Ten teens withdrew voluntarily while another five were deemed incapable of such volunteer activity. In all instances, such withdrawal or rejection was handled with sensitivity.

With the increase in aides, assignments were now more varied and differentiated. Beginning aides—those 13 and 14 years of age—were assigned to assist in social dancing, bowling, swimming and one-day trips to nearby places of interest. This selective use of the younger aide lessened the threat of working with a group. These experiences involved a one-to-one, or person to person, helping process such as teaching a retarded child or adolescent how to swim, or to bowl, or to keep score. This procedure proved extremely effective as a stepping stone to work with a group which required more experience and sophistication on the part of the aide. These opportunities for individual relationships helped to establish a new policy; that a new aide would begin in work with an individual retardate around a specific activity. Matching an aide with a retarded person became less difficult.

Those teenagers assigned to work with groups were placed nearer to their homes to lessen the travel involved. Training continued at the pace established during the previous year.

The staff found that the aides were not content merely to accept what was taught them and then to repeat it, as a first step in learning. Often many aides wanted to learn more than they could handle or integrate into their knowledge and skills.

In addition, they observed the professional staff's functioning, such as in making decisions about appropriate interventions, and noted how staff members consulted with colleagues and the director. The aides sometimes had views different from the professional staff regarding areas such as self-determination or limit setting. They had strong opinions on phases of the program, including the individual capacities of the retardates. They started to see and feel little signs or sparks which they made in the work with the individuals and groups.

With such a young and impressionable group of adolescents, close relationships were formed with the individual group leader—a trained social worker—who frequently became a role model for the young person involved. There were no major incidents involving lack of responsibility, interest or even a dropout.

In the spring of 1962, three of the aides were invited to participate in the agency's Summer Day Camp Program. This five-days-a-week program, six weeks in duration, was intensive in scope and served moderately and severely retarded children five to 15 years of age. In their performance the aides indicated an ability to cope with this sensitive and intensive situation by adding to the retardate's life experiences and contacts with youthful and enthusiastic persons.

Third Year's Developments

By 1962, the volunteer program seemed fairly well established and stabilized in its operations. As the program became known, inquiries came from friends of the aides, from parents, from high schools and from parents of the retarded who had normal adolescent children. A policy decision was made that volunteers had to come forth on their own; parent-initiated contacts frequently reflected more parental than adolescent concern for such activity.

A group of 28 teens was accepted this program year. About 60 were processed.

Those who were not accepted seemed incapable of establishing meaningful relationships with retarded persons while those who withdrew on their own could not meet time requirements, or found that such volunteer activity was not what they had envisioned. For the first time adolescent siblings of the retarded came into the program. Two of the three aides in the first year group returned while all 12 of the second year group came back.

Graduate social work students and a supervisor of group work were now part of the program staff and lent strength in the form of additional time and effort needed for screening, training and supervision.

The staff was concerned about recruitment of boys (now numbering four of 28) and involvement of minority group volunteers.

Efforts to recruit adolescent boys were not successful. While other social agency staffs reported similar experiences, AHRC staff could find only one plausible explanation for such difficulties—some boys had part-time employment. Contacts made with major community groups working with Negro and Puerto Rican youths were not productive as these young people wanted—and needed—paid employment. The staff had hoped that such recruitment would aid in better service to the retarded child and to the development of opportunities for the minority adolescent. While these initial efforts were not fruitful although considerable staff activity was invested in such recruitment, nevertheless such contacts and efforts were continued as staff felt that such young people were needed in the program.

Orientation and inservice training was now conducted on two levels: (1) for the new and (2) for the experienced aide. The experienced aide assisted the staff in orientation for the new group, and on other occasions, helped to conduct part of the monthly training sessions. Both groups met separately for orientation and training sessions.

During the second part of the year, after January, the staff noted the development of some group characteristics as indicated by a "we" feeling, cohesion and mutual support. Individual teens reported that some status was attached to their activities by friends, parents and teachers.

The young people themselves became involved in applying for a Parent's Magazine Youth Achievement Award. They, together with staff, wrote the application indicating the group's achievements. In the fall of the year the group and the AHRC were honored by the bestowal of the award.

With additional volunteer opportunities made available by Spring and Winter Day Camp programs during those holiday weeks, added meaning was given to the role of the aide who helped to provide additional concrete services for the retarded child.

As some aides were entering college in the fall, the agency agreed that such aides would be eligible for agency employment as assistant group leaders. This policy was established as the aide program was seen as one for high school students, but since the agency hired college students as assistant group leaders such employment it was felt should be available to aides in college.

Ten aides were used in Day Camp that summer. Those aides who were at camp for the first year received a $15 gift, while those who had been at camp the previous year received a $25 gift as a way of indicating the agency's recognition of the aide's contribution to the program.

Fourth Year's Progress

During 1963-1964, 32 young people were enrolled; 75 per cent were with the program the previous year.

Administratively the program was now fully established as part of the agency's ongoing Group Work Program. Commitment to proper processing and selection of applicants, training, supervision and meaningful assignments were maintained.

The first aide in the program recently informed the staff that she was planning to major in special education—teaching the retarded. Three additional aides were in undergraduate pre-social work programs. It is expected that these young people, and other aides, will move with confidence and competence into teaching and social work positions, as well as related helping activities.

The agency staff and lay persons, including the governing board and the Group Work Committee, now view the program as an integral part of the overall agency program.

What We Have Learned

For all involved in this volunteer program, considerable knowledge has been evolved from these experiences. This paper does not merely assume "success." There were false starts, mistaken design, the mishaps and the short views that characterize new developments and innovations. But lots of other things were learned from the hard effort by staff, lay persons and the aides, and from the retardates and families served.

These learnings included:

About the Adolescents: They feel that they have accomplished something useful in helping "somebody become someone." And we think they did. They realize that the "attractive people" are the ones who do something worthwhile when they have given of themselves. Consequently their lives have more meaning in terms of a value system which places stress upon human values. Most of the teenagers evaluated the experience in terms such as "most valuable," "worthwhile" and "great."

Who were the Teen Group Work Aides? As a group, the following characteristics emerged; these young persons were bright, articulate individuals, averaging 15 years of age and in the 10th year of school, from lower- and middle-income economic and social backgrounds. Of 78 volunteers, 12 or 15 per cent were boys while 66 or 85 per cent were girls. Such individuals were usually involved in extracurricular activities at school and provided leadership in school activities. They were highly motivated and had actually sought out such roles as the agency offered in this program. It is our considered judgment that there are many more such adolescents in the community, available for volunteer and community activity.

What kind of an adolescent makes for a good volunteer with the retarded? The least effective ones were those with lots of jargon and theories about mental retardation. The most effective ones thought of, and felt about, the retarded as people.

They showed a substantial interest in others. They were committed, pragmatic, not overly judgmental, optimistic, energetic, enthusiastic, giving freely and fully of themselves and able to accept supervision and criticism. The adolescent siblings of the retarded were in the effective group.

What have we learned from these adolescents?

Teen volunteers in a group work program for the mentally retarded have a significant part to play. They were partners in an enterprise of considerable proportions and they performed a function which was essential for the program participants and for them.

The role of the teenage volunteer was a varied one where he or she was able to take on a number of different assignments.

Each volunteer needs to be part of a well-defined and developed agency orientation and training program.

There was never a question of "exploiting" this volunteer as he or she was a "plus" factor who needed considerable training and supervision which was more costly than the assistance the teenager rendered if one were to venture into the erroneous path of measurement.

The aide needs to be held to limits. By limits we mean coming and leaving on time, proper attire, attendance at training and participation in special events. It was most important that volunteers were reliable and steady. Irregularity in attendance tended to be interpreted as rejection by the retardate and/or his family.

The agency must provide for a release of feeling which young volunteers have regarding the mentally retarded.

There were no problems of excessive emotional involvement as signs of such problematic behaviors were picked up in supervision; emphasis was placed upon the little but significant gains made by the volunteer. Not one teenage volunteer dropped out because of disillusionment, or anxiety. Nothing happened to a teen or retardate which could be construed as intensely upsetting.

Deep personal involvement was possible and not harmful. There are feelings of failure.

Volunteers need to get a genuine feeling of accomplishment, of worth and of enjoyment. Frustrations do and will occur; a sign of accomplishment will go far to balance the scale.

The volunteer learned that the mentally retarded do not need deep psychological understanding but rather encouragement, support and concrete assistance aimed at building up their self-images through development of a repertoire of social skills and other competencies.

The teenager learned that the mentally retarded child is like all children with needs, feeling, desires and aspirations. The volunteer saw and felt growth and change in such youngsters although this was sometimes difficult to create, and sometimes to perceive.

The teenager was part of a valuable life experience which had meaning for him. Commitment and interest on the part of the teenage volunteer carried him through to a good level of performance.

These young people learned that there are meaningful opportunities in the community around them for service to the less fortunate, that with training and supervision they can be helpful, that being held to the demands of the job was worthwhile as the retarded children needed the warmth and enthusiasm of the relationship.

The teenager learned, too, about mental retardation as a social problem in his own community and how the community needs to help by careful planning, by adequate funds, by human effort and with changing attitudes which accept the retardate as a person with dignity and worth. He also learned how he, as a volunteer, added to the worthwhile goal of improving conditions of living.

About the Retardate and His Family: The retarded person and his family welcomed the young volunteer who cared enough to give of himself to a "stranger" in need. The families appreciated the aide's ability to work with the retardate, to supply youthful spirit and enthusiasm that helped the retardate grow, change and achieve, as well as to provide reassurance that nurtured parental hope. The families viewed the companionship and extra attention made possible by the teenager as important as the program activity itself.

From the families and the retardates themselves, the aides learned of the family-center aspects of mental retardation (feelings and reactions, care and management, guidance and training and providing for the future) as well as its community-oriented components (lack of planning, fragmentation and paucity of services). The meaning of a defective child or sibling in the family was dramatically and vividly conveyed to the adolescent aide. The impact of the retardate upon his parents and siblings, as well as their effect upon the retarded member, made a strong impression upon the aide.

About Lay Agency Leadership: While the lay leaders of the AHRC developed conviction about the utilitization of adolescent volunteers in the agency's group work program, they learned that such efforts required careful development involving considerable professional time, money and activity. The building of continuity and tradition in such programs, as well as the *esprit d'corps* which emerged, were perceived by the lay leadership as important results. The major and overwhelming impact of the aide program to which the lay person responded was the increased and improved services made available to the retarded person.

Another significant and meaningful gain which they saw was the exposure of young people to possible career choices in professions involving work with the retarded. The lay leadership was able to see for themselves how pre-professional persons could work with the professional to provide concerted services to the retardate.

In observing the usefulness of the aide program, the AHRC Board and Group Work Committee evolved further firm belief in the program which culminated in providing funds, as well as participating in a meaningful recognition program for the group work aide. At the end of each program season, each aide was given a simple and well-written certificate presented at an agency party.

About the Professional Staff: The agency's full- and part-time professional staff members had to work through their feelings and doubts about whether all the time and effort to be invested in developing an adolescent volunteer program was worthwhile. Out of such planning considerations came a full commitment that this program merited their complete support. Teenage volunteers were seen as bringing with them endearing qualities such as enthusiasm, commitment and interest in people which the professional staff found exciting to behold.

From such experiences, the professional staff learned that: careful selection and training of the aide is the key to the program's success; structured experiences for the aides were helpful; peer and family involvement was important in giving support to the adolescent and in recognizing the value of the experience for him or her, and most important, the social needs of the individual retardate could be met by young people.

Staff learned, too, that additional effort is needed to recruit boys as well as members of minority groups and adolescents from low-income groups to give them a niche in the program and to assist in their participation which, for them, could lead to a career tryout.

With the shortage of workers in the helping profession, such as social work, the professional learned—or it was re-emphasized for him—that direct work with the adolescent provided a role model for the young person which stimulated interest in the retarded persons as well as developing career concerns in this helping profession.

Reports from the trained social workers, working with groups, as well as the full-time group work staff indicated that this group of adolescent aides was challenging, stimulating, innovating—and refreshing to work with.

A New Role for the Adolescent

The program is now established on its own merit as an integral part of the total agency's program. The agency's capacity to respect and nurture the individual aide's strength resulted in the production of an adolescent volunteer whose growth went to full potential. As these young people finish high school and college, we will learn of the impact of the experience on their career plans, upon their citizen roles. In the meantime, the impact upon their own self image and their value system has been demonstrated. Also, we are convinced—and we have reason to believe that the teenagers concurred—that their probing is their way of attempting to find some reality in their lives, some relevance to social problems.

One of the most civilizing features of adolescence is what some psychologists call the "psycho-moratorium" which provides a period of years free from adult pressures, commitments and responsibilities in which the young people may engage in "the search for identity." During this time adolescents may play and experiment with social roles in an attempt to find out who and what they are (Berger, 1965). Helping as a volunteer (in this instance with the retarded) seems to define a constructive and useful role for the adolescent.

Reference

BERGER, B. M. Teen Agers Are An American Invention. *The New York Times Magazine,* June 13, 1965.

EIGHTY-FOUR

Professional Staff and the Problem of Preciousness

SEYMOUR SARASON, MURRAY LEVINE, IRA GOLDENBERG, DENNIS L. CHERLIN, AND EDWARD M. BENNETT

We briefly discussed the tendency of mental-health professionals to view their technical skills in very precious kinds of ways, that is, to overestimate the differences in skills among the professions and to underestimate the communalities. This is an understandable tendency, perhaps inevitable, given the nature of training programs. . . . [and] it is certainly not our view that all boundaries among the fields should be broken down. Each field does have a core of distinctiveness, and this should be both recognized and treasured. It is one thing, however, to say that each field has a distinctive core of skills and it is quite another thing to say that *everything* a particular profession does is either distinctive or not, in part at least, learnable by the other professions in the settings in which they work together. The history of the child-guidance movement is a clear example of how professional preciousness was gradually dissipated, particularly in the face of the pressure of waiting lists. This dissipation was not always accomplished gracefully or smoothly, because having to alter a conception of professional distinctiveness can be experienced as something akin to a "narcissistic wound." The fact is that even if professional preciousness is not a problem, the unmet mental-health needs in our society confront the mental-health professions with serious questions about the appropriateness of the existing pattern of services and the inadequate numbers of graduates from existing training programs, factors about which Albee (1963, 1964) has written cogently and eloquently.

Within a clinic, usually because it is a relatively small social system facilitating interprofessional contact, professional preciousness tends not to be the problem it is in the larger institutional setting. Our earlier experiences in relatively large institutions made it clear that the pattern of staff organization was both a symptom and a cause of professional preciousness that had some unfortunate consequences. Typically, an institution for the retarded is made up of several "empires": social service, medical, psychological, educational, cottage life, vocational, and others. This pattern of staffing, by no means peculiar to institutions for mentally retarded children, tends to have the following consequences:

From *Psychology in Community Settings: Clinical, Educational, Social Aspects* (New York, John Wiley, 1966), pp. 587-591, 625-630. By permission of the authors and John Wiley & Sons, Inc.

1. Each of the departments is a little (or big) enclave within which there is far more communication than between departments.

2. Each department tends to view problems of policy and change primarily in terms of effects on its functioning, status, and role so that it has difficulty viewing problems in terms of larger issues.

3. The possibility that those in one department will truly understand the functions and problems of those in another department is drastically reduced.

4. The broadening of knowledge and skills of those within a department tends to occur within very narrow limits.

5. Each department has a responsibility for a "piece of the child," a tendency conducive neither to a comprehensive view of the child nor of the instititution's program.

6. Cold and hot wars can develop when one department perceives that another department is performing something similar to its functions. Such conflicts, unfortunately, tend to be complicated by considerations other than those reflecting preciousness.

These kinds of experiences and considerations led us to suggest to the Regional Center a rationale for staff functioning that had three aims: (1) to make explicit in the process of interviewing and hiring personnel the problems of professional preciousness and the need to combat them; (2) to maximize the amount of experience of professional staff with *all* aspects of the program of the Regional Center; (3) to provide a means whereby each of the professions could help those with different professional training gain experience in certain aspects of its traditional functions.

In its most simple form our suggestion was that *everybody would engage in similar activities.* By "everybody" we referred to social workers, physicians, psychologists, speech therapists, educators, and rehabilitation workers; by "engaging in similar activities" we meant that, to a certain extent at least, each of these people would take complete responsibility for a case shortly after the initial contact with the Regional Center was made and would continue such responsibility as long as the case was appropriate for the Regional Center. In other words the speech therapist would do more than speech therapy, a physician would do more than examine children and handle medical problems, a social worker would do more than visit homes and be concerned with extra-Center problems, and an educator would be concerned with more than the child in a school program.

The sense of our suggestion can be understood more clearly if we describe how it is implemented in practice.

1. All cases referred to the Regional Center are brought up for discussion at a conference of several hours duration. The professional staff is present at this conference, so that a dozen or more people may attend.

2. After the available information on a case is presented and discussed the question is routinely raised as to who should assume full responsibility for the case. "Full responsibility" means that, from that point on, the staff member assigned to the case is responsible for handling all problems, arranging for whatever subsequent procedures are deemed necessary, supervising the transition of the case from

the community to any of the Regional Center programs (residential or day care), and staying with the case for as long as it is in a Regional Center program.

3. The staff member responsible for a case can call on the services of any other staff member depending on the kinds of problems encountered and the information needed. However, and regardless of the number of other staff members called on, the "responsible" staff member is the one who coordinates these services and works with the family. In other words, from the standpoint of the family there is one staff member with whom they have primary contact and to whom they can come at any time.

4. The assignment of a case is determined by what the conference considers to be the most important features of the case, that is, those features, questions, or problems that will require understanding and solution if an appropriate program for that family is to be developed and implemented. For example, in a fair number of cases a variety of state and community agencies has been involved with a particular family so that it is clear it will require on the part of the staff member a degree of knowledge of and experience with the practices and traditions of these agencies that will allow him to be of maximum help to the family at the same time that inter-agency relationships are kept smooth, a task requiring exceptional skill. In these instances a social worker is assigned to the case. In a number of cases where the major questions center around the degree of speech and hearing possessed by a child and/or the family's understanding of and response to such problems in their child, the primary responsibility for the case is given to the speech therapist. There have been cases in which the conference has decided that the major problem is whether a problem in mental retardation is involved, or whether it is some kind of psychological disturbance in the child and the family. In these instances the clinical psychologist may be given responsibility for the case. Later in this chapter we describe in detail an instance in which the physician was given responsibility for a case. The important point here is that responsibility for a case—handling all aspects from the initial home visit to and after the point when the child is settled in a program—is not predetermined by professional labels.

5. The staff member responsible for a case is expected to bring it back to conference whenever a policy question has come up or when the staff member feels in need of some sort of guidance from the conference. The guidance of the conference is not, however, viewed as a substitute for the individual help and guidance a staff member may require of other staff members. We must emphasize that it is explicit in this process that each staff member has an in-service training responsibility to other staff members, and the failure to seek or to give such training is a serious matter.

6. When the staff member has decided tentatively about a program for child and family he brings the case back to conference. He presents his "prescription," that is, his answers to the following kinds of questions. When should the child be entered into a program? Is this a child who will experience separation difficulties when brought to what is for him a new physical and social setting? Should the child be brought several times for short visits to the Center before exposing him to full-

time residence or day-care programs? Will either of the parents experience separation difficulties? Is it indicated that the responsible staff member go to the home and actually participate in the transition to the Center? If the child is entering the residential program, in what living unit should he be placed and what should personnel in this unit know about the child, for example, feeding habits, food preferences, toilet habits, special behavioral characteristics, parental expectations and attitudes?[1] Into what training program should the children go? Should the parent be invited or strongly urged to become part of a parent group and, if so, which parent group and what should the group leader know about the parents? The answers to these and other questions constitute the prescription the staff member responsible for the case develops and brings to the conference.

There are advantages, dangers, and problems in giving this degree of responsibility to staff members whose training has not formally prepared them to assume the degree of responsibility described. . . .

At this point we present the first case in which this approach was used, a case in which a physician initially assumed full responsibility. The dramatic consequences of the physician's going into the home (rather than the social worker, as would traditionally be the case) are by no means typical but this case did serve to highlight for the staff the potential fruitfulness of the approach.

The Case of Joe

Joe, four and a half years of age, was one of many children on the waiting list of the State Office of Mental Retardation. Those children on the list who were in the greater New Haven area became the responsibility of the Regional Center. One year before the Center was scheduled to open, the Center's skeleton staff and members of the Psycho-Educational Clinic began the task of reviewing *each* case for which it would need to provide services.

Joe's case is illustrative of a number of things, for example, the need to be skeptical of previous findings and observations without falling into the trap of cynicism; the importance of seeing child and family on their home grounds; the productive effects of direction and support on their home grounds; the productive effects of direction and support of parental actions, when they are deemed appropriate and necessary; and the importance of correlating and using first-hand knowledge gained in one setting (e.g., Clinic) with that obtained in other settings (e.g., home, school), a procedure basic to the rationale employed in our work in the public schools. However, for our present purposes Joe's case is of primary significance for discussion of the view toward staff functioning presented earlier.

The consequences of using professional staff in ways unfamiliar to them, and for which their training did not directly prepare them, are not always as dramatic as in the case of Joe. Also, the fact that the Regional Center had not yet opened its doors prevented us from experiencing all the problems that might come up when a variety of professional personnel are given responsibility for a case beginning with the first home visit and continuing through and beyond adjustment of the child to a day-care or residential program. In short, our discussion of the advantages and limitations of our view toward staff functioning is based on pilot experiences in a situation (i.e., preparing to open an institution) that, while conducive to innovation, is not exactly conducive to systematic exploration. But we think the issues involved are of such importance as to justify reporting our view of our experiences.

Advantages

When we look at each staff member not only in terms of his professional label but also in terms of competencies and potentialities that are not necessarily discernible from the label, our views about and practices in hiring personnel undergo marked change. We do not view the psychologist only in terms of diagnostic testing or psychotherapy, or the physician only in terms of physical examinations, medication, and hospital affairs, or the teacher as one whose responsibilities are confined to a classroom and school building, or the speech therapist as one who works only with those having speech problems, or the social worker as one who focuses only on work with the family. It goes without saying that we look closely at training and competency in relation to what is distinctive in each field. In addition, however, we look for interests and potentialities that suggest that the individual could learn to assume skills more or less common to the work of all who help others, for characteristics and special competencies that maximize communalities rather than differences among the various professional fields. The process for achieving this begins at the point of hiring. As we shall see later, not everyone looks kindly at an attempt to stress what is or could become common to the different professions.

The most immediate advantage of our view of staff functioning is that it provides each member with opportunities to experience and be responsible for total service to a family. Rather than seeing problems only within the context of the practices and skills of a single profession, staff members are able to gain a more realistic picture of the complex and changing interrelationships among presenting problems, diagnostic evaluations, program planning, and the processes of implementation. Because of existing and proposed programs as well as relationships with personnel from other fields, the staff member gains a perspective not ordinarily attainable when he works only within the confines of his own profession or department.

One of the consequences of what the staff member gains by assuming responsibility and performing functions usually thought to be in the province of other professionals is that to the extent that staff members attain flexibility of role the agency has more people to call on as conditions require. If the Regional Center had been forced to assign responsibilities to staff members strictly in accord with their training and professional label, it would have hardly rendered any service in the period before its full professional staff had been hired and its facilities ready to open. In fact, even if the Regional Center had at a very early stage its full complement of staff, the pressure of new cases as well as the need to review old cases were sufficient to have created a long waiting list for social-casework service if, as is usually the case, it had been social workers who were solely responsible for home visits, collection and coordination of relevant information, and the rendering of whatever help was necessary and available.[2]

As we pointed out, ... the concept of the Regional Center embodies the aim of bolstering existing programs and helping to develop new programs in the community, that is, the Regional Center has not come into existence in order to facilitate the termination of ongoing programs in the community. *To achieve these aims requires a staff that knows the community in the sense that it is knowledgeable about available services, and is involved in the community in the sense that it represents the agency to certain families in the community. A community-oriented staff is not one that spends most, if not all, of its time away from the community and inside the walls of its own facility. A community-oriented staff is not one that experiences its problems in its institutional setting and rarely has the opportunity to see how the problems manifest themselves in their natural setting. A staff cannot be community-oriented if because of its own physical isolation from the community or lack of commerce with it, it knows only its own programs and has little interest in adding strength to programs other than its own. A community-oriented staff member is not one who talks only with people in his field, be they in his agency or elsewhere in the community.*

One of the most interesting and encouraging aspects of the implementation of our view about staff functioning was (with some notable exceptions) willingness, if not eagerness, on the part of individuals to engage in the venture and to assume the responsibilities involved, to be constantly aware of the help they would require and to be prepared to give help to others in regard to their own fields. We hardly need to emphasize that successful implementation of this approach depends in large measure on the seriousness with which the in-service training features are faced and handled. Our approach is not merely one of "spreading the work around" or equalizing levels of responsibilities because of some abstract conception of professional equality. It is also *not* part of our approach that everyone should be doing the same things in equal degree, but rather that all professional staff should, to some extent at least, share similar responsibilities.

There is no doubt in the case of the Regional Center that implementation of our approach resulted in more cases receiving more service more quickly than if the more traditional mode of staff functioning had prevailed. But what about quality of service? We must face squarely that for a period of time each staff member performing unaccustomed duties or assuming an unfamiliar degree of responsibility will probably not render the quality of service that a more experienced staff could render. With adequate supervision, however, this differential should decease. It is our impression, and it would be our prediction, that if this approach is implemented well it results in a professional growth of staff and in an interstaff relationship that makes for better service to the individual. In judging an institution or program we routinely ask about the quality of service to its clients; that is, to what extent have they changed in the desired direction? *It is our contention that an equally important question—the answer to which bears on quality of service to clients— concerns the opportunities for staff to grow, professionally and personally, in desired ways.*

We make no claim to have given our approach to staff functioning an adequate or extensive test. We do have sufficient experience with this approach to be able to say that the principles involved are worthy of further study. Parochialism of view and experience, shortages of professional personnel (now and in the foreseeable future), interprofessional conflicts and hostilities, the effects of institutionalization on staff (as well as patients) are but some of the consideration that should put a premium on innovation in and critical re-examination of existing practices.

Limitations

When we give people a degree of responsibility and/or ask them to discharge certain functions for which their training does not directly prepare them, we clearly run the risk of diluting quality of services and creating confused professional identities. When the welfare of patients is at stake we do not lightly tamper with the existing order. It may very well be a limitation of our approach that it requires for its successful implementation a degree of professional responsibility and of clinical sophistication, as well as a commitment to training, that are infrequently found in combination in one setting. Unfortunately, however, our experience suggests that where this combination is found the desire to innovate or the response to the innovations of others tends in the first instance to be weak and in the second instance violent or indifferent but rarely neutral. We cannot expect professional preciousness to be overcome or studied in settings in which adherence to the existing order is a source of satisfaction.

Even where there is agreement among staff, as there was in the case of the Regional Center, to view staff functions in the way we have described, we must expect that, when confronted with the realities inherent in change, some individuals will prefer to stay within a familiar tradition. This, of course, can present problems among staff, particularly if the difficulties are not verbalized. It is our experience that the more the staff members can verbalize problems, questions, and reservations about staff organization the more opportunity we have to discuss fundamentals: the significance of shortages in the different professions, the implications of a community orientation for staff functioning, the constricting effects to complete departmentalization of staff on professional growth, etc. However, we cannot deny that what at one time appeared to a staff member as a worthwhile experiment can become at a later time an intolerable situation toward which there is little likelihood of a change in attitude. Such changes in attitudes are to be expected and respected, but not accepted at the cost of impairing staff organization and efficiency. We consider this type of situation a limitation of our approach because it puts an additional burden on those in positions of leadership to be vigilant and sensitive to what is going on and to be prepared to take decisive action—characteristics in short supply among those who are in positions of leadership in mental-health settings (perhaps in short supply among leaders in other types of settings).

In and of itself innovation is neither good nor bad. When innovation becomes an end in itself, a way of achieving distinctiveness and recognition, or a way of denying that tradition has anything to offer, it is likely to be short-lived in time and space.

But innovation can be short-lived precisely because it requires an attitude toward change and experimentation, a search for rather than an avoidance of possibilities of growth and development, a kind of self-scrutiny which discriminates between issues of ideas and status, the capacity to entertain the possibility that what has been done may not be right, and confronting the fact that truth is an elusive commodity the possession of which allows certain people to avoid any further need to change or question. The nature of training in the mental-health and educational professions tends to extinguish—or at least not to reinforce—those characteristics necessary for productive innovation and this imposes a restriction on what we may hope to accomplish.

The opportunity we had at the Regional Center to try out ideas about staff functions and organization is rare, primarily because we were part of the Regional Center almost from its conception and because it had a director who on his own came to see the need for innovation. We have not spent this chapter on our ideas and experiences in relation to staff functioning because we have hard data about the effectiveness of our efforts or because we are completely secure in our feelings that we are correct. Our major aims have been to indicate the severe limitations of traditional patterns of staffing, to illustrate how this worked in a particular case, to make clear some of the pros and cons of our approach, and, most important, to convey to the reader our conviction that we are raising some legitimate and important questions that for too long have gone unraised and unstudied. If our impressions or intuitions are correct, we have raised questions that in the course of training and practice have occurred to many people in the different professions concerned with problems of help, be it help in a Regional Center for the mentally retarded, in a state hospital, a mental-hygiene clinic, or in a school. In some ultimate sense it is less important if in this chapter we have posed the right questions and given the right answers than if we helped start or continue a discussion about the characteristics and sources of professional preciousness and their consequences for the professional individual, for those whom he is supposed to serve, and for the larger issues surrounding the serving of the public welfare.

References

[1] Anyone who has worked in institutions for young or handicapped children is aware that it is by no means infrequent that the difficulties encountered by children (*and* the cottage or hospital personnel responsible for his care) in the weeks after admission are due to ignorance of personnel about the answers these questions provide.

[2] The traditional approach to staff functioning is seen in the following quotation from an article on psychiatric aspects of mental retardation (Menolascino, 1965): "Treatment considerations begin with the initial contact with our social worker, where the presenting problem is discussed; parental expectations from the evaluation are explored; and legal releases are obtained to allow for collation of data from previous medical records, evaluations or other significant contacts." The possibility that the first contact need not be with—and on occasion *should* not be with—the social worker is never raised or discussed. We consider it symptomatic of the problem of preciousness that questions about staff functions are rarely raised and true attempts at innovation amazingly rare.

PART TEN

Social Work Education for Better Services

EIGHTY-FIVE

Issues in Social Work Education Affecting the Teaching of Mental Retardation Content

WINIFRED E. SMITH

At some risk of seeming less than tactful, I can tell you that when I learned there was to be yet another institute on mental retardation and social work education I was not enthusiastic. My thoughts went like this: whatever may have been our past neglects and failures in social work education with regard to the retarded, surely by now we, along with other educators in the helping professions and society at large, have long since publicly confessed our sins of omission and have taken many and substantial steps toward inclusion of content related to the retarded in our curricula.

A second look at the title of this Institute—*Mental Retardation: A New Dimension in Social Work Education*—made me realize that this institute was different from others I had attended. It was starting on the premise that we were already teaching content from mental retardation and it was now time to assess its consequences for social work education. Then I wondered why I had reached the initial conclusion that this gathering would simply be one more exhortation to social work educators to meet their neglected responsibility to the retarded. A review of the literature on social work education and mental retardation revealed that much of it had been devoted to proving mental retardation as amenable to social work intervention and, hence, suitable and respectable content for inclusion in the social work curriculum. Those of us who were concerned with the neglected needs of the retarded had become not unlike the combative and embittered parent in his demand that his retarded child be viewed as a worthy human being, not as a social discard. The approach to our educator colleagues was often that of special advocate on behalf of the retarded. We charged the educators with neglect of social work values and humanitarian concern; we unduly stressed the difficulties of interesting students and faculty in the retarded; and we overwhelmed them with enough specialized information about retardation to fill a two-year curriculum. In the wisdom of hindsight it now seems we would have been more effective had we paraphrased mental retardation's most distinguished benefactor and asked not what social work educa-

Reprinted from *Mental Retardation: A New Dimension in Social Work Education* (Louisville, University of Louisville, Kent School of Social Work, 1967), pp. 27-42. By permission of the author and the Kent School of Social Work.

tion can do for mental retardation, but rather what retardation can do for social work education.

With this in mind I have come here to discuss with you how at UCLA certain aspects of mental retardation became significant in illuminating broader social work issues and their relation to our thinking and directions in curriculum construction. More specifically, I wish to show how the characteristics of mental retardation, and the point in time at which we were confronted with its introduction into our curriculum, led us to formulate the concept of the social problem as a major principle in curriculum design. Finally, I would like to share with you how we have used the social problem concept in achieving certain educational goals.

As you can readily see, I have set for myself a difficult assignment in the time allotted to me. For such are the complexities of the various elements involved, namely the exploration of mental retardation as a field of practice, the issues of social work education, and the analysis of the concept of the social problem, that each warrants a major discussion in itself. To attempt to interrelate them to one another and to curriculum construction is, indeed, a formidable undertaking. My only reason for attempting it at all is my hope that your familiarity with many of the themes of this presentation will enable you to add substance to issues to which I can only allude in passing. Also, I hope that by sharing our experiences at UCLA, unique as they may be to our school in our university and our community, they may be helpful in your workshop discussions and on your return home.

Issues in Education Classified

A review of the literature on issues in social work education reveals that they are essentially of three orders: (1) those relating to the criticism of social work practice, emphasizing its inadequacies as a problem-solving institution confronted with the demanding complexities and urgent needs of our society; (2) those concerned with how these inadequacies, in turn, stem from the failures of social work education in its definition of the social work task in society for which it prepares its graduates; and (3) those related to the difficulties and problems in curriculum construction, once the educational goal is defined.

Reduced to an extreme, some of the criticisms of social work practice and education may be rephrased as follows: We deal with society's problems retrospectively and upon assignment from others, since we lack a perspective that enables us to undertake prevention or to effectively engage in social change. Some have even asked if we cannot positively assist in changing the nature of the society which produces the problem, cannot we as a profession at least avoid the role of retarding positive change? It is alleged that we fail because we focus on persons rather than on populations in need. We promote our own professional goals as opposed to our social goals. We stress processes and methods rather than social purposes and function. We design social agencies and social programs more as a suitable setting for the exercise of our overly-refined methods than for the benefit of those whom we would serve. This preoccupation with method has led to the production of a few highly sophisticated professionals capable of serving relatively fewer and fewer individuals with low priority of need when compared to larger populations with much more urgent and desperate problems. In short, we have lost our connections with the larger society and have turned inward to the point that the self-oriented goal of social work becomes the practice of social work, with a blind faith that our inner image of our role somehow validates our existence.

To translate these criticisms into the educational issues they pose is far beyond the scope of our attention here. Perhaps they can be summed up in a few basic questions. How can we produce a social worker capable of practice as he finds it and at the same time capable of changing practice? How can we avoid educating a mere technician for a closed system—one incapable of responding or contributing positively to change, one whose knowledges and skills are frozen at a fixed point in time, and one who lacks either the perspective or means of incorporating or developing new knowledge and skills to meet rapidly changing needs? In other words, how can we educate a true professional with the vision and ability to take the current body of social work knowledge, skills, and value-orientation into the larger arena of society and adapt his expertise in such a fashion that he can join meaningfully with other institutions and professionals in the prevention, treatment, and control of the major social problems confronting us today, as well as those which are emerging?

In regard to timing, the year 1962 was a fateful one for mental retardation and social work education for in that year two landmark documents appeared which had crucial impact. One was that of the President's Panel on Mental Retardation culminating in the 1962 *Report to the President: A Proposal for National Action to Combat Mental Retardation* and the other was the 1962 Council on Social Work Education's *Curriculum Policy Statement*. While each of these was in effect merely the summation of an evolutionary development over a long span of time, by their reformulation and restatement of pertinent issues the reports themselves became major points of departure for subsequent action.

The President's *Panel Report* was a most remarkable document. It stung the conscience of the nation for gross neglect of a significant segment of our population; it crystallized into national social policy society's collective responsibility for the retarded; and it laid out a comprehensive program for combating mental retardation from which ensued extensive funding for service, research, and manpower training. Our presence here today is testimony to the fact that social work education heard its mandate.

This mandate came at a moment when social work education was being directed by the 1962 *Curriculum Policy Statement* to divest itself once and for all of efforts toward the preparation of social workers as specialists for particular fields of practice. Although many schools had long since made this change, as had ours, field instruction was still defined by some as the continuing commitment to specializations in the curriculum. But this interpretation seemed untenable in a curriculum which defined field instruction as a method of teaching and learning whose goals were, among others, to underpin the whole of the class instruction organized on the concept of the generic.

Experience at UCLA

Now I would like to describe what happened at UCLA and to identify those insights relevant to our discussion that were implicit in our experience. Our encounter with mental retardation began in 1961 when for the first time we placed five students in field instruction in an agency serving the retarded. At the time we were engaged in the perennial problem of improving the quality of our field placements, in the course of which we re-specified our goals for field instruction. We saw these goals as "ideals" and set about the task of finding any "agency setting" which would help us approximate them. What we decided upon was an agency serving the retarded. At the time the accepted criteria for selection of field placements were agency setting and method of practice.

Our success with that first placement led us to add two more agencies serving the retarded in the following year, making nine students in three agencies. Our experience that second year forced us to conclude that it was not agency setting or specificity of method practiced which was providing our students with such rich learning opportunities. Rather it was the subject matter of mental retardation. Viewed with reference to the criterion of agency setting, two of these agencies would have been defined as "secondary" and one was "primary." All three were private agencies but two were largely dependent on Federal funding and the third was supported by the consumer, namely the parent group, who also determined policy and provided a large cadre of sub-professionals and volunteers who assisted the professionals in rendering the services. As for the criterion of method for selecting a placement, here again there was little similar to our past experiences. In each agency the social workers practiced highly sophisticated casework, but it was by no means the only method they used. Confronted with the enormous task and shortage of trained workers, together with the fact that all three agencies were relatively new ones freed of ingrained and rigid patterns of service, the social workers were equally involved in work with groups and in community organization activities.

The range of services provided in the three agencies was indeed comprehensive. They offered diagnostic clinics, parent counseling and education, group and individual treatment for the retarded and their families, a residential home, a sheltered workshop, special education classes for the retarded, summer camps and on-going recreational programs, public education to interpret the needs of the retarded, and social action programs. Seemingly every helping profession possible was represented on the three staffs: physicians with specialties in pediatrics, neurology, psychiatry, and genetics; psychologists specializing in psychometrics and clinical practice; public health nurses; physical and occupational therapists; speech and hearing specialists; recreational workers; vocational rehabilitation specialists; lawyers concerned with the legal rights of the retarded and questions of guardianship; special educators, along with arts and crafts workers, musical therapists, and an expert in dance and physical fitness; consultants in religious education; and finally social workers who filled the roles of consultant and administrator while practicing social work in innovative combinations with sub-professionals.

Not only were the students in these placements engaged with a variety of professionals seldom encountered in two years of field instruction, they were practicing with them in decidedly new team alignments. For such were the complexities of the needs of the retarded that no specialty could lay sole claim to them.

The retarded were—as the title of the report prepared by our local Council on Social Agencies on their needs so aptly stated—"Everyone's Children." "Everyone's Children" not only in society's collective responsibility for them but in the sense they "belonged" to no one professional discipline more than to the next. And, while the practice was multi-disciplined, no one was host. New team patterns were emerging, constituted by the task at hand—not determined by status or vested interest of any single profession which predetermined the definition of the problem or the mode of intervention.

Classroom Teaching Unrelated

While we had seemingly discovered a gold mine in the richness of mental retardation as an area of practice for field instruction that second year, it was not without its problems. For there was little or nothing in the content of the classroom teaching specifically related to mental retardation as such. Since we no longer attempted to produce graduates skilled in specialization for any field of practice, it could be argued that these nine students were in no more difficulty in relating their class instruction to their field work than were other students in an agency concerned with problems of the mentally or physically ill, child welfare, family disorganization, the aged, the delinquent, or the poor.

Yet this was not quite the case. For these latter problems had long been of major concern to social work practice and education. As a result of their long history in our curriculum, some as areas of specialization, they had left an indelible imprint on our teaching and even on our curriculum construction, despite our commitment to the generic. So ingrained had content from these fields of practice become, we were hardly aware how much they had been the determinants of the concepts and theories which we taught or how heavily we drew upon them to illustrate and specify these. In contrast, seldom was mental retardation used to articulate a principle or to amplify or redefine it. Despite its richness and potential for specification of theories and principles, so unfamiliar and alien was mental retardation to most social work teachers that they could not introduce and weave it into their teaching with the same ease and success with which they used content drawn from long-familiar social problem areas. Further, the very vastness of the body of specialized knowledge relevant to mental retardation was so formidable that the initial task of relating it to social work practice seemed overwhelming.

In order to cope with the needs of those nine students and the problems of the three field instructors trying to help them relate classroom learning to their field instruction in mental retardation we hit upon the device of holding periodic meetings with all nine students from the three agencies. Initially our stated purpose was to teach them something about the specifics of practice with the retarded. At first we were not clear in our minds how to accomplish this. At times it seemed as if we were trying to teach them all of the accumulated knowledge we could acquire and transmit about the condition of retardation; at other times we seemed to be restating the whole of the social work curriculum, respecifying it to retardation. What we discovered and came to articulate was that in those sessions we were teaching the social problem approach to mental retardation, which was the only approach sufficiently holistic to comprehend the range and diversity of the material while providing a unifying identification with content taught elsewhere. Further, we were ordering the material by asking ourselves what was the social work task in the solution of the social problem of retardation. What skills, knowledges, and values did social work offer in prevention, treatment, and control of mental retardation as a social problem?

Here my report of our first encounter with mental retardation ends for the moment. With the advent of a new dean and a rapidly expanding student body and faculty, we used the opportunity afforded us by the change of the university from the semester to the quarter system to engage in a major curriculum revision. In the many educational issues confronting us in this complex task one major problem was that of integrating field instruction into the whole of the curriculum. The campus teaching was organized on the generic concept but the patterns of practice where we sent our students into placement for a large and crucial segment of their learning were organized by specializations of fields of practice. For there was not and could not be such a thing as a "generic agency" or a "generic client." However, each instance of social work activity occurs in the context of professional social work practice and is a definite and concrete manifestation of its responsibilities, its perception and definition of problems, its body of knowledge, its prescriptions of action and techniques for intervention, and its value perspective. Thus, the generic is realized in the specific. Nevertheless, for effective learning and practice in the field the student needed an increasing body of particular knowledge special to the needs of given agencies for their programs of service and their clients. Comprehensive programs of service in a given problem area helped to provide breadth of learning experiences and thus lessened the fragmentation of learning often experienced in the single functioned agency. But comprehensive service did not equate with the generic. On the contrary, it required, if anything, more specialized knowledge and skills related to the particular problem area, not less.

Difficulty in Translation

Other issues confronted us with regard to field instruction. The distance between field work and class was not only affected by the generic-specific issue, but in class the content was being organized and taught at increasingly higher levels of abstraction and theoretical conceptualization. This was the only way that the vast infusion of knowledge drawn from the social, behavioral, and life sciences, along with our own developing body of social work theory, could be either comprehended or conveyed in the time allotted in the ever-diminishing space of the two year curriculum.

As a result both students and field instructors, each for different reasons, were experiencing serious difficulty in the translation and application of what was taught in class to what was practiced in the field. Complicating these difficulties further was the directive from the *Curriculum Policy Statement* to broaden field instruction to include learning experiences which underpin and reinforce the whole curriculum rather than treating it as a mere extension of the methods sequences.

Thus in our efforts to better integrate field instruction with class teaching and learning we turned again to reconsider our experience with the nine students in the three mental retardation placements. In our review of that venture we began to see certain features of it which held promise of solution for problems facing us.

In reexamination of mental retardation itself as a field of practice we recognized that it had certain characteristics which were especially relevant to social work education in that they provided the student with learning opportunities which reinforced many of its major goals. As a field of practice: (1) it was an area in which social work skills, knowledge, and values were clearly established and applicable; (2) it demanded the skills of social casework, group work, and community organization, offering remarkable opportunity for the application of all of these methods either singularly or in combination; (3) it provided, by the very absence of well-established service programs, the opportunity to study new patterns of service in the light of increased knowledge and concern with more effective packaging and delivery of service, and to implement these programs free from the rigidities of past structures; (4) it presented problems, whose origins, consequences, and solutions seriously involved the psychological, the biological, and the social nature of man over his full life cycle; (5) it likewise presented problems which demanded for their solution the intervention of all helping disciplines and the utilization of the major social institutions of our society, with particular significance and consequence for the primary unit of society, the family; (6) it was concerned with a condition that affected all classes and strata of society, but at the same time had a unique relation to and impact on the poor; (7) it necessitated a reexamination of the values of the profession, forcing us to reconsider such issues as individual rights versus societal rights, the right of self-determination, and the obligation of society to provide for each of its members an opportunity to realize maximum potential and essential worth and dignity; (8) it forced us to look at our professional attitudes and those of a society which made a large segment of our population suffer the tyranny and penalties of prejudice, stigma, damaged self-image, and segregation, with all of their attendant consequences in social isolation and tragedy for the individuals concerned and the resultant costs to society; (9) in relation to the lifetime needs of the group affected it provided new perspectives on the application of such concepts as crisis, chronicity, rehabilitation, and anticipatory intervention; and (10) it required a highly specialized body of knowledge essential for effective practice with the retarded, which was distinguished from but related to the knowledges of social work generically conceived and applied wherever it is practiced.

These were some of the many characteristics of mental retardation which had made for success in our first field work placements.[1] It was these same characteristics which led us to see the social problem, or the social problem-area, as a central concept in social work education, particularly in the organization of field instructions. It may be asked why it was that we did not begin to think in social problem terms long before our encounter with mental retardation. Certainly it had a long history in our vocabulary and as a concept it was not new to us. Why did not its significance become equally clear to us in practice with the mentally and physically ill, the impoverished, and the delinquent, the deviant, to name only a few areas of social work practice readily defined as social problems? Why did mental retardation give the impetus to this insight? Two factors account it. One was the complexity of retardation which demanded a holistic approach to make it comprehensible to us and to our students. Further, it was the nature, saliency and range of the features and implications of mental retardation which enabled us to see its full ramifications as a major social problem and thus illuminated the social problem concept and its usefulness to field teaching and social work education.

Social Problem Concept Found Useful

At the same time, others working elsewhere with other issues and material were articulating the significance of the social problem concept to social work practice. I refer to that important contribution in social work literature which appeared in 1964, published by the NASW and edited by Nathan Cohen, *Social Work and Social Problems*. Also, the social scientist, especially the sociologist, had made the study and definition of the social problem as such a prime concern, along with extensive studies of major social problems as such a prime concern, along with extensive studies of major social problems such as family disorganization, poverty, crime and delinquency, housing, the aged, work and leisure, the inner-city, race relations, and many others. They have taught us that a social problem cannot be understood or solved except in the context of the whole society in which it is defined, taking into account at any given time its values, social institutions, arrangements for problem-solving, material resources, and state of technology and scientific knowledge. Also to be taken into account are the perspectives and methods of those professions and institutions that accept responsibility for problem solving.

I would like now to turn to our use of the concept of the social problem area in curriculum construction and other consequential decisions. To attempt to delineate fully how it has permeated our thinking would, of course, be futile. First, it is only one among many elements which shape our educational philosophy and goals. Secondly, like any truly useful and dynamic concept its distinctiveness and visibility are lost as it merges with other elements and forces in the reformulation of our educational goals and our processes for achieving them. However, a few examples should serve to illustrate how we have applied it to educational issues, allowing you to consider and evaluate its usefulness.

At present we are undertaking to specify those social problems which are of prime concern to social work considered in terms of their magnitude, their urgency and consequence for the individuals involved and for society, their interrelatedness to other social problems, such as poverty and family disorganization, and, finally, their amenability to social work intervention. We have used this identification as one of the central criteria for the selection of field instruction placements. When in the past we selected placements with primary concern for agency setting and method practiced we found we had a decided imbalance in the problem area represented, to the consequent impoverishment of the whole curriculum and neglect of our responsbility to large segments of society. Our ultimate goal is to have a more comprehensive representation of placements, at least with respect to the major social problem areas, defined in terms of the above criteria. Further, from these we hope to specify the general knowledge *about* these problems which should be taught to all students, regardless of where they are placed, not with the intent of providing them the full body of specialized knowledge essential for skilled practice but rather as an approach to any social problem.

Integrative Seminars Planned

The effect of the social problem concept on the development of particular course offerings and their content can best be seen in two new integrative seminars we shall be providing our second-year student in the final quarter of this year. The first, indirectly derived from the social problem perspective, is focused on "disadvantaged populations." Here the emphasis will be upon those conditions or circumstances inherent in many social problems which impair or preclude substantial participation of large numbers of individuals in many institutions of our society to their individual detriment and at risk and cost to society.

The second is an integrative methods seminar, combining students whose major concentration has been in casework or community organization. Using the context of the various social problems with which the students have become respectively familiar in two years of field work practice, we shall be examining the efficacy of a variety of strategies of intervention, the differential use of personnel in problem-solving, and new structures for more effective delivery of service. One objective in this seminar is to teach social accountability by asking in each instance of individual need whether our definition of the problem and the solution proposed is capable of being expanded to ever-widening populations in need by more imaginative use of our skills in combination with others and in new patterns of service. For it has become clear from practice today that, although the social worker will need a high degree of skill in a particular method, new patterns of practice require considerable proficiency in all methods of social work. We may not agree that there is as yet a single social work method but such is the interpenetration of methods that each can no longer be practiced exclusively. Further, if we are to meet the expanding demands for service, we must learn to apply our methods of innovative combinations with sub-professional as well as with other professional disciplines and social institutions.

Use of Concept in Faculty Selection

Another major use we have made of the social problem concept is in the recruitment and deployment of faculty. An important criterion in the selection of classroom faculty has been, and still is, competence to teach in the various sequences of the curriculum. However, in the case of our faculty-based field instructors we now look for, among other qualifications, substantial experience and expertise in given problem areas. We are using these field instructors to join in team-teaching with the sequence specialists. But, of equal importance, we rely heavily upon them for the application of theoretical concepts taught in the generic curriculum to a particular problem area and, in turn, for the respecification of these concepts for the enrichment of social work theory building and statement. For this is not only the best point of entry into the class teaching for specialized knowledge drawn from a particular field of practice, like mental retardation, but ultimately its greatest assurance of permanence.[2]

Finally, the place in our curriculum where the concept of the social problem has made the greatest impact has been in the construction of an experimental model of field instruction which we are implementing this year for the first time in the field of mental retardation by means of a grant from the Vocational Rehabilitation Administration. Our evaluation of its success to date confirms the validity of our decision to begin a second model in the field of mental health and illness next year. The model entails several key elements, which in their interrelatedness form the structure used to achieve its objectives.[3] They are:

1. The use of the social problem area as the organizing principle for the grouping of field instruction agencies into an educational unit or complex to be treated as a whole when planning the learning experiences for all the students placed in the several agencies constituting the cluster. This year we are using the same three agencies originally used with the nine students as described previously, with the addition of a fourth whose function is community organization in the field of retardation. Now there are ten second-year students with methods of concentrations in work with individuals and small groups (formerly casework) and in community organization.

2. The creation of a new faculty position designated as Field Instruction Specialist who has expertise in the given problem area, in this instance mental retardation, and who assumes administrative and educational direction of the project.

3. The utilization of two days per week of the three days allotted to field instruction in the second year to provide the student experience in rendering direct service to individuals and groups in one of the agencies in the cluster in which he is placed throughout the year. Here the teaching is primarily tutorial and the learning is by doing, with prime concentration on acquisition of methods skills.

4. One day of field instruction per week is devoted to group meetings with all the students in the four agencies, and to research which is a group project related to some aspect of practice with the retarded. The activities planned for these days vary. At the outset considerable time was used to acquaint all students with the

programs of the four agencies which comprise the cluster as a common base of understanding for future discussions. Field trips were made to other social agencies and institutions in the community also concerned with the retarded, such as state hospitals, public health services, churches, courts, recreational centers, schools, nursery and day care centers, vocational training projects, etc. Visits were made to official public hearings on pending legislation affecting the retarded and there was attendance at meetings and institutions for professionals and the lay public on various facts of retardation. However, in addition to research and assigned reading on mental retardation, the largest segment of time on these "third days" was devoted to on-campus seminars with all ten students. Here the Field Instruction Specialist, with the aid of the field instructors from the several agencies, and of others drawn from the faculty of the school, the larger university, and the community, together with the actively participating students themselves, presented various facets of mental retardation directed towards exploring its full ramifications as a major social problem. Although obviously a sharp distinction cannot be made between the student's learning in his agency and in the seminars, one of the prime objectives of the seminars is to assist him in that most demanding and creative task of integrating generic content from *all* the sequences of the curriculum with the specifics of practice with the retarded.

5. Regular seminars with the field instructors of the four agencies to acquaint them with content taught in the class and in the field instruction group meetings with the students, and to join with them in developing content to be taught in all facets of the model. Identification and ordering of learning experiences for achieving the educational goals of field instruction is a major endeavor of these meetings, along with consideration of methods and techniques of field teaching.

One might conclude that the result of the model I have just described is to use field instruction to prepare specialists for practice in the field of mental retardation. For it cannot be denied that these ten students will graduate with a high degree of specialized competence in social work with retardation. But this is not our objective, pleased as we may be to do our share in meeting the manpower crisis in this area. Rather, our goal is to educate a social worker ultimately capable of practice in any social problem area. In this endeavor we are using specialization in a given social problem to teach the generic as it ultimately must be understood in the concrete and applied in the specific.

Furthermore, we are using all components of the field learning to insure a holistic understanding of the social problem of mental retardation as a context for the articulation of the social work task. Our objective is to teach how the body of knowledge, skill, and value of social work is differently shaped and affected by the problem to which it is applied, and how it maintains its identity in all instances whatever the specific problem. Thus transferability and respecification of social work concepts and principles becomes a recurring theme in the teaching. Our aim in the model is to provide the student with a wide range of learning experiences in the field of mental retardation which will imbue him with the necessity for the continuing acquisition of the highly specialized knowledge related to the social problem in which he ultimately practices, as well as the developing knowledge of social work as a profession. We also aim to instill in him the respect and use of the rigorous intellectual discipline required of him to reorder and respecify these knowledges and skills to meet new problems. From the social problem focus we hope to widen his definitions of problems and solutions and to enable him to meaningfully relate his endeavors to societal concerns as well as to individual needs.

In sum, our goal in this model of field instruction is to give the student a social work perspective and approach which, focused on the given social problem, is effective wherever he may practice, and which will serve him well as a creative and productive social worker capable of adapting and contributing to change—a goal which, of course, is the objective of our whole curriculum and of the profession of social work.

References

[1] See Winifred E. Smith, "Services to the Retarded As Social Work Education," *Children,* Vol. 11, No. 5, September-October, 1964, pp. 189-192, for a delineation of the contributions to social work education of field placements in agencies serving the retarded and their families.

[2] See Bess Dana, "Enriching Social Work Education with Mental Retardation Content," *Journal of Education for Social Work* (New York: Council on Social Work Education, Fall, 1965), outlining a model for development of social work concepts and principles from the field of mental retardation for inclusion in the overall curriculum.

[3] Responsiblity for the development and statement of the model on behalf of the faculty was undertaken by a committee consisting of Dean Eileen Blackey, Dr. Maurice F. Connery and the writer.

EIGHTY-SIX

Student Learning Patterns and Problems in a Mental Retardation Setting

STEPHANIE BARNHARD

The task of this paper is to examine student learning patterns and problems in Mental Retardation field placement settings within the context of social work education. The statement calls for two foci in their separateness and in their interrelatedness, namely: the student in the process of becoming a social worker, some of the patterns and problems engendered, and the Mental Retardation setting as an impeding or energizing agent in the attainment of the profession's educational objectives.

The choice of the principle under whose aegis we can organize this presentation is troublesome. Are we to follow the beginning student through his two years of struggles and achievements? Would it be more meaningful to examine his patterns and problems in relation to the competencies he is to achieve or his metamorphosis from lay to professional identity?

It is proposed that we adopt as our frame of reference an examination of the student and the setting as the two interact in the process of education and professional acculturation. In the conciseness of professional language we separate the educational whole into values, knowledge, skill, and professional self; we separate the substantive and the affective learning tasks, which center around doing, thinking, and feeling. We separate the educational process into component tasks for the purpose of examination, but we are constantly aware of the artificiality of doing so, for they are in constant interrelatedness. They interact and influence each other and require an integration in the student. The educational formula has undergone a broadening, and the field setting as part of the total educational effort incorporates the teaching of accountability not only to the professional commitment but also to the larger social welfare planning—to a spirit of inquiry and testing and continued study. As Dean Blackey so aptly put it, "Social work and social work education [must be] responsive to the dual demands of continuity and change in our respective societies."[1] Slowly, or perhaps rapidly, social work education is evolving its

From Verd S. Lewis, ed., *Field Instruction in Mental Retardation Settings Serving Children* (Baltimore, The School of Social Work, University of Maryland, 1967), pp. 43-63. By permission of the author and the School.

goals from the preparation of students for responsible entry into a field of practice to the cultivation of professional entry into social work practice in a social welfare setting. If we accept this, the field setting carries expanded educational responsibility: (1) it must now provide the student not only with opportunities to experience and test his commitment, his knowledge, and his skills in the living reality, but also provide an active involvement with the client and societal institutions in the art of providing a helping service; (2) it must widen its obligations to society to identify and define social problem areas for the purpose of entry with appropriate social work intervention techniques; (3) it has an obligation for the refinement of existing knowledge and the development of new knowledge and methods appropriate to newly encountered human needs; (4) it must stimulate a spirit of experimentation and research; (5) it must possess the courage to point to gaps in services and to active participation in the creation of necessary new services.

This is a huge challenge, but an examination of current social work practice and education reflects the profession's progressive assumption of these responsibilities. Nor is our profession unique in this process. Similar trends are detectable in all professions: psychiatry and medicine are extending their horizons and obligations to the larger social scene in such fields as social medicine; law moves in the service of the poor; architecture recognizes the need for slum clearance.

Does the Mental Retardation field setting fulfill the practicuum requirement for the broadened educational goals? Can the increased learning demands be met in a Mental Retardation setting? One of the major problems encountered by students in an expanding educational program is the assimilation of the large body of knowledge and method. What role does the Mental Retardation setting play in the integrative process of the student?

This field setting is considered by those of us who have taught in it to be endowed with unusual potential for meeting the educational objectives identified above. Mental Retardation lends itself with great clarity to analysis as a social problem by means of the model proposed by Herman Stein and Irving Sarnoff.[2] Mental Retardation's comparative newness in the field increases its potential as an educational field setting, for no one traditional method has become firmly entrenched and the profession's entry into this social problem area coincides with broader educational goals. There are educational positives, but what learning patterns and problems does it evoke in the students?

Mental Retardation poses a conflict between the value systems of the profession and the larger society, and as a resolution emerges a sense of pioneering and excitement is present as the student feels himself a contributor as well as a learner. Similarly, the profession's knowledge of the special needs of the field is not as bound by conventional constructs which serve, rather, as guides which need testing and refinement.

The beginning student, who arrives on that first momentous day at the Mental Retardation field setting, may not share the appreciation of its educational potential. On the contrary, he may be rejecting of the setting and resistive to a beginning involvement and may exhibit this resistance in various patterns of behavior. My first year in a Mental Retardation field placement I greeted six students, five of whom announced that the agency was too removed from the center of the city for them to reach; there was no purpose in beginning, for they all expected to be relocated the very next day. The one unfortunate student who lived nearby sought solace as a lone survivor. This experience has been reported by other field instructors. Edith M. Baker writes, "In the District of Columbia we found that our first students came to us with reluctance. They had not asked for placement in a Mental Retardation clinic, and they thought they might perhaps secure a more meaningful experience in a different setting."[3] Clarke and Clarke report a similar phenomenon in England among students assigned to Mental Retardation.[4] The instructor's attempts to associate the manifest reluctance with Mental Retardation is usually met with initial strong defensive maneuvers, for the student has to maintain his self-image of a dedicated person, ready to accept any client and girded to battle for the richer social functioning of all. It is this image of an enabler, of a change agent, that first probably attracted him to social work and which received reinforcement through his admission process. It is precisely this dynamic which is the nucleus of his resistance to a Mental Retardation field setting, for most students bring the perception of Mental Retardation as a static, hopeless condition, unresponsive to intervention. Consequently they perceived the placement as contrary to their professed interests, and beginning resistance is heightened. The second-year student expresses his hesitation with greater educational acumen and specificity. He may point to the limited verbal communication and capacity for awareness and insight of the retarded as factors which will impede his learning. A group work student with prior work experience expressed this perception in terms of his need for concentration in selectivity of program appropriate to the needs of the individual group members and his doubt that this could be learned in Mental Retardation. The implication of this resistance is that retarded individuals are all the same, i.e., they possess a sameness of reactions, needs, interests, and ultimate potential.

The high premium placed by schools on higher student capacity and achievement for admission may be attracting young people who are not ready to accept blunted intellectuality. It is only the school's insistence that students remain in the chosen placement that enables us to break through the initial resistance to the Mental Retardation field setting. They do soon recognize the educational richness of their placement and as their growing satisfaction and enthusiasm is expressed to student colleagues the Mental Retardation setting becomes a respected and sought-for placement. The student becomes our best interpreter to his fellow-students.

The resolution of a significant educational conflict occurs within the context of process in which the students' acceptance of the Mental Retardation setting is but the first step. We should remember that all students enter field settings of all kinds with anxiety, in amount and extent. "Reality shock" describes the student's reactions of resistance and counter transference as he experiences beginning client contacts and the demands of clients and field instructor, agency, and his beginning professional self-concept. Isabel Stamm humorously describes the first-year students' movements through the gamut of client blame for agency limitations, or projected anger, or broken appointments.[5] We ask him "to reach out," and he asks of himself that he apply his classroom learning. She asks, "Is it surprising that he protects his ego against all this?" In the face of such pressure he uses his strength defensively, and we see withdrawal, reduced sensitivity, over-activity, intellectualization, and the whole gamut of protective measures. The second-year student also goes through somewhat similar throes of adjustment to a new and unknown field setting and field instructor. For the student, and the field instructor, this is made possible by a common underlying motivation—the knowledge that this too will pass and that we will somehow reach a calm for organized learning.

Mrs. Stamm asks a crucial educational question: "Is it enough to say that we expect anxiety and regression at the outset of the student's placement? Should we not try to differentiate between the anxiety which is an integral part of the beginning educational process and that which exists because we have not yet found ways to anticipate it and handle it? This makes a major difference in the degree and duration of debilitating shock."[6] The Mental Retardation setting lends itself to isolation and anticipation of an anxiety-engendering factor the handling of which can be significant in easing the ego-dystonic, debilitating atmosphere of the beginning field experience. That factor is retardation. It possesses the opposing polarities which we have learned to understand and to use fully and dynamically in our intervention techniques.

For the student in the Mental Retardation setting the beginning "reality shock" presents the unknown and different human condition—retardation—with its accompanying intellectual, social, and physical handicaps. The majority of our students come with stereotype images and attitudes. The retardate is an unknown quantity to them. Students' initial reaction to this unknown factor is a heightened anxiety reflected in their cautious and guarded requests for special help. Some find safety in strongly expressed self-assurances which deny differences. The students' diffused discomforts and the tensions generated by their beginning student-hood become attached to the alien condition with which they are to deal and through which they are to learn.

For the instructor this pattern presents a specificity endowed with rich educational potential, for here is the inter-play of anxiety, of feelings, of cognition. Underlying it is the student's motivation to learn to be a helping person. Immediate activity and structured exposure is our strongest armament. On the students' first day in the field, after a discussion of their concept of a retarded person the students spend the remainder of the day in institutional activities for direct exposure to and activity with the retardates. Structured assignments for observation channel the beginning anxiety into "the doing" activity guided to stimulate objectivity by the questions: What were your reactions to the mentally retarded? What social interactions did they have with peers, staff, and with you? How did they show feelings? Were they sensitive to what peers, staff, to what you said and how you acted? What can you say about their language, motor coordination, self care? How were they like other people? How did they differ? Did you see individual differences among the mentally retarded?

The following day the group meets to exchange observations and experiences. There are exciting moments for students and teacher because so many educational goals emerge. The sharing stimulates self-awareness and provides an atmosphere for free expression of doubts, distortions, counter-transference reactions, and newly gained insights. In the cognitive area numerous questions concern the relation of retardation to capacity and impairment of social functioning. Of crucial import for the student's entry into his own learning process is the predominant sense of a more ego-syntonic reaction, a consequence of the student's experience of activity with a client group, prior to assumption of responsibility for a specific client. The beginning anxiety is undergoing some resolution in the active interaction with the retardates and with staff. The presence of second-year students is most helpful, for they are freer in enunciating their feelings and attitudes.

Students, these days, exhibit a need for intellectual learning, which we can not always attribute to a flight from the impact of feelings. As educators we are also asserting the greater need for a sound knowledge base, for cognitive learning and curiosity. Consequently, the very next pattern we meet is a need to learn about Mental Retardation as a functional disease entity. This offers the instructor the opportunity to begin to develop learning about the individuality of man and the complexity of human behavior in response to relationships and environmental remediation. The role of the social worker is taught in the context of the professional relationship emphasizing the skills of observation, of differential diagnosis, and of concern for the functioning individual. I structure this process on the diagnosis of Mental Retardation and on student participation in arriving at the official A.A.M.D. diagnosis through an inductive method initiated with the question of "What is Mental Retardation and how does it manifest itself in the functioning of the retardate?" Usually there is student unanimity to the factor of "subaverage intellectual functioning," but the issue of including school under-achievers is met with strong opposition and with growing recognition of the complexities of a human condition and the need to acquire more rigorous knowledge. Identification of "developmental stages" emphasizes the importance of careful gathering of psycho-social and developmental history. The effects of socio-economic and emotional deprivation upon the development of cognition and ego functions find a natural point for initiation here. The concept of "impairment of adaptive behavior" permits a beginning examination of the relatedness of society expectations and demands to classification, especially of the individuals in the mildly retarded category.

The concept of chronicity and the acceptance of limited goals become educational issues whose manifestations and resolutions appear over and over in various disguises and on various levels of sophistication. The young student's difficulty in coming to terms with chronicity is more readily understandable than is the process of yielding and its eventual acceptance. Two contributing forces stand out and should receive mention. The life force, the organismic drive for homeostasis and adaptation which we experience and on which we rely as an ally in our interventive techniques, counters a comfortable acceptance of chronicity. Our culture values the vigorous individual who through sheer self-will and striving can overcome life's obstacles. The first-year student, especially the youthful one, usually is imbued with a strong sense of idealism which has not yet been tempered by life experience. It is antithetic for him to settle, without struggle, with the reality of partial healing and a more circumscribed social adaptation. A comfortable resolution would mean the abandoning of professional striving and search for new knowledge and new ways to overcome human tragedy. In the process of professionalization we learn how not to project our needs, our hopes, and our aspirations onto others. The value system we adopt and teach contains the appreciation of the individual, no matter what his capacity, and his right for help to fulfill that capacity. The student needs the experience of his own effectiveness. In the Mental Retardation setting we find a specific learning experience for his engagement with a client to give help. The partial attainment of client change and movement can be satisfying to the student and forms the basis for the attitudinal change regarding the immutable effects of retardation on functioning.

Chronicity or limited capacity for social functioning taught as concepts reach out into broad educational areas consistent with the more recent trends in social education. We can teach it within the frame of reference of the continuum of adaptive functions, establishing for the student the broader functional perspective of the term "adaptation." Choice of interventive techniques depends upon client needs rather than upon our historical divisions in methodology. A most exciting consequence has been our students' anger at gaps in services and an active demand for involvement in what we designate as the community organization method.

Social work education has been moving toward a more inclusive perspective of man as a bio-psycho-social being in transaction with his environment, abandoning the simplistic ordering of events on the basis of a strict cause and effect sequence. The students are receiving this theoretical base in class and actively search reinforcement in field.

It is my impression that his new scientific spirit and orientation received earlier and fuller support and acceptance in the field because Mental Retardation is a consequence of bio-psycho-social deficits and impairments. The advances of more recent biological research have led to new knowledge of the relationship between neuro-physiological functions and behavior, both normal and deviant, and to new insights being incorporated in curricula and in practice. The new knowledge may seem more crucial for medicine or neuro-physiology, but it has basic and pragmatic connection with social work practice and competence. The effect of perceptive difficulties, of hyperactivity and distractibility, of mild aphasic conditions and of impairments in spatial and time orientation on ego development, on maturation and on the sum total of adaptive functioning in transaction with environmental realities, now is being realized and studied. It is not the somatic impairment *per se* which is reflected in maladaptive behavior patterns, but rather how it affects development, interrelationships, and total functioning in the person's effort to compensate and adjust to the deficit. Work with parents has added a new facet for a sensitive helping process. This receives emphasis in Mental Retardation settings, and our students are recipients and participants in what promises to be a basic reorientation in theory, knowledge, and practice.

The concept and study of the wholistic man in his ontogenetic transaction with environment has stimulated refinements in three significant teaching and learning areas: (1) communication between client and student; (2) depth and clarity in understanding dynamics; (3) a spirit for research and validation.

The professional art of "communicating" with a client is frequently equated with the art of interviewing even though we are careful to stress affective communication. All this points to our heavy investment in the word-symbol in our professional relationship and interventive technique. One of the hallmarks of retardation is the limited and frequently impaired communication capacity reflected in language use, concreteness of thought process, perseveration, circumscribed understanding, and deficit in abstraction and conceptualization. These create reality problems for verbal, bright young students. Educational problems are posed by goals for second-year students who are learning the skills of exploration, clarification, interpretation, all based on the verbal exchange which leads to the clients' development of awareness and insight. These educational objectives can not be richly achieved with the retarded, but this gap can be filled by careful case selection to assign parent-clients capable of such involvement.

The Mental Retardation setting offers rich opportunities to learn the art of communication on a verbally limited scale, for communication does occur through actions, innovation of commonly shared experiences, and environmental alterations. The experiential process enables the student to introduce focus and direction in his immediate work with the retardate, and he discovers that awareness can be achieved by the mildly and moderately retarded person, painfully aware of his differences but able to verbalize this in a relationship of trust. He also is capable of a modified process of "working through" his feelings although it calls for much effort and patience. Mildly retarded youngsters offer opportunities to teach the concept of defenses and the interventive effort that develop healthier coping mechanisms.

The limited verbal communication ability of the retardate necessitates greater precision of knowledge and relatedness to the client's communicative and apperceptive capacity. The student must learn to test whether his verbalizations were understood, and do so in a manner that is not challenging or redundantly fatiguing. The student acquires skill in learning to seek out the nature and the extent of the client's cognitive deficit. This skill can be adapted to social work with disturbed children and adults whose lack of full understanding is at times disguised by a facade of restlessness and resistance, the genesis of which students or young workers may not be sufficiently experienced to recognize. A community organization practitioner has noted how very helpful the "vigil for understanding" or verbal communication, acquired in a Mental Retardation setting, proved to be in working with large community groups.

We now wish to consider the question: "greater depth in understanding dynamics" synonymous with "greater dynamic understanding in depth?" This paradox necessitates consideration of a student pattern so universal in its appearance during students' second semester and in its lingering and only partial resolution during the third and fourth semesters: the tendency to use professional terminology extensively and loosely and before it is fully assimilated. The achievement of understanding of dynamic formulations is a lengthy process which has a beginning in our early relationships and experiences. To understand them fully and to convert them into usable precepts the student has to think, feel, and associate them with familiar phenomena. Ideally, this is an on-going process necessitating continuous self-validation and professional validation. How then do we meet the student's need for time for introspective learning, and establish an educational timetable for the acquisition of sensitive understanding of dynamic concepts? I do not believe it can be accomplished fully, and we are all cognizant of a beginning worker's continued need for learning, for refinements and validations.

Research findings are casting doubts on some of our constructs while giving verification to others. To illustrate but a few—the recent publication of Rimland's—a most impressive work—disputes much of what we understood and practiced in our contact with the parents of autistic children, of the genesis of autism, and of currently known treatment methods.[7] The publications of Thomas, Chess, and Birch,[8] based on very fine research, will certainly modify and alter what we teach in our basic knowledge and skill courses.

Kadushin writes:"Systematic reviews of the literature regarding specific services, specific concepts, specific skills, undertaken under the direction of some central group, proposing some flexible commonality in approach, are feasible, are worth the effort involved, can give us what we need and do not now possess, a comprehensive, authoritative statement of our knowledge. Such material can act as a guide, a stimulus, a brake to our theoretical formulations. Unless we undertake such surveys side by side with attempts at delineating theoretical structures, we run the danger of formulations so divorced from our professional reality that in bringing the two together we do violence to both."[9]

I have gone far afield from my initial topic, but there is a relationship. In the Mental Retardation field setting it is somewhat more difficult for a student to feel secure with faultily assimilated formulations; the greater struggle for clarity and for differential diagnosis which marks the whole Mental Retardation field serves here as a censor. The comparative newness of this social problem to social work practice has left it clearer for an examination by means of more recent social work theory and thinking. To illustrate: the dynamic of resistance is encountered and generates in students anxieties and counter transference feelings similar to those in other field settings. However, here the student himself usually begins to question—how much of the retardate's uninvolvement is due to the lack of understanding and how much to his guardedness? It is a common student pattern to project with relative quickness a concept learned in class onto a behavioral manifestation of his client. One of the more frequent is the diagnostic label of "rejecting parent." This is not to deny that some parents do reject their retarded children. However, the reality of retardation and its accompanying social and management problems for parents introduce a teaching and diagnostic dynamic which helps a student to examine its behavioral manifestations and clarify with greater assurance his assessment, diagnostic formulations, and treatment direction.

Integration of knowledge is an inherent problem of student-hood, and the teaching profession has not established a smooth and incontestable method for its accomplishment in any profession. The complexity of teaching the "whole man"—the bio-psycho-social components which constitute him and his functioning—is a fortunate necessity in Mental Retardation field setting; however, it adds difficulty to the process of integration. The interrelationships of these significant systems during the developmental stages and as they manifest themselves at all times in social behavior can only be understood after one affirms their existence and interrelatedness. It is impossible to isolate them and teach them as separate entities because they do not exist as such. Therefore, the student becomes aware of them and learns about them as he encounters their manifestations in the client's functioning. Universally, our students have displayed an interesting pattern in their struggle to encompass this problem. They seem to be able to relate primarily to one component at a time. Much of a client's behavior is seen and understood in terms of the component system which has caught their attention and imagination for the time being. Dissatisfaction with such a monolithic orientation leads at first to the espousing of the next system and it is usually in the latter half of the first semester that students begin to show signs of a more comfortable beginning integration. Subsequent learning shows an accelerated tempo and a broader and richer approach to professional practice.

Students display various patterns and problems in learning the social work role on the interdisciplinary team. The first-year student, shaky in his knowledge base and in his identification with the profession, frequently endows the psychiatrist with magical healing powers and both the psychologist and psychiatrist with vastly greater understanding of the client. Traditionally, social work knowledge and practice have relied heavily on formulations and skills derived from other disciplines. The student is caught up in this and yet aware that we are also evolving our own knowledge base. Here there is an inherent risk for a young profession and its even younger student in the collaborative effort. The first-year student reacts with a need to incorporate in its totality what he hears, and the status of the other disciplines may take precedence over the social work knowledge and skills he is learning. The second-year student, although one expects him to be more selective, is caught between the classroom concentration on pathology and on his as yet not well assimilated role. It is on this "battle ground" that student and educator and perhaps profession find their identity and contributions. Interdisciplinary team-work offers much opportunity for testing, refining, and affirming social work's knowledge and identity despite its relationship to and reliance upon other disciplines.

Students in Mental Retardation residential settings—especially first-year students—exhibit a hesitation in beginning contact and involvement with parents and families. It is difficult to evaluate the factor of residential care and the young student's reaction to separation, since he is still in the throes of his own separation and achievement of independent adulthood.

The Mental Retardation setting as a stimulator of the spirit of inquiry flows naturally from the exposure of the student to the vital and vigorous ongoing research and remaining uncertainties as to causes, physical and social treatment, and social management of retardation. As stated before, the social work student is involved in a daily testing of his communicative techniques and observations, a questioning of assumptions, a search for clarity—all of which tend to create a climate of inquiry and encourage the student's creative and more scientific use of himself.

The highlighting of the socio-economic cultural components in the causation of Mental Retardation broadens for the student the horizons of social work accountability and its organic connection with social welfare and social work values. This area also lends itself to presentation of epidemiological studies and the consideration of social work participation in prevention.

The Mental Retardation setting also evokes problems which impede the educational effort, i.e., the first-year student's classroom work concentrates on normalcy and his field setting on deviation from the normal. This results in demands for harder and more intensive learning efforts. There are differences calling for reconciliation between what is taught in class and its practice application in such concepts as self-determination, the definition of a protective function and decision making—all consequences of clients' limited adaptive functioning.

To those who have experiences teaching in many field settings, the Mental Retardation field placement offers impressive educational opportunities for the utilization of the common and special student problems in the service of broadening the competence of the new generation of practitioners.

References

[1]Eileen Blackey, "Building the Curriculum: The Foundation for Professional Competence," Presented to the Thirteenth International Congress of Schools of Social Work, 1966.

[2]Herman Stein and Irving Sarnoff, *Social Work and Social Problems,* Nathan Cohen (ed.) 1964, NASW, pp. 9-14.

[3]Edith M. Baker, *Social Workers in Mental Retardation Programs,* Department of Health, Education and Welfare Publication.

[4]Ann M. Clark and A.D.B. Clark, *Mental Deficiency, The Changing Outlook,* 1965, Methuen & Co., Ltd., London.

[5]Isabel Stamm, "Educational Methods in Social Work Supervision," Presented to the Adelphi School of Social Work, 5/29/61.

[6]*Ibid.*

[7]Bernard Rimland, *Infantile Autism,* 1964, Appleton-Century-Crofts, New York City.

[8]A. Thomas, S. Chess, H. Birch, M. Hertzig, S. Korn, *Behavioral Individuality in Early Childhood,* 1963, New York University Press, New York City.

[9]Alfred Kadushin, "Assembling Social Work Knowledge, "NASW Publication, *Building Social Work Knowledge,* 1964.

EIGHTY-SEVEN

The Effect of Differences in Curricula and Experiences on Social Work Attitudes and Knowledge About Mental Retardation

MICHAEL J. BEGAB

The research reported in this project was concerned with the impact of differences in curricula and experiences on social work students attitudes and knowledge about mental retardation.

The Variables

The variables included in the study were classified into three categories: (1) *demographic-ecological variables*—age, sex, marital status, race, children, religious affiliation, socioeconomic status; (2) *antecedent life experiences*—personal life experience with retarded persons, the type of relationship (immediate family, relative, neighbor) and place of residence of the retarded person; professional work experience with retarded clients prior to graduate school admission; and (3) *the degree and type of educational exposure*—extent of classroom content and primary client group served in the field instruction placement.

These variables were investigated regarding their influence on student knowledge, attitudes and preferences for the retarded as a client group.

Sample

The sample consisted of 279 newly admitted and 288 graduating students in 7 schools of social work, selected on the basis of variations in the degree of their curriculum activity in mental retardation. All schools of social work were rated on a curriculum exposure gradient and a purposive sample was drawn incorporating additional criteria of size and scholastic standing to approximate national representativeness. Students were selected from each school according to random sampling procedures and the number of beginning and graduating students included from each school were near equal.

The two groups of students were highly homogeneous on demographic-ecologi-

Reprinted from Michael J. Begab, "The Effect of Differences in Curricula and Experiences on Social Work Student Attitudes and Knowledge About Mental Retardation" (Washington, The Catholic University of America, 1968), pp. 105-110. By permission of the author.

cal characteristics. The majority of students were under age 35, caucasian, female and of middle or upper social class status. Most of them are unmarried at school entrance and the majority of those married have no children. By religious affiliation, they approximate the general distribution of the population. A significant proportion of the students report personal life experience with retarded persons and approximately one-fourth have prior work experience with this group.

Procedure

The data in this study were collected through the use of a series of instruments, self-administered by each student. Instruments consisted of a personal data sheet, semantic differential rating scales, a knowledge inventory of 50 multiple choice and 50 true-false questions and a client preference rank order scale. Approximately 45 minutes was required to complete the total battery. In the analysis of data, parametric statistical tests were applied.

Results and Conclusions

Six hypotheses were tested. The results regarding each hypothesis have been presented in detail. The summary below includes the major findings which pertain to the general problems of the research. These problems are (a) the assessment of student knowledge and attitudes toward mental retardation upon admission to graduate schools of social work, (b) the relationship of knowledge and attitudes to demographic-ecologic variables, (c) the assessment of change in student knowledge and attitudes as a function of differences in graduate social work education.

KNOWLEDGE AND ATTITUDES OF BEGINNING STUDENTS

In general, the results support the hypothesis that student knowledge and attitudes toward the retarded are influenced by prior life experiences. The major findings follow:

1. Students with little or no direct contact or personal life experience with retarded persons demonstrate *moderately* unfavorable attitudes toward and limited knowledge of this group. Compared to the average person, the retarded are rated less favorably on all of the 21 semantic scales employed, at the .01 level of significance. Similar comparisons do not apply to other selected client groups served by social workers. Attitudes reveal the same configuration reported in other studies for the general public, but are less extreme.

2. Students vary considerably in their level of knowledge, but as a group, share many misconceptions about the nature and scope of the problem and the capacities of the retarded to profit from social work help. Their general image of the retarded seems based on the characteristics which predominate in the relatively small proportion of moderately and severely retarded persons—ill health, weakness, excitability, aimless behavior, physical handicap and extreme dependency.

3. The retarded are ranked sixth among ten client groups with respect to their

preference as clients. Less than 4% of the students select them as their most preferred choice.

4. Students with retarded siblings or relatives tend toward more extremeness in their attitudes and client preferences (generally in a favorable direction) and have significantly more knowledge about mental retardation than other students.

5. Except for the students whose knowledge appears derived in part from personal life experience, there is no significant correlation between level of knowledge and attitudes.

DEMOGRAPHIC-ECOLOGICAL VARIABLES

The role of demographic-ecological factors in attitudes about retardation is not part of the hypotheses tested. However, these factors are assessed to ensure confidence in the educational experience as the independent variable. The major findings follow:

1. Age, sex, marital status, religious affiliation and whether or not the student has children, are not significantly related to attitudes.

2. The socioeconomic status of students is significantly related to attitudes as reflected in semantic scale ratings and client preference choice (.05 level of significance). Students in the highest social class have less favorable attitudes and are least inclined to choose the retarded as a client group.

CHANGES IN STUDENT KNOWLEDGE AND ATTITUDES

The analysis of change in the student knowledge and attitudes was explored as a function of variations in curriculum exposure and nature of the learning experience. Comparisons were made between groups of students and within the graduating group, controlling for antecedent experiences. The major findings follow:

1. Graduating students show a trend toward more favorable semantic ratings than beginning students though not to a statistically significant degree on most scales. Comparisons between schools based on levels of exposure show no significant differences.

2. The general body of graduating students (field instruction students excepted) is not superior to beginning students in their knowledge about mental retardation and share identical misconceptions about the problem. The integration of content on mental retardation in other formal classroom courses is largely ineffective in increasing student knowledge or changing attitudes or client preferences.

3. Changes in client preference occur more frequently among students in high versus low exposure schools, but the rank ordering of client groups between beginning and graduating students remain unchanged by the educational experience.

4. Students in field instruction placements serving primarily retarded clients are significantly superior in knowledge about mental retardation to other students, and demonstrate greater changes in attitude and greater extremes in client preference choice. These changes are predominantly in a positive direction, though only one in six choose the retarded as their most preferred client group. The quality of the

agency placement and field instructor are important determinants of the direction of attitude change.

5. Field instruction students share a common level of knowledge and demonstrate a high level of agreement with similarly placed students in the same school, in their rankings of the retarded as a client group.

The data in this study strongly support the conclusion that cognitions, feelings and action tendencies are not consistently related except at the extreme valences of the attitude continuum. Knowledge derived through direct contact with retarded persons or their families, involving affective experiences, have greater impact on the changing of attitudes than knowledge alone. The sources of information are further determinants in the absorption of new knowledge and its integration in attitudes.

EIGHTY-EIGHT

A Teaching Record—Mental Retardation in a Child: the Impact on Parents in Therapy

CHARLES M. PATTERSON

This material was prepared in an adult mental hygiene clinic. The clinic was established in 1954 to provide outpatient psychiatric treatment to members of the community. Until October, 1960, the problem of mental retardation had never impinged on the clinic operation. At that time, a husband and wife, both patients in the clinic, learned that Kathy, their youngest child and only daughter, was mentally retarded.

The purpose of this paper is to describe the impact of mental retardation on the lives of the family, with the focus on how they reacted personally, toward each other, and toward their environment. Little emphasis is placed on the treatment process. For all intents and purposes, it ceased to exist for more than three months. The father simply stayed away from the clinic. He resisted our efforts to involve him by scheduling "important meetings," which conflicted with his clinic sessions. The mother arrived late when she kept an appointment. She, however, could not be "reached" by the therapist. Some of the reasons are revealed in the case material which follows. If, in the future, we are faced with a similar situation, our experience with this couple will enable us to handle it more effectively. We feel others might also profit by our sharing the material.

Mr. Evans applied for treatment at the clinic in November, 1959. He was at that time 35 years old, married, and the father of three children. He was a veteran of World War II, who, shortly before his release from the Army in 1946, reported to the station hospital complaining of "extreme nervousness and insomnia." He was hospitalized for 17 days, then discharged to civilian life. The physician, in writing his hospital summary, stated, "This soldier appeared to be suffering an acute anxiety reaction. The precipitating stress is unknown; however, his wife recently gave birth to the couple's first son, and the patient tried unsuccessfully to secure a furlough to be with her at the time of delivery." Had the doctor known that the child had been born with a congenital deformity, he might have been more sure of the precipitating stress. Several months later, surgeons corrected the deformity affecting the boy's feet, and Mr. Evans was adjusting well in civilian life.

In November, 1959, 13 years later, Mr. Evans contacted this clinic seeking outpatient psychiatric treatment for himself and, hopefully, for his wife. At intake, he

Reprinted by permission of the author, 1963.

complained of chronic fatigue, irritability, and insomnia. He added, "My wife has the same problems, only worse." He claimed that he tried to lose himself in his work at the office and spent most of his leisure hours doing church work. Mrs. Evans spent her time feeling sorry for her invalid mother and crying about Kathy, the couple's 2-year-old daughter. Kathy had been born with a cleft palate. She is the third child and has two older brothers, ages 11 and 14. Since his discharge from the Army, Mr. Evans has progressed from warehouseman to office manager of a successful lumber and hardware company. He is buying his home in a suburb of a western city of 150,000 people.

The couple began individual sessions at the clinic in December, 1959. Each dated the onset of the marital difficulty to shortly after Kathy's birth. At that time, a member of the family told Mrs. Evans that her husband's grandfather had a cleft palate and deformed feet. "I wondered why the family never talked to me about his grandfather. If it hadn't been for Marie, I'd never have known it came from his side of the family." Mrs. Evans didn't share with her husband the information, nor did he approach her in an effort to communicate what he was feeling. At the time of intake, neither had discussed with the other the feeling about Kathy's handicap. Mr. Evans had invested more time away from home, and she virtually withdrew from social contacts. Treatment was geared toward enabling them to re-establish effective communication one with the other.

This couple had first met while attending high school. Mr. Evans was the son of the "town handy man." He supported his wife and four children by doing odd jobs for individuals and families in the community. They were "poor" but clean." Mr. Evans was the youngest of the family of four boys. He felt very keenly the difference in living standards between himself and his friends and related to the kids in the neighborhood and at school by being a "nice guy." He was passive, shy, and deferent—"I didn't have an enemy in the world." Mrs. Evans was the third in a family of four girls. Her father was a successful insurance agent. They lived in a large, comfortable home. He was respected by members of the community; however, on the weekends would often stay in bed drinking as much as a fifth of bourbon a day. Mrs. Evans' mother developed a heart condition shortly after Mrs. Evans was born and has lived for the past 35 years an "invalid." Mrs. Evans suggests that her three sisters were encouraged to date, have friends, and "make a life for themselves." Mrs. Evans, however, was "mother's nurse. 'You may envy your sisters now, but you'll get a special reward later on.' " In high school, Mrs. Evans liked "the boy from the wrong side of town," because of his willingness to please her at every turn. Their dates consisted of working at the home of her parents. They did the gardening, painting the house, or "just visiting with mother." He seemed to be eager to please her mother and father and enjoyed the acceptance he received.

At the time of intake, Mrs. Evans still spent part of every day cleaning her mother's house, taking her mother to the doctor and running errands; and the couple's oldest son spent part of each Saturday doing little tasks for "Mumma." Mr. Evans had grown to resent the tie to his wife's family, yet had completely rejected his own.

Both Mr. and Mrs. Evans were given individual appointments scheduled on a weekly basis. The clinic staff and the two therapists involved agreed on the following plan of treatment. Mr. Evans was viewed as a very capable individual. When left to his own resources, he was ambitious and dependable, especially on the job and in the church; however, at home, he rarely if ever took a stand with his wife. She often reminded him that she served as both mother and father to the children, "You're more like a piece of furniture." He recognized early in his treatment experience that he had looked to his wife and her family for social position and respectability, and furthermore could see a need for becoming more agressive in relation to his two sons, "They think I'm a jellyfish." He described a somewhat nagging antagonism toward his wife, but claimed to be unable to deal with her in a verbally agressive way. He described a plot of ground in their back yard, 50'x50', "She always wanted me to plant something there, so I told her I had transformed the weed patch into a garden." He planted it all in corn. "She thought I was going to plant flowers, and she hates corn." In retaliation, Mrs. Evans withdrew from church contacts and spent more time at the home of her mother, and often forgot to inform him of telephone messages and scheduled church meetings. Mrs. Evans pampered the children and often criticized their father as being irresponsible in their presence. During individual sessions with Mrs. Evans, she began to look at the fear she experienced in permitting him to be "the head of the house." She described a fear of people she encountered when she accompanied her husband to various parts of the state on church business. She talked about a fear that she couldn't measure up in public. She began to look at "taking care of Mamma as a way of life for me. It's all I know, and I've used it to avoid growing up." Mrs. Evans began to spend less time at the home of her mother. Rather than driving mother all over town to pay her monthly bills, buy her groceries, etc., she made other arrangements. She opened a checking account and paid mother's bills by mail. She found a grocery store that would deliver mother's groceries to the door, and thus was freed to devote more time to her home, friends and neighbors. This was a threatening shift for Mrs. Evans, in that her mother resisted any shift in the relationship. She often accused her daughter of "becoming too interested in the lives of others to look in on the one who always loved you the most." She again referred to the "special reward" and that this would certainly be withdrawn. During June of 1960, the Evanses with their children visited Yellowstone Park. They were gone seven days. This was the first time in their married life that they had had a vacation. They all enjoyed themselves, and the children were especially "happy to get away as a family." On their return, Mumma greeted them with, "Would it have hurt you to include me?" Mrs. Evans spent two weeks soothing her feelings and reassuring her mother. For the next four weeks, she dealt with her ambivalence toward the shift away from mother. Her younger, unmarried sister had moved back into the home with mother, and both criticized Mrs. Evans for rejecting her responsibilities.

As Mr. Evans was able to risk a more direct approach to his wife, there were occasional verbal encounters that left both individuals somewhat frightened and angry. They were, however, able to resolve most of the arguments without either of them withdrawing and refusing to face their problems. They talked together about

Kathy's cleft palate. They consulted their pediatrician about the possible hereditary factors in Kathy's condition. Both shared with their respective therapists conflicting feelings about "getting closer together." Mr. Evans seemed able to risk more of himself than she.

During the month of September, Mrs. Evans' older sister arrived in the city from a neighboring state, where she had resided with her husband and two children for ten years. Mrs. Evans was invited one day to have lunch with her two sisters and mother. What started out to be a friendly visit turned into a bitter, prolonged argument. Mrs. Evans came away from the four-hour affair shaken and despondent. The two sisters and mother had accused her of "letting us all down." She was told that clinic personnel had "brain-washed" her, and she had become a selfish, irresponsible person. When she shared with her husband that evening the episode of the afternoon, he wanted to "get up there and settle this once and for all." She restrained him, suggesting that "much of what they said is true. I don't want you to make matters worse."

During the next several hours at the clinic, Mrs. Evans questioned her behavior. She doubted that she could ever depend on Mr. Evans as husband, father, and breadwinner, "He's never been very well. He could die tomorrow, and I'd be alone."

Mr. Evans described similar doubts about the changes he was attempting to make in the marriage, "My old self may not have been better, but at least I was more comfortable."

The greatest crisis this marriage has faced occurred in October, 1960. Kathy, now three years old, didn't talk, she wasn't toilet trained, nor could she feed herself. The pediatrician became concerned and referred Kathy to a speech therapist at the University Medical School, who in turn consulted with other specialists. After a series of examinations spread over a three-week period, the couple were told Kathy's problem was neither a speech nor hearing defect, but that she was mentally retarded. Three specialists spent an hour with the parents, describing the techniques employed in arriving at their diagnosis. The team explained in detail the preliminary investigation and the evidence that substantiated the findings. A plan for further testing and treatment was outlined and scheduled to begin six months hence, when Kathy would be nearing her fourth birthday.

Judging from what has occurred since the conference in October, the Evanses heard little of what had been said. Both regressed to their characteristic way of handling a personal crisis. Mrs. Evans almost lost control of herself. For a period of five weeks, she remained at home. She kept only two appointments at the clinic. During the two hours she spent here, she cried incessantly. When able to talk, she described an overwhelming resentment toward her husband. A delegation of women from the church called on her to offer their help and spiritual support. During their visit, she buried her head in a pillow and cried. She was aware of an intense resentment toward them and the church. Most of the household responsibilities were turned over to the older children. She sat for several hours a day with Kathy on her lap.

Mr. Evans became belligerent toward her. He slept on the couch, ate many of his meals away from home. He extended his work in the church to five nights a week and most of the day on Sunday.

During the latter part of November, an elderly neighbor dropped in and shared with Mrs. Evans information concerning a friend, whose child was a cerebral palsy victim. The child had been "greatly helped" by a non-medical healer in the community. A week later, Kathy was started on a series of treatments in the office of this "doctor." The parents contracted for eight weeks of treatment at a cost of $175. Fearing to advise her pediatrician about the treatment, when Kathy developed a throat infection, Mrs. Evans took Kathy to "our old family doctor for a shot." From the family doctor, she was referred to an ENT specialist, who, after hearing what Mrs. Evans chose to tell him, recommended referral to a child psychiatrist, who could give them "some idea about the prognosis." Before this referral was effected, she was contacted by the family doctor, who had arranged an appointment for Kathy with a neurologist. This flurry of activity took place over a two-week period in December. Clinic appointments were canceled by both individuals during this period of time. At no time in this couple's treatment experience was a home visit made, nor was it considered at this critical period.

Mrs. Evans arrived for her appointment on December 28 and, for the first time, shared with her therapist the "confusing feelings" of the past two months. For the next four sessions, she described and examined the inner chaos as follows: Beginning the day she heard the verdict "mentally retarded," she and Kathy were doomed. As she perceived the situation, it was absolute. God had made a judgment. She and Kathy were sentenced to suffer for some unrevealed transgressions against Him. She had tried desperately to be a good wife and mother; Kathy was an innocent child. Though they must suffer, she felt they were paying for the sins of others. Parents and grandparents on both sides of the family were viewed as partially responsible for the tragedy. On several occasions, she wondered to herself whether or not her unexpressed resentment toward her chronically ill mother accounted for her plight. She had often secretly supported her alcoholic father when he dared to argue with her mother. On one occasion, she escaped the inner turmoil for eight hours by imagining that this was God's way of making sure "I'll always have a baby with me."

She couldn't allow her husband to share her suffering. She had only to look at him to blame him. When she permitted herself to recognize that he, too, might be 'hurting,' she quickly negated it with, "He has his church."

When the neighbor suggested the non-medical healer, Mrs. Evans scheduled the first appointment without informing her husband, and considered keeping him uninformed. With the neighbor, she conspired to borrow the money to pay for the treatment. Her therapist succeeded in getting her to share with her husband the decision to contract for the treatments. She resisted, however, his attempts to refer her again to the Medical School Clinic for further clarification on their findings and treatment plans. She stated later that she wanted someone to do something. She was afraid they would convince her to wait the six months, "I couldn't stand to wait; I've never felt so helpless."

She happened onto an article on cerebral palsy, and interpreted it in a way that permitted her to discount one statement made by the speech therapist. "They were wrong there; maybe they don't know everything." Armed with this and Kathy's throat infection, she embarked on a two-week crusade designed to make Kathy, a "normal, healthy child."

After five weeks of treatment with the non-medical healer, Mrs. Evans reported encouraging shifts in Kathy's condition. "Her eyes seem clearer; they focus better. She has regular bowel movements. Both of us agree that she seems better coordinated." Two weeks later, the treatments were discontinued on the advice of the family doctor. About the non-medical healer, who practiced a form of physical therapy, she said, "We'll always be grateful to him. He gave us hope; his treatments may not have helped her, and they certainly didn't hurt her. The $175 was money well-spent."

On New Year's Day, Mrs. Evans received a call from a woman, a member of the church, about whom she knew very little. The woman had to take her son to the doctor the following day. Her car wasn't running, and she asked if Mrs. Evans would drive her to keep the appointment. She agreed and called for the woman the following morning at her home. The seven-year-old boy climbed in the back seat and sat quietly while the two women chatted up front. Prefacing her remarks with, "I know what you have been going through," the woman mentioned that her son was mentally retarded, and they were on their way to a clinic conducted by the Scoiety for Mentally Retarded Children. The events of that morning have had a profound effect on Mrs. Evans. She witnessed a group of parents, volunteers, and professional people working together to provide care and training for a group of mentally retarded children. "Most were much worse than Kathy. I went back yesterday, and I'm going again next week. I've already picked up some ways of helping Kathy."

On February 7, Kathy was hospitalized. A pneumoencephalogram was performed. Mrs. Evans shared with her therapist the session that followed with the neurologist. It was much like the one in October. "Kathy has brain damage; she is mentally retarded. She appears to be educable. Treatment will be continuous, and the results won't be dramatic." The couple cried together, and that evening the family prayed together. Mrs. Evans summed it up with, "We've all accepted it. Now we know where we are going."

For more than three months, our treatment efforts failed to reach this couple. They canceled or failed 60 percent of their scheduled appointments. Prior to October, there were no failures, and cancellations were negligible. Mrs. Evans seemed so closely identified with the problems of her child that she was completely ineffectual as a parent. She is a dependent, masochistic individual. Shortly before Christmas, her therapist made the observation, "I suspect I could communicate with Kathy easier than I can with you." She wailed like a lost child for a few minutes, then left the office claiming that she felt "too sick" to continue. Several weeks later, she mentioned the incident in connection with a feeling that no one could help her until Kathy was also being helped. In retrospect, we can see that had we collaborated with the pediatrician, the speech therapist at the Medical Center, or the Society for Mentally Retarded Children, a more unified approach to the problem could have been inaugurated.

Mrs. Evans had told no one but her mother that she was being seen at the clinic. She continually compares the statements of various authorities; i.e., the neurologist, the pediatrician, the social worker, the psychologist, the speech therapist. If she can find any discrepancy in their statements regarding treatment or prognosis, she becomes frustrated and annoyed. She has used one authority against another, "Dr. Smith says to be optimistic about her future." Dr. Brown, who worked in a State Training School for five years, is "very pessimistic and talks about an institution. You can't believe anybody. We should stop coming to the clinic, because our problems are different than they were when we started."

Neither of these individuals is equipped emotionally or psychologically to accept and deal realistically with a retarded child. As Kathy matures, the parents will need continued support and encouragement. Every healthy influence available must be brought to bear if Kathy is going to progress. The efforts of individuals and agencies could well be sabotaged by the individual problems of these parents. Our treatment goals have been expanded. To the degree that we are able, we will protect against this contingency.

PART ELEVEN

Social Research and Outcome Studies

EIGHTY-NINE

Factors in Child Placement: Parental Response to Congenital Defect

NELLIE D. STONE AND JOSEPH J. PARNICKY

The parents of a child born with an obvious impairment, such as mongolism, are immediately confronted with a crisis that raises the question of whether the family's welfare may best be served by institutional or home care of the defective infant. The visibility of the physical stigmata of mongolism (also referred to recently as Down's syndrome) heightens its impact and evokes pressures toward placement at a time when the parents are experiencing turbulent emotional reactions to this personal calamity. Because their self-regard and ego capacities have been severely threatened, parents are quite vulnerable to authoritative suggestion at this point, and are not in a position to make a sound decision about care of the mongoloid child. Such vital planning requires cognitive and emotional clarity that cannot be achieved by parents until their chaotic feelings are resolved and their ego capacities released to seek a sound and realistic solution.

During this initial crisis impact these parents are most in need of the kind of help social casework counseling and guidance can offer, through assisting them to sort out their conflicting feelings, regather their strengths, and consider alternative ways of dealing with the problems presented by the defective child. However, in many instances such preventive intervention is not available to help parents move toward a sound crisis resolution. Instead they are often subjected to pressures from physicians, relatives, and other significant persons in their social networks, who advise them to take immediate steps toward institutional placement of the infant. The parents frequently acquire a faulty conception of the mongoloid's condition as being completely hopeless and offering little or no potential for human development or response. Often, also, the parents are warned that their other, normal children will be harmed by the presence of the mongoloid child in the home. Under such circumstances it is not surprising that premature and unstable placement decisions may be made, leaving the parents with unresolved ambivalence, inadequate cognitive understanding, and impaired ego capacity with which to meet the strain of the child's care during the extended waiting period before the child may be admitted to the institution.

Reprinted by permission of the authors and the National Association of Social Workers from *Social Work*, Vol. 11, No. 2 (April, 1966), pp. 35-43.

The way in which parents resolve the initial crisis affects their ability to cope constructively with the continuing stress and succeeding crises that arise at strategic life stages of the defective child. It is therefore important to help parents make sound placement decisions by assisting them to meet the birth crisis with adaptive rather than maladaptive responses.

Approach of the Study

In an effort to learn more about the factors entering into parental decisions concerning institutional or home care, the experiences of 103 northern New Jersey families with young mongoloid children at home were studied. Fifty of these families had applied for institutional care and were on the state waiting lists, while the remaining 53 families were nonapplicants. The experiences, characteristics, reactions, and strengths of the applicant and nonapplicant parents were compared, with the aim of identifying factors associated with sound placement decisions and healthy crisis response for each group of families.

Although there has been some study of parental decisions concerning placement of mongoloid and other types of retarded children, it was felt that further empirical investigation was needed to substantiate and add to the previous indications. Kramm's case studies of 50 families with mongoloids covering a broad age range indicated that the nonapplicants appeared to have made a better adjustment, in general, than the applicants, although no statistical analysis was carried out.[1] Kelman compared the living patterns of families containing a mongoloid child with a matched sample of families having only normal children, and concluded that there was not sufficient basis for categorically recommending placement of these retardates.[2] The findings of other investigators, such as Farber, Saenger, and Tizard and Grad, have produced varying conclusions about placement of retarded children, which call for further clarification.[3]

The important role social work counseling can have in helping parents face crises centering around congenitally defective children has been discussed by Cohen and Kozier, while Goodman has described the nature and impact of the crisis of mongolism, outlining the tasks required for successful resolution.[4] The effectiveness of casework counseling in helping parents who had made early application for institutionalization of their mongoloid infant to reassess their decision was demonstrated by Giannini and Goodman's project.[5] However, the need remains for systematic inquiry as a basis for deriving clear-cut practice guides.

The present study adds the dimension of both parents' reports to the judgments of the casework interviewers as data for examining family response to the particular crisis represented by the birth of a mongoloid child. As a framework, this study draws on the concepts concerning crisis response developed by public health investigators such as Caplan, and as applied by Rapoport and Caplan and Parad respectively in intervention directed toward the family threats of prematurity and tuberculosis.[6] The parents' reactions to the crisis and continuing stress, their initial resolution and subsequent adjustment, their social situations as well as their family relations were all brought under the purview of the investigation discussed here. The dynamic behavioral concepts underlying psychosocial casework diagnosis were utilized in the assessment of family functioning, while implications for preventive intervention were derived from the insights of social work practice.

Procedures

The study population included those families in northern New Jersey who could be identified by intensive case-finding as meeting the criteria and who agreed to participate. Eligible families were required to include intact parental pairs plus one mongoloid retardate under the age of 9 years living in the home at the end of 1963. Fifty families who were on the state institutional waiting lists participated, along with 53 nonapplicant families, representing about 70 percent of those identified as eligible for study.

Data were collected by four trained caseworkers experienced in working with the mentally retarded. The father and mother in each family were interviewed successively in the home and alternately completed questionnaires designed to tap their attitudes and knowledge about the child's handicap and to reflect the nature of family interrelationships, as well as to indicate their current adaptation to the situation. The structured interview covered the parents' reactions and experiences following the birth of the mongoloid child, focusing on influences perceived as affecting the decision for or against application for institutional placement and also reporting the parents' degree of willingness to proceed with placement at the time of the visit.

On the basis of his observations and casework judgment, the interviewer rated the adequacy of family functioning on an eight-point scale, using the anchor points for inadequate, marginal, or adequate social functioning specified by Geismar and Ayres.[7] The study director made a second, independent rating based on the interviewer's recorded observations and the parents' response to the interview. Agreement within one point was obtained on 98 percent of the ratings. Other steps taken to reduce the bias introduced by the interviewer's knowledge of the families' application status were the assignment of equal numbers of applicants and nonapplicants to each interviewer and the obtaining of objective data directly from the parents.

Because of the cross-sectional method of study, the families were examined at varying points in time after the birth crisis, since their mongoloid children ranged from under a year through 8 years of age. In an effort to offset this time differential to some extent, the data were analyzed separately for families whose mongoloid children were under or over 5 years of age. By this means it was possible to obtain some impression of the early impact as against the continuing impact on the family of the mongoloid's presence. Nevertheless, the limitations of retrospective data must be recognized in evaluating the findings of the study.

The major variables consisted of sociodemographic data; interview responses of each parent; indices of parental knowledge and of current placement willingness;

parents' self-reports concerning the level of their own current adaptation and degree of family role concord; expressions of parental attitudes toward care of the child, his condition, and life in general; and the professional ratings of family functioning level. Since the interview responses indicated that many applicants were not then willing to proceed with institutionalization, the applicants were divided into two groups: the thirty families who were reluctant to place are called the "Postponers," and the twenty families who expressed willingness for placement are called the "Placers." These two groups, along with the third group of nonapplicants, were compared with reference to the above variables by analyzing the variance of the quantified data through use of IBM equipment. Pearsonian correlations were computed on the data for all families in order to determine strength of association between variables. Data obtained from fathers and mothers were subjected to parallel analyses to show similarities or differences. The parents' scores on the attitude items were reduced by factor analysis to fifteen sets of highly intercorrelated responses, designated "attitude factors."

Practice Implications

Certain results have been selected from the total findings as having pertinence for social work practice with families facing the problems that center around the birth and presence of a child with a congenital defect such as mongolism. This discussion focuses on the areas of family life and experience that comprise crucial elements in parental resolution of their separation dilemma and that indicate the need for effective methods of preventive intervention.

Validity of the application. Perhaps the most noteworthy finding was that 60 percent of the parents whose children's names appeared on the institutional waiting list were, at the time of the interview, unwilling to place them if admission were offered. This reveals that a large proportion of these applications were not valid and binding, since they no longer represented the parents' wishes. That most of these parents did not initially have deferment of admission in mind is confirmed by the statements of 40 percent, indicating that originally they had favored institutional care.

The need for preventive intervention in these situations seems evident if premature decisions are to be avoided and favorable adaptation fostered. Parad has emphasized:

> Persons in crisis states are usually more ready for, and amenable to, interventive help if it is offered at the right time and at the right place; that is, during the throes of crisis before rigid defenses and related maladaptive solutions have become consolidated by the ego.[8]

Since 40 percent of the applicants who favored placement at the time of the interview also reported a shift from their original disposition toward home care, perhaps casework counseling could have helped them reach their placement decisions more promptly and surely, or else have made available social supports that would have increased their capacity to cope with the child at home.

The finding that only 10 percent of the nonapplicants had shifted from their initial inclination toward home care leads to the feeling that their decisions were largely sound and stable. Since significantly fewer applicants than nonapplicants reported that they had found helpful community services during their crisis period, the need to provide more assistance to applicant families appears to be supported.

The indicated shrinkage of the nominal waiting list has an important administrative connotation, since planning for additional institutional facilities could thereby be affected markedly. The high degree of placement reluctance also suggests the need for reviewing application procedures, in order to assure valid intentions by applicants. Those applications that are filed for the purpose of insuring a plan for the child's care in case of future contingency should be categorized as provisional rather than active. Periodic casework review of the applicants' situations would not only help to keep the waiting list accurately classified, but could also provide reassessment of the family's needs for referral to other community resources. Such casework service might serve to prevent family deterioration under the continued stress of the child's care by making promptly available the social bulwarks offered by supportive programs or by arranging for institutional admission if needed to relieve the situation.

Sociodemographic factors. The mongoloids in the two applicant groups were significantly younger than those of the non-applicants, their ages averaging 3.1 years among the Postponers and 3.6 years among the Placers, in contrast to 4.5 years for the nonapplicants. This difference was attributed to community conditions that resulted in an overrepresentation of younger applicant mongoloids because of the state institutions' practice of deferring their admission until after the age of 5 years. In addition, the nonapplicant mongoloids were more likely to be identified after the usual school age than during their more anonymous preschool period. This uneven age distribution was partially offset by the separate analysis of data for families with younger mongoloids (under 5 years of age) and older ones (5-8 years).

Although the applicants and nonapplicants did not differ significantly with respect to socioeconomic status, there was a statistically significant variance when the applicants were subdivided and all three groups compared. According to Hollingshead's Index, the Placers achieved the lowest level, that of lower middle class, while the Postponers were rated as the highest, in the middle class, with the nonapplicants located in between.[9] However, neither social status nor age of the mongoloid differentiated between the families studied in regard to placement willingness. The applicants did not differ significantly from the nonapplicants on other social characteristics (such as religion) or ordinal position of the mongoloid (who tended to be the youngest, since parents are likely to curtail child-bearing after the birth of such a child).

Age-related differences. In the judgments of the interviewers older mongoloids were significantly more severely retarded than younger ones, which concurred with the clinical observations of other investigators that the developmental lag of mongoloid children becomes increasingly apparent and measurable as they reach the

696 · *Social Research and Outcome Studies*

usual school ages.[10] This phenomenon means that families will probably feel the impact of the mongoloid's deficiency more strongly after his infancy and preschool stage, with resulting increase of pressure on relationships and functioning, as indicated both by parents' reports and professional ratings.

When the mongoloid's sex was considered in conjunction with his age, the preponderance of older boys found among the Placers pointed to an association between this age-sex combination and parental attitudes toward placement. However, parental willingness to place mongoloid girls did not appear to be related to their age. These results suggest that parents find it more difficult to tolerate the deficiency of the mongoloid boy as it becomes more obvious with time. Societal expectations for male achievement seem to be reflected in these differential parental attitudes toward younger-older, male-female mongoloid retardates.

An awareness of these patterns of role expectations can alert the social worker to signs of lessening parental tolerance as the mongoloid passes into the school years. This critical period calls for careful casework review of the family's capacity for withstanding the continuing stress of the child's limitations on the adjustment of all members. The advisability of such evaluation is indicated by the finding that family relationships, particularly between the mother and her normal children (as well as with the retarded child), were significantly less compatible in those families with older, as compared to younger, mongoloids. The parents' own reports furnished the basis for this conclusion, which was also supported by the interviewers' judgments regarding family relationships.

By their own reports, fathers of the older mongoloids in the Postponer group of families revealed that their adjustment was markedly poorer than that of fathers of younger mongoloids in this segment. One may therefore question the adaptiveness of these applicants' reluctance for placement, since the welfare of the family may not be promoted by the continued presence of the retardate in the home. Unless the parents' capacity to cope with the increasing pressures can be bolstered by additional social supports, placement may need to be considered in order to reduce the strain for the family. The caseworker's judgment can be useful in weighing these alternatives and in counseling the family.

Parental reactions and experiences. The parents who applied for placement reported that their experiences and situations were appreciably less encouraging and sustaining of a plan for home care of the handicapped child than were those of the nonapplicants. According to the applicants, the advice they received strongly favored institutional care, while the nonapplicants indicated that they had been largely encouraged by their advisers to care for the retarded child at home. The applicants attributed most of the advice favoring institutionalization to their physicians, clergymen, and relatives.

In view of the high proportion of subsequent change in the placement intentions of the applicants, it seems obvious that much of the advice that initially influenced them to file for institutionalization proved not to represent their continuing wishes. This interpretation upholds the parents' need for sensitive and competent counseling during the birth crisis to enable them to arrive at sound rather than precipitous decisions about care of their child. If this need is to be met, hospital social workers must be available who are competent to provide the emotional support, clarification, information, and planning help that is required for effective crisis intervention.

An additional and important function of the social worker in such situations is to put the family in touch with other community resources that may furnish continuing support after the intial resolution. One of the most effective resources is parents' organizations. Those parents who were affiliated with other parents in such groups reported that they obtained significant enlightenment and encouragement toward coping with the stresses of home care of the retarded child. In fact, it appears that active participation of the Postponers in parents' organizations was probably an important factor in their changing attitude toward placement, while the failure of the Placers to avail themselves of this source of help may have been associated with their eventual readiness for institutionalization.

In either case, early contact with other parents facing a similar situation is an important means for strengthening parental capacity to care for the handicapped child. According to Giannini and Goodman, most parents of mongoloid infants "are not unable or incapable of caring for their children at home—but yet they are blocked from doing so from inner pressures and external influences."[11] Early casework services may indeed provide preventive intervention by enabling parents to achieve their potential adaptation to this kind of situation.

Family relationships. The importance of warm and close marital relations between parents when meeting adversity was shown by the finding that the parents who were least willing to institutionalize their mongoloid children were the most empathic and accurate in their perception of each other's feelings and wishes. Specifically, the mothers who reported that their husbands had been the most sympathetic and supportive toward them during the birth trauma were the most willing to cope with care of the handicapped child at home. Concomitantly, those fathers who indicated the greatest ability to withstand the impact of the defective child's birth were the ones who were able to be most accepting and encouraging toward their wives. The mutual dependence of both spouses in dealing with crisis is illustrated and points up the major role of fathers, as well as mothers, in the helping process.

The interrelationship of all family members in responding to this crisis was revealed in the finding that the harmony of the whole unit was seen by the fathers to depend on the mother's compatibility with the retarded child, while the mother's feelings of acceptance toward the child were closely related to the family's willingness to keep him at home. The parents' own opinions that close and harmonious family relations were required to cope with the child corroborated the judgments of the social work interviewers in their ratings of family functioning. The mental health principle that the surmounting of personal adversity and regaining of family equilibrium following a crisis depends largely on parental strengths seems confirmed by these results.[12]

Knowledge about mongolism. The study revealed that adequate parental knowledge about the retardate's condition and outlook was a powerful factor. At the time of the interview, the parents who indicated the most accurate information were not only those who wished to care for their mongoloid children at home, but also those who reported the most favorable adaptation to their situations and had participated most actively in parents' organizations. These significantly associated factors attest to the effectiveness of informational counseling as a tool with which the physician and social worker can assist parents to withstand stress and crisis.

Lack of adequate information at the time of the birth was cited by a majority of the parents as adding to their confusion and distress. The significantly diminished hopefulness reported by applicant mothers with respect to their expectations for the mongoloid baby's development may be traced to inaccurate or inadequate diagnostic and prognostic explanations, which may well have influenced their decision to apply for institutional care. The sooner and better the cognitive understanding achieved by the parents, the more adequately equipped they are to face and deal with each succeeding step in their crisis situation. The parent needs and is entitled to receive from his medical and other counselors a correct and realistic appreciation of what he may expect of the retarded child at various steps in his development.

Professional evaluation of family functioning. The general concurrence between the interviewers' ratings of the family's functioning and the parents' self-reports concerning their adjustment to their situations provides a sense of validity and confidence in professional judgments. The family relationship was found to be the most sensitive area with regard to plans for home or institutional care of the mongoloid child, as well as with respect to continued adjustment of the whole family, since those families who favored home care were rated as having the most adequate individual and family adjustment. The most positive and least pathological attitudes were displayed by parents in those families the interviewers evaluated as having the best over-all functioning.

Summary Profiles

The differential levels of functioning displayed by the three groups of families studied provide distinctive profiles that help to explain their placement decisions and indicate the appropriateness of their subsequent intentions.

The Placers. The extensive findings indicated that these parents were not able to absorb the defective child into their family circles without adverse effects and hence felt that his removal was necessary. The least adequate social situations and personal resources were reported by these families in comparison with the other groups. Their relationships were the least harmonious and supportive and their over-all adjustment was at the lowest level, on the average, according to their own as well as professional judgment. Despite this negative comparative picture, it must be understood that these families cannot be classified as severely disadvantaged, since they were rated on the average as functioning above a marginal level. Therefore one wonders whether their coping abilities might not have been improved through provision of more adequate counseling and social supports. If such preventive intervention had been furnished, both initally and subsequently, perhaps many of these parents need not have reached the point of discouragement that may have led them to seek relief from the pressures of the mongoloid child by placing him. Adequate professional and community services can, instead, help to preserve and promote family integrity at the time of crisis.

The nonapplicants. The generally adequate situations, resources, and functioning capacities shown by these families seem to confirm the appropriateness of their consistent desire to care for their mongoloid children at home. Because of the unity of the parents' wishes and their marital closeness, as well as the positive nature of their family and social relations, these families were able to integrate the defective child into their ranks without appreciably adverse consequences. The older average age of these mongoloid children, with their increasingly obvious deficiency, suggests that their families must have had superior strength with which to withstand the continuing pressure of their care.

The Postponers. These families presented a mixed picture, with their many positive resources and capacities measured against significant weaknesses which implied that their crisis conflict had not been fully resolved. The lack of unity in the spouses' placement wishes at the time of the birth, along with marked maternal insecurity and paternal susceptibility to authoritative placement advice, seemed to point to an unsound application decision with impending emotional repercussions. However, the subsequent adaptation of these parents showed a positive gain, in that they acquired a good cognitive understanding of their child's handicap and obtained the support of other parents and programs that encouraged them toward home care.

On the whole, these parents appeared to represent a state of transition from their initial ambivalence toward greater awareness of their own wishes and coping capacities. However, their ambiguous status as "unwilling applicants" suggested that they had yet to come to grips with their conflicts. Since their mongoloid children were the youngest in average age and mostly of preschool level, it appeared that these parents had not yet faced the full impact of their divergence from normality or experienced the extended pressure of their care and presence over time.

If preventive social services had been available to these parents at the time of their child's birth, they might have been helped to avoid the wrenching and precipitate decision to place their baby and instead have been enabled to resolve their reactions more fully and constructively. Their favorable situational and personal resources make these parents especially good candidates for the guidance that social casework should offer at the time of crisis.

Conclusions

The interaction of social, cognitive, experiential, and relational factors was revealed by the study of the application decisions and subsequent intentions of 103 parents, concerning institutional or home care of their mongoloid children. The critical nature of the family's experiences following the child's birth emphasized the need for early casework counseling and crisis intervention. The importance of strong family relations in surmounting crisis was confirmed by the concurrence of the parents' reports with the casework judgments of the interviewers. Periodic casework evaluation and the provision of social supports to the family during the crucial period of the early school years seemed to be called for by the indication that the retardate's age and sex influenced parental attitudes toward placement. The apparent effectiveness of cognitive understanding as an aid to parents in withstanding crisis and arriving at sound plans suggested the importance of informational counseling by physicians and other professional advisers.

References

[1]Elizabeth R. Kramm, *Families of Mongoloid Children,* Children's Bureau Publication No. 401 (Washington, D. C.: Children's Bureau, U.S. Department of Health, Education, and Welfare, 1963).

[2]Howard R. Kelman, "The Effects of a Group of Non-institutionalized Mongoloid Children upon Their Families as Perceived by Their Mothers." Unpublished doctoral dissertation, New York University, 1959.

[3]Bernard Farber *et al., Family Crisis and the Decision to Institutionalize the Retarded Child,* Research Monograph Series A, No. 1 (Washington, D.C.: Council for Exceptional Children, 1960); Gerhart Saenger, *Factors Influencing the Institutionalization of Mentally Retarded Individuals in New York City* (Albany, N. Y.: New York State Interdepartmental Health Resources Board, 1960); Jack Tizard and Jacqueline C. Grad, *The Mentally Handicapped and Their Families* (London, England: Oxford University Press, 1961).

[4]Pauline C. Cohen, "The Impact of the Handicapped Child on the Family," *Social Casework,* Vol. 43, No. 3 (March 1962), pp. 137-142; Ada Kozier, "Casework with Parents of Children Born with Severe Brain Defects," *Social Casework,* Vol. 38, No. 4 (April 1957), pp. 183-189; Lawrence Goodman, "Continuing Treatment of Parents with Congenitally Defective Infants," *Social Work,* Vol. 9, No. 1 (January 1964), pp. 92-97.

[5]Margaret J. Giannini and Lawrence Goodman, "Counseling Families During the Crisis Reaction to Mongolism," *American Journal of Mental Deficiency,* Vol. 67, No. 5 (March 1963), pp. 740-747.

[6]Gerald Caplan, "An Approach to the Study of Family Mental Health," *U. S. Public Health Reports,* Vol. 71, No. 10 (October 1956), pp. 1027-1030; Lydia Rapoport, "Working with Families in Crisis: An Exploration in Preventive Intervention," *Social Work,* Vol. 7, No. 3 (July 1962), pp. 48-56; Gerald Caplan and Howard J. Parad, "A Framework for Studying Families in Crisis," *Social Work,* Vol. 5, No. 3 (July 1960), pp. 3-15.

[7]Ludwig L. Geismar and Beverly Ayers, "Measuring Family Functioning" (St. Paul, Minn.: Family-centered Project, 1960). (Mimeographed.)

[8]Howard J. Parad, "Preventive Casework: Problems and Implications," *The Social Welfare Forum 1961* (New York: Columbia University Press, 1961).

[9]August B. Hollingshead, "Two-Factor Index of Socioeconomic Status" (New Haven: published by the author, 1957). (Mimeographed.)

[10]Karol Fischler *et al.,* "Adaptation of Gesell Developmental Scales for Evaluation of Development in Children with Down's Syndrome (Mongolism)," *American Journal of Mental Deficiency,* Vol. 68, No. 5 (March 1964), pp. 642-646.

[11]*Op. cit.*

[12]Gerald Caplan, *Principles of Preventive Psychiatry* (New York: Basic Books, 1964).

NINETY

Self-Maintenance and Community Behavior of Adult Retardates

VIVIAN WOOD and JEANNE MUELLER

What are those who were once considered retarded doing as adults in the community? There are those among us who speculate about criminality, sexuality, and lassitude (public welfare). There are others who doubt the adequacy of tests and examinations given in childhood for predicting social adaptation in adulthood, and who speculate on what the reputed retardates are doing as workers, citizens and family members.

This study was focused on reputed retardates who have survived the hazards of childhood and the rigors of school and have managed somehow to stay outside the institutions. To what extent do they take care of themselves, perhaps even assume family responsibilities of their own, and to what extent are they dependent on others and/or community services, to support their independent living? For this purpose a role analysis frame of reference was used and behavior was categorized into major roles, such as family roles and work roles. Information was obtained also on income, health status and use of community services.

Previous Studies

This is not a new problem; early in this century Fernald (1919) initiated the first of a series of studies which examined the adjustment of retardates who were formerly residents of institutions or students in special education classes. These studies gave evidence to refute the notion that retardates are not able to make a satisfactory adjustment to community living (Fairbanks, 1933; Baller, 1936; Kennedy, 1948; Charles, 1953). They also tend to show that the level of intelligence, aside from the most severe retardation, is not highly related to either success on the job or amount of income earned. These investigators reported primarily on marital and occupa-

Reprinted by permission of the authors, 1968. This study was co-sponsored by the University of Wisconsin School of Social Work and the Jefferson County Association for Retarded Children. It was financed in part by the grant made by the Wisconsin State Association for Retarded Children to the County Association. Social work graduate students who participated in the study and carried out the interviewing were: Lillian Cheng, Norma Nesbitt, Carol Sherfinski, Eleanor Sparks, Patricia West, Elizabeth Brandt, Lana Cue, Carol Dargatz, Jo Anne Hugunin, Roger Schmidt, Judy Sokolow, Bernice Straub, Nancy Weinberg, Karen Gilbertson.

tional status, income, and police records. The important findings were that most retardates whose IQ was 50 or above held jobs as unskilled laborers, jobs in which they performed about as well as anyone else working at the same level of skill. They had more minor encounters with the law, needed more help from social services, and participated less than the general population in civic and recreational activities.

More recent and more sophisticated research studies, such as those by Windle (1962) and Edgerton (1967) show far less hopeful outcomes and point to the weaknesses of earlier studies in adequately defining "adjustment." When Edgerton (1967) followed up on the most hopeful and carefully selected cases after they were discharged from Pacific State Hospital, he found them living in slum neighborhoods, in the most dilapidated dwellings. The retardates had few marketable skills, many were heavily in debt, and much of their time and energy went into elaborating subterfuges to deny and conceal their spoiled identities. They were also highly dependent on benefactors to help them meet the very ordinary demands of everyday living.

The Peterson and Smith (1960) study compared a group of normal subjects from a low socio-economic level who had been in regular classes with a group of retardates who had been in special education classes during the same period of time. The educable retarded were employed primarily in service occupations or as unskilled laborers, while the normals had clerical, semi-skilled or skilled jobs. Median income for the normal group was higher; female normals earned slightly more than male retardates and female retardates earned least of all, $1,002 annually. These low median incomes bring into question the use of the adjective "satisfactory" in describing adjustment. Also, contrary to popular notion, was the evidence that retarded females earn lower incomes than retarded males.

The Study Population

The setting for the study reported here is a semi-rural Wisconsin county with a population of about 51,000 residents. It is located between two metropolitan areas where there are health, vocational training and other services and, in addition, the county has several resources of its own. This include a county home, county mental hospital, family counseling center, sheltered workshop, day care for young retarded children, two private residential care facilities for retardates, special education classes, and a county association for retarded children.

This County Association is a long established and very active group who have broadened their focus of concern to include older retardates who have lived beyond the age of childhood. Understanding the need for families and communities to work together to create, expand or improve resources where they are lacking or inadequate to the demand, the County Association looked to the findings of this study to help in planning their community action program.

In order to locate the study population, interviews were held with teachers, school principals, staff of the county department of health and social services, the sheriff, police chief, county nurse, agricultural extension agent, vocational rehabilitation counselor, workshop director, town clerks and supervisors, and members of the local selective service board. In all, a total of 25 local agencies or key professionals and two state level agencies, Department of Public Instruction and Department of Health and Social Services, contributed to the initial list of retardates or furnished useful information for identifying and locating them. The Wisconsin State Employment office had no way to distinguish mentally handicapped from other clients, and the Vocational Rehabilitation supervisor was concerned about possible breaches of confidentiality and therefore would not give clearance to the district office to release information.

The population list of 275 retardates represents an age range from 20 years to over 65; there are 192 males and 103 females. The proportion of persons in the younger age ranges was larger than in the older group. All persons in the older age range who would consent to be interviewed were included in the study a d a sample was drawn from the youngest group (20-25). One hundred forty-eight names were drawn from the list ot secure a quota sample of 61 respondents. There were 30 refusals, 16 by men and 14 by women, which were evenly distributed over the age categories. Approximately 40 persons were not interviewed because they had moved or could not be located. The remaining 17 who were not interviewed were ill, deceased, institutionalized, or did not fit the criteria for inclusion in the sample.

The 43 men and 18 women who were interviewed included both diagnosed and perceived retardates. The diagnosed retardate has been (1) labeled by a professional service agency, and/or (2) has scored below 85 on a test of intelligence and/or (3) has attended special education classes and/or (4) been institutionalized as a retardate during childhood. The perceived retardate was seen by those in his community as being "slow," "a bit dense," or "not too bright"; he also may have been diagnosed as retarded, in which case he was included in the "diagnosed" category for purposes of this study.

It is interesting that the interviewer judged only one of the five persons 60 or older to be retarded. For example, one 63-year-old woman was physically disabled and had attended school only from ages 13 to 18 because of this disability but she appeared to be of normal intelligence, judged by her responses to the interview questions and to the interviewer. The 78-year-old man whose caseworker identified as being retarded, and who was judged so by the interviewer and the 82-year-old sister with whom he lives, has two mood swings annually: for six months he becomes depressed, nervous, and unable to cope with life. All five of the older persons had limited educations, and two were foreign born.

The age distribution and other general characteristics of the 61 principal respondents (PRs) are shown in Table 1. Although males make up 50 percent of the county population, they represent 65 percent of the population pool of identified retardates and 70 percent of the study population. It is not clear whether this was a random error, or whether families and friends of female retardates are more protective, making it more difficult to locate and get permission to interview them. The proportion of each sex who had never married was about the same, 69 percent of the males and 72 percent of the females. Most of the study population lived in the small towns (72 percent) where most of the county population is concentrated.*

TABLE 1 CHARACTERISTICS OF RETARDATES: BY SEX

	MALE (N = 43)	FEMALE (N = 18)	TOTAL (N = 61)
Age			
20-25	13	7	20
26-40	15	7	22
Over 40	15	4	19
Marital Status			
Single	30	13	43
Married	12	2	14
Divorced or Separated	1	3	4
Residence			
Rural or Village	10	7	17
Town	33	11	44
Level of Retardation			
(Interviewer's Estimate)			
Severe or Moderate	12	10	22
Mild	12	5	17
Not retarded	9	2	11
Can't judge	10	1	11
Identification			
Diagnosed	25	11	36
Perceived	15	7	22
Unknown	3	0	3

A larger proportion of females than males are rated as severely or moderately retarded by the interviewers and, even though the numbers are small, one can speculate the adult females who are only mildly retarded may not be visible as deviants in the community because of lesser demands for work role performance.

For each of the retardates a significant other person was also interviewed. These were persons to whom the retardate could turn for help in time of trouble, persons called "benevolent conspirators" by Edgerton (1967). The significant other was asked questions which would, in part, verify answers given by the retardate with whom he had a relationship. Additional questions were aimed at assessing the burden of caring on others. During the interviewing process we became aware of an extensive lack of knowledge about community resources which were already available to lighten this burden of care.

*The difficulty of finding and scheduling interviews with persons who are without phones and who live on unmarked country roads probably accounts for the smaller number in our sample from rural areas and villages.

In most instances the retardates lived in the same household as the significant other respondents, and whenever possible a team interviewed the respondents simultaneously. This prevented the significant other, usually a parent, from answering for the retardate or from becoming overanxious or overprotective on his behalf. Retardates reported more health problems than their respective significant others, usually as a rationalization for unemployment. They also tended to overestimate income compared to the figures given by the significant others. This may be a response to felt status pressures. On the other hand, the retardates mentioned police and courts among community services they had made use of or been involved with, more often than did the significant others.

In line with the major objective of determining how respondents are getting along in the community, a measure was devised to determine level of self-maintenance and morale. Respondents were rated on each of six criteria and ratings were summed to get a combined self-maintenance and life-satisfaction score.* Brief consideration will be given to outcomes for each of the index items and a comparison of groups whose scores on the index fell into the high, middle and low ranges.

Major Findings

Meeting everyday needs: According to the significant others' reports, all respondents were able to perform the simplest tasks of everyday living; they were able to feed, dress, bathe, and go to the bathroom alone. A smaller number were able to perform more complex tasks as the following list shows:

TASK	NUMBER OF RETARDATES
Spend evenings without supervision	55
Shave self or shampoo hair	53
Choose own clothing	53
Get around in neighborhood alone	52
Do some or all of household chores	51
Pay his own bills	43
Have a bank account	33
Read magazines and papers regularly	33
Take trips alone	27
Have a driver's license	20

*Self-maintenance Index items included: (1) Level of functioning with regard to meeting everyday personal and social needs; (2) Employment record; (3) Adequacy of income; (4) Living arrangements; (5) Social adjustment: relations with others; (6) Personal adjustment or life satisfaction of adult retardates (Wood, Wylie, and Sheafor, 1966). Responses for each set of interviews were coded and punched on IBM cards. Inter-coder reliability was 95.4. Of a total of 2,373 compared judgments, disagreement occurred on only 108, or 4.6 percent of the comparisons. Disagreements were resolved by discussion.

Although the differentiation between savings and checking account was not made in the present study, Edgerton (1967) found that none of his 53 respondents had a checking account and those who had savings accounts were always assisted in its use. Perhaps none of the 33 from the present study who were said to have bank accounts actually handled them independently, but the fact that over half of the PRs had bank accounts seems rather remarkable. Even more unusual in relation to Edgerton's study is that 20 of the retarded respondents in this sample were said to have driver's licenses. Only one of the 53 in the Edgerton study ever had a license, and only three others had attempted to pass the driving tests. The respondents in the present study, of course, lived in a rural area where the need for driving skills and criteria for licensing were probably less demanding and more urgent than in the urban area where Edgerton's population was located.

Employment: Forty-three of the 61 principal respondents were employed at the time of the interview, the majority (N = 29) were doing service, unskilled, maintenance or farm work.* Only 16 (25 percent) had never worked; 21 (35 percent) had an irregular work history; while 24 (40 percent) had worked regularly. The major reason given for not working was poor health or physical disability. Twenty-two (37 percent) of the respondents had special training, and of these 12 were working at service or farm jobs or other unskilled or semiskilled jobs; five had skilled jobs and five were unemployed. Most claimed to have secured their present jobs by applying in person (N = 13) or through a relative or friend (N = 15). Most of them were reasonably well satisfied with their jobs and work conditions. Twenty-two said "nothing" when asked what they did not like about their work as compared to 18 who mentioned some aspects of the work situation with which they were dissatisfied; the most frequent mention was of factors affecting physical comfort.

Income: Both the principal respondents and significant others were asked about the amount of the retardate's monthly income. The significant others tended to name a lower figure for monthly income than that reported by the reputed retardates and we have used the SO's figures. Forty-four percent of the retardates, compared to eleven percent of the general population, had incomes at or below the poverty level. Ten percent of the retardates, however, had incomes above the median for the county. (For 18 percent of the respondents income could not be ascertained.) Sources of income include earned wages (36), family (14), and public funds (11). Sixteen mentioned a second source, usually family or public funds. Of the 46 retardates from whom responses were obtained, 30 said they were getting along "fairly well" on their income, 15 said "very well," and only one said "not well at all."

Living arrangements: Seventy-two percent (N = 44) of the retardates live in the towns and 28 percent live in villages or open country. Of the 231 whose residence

*A report of major occupational groupings for 2,942 retarded persons vocationally rehabilitated through Federal-State programs in the period 1954-57 shows a similar percentage distribution: service workers, 30.0%; unskilled workers, 21.2%; semi-skilled workers. 19.3%; clerical, sales, kindred, 12.0%; family workers, homeworkers, 6.2%; agricultural workers, 5.9%; skilled employees, 5.4% (The President's Committee on Employment of the Handicapped, *Guide to Job Placement of the Mentally Retarded* (Washington: U.S. Government Printing Office, 1964), p. 5.

location was determined and from which the sample was drawn, 56 percent lived in towns. Our sample, therefore, under-represents rural residents.

Most of the respondents (52) lived in houses; seven were apartment dwellers and only two lived in single rooms. While quality of housing varied greatly, it was generally substandard as is typical of housing conditions reported in the studies reviewed above.

Most of the people were long-time residents of the county, many for most of their lives and none for less than a year. Residents in the retardates' home communities reportedly give assistance ranging from active help ("people around here save all their odd jobs for him") to a benevolent tolerance ("the community has been kind to him"). Fewer social skills are needed to manage life in a rural area and this factor may also contribute to stability in residence.

About one third of the retardates were married, living with spouse and had children. There was only one instance of unmarried parenthood. Except for three cases, all children were living at home.

The majority (33) of the PRs lived with their parents; four lived alone, six with siblings, one with another relative and only one with non-relatives. They contributed help with such tasks as household repairs (26), shopping (25), laundry (20), gardening (19), care during illness (14), and baby-sitting (10).

Use of leisure time and social relations: The use of leisure time by the single retardates in this study was probably not basically different from other single adults in the county. There appears to be a lack of recreational facilities and social groups for young adults; in addition, retardates seem to avoid going to what is available for fear of being rejected. Several parents mentioned the need for a place for the retardates to go where they knew they would be accepted.

About 40 percent (24) of the retardates had time on their hands, according to the significant other respondents, but only seven saw this as creating problems for the family or others. When asked what the retardate did for enjoyment, the most frequent mention was of activities carried out alone at home, and community activities in company with others had the second highest mention. When asked about their weekday activities, somewhat more than half of the retardates mentioned only going to work or doing household chores and errands. Only ten of the 61 PRs said they belonged to any church group or social club and only three mentioned belonging to a second group. All but nine of the PRS said they attended church but fewer than half attended regularly. Somewhat over half of the retardates claimed to have friends that they got together with regularly. Most said these were friends from school days or from work. When asked how they spent most of their spare time, the most frequent mention was with family members; spending time alone was mentioned second most often, with friends third. Only eleven of the 47 unmarried retardates said they dated. Twelve said they had thought of getting married at one or another time, but none had any special plans for marriage.

The most common evening activity was watching television. Less frequent was the mentioned recreation or visiting outside the home. In general, activities other than work were home-centered during the week, with church and recreational pursuits the most often mentioned outside-the-home activities for Sunday. The most often mentioned leisure-time activities other than watching TV or listening to the radio or phonograph were watching sports, playing cards and other games, and visiting friends and neighbors. These activities correspond to those found among the discharged retardates studied by Edgerton (1967). The basic leisure-time pattern for the retardates in his study was a combination of conversation and television. As Edgerton (1967) points out, it is difficult to find a comparable group of normal persons with which to contrast the leisure patterns of the retardates to determine whether the latter are impoverished in their leisure life. He concluded with regard to the ex-patients in his study population that "they do not differ greatly from the 'normal' persons who live near them in lower socio-economic status neighborhoods" (Edgerton, 1967, p. 141). This concurs with our impression that the leisure life at least of the single retardates in the present study did not differ too greatly from other single adults in the community.

Life satisfaction: In trying to determine how well the retardates maintain their morale in the face of their difficulties, we used a measure of positive self-evaluation in their life circumstances.* There was a clear tendency for low life satisfaction scores to be associated with a low score on the total self-maintenance index. Three-fourths of the respondents with low life satisfaction scores were at the poor self-maintenance level. On the other hand, two-thirds of those with high life satisfaction were at the highest of the three self-maintenance levels.

Self-maintenance levels: A higher proportion (75 %) of retardates encouraged by significant others to be independent by using instrumental means (setting up tasks, teaching by example) were at a low level of self-maintenance compared to those with whom verbal encouragement was used (53 %). Probably verbal encouragement was not used with the more severely retarded because it was believed it would not help; consequently, instrumental means were used with these persons.

Two thirds (N = 12) of the females but only one-fourth (N = 11) of the males had low ratings on self-maintenance. This is probably because a larger proportion of the females were severely or moderately retarded. The self-maintenance ratings are biased against females on two criteria: employment record and adequacy of income. While there is probably no inherent superiority in the ability of retardates of either sex to meet these criteria, social expectations for females do not include holding a steady job and earning enough for self-support, with the probable result being that female retardates are less often employed than are males. Four of the 18 women in the study population were employed at the time of the interview, and of these, only two had a regular work history. An additional five women said they had worked in the past, all but one in service occupations.

---

*The measure used was the Life Satisfaction Index Z (Wood, Wylie and Sheafor, 1969) which is a modification of the LSI-A developed by Neugarten, Havighurst and Tobin (1961). The LSI-Z was adapted for use in the present study by phrasing 12 of the 13 statements as questions.

Married respondents (N = 14) scored high on the self-maintenance index. Married status, of course, is a part of the self-maintenance rating, but in addition most of these respondents scored high on the other criteria. For example, one of the two women with a regular work history was married and had one child. This 22-year-old woman takes care of her home and family and works nights grinding knives in a factory, a job which her mother feels is too hard for her. Her husband had been unemployed for some months, and her earnings were supplemented from public funds. The interviewer judged the principal respondent to be only mildly retarded and reported that she maintained a sense of humor and was doing relatively well in difficult circumstances, although she looks "worn out."

Years of school completed, which is again an indication of severity of retardation, is also related to level of self-maintenance. For example, one-half of the retardates who did not get as far as high school or who were only in ungraded special classes were in the lowest group in self-maintenance behavior.

Use of community services: Each principal and significant other respondent was presented with a list of community services and asked whether he had ever used each of them, and whether the service given was helpful.

The services least often used are counseling, services for the handicapped and retarded, and youth groups. The most frequent comment given to explain why services were not used related to lack of need for them. Usually it was said that there was no problem or that any problem existing could be handled with no outside help. Employment and training services were most frequently mentioned both for use and helpfulness. Most of the significant other respondents had favorable comments about special programs of all types, especially with regard to vocational school and sheltered workshop programs.

When retardates were asked whether they thought other community services were needed and if so, what types, 17 of them said they did not think additional services were needed and 21 replied, "don't know." The only service mentioned with any frequency by the 21 retardates who did respond was a need for recreation for youth, a need which is probably as urgent for the normal as for the retardate population of the county.

Respondents in this study who use community services are most likely to be severely or moderately retarded, to have been diagnosed as retarded, to have a low self-maintenance level, an income under $200 a month, and an irregular work history. With the exception of some of the employment and training programs, only a minority are reported to have used services designed to meet the special needs of retardates. Of those who used day care and sheltered workshop programs, two-thirds were aged 20-30 and over half of those with vocational school training were in this younger age group. This indicates that younger retardates are making better use of special services for the handicapped than are the older ones. This is probably due in part to the relative newness of many of the services; the older retardates are often not aware of the existence of such services or what they actually provide. Younger retardates and their families are likely to have been made aware of the services through the schools which have had more aggressive information programs in recent years. The recency of many of these services probably accounts in part for the fact that adult retardates in general are making relatively minimal use of community services available to them. Another factor related to age is the philosophy that prevails, especially among older persons, that "we can take care of our own." Another variable involved is the reluctance on the part of the retardate and his family to have him identified and labeled by the community as retarded. Hence the denial of need and attempt to normalize problem situations.

Significant others: The typical significant other person was a retardate's mother who was over 50 years of age. A common refrain of these persons was "What will happen to him when we are gone or unable to take care of him?" For some parents the prospect was too painful and agonizing to discuss. For most, the problem was still one for the future, but a few were already face-to-face with the problem. One couple in their 70's had to put their retarded and physically handicapped son in the county home after the father suffered a stroke and the mother broke a leg. They were hopeful that it was a temporary arrangement, but knew realistically that it might not be. Some parents hoped that one of the retardate's normal siblings would undertake the care-taker role when they were dead, while others fiercely resisted the idea of siblings having to take on this responsibility. A few parents felt they had made adequate financial arrangements for their retarded offspring, but were still very concerned about possible living arrangements for them after their deaths. Some were resigned, but unhappy, that the retardate would end up in the county home. While some stated with fierce pride that they "didn't need the community's help," many of those who were able to articulate a response, spoke of the need for some kind of protective living arrangement for retardates without families. One 84-year-old widow had made financial arrangements for her mongoloid son to become a permanent resident in a religious-sponsored retardation facility in the county after her death, but she was still quite concerned about who would make the final arrangements if she should die suddenly. That other family members do sometimes take over responsibility for the retardate after his parents die is indicated by one case in this study. Two nieces in their late 20's had the retardate and her illegitimate child come to live with them after her mother's death. They felt the mother "ran her life" and that they are helping her to become more independent and to be able to take care of herself. Yet they too expressed concern about what will happen to her in her later years.

Two retardates in this study have married persons considerably older than themselves. While this may not be a common occurrence, it may occur with more frequency than we think. It seems likely that an older person who may feel he is no longer needed will be attracted to the idea of taking care of a retardate, someone who so obviously needs him. While the needs of each are fulfilled in a symbiotic relationship, the death of the older person may be quite devastating to the retardate. At the very least, it will precipitate the need for a new living arrangement. In this study a 49-year-old retardate had married an 82-year-old woman because each was lonely and sympathetic to the other's needs. She seemed quite essential to the retardate in terms of making decisions for him. One wonders, as the wife does, what will happen to him when she dies. Another retardate in her 50's is married to a 75-year-old man. This couple live in very poor housing and seem to be quite isolated from the community. As they become older and the possibility of disability increases, one wonders what will happen if their already substandard living conditions deteriorate further. The death of either one will result in the need for a protective living arrangement for the remaining one.

Summary and Implications for Social Work Practice

In summary, the ability of most of those retardates to live in the community is dependent on the continued help of relatives, usually parents or spouses. A common and realistic concern of these significant other persons in the retardates' lives is with living arrangements when the caretakers become disabled or die. Moreover, most of these relatives have limited incomes and cannot make provision for continued economic support of the retardate through leaving an estate. A community organization task suggested by this need is the mobilization of support for a contract between families and state and local communities for sharing responsibility for the lifetime care of the retardate (Loeb, 1965). Under such a contract arrangements would be made for the family to assume responsibility for the care of their retarded member for as much of the time and for as long a time as possible. In turn, there would be established resources in the community for intermittent care for use in times of family crises, for vacations from the burden of 24-hour supervision and for that time when the family is no longer there.

The second major problem identified was health status. Sixty-two percent of the significant others report that poor health of the retardate has been or is now of concern to them. About a third of the group has gone to one of the larger nearby metropolitan areas for special services, including health care. There is much left to be done, however, for more comprehensive identification and treatment of illness and disability, especially among the older retardates. The widespread ignorance among respondents about help that already exists in the community suggests the need for more aggressive case-finding, for a reaching out to find those who, because of advancing age, poor health, lack of knowledge about resources, or rural isolation have more than the usual difficulties in finding the path to the appropriate social agency. Sometimes failure to seek out retardates or others with special needs reflects an administrative decision to keep county health and welfare budgets to a minimum. In such instances social workers must look critically at agency values and at times they must act as advocates for their clients, particularly for those from low-income groups who have few articulate representatives to speak on their behalf.

It is not proper to ask an individual social worker to take risks alone. Local N.A.S.W. chapters can play a more active role, joining with local associations for retarded children to plan comprehensive community services for the mentally retarded of all ages. Action programs, suggested by findings of this study, would include more adequate income maintenance provisions (44 percent of incomes were below the poverty level); more extensive case-finding and recruitment into vocational training (only 37 percent had special work training, yet this was the service most used and found helpful); more adequate delivery of health services; and the establishment of supervised living situations with social work services available to sustain those retardates who can manage in such circumstances to live outside an institution. Also, for the 40 percent who have "time on their hands," recreation services are either inadequate for their particular needs or not available at all. These problem areas call for interventions that make use of group work and community organization as well as casework skills.

Public education efforts must extend not only to potential users of service, but also to the helping professionals. The failure of public agencies to keep records in such a way that retardates could be readily identified and information gathered concerning place of residence, age, marital status, health, income and work history makes it nearly impossible for community planners to assess the extent and kinds of needs that exist in this special population. Without this knowledge, adequate provision for meeting these needs cannot be established. It took several months of investigative efforts to locate the sample of respondents for this study. Part of the difficulty arose from agencies' efforts to prevent stigmatization of their clients by avoiding the mental retardation label. The value of this practice may be questioned as it sometimes seemed to result in the hiding of clients from their would-be benefactors—the agency staff itself. The stigma that may be attached to positions labeled "mental retardate" or "welfare client" deters many families from asking for much needed help. Among the respondents in the present study were many who would insist sometimes with fierce pride that they "could take care of their own." This insistence leads to the under-utilization of services. Without the mental retardation label, services designed for this group are often not available to them. As this study has shown, individuals once labeled as retarded, for example by the schools, may not be labeled as such in adulthood. Yet these persons often turn up in the general population as more or less dependent people as a result of their inadequacies in fulfilling family and community roles. They usually are not seen as eligible for mental retardation services or, for that matter, for many other social services. This suggests that social work efforts directed to establishing a less stringent definition of social dependency and to guaranteeing to everyone the right to social and rehabilitation services (just as there is now a right to public health services without having to submit to a means test) is one way to make it possible for these persons both to receive social work services and to achieve the de-stigmatization of the client position.

Social work services can also be directed toward helping significant other persons in the retardates' lives overcome their resistance to the use of services presently available for help with the inevitable family life-cycle crises. Programming for the needs of the mentally retarded has focused on retarded children. This study points up the need for social workers, as well as other professions working in the mental retardation field, to consider the whole life span of the individual. A good beginning point for planning services for the adult retardate is a consideration of the crisis points in the family life-cycle where assistance is likely to be needed. Effective case finding is required if these clients are to receive help. Most of them will not be aware of the available services and would probably would not ask for them even if they did know about them. In short, if the community waits until services for the adult retardate are demanded before making them available, nothing will happen. The social work profession has the opportunity, if not the responsibility, to take the lead in determining what services are needed for adult retardates in the community and in getting the services to them.

To date, most special education and training for retardates has centered on vocational training. While there is a clear need for this, it does ignore the home-making role for women and the need for both sexes to have training in managing their personal affairs and living independently or at least semi-independently. Our educational system is designed to train individuals in youth for their adult roles in the family and community; there is the expectation that this training will provide adequate guidance for the individual throughout his life span. We are beginning to question this assumption even for the normal individual; certainly there is little reason to believe that training in youth prepares the retardate for meeting even the everyday demands of living in his adult and later life.

In this study, social work services which could have lessened the stress for both the retardate and his family were greatly under-used. Also lacking was the important element of integration and coordination of services to provide for continuity of care in cases where a variety of resources are involved. This responsiblity is often assumed by a social worker who acts as liaison between family and community agencies or institutions, and who emphasizes the social work value that service must be adapted to people, not people to services. At an organizational level, information and referral centers which are open to all citizens and therefore not stigmatizing are one possible way to furnish coordinating services and to provide for continuity in care.

Questions yet to be answered for social workers who are concerned with adequacy of the social role performances of adult retardates are: What are the criteria for judging optimal role performance of the adult retardate in varying circumstances? What demands should be placed on him to help him realize his potential for adequate social behavior? In this study the scores on an index of self-maintenance and life satisfaction were related to judged level of retardation in most cases but there were exceptions. There are those who feel isolated and rejected by their community but there are others for whom the whole community acts as a sheltered environment, providing them with acceptance and "odd jobs" as well as making demands for appropriate performance. The lower social expectations set for females may account in part for their low scores on self-maintenance, but for both males and females it may be that concern for overtaxing capabilities has prevented the community from setting social expectations that would effect more adequate social functioning.

The problem of determining the optimal social expectations that should be placed on the adult retardate is but one of the many challenges to social work in the mental retardation field. It is not only a question of meeting human needs but also of creating a community where every individual is able to perform at the highest level possible for him.

References

BALLER, W.R. "A Study of the Present Social Status of a Group of Adults Who, When They Were in Elementary School Were Classified as Mentally Deficient," *Genet. Psychol. Monog.*, 1936, 18: 165-244.

CHARLES, D.C. "Ability and Accomplishment of Persons Earlier Judged Mentally Deficient," *Genet. Psychol. Monog.*, 1953, 47: 3-71.

EDGERTON, ROBERT B. *The Cloak of Competence.* Berkeley: University of California Press, 1967.

FAIRBANK, R.E. "The Subnormal Child-Seventeen Years After," *Mental Hygiene*, 1933, 17: pp. 177-208.

FERNALD, W.E. Aftercare Study of the Patients Discharged from Waverly for a Period of 25 Years. *Ungraded*, 1919, 5: 25-31.

KENNEDY, JAMES. "The Social Adjustment of Morons in a Connecticut City," Hartford: Mansfield-Southbury Training School, pp. 38.

LOEB, MARTIN B., "Shared Responsibility of the Mentally Retarded—One Approach to the Prevention of Institutionalism," *Am. J. of Orthopsychiat.*, 1965, 35: 903-905.

NEUGARTEN, B.L., R.J. HAVIGHURST, and S.S. TOBIN. "The Measure of Life Satisfaction," *J. Geront.* 1961, 16: 134-143.

PETERSON, L., and L. SMITH. "The Post-school Adjustment of Educable Mentally Retarded Adults Compared with That of Adults of Normal Intelligence." *Exc. Child*, 1960, 26: 404-408.

President's Committee on Employment of the Handicapped, *Guide to Job Placement of the Mentally Retarded.* Washington, D.C.: U.S. Government Printing Office, 1964.

WINDLE, C.D. "Prognosis of Mental Subnormals." *Amer. J. Ment. Defic. Monogr. Suppl.*, 1962, 66: 1-180.

WOOD, VIVIAN, MARY WYLIE and BRADFORD SHEAFOR, "An Analysis of a Short Self-Report Measure of Life Satisfaction: Correlation With Rater Judgments." *Journal of Gerontology*, 1969.

Effects of Adoption on Children from Institutions

HAROLD M. SKEELS

The National Institute of Mental Health is presently carrying on three followup studies of adults who were reared away from their own parents. The purpose is to determine the adult status of children previously studied by the Iowa Child Welfare Research Station, State University of Iowa, in cooperation with the Children's Division, Iowa Board of Control of State Institutions, which initiated modes of intervention in infancy or early childhood. These include followup studies of—

I. A longitudinal study of 100 adopted children.[1] The followup of this study is being carried on by the original investigators.

II. A study of the effects of differential stimulation on mentally retarded children.[2] The followup of this study is also being carried on by the original investigator.

III. A study of the mental development in adoptive homes of children whose biological mothers were mentally retarded.[3] The followup of this study is being carried on by Lowell W. Schenke, psychologist, Iowa Board of Control of State Institutions, with one of the original investigators (the writer) serving as consultant.

In all three of these studies, the children selected for study were considered to be biologically sound and without demonstrable abnormality as determined through diagnostic evaluation by competent pediatricians. With the inclusion of the present followup studies, they cover a life span of 30 years, the present ages of the subjects being within a range of 25 to 35 years.

Adopted Children

In regard to the followup of Study I, all adoptive parents and adopted children have been located after a lapse of 16 years since the last contacts of the earlier study. Interviews with adoptive parents and their adult adopted children are nearing completion. Analysis of the data will start in the near future.

From *Children,* Vol. 12, No. 1 (January-February, 1965), pp. 33-40, by permission of the author and The Children's Bureau.

Preliminary indications are that these adoptive children as adults are achieving at levels consistently higher than would have been predicted from the intellectual, educational, or socioeconomic level of the biological parents, and equal to the expectancy for children living in the homes of natural parents capable of providing environmental impacts similar to those which have been provided by the adoptive parents.

Mentally Retarded Children

In regard to followup of Study II, all subjects have been located after a lapse of 21 years, all interviews completed, with the data presently being processed.

Preliminary findings of this followup study are particularly startling. In the original study, 13 children in an experimental group, all mentally retarded at the beginning of the study, were at an early age transferred from one institution to another which provided a much higher degree of one-to-one emotional relationship between mother-surrogates and the children. Later, 11 of these children were placed in adoptive homes.

A contrast group of 12 children, initially at a higher level of intelligence than those in the experimental group, remained in a relatively nonstimulating institutional environment over a prolonged period of time. In the initial study, the children in the experimental group showed a decided increase in rate of mental growth, whereas the children in the contrast group showed progressive mental retardation.

In the adult followup study, the two groups continued to be remarkably divergent. All 13 children in the experimental group are self-supporting, and none is a ward of any institution, public or private. Eleven of the 13 children are married, and 9 of these have children.

Of the 12 children in the contrast group, 1 died in adolescence following continued residence in a State institution for the mentally retarded; 4 are still wards of institutions—1 of these is in a mental hospital, and 3 are in institutions for the mentally retarded. Among those no longer wards of institutions, only two have married, and one of these is divorced. Two of the four females in the contrast group were sterilized in late adolescence to preclude the possibility of procreation if later placed out to work.

In education, disparity between the two groups is great. In the experimental group, the median grade completed is the 12th; in the contrast group, the 3d. Four subjects in the experimental group have had one year or more of college work, one of the boys having received a B.A. degree. Occupationally, the experimental group ranges from professional and semiprofessional positions to semiskilled labor or domestic work. In the contrast group, 50 percent of the subjects are unemployed, and those that are employed are, with the exception of one person, unskilled laborers.

One girl in the experimental group who initially had an IQ of 35 has subsequently graduated from high school and taken one semester of work at a college.

She is married and has two boys. These boys have been given intelligence tests and have achieved IQ scores of 128 and 107.

If this girl had had the continuing experience characteristic of those in the contrast group, she would have remained all these years on a custodial ward in an institution for the mentally retarded, or have been sterilized in late adolescence or early adulthood and subsequently placed out on a nonskilled labor type of domestic employment.

In fact, "but for the grace of God," any one of the cases in the experimental group might have experienced the impact of deprivation of those in the contrast group, and vice versa.

Cost to the State

We are also studying the cost to the State of each subject in the experimental group and the contrast group of Study II—based on information as to per capita cost for institutional care per month or year for each of the years from 1932 to 1963. Preliminary indications are shocking.

In the experimental group the median total cost is less than $1,000, whereas in the contrast group it is 10 times that, with a range from $7,000 to $24,000. One case in the contrast group can be cited of a person who has been a ward of the State institution for over 30 years. The total cost to the State in this instance has been $24,113.

In the 1930's, the monthly per capita cost at State children's institutions and at mental hospitals ranged around $17 per month. This has progressively increased over the years until the present figure is considerably more than $200 per month. We can speculatively extrapolate on the cost to the State of the subjects in Study II had our comparisons started in 1963 instead of 1932. Assuming that costs were constant from 1963 to 1993, the case in the example cited would have cost the State $100,000.

Mentally Retarded Parents

As already mentioned, Study III involved children whose biological mothers were considered to be mentally retarded. The children had been separated from their natural mothers in early infancy, either by voluntary release or by court commitment, and has been placed in adoptive homes before they were 2 years old. The study included a total of 87 cases. IQ scores were obtained on each of the mothers, none of whom achieved higher than 75. The range extended down to an IQ of 32.

After a time interval of 21 years, efforts are under way to locate the adoptive parents and children of this study, and indications are that all or most of them will be found. Several interviews have already been completed.

In the followup, in addition to securing information on the adult status of the children, intelligence tests are being administered to the second generation—the grandchildren of the mentally retarded, biological grandmothers.

Preliminary findings in this followup study suggest that the first generation (the children of the original study) compares favorable in occupational status as adults with the Iowa population of comparable ages according to 1960 census figures. The second-generation children are scoring average and above on intelligence tests.

Some Implications

Since the preliminary findings of these three followup studies are substantiated by reports of many supporting studies published in the past 20 years, it would seem that we have adequate knowledge for designing programs of intervention to counteract the devastating effects of poverty, sociocultural deprivation, maternal deprivation, or a combination of these ills. This means making expenditures for prevention, rather than waiting for the tremendous costs of a curative nature. It does not, of course, preclude further research and exploratory studies to determine the optimum modes of intervention and the most appropriate ages for initiating such procedures.

References

[1]Skodak, Marie; Skeels, Harold M.: A final follow-up study of one hundred adopted children. *Journal of Genetic Psychology,* September 1949.

[2]Skeels, Harold M.: Dye, Harold B.: A study of the effects of differential stimulation on mentally retarded children. (Proceedings and addresses of the American Association on Mental Deficiency.) *Journal of Psycho-asthenics,* vol. 44, no. I, 1938-39.

[3]Skeels, Harold M.; Harms, Irene: Children with inferior social histories; their mental development in adoptive homes. *Journal of Genetic Psychology,* June 1948.

NINETY-TWO

Review of Group Methods with Parents of the Mentally Retarded

GLENN V. RAMSEY

Group methods used for meeting some of the needs of patients and clients in the mental health field is expanding rapidly (Rosenbaum & Berger, 1963). This development, combined with the current emphasis of extending counseling and therapeutic services to the "total family," logically leads to more extensive use of group methods with family members of a disturbed or handicapped individual. This paper presents a review of selected articles which report on the use of group methods to meet some of the needs and problems of parents who have a mentally retarded child.

Probably the first major studies to report on the use of such group approaches were made by Weingold and Hormuth (1953) and Coleman (1953). Fifteen publications in all were located which deal primarily with the use of various group methods to help parents meet their various anxieties, frustrations, and problems which arise because of a retardate in the family. In addition to the two studies previously mentioned, the other studies found include: Anderson (1962); Appell, Williams and Fishell (1964); Bitter (1964); Blatt (1957); Cummings and Stock (1962); Goodman and Rothman (1961); Nadal (1961); Popp, Ingram and Jordan (1954); Rankin (1957); Roche (1964); Rosen (1955); White (1959); and Yates and Lederer (1961).

Published studies in this area permit some consideration of such issues as the structure and composition of groups; selection criteria for membership; type of leaders employed; size and composition of groups; frequency and duration of sessions; parental issues and problems considered; and reports of outcomes. In the final section of this paper, the writer discusses several issues which seem relevant to any future planning for use of group methods in meeting some of the needs of parents of the retardate if any systematic advancement of knowledge in this field of endeavor is to be achieved.

Many parents of a retardate openly express a strong need for counseling assistance and guidance to assist them in dealing with their child as well as with the fam-

Reprinted from the *American Journal of Mental Deficiency*, Vol. 71, No. 5 (March, 1967), pp. 857-863. By permission of the author and the *Journal*. Copyright 1967, American Association on Mental Deficiency.

ily's adjustment, both within and outside the home. Professionals in clinics, special schools, institutions, and private offices usually make some effort to meet the more pressing needs of such parents on an individual family basis, but most of these workers admit that, because of the time factor and needs of the handicapped child, their services to parents are often limited and usually far from adequate.

Analysis of Studies

The studies surveyed on the use of groups for meeting various emotional needs and problems of parents of retardates were analyzed for such factors as: composition and organization of the groups; the number of members; length of a given session; total number of sessions; criteria for selecting group members; type of the group leader; nature of the group's structure; and reported outcomes. In the following section each of these factors will be considered.

Recruitment and Composition

Members for groups were recruited in several ways. Parents were often referred by a physician or clinic staff who was treating the retardate. In one project, parents were required to attend as one of the conditions set for admission of their handicapped child to the treatment program. Another group was easily organized by writing letters of invitation asking parents to join. Still other parents requested they be permitted to join a group when it was opened to new members. None of the writers reported any difficulty in recruiting a sufficient number of members except Cummings and Stock (1962). A large majority of the groups were developed for mothers while the remainder were organized for both parents.

Number of Group Members

The number of members in the groups ranged from three to thirty-six with the median number being ten. Groups having over ten members were to a large extent quite formal and organized. They were primarily designed as educational-informational meetings in which the parent role was primarily that of a listener. On the other hand, those groups composed of ten or less were largely informal and unstructured. These smaller groups were considered primarily as counseling and therapeutic sessions in which parent participation and discussion were encouraged.

Length of Session

Practically all studies stated that group sessions were scheduled for one and a half hours in duration. There was often some variation, as the time limit was not rigid. The sessions designed primarily for mothers were usually held in the daytime, while those for both parents met in the evenings.

Total Number of Sessions

The total number of sessions held for any one group ranged from three to sixty, with a median number of ten. Those groups involving the higher number of sessions were usually more therapeutic in nature. Those of ten or less were usually of the educational-informational type. One exception was the three session study of Yates and Lederer (1961) which was designed as a therapeutic project. The most frequently used schedule of meetings was weekly, but one series was held semi-monthly and another monthly. Only about half of the studies reported on the time interval between sessions.

Criteria for Selection of Group Members

The studies surveyed were far from precise in describing the selection criteria for admission of parents into a group. The failure to delineate the selective process is clearly evident in the following excerpts from the studies. Generally, the groups were described as composed of mothers or parents of a: "mentally retarded child," "a trainable retarded child," "a child on a clinic waiting list," "a child involved in clinic diagnosis," "a retarded child not acceptable to the public school," "a child diagnosed as mongoloid," "a child in a private school," or a "child under age 18 (12 or 10)." Another factor sometimes figuring in the admission criteria was the clinical judgment of a professional or of clinic staff members as to the suitability of the parent for group memberships. Seldom were the criteria for clinical judgments stated. One stated he excluded parents who were psychotic, psychopathic, or severely neurotic. A few established some specific qualifications for admission such as acceptance by parents of the medical diagnosis of their child's mental retardation. In another, divorced parents were not accepted. In general, studies, while listing some of the factors which excluded parents from groups, seldom listed any positive selection criteria on which admission was based.

Type of Group Leadership

Most groups had one person as leader. A few were joint enterprizes involving two professionals. The professional title of the various group leaders was reported as follows: Psychologists, listed five times; social workers, five; physicians, three; psychiatric nurses, twice; and a special education teacher, once. In groups designed to be more therapeutic in nature, the leaders were usually psychologists and psychiatrists. Other professionals were more frequently cited as leaders in the educationally oriented groups. In several of the educational-informational types of group programs, the leader often called upon various other specialists to lecture on topics related to mental retardation. Most of the studies gave little or no information regarding the special qualifications, if any, of the leader's training, experience and skill in directing such groups.

Structure of the Group

The organization of the various groups which parents attended ranged at one end from highly organized and formal meetings to very informal and unstructured groups at the other. About half the studies, however, attempted to combine both formal presentation and informal discussion in their structure. These three types were generally related to the goals set for each group.

The purpose of the more formal and organized type of program was to give parents facts about the retardate's care and training, sources of help, causes of mental deficiency, clinic procedures, and so on. The primary role of the parents in such groups was to listen and be informed. Programs of this type are reported by Bitter (1964) and Rosen (1955).

The informal and unstructured type of group, which was essentially designed to offer counseling and psychotherapy, was at the other end of group organization. The focus here was primarily upon the attitudes, feelings, and emotional problems of the parents. The goal of these groups was seen as release of tension, insight into difficulties, more constructive planning, and so on. A description of this type of group organization is given by Cummings and Stock (1962) who state, ". . . the group sessions would consist of open, unstructured discussions intended to provide opportunities for exploration and increased understanding of each member's feelings about herself and her child, her relatives and neighbors. . . ." Studies surveyed which involved the informal and open type of group structure are those reported by Appell, Williams, and Fishell (1964), Blatt (1957), Cummings and Stock (1962), Rankin (1957), and Yates and Lederer (1961).

The third type of group organization was a combination of the structured and formal with the unstructured and informal. In these groups, the goals were both the presentation of facts by experts and some controlled participation by parents. The latter aspect was attained by providing the parents with a question and answer period following a lecture or film, or allowing them some limited expression of attitudes and feelings through directed group discussions. White (1959), whose study follows these lines, states the structure of his group in these words: "Our groups are a compromise between the predominantly affective experience of group therapy and the intellectual experience of educational lectures." Such an approach is characteristic of the studies of Anderson (1962); Coleman (1953); Goodman and Rothman (1961); Nadal (1961); Popp, Ingram and Jordan (1954); and White (1959). The topics covered in informational sessions have been fairly adequately reported by Popp, Ingram and Jordan (1954) and Coleman (1953).

Reported Outcomes of Group Sessions

Evaluation of outcomes of the fifteen studies is based on subjective claims in twelve of them, while the other three offered some objective data to support their findings. All studies, however, report that the group sessions did meet some of the salient needs of the parents rather successfully. Most reports gave an enthusiastic endorsement of the use of group methods and were considered as effective approaches in meeting many of the needs of parents of retardates. All writers encouraged a more extensive use of group methods in designing programs in the future.

In reviewing the outcomes of group sessions, attention is directed first to those based primarily upon subjective evaluation. Among the unstructured groups involving counseling and psychotherapy, the subjective report given by Blatt (1957) is representative. He states: "Through catharsis, emotionally facing each other, identification of feelings of other group members, support from group members and from the therapist, they are able to derive maximum benefits." Another typical subjective report, based on the outcomes of a semi-structured project, is given by

Weingold and Hormuth (1953), who state: "Our work with parents of the mentally retarded has definitely established the value of the group guidance for parents of the mentally retarded children as one of the most effective tools to bring about more adequate adjustment of the family to such a child, as well as reintegrating the family into the community."

Studies by Appell, Williams and Fishell (1964); Bitter (1964); and Cummings and Stock (1962) introduced various test instruments into their groups in order to provide a more objective basis for assessment purposes. Among the more informal and unstructured types of programs is the one reported by Cummings and Stock (1962). They claim their objective data support such outcomes as providing ventilation, sharing practical advice, giving reassurance to one another, and achieving a more appropriate recognition of reality. Another program involving objective measurements and designed along the general lines of an unstructured group is the study made by Appell, Williams, and Fishell (1964). They report their data support such desired group outcomes as providing catharsis for parents; helping them accept the diagnosis of mental retardation; assisting them to shift from short-term goals to long-term goals; helping them realize others were sympathetic; and providing them with a greater optimism regarding the child's future. Among the more semi-structured group projects, the report of Nadal (1964) is based upon some objective data as well as clinical opinion. She states: ". . . on the basis of clinical and raters' judgment, it can be said that genuine improvement was made in such areas as attitudes toward the child, child-rearing practices, ability to handle the child, and general level of the mother's communication of her concern and problems." Among the fairly structured groups in which objective data was used to assess outcomes was the one conducted by Bitter (1964). He states: "The objective evidence, although not conclusive, would seem to indicate that a series of parent discussion sessions is effective in changing attitudes of parents of trainable mentally retarded children toward their retarded child and toward family problems occasioned by the retardation."

Discussion

The opinions and evidence presented by the fifteen studies covered in this review, in which group methods were used to meet emotional and other needs of parents of retardates, testify to the general value of such procedures and also support more extensive use of them in the future. No attempt is made here to question the successful outcomes reported in the published studies, as the nature of the reports and data do not lend themselves to such an evaluation. This statement is made because practically all studies were so poorly designed as research projects or so inadequately reported that any precise repetition of them, which would warrant comparison or results, appears improbable. However, the reports did provide a basis for other analyses and revealed certain issues and factors which demand more critical attention in planning future studies if any systematic understanding of the effectiveness of such groups is to be attained. Some of the deficiencies revealed in the design of these studies are discussed in the following paragraphs.

A most elementary requirement indicated for future studies is a more comprehensive taxonomic description of the population variables which might be related to outcomes. For example, the parent populations involved in such studies can be more clearly defined by citing data concerning age, sex, years married, number of children, ordinal position of retardate, socio-economic status, parental educational level, and so on. Also descriptive data regarding the retardate in each family needs to be more adequately reported such as age, sex, general degree of mental deficiency, resident at home or in an institution, additional handicaps, and other variables. Such simple taxonomic data premits at least some study of the relationship of such variables and outcomes as well as certain comparisons between different groups and outcomes. None of the studies presented any bearing upon the relationship of such taxonomic variables and reported results.

Another major variable which demands more detailed attention and more precise description is the nature of each group's structure, functioning, and goals. First, such simple descriptive data is needed as to the length of sessions, frequency of sessions, and total number of sessions. Second, a more adequate statement needs to be given concerning the nature of the group process to which the parents are exposed. In most of the studies reviewed, the group activity employed was simply described as group guidance, counseling, or psychotherapy. Does this mean directive, nondirective, psychoanalytic, or other theoretically based therapy or group process? Many questions concerning theory and practice can also be raised. Is one group method superior to another? Is there an optimal number of sessions for any one method? Is there an optimal size for groups? Is the time interval between meetings important? What is the difference in outcomes between structured and unstructured group projects?

The studies also did little to describe the nature of the group leader other than to give his professional title. Many questions about group leaders can be raised. Should the leader be a professional mental health specialist? Does he need special training in group therapy or group process? Can semi-professionals be trained to become group leaders? Does the group leader need to have direct information about the retardate in the family? Do different group goals require a different set of leader qualifications? The qualifications of the group leader and the types of group leadership skills he exerts are undoubtedly variables related to outcomes and, therefore, invite systematic study.

Another salient issue largely neglected except by Anderson (1962) concerns the immediate family situation and the time of group intervention. Are there times when a given group method is more effective with parents than at other times? Do groups function more effectively during crisis situations, such as when the parents go on the "waiting list," or when their child is given a medical diagnosis of mental retardation, or when the child is placed in an institution, or when the retardate becomes adolescent? Should certain types of groups for parents be scheduled at times of crisis? Should another type be offered parents who face long standing problems?

The greatest research need in this field is to introduce more objective measures so that more quantitative types of data can be secured. Such instruments could be used in selecting parent groups, measuring changes during group procedures, and assessing final outcomes. A beginning has been made in the use of objective instruments for such evaluation as seen in studies made by Appell, Williams, and Fishell (1964); Bitter (1963); Cummings and Stock (1962); and Rankin (1957). Even these investigations, with the possible exception of the Bitter study, cannot be satisfactorily repeated by others because of inadequate research design or description in certain parts of each study. Therefore, most of the findings reported cannot be checked by independent investigators.

None of the studies used objective measures to aid in the selection and description of the populations admitted to group projects. Three studies administered certain tests, questionnaires, and rating scales to participants after they were engaged in group activities but only incidentally were the data obtained related directly to outcomes. The Bitter study (1963) was the only one which administered objective instruments before and after the group intervention and is possibly the only one that could be repeated again and results compared.

Cummings and Stock (1962) reported making tape recordings of group sessions. While these writers do not make any report of analysis of their tapes, the procedure certainly seems to offer a valuable source of data regarding the content and issues which evolve in group sessions, the nature of group and family dynamics, types of interventions by leader, and other variables which appear related to outcomes. More extensive use of tapes seems promising.

Another research design factor which needs to be incorporated in such studies is the use of control groups. None of the studies reviewed reported the use of such groups. It is essential to obtain subjective and objective types of data based on control groups if any substantial support is claimed for the efficacy of group projects. The best design for measuring outcomes would involve before and after measurements of selected variables for both the experimental and the control group. Research designs involving only measurements after a study is completed are difficult to evaluate. Another possible use of two or more groups is to compare them by measurement of self-reports for some major variation to which each is exposed, such as introducing different types of group leadership. Such studies can provide valuable comparative inferences and offer promising leads for further studies.

There are many basic issues which only control groups can begin to answer. Do different types of group structure produce different results? Is one type of leadership proven more effective than another? Is it really the group intervention that brings about claimed results or is it simply the passage of time which solves many of the parents' problems, whether they are "in" or "out" of such groups? Do the professional qualifications of the leader elicit certain types of agenda and processes?

Finally, the need for long-term follow-up studies of results is beyond question. None of the studies reported any such attempts. Which changes noted at the end of group intervention tend to hold and which fade away? Are some changes not apparent until after six months or a year? Do parents who made gains through group interactions continue to increase in self-sufficiency and self-direction? Only long-term studies can answer a whole range of basic inquiries into the lasting effectiveness of such groups.

This review and discussion attempts to point out some possible improvements in designs of group projects which could aid in furthering our knowledge of the effective use of groups in meeting emotional needs and other problems of parents of retardates. It is hoped that this report will encourage a more extensive use of empirically planned group procedures as well as more tightly designed investigations.

References

ANDERSON, A.V. Orientating parents to a clinic for the retarded. *Children.* 1962, 9, 178-182.

APPELL, M. L., WILLIAMS, C. M., and FISHELL, K. N. Changes in attitudes of parents of retarded children effected through group counseling. *Amer. J. Ment. Defic.,* 1964, 68, 807-812.

BITTER, J. A. Attitude changes by parents of trainable mentally retarded children as a result of group discussion. *Except. Child.,* 1964, 30, 173-176.

BLATT, A. Group therapy with parents of severely retarded children: a preliminary report. *Group Psychotherapy,* 1957, 10, 133-140.

COLEMAN, J. C. Group therapy with parents of mentally deficient children. *Amer. J. Ment. Defic.,* 1953, 57, 700-726.

CUMMINGS, S. T., and STOCK, D. Brief group therapy of mothers of retarded children outside of the specialty clinic setting. *Amer. J. Ment. Defic.,* 1962, 66, 739-748.

GOODMAN, L., and ROTHMAN, R. The development of a group counseling program in a clinic for retarded children, *Amer. J. Ment. Defic.,* 1961, 65, 789-795.

NADAL, R. A counseling program for parents of severely retarded preschool children. *Social Casework,* 1961, 42, 78-83.

POPP, CLEO B., INGRAM, V., and JORDAN, P. H. Helping parents understand their mentally handicapped child. *Amer. J. Ment. Defic.,* 1954, 58, 530-534.

RANKIN, J. E. A group therapy experiment with mothers of mentally deficient children. *Amer. J. Ment. Defic.,* 1957, 62, 49-55.

ROCHE, T. A study of the impact on child-family relationships of group counseling of mothers of mentally retarded. In: *Maintaining the integrity of the individual, the family, and the community: a nursing responsibility.* New York: Amer. Nurses Assoc., 1964.

ROSENBAUM, M., and BERGER, B. *Group psychotherapy and group function.* New York, Basic Books, 1963.

ROSEN, L. Selected aspects in the development of the mother's understanding of her mentally retarded child. *Amer. J. Ment. Defic.,* 1955, 59, 522-528.

WEINGOLD, J.T. and HORMUTH, R.P. Group guidance of parents of mentally retarded children. *J. Clin. Psychol.,* 1953, 9, 118-124.

WHITE, B. L. Clinical team treatment of mentally retarded child and his parents: group counseling and play observation. *Amer. J. Ment. Defic.,* 1959, 63, 713-723.

YATES, M.L. and LEDERER, R. Small, short-term group meetings with parents of children with mongolism. *Amer. J. Ment. Defic.,* 1961, 65, 467-472.

PART TWELVE

The New Threshold

Prevention as a Goal for Social Work: Is Social Work Ready to Meet the Challenges of Mental Retardation?

GUNNAR DYBWAD

The most striking development in the field of mental retardation during the past ten years has been the growing recognition of the complexity of this problem. Once shunned as a dead field for scientific inquiry, save for the pathologist, and as a hopeless field for intervention because of its generally assumed irreversibility, mental retardation today is a subject of a rapidly growing professional literature and of a veritable avalanche of research studies and, in both cases, participation comes from a wide cross section of disciplines.

It is, indeed, intriguing that at the very time that mental retardation is so heavily courted by the professional community (not to mention the impact it has made at the same time on all levels of public life) there are those who deny with increasing vehemence that there is such a thing as mental retardation. The argument is that what is commonly referred to as mental retardation actually comprises such a wide array of divergent factors and circumstances relating to such separate areas of biological or cultural origins that a single term, no matter how carefully qualified, cannot possibly encompass them all. There are those who will settle for terming mental retardation a condition of widely varying etiology and widely differing manifestations. But others, such as Michael Begab (1966), the luncheon speaker today, maintain that the only rational terminological conceptualization is one that refers to mental retardation as a complex of symptoms deriving from a variety of causes.

In the mid 1950's an Expert Committee called by the World Health Organization (1954) arrived at the conclusion that for practical purposes a clear-cut distinction was possible between retardation related to biological factors and that related to sociocultural factors, and even recommended that the first be referred to as mental deficiency, the second as mental retardation, with mental subnormality serving as the generic term embracing both. Subsequently, others introduced as a desirable dichotomy that between organic and functional mental retardation. Today we know that these proposals are definitely lacking in practicability because our widening knowledge has brought to us an increasing understanding of the frequency of

Presented at a conference sponsored by the Graduate School of Social Work, University of Pittsburgh, 1968. By permission of the author and the School.

cases where biological and sociocultural, organic and functional factors are intertwined beyond recognition. Biological factors identified as causative in a given case of mental retardation may themselves be the result of socioeconomic deprivation.

In general, of course, our search for etiological factors is predicated on the insight that it points a way to appropriate intervention. Yet, here too, mental retardation proves its complexity: While mongolism (Down's Syndrome) has a clear-cut biological causation, yet the required intervention is primarily in the social and educational area. On the other hand, President Kennedy's Panel on Mental Retardation (1962) stressed that a promising approach to early amelioration in cases of mental retardation due to socioeconomic deprivation was in the area of maternal and child health.

Thus, one way of underlining the complexity of mental retardation is by pointing out that it does not belong to, nor is it encompassed by any one discipline or professional group. Its manifestations and the necessary preventive and remedial actions involve education, medicine, psychology, sociology and social work, rehabilitation, law, nursing, and a host of other disciplines in such a way that it is impossible to put them down in a definite order of priority—the function of any one of these disciplines and professional groups changes with the type and degree of mental retardation, the age group involved and, indeed, the individual characteristics of the mentally retarded person in a particular life situation. Thus, in contrast to rigidly held earlier views, which had such a pernicious limiting effect on the field, we now know that mental retardation is a dynamic, not a static entity, regardless of its origin, and, therefore, is developmental not only in terms of the life stage of its origin, but remains developmental as it reflects the growth steps of a human being (Dybwad, 1964).

From the foregoing, it follows that there are many ways of viewing the problem of mental retardation but foremost and forever it is a social problem, significantly affecting not only the person characterized, but his family, the neighborhood, the community. As Stanley P. Davies (1968) expressed it: "We know today that prevention in mental retardation is intimately related to the removal at their source of the acute problems of our entire society. It involves essentially united action on the part of all of us to make amends for the shortcomings of our whole social order with respect to race and poverty, material and cultural deprivation and glaring inadequacies in health, education and justice." Clearly, mental retardation presents a major challenge to social work.

At this point it is necessary to make some explanatory comments regarding my use of the term "mental retardation" since there is much uncertainty as to the dimensions of this concept. Indeed, it is very interesting that at this stage of development one still faces in this country, and in other countries as well, widely varying opinions when the simple question is raised "Who are the mentally retarded?" I proceed from the following modification of the definition proposed by the American Association on Mental Deficiency: "Mental Retardation refers to *significant* subaverage general intellectual functioning which originates during the developmental period and is associated with *substantial* impairment to adaptive behavior." I have emphasized two qualifying adjectives—significant and substantial—because, by using them, I am delineating mental retardation more narrowly than some people in this country have suggested. Specifically, I am very much in disagreement with the American Association on Mental Deficiency which has proposed to include a very broad gray borderline area which formerly was known as borderline intelligence and which the AAMD now has chosen to call borderline mental retardation. To you as social workers, it will be immediately apparent that this shift from the term borderline intelligence to the term borderline mental retardation has a very far-reaching social impact as well as an undesirable and often devastating effect on the individuals involved.

The significance of the AAMD definition, first introduced in 1959, rests in its departure from the previously prevailing view which delimited mental retardation essentially in psychometric terms, that is by the scores on some standard intelligence tests. Based on earlier work done by William Sloan and Jack Birch, now the Associate Dean of Education at this University, the AAMD classification added another dimension—that of adaptive behavior. In other words, it proposed that a diagnosis of mental retardation can no longer be justified merely by a demonstrably low intellectual performance but must also be related to a distinct impairment of adaptive behavior, that is to say of the social performance in day-to-day living normally expected from a person of a particular age by the community (or culture) of which he is a part.

In the wake of increasing general awareness of the debilitating effects engendered by socioeconomic and cultural deprivation, objections have recently been raised to this criterion of adaptive behavior on the grounds that this meant that the presence or absence of mental retardation would be judged by culturally biased middle class professional workers on the basis of conventional middle class standards. Those who express this objection have overlooked that adaptive behavior can and must be stressed not in terms of any set conventional standards but rather in terms of the individual under assessment, taking into consideration, as was already stated earlier, the mode of the day-to-day living normally expected from a person of a particular age by the community or culture of which he is a part and this certainly means his immediate community or subculture—whether it is that of an urban ghetto slum, an isolated rural poverty area, or the restrictive rigidity of an extremist religious sect.

From that viewpoint, it is not at all undesirable that assessment of adaptive behavior so far has to be done without the help of a standardized instrument. Such instruments are now being constructed—whether they will lend themselves for use with cultural and socioeconomic subgroups in our complex society remains to be seen.

It was necessary for me to make these introductory comments to my presentation today to clarify the frame of reference from which I am making this presentation. However, in view of my particular assignment this morning, I do not think that it is necessary for me to address myself in the same fashion to the question "How many mentally retarded are there?" Let me just briefly emphasize that it is no longer justifiable to use the long established and much quoted figure of 3% as the general prevalence of mental retardation in this country. Neither the more recent epidemiological studies nor the inquiries made in connection with the nationwide effort in comprehensive statewide mental retardation planning under the Kennedy-inspired federal legislation of 1963, furnish a basis for such a high estimate within the conceptual framework of mental retardation I have previously outlined. To be sure, in some specific population groups and in certain specific age groupings there has been found evidence of a much higher percentage but even so the 3% as an overall figure is untenable.

Unfortunately, we have not yet arrived at a substitute figure in terms of the overall national prevalence of mental retardation but we do have not only national but rather substantial international agreement on two more specific figures. We know that in this country and in several other countries with well developed mental retardation programs, between one and two per thousand of population are so severely handicapped by mental retardation that under the present conditions and our present state of knowledge (and this qualification needs to be underlined) they need some type of residential service. This term includes far more than the tradtional institution—as a matter of fact, there are many who hope that it soon will no longer include the traditional institution. It extends, among other things, to group homes, boarding homes, hostels, nursing homes, specialized medical facilities, etc., etc. In other words, any and all residential services away from home.

Secondly, there is a rather remarkable international agreement (from such different countries as Poland, U.S.A., Denmark or England, for instance) that between 3.5 and 5 persons per thousand population are moderately, severely, or profoundly retarded constituting a group which both in terms of intellectual performance (usually below fifty I.Q. on a standard intelligence test) and in adaptive behavior is seriously limited. Educationally, it is from this group that the public schools draw the pupils for classes on the so-called "trainable" level, and saying this affords me a good opportunity to exhort you not to use the terms "educable" and "trainable" unless you are referring to educational assignments and performance. By no means, are all children classified moderately retarded in classes on the trainable level—some manage to get along in the higher, educable level, while others for various and sundry reasons may not be considered as suitable for schooling at the particular stage of their development that may be under discussion. To use the terms "educable" and "trainable" in the area of vocational training and sheltered workshops or with regard to adults in general, is completely indefensible and badly confusing.

When, in 1961, President Kennedy appointed a special panel to submit to him a proposed program for national action to combat mental retardation, he specifically instructed the Chairman, Dr. Leonard Mayo, to investigate what the United States had to learn from other countries in the handling of this problem. In the course of its studies, it became obvious to the panel that, while many countries were ahead of us in this field, it was from the Scandinavian countries that we had the most to learn. However, even though some professional leaders had been in the Scandinavian countries for a study of their mental retardation programs long before the Kennedy campaign, and a large number of professional individuals and groups traveled there after the report of the Task Force of the President's Panel was published, it has only been in the most recent past that we have gained a clear notion in what way the great accomplishments of the Scandinavian countries can be conceptualized in terms that not only have meaning for us but lend themselves to planful change through governmental action.

I am fully aware that what I have to say in this regard may sound to this distinguished learned audience offensively elementary and oversimplified. May I then be permitted to remind you that in mental retardation you face an area of activity that in our Nation's steady progress has been left far behind in a state of unbelievable primitivity. Only a few weeks ago, the President's Committee on Mental Retardation (1968) submitted to the White House a report in which it stated: "Many of the nearly 200,000 residents in state institutions for the mentally retarded live in disgraceful conditions that the states' own regulatory agencies would not tolerate in privately operated facilities for anyone."

"Moreover, the facilities in which these retarded persons live are in many cases in a state of decay."

Those of you who have had the courage to visit the state institutions, which you as taxpayers maintain for the care of the mentally retarded in Pennsylvania and who made sure to see the entire institution and not just carefully selected parts of it, know that, if anything, the language of this presidential commission is an understatement of the intolerable conditions you continue to condone in your State.

It is against this background of inhuman and degrading conditions in existence in our institutions, of our denial of basic human rights to the mentally retarded and of our continued refusal to allow them access to basic community services that you must judge the significance of the cornerstone of Scandinavian services for the mentally retarded: the principle of normalization. It represents a conscious effort in all that is being done and planned for and with the mentally retarded and their families to come as close to normal living conditions as is feasible considering the degree of intellectual, physical and social disability of the retarded person or persons involved.

When American visitors see Danish or Swedish institutions, they invariably say that in this country one could not possibly obtain public funds for such extravagant buildings and equipment. The Danes and Swedes merely respond that all they have done is to create living quarters that are as close as possible to normal living institutions in their country. Thus they provide increasingly single rooms, particularly for adults, because that is what they would have in normal life, they have tables and chairs in the bedrooms so that people can retire to their own rooms even if they are moderately or severely retarded, windows mostly have normal window glass, eating is done in small groups and at normal meal hours. *Normalization* implies opportunities for men and women, boys and girls, to join in activities that are appropriate for the particular age group (something we call awkwardly and fearfully "mixing of the sexes") and normalization should be reflected in the rhythm of the day's activities whether at work or at leisure.

There are several associated concepts which put the broad principle of normalization into a more concrete frame of reference. The first one of these is *integration* —the conscious effort to stimulate a retarded person's participation in appropriate community affairs and an effort to prevent his being shut out on a prejudicial basis. Integration means that the retarded child living in a community must be accepted by a community hospital when he becomes acutely ill or is in need of surgery. The mentally retarded adult should be accepted at work as long as he can perform at a reasonable minimal level, should have the use of normal recreational facilities, etc., etc. Of course, it is understood that many mentally retarded must be restricted in certain ways or excluded from certain activities. However, one essential point in the normalization principle is that such a restriction, exclusion or limitation should not automatically lead to a host of other restrictive exlusions or limitations merely because of certain categorical preconceptions. One can well say that "categorization," which is such a cornerstone of our traditional approach to the mentally retarded whether within or without an institution, runs counter to the concept of integration. All too often, we categorize in order to segregate and this certainly is a case in mental retardation.

The second concept is that of *dispersal* of services and facilities for the mentally retarded. Nothing is more abnormal than the vast congregate instiutions which Pennsylvania, like other States, has erected, usually away from centers of population and often far away from the mentally retarded person's home. That the aggregation of so many people, residents and staff, in one place creates innumerable problems of the most serious nature is well documented. Therefore, what we should be aiming for in our country are small facilities, small enough to allow for good human interaction between residents and staff, small enough to find space for them even in metropolitan areas, small enough to be accepted by and integrated into the neighborhood.

The next concept is that of *specialization*. Indeed, dispersal is almost dependent on specialization of facilities. With our fixation on organization, structure and mechanization, we have been seduced into establishing community services for the mentally retarded akin to those for the mentally ill centered in a new type of congregate facility known as the comprehensive community mental health or mental retardation center and housing a mish-mash of divergent activities—a worthy counterpart to the old congregate institution.

To a sociological observer this development will not come as a surprise because he is well acquainted with the phenomenon of *system maintenance* and with another force known as the *momentum of the current service pattern*, both of which effectively stand in the way of planned change. What needs to be kept in mind here is that the development of comprehensive mental health or comprehensive mental retardation centers (or a combination of the two) is engineered by a subgroup of the same power structure that has so effectively resisted change in the institutional field and is so insistent on preserving what it considers its professional and hierarchical prerogatives.

There is nothing basically wrong, of course, with the model of dispersal presently being developed in several states in this country, namely decentralization by regionalization. What is wrong, however, is that under the impact of the momentum of current service patterns in many states, as I have just pointed out, the regional center was not seen as conceptualization of the planning, direction and coordination of services, but rather in terms of brick and mortar as a massive structure, housing an irrational conglomeration of divergent services.

I am emphasizing this point before this particular audience of social workers because social work has long been interested in the development of sound approaches to planning and social work planners would be expected to focus on the needs of client groups to be served.

Unfortunately, the powerful and tremendously beneficial impact of President Kennedy's program in the field of mental retardation has had here a very serious shortcoming: it continues to spawn what I consider planning disaster, namely the seduction of state planners by making available large amounts of matching funds for the construction of buildings, large, in any case, in relation to the very limited availability of funds for the development of the so long and so persistently neglected non-residential services, many of which bear a direct relation to the topic to which we are to address ourselves today, that of prevention.

The final concept supportive of the principle of normalization is that of *continuity*. As you know, this concept itself was clearly recognized by the President's Panel on Mental Retardation in its 1962 report when it made the demand for a continuum of services one of its main recommendations. However, once again thinking of the focus of today's institute on prevention, and the social worker's role in it, it needs to be underlined that unquestionably the most serious void in the continuum of services typically available in this country in general and in your State specifically lies in its beginning stage, the early years of life when, in any case secondary, but largely also primary preventive action offer promising results. Once again, social workers have a particular opportunity of making a contribution here because the problem encountered is that of service delivery, long of interest to the social work profession. Service delivery is, of course, easiest accomplished where it can utilize existing strong societal mechanisms such as the public schools, hospitals and other avenues of medical care, the organized ways of production and distribution of goods, the organized forms of recreation and entertainment, the organized activities of religious groups, public welfare, and the system of law enforcement and the judicial process, etc., etc. But the life of the infant and very young child is rarely touched by these systems, he exists largely within the confines of the home and it is the long standing principle of the inviolability of the home, the privacy of family life, that stands in the way of service delivery. It is only fair and necessary to add here that the professionalization of social work has rationalized increasingly during the past quarter of a century within its own context a reemphasis of this inviolability of "the family's castle"—many of our foreign colleagues are amused at the disdain we have developed for any home visiting or, as we would call it, intrusion into the home, and wonder why we are so dependent on the protective cover of the agency's office.

Let me now turn to the essence of this institute today, the Social Worker's Role in Prevention of Mental Retardation. This is a topic that must be approached with some caution—in spite of frequent optimistic predictions which have become an inevitable part of public pronouncements on mental retardation, we have not yet developed adequate strategies to deal effectively with the promising leads toward prevention scientists have supplied in recent years (Dybwad, 1968). Thus an Expert Committee of the World Health Organization (1968) recently stated: "It is generally recognized that prevention is the ultimate goal of all efforts to combat mental retardation. Identification of etiological factors in mental retardation is essential to a sound programme of prevention. Recent developments in knowledge about the numerous causative factors responsible for defective intelligence make possible some tentative inferences regarding prevention."

This cautious comment is in striking contrast to the often quoted comment emanating from the President's Panel on Mental Retardation to the effect that if only we would apply what we know, we could prevent 50% of mental retardation. In answer to that I am invariably quoting the classic comment of Kingsley Davis (1967) who said in a paper entitled "The Perilous Promise of Behavioral Science": "Given the great promise that social science holds out for solving our problems, one is puzzled by what appears to be a mocking reality. I have observed, for example, that solutions to social problems tend to have three characteristics: First, they are extremely simple, especially compared to technological solutions. Second, they are foolproof—that is, if they were applied, they would solve the problem. Third, they are not being applied." This comment, by no means, should imply a pessimistic outlook. To the contrary, I sincerely believe that if we take the words of Kingsley Davis to heart, we will see a way clear for social workers to make a particular contribution in the field of mental retardation prevention. Granted that we are still in the dark about the etiology of much of the biological aspects of mental retardation, we do have a substantial body of knowledge but the problem lies in its application. We have identified numerous conditions transmitted genetically. The problem lies in finding the cases, and effecting genetic counseling. Social work has a special contribution to make through its knowledge of case finding and counseling. Measles and other infectious diseases suffered during pregnancy can do serious damage to the child, as can improper drugs and medications. Lack of adequate prenatal care can contribute to complications resulting in mental retardation and lack of prenatal care is particularly frequent in population groups which are (or should be) of concern to social workers. Inadequate nutrition (i.e., not just lack of food) is increasingly identified as a contributing factor—there was a time when social workers were quite conscious of the importance of nutrition and their responsibility in this area. Risk factors occur in the circumstances surrounding delivery of the child and during the child's early developmental period. We know a lot about prevention scientifically but we are short in practical application. The key lies in a subject area that has been of increasing interest to social work, in particular social planners—service delivery. How to bring service to people, how to create receptivity for the service, how to offer it in a form, at a place and at a time appropriate to the different population groups to be addressed —here lies one of the most tangible roadblocks to effective prevention and here is an opportunity for social work to contribute its skills and experience.

In discussing prevention of mental retardation and other disabilities, some physicians have recently reactivated proposals for elaborate registers of high risk cases. Social work has had experience with case registers and, in most instances, found reason to discontinue them. Social work can make a valuable contribution in pointing out the social components of risk registers and in identifying the social risks when such registers become administrative instruments and are used for inappropriate decision making.

It should become clear by now that in making its contribution to prevention of mental retardation, the field of social welfare will meet up with the field of public health. The pregnant fifteen-year-old high school dropout recently arrived from Puerto Rico, who, due to her age and other circumstances surrounding her pregnancy (including ignorance of many available services and fear of using those which are known to her), decidedly presents a risk, is a challenge to both social welfare and public health. That recognition is nothing new—but the ever expanding services and service conceptualization of public health raise some interesting questions about the interaction between these two fields, which have long utilized each other's professional staff but have been hesitant to take a fresh look at their mutual administrative and planning interaction.

Undoubtedly, a complicating factor here has been the uncertain status of mental health vis-à-vis public health. The psychiatric aura of mental health has always been seductive to social workers and they have—seen as a professional group—readily accepted the claim of mental health authorities that mental retardation was within the mental health game preserve, a claim the public health authorities of the past (that is, in the forties and fifties) were hardly eager to dispute.

But the present situation is different—comprehensive health planning is threatening to supersede comprehensive mental health planning—the comprehensive health center aims at encompassing the comprehensive mental health center and all this only reinforces the just referred to need for social work to take a fresh look at these interactional processes.

It might appear to you as if I were placing too much emphasis on these external organizational factors. Yet, they are surely a major reason for the failure to translate into effective action the knowledge we have on prevention, knowledge I am not presenting here today in great detail because it has already been presented innumerable times. However, there is reason for me to point up for you the availability of some recent materials which specifically address themselves to the interrelationship of poverty and mental retardation.

Rodger L. Hurley's (1968) monograph on Poverty and Mental Retardation: A

Causal Relationship, cogently shows how poverty can "actively imperil the physical well being of the individual and make it doubly unlikely that his mental development will be satisfactory" (p. 6). By sharply highlighting how faulty functioning of the systems of public health, public welfare, public schooling and urban planning (and, implicitly, the societal pressures which give these services their planned inadequacy) contribute to a deficient developmental process resulting in social and intellectual inadequacy of children in poverty areas, he clearly points up the avenues of preventive action. The Mental Health Planning Committee of Milwaukee County (1968), in a more limited but also more specific approach to this problem, has developed what it calls a comprehensive mental retardation prevention program for low income communities, pointing up specific targets to initiate definite action programs—the one is the health and cultural environment of the woman of child bearing age—the other, the young child as he develops organically and socially within the culture of poverty (p. 21). Charles Meisgeier (1966), in a significant monograph entitled The Doubly Disadvantaged —A Study of Socio-Cultural Determinants in Mental Retardation, specifically deals with the problem of mental retardation among the two ethnic minority groups in Texas, the Negroes and the Latin Americans, adding a special chapter on Migrancy and Mental Retardation. He states: "Texas has both the resources and the knowledge to abolish the conditions which are the breeding ground of certain kinds of mental retardation and other crushing afflictions" (p. iii). But how long will we have to add Kingsley Davis' devastatingly lucid observation: "they are not being applied." A challenge to social work? Only to the extent that social work can free itself from its self-imposed stricture as the obedient servant and implementer of the prevailing establishment.

May I inject here a conceptual-terminological note. Hurley and others claim that when it comes to the culturally and socioeconomically disadvantaged we should speak of pseudo-retardation. This is an old and often refuted term (Benton, 1956) which implicitly still harks back to the now discarded notion of the irreversibility of mental retardation. Retardation of the poor *is* retardation but to a considerable extent remediable (limited, of course, e.g. by the influence of concomitant causative factors of genetic origin). This, of course, does not deny the fact that some children are wrongly diagnosed as retarded. But then we must refer to them as non-retarded rather than pseudo-retarded.

It is obviously impossible to include in this introductory presentation all the aspects of mental retardation prevention to which this institute might address itself. In particular, I have had to exclude broad areas of secondary prevention to which social workers can make distinct contributions. Among these areas are the impact of the problem on the family (both in terms of deleterious factors aggravating the child's disability and of positive supportive and thereby remedial factors); the role of auxiliary services to the home to lessen the burden imposed by the impact of severe and profound mental retardation, a burden which debilitates the total family, including the afflicted child; new concepts of crisis intervention; emergency services, such as short-term residences, which prevent avoidable long-term institutionalization with its aggravating effects; parent education and counseling, including the newer group approaches and similar services directed at siblings of the retarded child; community and neighborhood education and, where need be, intervention in order to neutralize prejudicial pressures arising out of misconceptions and fear of the mentally retarded.

A particular problem area is that of the adult retarded and his problem to deal on his own terms with a world that little understands him, and, indeed, even now is inclined to see in him the eternal child (Dybwad, 1960). The adult retarded in particular suffers from his traditional status of a second class citizen, a stigma which he tries to cover up under a "cloak of competence," to use the title of Robert B. Edgerton's (1967) highly significant book on the problems of community living encountered by retarded adults released, after years of confinement, from the constraints and dehumanization of the state institution. An important aspect of secondary prevention can be mobilized through recognition of the basic human rights of the mentally retarded, adults as well as children—a subject matter, heretofore hardly discussed and, indeed, quite controversial. Yet, anyone involved in social planning in this area should be acquainted with the conclusions of a symposium on legislative aspects of mental retardation convened 1967 in Stockholm by the International League of Societies for the Mentally Handicapped (1967).

Almost ten years ago, Benjamin Pasamanick (1959) concluded already: "However, as far as the determination of etiology in the socioculturally retarded is concerned, I must confess that I consider this area pretty much a closed affair. Most of the variables have already been well and intensively investigated and definitely incriminated. It remains for the statesmen, social welfare workers and educators to institute the proper preventive measures which, if they so desire, can be programmed on an experimental basis so that the last bit of definitive evidence may be acquired." Organized social work, however, remained strangely unresponsive to this challenge, notwithstanding the superior contributions of individual members of the profession. Even though the Chairman of the President's Panel on Mental Retardation, Dr. Leonard Mayo, appointed by John F. Kennedy in 1961, was a former president of the Child Welfare League of America, it was only six years later that the League released to its members a first statement on child welfare's role in mental retardation. The Family Service Association of America for years rejected all efforts to enlist their interest in the problem—it was in 1966 that they finally prepared a member bulletin on Mental Retardation and the Family Service Agency. The same unresponsiveness was encountered from the National Association of Social Workers whose staff stoutly maintained, all through the nationwide mental retardation planning effort initiated by President Kennedy, that this problem was outside their sphere of activity. There is good reason to surmise that, in large part, this refusal to recognize the social aspects of mental retardation as a responsibility of the profession was due to social work's middle class orientation—reflecting all the age-old popular prejudices—and social workers' preference for settings (and clients) where greater emotional reward is available (DeHoyos, 1968). This factor came even stronger into play where mental retardation coincided with the problem of socioeconomic deprivation. It is to the credit of two of our colleagues, Michael Begab and Meyer Schreiber, that they undertook a persistent and not unsuccessful effort to enlist the interest of the Schools of Social Work in the field of Mental Retardation.

The challenge is here—stronger than ever—backed by more solid knowledge, by greater commitment of the public agency and by more tolerant, if not a more accepting attitude of the public. Will the profession answer the challenge?

References

BEGAB, MICHAEL, Some Central Concepts in Mental Retardation, in: Institute on Mental Retardation, June 22-26, 1966. St. Louis School of Social Service, St. Louis University, 1966.

BENTON, A. L., The concept of pseudo-feeblemindedness, *AMA Arch. Neurol. Psychiat.*, 75: 379-88, 1956.

DAVIES, STANLEY P., Social Work and Mental Retardation—Past, Present and Future, address at Social Work Section Annual Luncheon, American Association on Mental Deficiency, Boston, May 2, 1968 (mimeographed).

DAVIS, KINGSLEY, The Perilous Promise of Behavioral Science, in: Research in the Service of Man: Biomedical Knowledge, Development and Use, Washington, D.C., Superintendent of Documents, 1967.

DEHOYOS, ARTURO and GENEVIEVE, The Professional Mobility in Social Work and its Middle Class Orientation, *American Journal of Orthopsychiatry*, 38,1, pp. 18-24, 1968.

DYBWAD, GUNNAR, Developing Patterns for Aid to the Aging Retarded and Their Families, in: Outlook for the Mentally Retarded, Langhorne, Pennsylvania, The Woods Schools, pp. 24-33, 1960.

DYBWAD, GUNNAR, The Dynamics of Mental Retardation, U.S. Department of Health, Education and Welfare, Public Health Service Publication No. 1267, Washington, D.C., Superintendent of Documents, 1964.

DYBWAD, GUNNAR, The Importance of Prevention in Mental Retardation, paper presented at the 92nd Annual Meeting, American Association on Mental Deficiency, April, 1968.

EDGERTON, ROBERT B., The Cloak of Competence—Stigma in the Lives of the Mentally Retarded, Berkeley, University of California Press, 1967.

HURLEY, RODGER L., Poverty and Mental Retardation—A Causal Relationship, Trenton, New Jersey, Department of Institutions and Agencies, 1968.

International League of Societies for the Mentally Handicapped, Legislative Aspects of Mental Retardation, Brussels, International League of Societies for the Mentally Handicapped, 12 rue Forestiere, Bruxelles 5, Belgium, 1967.

MEISGEIER, CHARLES, The Doubly Disadvantaged—A Study of Socio-Cultural Determinants in Mental Retardation, Austin, Division of Extension, The University of Texas, 1966.

Milwaukee County Mental Health Planning Committee, Poverty and Retardation—A Comprehensive Program of Mental Retardation Prevention, Interim Report, Milwaukee, Wisconsin, 1968.

PASAMANICK, BENJAMIN, Research on the Influence of Sociocultural Variables upon Organic Factors in Mental Retardation, in: Approaches to Research in Mental Retardation, Langhorne, Pennsylvania, The Woods Schools, 1959.

President's Committee on Mental Retardation. M.R. 68—The Edge of Change, Washington, D.C., Superintendent of Documents, 1968.

President's Panel on Mental Retardation, A Proposed Program for National Action to Combat Mental Retardation, Washington, D.C., Superintendent of Documents, 1962.

World Health Organization, The Mentally Subnormal Child, Geneva, World Health Organization, 1954.

World Health Organization, Organization of Services for the Mentally Retarded, Geneva, World Health Organization, 1968.

NINETY-FOUR

Process and Tasks in Hoping

BEATRICE A. WRIGHT AND FRANKLIN C. SHONTZ

That hoping is fraught with great significance is dramatically expressed in our aphoristic language, where both highly negative and highly positive consequences are predicted. "When hope leaves man, despondency begins to subude him" *(Plato)* reveals truth, but so does "Who lives by hope will die of hunger."

However such wisdoms are to be reconciled, one is struck by the scientific neglect of so consequential a human phenomenon as hoping, although philosophers have always given much thought to hope and despair. Fifty years ago Shand[7] wrote an impressive volume in which he used literary evidence upon which to base laws concerning a wide range of emotions, including hope. More recently, French[3] dealt with hopes as significant for planning and therefore central to the integration of behavior. Tamara Dembo[1] has stressed the importance of hoping in coping with misfortune. Karl Menninger,[6] in an eloquent plea for recognizing the essential place of hoping in man's nature, decried the lack of scholarly attention given to this problem.

Common usage suggests that the distinction between *hopes* and *wishes* reflects the degree to which the person believes that a desired outcome could actually occur. Wishes are most likely to reflect a low level of probability (I wish I could be young again; I wish the Athletics would win the pennant). When a wish comes true, it is cause for surprise and sometimes incredulity. In adults, the inability to distinguish between wishes and reality is regarded as evidence of cognitive immaturity or disorganization. Hopes are, in effect, "wishes that might come true." When a hope is realized, there is relief from tension and a feeling of satisfaction, but rarely amazement. Only when one "hopes against hope" (when one wishes) is a favorable outcome surprising. Since the difference between hopes and wishes is subjective, there is no clear-cut line that separates the two. The gambler who is riding a wave of luck *hopes* to roll a seven on the first throw of the dice. The gambler who has been losing regularly may only *wish* that his luck would change. People in desperate straits may wish for things for which they "do not dare" to hope. In contrast to hopes and

From *Rehabilitation Literature*, Vol. 29, No. 11 (November, 1968), pp. 322-331, with permission of the authors and the National Easter Seal Society for Crippled Children and Adults.

wishes, expectations always have a high subjective probability of actualization and may refer to negative as well as positive eventualities.

The Research

It was felt that hopes concerning children with disabilities would be especially suitable for advancing understanding of the psychology of hoping, since these hopes would not glibly reflect ready-made hopes provided by the culture and might therefore be expected to reveal important aspects of hoping. The present report is based on tape-recorded interviews with parents, teachers, and therapists of children attending a school for crippled children, and with the children themselves. The 14 children varied in age (5 to 19 years), sex (10 boys, 4 girls), and medical diagnosis (cerebral palsy, spina bifida, and achondroplasia, among others).

The 25 parents (or guardians) of these children were interviewed in their homes when feasible, both parents being interviewed together. The therapist and teacher who knew the child best were interviewed individually. The four therapists involved in the study (two physical therapists, one occupational therapist, and one speech therapist) were employed by the school. The six teachers interviewed ranged from preschool through high-school grade levels.

The adult interviews, lasting from 1 to 2 hours, included one set of questions that directly pertained to hope concerning the child:

1. What are your hopes for ——— when he becomes an adult?
2. How far in school do you hope he can go?
3. As far as marriage is concerned, what are your hopes?
4. What are your hopes in regard to his physical health and condition?
5. Now, about an occupation, what are your hopes there?
6. Do you think any of these hopes are unrealistic?
7. How have your hopes changed since ——— was born (or "since you started working with him")?

Other questions raised in the interview were concerned with different topics, e.g., the child's progress in school. In the case of the child interviews, which lasted from 15 minutes to one hour, appropriate modifications to fit the child's role and level of comprehension were made in the wording of the questions. Because of the temporary relationship between interviewer and subject, the interviewer did not press for feelings and beliefs beyond those the subject was ready to give.

The basic methods of treating the interview data involved an analysis of the psychological forces that may be presumed to guide the thoughts and feelings expressed therein as well as rating scales that were designed to measure several important dimensions.

Child and Adult Hope Structures

The highly differentiated and complex interdependent processes involved in adult hoping contrasts with that in children. The simplest hope structure may be thought of as involving a single characteristic, that of positive valence. Because the time perspective of very young children is undifferentiated, their hopes can be expected to be expressed without reference to a future state. Thus:

HOPE STRUCTURE I: CHILD

1. Positive valence

2. Present orientation

A somewhat more complex structure emerges when the child's time perspective becomes differentiated into a future and a present, allowing his hopes to be future-oriented, thus:

HOPE STRUCTURE II: CHILD

1. Positive valence

2. Future orientation

The children in the present study were mature enough to express their hopes in terms of the type II (future-oriented) structure. The following examples sample replies given by subjects 5 to 8 years of age to the question "What are your hopes when you are grown up?" (For clarification, as needed, "What do you hope to be like when you are grown up?" was added):

"Next year!" [*Q repeated*] "I would like to be a policeman." *(age 5)*
"Then I'm going to high school then." (*age 7*)
"A bachelor." *(age 8)*
"I hope I'm gonna be a nurse." (*age 8*)

What is striking in these replies is that the child directly expresses a desire for some future state of affairs without considering reality questions in any way. Even when the hope was challenged by such follow-up questions as "Do you know what kinds of things you have to do to be a policeman" or "Are there any of these things that you hope for that you don't think you'll be able to do?" the lack of concern of the child with such issues was dramatic. In the few instances where he acknowledged that he might not achieve his hope, he simply let it go at that.

The impressive difference between children and adults in the degree to which reality considerations are brought into the hoping process is shown in the rating of the replies to the open-ended question regarding "hopes when adult" on a dimension of "reality surveillance." A four-point scale was used, rating 1 indicating no evidence of any reference to reality (see examples above) and rating 4 giving evidence of considerable surveying of reality. A rating of 4 was given when the subject considered at least three separate areas of reality with an elaboration of at least one of them, or at least four separate reality areas with no elaboration, or a single, crucial, all-encompassing reality factor. (See for example the reply of Donald's parents to the open-ended question.) The ratings of two judges yielded a reliability of r_s = .78. For examplification of a rating of 4, the reply of a teacher to the open-ended questions about her hopes for Sophie as an adult is divided according to the criterion units.

(Sophie: 8 years old, cerebral palsied):

    T: Well, I think she could hold a job. There is no doubt in my mind that she could do this [reality area 1, the use of "could" referring to the child's abilities, an important reality area]. I don't know if she could do any type of skilled hand work [elaboration]. But she could, if she continues to develop [reality area 2], and if her parents could support it [reality area 3], I think she could maybe—a year, maybe two, of college [reality area 4].

Of the 12 child interviews in which replies to the open-ended question were ratable, all were given a rating of 1. In contrast, this absence of reality consideration was found in only 7 percent (2 mothers and 1 teacher) of the 46 adult interviews (teachers and therapists were interviewed about more than one child):

	Degree of Reality Surveillance			
	NONE	SLIGHT	MODERATE	CONSIDERABLE
Child (N = 12)	100%			
Adult (N = 46)	7%	15%	35%	43%

The characteristic hope structure of adults, in contrast to that of children, is thus seen to include reality surveillance as an important third attribute. In accounting for this difference, use can be made of Lewin's[5] conceptualization of the child's life span as having little differentiation between levels of reality and unreality. In addition to this factor, presumably biologically determined, role expectations appear to be important in the cognitive differentiations of levels of future reality and unreality.

To the child, the future is not part of his responsible sphere of action, and as such he can express hopes without needing to be concerned about outcome probabilities. The future is far off and will be taken care of by omnipotent adults. Even the adolescents in the study tended to be indifferent to reality issues, perhaps because all their lives important decisions were not theirs to make. Of the 5 subjects 14 to 19 years of age who were ratable on the Reality Surveillance dimension, all were rated 1, i.e., no evidence of any survey of reality. However, on a second dimension, "doubt as to the realizability of hope," the two children who were rated as showing "slight doubt" were both adolescents, suggesting a beginning orientation to the reality issues. All other children were given a rating of 1, "no doubt." It can be posited that, when decision-making and personal responsibility for the future are delayed, for whatever reason (whether because the child has a disability, is mentally retarded, is overprotected) reality orientation may be expected to play a relatively unimportant role in the hoping process.

Developmentally, then, the hoping process appears to progress through several stages. The most primitive hopes may be expected to be equivalent to desires that are neither time- nor reality-dependent. With further maturation, the hopes of the young child become future-oriented. The reality issue, however, does not yet enter. The wish is so much "father to the thought" that hopes are assumed to be the future reality. When the hopes of an older child are challenged by an outsider, reality thoughts are only tenuously forced, for at best the child remains content simply to acknowledge that his hopes may not come true. However, when the young person begins to take charge of his future, then one can expect a more substantive surveying of reality and a launching of the adult hope structure. Several types of adult hope structures are distinguished below.

Reality Surveillance, Reality Grounding, and Uncertainty

Upon reality surveillance hinges many further complexities of the hoping process. The person surveys reality because he realizes that hopes must have a realistic base if they are to come true. Not only is the person threatened by the prospect of false hopes, but he also recognizes that the actualization of his hopes requires action on his part, action that must be coordinated with reality during the time intervening between the present and the future. The adult expression, "There is hope," implies a reality base, however weak. If the person is fortunate, his scanning of reality finds sufficient grounds to support his hopes and he can remain content, at least until intervening events disturb the equilibrium. This type of adult hope structure may be represented as follows:

HOPE STRUCTURE III: ADULT

1. Positive valence   *3.* Reality surveillance
2. Future orientation   *4.* Reality grounding

It is seen in the following remarks of Sandra's physical therapist.

(Sandra, 8 years old, cerebral palsied):
   PT: (Hopes when adult) I would hope that Sandra could take a pretty good place in society. She will have to do something, probably not too difficult a job and with some supervision, but I would think that she would make a good enough appearance that she could meet people and be socially acceptable.

A more typical adult hope structure, at least in regard to the hopes tapped in the present study, is characterized by a continuing sense of certainty in spite of whatever reality grounding is forthcoming. Evidence for this is revealed in the ratings of the open-ended question on two dimensions other than that of degree of reality surveillance. These were the amount of reality supports uncovered and the amount of doubt expressed as to the realizability of the hope. Each of these dimensions was rated on a four-point scale ranging from none to considerable. The ratings of two judges yielded a reliability of $r_s = .83$ for the support dimension and a reliability of $r_s = .76$ for the doubt dimension. Of the 35 adult interviews in which the respondent surveyed reality in regard to an *explicit* hope (cases in which no special hope or no survey of reality was noted being excluded), 91 percent revealed at least some support for the hopes expressed, but only 29 percent revealed no doubt about the realizability of the hope:

	NONE	SLIGHT	MODERATE	CONSIDERABLE
Support	9%	14%	46%	31%
Doubt	29%	43%	29%	____

Parenthetically, not one of these interviews received a rating of considerable doubt. In five interviews in which there were no explicit hopes, the respondent gave evidence of considerable doubt about possibilities for the future, as, for example, the case of Donald, in which the outlook for the child in general was dismal.

Adult hopes are typically supported by both the person's desires and reality considerations. The desires are expressed in the hopes themselves and exert a force to sustain the hopes in spite of less than complete reality grounding. Based on Dembo's[1] theoretical analysis of "realistic" versus "wishful" expectations, two types of reality surveillance in the face of uncertain realization may be distinguished. In the first, reality grounding is accomplished within the framework of "realistic expectations" determined by probabilities and natural law. In the second, grounding takes place in terms of possibilities that do not have to conform to the laws of nature, thereby allowing even fanciful or the slightest evidence to support a hope. The fourth type of hope structure is therefore differentiated into subtypes that differ essentially in the kind of reality grounding that takes place (the fourth characteristic in the following lists):

HOPE STRUCTURE IV A: ADULT

1. Positive valence
2. Future orientation
3. Reality surveillance
4. Partial reality grounding: realistic expectations
5. Uncertain realization

HOPE STRUCTURE IV B: ADULT

1. Positive valence
2. Future orientation
3. Reality surveillance
4. Partial reality grounding: wishful expectations
5. Uncertain realization

It is not supposed that these characteristics appear in an orderly sequence of psychological events. As a rule, hopes emerge as whole units of mental activity, as molar entities or gestalts, which may or may not be subjected to later differentiation and elaboration. The process giving rise to explicit hopes sometimes appears in slow motion when the survey of reality does not immediately lead to sufficient grounds (realistic or wishful) on which to base them. Such hesitancy appears in the remarks of Dale's mother.

(Dale: 8 years old, achondroplastic dwarf):

M: (Hopes when adult) To make money. No, I would like to see him get in a field—well, I *more or less* really expect him to. He would have to do something more or less sitting at a desk. *Maybe* later on he could take typing or something. Now for example, take—. He's a crippled man. [F intersperses some remarks] M: He *might* grow up to be like Mike, to be good in electronics.

The italicized phrases point up the doubts prodding Dale's mother to explore the reality base for her hopes. The process here seems to be one in which uncertainty and reality surveillance are interdependent, uncertainty being not only a product but also a prompter of reality surveillance.

If the time dimension is extended, one may discern additional hope structures stemming from the way in which the uncertainty is handled. First, the person may rest from the strain of reviewing a troubling reality, temporarily pushing it out of his mind. The rest seems to enable him once again to confront the reality issue, an issue kept astir by the unresolved tension of uncertain hopes. Thus it is that periods of escape from reality become interspersed with efforts at its appraisal, indicating the following hope structure:

HOPE STRUCTURE V: ADULT

1. Positive valence
2. Future orientation
3. Intermittent reality surveillance
4. Partial reality grounding
5. Uncertain realization

Intermittent scanning of reality prepares the person for the task of substituting a new hope for one that eventually will be abandoned. It is apparently easier to give up a hope if a hope that can be supported by reality is there to take its place. The process of surveying and resurveying reality for support of one hope may serendipitously provide support for other possibilities. Surveying reality, therefore, serves the important function, not only of finding support for present hopes, but of laying the groundwork for substitute hopes, thus:

Reality Surveillance $\begin{cases} \longrightarrow \text{Reality grounding of present hopes} \\ \longrightarrow \text{Reality grounding of substitute hopes} \end{cases}$

A second approach to the problem of insufficiently grounded hopes is to hold the specification of hopes in abeyance until a definite time when there will be more evidence to marshal. By setting an explicit time for the review of reality, the person gives himself assurance that his hopes will be kept unformulated or tenuously formulated and ungrounded for only so long. Such a structure may be characterized as follows:

HOPE STRUCTURE VI: ADULT

1. Unspecified hopes
2. Future orientation
3. Timed postponement of reality surveillance
4. Uncertain realization

Such an attempt to cope with the problem of hoping is seen when Mary's mother deferred specifying her hopes for Mary as an adult by saying, "She's going to public high school next year. I think we'll probably have to wait and see if she can make that. I am kind of doubtful." *(Mary: age 16, cardiac disability).* Grounds for supporting a hope may be found in the new evidence, but, if this proves not to be the case, the person is again faced with the precarious structure of hopes, however vaguely specified, that remain ungrounded.

Finally, instead of timing the review of reality, it may be indefinitely postponed, not because one lacks sufficient information, but, on the contrary, because one knows enough to wish to avoid a fruitless confrontation with a frightening reality. The future is pushed farther and farther back, its differentiation avoided. Instead, stress is put on the present. The essential features of such a hope structure may be listed as follows:

HOPE STRUCTURE VII: ADULT

1. Unspecified hopes
2. Dedifferentiation of future
3. Positive valence of present
4. Reality surveillance of present
5. Uncertainty of future

And still the person hopes. How this is accomplished is reserved for later discussion under the heading, "The Unpromising Future."

It is not supposed that the several types of hope structures that have been delimited in this paper are the only ones, or that only one of them can occur at any one time in the life space of the person. For example, certain aspects of the future may intentionally be blocked from view (dedifferentiation) while the person details other aspects (reality surveillance), in this way either manifesting a new hope structure or combining two hope structures (e.g., VII and IV). Moreover, it is psychologically possible for the person to be operating at two levels at the same time, actively testing his hopes against reality for example, while at another level maintaining the earlier structure of childhood (II) where future hopes remain equivalent to desires.

Reality Grounding Methods

The importance of reality grounding in sustaining hopes is seen below in the qualitatively rich variety of ways in which this is accomplished. We wish to stress that it is *phenomenal* grounding in reality that is of concern here, and not the issue of whether the person is actually being realistic, for, so long as the person *believes* that he has grounds on which to rest his hopes, he feels assured. That is to say, phenomenal grounding can be based on realistic or unrealistic expectations.

The following categories delimit methods for achieving reality grounding but are not mutually exclusive. The exemplification is taken from the adult interviews about Jed, a 14-year-old boy who had sustained a suprapubic cystotomy at 1 week of age and had had poliomyelitis at age 5. He now wears a drainage catheter inserted into the abdominal wall, emptying into a urinal bag strapped to his leg. With the use of bilateral long-leg braces that lock at the knees, he is able to walk a little without crutches. He is independent with respect of dressing and feeding himself and his speech is adequate. Intelligence is low average. Where only part of the example is especially relevant to the category, it is italicized. (*F* = Father, *T* = Teacher, *ST* = Speech Therapist; Jed's mother, though present with the father, did not express her hopes).

1. Environmental Conditions. Conditions in the environment that support the realistic basis of hope are emphasized. They may refer to present or future conditions. Sometimes the future is anticipated or is a mere extrapolation of present conditions as in the following example.

Example: Hopes for Jed as an adult?

> *F:* Well, I think, if we can get him through high school, I can send him to Horkins School. They have business courses out there, which I think would be the best thing for him. I graduated twice out there, from high school and from the vocational program, and they do have a two-year business course—typing, shorthand, bookkeeping, but generally I think that, once I get him through high school, why they'll be able to more or less teach him a trade, so he can earn a living, which is not impossible.

2. Assets of the Child. Characteristics of the child, usually implicitly assumed to continue into the future, are presented in support of the hope.

Example: Hopes for Jed as an adult?

> *T:* Actually, I hope that Jed can go on through school to receive the type of certificate or diploma that would mean that he would be able to get some type of training, because his *upper extremities are good, his hands are good, and he should be able* to go into some trade or vocation that would, you know, give him a nice livelihood.

3. Growth Forces. The natural stages of development in the child are called upon to support the hopes.

Example: Hopes as far as marriage?

> *T:* (After much hesitancy and avoidance of the issue) Maybe as he grows more and becomes more emotionally stable, he will find someone with whom he could be compatible.

4. Group Comparison. The assets of child are verified through comparison with other children.

Example: Hopes for Jed as far as health?

> *F:* I think it can be good. He's been, other than this paralysis, bladder trouble, he's been one of our healthiest children.

5. Consensual Validation. Other people are called upon for a verification of reality statements.

Example: Hopes as far as health?

> *F:* (Seeking confirmation from wife in support of his affirmation that Jed's health can be good) Strictly speaking, has he ever come down with anything the other children have not had?

6. Responsible Action: Responsibility for maintaining favorable reality conditions is assured.

Example: Hopes as far as health?

> *F:* (Adding in support of his affirmation that Jed's health can be good) Around here, if we get a bad cold, and the aspirin won't break it up, we run for the penicillin.

7. Negation of Countervailing Possibility. The survey of reality spotlights a negative condition or possibility, which is then discounted or denied.

Example: Hopes as far as school?

> *ST:* I, of course, would hope that he could graduate, but I also hoped that Doug could, and Doug didn't make it. I don't see why Jed can't make it though.

8. "If . . . Then" Conditional Events. Hope rests on the occurrence of specific events that are reasonably possible, although not certain.

Example: Hopes for Jed as an adult?

> *ST:* I think that, if he . . . his speech is good, he could certainly take care of himself physically, I mean walk around, this sort of thing and get from place to place. I feel that he could lead a pretty normal life. This is what I hope, *if he gets some help in the areas where he really needs it.*

9. Speculative Coercion of Reality. The constraints of realistic cause-effect relations are loosened as one fantasies what conceivably could occur to support a hope.

Example: Hopes as far as marriage?

> *F:* (After asserting the unfeasibility of marriage for Jed from the practical point of view) Unless they do something else with the bladder trouble. To me, I've got a different way. I think they could run it through the penis and do it that way and put a regular male urinal

bag on him. I've talked to the doctors before about that. But eventually, let's say, I'm hoping that they can, because then they can remove this tube from the bladder and, like I say, give him a regular male urinal, and then he'll be able to consummate marriage and maybe have some children.

10. Maybe Someday, Something. The possibility of future undefined discoveries that will support hopes, however tenatively, is expressed.
Example: Hopes as far as marriage?
> *F:* Well someday, maybe he can, but from all practical viewpoints, I doubt it. (F then continues speculatively coercing reality; see previous example.)

11. Truism. An uncontestable generality that applies to everyone is introduced in support of hopes.
Example: Hopes for Jed as adult?
> *T:* (After presenting Jed's assets that will enable him to earn a nice livelihood, adds) Now, what job area, this still has to be determined. *But I do feel that he's capable of leading as normal a life as is possible for him with his disability.*

12. Hope Commendation. The hope is supported by affirming its value for the child.
Example: Hopes as far as marriage?
> *T:* (After saying that Jed might become more stable and find someone with whom he could be compatible, adds) This, I think would be good for him if it's ever realized.

These 12 categories are by no means exhaustive of the ways in which hopes are cognitively grounded in reality, but they are the ones that were applied in Jed's case. Difference in cognitive hoping styles are revealed by both the categories used and the emphasis given to them. Jed's father made use of 11 categories with special weight given to #1 and #9 *(Environmental Conditions and Speculative Coercion of Reality);* the teacher invoked 4 categories with emphasis on #2 and #3 *(Assets of the Child* and *Growth Forces);* the speech therapist relied on 3 categories, #8 being especially prominent *("If . . . Then" Conditional Events).* A relatively frequent reality-grounding method, *Testimonial,* not used in Jed's case, offers in support of one's hopes the achievements of someone with a disability similar to that of the child.

The significance of cognitive hoping styles is suggested by the following:

1. As seen within the framework of developmental hope structures, cognitive hoping styles are a function of age.

2. They may also be expected to be influenced by the role relation of the hoper to the child. For example, parents to a greater degree than staff members are inextricably a part of the child's future, a situation that forces thoughts about hopes for the future as well as vigilance against the threat of disappointed hopes. This may be one reason for the tendency of parents in the present study to devote a greater proportion of reality surveying in the service of supporting their hopes than did the staff members. Parents were also more reluctant than staff to acknowledge the possibility that any of their hopes might be unrealistic when asked about this (24 % vs 65 %; $X^2 = 7.21$; 1 df, p $<.01$).

3. Like other types of individual differences, cognitive hoping styles may be expected to reflect personality variables.

4. An analysis of the cognitive hoping styles of a particular person would appear to provide leads as to where and how to shift the focus should a reevaluation of his hopes seem indicated. For example, because Jed's father paid little attention to the child's characteristics, relying rather on factors outside the child, concentration on Jed himself, as a person with strengths and limitations, might be encouraged.

5. Cognitive hoping styles may also be expected to vary with how bleak or hopeful the future reality appears. In the extreme case, where the future holds little promise, a different type of hope structure emerges, as will be seen below, one uniquely important in highlighting the function of hoping in avoiding despair.

The Unpromising Future

If the person's repeated reviews of reality do not lead to adequate reality grounding of even substitute hopes, he is faced with the difficult task of bolstering his morale. Reality notwithstanding, he tries to achieve a hopeful attitude by intentionally taking "each day as it comes" and dedifferentiating the future, while at the same time preserving its positive cast. Thoughts of "someday, something" may provide at least the minimal amount of reality-grounding for the future to generate its own positive valence, but additional support for maintaining a hope attitude appears when the person is able to concentrate on meaningful and positive values in the present. Stripped of its own definition, the future glows from the illumination of the present.

The case of Donald well illustrates the struggle of his parents to keep the future undifferentiated in the face of a forbidding reality. Donald is a 14-year-old boy with congenital amyoplasia, a progressively debilitating disease. He is completely dependent on others for ambulation in a wheelchair, for toileting and dressing, and is almost completely dependent for feeding. His speech is good, but his low vital capacity makes his voice extremely weak. He is of average intelligence and is emotionally mature.

The interview with his parents started off with a number of attempts to keep the future undifferentiated, e.g., the parents claimed lack of knowledge, constricted the time perspective, and shifted the topic to Donald's needs:

I. Now what are your hopes for Donald when he becomes an adult?

M: Well, I just don't know. We just [pause] I just don't quite think that far ahead. We just [pause].

F: We keep building him up, but, you know, we don't know what [pause].

M: We'll just more or less have to wait until we face that time and, I mean, we can't talk to him about it because he gets his feelings hurt, too. I mean, when he discusses things that he likes to do when he gets older, and you would say, well, he couldn't do it, why he couldn't do it, why he would just give up completely, and you can't, you can't, you have to keep building their hopes. However, you just never know. . . .

F. He has big interests and everything, but I mean, we all know that it can't turn out that way, I mean, being that his handicap is the way it is, so we really don't expect too much. I don't know how to say [pause].

When some differentiation of the future was encouraged by the question about hopes regarding school, the father then made use of a truism to provide some slim basis upon which to support his hope, saying that he "hopes he can go far enough so he'll know what it's all about and that he can enjoy it." The mother also found some tenuous reality grounds by adding, "Maybe someday there might be something that would help him in, you know, making his own living. If things would be available for his handicap at the time."

The special role of focusing on the present in the effort to maintain a hopeful attitude is revealed when the parents were asked how their hopes have changed since Donald was born. The parents first talked about the absolute necessity of keeping on hoping, hope substitution being one way so long as there was even slight reality support.

I: How have your hopes for Donald changed since he was born?

M: Well, I mean as far as hoping, we've just never [pause].

F: We've never given up hoping [pause].

M: You never give up, I mean, to a certain extent he might be handicapped in one way [note the understatement here] but you hope that eventually he will gain more in another part, that someday [pause].

The lack of adequate reality support shortly shifted the conversation to the need for living in the present:

M: There was a time when he [Donald] worried terribly about what he was going to do when he was going to get old, whether, you know, about making his own living and of course it shocked me. That was about two or three years ago. And I just told him that he shouldn't worry about it, because, I said, "We don't even worry." And he asked me how he would make his own living, and I said, "Well, that I don't know/That's just too far ahead," I said. "Even if I would say you're going to make it this way, by the time you get that age, you'd be doing something different, because," I said, "we don't even know what we'll be doing when we get that old." I said, "You don't want to think that far ahead, you just live today, and then tomorrow morning when you get up, you live for that day." I said, "Don't live so many years in advance." Well, now, ever since that he's kinda, you know, lived for the present, not for the future so much.

The father then continued the conversation still focusing on the present and thereby renewing his own morale:

F: As far as his interests go, he's still as, just as much a normal kid, I mean. He's crazy about baseball, and he likes football, basketball, and he's always had a great thrill for racing, building model racers, and stuff like that like most boys his age. As for as his morale, it's always pretty good, I mean, he's never let himself down in the dumps to think that, "Well, it's just here and that's it." So he's got high hopes.

The essential features of this hope structure were listed in *Adult Hope Structure VII*. Theoretically, its efficiency rests on the proposition that lack of differentiation of the future is the feature par excellence that enables it to borrow, as it were, the affective tones of the present. Fluctuations between good morale and despair are to be expected, inasmuch as an undifferentiated outlook could also be expected to be especially vulnerable to negative affects in the present. Despair bespeaks a state where *both* future and present are overwhelmed by negatives. Despair does not flourish when the present is bleak and the future is bright, nor when' the present is bright and the future is held in abeyance.

Cognitive-Affective Tasks in Hoping

Thus far we have examined hoping, primarily as a cognitive process in which the adult seeks to coordinate his hopes with reality, thereby better guaranteeing the actualization of his hopes. Where adequate grounds are not to be found, he continues to survey and test reality within a framework of realistic or wishful expectations or both, modifying and substituting hopes in the process. Even when the grounds on which to rest hopes have been gained by loosening the constraints of reality, the person feels reassured that his hopes have a good chance of coming true. Should future reality as he sees it still remain unsupportive of any specific hope, he dedifferentiates and constricts the future, seeking reality supports for positive values in the present. The main task of the cognitive part of the hoping process can thus be seen as *reality surveillance* in order to find grounds upon which to hope.

The process of hoping also involves a number of affective tasks, namely the task of encouragement, worrying, and mourning. They interlard the hoping process as both products and instigators of attempts at reality surveillance.

Encouragement becomes the affective counterpart of reality surveillance when the person finds some basis on which to rest his hopes. It is positive, sustaining, and comforting and provides the emotional feedback that one is on the right track (even though, objectively, one may not be). It also provides motivation to continue striving and therefore commands an enormously important function in the psychic economy. Physicians have long observed how quickly some patients succumb once they believe their case is hopeless.

Uncertainty regarding possibilities for realizing hopes commonly remains as part of the adult hope structure. This uncertainty, in turn, provokes an anxious, apprehensive, affective experience that expresses itself in *worrying*. Worrying about the future presses the person to think about how hoped-for eventualities can be better guaranteed; it forces him to face the reality that at the same time he fears and to consider it soberly as well as fantastically. Although experienced as discomfort, worry can therefore be beneficial. Janis[4] has described worry as preparation for anticipated stress. He sees the "work of worrying" as necessary for successful adjustment to potentially dangerous situations and points to the psychological problems that frequently arise when worrying fails to occur.

When worry brings about reexamination of reality, the person may discover new supports for his hopes, new actions that can be taken toward their realization. Or as Dembo[1] has pointed out, the person may abandon "realistic expectation" for "wishful expectation," where even remote possibilities become sufficient as evidence, for they do not have to answer to lawfulness and probability as criteria. In either case, encouragement is fed and worry assuaged.

But worrying does not always sustain hopes. Reality conditions may dissolve hopes in spite of repeated efforts to reappraise the situation or to retreat to wishful expectation. It is then that *mourning*, a state of sorrow over deeply felt loss, replaces worrying as hopes are given up or seriously modified. (For a more detailed analysis of mourning as a value loss see Dembo, Leviton, and Wright[2] and Wright.[8]) In case of the child's disability the parent grieves over the personal and social·satisfactions associated with a healthy body or mind that are now felt to be denied the child and himself.

As with other emotions, the sorrow of loss is satiable. The person is gradually released from his intense emotional involvement with the hope that had to be given up. Forced by the intolerability of mourning forever, the person eventually considers other possibilities on which to construct and nurture hopes. Where the groundwork for substitute hopes had been laid in previous surveys of reality, recovery is speeded.

Sometimes, however, previous reviews are of little avail because a major alteration in the person's value system is required before he is able to scan reality with the kind of new look that will allow the support of meaningful new hopes. New thinking about and evaluation of what is important then assume primacy. Where future reality remains too threatening, the new thinking may focus on the present, dedifferentiating and constricting the future, so that the satisfactions of the present can affectively support hopes for a future otherwise undefined. These are some of the outcomes of the period of mourning, and, for all of them, the need to feel that "all is not lost," the need to hope, eventually reconstitutes the cognitive-affective processes involved in the interplay between hoping and reality surveillance. Mourning becomes displaced by once again worrying and being encouraged.

This psychological analysis of process and tasks involved in hoping provides some guidelines for counseling parents in regard to difficulties the future may hold for their child. The most general principle is that weight be given to each of the four tasks involved in hoping, none being supported so completely as to preclude another. This leads to the conclusion that encouragement should not be so all-important as to bypass the productive outcomes of worrying and mourning. Conversely, it also leads to the conclusion that objective reality considerations should not be pursued in a highly differentiated way if so doing would destroy encouragement. Sometimes wishful expectations may have to be countenanced and realistic expectations muted in order to keep encouragement alive.

It is further proposed that the proper balance and phasing among the four tasks involved in hoping can be most adequately maintained when the parent becomes actively involved with the child's rehabilitation in an atmosphere of mutual respect and sharing with the specialist as well as with other parents. The very act of trying to do something on behalf of the child implies goals that are worth striving for. Doing something for the child can also serve as restitution for guilt, a feeling that so often troubles the parent, especially in his initial reaction to the child's disability. Having the specialist discuss questions with him and sharing his feelings and concerns with other parents can give the parent the feeling that he is not alone and that he will be able to cope with the problems that lie ahead. Seeing other children in the hospital or rehabilitation setting who are "worse off" can dramatically remind the parent that, in fact, all is not lost.

The value of active involvement in the rehabilitation enterprise during the early stages of the period of mourning is expressed in the words of the mother of Sandra, an 8-year-old child whose cerebral palsy was discovered at the age of 6 months. When asked how her hopes had changed since that discovery the mother replied:

> Well, really at that time, I didn't know too much about it [pause] nothing like that. In fact I didn't know anything, and I thought it was just horrible and I just figured she was going to be in such bad condition and everything. But after I was taking her back and forth to the hospital and things like that and her with other kids, why then I realized that she was pretty well off [pause] all considering.

To be sure, the parent will continue to worry and to mourn, to resist and to resent, to blame and to deny, but these feelings have a better chance of being worked through to the end of accepting the child's disability and regaining hope when he is part of, rather than excluded from, the rehabilitation process.

Summary

Seven types of hope structures have been delineated, two applying to children and five to adults. The main feature distinguishing child and adult hope structures is the absence of reality surveillance in the former. Whereas children's hopes are equivalent to desires, both desires and reality considerations support adult hopes.

Adult hope structures were seen to vary according to the manner in which the person copes with the problem of uncertainty regarding the realizability of his hopes. Where the reality base is found wanting, the person may seek grounding in terms of wishful expectation as well as realistic expectation; he may intermittently review reality, postpone its review, or confine reality to the present while dedifferentiating the future. The variety of ways in which reality evidence is brought to bear on hopes underscores how important it is for the person to believe that there is a reality base for his hopes. It also suggests how to reorient the reality focus should this be desirable. Reality surveillance provides support, not only for existing hopes, but also for hopes that eventually may be substituted.

The process of hoping involves four cognitive-effective tasks, namely:

1. Reality surveillance: a cognitive function directed toward coordinating hopes with reality in order to insure the fulfillment of hopes. It also serves as a base for substitute hopes.

2. Encouragement: the affective side of coordination of hopes with reality as the person sees reality. It motivates, sustains, and comforts the hoper.

3. Worrying: the affective counterpart of cognitive uncertainty. It forces the person to reexamine reality.

4. Mourning: the affective consequence of having to relinquish hopes. Mourning prepares the person for the task of reappraising values and accepting hope substitutions.

The proper balance among these four tasks can best be effected when parents become actively involved with the child's rehabilitation and share questions and concerns with specialists and other parents in an atmosphere of mutual respect.

ACKNOWLEDGMENTS

Grateful acknowledgment is made to the staff and parents of children at the Capper Foundation, Topeka, Kan., who cooperated in the execution of research reported in this paper.

References

[1]DEMBO, TAMARA. *Suffering and Its Alleviation: A Theoretical Analysis.* Report submitted to the Association for the Aid of Crippled Children. New York: 1955.

[2]DEMBO, TAMARA, LEVITON, GLORIA LADIEU, and WRIGHT, BEATRICE A. Adjustment to Misfortune—A Problem of Social-Psychological Rehabilitation. *Artificial Limbs.* Autumn, 1956. 3:2:4-62.

[3]FRENCH, THOMAS M. *The Integration of Behavior.* Chicago: Univ. of Chicago Pr., 1958.

[4]JANIS, IRVING L. *Psychological Stress: Psychoanalytic and Behavioral Studies of Surgical Patients.* New York: John Wiley, 1958.

[5]LEWIN, KURT. *A Dynamic Theory of Personality; Selected Papers.* New York: McGraw-Hill, 1945.

[6]MENNINGER, KARL. *Hope.* Lecture given at the 115th Annual Meeting of the American Psychiatric Association, Philadelphia, Pa., 1959.

[7]SHAND, ALEXANDER F. *The Foundations of Character.* London: Macmillan and Co., 1914.

[8]WRIGHT, BEATRICE A. *Physical Disability—A Psychological Approach.* New York: Harper & Row, 1960.